Advance Praise for *The Long Game*

"The Long Game brings what's been largely missing from debate on US-China relations: historically informed insight into the nature of China's Leninist system and strategy."

—**Kevin Rudd**, President of the Asia Society and former Prime Minister of Australia

"The Long Game is essential in understanding China's approach to the evolving US-China relationship and global order. Unique in scope and unmatched in substance, Rush Doshi's masterfully researched work describes clearly the economic, political, and military contours of China's strategic approach. The observations, analysis, and recommendations of this superb work must be foundational to any China playbook—business, political, or military."

—**Admiral Gary Roughead**, U.S. Navy (Retired)

" 'What does China want?' Rush Doshi makes such a cogent case, based on a wealth of Chinese textual and behavioral evidence, that China's consistent strategy has been to displace the United States that he persuades me to re-examine my view that China's aims are open-ended and malleable. His compelling book should become an instant classic in the China field and required reading for everyone trying to figure out America's own best strategy toward China."

—**Susan Shirk**, Professor and Chair of the 21st Century China Center, University of California-San Diego

"A must-read for anyone wrestling with the China Challenge. Doshi's careful analysis of Chinese language documents make a powerful case that China is pursuing a coherent grand strategy to overturn the US-led international order."

—**Graham Allison**, Professor of Government, Harvard Kennedy School

"Doshi has brilliantly limned a new framework for understanding both the global ambition and the strategic challenges posed by Xi Jinping and his 'wolf warrior diplomacy.' If you're looking for the one book that best illuminates the historical logic of his unrepentant 'China Dream,' The Long Game is it."

—**Orville Schell**, Director, Center on US-China Policy, the Asia Society

"Drawing from a vast array of Chinese sources, Rush Doshi presents a novel account of the evolution of Beijing's grand strategy. Doshi argues persuasively that shifts in China's behavior are driven by the Communist Party's collective assessment of trends in the global balance of power rather than by the personalities of individual leaders. The implications are not reassuring: China's increasingly aggressive attempts to displace the US and transform the international system began before Xi Jinping took power and will likely persist after he is gone. This should be required reading for scholars and policymakers alike."

—**Aaron L. Friedberg**, Professor of Politics, Princeton University

"The debate over whether China has a strategy to displace American leadership in Asia is over. Now comes the first authoritative account of what that strategy is. Using a vast array of original sources, Rush Doshi does unprecedented forensic work on the origins of Chinese grand strategy and its prospects for success."

—**Michael J. Green**, author of *By More than Providence: Grand Strategy and American Power in the Asia-Pacific since 1783*

"If you doubt that China has been pursuing a long-term, comprehensive strategy to achieve global primacy, read Rush Doshi's book. In this brilliant, definitive work, Doshi details the vaulting ambition of Beijing's agenda. Everyone interested in the future of American power and world order should read it now—or weep later."

—**Hal Brands**, Johns Hopkins University and American Enterprise Institute

The Long Game

China's Grand Strategy to Displace American Order

RUSH DOSHI

OXFORD
UNIVERSITY PRESS

OXFORD

UNIVERSITY PRESS

Oxford University Press is a department of the University of Oxford. It furthers
the University's objective of excellence in research, scholarship, and education
by publishing worldwide. Oxford is a registered trade mark of Oxford University
Press in the UK and certain other countries.

Published in the United States of America by Oxford University Press
198 Madison Avenue, New York, NY 10016, United States of America.

© Rush Doshi 2021

Library of Congress Control Number: 2021938602
ISBN 978–0–19–752791–7

DOI: 10.1093/oso/9780197527917.001.0001

1 3 5 7 9 8 6 4 2

Printed by LSC Communications, United States of America

Cover illustration by Jonathan Bartlett.

All statements of fact, opinion, or analysis expressed are those of the author and do not reflect the official
position or views of the National Security Council (NSC) or the US Government. No content should be
construed as asserting or implying US Government or NSC authentication of information or endorsement
of the author's views. The author's work on this report was completed prior to his government service.

For Kurt
For Parshu, Rupa, Uday, and Sohum
And for Jennie

CONTENTS

ACKNOWLEDGMENTS

No book is a solitary effort, and I owe a debt of gratitude to so many who made this book possible.

My earliest tutors in Chinese foreign policy and political science were at Princeton. Were it not for them, I would never have written this book nor pursued this career. Gilbert Rozman provided the initial spark with his classes on Asian geopolitics. Tom Christensen kept it burning, and I can still quote from his lectures on Chinese foreign policy and on the importance of public service. Robert Keohane provided the kindling by teaching me the craft of research and patiently showing me how to be a social scientist. And Aaron Friedberg, to whom I owe a great professional and intellectual debt, fanned the flames by taking me on as a research assistant and then turning me loose on a wide array of professional challenges. I am grateful for his nearly fifteen years of constant support and thoughtful advice.

This book also owes a debt to many professional mentors, all of whom took a chance on me. Susan O'Sullivan, a tireless advocate for human rights in China, gave me my first opportunity to serve in government and changed the way I understood China and foreign policy. Josh Bolten offered me my first full-time job in Washington, provided me an early model of service and character, and placed me into the company of mentors like Dan Price, Mike Smart, and Clay Lowery who have taught me so much over the years. Jackie Deal and Steve Rosen offered me my first job in defense research, and that experience led me to pursue graduate school and a career at the intersection of China and foreign policy.

I was fortunate in graduate school to benefit from three extraordinary teachers and dissertation advisers: Steve Rosen, Iain Johnston, and Josh Kertzer. They taught me how to write a dissertation, and their patience, guidance, and generosity made this book possible. Along with them, I owe thanks to many other faculty who guided and supported me through my graduate studies, including Taylor Fravel, Vipin Narang, Beth Simmons, Judith Kelley, Barry Posen, and

Owen Cote. I am also grateful to Charlie Glaser, who offered me an opportunity to spend a year exclusively on research and writing at George Washington University.

I wrote much of this book while serving as a resident tutor at Harvard's Quincy House, where I found welcome fellowship and community during the otherwise solitary process of research and writing. I am grateful to Lee Gehrke, our faculty dean, and his wife Deb—the irrepressible heart and soul of Quincy—who made that House a home. Her memory lives on in the thousands of students and staff like me whose lives she touched.

Over the last few years, I am grateful to have called Brookings and Yale Law School's China Center my intellectual homes. I am indebted to John Allen, Bruce Jones, Suzanne Maloney, and Tarun Chhabra for bringing me aboard Brookings and entrusting me with the opportunity to build its China Strategy Initiative. Our center directors Mike O'Hanlon, Cheng Li, Mireya Solis, Richard Bush, and Tom Wright provided guidance, advice, and support along the way. So many other colleagues made my time at Brookings unforgettable and provided encouragement on this project, including Jeff Bader, Celia Belin, Dan Byman, David Dollar, Lindsey Ford, Ryan Hass, Shadi Hamid, Mara Karlin, Ken Lieberthal, Tanvi Madan, Chris Meserole, Jung Pak, Ted Piccone, Alina Polyakova, Frank Rose, Natan Sachs, Constanze Stelzenmüller, Jonathan Stromseth, Strobe Talbott, Joshua White, and Tamara Cofman Wittes, among others. Andy Moffat, Kevin Scott, Emilie Kimball, Jennifer Mason, Ted Reinert, Ryan McElveen, Leah Dreyfuss, Anna Newby, Miguel Vieira, and Patrick Cole kept the ship afloat and made our work possible. I'm particularly grateful to Jacob Helberg, the co-chair of the Brookings China Strategy Initiative, for his passion for this project and for his counsel on matters ranging from technology to politics.

I owe a special debt to Paul Gewirtz, who brought me to Yale, supported my research, and whose encouragement over the years helped push this book across the finish line. Rob Williams, our executive director, was a sounding board and enthusiastic champion of almost every research project I ever considered at Brookings and at Yale. I also benefited enormously from the fellowship of Jeremy Daum, Jamie Horsley, Mia Shuang Li, Darius Longarino, Karman Lucero, Mira Rapp-Hooper, Samm Sacks, Susan Thornton, and others at Yale. Concetta Fusco, Severine Debaisieux, and Lisa Wade made everything possible.

The Center for a New American Security (CNAS) has been another intellectual home, and I am so fortunate that Michele Flournoy, Richard Fontaine, Patrick Cronin, and Dan Kliman brought me on as an adjunct fellow and invited me to join a range of CNAS projects. I'm grateful to Ely Ratner for years of advice, for his encouragement when this project was still just a research proposal, and for the privilege of working for him on several key initiatives.

So many others also deserve special thanks. Mike Green has been my guide on crafting a career that spans policy and academia and an early champion of this project. Hal Brands was also enthusiastic about this book, provided advice on framing, and convened a roundtable to help me test the argument. Ashley Tellis was supportive of the project from the first time we discussed it. He brought my career full circle when he offered me the chance to write a chapter for *Strategic Asia*—the very same series that helped kickstart my interest in Asian geopolitics in Gilbert Rozman's class over a decade earlier. Andrew May and David Epstein pulled me into a range of studies and projects over the years that have shaped the arguments made here. Abe Denmark brought me on as a Wilson China Fellow and introduced me to the institution's incredible bench of Asia expertise. I'm also very grateful to Mira Rapp-Hooper, Zack Cooper, and Tarun Chhabra, whom I've repeatedly turned to over the years for advice at critical professional junctures.

So many others in the academic and policy worlds are also owed a debt of gratitude: Jude Blanchette, Chris Brose, Mike Chase, Elizabeth Economy, Charlie Edel, Andrew Erickson, Julian Gewirtz, Bonnie Glaser, Sheena Greitens, Melanie Hart, Oriana Mastro, Jason Matheny, Evan Medeiros, Sarah Miller, Siddharth Mohandas, Nadege Rolland, Laura Rosenberger, Gary Roughead, Sophie Richardson, Eric Sayers, Orville Schell, David Shambaugh, Victor Shih, Susan Shirk, Matt Stoller, Joseph Torigian, Matt Turpin, and George Yin—to name just a few.

It took a team of people to transform this project from a dissertation to a book. Bridget Matzie and Karen Murgolo from Aevitas Creative Management had faith in the project even at the moments when mine was flagging. Jim Goldgeier brought the book into his Bridging the Gap series and has been a tireless cheerleader for it from the beginning. David McBride, my editor at Oxford, was convinced the book could be a success and patiently put up with my questions and requests while dispensing advice and wisdom along the way. Jonathan Bartlett, Brady McNamara, and Nisha Iyer each made significant contributions to the cover. Finally, I'm grateful to Cheryl Merritt for somehow managing an incredibly tight production timeline.

In this project as in so much else, I owe an enormous debt of gratitude to Kurt Campbell—my supervisor, mentor, collaborator, and supporter for the last several years. Kurt has mentored enough Asia hands over the last twenty-five years to staff a half dozen think tanks, and it is my great privilege to be counted among them. His wisdom, creativity, generosity, and dedication to service are a Washington legend. In this case, the legends are true. Thank you, Kurt, for your guidance through the ups and downs of politics, policy, and life these last six years. Your influence can be found on every page of this book.

Nothing in life would be possible without the unconditional love and support of my parents, Rupa and Uday. They came to the United States alone, found each other, and built a home for Sohum and for me. The greatest stroke of luck in my life has been to be their son. I owe them everything, and I am so very proud of them too. I also owe a special debt to my brother Sohum, my most loyal and steadfast supporter whose advice and support I solicit on all things in life, big and small.

Finally, I owe more than words can convey to the love of my life, Jennie. This book exists because of your counsel and sustenance throughout this long and winding process. You are my partner in all things, and it is my great fortune that we found each other at the same time we found our passion for China and Asia. I am grateful for so much in life, but especially that you said yes.

Introduction

It was 1872, and Li Hongzhang was writing at a time of historic upheaval. A Qing Dynasty general and official who dedicated much of his life to reforming a dying empire, Li was often compared to his contemporary Otto von Bismarck, the architect of German unification and national power whose portrait Li was said to keep for inspiration.[1]

Like Bismarck, Li had military experience that he parlayed into considerable influence, including over foreign and military policy. He had been instrumental in putting down the fourteen-year Taiping rebellion—the bloodiest conflict of the entire nineteenth century—which had seen a millenarian Christian state rise from the growing vacuum of Qing authority to launch a civil war that claimed tens of millions of lives. This campaign against the rebels provided Li with an appreciation for Western weapons and technology, a fear of European and Japanese predations, a commitment to Chinese self-strengthening and modernization—and critically—the influence and prestige to do something about it.

And so it was in 1872 that in one of his many correspondences, Li reflected on the groundbreaking geopolitical and technological transformations he had seen in his own life that posed an existential threat to the Qing. In a memorandum advocating for more investment in Chinese shipbuilding, he penned a line since repeated for generations: China was experiencing "great changes not seen in three thousand years."[2]

That famous, sweeping statement is to many Chinese nationalists a reminder of the country's own humiliation. Li ultimately failed to modernize China, lost a war to Japan, and signed the embarrassing Treaty of Shimonoseki with Tokyo. But to many, Li's line was both prescient and accurate—China's decline was the product of the Qing Dynasty's inability to reckon with transformative geopolitical and technological forces that had not been seen for three thousand years, forces which changed the international balance of power and ushered in China's "Century of Humiliation." These were trends that all of Li's striving could not reverse.

Now, Li's line has been repurposed by China's leader Xi Jinping to inaugurate a new phase in China's post–Cold War grand strategy. Since 2017, Xi has in many of the country's critical foreign policy addresses declared that the world is in the midst of "great changes unseen in a century" [百年未有之大变局]. If Li's line marks the highpoint of China's humiliation, then Xi's marks an occasion for its rejuvenation. If Li's evokes tragedy, then Xi's evokes opportunity. But both capture something essential: the idea that world order is once again at stake because of unprecedented geopolitical and technological shifts, and that this requires strategic adjustment.

For Xi, the origin of these shifts is China's growing power and what it saw as the West's apparent self-destruction. On June 23, 2016, the United Kingdom voted to leave the European Union. Then, a little more than three months later, a populist surge catapulted Donald Trump into office as president of the United States. From China's perspective—which is highly sensitive to changes in its perceptions of American power and threat—these two events were shocking. Beijing believed that the world's most powerful democracies were withdrawing from the international order they had helped erect abroad and were struggling to govern themselves at home. The West's subsequent response to the coronavirus pandemic in 2020, and then the storming of the US Capitol by extremists in 2021, reinforced a sense that "time and momentum are on our side," as Xi Jinping put it shortly after those events.[3] China's leadership and foreign policy elite declared that a "period of historical opportunity" [历史机遇期] had emerged to expand the country's strategic focus from Asia to the wider globe and its governance systems.

We are now in the early years of what comes next—a China that not only seeks regional influence as so many great powers do, but as Evan Osnos has argued, "that is preparing to shape the twenty-first century, much as the U.S. shaped the twentieth."[4] That competition for influence will be a global one, and Beijing believes with good reason that the next decade will likely determine the outcome.

As we enter this new stretch of acute competition, we lack answers to critical foundational questions. What are China's ambitions, and does it have a grand strategy to achieve them? If it does, what is that strategy, what shapes it, and what should the United States do about it? These are basic questions for American policymakers grappling with this century's greatest geopolitical challenge, not least because knowing an opponent's strategy is the first step to countering it. And yet, as great power tensions flare, there is no consensus on the answers.

This book attempts to provide an answer. In its argument and structure, the book takes its inspiration in part from Cold War studies of US grand strategy.[5] Where those works analyzed the theory and practice of US "strategies of containment" toward the Soviet Union during the Cold War, this book seeks to analyze the theory and practice of China's "strategies of displacement" toward the United States after the Cold War.

To do so, the book makes use of an original database of Chinese Communist Party documents—memoirs, biographies, and daily records of senior officials— painstakingly gathered and then digitized over the last several years from libraries, bookstores in Taiwan and Hong Kong, and Chinese e-commerce sites (see Appendix). Many of the documents take readers behind the closed doors of the Chinese Communist Party, bring them into its high-level foreign policy institutions and meetings, and introduce readers to a wide cast of Chinese political leaders, generals, and diplomats charged with devising and implementing China's grand strategy. While no one master document contains all of Chinese grand strategy, its outline can be found across a wide corpus of texts. Within them, the Party uses hierarchical statements that represent internal consensus on key issues to guide the ship of state, and these statements can be traced across time. The most important of these is the Party line (路线), then the guideline (方针), and finally the policy (政策), among other terms. Understanding them sometimes requires proficiency not only in Chinese, but also in seemingly impenetrable and archaic ideological concepts like "dialectical unities" and "historical materialism."

Argument in Brief

The book argues that the core of US-China competition since the Cold War has been over regional and now global order. It focuses on the strategies that rising powers like China use to displace an established hegemon like the United States short of war. A hegemon's position in regional and global order emerges from three broad "forms of control" that are used to regulate the behavior of other states: coercive capability (to force compliance), consensual inducements (to incentivize it), and legitimacy (to rightfully command it). For rising states, the act of peacefully displacing the hegemon consists of two broad strategies generally pursued in sequence. The first strategy is to *blunt* the hegemon's exercise of those forms of control, particularly those extended over the rising state; after all, no rising state can displace the hegemon if it remains at the hegemon's mercy. The second is to *build* forms of control over others; indeed, no rising state can become a hegemon if it cannot secure the deference of other states through coercive threats, consensual inducements, or rightful legitimacy. Unless a rising power has first blunted the hegemon, efforts to build order are likely to be futile and easily opposed. And until a rising power has successfully conducted a good degree of blunting and building in its home region, it remains too vulnerable to the hegemon's influence to confidently turn to a third strategy, global *expansion*, which pursues both blunting and building at the global level to displace the hegemon from international leadership. Together, these strategies at the regional and then global levels provide a rough means of ascent for the Chinese Communist Party's nationalist elites, who seek to restore China to its due place and roll back the historical aberration of the West's overwhelming global influence.

This is a template China has followed, and in its review of China's strategies of displacement, the book argues that shifts from one strategy to the next have been triggered by sharp discontinuities in the most important variable shaping Chinese grand strategy: its perception of US power and threat. China's first strategy of displacement (1989–2008) was to quietly *blunt* American power over China, particularly in Asia, and it emerged after the traumatic trifecta of Tiananmen Square, the Gulf War, and the Soviet collapse led Beijing to sharply increase its perception of US threat. China's second strategy of displacement (2008–2016) sought to *build* the foundation for regional hegemony in Asia, and it was launched after the Global Financial Crisis led Beijing to see US power as diminished and emboldened it to take a more confident approach. Now, with the invocation of "great changes unseen in a century" following Brexit, President Trump's election, and the coronavirus pandemic, China is launching a third strategy of displacement, one that *expands* its blunting and building efforts worldwide to displace the United States as the global leader. In its final chapters, this book uses insights about China's strategy to formulate an asymmetric US grand strategy in response—one that takes a page from China's own book—and would seek to contest China's regional and global ambitions without competing dollar-for-dollar, ship-for-ship, or loan-for-loan.

The book also illustrates what Chinese order might look like if China is able to achieve its goal of "national rejuvenation" by the centennial of the founding of the People's Republic of China in 2049. At the regional level, China already accounts for more than half of Asian GDP and half of all Asian military spending, which is pushing the region out of balance and toward a Chinese sphere of influence. A fully realized Chinese order might eventually involve the withdrawal of US forces from Japan and Korea, the end of American regional alliances, the effective removal of the US Navy from the Western Pacific, deference from China's regional neighbors, unification with Taiwan, and the resolution of territorial disputes in the East and South China Seas. Chinese order would likely be more coercive than the present order, consensual in ways that primarily benefit connected elites even at the expense of voting publics, and considered legitimate mostly to those few who it directly rewards. China would deploy this order in ways that damage liberal values, with authoritarian winds blowing stronger across the region. Order abroad is often a reflection of order at home, and China's order-building would be distinctly illiberal relative to US order-building.

At the global level, Chinese order would involve seizing the opportunities of the "great changes unseen in a century" and displacing the United States as the world's leading state. This would require successfully managing the principal risk flowing from the "great changes"—Washington's unwillingness to gracefully accept decline—by weakening the forms of control supporting American global order while strengthening those forms of control supporting a Chinese alternative. That order would span a "zone of super-ordinate influence" in Asia as well as "partial hegemony" in swaths of the developing world that might gradually expand to encompass the world's industrialized centers—a vision some Chinese popular writers describe using Mao's revolutionary guidance to "surround the cities from the countryside" [农村包围城市].[6] More authoritative sources put this approach in less sweeping terms, suggesting Chinese order would be anchored in China's Belt and Road Initiative and its Community of Common Destiny, with the former in particular creating networks of coercive capability, consensual inducement, and legitimacy.[7]

Some of the strategy to achieve this global order is already discernable in Xi's speeches. Politically, Beijing would project leadership over global governance and international institutions, split Western alliances, and advance autocratic norms at the expense of liberal ones. Economically, it would weaken the financial advantages that underwrite US hegemony and seize the commanding heights of the "fourth industrial revolution" from artificial intelligence to quantum computing, with the United States declining into a "deindustrialized, English-speaking version of a Latin American republic, specializing in commodities, real estate, tourism, and perhaps transnational tax evasion."[8] Militarily, the People's Liberation Army (PLA) would field a world-class force with bases around the world that could defend China's interests in most regions and even in new domains like space, the poles, and the deep sea. The fact that aspects of this vision are visible in high-level speeches is strong evidence that China's ambitions are not limited to Taiwan or to dominating the Indo-Pacific. The "struggle for mastery," once confined to Asia, is now over the global order and its future. If there are two paths to hegemony—a regional one and a global one—China is now pursuing both.

This glimpse at possible Chinese order maybe striking, but it should not be surprising. Over a decade ago, Lee Kuan Yew—the visionary politician who built modern Singapore and personally knew China's top leaders—was asked by an interviewer, "Are Chinese leaders serious about displacing the United States as the number one power in Asia and in the world?" He answered with an emphatic yes. "Of course. Why not?" he began, "They have transformed a poor society by an economic miracle to become now the second-largest economy in the world—on track . . . to become the world's largest economy." China, he continued, boasts "a culture 4,000 years old with 1.3 billion people, with a huge and very talented pool to draw from. How could they not aspire to be number one in Asia, and in time the world?" China was "growing at rates unimaginable 50 years ago, a dramatic transformation no one predicted," he observed, and "every Chinese wants a strong and rich China, a nation as prosperous, advanced, and technologically competent as America, Europe, and Japan." He closed his answer with a key insight: "This reawakened sense of destiny is an overpowering force. . . . China wants to be China and accepted as such, not as an honorary member of the West." China might want to "share this century" with the United States, perhaps as "co-equals," he noted, but certainly not as subordinates.[9]

Why Grand Strategy Matters

The need for a grounded understanding of China's intentions and strategy has never been more urgent. China now poses a challenge unlike any the United States has ever faced. For more than a century, no US adversary or coalition of adversaries has reached 60 percent of US GDP. Neither Wilhelmine Germany during the First World War, the combined might of Imperial Japan and Nazi Germany during the Second World War, nor the Soviet Union at the height of its economic power ever crossed this threshold.[10] And yet, this is a milestone that China itself quietly reached as early as 2014. When one adjusts for the relative price of goods, China's economy is already 25 percent larger than the US economy.[11] It is clear, then, that China is the most significant competitor that the United States has faced and that the way Washington handles its emergence to superpower status will shape the course of the next century.

What is less clear, at least in Washington, is whether China has a grand strategy and what it might be. This book defines grand strategy as a state's theory of how it can achieve its strategic objectives that is intentional, coordinated, and implemented across multiple means of statecraft—military, economic, and political. What makes grand strategy "grand" is not simply the size of the strategic objectives but also the fact that disparate "means" are coordinated together to achieve it. That kind of coordination is rare, and most great powers consequently do not have a grand strategy.

When states do have grand strategies, however, they can reshape world history. Nazi Germany wielded a grand strategy that used economic tools to constrain its neighbors, military buildups to intimidate its rivals, and political alignments to encircle its adversaries—allowing it to outperform its great power competitors for a considerable time even though its GDP was less than one-third theirs. During the Cold War, Washington pursued a grand strategy that at times used military power to deter Soviet aggression, economic aid to curtail communist influence, and political institutions to bind liberal states together—limiting

Soviet influence without a US-Soviet war. How China similarly integrates its instruments of statecraft in pursuit of overarching regional and global objectives remains an area that has received abundant speculation but little rigorous study despite its enormous consequences. The coordination and long-term planning involved in grand strategy allow a state to punch above its weight; since China is already a heavyweight, if it has a coherent scheme that coordinates its $14 trillion economy with its blue-water navy and rising political influence around the world—and the United States either misses it or misunderstands it—the course of the twenty-first century may unfold in ways detrimental to the United States and the liberal values it has long championed.

Washington is belatedly coming to terms with this reality, and the result is the most consequential reassessment of its China policy in over a generation. And yet, amid this reassessment, there is wide-ranging disagreement over what China wants and where it is going. Some believe Beijing has global ambitions; others argue that its focus is largely regional. Some claim it has a coordinated 100-year plan; others that it is opportunistic and error-prone. Some label Beijing a boldly revisionist power; others see it as a sober-minded stakeholder of the current order. Some say Beijing wants the United States out of Asia; and others that it tolerates a modest US role. Where analysts increasingly agree is on the idea that China's recent assertiveness is a product of Chinese President Xi's personality—a mistaken notion that ignores the long-standing Party consensus in which China's behavior is actually rooted. The fact that the contemporary debate remains divided on so many fundamental questions related to China's grand strategy—and inaccurate even in its major areas of agreement—is troubling, especially since each question holds wildly different policy implications.

The Unsettled Debate

This book enters a largely unresolved debate over Chinese strategy divided between "skeptics" and "believers." The skeptics have not yet been persuaded that China has a grand strategy to displace the United States regionally or globally; by contrast, the believers have not truly attempted persuasion.

The skeptics are a wide-ranging and deeply knowledgeable group. "China has yet to formulate a true 'grand strategy,'" notes one member, "and the question is whether it wants to do so at all."[12] Others have argued that China's goals are "inchoate" and that Beijing lacks a "well-defined" strategy.[13] Chinese authors like Professor Wang Jisi, former dean of Peking University's School of International Relations, are also in the skeptical camp. "There is no strategy that we could come up with by racking our brains that would be able to cover all the aspects of our national interests," he notes.[14]

Other skeptics believe that China's aims are limited, arguing that China does not wish to displace the United States regionally or globally and remains focused primarily on development and domestic stability. One deeply experienced White House official was not yet convinced of "Xi's desire to throw the United States out of Asia and destroy U.S. regional alliances."[15] Other prominent scholars put the point more forcefully: "[One] hugely distorted notion is the now all-too-common assumption that China seeks to eject the United States from Asia and subjugate the region. In fact, no conclusive evidence exists of such Chinese goals."[16]

In contrast to these skeptics are the believers. This group is persuaded that China has a grand strategy to displace the United States regionally and globally, but it has not put forward a work to persuade the skeptics. Within government, some top intelligence officials—including former director of national intelligence Dan Coates—have stated publicly that "the Chinese fundamentally seek to replace the United States as the leading power in the world" but have not (or perhaps could not) elaborate further, nor did they suggest that this goal was accompanied by a specific strategy.[17]

Outside of government, only a few recent works attempt to make the case at length. The most famous is Pentagon official Michael Pillsbury's bestselling *One Hundred Year Marathon*, though it argues somewhat overstatedly that China has had a secret grand plan for global hegemony since 1949 and, in key places, relies heavily on personal authority and anecdote.[18] Many other books come to similar conclusions and get much right, but they are more intuitive than rigorously empirical and could have been more persuasive with a social scientific approach and a richer evidentiary base.[19] A handful of works on Chinese grand strategy take a broader perspective emphasizing the distant past or future, but they therefore dedicate less time to the critical stretch from the post–Cold War era to the present that is the locus of US-China competition.[20] Finally, some works mix a more empirical approach with careful and precise arguments about China's contemporary grand strategy. These works form the foundation for this book's approach.[21]

This book, which draws on the research of so many others, also hopes to stand apart in key ways. These include a unique social-scientific approach to defining and studying grand strategy; a large trove of rarely cited or previously inaccessible Chinese texts; a systematic study of key puzzles in Chinese military, political, and economic behavior; and a close look at the variables shaping strategic adjustment. Taken together, it is hoped that the book makes a contribution to the emerging China debate with a unique method for systematically and rigorously uncovering China's grand strategy.

Uncovering Grand Strategy

The challenge of deciphering a rival's grand strategy from its disparate behavior is not a new one. In the years before the First World War, the British diplomat Eyre Crowe wrote an important 20,000-word "Memorandum on the Present State of British Relations with France and Germany" that attempted to explain the wide-ranging behavior of a rising Germany.[22] Crowe was a keen observer of Anglo-German relations with a passion and perspective for the subject informed by his own heritage. Born in Leipzig and educated in Berlin and Düsseldorf, Crowe was half German, spoke German-accented English, and joined the British Foreign Office at the age of twenty-one. During World War I, his British and German families were literally at war with one another—his British nephew perished at sea while his German cousin rose to become chief of the German Naval Staff.

Crowe, who wrote his memorandum in 1907, sought to systematically analyze the disparate, complex, and seemingly uncoordinated range of German foreign behavior, to determine whether Berlin had a "grand design" that ran through it, and to report to his superiors what it might be. In order to "formulate and accept a theory that will fit all the ascertained facts of German foreign policy," Crowe argued in his framing of the enterprise, "the choice must lie between . . . two hypotheses"—each of which resemble the positions of today's skeptics and believers with respect to China's grand strategy.[23]

Crowe's first hypothesis was that Germany had no grand strategy, only what he called a "vague, confused, and unpractical statesmanship." In this view, Crowe wrote, it is possible that "Germany does not really know what she is driving at, and that all her excursions and alarums, all her underhand intrigues do not contribute to the steady working out of a well conceived and relentlessly followed system of policy."[24] Today, this argument mirrors those of skeptics who claim China's bureaucratic politics, factional infighting, economic priorities, and nationalist knee-jerk reactions all conspire to thwart Beijing from formulating or executing an overarching strategy.[25]

Crowe's second hypothesis was that important elements of German behavior were coordinated together through a grand strategy "consciously aiming at the establishment of a German hegemony, at first in Europe, and eventually in the world."[26] Crowe ultimately endorsed a more cautious version of this hypothesis, and he concluded that German strategy was "deeply rooted in the relative position of the two countries," with Berlin dissatisfied by the prospect of remaining subordinate to London in perpetuity.[27] This argument mirrors the position of believers in Chinese grand strategy. It also resembles the argument of this book: China has pursued a variety of strategies to displace the United States at the regional and global level which are fundamentally driven by its relative position with Washington.

The fact that the questions the Crowe memorandum explored have a striking similarity to those we are grappling with today has not been lost on US officials. Henry Kissinger quotes from it in *On China*. Max Baucus, former US ambassador to China, frequently mentioned the memo to his Chinese interlocutors as a roundabout way of inquiring about Chinese strategy.[28]

Crowe's memorandum has a mixed legacy, with contemporary assessments split over whether he was right about Germany. Nevertheless, the task Crowe set remains critical and no less difficult today, particularly because China is a "hard target" for information collection. One might hope to improve on Crowe's method with a more rigorous and falsifiable approach anchored in social science. As the next chapter discusses in detail, this book argues that to identify the existence, content, and adjustment of China's grand strategy, researchers must find evidence of (1) grand strategic concepts in authoritative texts; (2) grand strategic capabilities in national security institutions; and (3) grand strategic conduct in state behavior. Without such an approach, any analysis is more likely to fall victim to the kinds of natural biases in "perception and misperception" that often recur in assessments of other powers.[29]

Chapter Summaries

This book argues that, since the end of the Cold War, China has pursued a grand strategy to displace American order first at the regional and now at the global level.

Chapter 1 defines grand strategy and international order, and then explores how rising powers displace hegemonic order through strategies of blunting, building, and expansion. It explains how perceptions of the established hegemon's power and threat shape the selection of rising power grand strategies.

Chapter 2 focuses on the Chinese Communist Party as the connective institutional tissue for China's grand strategy. As a nationalist institution that emerged from the patriotic ferment of the late Qing period, the Party now seeks to restore China to its rightful place in the global hierarchy by 2049. As a Leninist institution with a centralized structure, ruthless amorality, and a Leninist vanguard seeing itself as stewarding a nationalist project, the Party possesses the "grand strategic capability" to coordinate multiple instruments of statecraft while pursuing national interests over parochial ones. Together, the Party's nationalist orientation helps set the ends of Chinese grand strategy while Leninism provides an instrument for realizing them. Now, as China rises, the same Party that sat uneasily within Soviet order during the Cold War is unlikely to permanently tolerate a subordinate role in American order. Finally, the chapter focuses on the Party as a subject of research, noting how a careful review of the Party's voluminous publications can provide insight into its grand strategic concepts.

The book then divides into three parts, each of which focuses on a different Chinese strategy of displacement. Part I discusses China's first strategy of displacement, which was to *blunt* American power under the broad strategic guidelines of "hiding capabilities and biding time."

Part I begins with Chapter 3, which explores the *blunting* phase of China's post–Cold War grand strategy using Chinese Communist Party texts. It demonstrates that China went from seeing the United States as a quasi-ally against the Soviets to seeing it as China's greatest threat and "main adversary" in the wake of three events: the traumatic trifecta of the Tiananmen Square Massacre, the Gulf War, and the Soviet Collapse. In response, Beijing launched its *blunting* strategy under the Party guideline of "hiding capabilities and biding time." This strategy was instrumental and tactical. Party leaders explicitly tied the guideline to perceptions of US power captured in phrases like the "international balance of forces" and "multipolarity," and they sought to quietly and asymmetrically weaken American power in Asia across military, economic, and political instruments, each of which is considered in the subsequent three book chapters.

Chapter 4 considers *blunting* at the military level. It shows that the trifecta prompted China to depart from a "sea control" strategy increasingly focused on holding distant maritime territory to a "sea denial" strategy focused on preventing the US military from traversing, controlling, or intervening in the waters near China. That shift was challenging, so Beijing declared it would "catch up in some areas and not others" and vowed to build "whatever the enemy fears" to accomplish it—ultimately delaying the acquisition of costly and vulnerable vessels like aircraft carriers and instead investing in cheaper asymmetric denial weapons. Beijing then built the world's largest mine arsenal, the world's first anti-ship ballistic missile, and the world's largest submarine fleet—all to undermine US military power.

Chapter 5 considers *blunting* at the political level. It demonstrates that the trifecta led China to reverse its previous opposition to joining regional institutions. Beijing feared that multilateral organizations like Asia-Pacific Economic Cooperation (APEC) and the Association of Southeast Asian Nations Regional Forum (ARF) might be used by Washington to build a liberal regional order or even an Asian NATO, so China joined them to blunt American power. It stalled institutional progress, wielded institutional rules to constrain US freedom of maneuver, and hoped participation would reassure wary neighbors otherwise tempted to join a US-led balancing coalition.

Chapter 6 considers *blunting* at the economic level. It argues that the trifecta laid bare China's dependence on the US market, capital, and technology—notably through Washington's post-Tiananmen sanctions and its threats to revoke most-favored-nation (MFN) trade status, which could have seriously damaged China's economy. Beijing sought not to decouple from the United States but instead to bind the discretionary use of American economic power, and it worked hard to remove MFN from congressional review through "permanent normal trading relations," leveraging negotiations in APEC and the World Trade Organization (WTO) to obtain it.

Because Party leaders explicitly tied *blunting* to assessments of American power, that meant that when those perceptions changed, so too did China's grand strategy. Part II of the book explores this second phase in Chinese grand strategy, which was focused on *building* regional order. The strategy took place under a modification to Deng's guidance to "hide capabilities and bide time," one that instead emphasized "*actively* accomplishing something."

Chapter 7 explores this *building* strategy in Party texts, demonstrating that the shock of the Global Financial Crisis led China to see the United States as weakening and emboldened it to shift to a *building* strategy. It begins with a thorough review of China's discourse on "multipolarity" and the "international balance of forces." It then shows that the Party sought to lay the foundations for order—coercive capacity, consensual bargains, and legitimacy—under the auspices of the revised guidance "actively accomplish something" [积极有所作为] issued by Chinese leader Hu Jintao. This strategy, like blunting before it, was implemented across multiple instruments of statecraft—military, political, and economic—each of which receives a chapter.

Chapter 8 focuses on *building* at the military level, recounting how the Global Financial Crisis accelerated a shift in Chinese military strategy away from a singular focus on blunting American power through sea denial to a new focus on building order through sea control. China now sought the capability to hold distant islands, safeguard sea lines, intervene in neighboring countries, and provide public security goods. For these objectives, China needed a different force structure, one that it had previously postponed for fear that it would be vulnerable to the United States and unsettle China's neighbors. These were risks a more confident Beijing was now willing to accept. China promptly stepped up investments in aircraft carriers, capable surface vessels, amphibious warfare, marines, and overseas bases.

Chapter 9 focuses on *building* at the political level. It shows how the Global Financial Crisis caused China to depart from a blunting strategy focused on joining and stalling regional organizations to a building strategy that involved launching its own institutions. China spearheaded the launch of the Asia Infrastructure Investment Bank (AIIB) and the elevation and institutionalization of the previously obscure Conference on Interaction and Confidence-Building Measures in Asia (CICA). It then used these institutions, with mixed success, as instruments to shape regional order in the economic and security domains in directions it preferred.

Chapter 10 focuses on building at the economic level. It argues that the Global Financial Crisis helped Beijing depart from a defensive blunting strategy that targeted American economic leverage to an offensive building strategy designed to build China's own coercive and consensual economic capacities. At the core of this effort were China's Belt and Road Initiative, its robust use of economic statecraft against its neighbors, and its attempts to gain greater financial influence.

Beijing used these blunting and building strategies to constrain US influence within Asia and to build the foundations for regional hegemony. The relative success of that strategy was remarkable, but Beijing's ambitions were not limited only to the Indo-Pacific. When Washington was again seen as stumbling, China's grand strategy evolved—this time in a more global direction. Accordingly, Part III of this book focuses on China's third grand strategy of displacement, global *expansion*, which sought to blunt but especially build global order and to displace the United States from its leadership position.

Chapter 11 discusses the dawn of China's *expansion* strategy. It argues that the strategy emerged following another trifecta, this time consisting of Brexit, the election of Donald Trump, and the West's poor initial response to the coronavirus pandemic. In this period, the Chinese Communist Party reached a paradoxical consensus: it concluded that the United States was in retreat globally but at the same time was waking up to the China challenge bilaterally. In Beijing's mind, "great changes unseen in a century" were underway, and they provided an opportunity to displace the United States as the leading global state by 2049, with the next decade deemed the most critical to this objective.

Chapter 12 discusses the "ways and means" of China's strategy of expansion. It shows that politically, Beijing would seek to project leadership over global governance and international institutions and to advance autocratic norms. Economically, it would weaken the financial advantages that underwrite US hegemony and seize the commanding heights of the "fourth industrial revolution." And militarily, the PLA would field a truly global Chinese military with overseas bases around the world.

Chapter 13, the book's final chapter, outlines a US response to China's ambitions for displacing the United States from regional and global order. It critiques those who advocate a counterproductive strategy of confrontation or an accommodationist one of grand bargains, each of which respectively discounts US domestic headwinds and China's strategic ambitions. The chapter instead argues for an asymmetric competitive strategy, one that does not require matching China dollar-for-dollar, ship-for-ship, or loan-for-loan.

This cost-effective approach emphasizes denying China hegemony in its home region and—taking a page from elements of China's own blunting strategy—focuses on undermining Chinese efforts in Asia and worldwide in ways that are of lower cost than Beijing's efforts to build hegemony. At the same time, this chapter argues that the United States should pursue order-building as well, reinvesting in the very same foundations of American global order that Beijing presently seeks to weaken. This discussion seeks to convince policymakers that even as the United States faces challenges at home and abroad, it can still secure its interests and resist the spread of an illiberal sphere of influence—but only if it recognizes that the key to defeating an opponent's strategy is first to understand it.

1

"A Coherent Body of Thought and Action"

Grand Strategy and Hegemonic Order

"We're a nation of specialties. We tend to think a problem is either economic or political or military. . . . It is hard for us to understand we have to be able to do military and political and economic . . . all simultaneously."[1]

—*Henry Kissinger, 1958*

Three hundred years ago, the word *strategy* would have generated blank stares from statesmen across Europe and the Americas for one simple reason: it did not exist. The closest analog was the forgotten word *strategia* in a few ancient Greek texts, and that word referred narrowly to "the means by which the general may defend his own lands and defeat his enemies."[2] It was not until a French soldier and scholar translated an old Byzantine military treatise in the eighteenth century that the word reemerged and took on a broader meaning in Western circles. Now, *strategy* and its cousin, *grand strategy*, have become indispensable to thinking about world politics—even as the definitions remain elusive.

The concepts "grand strategy" and "international order" are at the center of this book's argument, which is that China has wielded the former to displace American leadership over the latter. To lay the foundation for this argument, this chapter explores both concepts across three short sections. First, it seeks to explain what grand strategy is and how to find it. Second, it explores what international order is and why it is at the center of US-China competition. Finally, it asks what grand strategies rising powers might use to shape order and which variables might cause them to shift from one strategy to another.

In Search of Grand Strategy

What is *grand strategy*? The term is "one of the most slippery and widely abused terms in the foreign policy lexicon," notes Johns Hopkins professor Hal Brands.[3] Most definitions of the term fit into two broad categories. One restricts grand strategy to a focus only on military means, which is problematic because it converts "grand strategy" into "military strategy" and ignores economic and political tools. The other defines grand strategy as the use of any means to accomplish any ends, but this makes grand strategy no different from strategy itself.

A better approach—one that keeps "grand strategy" distinctive as a concept—is to view it as an *integrated security theory*. Security is defined here as "sovereignty [i.e., freedom of maneuver or autonomy], safety, territorial integrity, and power position—the last being the necessary means to the first three."[4] A grand strategy is a state's theory of how it can achieve these security-related ends for itself that is intentional, coordinated, and implemented across multiple means of statecraft, such as military, economic, and political instruments.

This definition is also rooted in the term's historical evolution over the last two centuries. As strategists and scholars watched the emergence of the modern industrial state and its multiplying set of capabilities and instruments—from the Napoleonic era through the age of steamships and into the total wars of the twentieth century—they too gradually broadened their conception of the *means* of grand strategy from military to other tools even as they continued to see the *end* of grand strategy as grounded in security, arriving at a definition similar to that employed here.[5]

How might we divine China's grand strategy from its seemingly disjointed behavior? As the Introduction noted, this is not an entirely new challenge. In 1907, the British diplomat Eyre Crowe wrote a lengthy and influential memo that attempted to explain the wide-ranging behavior of a rising Germany.[6] While Crowe's memo is still debated today, it nonetheless provided a useful foundation for studying grand strategy that we can improve upon with a more rigorous and falsifiable approach anchored in social science.

Crowe argued that German strategy could "be deduced from her history, from the utterances and known designs of her rulers and statesmen" and from "ascertained facts of German behavior"—that is, texts and behavior. To Crowe's emphasis on these two factors, we might add one more factor—national security institutions. Pulling these approaches together yields a focus on three elements. States must have a set of:

(1) *grand strategic concepts* about how the ends, ways, and means of strategy fit together;

(2) *grand strategic capabilities* in national security institutions to coordinate diverse instruments of statecraft to pursue national interests over parochial ones; and

(3) *grand strategic conduct* that is ultimately consistent with a state's strategic concepts.

The alternative to these rigorous criteria for identifying grand strategy is to adopt a "know-it-when-you-see-it" approach that is common but risks misdiagnosis, which can be dangerous if it influences policy. To determine whether the preceding criteria are met requires a social-scientific focus on three elements: the *texts* that contain grand strategic concepts; the *institutions* that demonstrate grand strategic capability; and the *behavior* that evinces grand strategic conduct.

With respect to *texts*, the core foundation of the book is its focus on authoritative documents through an original and fully digitized database of Chinese-language Communist Party documents personally excavated over the last three years from libraries; bookstores in Taiwan, Hong Kong, and mainland China; and Chinese e-commerce sites (see Appendix). These texts not only provide insight into grand strategic concepts, but they also touch on grand strategic capabilities by highlighting how institutions work, as well as on grand strategic conduct by showing why certain decisions were taken.

This leads to the second major method. In addition to texts, the book focuses on Chinese national security *institutions* as evidence of China's grand strategic capability. Some of the key Party institutions in foreign policy—the General Secretary's office, the Politburo Standing Committee, the Leading Small Groups (many now called Central Commissions), and the Central Military Commission—publish virtually nothing directly and are extremely challenging to study given the secretiveness surrounding their activities. Sometimes various Party texts—including memoirs, selected works, compendiums, and readouts—can provide important, limited insights into key speeches, decisions, study sessions, and debates within these institutions. And these in turn offer insight into China's grand strategy.

Finally, the third method looks at *behavior*. As Crowe observed, great powers undertake a wide range of activities across every domain. It is not always easy to separate signal and noise and determine what is strategically motivated and what is not. Given this challenge, a social-scientific approach can help. Scholars can look at military, economic, and political behavior; determine whether puzzling behavior in each domain is best explained through grand strategic logic; look for synchronized shifts across policy domains as evidence of coordination; and consult Party texts to understand why China acted the way it did. These efforts shed light on China's grand strategic conduct.

Taken together, the preceding approach yields several key questions critical to identifying China's grand strategy listed in Table 1.1. Massachusetts Institute of Technology professor Barry Posen once said that to find grand strategy we must look for "a coherent body of thought and action," and the questions below structure the search for it.[7]

Moreover, these questions assist not only in identifying whether a grand strategy exists, but also in determining *what* it is as well as *when* and *why* it changes. Grand strategy is rare, and changes in grand strategy are rarer still. As the Tufts University scholar Daniel Drezner notes, changing grand strategy "is like trying to make an aircraft carrier do a U-turn: it happens slowly at best," leaving "grand strategy a constant rather than a variable."[8] The "stickiness" of a state's grand strategy comes from both psychological and organizational factors. Research in psychology suggests that "people do not readily alter their beliefs

Table 1.1 **Questions for Identifying Grand Strategy**

Identifying Grand Strategy:
Key Questions

Concepts **(Texts)**	1. Ends: Is there a consistent view on which security threats, of all those a country faces, are most significant or fundamental?
	2. Ways: Is there a consistent set of ideas about how to address those significant or fundamental threats in core texts?
	3. Means: Is there a theory of what role each of the major means of statecraft plays in addressing a given security threat in core texts?
Capability **(Institutions)**	4. Coordination: Do we see evidence that policymakers have bureaucratic institutions they can use to coordinate multiple instruments of statecraft?
	5. Autonomy: Do foreign policy institutions and the broader state have a degree of autonomy from the society and various domestic forces that might supersede grand strategy?
Conduct **(Behavior)**	6. Variation within Means: Does our theory of a given state's grand strategy explain variation in behavior in specific policy domains better than prevailing theories of state behavior in those domains?
	7. Variation across Means: Does our theory of a given state's grand strategy apply not to one but to multiple policy domains, such as military, economic, and political domains?
	8. Synchronized Variation: When grand strategy changes, do we see changes in behavior synchronized across each of the three means of statecraft?

about the world and do not easily confront their own mistakes," and that "once they are committed to a particular perspective, judgment, or course of action, it is difficult to get them to change their mind."[9] Organizational research finds that "resource constraints, transaction costs, internal politics, and the domestic environment in which organizations operate," combined with formal rules and standard-operating-procedures, together help explain "why decision makers will typically feel pressure not to deviate radically from the status quo."[10] Together, these factors lock in grand strategy.

If grand strategies are "sticky," what then causes them to shift? This book argues that grand strategies rest on perceptions of power and threat, and that shifts in these perceptions "are driven more by events, especially shocks, than statistical measures" like gradually changing GDP growth rates or fleet sizes.[11] By comparing descriptions of power and threat in Chinese texts before and after foreign policy shocks—such as the Tiananmen Square Massacre, the Gulf War, the Soviet collapse, and the Global Financial Crisis, among others—one can determine whether perceptions of power and threat changed and produced strategic adjustment too.

The Contest for Order

As US-China competition intensified over the last few years, a number of policymakers and scholars have frequently returned to the same question: "What is this competition over?" This book argues that US-China competition is over who will lead regional and global order.[12]

Although international relations scholars have generally assumed the world to be anarchic, the reality is that it has often been hierarchic, with some states exercising authority over other states.[13] The number, scope, and density of these hierarchical relationships produce order, or "the settled rules and arrangements between states" that can govern both their external and internal behavior.[14] In a hegemonic order, the preeminent state "mobilizes its leadership" atop the hierarchy to structure relations between states and within them.[15] Hegemonic orders involve what former Princeton professor Robert Gilpin called some "form of control" by a dominant state to regulate its subordinates, and that control often involves a mixture of coercive capability (to force compliance), consensual inducements (to incentivize it), and legitimacy (to rightfully command it).[16]

Coercion emerges from the threat of punishment. Coercive capability can flow from a state's military strength or its structural power over key chokepoints in the system, including currency, trade, and technology, among others. Consensual inducements involve the ability to incentivize or even "bribe" cooperation through mutually beneficial bargains or enticements. It often involves voice opportunities, security guarantees, public or private goods provision, or elite capture. Finally, legitimacy is the capability to command simply by virtue of the dominant state's identity or ideology. Legitimacy can flow from ideological affinity, symbolic capital, or other sources and can function as a kind of authority. For example, centuries ago the Vatican was able to command states over which it exercised little material power simply due to its theological role. Together, coercive capacity, consensual inducements, and legitimacy secure the deference of states within order.

This mixture of coercion, consent, and legitimacy is hardly uniform, and accordingly, hegemonic orders can vary in their content and geographic reach. Some forms of order, like empire, rely more on coercion; others, like the American liberal order, emphasize consensual inducements and legitimacy. Most orders are stronger in some regions than in others, and most eventually face competitive challenges that can cause them to change.

The question of how orders change is a perennial one with relevance today. Hegemonic orders like the one the United States leads today are believed to change primarily through massive great power war, with conflicts like the Second World War ending one order and launching another. Since great power war is now less likely given the nuclear revolution, some mistakenly see the present order as fundamentally stable. That perspective discounts the nature of peacetime great power competition and the possibility of order transition short of war. Orders can change peacefully when their forms of control—coercive capability, consensual inducement, and legitimacy—are undermined, and they can strengthen when these forms of control are bolstered. These processes can occur gradually or all at once, but like the relatively peaceful collapse of the Soviet Union, they need not require war.[17]

Strategies of Displacement

How might a rising power like China seek to displace an established hegemon like the United States short of war?[18] If a hegemon's position in order emerges from "forms of control" like coercion, consent, and legitimacy, then competition over order revolves around efforts to strengthen and weaken these forms of control. Accordingly, rising states like China can peacefully displace hegemonic powers like the United States through two broad strategies generally pursued in sequence:

I. The first is to *blunt* the hegemon's exercise of its forms of control, particularly those that are extended over the rising state; after all, no rising state can displace the hegemon if it remains largely at the hegemon's mercy.

II. The second is to *build* forms of control over others, as well as the foundations for consensual bargains and legitimacy; indeed, no rising state can become a hegemon if it cannot constrain the autonomy of others or entice them with consensual bargains and legitimacy to ensure that they follow the rising state's preferences.

For rising powers, the decision to deploy these grand strategies takes place in the shadow of the hegemon's power and influence, which presents considerable risks. A rising power that openly pursues order-building too soon might cause the hegemon to intervene in the rising power's home region, rally the rising power's neighbors to encircle it, or cut off the rising power from the goods that the hegemonic order provides. For these reasons, blunting strategies that seek to weaken a hegemon's order generally precede building ones that seek to erect a rising power's own order. Moreover, both strategies are often pursued at the regional level before a rising power turns to a third strategy, global *expansion*, which involves both blunting and building at the global level to displace hegemonic order.

When might a power pursue *expansion*? While some scholars like University of Chicago professor John Mearsheimer argue that a rising power like China must first achieve regional hegemony before pursuing wider global ambitions, this criterion is perhaps too narrow.[19] As other scholars like former Princeton professor Robert Gilpin would argue, a rising power lacking regional hegemony could still challenge the hegemon globally over the crosscutting "forms of control" that sustain its global hegemonic order, such as economics, finance, technology, and information. Germany challenged Britain's global dominance in these domains before the First World War despite lacking regional hegemony in Europe, and China appears to be doing so as well today.[20] What matters is not whether a rising power like China has full regional hegemony but rather whether it has done enough blunting and building in its home region to have confidence that it can manage the risks of hegemonic intervention if it pursues global *expansion*.

Some might be skeptical that a rising state like China would do any of this, but rising powers—like most states—are generally revisionist. Some might consider this a controversial claim, but the fairly modest assumption that most states have their own thoughts about how regional and global order should function and would act to realize them if the costs of doing so were low should be unsurprising. Indeed, when costs are low, great powers exhibit what we might call "hegemonic drift" toward order-building in one's neighborhood or elsewhere. Even when the United States was reluctant to act as a great power abroad in the nineteenth century, it nonetheless drifted toward exercising hegemony in the Western Hemisphere. The key question is not whether rising states have alternate preferences for order but instead whether, when, and how they choose to act on them.

Because the hegemon looms largest in the strategic calculations of a rising power, this book argues that the choice to "revise" order is based on perceptions of the hegemon. Two variables are critically important: (1) the size of the *perceived relative power gap* with an external hegemon, which refers broadly to the hegemon's *capacity* to harm the interests of the rising power; and (2) the *perceived threat* from the external hegemon, which applies to the hegemon's perceived *willingness* to use that power to cause harm.[21] Defining these variables perceptually is critical because what is most relevant to strategic formulation is not an objective measure of power and threat (which is elusive in any case) but instead a state's own assessment of a rival's power and threat. For simplicity, both these variables are rendered in Table 1.2 as high or low. Finally, while blunting and building are strategies for revising order, great powers can also pursue other strategies, definitions of which will follow.

First, when the rising power views the hegemon as much more powerful than it but not particularly threatening, the rising power tends to *accommodate* hegemonic order even when its own preferences differ from those of the external hegemon. Accommodation can be driven by the desire to avoid turning the external hegemon into a hostile force or to benefit from partnership with the hegemon against a third party. Accordingly, a rising power might tolerate or even support a hegemon's regional military presence, leadership of regional organizations, and sponsorship of regional economic initiatives. One example of this strategy is India's accommodation of the United States within South Asia because it perceives the United States as powerful, not particularly threatening, and helpful against China. Another might be China's policy toward the United States in the 1980s.

Second, when a rising power thinks the hegemon is much more powerful than it and also very threatening, then the rising power will pursue a *blunting* strategy that targets the hegemon's forms of control—coercion, consent, and legitimacy—regionally or globally. In this scenario, the rising state cannot accommodate a hegemon it sees as threatening nor can it overtly oppose a hegemon

Table 1.2 **Grand Strategies of Rising Powers toward Hegemonic Order**

		Perceived Relative Power Gap with External Hegemon	
		High	*Low*
Perceived External Threat from External Hegemon	*High*	Blunting	Building
	Low	Accommodation	Dominance

it sees as powerful, forcing the rising power to resort to "weapons of the weak" to blunt the hegemon's leverage.[22] At the military level, it might pursue defensive military capabilities to deter the hegemon from regional intervention while eschewing capabilities that would alarm the rising state's neighbors and trigger encirclement; in political terms, it might seek to reduce the external hegemon's role in regional bodies; and in economic terms, it might seek to protect itself from the hegemon's use of economic statecraft. China pursued a version of this strategy throughout the 1990s until roughly 2008.

Third, when a rising power thinks the external hegemon is only modestly more powerful than it but still very threatening, the rising power will pursue a *building* strategy to construct the foundations for its own order by investing in its own forms of control—coercive capability, consensual inducements, and legitimacy. The rising power is powerful enough to accept the risk of hegemonic opposition but not so powerful that it can freely dominate its region since doing so might create an opening for the external hegemon. At the military level, it might pursue capabilities that allow for coercion, intervention, power projection, and control (rather than denial) of the land, air, and sea; politically, it might establish new institutions to govern the region and sideline the hegemon; and economically, it might deliberately cultivate asymmetric interdependence that appears beneficial but actually constrains others. These efforts may even resemble the kinds of liberal order-building strategies that scholars like Princeton professor John Ikenberry believe secure the consent of weaker states and avoid balancing. And when undertaken successfully in a state's home region, they can allow the rising power to pursue *expansion* at the global level. China has pursued this strategy from 2008 onward, and it formed the foundation for the strategy of *expansion* it pursued after 2016.

Fourth, when a rising power thinks the external hegemon is only slightly more powerful and not particularly threatening, then the rising power has greater freedom to pursue dominance over others in the order because it is unconcerned about rival order-building efforts or hegemonic intervention. While building might involve a mixture of coercion and consensual inducements, dominance might overweight coercive tools given the lack of a challenge to order or possible balancing coalition. In military terms, a rising state may more frequently deploy force; in political terms, it may create rules and norms to "lock in" the rising state's interests and undermine all competing institutions; and in economic terms, it may pursue extraction in addition to the cultivation of asymmetric interdependence. US strategy in Latin America during the late nineteenth and early twentieth centuries, when European relative power was low and when European threats in Latin America were less serious than they had been decades earlier, might serve as an example of this strategy.

These four strategies generally occur sequentially from accommodation to blunting to building and then to dominance, but there are exceptions: a state may move from blunting to accommodation after a rapprochement with the external hegemon; or it may move from accommodation to dominance if a benign hegemon is perceived as having weakened.

In China's case, the conventional sequence appears to be at work: China initially accommodated a powerful but non-threatening United States after normalization; sought to blunt it after the Cold War's conclusion led it to see the United States as more threatening; began to build its own order after the Global Financial Crisis led it to see the United States as weakening; and may pursue regional dominance if the United States acquiesces or is defeated in a regional conflict. Much of the theory, practice, and empirical evidence of this Chinese grand strategy is intertwined with the Chinese Communist Party and its worldview and organization. We now turn to that institution and the role of nationalism and Leninism in shaping the Party, and in turn, China's grand strategy.

2

"The Party Leads Everything"

Nationalism, Leninism, and the Chinese Communist Party

"The Soviets can do something after just one Politburo meeting. Can
the Americans do that?"[1]

—*Deng Xiaoping to China's Politburo, early 1980s*

In June 1987, China's de facto leader Deng Xiaoping was in a meeting with
Yugoslav officials, and he was worried. China was in the midst of "reform and
opening," a series of market reforms propelling China's economy forward
and ultimately laying the foundation for its rise to superpower status. But the
journey was far from smooth. A few months earlier, China had faced some of
its worst political instability and unrest since the Cultural Revolution—which
led Deng to purge the Party's general secretary, Hu Yaobang, for his reformist
sympathies.

During his meeting, Deng's mind kept turning to China's political situation,
and he routinely drifted away from talk of economic reform and instead held forth
on the benefits of the Leninist party-state for policymaking. "One of the greatest
advantages" of Leninist systems, he told his guests, "is that, as long as something
has been decided and a resolution has been made, it can be carried out immediately without any restrictions."[2] Unlike the Americans, he declared, "our effi-
ciency is higher; we carry things out as soon as we have made up our mind. . . . It is
our strength, and we must retain this advantage."[3] Deng's handpicked lieutenant,
Zhao Ziyang, noted years later that Deng would return to this point throughout
his leadership: "Deng regarded a system without restrictions or checks and balances, and with absolute concentration of power, as our overall advantage . . . he
adored the high concentration of power and dictatorship."[4]

Deng's love affairs with Leninism began some sixty years earlier. Like so many
of the Chinese communists of his generation, Deng entered politics through nationalism. He had participated in the ferment of the May 4th movement and

traveled to France to learn, in his words, how to "save China."[5] And like so many of the nationalists of his generation, Deng found an instrument for realizing his political project in Leninism. After his entry into communist organizing in France, Deng enrolled in his early twenties at Sun Yat-sen University in Moscow, where he learned the theory and practice of Leninist party-building and organization. "Centralized power flows from the top down," he wrote in an essay at the time on why democracy was ill-suited for China and Russia; "it is absolutely necessary to obey the directives of the leadership."[6] As the MIT political scientist Lucian Pye observed, through these and other experiences, "Deng was socialized to be a true Leninist" dedicated to sustaining "the organizational integrity, and hence the power monopoly, of the Party."[7] And Deng was hardly alone in "adoring" Leninism, as his lieutenant Zhao had put it. Other leading nationalists, including Sun Yat-sen and his successor Chiang Kai-shek, similarly adopted Leninist precepts. For them as for Deng, Leninism was the means by which to achieve their vision of a wealthy and powerful China.

The high-level coordination, integration, and implementation of policymaking that Deng and other Chinese communists valued certainly has advantages for China's grand strategy. The Party sits above the state and penetrates every level of it as well. In this way, it serves as an instrument for *coordinating* grand strategy and gives policymakers relative *autonomy* from parochial interests in foreign policy matters so that they can pursue grand strategic ones. As Mao once put it, and Xi recently reiterated, "Party, government, military, civilian, and academic, north, south, east, west, and center, the Party leads everything."[8]

This chapter focuses on what the Party's leadership means for Chinese grand strategy. In so doing, it draws from an original collection of Party compendiums, memoirs, selected works, articles, and other materials.

The focus on the Party may at times feel anachronistic to some in the press or media, but not long ago it was widely understood that such a focus would be important. "Western elites were once familiar with the order of battle in communist politics" during the struggle with the Soviet Union, notes the journalist Richard McGregor, and they benefited from and invested in "the mini-industry in academia, think-tanks and journalism known as Kremlinology."[9] But "the collapse of the Soviet empire in the early 1990s took with it much of the deep knowledge of communist systems," with a steadily diminishing number of experts from academia and the intelligence community left to pass on that knowledge as funding declined.[10] China's economic ascent, for a time, obscured public interest in the Party's inner workings too, though all this has begun to change. There is now a renewed understanding that, as the scholar David Shambaugh once observed, "Few, if any, issues affect the future of China—and hence all the nations that interact with it—more than the nature of its ruling party and government."[11]

In exploring the Party's relationship to grand strategy, this chapter undertakes three broad tasks. First, it focuses on the Chinese Communist Party (CCP) as a nationalist party, one that emerged from the patriotic ferment of the late Qing period and has sought to restore the country to its rightful place. Second, it focuses on the CCP as a Leninist party, one that has built centralized institutions—blended with a ruthless amorality—to govern the country and achieve its nationalist mission. Together, the Party's nationalist orientation helps set the ends of Chinese grand strategy, while Leninism provides an instrument for realizing them. Finally, the book focuses on the CCP as a producer of paper and a subject of research, noting how a careful study of the Party's own voluminous publications can provide insight into its grand strategic concepts. That section outlines much of the textual research strategy employed in the rest of this book.

A Nationalist Party

It can be controversial to argue that the Chinese Communist Party is a nationalist party. Many see its public focus on nationalist credentials as instrumental, a part of a broader search for new sources of legitimacy after the tarnishing of communist ideology. The reality is more complicated. While China did indeed launch a "patriotic education" campaign after the Tiananmen Square Massacre and the Soviet collapse to amplify nationalist themes publicly, other scholars note that nationalism has long been ingrained in the Party's ideology and identity, with a long historical line connecting the Party of today with the nationalist ferment of the late Qing Dynasty.

The core theme animating the Party across that stretch is the search for something that could restore China to its former greatness and would help it achieve the goal of "national rejuvenation." Today, that phrase is at the center of Xi Jinping's political project, but it has a deep history that has pervaded China's political exertions for almost two centuries. As Zhen Wang notes, the concept "goes at least as far back as Sun Yat-sen, and has been invoked by almost every modern Chinese leader from Chiang Kai-Shek to Jiang Zemin and Hu Jintao."[12] Rejuvenation provides a sense of mission not only for China's domestic reforms but for its grand strategy as well.

Wealth and Power

In the 1790s, as George Washington was settling into his first term of office in the United States, the Qing Dynasty was at its height. But over the next few decades, repeated provincial unrest, foreign depredations, and a sclerotic government led some officials to sense that China was entering decline.

Wei Yuan was one of those officials, and he resurrected a tradition in Chinese intellectual history that focused on the state's pursuit of "wealth and power" (富强) as opposed to the more typical Confucian tradition of "rule of the virtuous"(德治). When China's domestic decay collided with European imperial ambition in the disastrous First Opium War, what China calls its "Century of Humiliation" began. As the country declined, a growing intellectual focus emerged on how to gain strength to recapture past glory. As Orville Schell and John Delury note in their sweeping intellectual history of China's obsession with "wealth and power," Wei Yuan's resurrection of the 2,000-year-old phrase came at the right time, and it has "remained something of a north star for Chinese intellectual and political leaders" ever since.[13]

In the century that followed the First Opium War, China suffered a series of humiliating defeats that cracked the edifice of the Qing Dynasty and gave rise to generations of scholars and activists who built on Wei Yuan's "wealth and power foundations." Feng Guifen, an intellectual successor to Wei Yuan, watched the Second Opium War and the Taiping Rebellion that almost toppled the Qing and helped launch the Self-Strengthening Movement. He influenced a generation of scholars as well as Li Hongzhang, the general and statesman discussed in this book's Introduction.

Two decades after Feng Guifen's death, the situation had little improved, and Japan then shocked China by defeating it in the first Sino-Japanese War. That defeat proved traumatic for scholars like Kang Youwei and Liang Qichao, as well as nationalist revolutionaries like Sun Yat-sen, who were spurred on to offer their own paths for China to pursue, all with the ultimate aim of self-strengthening.

These individuals and the broader nationalist discourse of which they were a part were dedicated to rejuvenating China and catching up with the West, and their words and deeds formed the soil in which China's Communist Party would grow. Many of the CCP's early leaders were patriotic youth drawn to what was essentially a restorative nationalist project. Some, like Deng Xiaoping, participated in nationalist events like the May 4th movement and were drawn "to the national effort to rid China of the humiliation it had suffered" and "to make it rich and strong."[14] Like many future communists, Deng went abroad to study, and he explained his reasoning with an answer right out of Wei Yuan's focus on "wealth and power": "China was weak and we wanted to make her stronger, and China was poor and we wanted to make her richer. We went to the West in order to study and find a way to save China."[15]

In addition to travel and protest, many leading communist figures, including Chen Duxiu, Zhou Enlai, and Mao Zedong, found their way to nationalism through authors like Kang Youwei and Liang Qichao. Mao later recounted that he "worshipped Kang Youwei and Liang Qichao" and "read and re-read them" until he had memorized their works, and that when he was young, he put up posters advocating that Sun Yat-sen be made China's president, Kang its premier, and Liang its foreign minister.[16] Deng Xiaoping's own father was reportedly a member of Liang Qichao's political party, which undoubtedly shaped Deng's early nationalist worldview.[17] Many future communists were drawn to Sun Yat-sen, who is still revered by the CCP. Indeed, Sun Yat-sen's nationalists had set up a government and military academy in Guangzhou that "attracted promising patriotic youth" to the city, including many who rose to prominence like Zhou Enlai, Ye Jianying, Lin Biao, and Mao Zedong.[18]

Once in power, and even as they pursued policies in line with their own communist ideology, the Party nonetheless remained motivated by an unmistakably nationalist mission, and closing the wealth and power gap with the West was at its center. Mao-era industrial modernization, the failed Great Leap Forward, the desire for "two bombs, one satellite," and the extraordinarily dangerous move to step out from Soviet order and claim the mantle of ideological leadership from Moscow were all motivated by these nationalist impulses. Deng Xiaoping's reform and opening, and his emphasis on economic and technological advancement, explicitly emulated the language of an earlier generation of self-strengtheners. His successors, including Jiang, Hu, and Xi, have carried forward the nationalist project and focused on rejuvenating China and restoring it to its rightful place in regional and global order.

Rejuvenation

"Sun Yat-sen," Jiang Zemin once noted, "was the first man to put forward the 'rejuvenate China' slogan."[19] And it was indeed from Sun Yat-sen that the CCP took up the language of rejuvenation [振兴中华 or 复兴] that has been a mainstay ever since.

In 1894, as China and Japan went to war, Sun Yat-sen founded the Xingzhonghui, which roughly translates as the Revive China Society, and declared as its mission rejuvenating China. Even amid the Second Sino-Japanese War, Deng and other Party members encouraged cadres to focus on the "road to rejuvenation," and when the Communists were victorious, Mao declared that "only the CCP can save China."[20] When China began reform and opening in 1978, Deng and his deputies Hu Yaobang and Zhao Ziyang repeatedly made clear that the purpose was to "rejuvenate China" [征信中华] and ensure it achieved "wealth and power." In 1988, Jiang Zemin stated that the Party's mission was to "realize the great rejuvenation of the Chinese nation."[21]

The centrality of these sentiments to the Party is confirmed by the fact that they appear in virtually every Party Congress address, which as we will soon see, are among the Party's most authoritative texts. Hu Yaobang's 12th Party Congress address in 1982 bemoaned the "century or more between the Opium War and liberation" and pledged China would "never allow itself to be humiliated again."[22] His successor, Zhao Ziyang, gave the 13th Party Congress address in 1987 using the language of "wealth and power" and arguing that "reform is the only way China can achieve rejuvenation."[23] Jiang Zemin's addresses across the 14th, 15th, and 16th Party Congresses recounted the Opium Wars and Century of Humiliation, praised the Party for having "put an end to the Chinese nation's tragic history," and reminded audiences that "the Chinese Communist Party is deeply rooted in the Chinese nation" and has "shouldered the great and solemn mission of national rejuvenation since the day it was founded."[24] Hu's 17th and 18th Party Congress addresses repeated these themes and added that the Party was "striving for the great rejuvenation of the Chinese nation for which count-less patriots and revolutionary martyrs yearned."[25] Most recently, Xi Jinping's 19th Party Congress in 2017 put rejuvenation at the center of his "China Dream" and his "new era" for China. He referenced the tragedy of the Opium Wars, and declared rejuvenation as "the original aspiration and mission of the Chinese Communists"—one only the Party could achieve.[26]

The Party has from its founding wrapped itself in the exertions of the nationalists who came before it. Top leaders have declared for almost a century that "the Chinese Communist Party has inherited and developed the spirit of the May 4th movement" and was striving to "learn from and carry forward" the legacy of Sun Yat-sen.[27] As Hu Jintao noted on the centennial of Mao's birth, the Party is in a relay race toward rejuvenation. "History is a long river," he declared. "Today developed from yesterday, and tomorrow is a continuation of today."[28] "The great rejuvenation of the Chinese nation is the great ideal of Mao Zedong, Deng Xiaoping, their comrades, and millions of revolutionary martyrs.... Today, the baton of history has reached our hands."[29]

The "baton of history" must be carried by successive leaders until mid-century, or the centennial of the Party's assumption of power. For at least forty years, China's top leaders have all indicated that this is the target date for achieving re-juvenation, a goal that has generally involved closing the gap with the West, and in some cases, shaping the global system. The focus on the middle of the century emerged in the mid-1980s when Deng and his lieutenants put it forward as the date for reaching the level of "moderately developed countries" or completing "socialist modernization."[30]

Success in this goal would have enormous implications. In 1985, in an impor-tant address to China's second-ever "National Congress" (中国共产党全国代表会议) convened to adjust national policy, Deng declared, "By the middle of the next century, when we approach the level of the developed countries, then there will have been really great changes. At that time the strength of China and its role in the world will be quite different."[31] This timeline effectively became China's timeline for rejuvenation shortly thereafter. As Deng's successor Jiang put it, "our goal is by the middle of this century to . . . realize the great rejuvenation of the Chinese nation."[32] In a major speech commemorating the eightieth anniversary of the Party, Jiang elaborated on the timeline: "In the 100 years from the middle of the 20th century to the middle of the 21st century, all the struggles of the Chinese people have been to achieve wealth and power for the homeland . . . and the great rejuvenation of the nation. In this historic cause [of rejuvenation], our party has led the people of the country for 50 years and made tremendous progress; after another 50 years of hard work, it will be successfully completed."[33]

What might completion mean in practical terms? Deng had suggested it would change China's relationship with the world, and later that it would have critics "completely convinced" of the superiority of China's socialist system.[34] Jiang agreed, and stressed that it was a kind of restoration relative to the West. Before its fall under the Qing, Jiang noted, "China's economic level was leading in the world" and "China's economic aggregate ranked first in the world."[35] Accordingly, rejuvenation would involve "narrowing the gap with the world's advanced level" and making China "wealthy and powerful" again.[36]

Restoration would also involve a more global role. After achieving rejuvenation mid-century, Jiang noted, "a wealthy and powerful, democratic, and civilized socialist modern China will stand in the east of the world, and the Chinese people will make new and greater contributions to humanity."[37] Hu Jintao quoted Sun Yat-sen to define rejuvenation's global dimension: "if China becomes strong, we should not only restore our national status but also bear a big responsibility for the world," adding that this would involve efforts to "promote the development of the international political and economic order in a more just and reasonable direction."[38] Rejuvenation, Hu made clear, would allow China to "stand in the forest of nations with an entirely new bearing."[39] At the 19th Party Congress, Xi Jinping was the most specific of any Chinese leader on what rejuvenation by mid-century would mean: "China would become a global leader in terms of composite national strength and international influence," construct a "world-class army," be actively involved in "global governance," and foster "a new type of international relations and build a community with a shared future for mankind."[40]

Xi Jinping's brash vision of mid-century rejuvenation is the product not simply of personality or parochialism but something more powerful: a nationalist Party consensus that stretches back through time to the self-strengthening focus of the late Qing reformers. The CCP has had its internal disagreements, struggles, factionalism, and extended descents into ideological extremism, but its founders and their successors have consistently understood it as the vehicle for rejuvenating China. Disagreements about the ways and the means have surfaced at times, but the end goal is relatively clear and has imposed consensus on China's post–Cold War grand strategy.

That goal is now within reach. The same Party that sat uneasily within Soviet order is unlikely to willingly defer to American order. China's pursuit of rejuvenation and the nationalist engine that drives it puts it at odds with US hierarchy, within Asia and worldwide. As later chapters will discuss in greater detail, China has sought to displace the United States from these orders and to create its own equivalent. One of its key assets in this pursuit, it believes, is its Leninist structure, and we turn now to consider it.

A Leninist Party

The Chinese Communist Party was founded under the influence of the Soviet Union and built on Leninist principles for structuring the state and governing society. Marxism may have provided the theory, noted the pioneering scholar of the Party Franz Schurmann, but Leninism provided the practice—the principles of organization related to gaining and wielding power that have endured even as Marxism has withered.[41]

China's Communist Party is a Leninist party. The namesake of this political approach, Vladimir Lenin, believed a vanguard of professional revolutionaries with tightly centralized political power could reshape history. He was committed to the centralization of authority, and he repeatedly stressed that the "important principle of all Party organization and all Party activity" was "the greatest possible centralization" of leadership.[42] Lenin's Bolsheviks structured their party in this fashion, and when they seized power after the Russian Revolution, they built a Leninist fusion of the party and state that China imported almost wholesale. "The names of the bodies through which the [Chinese Communist] Party exercises power, the Politburo, the Central Committee, the Praesidium and the like," notes Richard McGregor, "all betray one of the most overlooked facts about the modern Chinese state—that it still runs on Soviet hardware."[43]

That hardware is essential to understanding China's grand strategic capability. To wield a grand strategy, this book argues that states must have foreign policy institutions that are capable of (1) *coordinating* multiple instruments of statecraft in service of grand strategy and (2) exercising *autonomy* by overcoming parochial interests that would interfere with national grand strategic objectives. It is likely that Party institutions provide both coordination and autonomy better than institutions in most other states, particularly so in the foreign policy domain.

Coordination

A "red phone" sits on the desks of roughly 3,000 of the highest-level Party members, a quaint but concrete sign of the Party's ability to coordinate multiple instruments of statecraft.[44] Operated by a mysterious sixty-year-old military unit, this special "red phone" network directly connects the Party's senior-most cadres in government, the military, academia, state-owned enterprises, state media, and other sectors to each other without the need for any phone numbers.[45] The red phone system not only signifies that an official "has qualified for membership in the tight-knit club" that runs the country; it also provides the Party a "direct hotline" into the arms of the state and the various sectors of society that can be used for both information gathering and providing directives.[46] And like so much of China's system, it too was borrowed from the Soviet Union.

The "red phone" provides a tangible metaphor for Leninist governance, but that effort goes far beyond it to include institutions, meetings, and documents that together coordinate strategy.

With respect to institutions, China's critical foreign policy decision-making bodies are all within the Communist Party and sit above the state, providing centralized coordination and direction. The highest body is the General Secretary and its office. Next follow the seven to nine members of the Politburo Standing Committee, who are nominally selected from the 25-member Politburo, which is in turn selected from the 370 members of the CCP's Central Committee. These institutions are informed by a variety of groups that are believed to be tasked with formulating long-term strategy, such as the Central Policy Research Office of the CCP Central Committee. On military matters, the Central Military Commission, which is chaired by the General Secretary, is the leading institution. There is also a National Security Commission, though it "has struggled to find its footing" and may be more focused on domestic security than international security.[47]

Of critical importance in foreign policy are a series of often ad hoc Party bodies known as "leading small groups" [领导小组] or in some cases as more institutionalized "central commissions" [委员会], such as the Central Foreign Affairs Commission. Comprising very high-level Party officials—and often chaired by the General Secretary himself or by members of the Politburo Standing Committee—these bodies sit above the state ministries and issue guidelines for policy in virtually all critical domains.[48] As leading China scholar Alice Miller notes, these institutions engage in both "policy formulation and policy implementation" across Party, state, and society. They often coordinate "Central Committee departments, State Council ministries and agencies, components of the Chinese People's Political Consultative Conference, and other institutions."[49] These bodies are becoming more institutionalized too as the Party takes on more authority from the state, and the result is a greater centralization of policy formulation and implementation.[50]

Together, these institutions—the General Secretary, the Politburo Standing Committee, the Central Foreign Affairs Commission, and the Central Military Commission—run foreign policy. What is notable about this structure is how well suited it is for coordinated, top-down decision-making. Every key institution, particularly for foreign policy, is *within* the Party itself, has the General Secretary at its center, and sits above the state. Together, these factors provide these institutions the capability and the authority to bring together military, political, and economic instruments in coordination.

Some experts argue a seemingly centralized system like this one can still fail to coordinate properly. The scholar Ken Lieberthal argues that China exhibits "fragmented authoritarianism" among competing institutions and actors. Another scholar, David Lampton, notes that leading small groups may conflict with each other and may be "analogous to the 'principal' and 'deputies' meetings" of the US National Security Council, which sometimes fail to coordinate properly.[51]

Others like Wang Zhou, one of the top Chinese experts on the still rather opaque leading small groups, take the opposite view. Writing with Taiwanese scholar Wen-Hsuan Tsai, Wang Zhou uses case studies, new sources on the organizational structure of leading small groups, and an unprecedented televised proceeding of one such meeting.[52] Tsai and Zhou contend that these groups are fully embedded in the Party, which allows the head of the leading group to leverage Party authority—such as formal or informal influence over promotion—and not just state authority to produce state compliance. This is particularly true in foreign policy, where the head is almost always Xi Jinping or a member of the Politburo, and where there are fewer relevant groups compared to domestic policy. Moreover, Tsai and Zhou note that leading small groups usually have a dedicated office and office director working with the group head to coordinate internally and externally, making these bodies more institutionalized than the convening of individual " 'principal' and 'deputies' meetings."

While these bodies may marginalize the state or lack adequate professional staffing, they are nonetheless able to function as Leninist instruments for top-down, coordinated policy. As Zeng Peiyuan, former deputy premier of China's State Council, notes, these groups are "an effective method that our Party and government have developed through a long period" and are used to "implement major strategic tasks."[53] Rather than "fragmented authoritarianism," some see instead a kind of "integrated fragmentation" because of the Party's control over its subordinates—and this likely helps coordinate grand strategy.[54]

The second major instrument that imposes coordination and discipline on policy is Party meetings and the texts that emerge from them. To steer the ship of state, as this chapter discusses in greater detail later, the Party relies on a rigid hierarchy of guidances—such as the Party line, guideline, and policy (路线，方针，政策)—which cadres must follow. These guidances are repeated or revised in authoritative speeches or readouts from major meetings and conclaves, and they are also taken extraordinarily seriously. In the foreign policy domain, the line, guideline, and policy are often outlined in key addresses, such as at the Party's most important gathering, the Party Congress, held every five years; the Ambassadorial Conferences, which are held on average every six or so years (and now far more frequently under Xi); the Central Foreign Affairs Work Conferences, which have only been held five to six times ever; and other more ad hoc conclaves.

These kinds of foreign policy meetings, notes scholar Suisheng Zhao, "build policy consensus on China's national security strategy and foreign policy agenda while synthesizing China's official analysis of international trends."[55] The speeches and texts they produce—among others discussed later—are the ways the Party directs its cadres and the state, and they often indicate that their judgments have emerged from high-level Party consensus at the level of the Central Committee or Politburo Standing Committee. One indication of the importance of high-level Party guidances, and particularly those published by Xi Jinping, is that officials are required to regularly examine and reflect on them in organized "study sessions" that now take up as much as 30 percent of their time.[56]

Autonomy

It is of course not enough for the Party to merely coordinate and broadcast policy; it must also be able to ensure its implementation. As Lenin wrote in his discussion of political organization, "For the center . . . to actually direct the orchestra, it needs to know who plays which violin and where, who plays a false note and why, and how and where it is necessary to transfer someone to correct the dissonance."[57]

This the Party does in part by thoroughly penetrating both state and society. The Party sits above the state, runs parallel to the state, and is enmeshed in every level of the state. Virtually all important officials in the country are members of the Party: ministers and vice ministers, provincial leaders and mayors, generals and diplomats, chairmen of state companies, and university presidents, etc. So too are the millions of junior officials that work beneath them. The more than 90 million members of the Party are spread out across society and instrumental to policy implementation. Outside of the state, Party cells can be found in almost all institutions—as wide-ranging as law firms, private companies, and nonprofit organizations—which work to ensure that the Party's preferences are accommodated in both the state and society. Together, with leadership at the top and institutional penetration virtually all the way through to the bottom, the Party has the ability not only to coordinate and direct state behavior but in many cases to monitor it. This is by design.

In addition to directing and monitoring Party members, the Party also has mechanisms to enforce compliance. At the extreme end, this involves wielding the Party's disciplinary infrastructure to punish errant cadres. But it also involves less openly coercive tools that were also borrowed from the Soviet Union and provide power over careers, promotions, and postings through the personnel system. The critical institution in this system is the Party's secretive and extremely powerful Central Organization Department. The Organization Department determines who will fill tens of millions of posts, and in this way can powerfully shape the lives of cadres and provides yet another reason for them to follow Party guidances or else risk their careers.[58] This makes it difficult and costly for actors to steer major policy in rogue directions.

No state is fully autonomous from society, but in China foreign policy is probably more centrally directed and protected from vested interests and from social forces than domestic policy. Domestic policy is vast and cuts from ministries and provinces at the top to villages and counties at the bottom. Because it involves a wide range of actors and directly impacts public interests and opinion in tangible ways, autonomy can sometimes be reduced. By contrast, foreign policy is comparatively more centralized, narrower in scope, and involves fewer actors and therefore fewer parochial interests. Apart from highly salient issues, it also likely attracts less sustained interest than the bread-and-butter issues implicated by domestic policy, and what awareness there is can be shaped by Party censorship and media framing.[59]

The key exceptions to this are issues that touch on nationalist sensitivities. Research suggests, however, that nationalist outcries are not necessarily determinative.[60] The Party is willing to arrest nationalist critics and suppress their dissent in some cases while amplifying them in other cases to send signals to external audiences.[61] None of this is to say that nationalist public opinion is irrelevant—instead, as the scholar Joseph Fewsmith argues, it probably matters most at times when elite consensus falters.[62] Rather, the argument is that rather than be controlled by popular nationalism, the Party is often able to wield it as a tool—providing the state adequate autonomy in most cases to pursue grand strategy even when it conflicts with public sentiment.

Despite these strengths, there are limits to a Leninist system's ability to maintain state autonomy. Scholars like Thomas Christensen and Linda Jakobson argue persuasively that the proliferation of foreign policy actors within China and the complexity of international behavior outside of China together provide some space for autonomous action among officials and agencies.[63] Other researchers like David Shambaugh note the atrophy of Party institutions, while Minxin Pei emphasizes how corrupt heads of provinces, ministries, or state-owned enterprises may pursue their own agendas over those of the state's.[64]

These critiques capture something important and valid about the Party, but they do not preclude grand strategy capability. Coordination and autonomy are not a binary but a spectrum, and they are likely greatest at strategic levels and weaker at more tactical levels of policymaking (e.g., deployments along the Sino-Indian border or a particular infrastructure investment). At the lowest levels of policymaking, coordination across instruments may be minimal, monitoring is challenging, instruction is lacking, and resistance to the central government's dictates may be undetected and may go unanswered. This book does not argue that one theory can explain all Chinese behavior down to these most granular levels; rather, it hopes to explain costly strategic efforts such as major military investments, economic initiatives, and participation in international organizations—arguing that they are generally undertaken as part of a broader grand strategy. The question of whether one sees chaos or purpose in foreign policy can sometimes be about the level of analysis. And as the scholar Suisheng Zhao argues, despite "the increasing number of stakeholders and the requirement of specialized knowledge," as well as the role of public opinion, China's top leaders "have retained absolute latitude in shaping China's overall foreign policy direction."[65] Coordination and autonomy is likely possible where it matters most, and as the next section demonstrates, the Party's unquestioned control over foreign policy is a key theme in its internal messaging.

The Party Leads Foreign Policy

For decades, China's most authoritative foreign policy addresses delivered by its most senior leader—often to the assembled foreign policy apparatus—have repeatedly emphasized one common feature: that China's grand strategy is set at the highest levels of the Party itself. This has long been the case, though the centralization has intensified under Xi.

In addresses before the 6th Chinese Ambassadorial Conference in 1986, then premier Zhao Ziyang declared that "The adjustment of foreign policy must be highly centralized and must be decided by the Politburo Standing Committee."[66] Zhao's remarks made clear that grand strategy and strategic adjustment are the domain of the Party, not the state. To the assembled diplomats, he declared that they could "offer suggestions, but they must of course act in accordance with the decisions of the center. What is most important now is to understand and implement the general intention of the center and carry out the work."[67]

At the 8th Annual Ambassadorial Conference, Chinese leader Jiang Zemin made a similar point to the assembled foreign policy apparatus. "In external work, the guidelines and policies formulated by the center should be implemented with determination and unswervingly; there cannot be the slightest bit of ambiguity about this."[68] Indeed, "diplomacy is highly centralized and unified," and must take place "under the guidance of the center's diplomatic guideline [外交方针]."[69] "You should also see that diplomacy is no small matter and that diplomatic authority is limited," Jiang told the assembled officials, and "all the departments must resolutely carry out the central government's diplomatic guideline [外交方针], they cannot go their own separate ways [不能政出多门、各行其是]. Otherwise, there may be a big problem, one that could become a major issue that will affect our reputation."[70]

Jiang's successor also stressed these themes. In a 2003 speech to a major Foreign Ministry symposium, Hu Jintao argued, "Comrades in the diplomatic front must persist in . . . comprehensively implementing the principles and policies of the central line."[71] "To be good central government foreign policy advisors," Hu continued, "it is necessary . . . in any and all circumstances to be unwavering in implementing the central government's line (路线), guidelines (方针), policies (政策), and work."[72] Here, Hu makes clear that the line, guidelines, and policies that Party institutions put forward should guide state behavior.

Hu's successor, General Secretary Xi, has further strengthened Party control over the state and reemphasized the Party's central role in Chinese foreign policy work. In his 2013 Peripheral Diplomacy Work Forum address, Xi stated that centrally dictated "policies and tactics are the life of the party and the life of diplomatic work."[73] In his next major foreign policy address, the 2014 Central Foreign Affairs Work Conference address, Xi stated, "In order to comprehensively promote external work in the new situation, we must strengthen the Party's central and unified leadership" over foreign affairs.[74] State Councilor Yang Jiechi elaborated on Xi's thinking in a major Party journal, noting that China's grand strategy is planned at a high level by the Party Central Committee with a long time horizon in mind and centrally implemented. "Comrade Xi Jinping has repeatedly stressed that it is necessary to make a strategic plan for medium and long-term external work from the highest-level design perspective," he said, with the Party "integrating" activities involving "great powers, neighboring countries, developing countries, and multilateral organizations."[75]

Five years later, at China's sixth ever Foreign Affairs Work Conference, Xi expanded on these themes at surprising length, and his remarks are worthy of scrutiny. "Diplomacy is a concentrated representation of the will of the state," he declared, "and diplomatic authority must stay with the CCP Central Committee" and its "centralized and unified leadership."[76] Across all foreign policy domains, he noted, "all must consciously maintain unity with the CCP Central Committee, ensuring strict enforcement of orders and prohibitions [令行禁止], and that all march in lockstep [步调统一]."[77] The Party had formulated a long-term systematic strategy that others were expected to implement. "External work is a systematic project [系统工程]" that involved coordination among "political parties, governments, people's congresses, the CPPCC, the military, localities, public, etc."[78] Through the synchronized labors of these groups "the party takes overall responsibility and coordinates the foreign work of each group to ensure that the CCP Central Committee's foreign policy guidelines, policies, and strategies, and plans are implemented."[79] Here, Xi was listing a rough hierarchy of CCP policy dictates and the various parts of the state, society, and Party expected to advance them. Finally, Xi also focused on the people involved in foreign policy. "After the political line is determined, cadres are the decisive factor," he noted, "so we must build a strong contingent of foreign affairs personnel that are loyal to the CPC, the country and the people."[80] His speech emphasized Party control over foreign policy institutions and Party-building within them—which these loyal individuals would advance.[81]

These texts show that China's leaders have taken the Party's guiding role in foreign policy extremely seriously for decades. They also indicate that foreign policy is directed centrally, formulated at high levels, coordinated across state and social sectors, and often long-term. It is rare, and extremely costly, for Party officials to buck authority or innovate in foreign policy, and multiple generations of leaders have indicated stark punishments if they do so. Together, these attributes suggest the existence of grand strategic capability.

Grand Strategic Concepts

To gain insight into the thinking of the otherwise opaque CCP, the starting point must often be authoritative texts. The Party believes its official speeches and texts are of critical importance, and for that reason, many of the most astute observers of China have long taken them seriously.

One of the pioneers of this approach was Father Lazlow Ladany. Ladany was a Hungarian-born Jesuit priest and "one-man think tank" who spent a lifetime poring through official Party sources, central and provincial newspapers, radio broadcasts, and a variety of other open source materials.[82] He was the son of a

physician, received a doctorate in law, and studied violin in a conservatory before joining the Jesuit order and being sent to China in 1940. Expelled from
China when the Communists came to power, he retreated to Hong Kong. Four
years later, he launched "China News Analysis," a weekly newsletter he spent
the next thirty years publishing from a few basement rooms in a Jesuit-run dor-
mitory at Hong Kong University. His legendary newsletter's more than 1,200
issues, each roughly six to eight pages in length and generally organized around a
singular theme, were disseminated to China experts around the world and to US
allies and Soviet states alike. They also went to the CIA. None other than James
Lilley—a thirty-year CIA analyst who rose to become the highest-level intelligence officer for China and later the US ambassador in Beijing—believed that
China News Analysis provided the very best intelligence available to the United
States before normalization.[83]

Father Ladany's success was the product of a singular focus almost entirely
on the way the Party communicates with itself and to others. This approach was
austere in principle but arduous in practice, and it required painstaking analysis
of Party material. The sinologist Simon Ley argues that this kind of close reading
of Party texts is "akin to munching rhinoceros sausage, or to swallowing saw-
dust by the bucketful" and it requires one to not only learn Chinese but also to
"crack the code of the Communist political jargon and translate into ordinary
speech this secret language full of symbols, riddles, cryptograms, hints, traps,
dark allusions, and red herrings."[84] While Father Ladany was one of the earliest
and most experienced practitioners of this approach, others carried it out too.
Within the CIA, the Foreign Broadcast Information Service (FBIS) absorbed
vast quantities of Chinese open sources, translated them, and made them available to others. In the process, it built institutional experience in understanding
the CCP and trained a generation of scholars in these methods.

One of those scholars is Alice Miller, a leading expert on CCP open sources
who defends the close reading of Party texts even though the approach has
grown increasingly complicated. Miller notes that there has been an explosion in
China's print media from 300 outlets when Father Ladany first began publishing
in 1952 to roughly 2,000 today; radio and television broadcasts have likewise
dramatically increased, overwhelming the capacity of individuals to track all of
it. Access to Chinese academics, diplomats, researchers, bureaucrats, journalists,
leaders, and government institutions also provides more opportunities for information.[85] And foreign journalists—with significant limitations—are able to
explore a range of stories. We are a long way from the era of Father Ladany and
FBIS, when China was isolated from the world. It is reasonable to ask why a
focus on Party texts is still useful.

But although much has changed, not everything has. The Party remains
the critical institution in China, and its line, guidelines, and policies continue

to shape China's behavior. There has indeed been an explosion in media, but not necessarily an equivalent growth in the most *authoritative* media, and the Party continues to use key speeches, statements, and commentaries—as well as key gatherings—to communicate its policy preferences to itself and others. And in some of the areas where authoritative material has increased, it is often narrow enough in scope to avoid overwhelming analysts. Unlike the days of Father Ladany and FBIS, when the textual base was narrow and the conclusions were broad, the arrival of new sources (e.g., books or journals from the presses of key state ministries) means paradoxically that the base is now so broad it can allow for narrower conclusions based on specialized sources. For example, scholars can use journals from the Ministry of Industry and Information Technology to understand decision-making in telecommunications policies too granular to receive sustained attention in the Party's flagship papers.

At the same time, even as some materials grow, China itself is clearly retreating from what openness it had recently allowed: journalists are being expelled, archives have closed, and many in-person meetings are now too sensitive to yield rich insight. As a result of these trends, notes the Australian sinologist Geremie R. Barmé, "the long-overlooked, or underestimated, skills of being able to read, listen to and understand the bloviations of the Chinese party-state are, perhaps, in vogue once more."[86] Indeed, the Party remains a deliberately secretive and opaque institution, and its texts remain one of the only narrow windows into it. "Political communication is a variety of deliberate political behavior," Miller argues convincingly, and "all political behavior says something about the actors that engage in it."[87]

When applied to foreign policy—a domain that is still centrally controlled and in which parochial interests appear to have relatively limited influence— these insights ring even truer. Foreign policy is largely communicated in a series of key addresses. What is said by senior leaders at the Party Congress, at the Central Foreign Affairs Work Forum, at the Ambassadorial Conferences, in Central Military Commission meetings, and in a variety of other occasions that are used to set or adjust foreign policy remains as critical now as it ever has. The commentaries on these sometimes incomplete or inscrutable speeches, often published by senior officials in key Party journals, are authentic and authoritative—as they have been for decades. And the key judgments in these texts about the "international balance of forces" or the "strategic guideline" continue to be of great relevance to grand strategy. Meanwhile, below this high-level stratum of the most authoritative texts lies an ocean of material of varying degrees of authoritativeness. When carefully analyzed, that material too can yield still greater insight into Chinese grand strategy. We now turn to how this kind of research can be undertaken.

Research Method

Which specific documents form the foundation of this book's inquiry into Chinese grand strategy? A textual approach to Chinese grand strategy relies on establishing a hierarchy of open source and classified Chinese sources in order of authoritativeness and drawing from them accordingly. The most authoritative of these are leader-level memoirs, doctrinal texts, archival sources, official speeches, classified materials, and essays by senior leaders. They better reflect Party thinking than more frequently cited but often less reliable sources like Chinese journal articles and think tank reports.

This raises an important question: how does a scholar differentiate among sources broadly believed to be authoritative? It helps that not all authoritative materials are of the same kind, allowing for us to divide them into a variety of categories, as Table 2.1 demonstrates.

Sources can be divided into five rough categories, in descending order of authoritativeness. (See the Appendix for a detailed discussion of this book's textual methodology.) The first is leader-level speeches that set the line, guideline, and policy on major issues—particularly speeches at the Party Congress, at Foreign Affairs Work Conferences, and at Ambassadorial Conferences, among other domestic and foreign venues. The second category is Chinese government documents and speeches, such as White Papers on foreign policy or defense or diplomatic addresses, that are intended for foreign audiences. The third category

Table 2.1 **Hierarchy of Primary Sources**

Hierarchy of Documents for Insight into the Party's Foreign Policy Judgments	
Leader Speeches	Party Congress Reports
	Major Internal Foreign Policy Addresses
	Other Internal Leader Party Speeches
External-Facing Foreign Policy Documents	Addresses to Foreign Audiences by Leaders or Senior Officials
	Government White Papers
Party Media on Party Judgments	Renmin Ribao Pseudonymous Editorials and Commentaries
	Qiushi and Xuexi Shibao Commentaries
Functional Sources	Ministry and Military Documents and Statements
	Material from Ministry and Military Publishing Presses
Think Tank and Academic Commentary	Comments from Well-Connected Scholars
	Comments from Government-Affiliated Programs

is the Party's authoritative newspapers such as the *People's Daily* [人民日报] and magazines like *Seeking Truth* [求是], published by the Party Central Committee, and *Study Times* [学习时报], published by the Central Party School. These publications express official Party views, broadcast some Party debates, and also contain detailed authoritative commentaries on official speeches. The fourth category is functional sources, such as the selected works and memoirs and other publications produced by presses affiliated with key agencies or the military. This book draws significant content from memoirs of generals, diplomats, and other senior officials. The fifth category is think tank and academic commentary of varying degrees of authoritativeness. These sources sometimes illustrate the scope of key elite debates that might guide statecraft.

This book relies on an original database of these kinds of documents. The core of this database includes major regularly published Party document compilations, such as the official publications of selected works of all major leaders after Mao as well compilations of Party documents published in three volumes between Party Congresses, among others. These sources are used to establish longitudinal comparisons because they are regularly published and exhibit some consistency in document selection. In addition, a number of other sources that are not regularly published were also consulted on a case-by-case basis. Most of these are drawn from other thematic Party compilations published by the Central Documentation Press; in addition, state White Papers, minister remarks, Party media, functional sources from ministries or ministry presses, memoirs, and academic and think tank commentary are also consulted. Several leaked documents are also included as well.

How do we know whether Party documents are biased? Authoritative Party and state documents compiled by official presses are, after all, edited and manipulated in ways that leaked documents are not. But rather than overstate China's ambitions or threat perceptions, these documents should be seen as likely to understate them and as providing "hard tests" for the book's arguments. These texts are *less* likely to contain authoritative explications of China's efforts to blunt American power or build regional hegemony since these are goals China does not generally emphasize publicly. Moreover, China often screens its publications for terms likely to be picked up by Western observers that would contribute to anxieties about China's rise. For example, following the U.S. trade war with China in part over China's support for the industrial policy initiative "Made in China 2025," the Propaganda Department ordered the term no longer be used and its mentions in *Xinhua* promptly plummeted.[88] Phrases like "Tao Guang Yang Hui" (i.e., Deng's admonition that China must "hide capabilities and bide time") are similarly considered sensitive. In addition, these texts are unlikely to play up China's ambitions for nationalist audiences because they are not widely read outside of Party audiences, and they are restrained relative to more popular and forceful think tank or media commentary. Finally, leaked documents appear to be much more frank about the US threat and about Chinese ambitions than officially published ones.

Although these documents make it difficult to detect Chinese strategy, they nonetheless play a useful coordinating role within the Party-state apparatus. As a result, the "signal" of Chinese strategy can still be detected through the "noise" of official edits, especially when the documents are compared *longitudinally over time*. For example, one can look at differences in Party Congress work reports, Ambassadorial Conference addresses, Central Foreign Affairs Work Forums—as well as in key concepts like the strategic guideline [战略方针] or the assessment of multipolarity [多极化]—to detect shifts in strategy.

The analytical approach described here for sifting through Party material is not easy to implement and it cannot always be perfectly implemented, but it is nonetheless necessary because understanding Chinese foreign policy requires taking the Party seriously. Since the end of the Cold War, however, it has been challenging for nonexpert Western observers to focus much on the Party. The institution is alien, its institutions seem obsolete, and its texts are often stale and wooden. And yet, those institutions are an extraordinarily powerful vehicle for Chinese nationalism and for coordinating grand strategy and providing the state some autonomy from society. Those texts too provide a unique window into an otherwise secretive organization. And a look at both can help illustrate the contours of China's grand strategy. We turn now to the first chapter that applies this approach and that examines how the traumatic trifecta of Tiananmen Square, the Gulf War, and the Soviet collapse gave rise to China's first displacement strategy: a grand strategy to *blunt* American order.

PART I

"HIDING CAPABILITIES AND BIDING TIME"

Blunting as China's First Displacement Strategy (1989–2008)

"New Cold Wars Have Begun"

The Trifecta and the New American Threat

"I looked forward to the end of the Cold War, but now I feel disappointed. It seems that one Cold War has come to an end but that two others have already begun."[1]

—*Deng Xiaoping, 1989*

Four decades ago, on the windswept edges of Soviet empire, an improbable partnership was forged. With Beijing's approval, the United States built and operated two signals intelligence facilities at Korla and Qitai that sat astride old Silk Road caravan routes in western China. These stations were used to monitor Soviet missile testing in Kazakhstan, and within their walls, American intelligence professionals worked shoulder to shoulder with their counterparts in China's People's Liberation Army (PLA) to keep tabs on the Soviet threat.[2]

The stations at Korla and Qitai were physical proof of something that now seems hard to believe: the United States and China were once quasi-allies. Over the course of the 1980s, Washington worked with Beijing to oppose the Soviet invasion of Afghanistan and Soviet influence in Southeast Asia. It sold China weapons, including "artillery equipment and ammunition, antisubmarine torpedoes, artillery-locating radar, advanced avionics, and Blackhawk helicopters."[3] And it even permitted its allies to sell China an old carrier hull for study—one that was complete with a steam catapult, arresting equipment, and mirror landing systems.[4] China's leaders welcomed these ties. In meetings with China's Central Military Commission, Deng had stated that "threat of Soviet hegemonism" caused it to form "a strategic 'line' of defense—a 'line' stretching from Japan to Europe to the United States" for security.[5] Military, economic, and political cooperation with the West was widespread and deep, and some in Beijing also hoped Washington would intervene in a Sino-Soviet war.

All of this changed abruptly following what this book calls the "traumatic tri-fecta" of Tiananmen Square (1989), the Gulf War (1990–1991), and the Soviet collapse (1991). These three short but historic years reshaped the United States, China, and the international system, and each heightened Beijing's anxieties about the United States. The Tiananmen Square protests reminded Beijing of the American ideological threat, the swift Gulf War victory reminded it of the American military threat, and loss of the shared Soviet adversary reminded it of the American geopolitical threat. In short order, the United States quickly replaced the Soviet Union as China's primary security concern, that in turn led to a new grand strategy, and a thirty-year struggle to displace American power was born.

As the socialist world crumbled in the late 1980s and a new order came into being, Deng Xiaoping put forward a "strategic guideline" [战略方针] to re-duce the risk of American-led balancing and containment, to blunt American leverage over China, and thereby to secure conditions for China's development and autonomy. The guideline was eventually encapsulated in a twenty-four-character guidance often summed up in a four-character instruction: China needed "to hide one's capabilities and bide one's time," or "Tao Guang Yang Hui" [韬光养晦].[6] This guideline served as the high-level organizing principle for Chinese foreign policy. In that way, it functioned as a grand strategic concept and set China off on a grand strategy to quietly and carefully *blunt* American military, political, and economic leverage over it, all with the goal of enhancing Beijing's own freedom of maneuver.

This chapter explores China's changing view of the United States at the end of the Cold War and the ends, ways, and means of its subsequent grand strategy. It argues that although some believe the phrase "Tao Guang Yang Hui" receives excessive attention among foreign audiences, such a perspective is misguided. The phrase's appearances across a wide range of leader-level speeches, memoirs, and semi-official commentaries makes its importance and contours clear. It also reveals that the non-assertive strategy it inaugurated was never meant to be permanent. "Tao Guang Yang Hui" was explicitly tied to China's assessment of the "international balance of power" [国际力量对比]. When that balance of power changed, the strategy was to change too.

Under this strategy, China chose not to *build* the foundations for Asian he-gemony because it feared doing so would unsettle the United States and its own neighbors. It avoided major investments in aircraft carriers, ambitious interna-tional organizations, and regional economic schemes and instead—as the next three chapters demonstrate—pursued *blunting*. At the military level, Beijing shifted from a "sea control" strategy increasingly focused on holding distant maritime territory to a "sea denial strategy" focused on blunting the ability of the US military to traverse, control, or intervene in the waters near China. At the political level, Beijing decided to join and then stall regional institutions, blunting Washington's ability to use them to promote Western ideology or organize an Asian NATO. And at the economic level, unnerved by Tiananmen-era sanctions, Beijing fought to preserve access to American markets, capital, and technology through bilateral and multilateral agreements that blunted the discretionary use of American economic coercion. Together, China's *blunting* strategy was remarkable both for its sweep and subtlety across multiple instruments. As Deng had once stated, China's leaders knew that the Cold War had ended, but they feared another one had already begun. They prepared accordingly.

A Shift in the Perceived US Threat

Under the cover of dark on a cool Friday morning in June 1989, National Security Advisor Brent Scowcroft boarded a C-141 military cargo plane at 5 A.M. and took off from Andrews Air Force Base for a secret mission to Beijing. The trip was intended to stabilize bilateral ties roughly three weeks after the People's Liberation Army had opened fire on student protesters in Tiananmen Square, and much about it was unusual. To maintain secrecy, Scowcroft needed a plane like the C-141 that could be refueled midair and that would not need to land. To accommodate Scowcroft and his two companions, the C-141 needed to be specially outfitted with a deceptively named "comfort pallet" with bunks and seats. And to reduce the risk of a military incident, the plane needed to have its Air Force markings removed and its military crew outfitted in civilian attire.[7] That last measure proved only modestly successful. The mission was so secretive that China's local air defense units had no knowledge of it and almost fired on Scowcroft's plane, but decided to call President Yang Shangkun's office first. "Fortunately for us," Scowcroft later recounted, "the call went right through and Yang advised them it was a very important mission and they should hold their fire."[8]

When the plane landed in the afternoon on July 1, it was hidden behind an old terminal away from prying eyes. The next morning, Scowcroft met with Deng Xiaoping, Li Peng, and other officials, as well as a photographer who happened to be the son of President Yang. Before Scowcroft's visit, President George H. W. Bush had sent an apologetic and solicitous secret letter to Deng Xiaoping on the importance of bilateral ties; now, Scowcroft would carry a similar message in person to reassure China's paramount leader that despite the tough measures the United States was forced by public opinion to take in response to China's crackdown, Washington would keep its actions limited to preserve the relationship.

Ultimately, the effort made little difference.[9] Deng initially praised the Bush administration for its "cool-headed attitude" but then turned sharply critical, arguing that "U.S. foreign policy has actually cornered China."[10] Tiananmen Square "was an earthshaking event," he said, "and it is very unfortunate that the United States is too deeply involved in it."[11] Deng argued that US sanctions and criticism from Congress and the media were "leading to the break up of the relationship," and it was up to Washington to "untie the knot."[12] The Bush administration's efforts apparently failed to adequately reassure Deng, who instead repeatedly stressed that the protests and their aftermath were an existential threat to the Party. "The aim of the counter-revolutionary rebellion was to overthrow the People's Republic of China and our socialist system," he said, and Washington appeared willing to "add fuel to the fire."[13] Scowcroft tried again to stress the American perspective, but Deng had apparently made up his mind. "I don't have much time," he responded despite his otherwise warm reception of Scowcroft, and he stressed that he disagreed with "a considerable portion" of the national security advisor's remarks.

A decade later, Scowcroft reflected on these meetings and noted the challenge he faced in reassuring Beijing. "I explained over and over again . . . how our system worked, but I think they never really believed it," he said of his attempt to explain the split between Congress and the Bush administration on Tiananmen sanctions.[14] The difference in culture and political systems "had created a wide divide between us," and while "they were focused on security and stability," Scowcroft observed, "we were interested in freedom and human rights."[15] It was precisely this ideological gap—with liberal values posing a danger to the CCP—that had made the United States too threatening to Beijing and that made Beijing too difficult to reassure.

Only a few months before Tiananment, however, the situation had been entirely different. In a February 1989 meeting with President Bush, Deng focused intently on the Soviet threat. Border clashes, nuclear weapons, and the presence of thirty Soviet divisions on China's border made large-scale war possible. He wrapped his concerns in history. "Japan did the most damage" to China, Deng recounted to Bush, but it was the Soviet Union that took "three million square kilometers" of Chinese territory.[16] "Those over fifty in China remember that the shape of China was like a maple leaf. Now, if you look at the map," Deng explained, "you see a huge chunk of the north cut away" by the Soviets.[17] Even so, he observed that Soviet leader Joseph Stalin was a friend of China who supported its modernization, but his successor Nikita Khrushchev "scrapped several hundred Sino-Soviet contracts overnight" and sought to encircle China. "All along the Sino-Soviet border, in the west and the east, the Soviet Union stationed one million men and deployed about one-third of all its nuclear missiles," Deng said.[18] As part of this Soviet encircling coalition, "India was added and then Vietnam [as well as Afghanistan and Cambodia]. Now the Soviets have military air transit rights over North Korea, which allow them to connect to Cam Ranh Bay [in

Vietnam]. Their planes can now conduct air reconnaissance over China."[19] Deng was clear that this assessment necessitated "the development of its relations with the United States." He then delivered the key point: "how can China not feel that the greatest threat comes from the Soviet Union?" This assessment of the Soviet threat was not simply for Bush's benefit. When the Soviet Union's leader Mikhail Gorbachev visited Beijing a few months later, Deng conveyed this same assessment of the Soviet threat directly to him.[20]

Although Beijing at times sought improved ties with the Soviet Union and stressed its interest in an "independent" foreign policy in the early 1980s, it clearly leaned heavily toward Washington.[21] China cooperated closely with the United States on security matters, and its military and doctrinal texts still focused primarily on the possibility of war with the Soviet Union and not the distant United States.[22] When the American journalist Mike Wallace asked Deng during an interview in 1986 why China's ties with capitalist America were superior to its ties with Soviet communists, Deng did not dispute Wallace's assessment. "China does not regard social systems as a criterion in its approach to problems," he explained, but focuses instead on the "specific conditions" of those problems.[23] Throughout the 1980s, the risk of war with the Soviet Union remained a significant problem for Beijing.

As the 1980s came to a close, and as the meeting with Scowcroft revealed, China's assessment was changing. Tiananmen Square in 1989, the Gulf War in 1990-1991, and then the Soviet collapse in 1991 led China to see the United States and not the Soviet Union as China's primary threat, as authoritative documents make clear.

Despite the Bush administration's efforts, Deng's comments about the United States changed dramatically beginning in 1989. Throughout most of the 1980s, as a review of his *Selected Works* makes clear, Deng would occasionally chide the United States for democratic arrogance or for interference in Taiwan, yet he did not refer to the United States as a threat. After 1989, he frequently denounced the United States in ideological terms. For example, in a private talk with several members of the CCP Central Committee just two months after his meeting with Scowcroft, Deng said there was now "no doubt that the imperialists want socialist countries to change their nature. The problem now is not whether the banner of the Soviet Union will fall—there is bound to be unrest there—but whether the banner of China will fall."[24]

The sentiment became a common feature of Deng's remarks, even his public ones. "The West really wants unrest in China," Deng declared later that same month, "it wants turmoil not only in China but also in the Soviet Union and Eastern Europe. The United States and some other Western countries are trying to bring about a peaceful evolution towards capitalism in socialist countries."[25] In Deng's mind, this threat to China was a form of warfare. "The United States has coined an expression: waging a world war without gunsmoke," he argued. "We should be on guard against this. Capitalists want to defeat socialists in the long run. In the past they used weapons, atomic bombs and hydrogen bombs, but they were opposed by the peoples of the world. So now they are trying peaceful evolution."[26] In a meeting with Richard Nixon after Tiananmen, Deng declared that the "United States was deeply involved" in "the recent disturbances and the counter-revolutionary rebellion" of the students and that "some Westerners" were "trying to overthrow the socialist system in China.[27] In a November 1989 address, he warned, "Western countries are staging a third world war without gunsmoke."[28] Then, in a talk with a visiting Japanese delegation, Deng elaborated on Western responsibility for the Tiananmen incident. "Western countries, particularly the United States," he argued, "set all their propaganda machines in motion to fan the flames, to encourage and support the so-called democrats or opposition in China, who were in fact the scum of the Chinese nation. That is how the turmoil came about."[29] Not only was the United States responsible, in Deng's view, but its objectives were hostile: "In inciting unrest in many countries, they are actually playing power politics and seeking hegemony. They are trying to bring into their sphere of influence countries that heretofore they have not been able to control. Once this point is made clear, it will help us understand the nature of the problem."[30]

Amid these fears, the US demonstration of force in the Gulf War in early 1991—as the following chapter makes clearer—was disturbing to Beijing. At the outset of the war, Chinese analysts and leaders remained convinced that the United States would suffer high casualties and may even fail to secure its objectives. They noted that US "aggression" against Iraq would be less effective than against Grenada, Libya, and Panama; that Iraq, with equipment similar and in some cases superior to China's, would wage a successful form of "People's War under Modern Conditions"; and that the United States would be pulled into a long ground war that would result in its political defeat.[31]

All of this was revealed to be extraordinarily overstated, and when the United States prevailed spectacularly in the conflict, a stunned Chinese leadership saw a frightening similarity between Iraq's defeat and China's possible fate in a conflict with the United States. Some Chinese figures wrote publicly that the Gulf War was an example of US "global hegemonism" and that "the U.S. intended to dominate the world," including China.[32] The conflict not only amplified China's fear of the United States, it also led the Central Military Commission to launch a major initiative to study the conflict and how to build asymmetric weapons to deal with the US military, efforts paramount leader Deng discussed and in which his successor Jiang Zemin directly participated.

The Soviet collapse the following year marked the final leg of the trifecta. By then, much of the socialist world was gone, and China stood increasingly alone.

As George Washington University professor David Shambaugh chronicles in his work *Atrophy and Adaptation*, the Soviet collapse had a profound impact on the Party, inspiring a way of studies on what went wrong and much handwringing about US subversion.[33] Decades later, China's leaders remain consumed by the event, with paramount leader Xi Jinping continuing to support study of the event and offering his own thoughts on it—particularly the importance of resisting Western liberalism.[34]

Together, these excerpts demonstrate the remarkable adjustment brought about in China's threat perception. Deng's judgments on the US threat were effectively official Party judgments, and they were echoed in countless narrower military, economic, and political documents. This threat perception formed the crucible in which a new Chinese grand strategy would be formed—one focused on surviving the US threat.

Ends—Surviving US Threat

In AD 780, the thin and sickly poet of "devilish talent" Li He (李贺) was born "to a minor branch of the imperial house of Tang" whose fortunes had long ago declined.[35] Li was a poetic savant at age seven, but his life was difficult. His father died when he was young, and Li was then excluded from the Imperial Examination on a technicality, preventing him from gaining an office to support his family and their crumbling estate and pushing him into a military career that led to his untimely death at twenty-six from tuberculosis. Li's vivid and often pessimistic poetry might have been lost to history had he not attracted the attention of the eminent poet and official Han Yun, who met Li at nineteen, read the first line of one of his poems, promptly recognized his genius, and likely helped preserve his work.[36]

Centuries later, that work inspired Mao Zedong, who was known to hold Li He as one of his most favorite poets. And it may be that precise association with Mao that led Chinese leader Jiang Zemin in a 1998 speech to the Central Military Commission to incongruously invoke one of Li He's lines as Jiang warned that Western forces sought China's collapse. By pure coincidence, Jiang chose the *exact* same line believed to have dazzled Han Yun centuries earlier. "Black clouds press heavy on the city," Jiang said, "and the city is on the verge of caving in."[37]

Jiang's warnings were hardly anomalous. The belief that the United States was China's primary threat, and that China's grand strategy should focus on surviving that threat, was affirmed for nearly two decades in leader-level speeches found in Party compendiums. This section explores some of the most authoritative of these, particularly the important and infrequent Ambassadorial Conferences held roughly every six years to reiterate or alter foreign policy judgments.

The first Ambassadorial Conference after the traumatic trifecta was held in 1993, and it was only the eighth in China's history. In his address, Jiang Zemin outlined a sentiment that departed dramatically from earlier Ambassadorial speeches delivered in 1986 by Zhao Ziyang and Hu Yaobang. "From now on and for a relatively long period of time, the United States will be our main diplomatic adversary [对手]. . . . The status and role of the United States in today's world determines that it is the main adversary in our international dealings," Jiang argued.[38] The United States, he clarified, had hostile intentions:

> The U.S. policy on China has always been two-sided. The peaceful evo-lution of our country is a long-term strategic goal for some in the United States. In essence, they are reluctant to see China's reunification, devel-opment, and strengthening. They will continue to keep pressure on our country on issues of human rights, trade, arms sales, Taiwan and the Dalai Lama. The United States is domineering in its dealings with our country and possesses the posture of hegemonism and power politics.[39]

And yet, Jiang argued before the assembled diplomats, there was a second side to US policy toward China. "On the other hand, the United States out of consid-eration for its own global strategy and its fundamental economic interests, will have to focus on our country's vast market and has no choice but to seek cooper-ation with us in international affairs."[40] In other words, Jiang argued, Washington "needs to maintain normal relations with us."[41] Even so, China could not adopt an overtly confrontational strategy because, as Jiang observed, "The United States is our principal export market and an important source for our imported cap-ital, technology, and advanced management experience."[42] Instead, "protecting and developing Sino-U.S. relations was of strategic significance" to China. By cooperating with the United States in some areas and avoiding confrontation in others, China could minimize US antipathy, continue to develop economically, and increase its relative power.[43]

Five years later, at the next Ambassadorial Conference in 1998, Jiang con-tinued to emphasize the US threat. "Some in the United States and the other Western countries," he declared, "will not give up their political plot to west-ernize and divide our country. It doesn't matter whether it is adopting a 'con-tainment policy' or a so-called 'engagement policy,' all of which may vary in 10,000 different ways without ultimately departing from their central aim [万变不离其宗], which is to try with ulterior motives [企图] to change our country's socialist system and finally bring our country into the Western capi-talist system."[44] The contest with Washington would be an enduring one. "This struggle is long-term and complex," Jiang declared, and "in this regard, we must always keep a clear head and must never lose our vigilance."[45] In his mind, there was also a fear that Washington might work with China's neighbors, and he added that, like the United States, "some of our neighboring great powers also want to contain us in different ways."[46] Jiang then offered the diplomats an extraordinary, official review of Sino-American relations, with the emphasis being on the hostility and threat posed by the United States:

> In November and December 1989, former U.S. Secretary of State and the president's National Security Advisor Brent Scowcroft visited China successively, and comrade Deng Xiaoping met with them both and put forward a wholesale plan for restoring Sino-U.S. relations. This plan ultimately found its realization in my [Jiang's] state visit to the United States. At the time, the visit received the approval of the American side, but then the United States changes its mind and went back on its word. Because of the drastic changes in Eastern Europe, some in the United States pinned their hopes on us "changing." In 1991, there was a serious flood in East China, and some in the United States set their minds on us having chaos. In December of that year when the Soviet Union dissolved, some in the United States thought we should "collapse." In 1992, the United States sold Taiwan F-16 fighter jets, in 1995 they permitted leaders of Taiwan to visit the United States. Some in the United States with respect to the so-called "post-Deng China" made all kinds of speculation and put pressure on us in an attempt to overwhelm us and put us down.[47]

Although many in Washington believed relations had improved in the 1990s, Beijing saw things differently, and Jiang emphasized his skepticism about US intentions to the assembled foreign policy establishment. "When I was in New York with Clinton, he clearly told me that the U.S. policy on China is neither isolation nor deterrence nor confrontation, but full engagement," Jiang stated.[48] But Jiang immediately emphasized to the audience that he did not believe these assurances: "we must realize that the U.S. policy on China is still two-sided. The attempt by the U.S. anti-China forces to evolve us will not change."[49] Moreover, Jiang argued that "the United States is trying to construct a unipolar world . . . and dominate international affairs" and that, instead of declining, "for a long time, the United States will maintain significant advantages in politics, economics, science and technology, and military affairs."[50]

The continuity of these views across two of China's most important foreign policy speeches was remarkable. Then, in a speech to the Central Military Commission roughly ten years after Tiananmen, Jiang emphasized that these themes had not diminished in salience. "After undergoing drastic changes in Eastern Europe, the dissolution of the Soviet Union, and the end of bipolarity in the late 1980s and early 1990s," he remarked, "setbacks in the development of worldwide socialism caused us to face unprecedented pressure."[51] In particular, "hostile international forces have threatened to bury communism in the world, arguing that China will follow the footsteps of the Soviet Union and Eastern European countries and will soon collapse. They have exerted comprehensive pressure on China and openly support our domestic anti-communist, anti-socialist forces, and separatist forces as they engage in sabotage and subversion."[52] Hostile foreign forces, he continued, were "intensifying all kinds of infiltration and destruction activities aimed at the Westernization and splitting-up of our country, and continuing to use so-called 'human rights,' 'democracy,' 'religion,' the Dalai Lama, Taiwan, economic and trade instruments, and arms sales all to stir up trouble."[53] In summing up the situation, he declared that "China's security and social and political stability are facing serious threats" from the United States.[54]

In another Central Military Commission speech two years later, Jiang was more explicit that the cause of China's troubles was the United States, and he confirmed that rocky relations with the United States were perceived in Beijing to have begun with the trifecta: "After the end of the Cold War, Sino-American relations have continuously been very unsteady, sometimes good and sometimes bad."[55]

Jiang's successor, President Hu Jintao, continued to stress the US threat. In speeches to the Foreign Ministry in 2003, Hu argued that although "the United States and other large Western countries need to seek China's cooperation on major international and regional issues, we must also recognize the grim reality that Western hostile forces are still implementing Westernization and splittist political designs on China."[56]

Top figures were sometimes even blunter. In an exhaustive review of what appears to be leaked documents from China's 16th Party Congress held the previous year, Andrew Nathan and Bruce Gilley conclude that "managing relations with the United States is seen as a looming threat" to China's security.[57] The full text of the documents is quite revealing, with Hu Jintao and other top Chinese elites and Politburo Standing Committee members deeply anxious about US power and intentions. Hu Jintao identified the United States as "the main line [i.e., the central thread] in China's foreign policy strategy."[58] He also argued that the United States sought to encircle China:

> Many people in the United States have always regarded China as a latent strategic opponent, and from a geopolitical perspective have adopted a two-faced engagement and containment approach. . . . The United States has strengthened its military deployments in the Asia-Pacific region, strengthened the US-Japan military alliance, strengthened strategic

cooperation with India, improved relations with Vietnam, wooed Pakistan, established a pro-American government in Afghanistan, increased arms sales to Taiwan, and so on. They have extended outposts and placed pressure points on us from the east, south, and west. This makes a great change in our geopolitical environment.[59]

In those same files, Premier Wen Jiabao saw the United States as seeking to contain China:

> The United States is trying to preserve its status as the world's sole superpower and will not allow any country the chance to pose a challenge to it. The US will maintain its global strategy based in Europe and Asia, and the focus will be on containing Russia and China and controlling Europe and Japan. The core of American foreign policy toward China is still to "engage and contain." Some conservative forces in the US are sticking stubbornly to their Cold War thinking, stressing that the rise of China must harm American interests. The US military is planning to move the focus of military planning from Europe to the Asia-Pacific region. The US will continue to exert pressure [on us] on Taiwan, human rights, security, and economics and trade.[60]

Other prominent figures, like Jiang Zemin's right-hand adviser Zeng Qinghong, declared similarly that "the Americans constantly worry that a strong China will threaten their position of primacy. So the US wants both to dominate China's market and to find every possible way to contain its development."[61] Even Li Ruihuan, a Standing Committee member who had been a supporter of modest political liberalization, saw US intentions as hostile:

> To tell the truth, the United States is very clear about our power. It knows that China today is not a direct threat to the United States. But as for America's long-term development strategy, when it looks at our latent developmental strength, if the Chinese economy keeps developing for a few more decades, it will be big enough to be able to balance with them. So they want to contain us, they want to implement a carrot-and-stick policy. It's useless for us to use a lot of words to refute their "China threat theory." The Americans won't listen to you.[62]

In the years after the 16th Party Congress, as Washington became increasingly preoccupied with the Middle East, China continued to be concerned about the US threat. In 2006, Hu Jintao hosted the Central Foreign Affairs Working Conference—only the third time in the entire PRC's history that this kind of meeting had been convened. At it, he emphasized the US threat and discussed China's fear of encirclement by the United States in concert with its allies: "the United States and other Western countries have vigorously promoted the establishment of a 'democratic nations alliance,'" he warned.[63] Later, repeating language from previous General Secretaries in similar settings, Hu stressed that "the United States remains the main adversary that we need to deal with internationally."[64]

Together, all of these accounts suggest that the United States was the defining focus of China's strategic planning. Chinese leaders consistently labeled the United States as China's chief opponent, defined it explicitly as China's main threat, and raised concerns about the need to manage US ties. We now turn to the *ways* China sought to avoid US containment and to blunt American power.

Ways—Deng's "Tao Guang Yang Hui"

In roughly 494 BC in what is today Zhejiang and Jiangsu province, the rising powers Yue and Wu struggled for advantage. When Yue's overconfident King Goujian decided to attack the much stronger King Fuchai of Wu, the result was a disastrous defeat for Yue. To save Yue from extinction, the humiliated King Goujian placed himself into captivity and servitude at the court of Wu's King Fuchai, where he lived as a commoner and cleaned the stables. While he harbored hopes for retribution, the defeated Goujian never showed resentment, and his quiet dignity and ostentatious displays of loyalty earned him a pardon from the now trusting King Fuchai.

When Goujian returned home to lead Yue, he slept on brushwood and licked a slaughtered animal's gallbladder daily to remember his humiliation and fortify his determination. While he publicly still showed deference to King Fuchai, he quietly set about building his state's strength and subverting King Fuchai's decadent kingdom by bribing his ministers, encouraging him to take on debt, emptying his granaries, and distracting him with women and wine. Roughly a decade later, a vastly stronger Yue that had borne its humiliation well invaded and conquered a declining and unsuspecting Wu.[65]

This story, notes historian Paul A. Cohen, is more parable than history and has enduring cultural impact. It has produced positive idioms like "sleep on brushwood and taste gall" [卧薪尝胆] to encourage hard work and discipline in school or business, as well as more dark expressions like "for a gentleman's revenge, ten years is not too long to wait" [君子报仇，十年不晚]. The parable was frequently cited by Chinese nationalists during the Century of Humiliation, the self-strengthening movement that followed it, and—critically—in Chinese discourses on Deng's post–Cold War strategic guideline that China must "hide its capabilities and bide its time" (Tao Guang Yang Hui), with the parable forming part of the "cultural knowledge" from which the guideline emerged and later appearing in many scholarly discussions of it.[66] That association should hardly be surprising. Japanese and Vietnamese nationalists also turned to the story at times for a similar purpose.[67] Nor should the linkage be taken as literal evidence that China somehow harbors designs as brutal and deceptive as those of King Goujian of Yue.[68] What the parable does suggest is that Deng's guideline should be taken seriously, understood within a larger nationalist context, and not dismissed as a mere Party pablum.

Tao Guang Yang Hui was a shorthand that referred to a longer twenty-four-character admonition from Deng: China should "observe calmly, secure our position, cope with affairs calmly, hide our capabilities and bide our time, maintain a low profile, never claim leadership, and accomplish something."[69] This was a conscious strategy of non-assertiveness. China did not pursue region-building enterprises that might unsettle the United States; instead, it focused on non-assertively blunting the foundations of US power.

Tao Guang Yang Hui appeared after the traumatic trifecta of Tiananmen, the Gulf War, and the Soviet collapse. Several Chinese sources, including articles on the website of the Party newspaper *People's Daily*, recount the guideline's history:

> [Tao Guang Yang Hui] was put forward by Deng Xiaoping during the "special period" of drastic changes in Eastern Europe and the disintegration of the socialist camp there in the late 1980s and early 1990s. At that time, China faced questions about "what to do" and "in what direction to go" as well as others that it urgently needed to answer, and Deng Xiaoping put forward a series of important thoughts/ideology and countermeasures.[70]

Another article on the *People's Daily* site says the same, dating the concept after Tiananmen: "At the beginning of the end of the Cold War, when China was sanctioned by Western countries, Comrade Deng Xiaoping put forward . . . Tao Guang Yang Hui."[71] Party officials ranging from paramount leaders like Hu Jintao to Politburo Standing Committee members like Liu Huaqing echo this history.[72]

The earliest official reference to Tao Guang Yang Hui's core tenets came after the Tiananmen Square Massacre. In a 1989 speech to the CCP Central Committee, Deng laid out much of it: "In short, my views about the international situation can be summed up in three sentences. First, we should observe the situation coolly. Second, we should hold our ground. Third, we should act calmly. Don't be impatient; it is no good to be impatient. We should be calm, calm and again calm, and quietly immerse ourselves in practical work to accomplish something—something for China."[73] Together, these constitute four of the key portions of what eventually became Tao Guang Yang Hui. As Chinese scholars Chen Dingding of Jinan University and Wang Jianwei of the University of Macao write in an analysis of this speech, "Although Deng did not use the precise TGYH [Tao Guang Yang Hui] phrase, the spirit of TGYH was clear in his talks."[74]

As time passed, Deng gave several speeches elucidating Tao Guang Yang Hui and placing it at the center of China's foreign policy in language that strongly suggested that the concept was intended to encourage Chinese self-restraint at a time when its relative power was low. For example, in a speech summarized in Deng Xiaoping's official chronicles, Deng declared Tao Guang Yang Hui the central component of his strategic vision for China's foreign policy and said it was shaped by perceptions of China's relative power: "Only by following Tao Guang Yang Hui for some years can we truly become a relatively major political power, and then when China speaks on the international stage it will make a difference. Once we have the capability, then we will build sophisticated high-tech weapons."[75] Here, Deng links China's limited diplomatic activism and delayed military investment to his Tao Guang Yang Hui strategy, and specifically, to China's temporary weakness.

Tao Guang Yang Hui continued to be China's official strategy even as top leadership changed. Not long after taking power, Jiang Zemin gave a speech on resisting "peaceful evolution" at an expanded meeting of the Politburo Standing Committee in 1991 that reinforced Tao Guang Yang Hui. "Under the current international situation of constant changes, we must stick to carrying out Comrade Deng Xiaoping's strategic guideline of 'observe calmly, stabilize our position, cope calmly, hiding capabilities and biding time [Tao Guang Yang Hui], and be good at defending yourself.' "[76] Jiang declared. "Practice has shown that this is the right guideline. Implementing this guideline is by no means an indication of weakness or that we are giving in, let alone abandoning our principles," he caveated, "instead, it is a realization that we face a complex international structure and we cannot cultivate enemies everywhere."[77] Similarly, a few years later at a smaller gathering of ambassadors, Jiang reiterated these views: "We must implement Comrade Deng Xiaoping's policy of Tao Guang Yang Hui and never taking leadership—this is without doubt."[78] He further stressed, "we cannot go beyond our reality in trying to do things" on the international stage.[79] The goal was to ultimately increase China's autonomy, he said to the Central Military Commission in 1993. "One of the important issues in our strategic guidance is to make good use of contradictions, flexibility, and initiative," Jiang declared, "In the struggle against hegemonism and power politics. . . . We use all possible contradictions to expand our freedom of maneuver."[80] That effort would be long-term, he stressed in another address. "In dealing with international relations and carrying out international struggle, there is a question of the relationship between long-term and short-term interests," he observed. "Sometimes there is a conflict between these short-term and long-term interests, and we will not hesitate to subordinate short-term interests to long-term interests."[81]

In a major foreign affairs address delivered by President Jiang Zemin in 1998 to the 9th Ambassadorial Conference, he continued to commit China to Deng's foreign policy because China was weaker than its competitors, reiterating—as Deng had—that adherence to the guideline was rooted in China's low relative power.

> At this important historical period at the turn of the century, we must unswervingly implement Deng Xiaoping's diplomatic thinking . . . first, we should continue to adhere to the "strategic guidelines" [战略方针] of "calmly observe, calmly deal with the situation, never take leadership, and get something done." [冷静观察、沉着应付、绝不当头、有所作为的战略方针] We should hide our capabilities and bide our time, drawn in our claws, preserve ourselves, and consciously plan our development. [韬光养晦，收敛锋芒，保存自己，徐图发展] *The contrast between our country's conditions and international conditions determines that we must do this.*[82]

Jiang's successor, Hu Jintao, likewise continued to emphasize Tao Guang Yang Hui in multiple speeches. For example, in a major 2003 speech to the Foreign Ministry, he dedicated an entire section to speaking about its fundamental importance: "We must correctly handle the relationship between Tao Guang Yang Hui and accomplishing something," which was a reference to being more active.[83] Tao Guang Yang Hui, along with "observing calmly, calmly coping with challenges, not leading, making a difference," Hu reminded his audience, "is a high-level summary of Comrade Deng Xiaoping's series of important strategic policies for China's diplomacy after the sudden change of international politics in the late 1980s and early 1990s."[84] Following this guideline meant providing China time to develop through non-confrontation, and he warned the assembled foreign policy apparatus that China must not delay development "by sinking into the whirlpool of international conflict."[85] He concluded that "we must adhere to this principle [Tao Guang Yang Hui] without wavering."[86] Indeed, that decision was based on the perception of China's relative power. As Hu argued, "Considering the current situation and development trend of China's national conditions, as well as the international balance of power, *this is a long-term strategic policy.*"[87]

Similarly, in leaked documents prepared for the 16th Party Congress, Hu made clear that China's restraint was influenced by its power. " 'Holding back differences' [存异] is in the common interest of both China and the United States," Hu stated, but this was only because China was weak. "With the development of China's economy and the enhancement of our comprehensive national strength," Hu stressed, "we will be more flexible and confident in handling Sino-US relations."[88]

Perhaps the most thorough and consequential discussions of the concept came in 2006 at the Central Foreign Affairs Working Conference. This was a foreign policy meeting so significant it had previously only ever been held twice before. China must "adhere to the strategic guideline of Tao Guang Yang Hui and getting something done," Hu said at the conference, and he further made clear that "this principle cannot be forgotten at any time."[89] He warned that China's growth might create new attention and complicate the strategy. "Now, some countries are optimistic about us and hope that we can play a greater role and bear more responsibilities.... For this reason, we must keep a clear head, we cannot let our minds get heated because we are living a little better. We must insist on not speaking too much and not doing too much, and even if our country develops further, we must insist on this point."[90]

Hu's address made clear that while China needed to keep its head down, to the extent it tried to "accomplish something," it would focus primarily on blunting. "We must place the basis for 'accomplishing something' on the maintenance and development of our interests, on improving our strength . . . *and reducing and eliminating external resistance and pressures.*"[91] He also put forward a clear articulation of blunting: "it must be seen that the more developed a country is, the more likely it is to encounter external resistance and risky challenges . . . it is necessary to use various contradictions to check external hostile forces' strategic containment of China and to minimize the strategic pressure of external forces on China."[92]

Finally, Hu further argued that Tao Guang Yang Hui required compromise on major interests, using language that suggested openness on territorial questions that he would reverse some years later. "In particular," Hu declared, "we must pay attention to differentiating and grasping core interests, important interests, and general interests. We must prioritize, focus, and do what we can.... For issues that do not impede the overall situation, we must embody mutual understanding and mutual accommodation so that we can concentrate our efforts on safeguarding and developing longer-term and more important national interests."[93] As part of Tao Guang Yang Hui, China would not pursue the kind of coercion or order-building that might otherwise allow it to achieve these interests.

The Tao Guang Yang Hui Skeptics

From the preceding leader-level excerpts, it should be clear that Tao Guang Yang Hui was a Chinese grand strategy to make China less threatening and to avoid encirclement that was based on China's relative power vis-à-vis the United States. A few writers disagree with this view: some perhaps for political reasons, and others for substantive ones. Disagreements take two forms: first, that the phrase does not refer to temporary strategy based on China's power; second, that it is unrelated to blunting the United States.

With respect to the first argument, a few Chinese authors argue that Tao Guang Yang Hui is not a tactical or time-bound instrumental strategy but rather a permanent one. This debate emerges from the mixed uses of Tao Guang Yang Hui in China's own strategic and classical canon. In many cases, the use of the phrases "Tao Guang" and "Yang Hui" whether separately or whether combined into one idiom generally referred to the decision of hermits to retire into seclusion to develop themselves morally or intellectually. "Based on the usages of 'Tao Guang Yang Hui' by our forefathers," argues Yang Wengchang, a retired vice minister of foreign affairs in a prominent essay excerpted later by the Western-facing propaganda outlet *China Daily,* "the term described a low-key lifestyle" and strategic reflection and was not an "expedient tactic."[94] In this view, he argues, Tao Guang Yang Hui "can apply to both good times and bad times" and whether one is weak or strong since it is not determined by external factors or variables.

And yet, as the parable of King Goujian suggests, another strain of literature from which Tao Guang Yang Hui may have arrived is far more tactical and clearly situates Tao Guang Yang Hui as an instrumental strategy affixed to questions of power and threat. Even if linking Tao Guang Yang Hui to this story is overstated, the ultimate provenance of the phrase is not the sole arbiter of its current political meaning. Indeed, as the preceding excerpts from leader-level speeches demonstrate, Deng, Jiang, and Hu all made clear that Tao Guang Yang Hui was a strategy China had to adhere to precisely because of its material inferiority relative to the "international standards" and the international balances of power [力量对比], conceptual stand-ins for the West and Western hegemony, respectively. Deng himself said it was not a fixed strategy. This context demonstrates that Tao Guang Yang Hui is not a permanent grand strategy but an instrumental and time-bound one, contrary to Yang Wengchang's statement.

Second, some skeptics agree that the strategy is instrumental and conditional rather than permanent, but take issue with the notion that it is focused on the United States or constitutes some broader organizing principle. As Michael Swaine argues when discussing Tao Guang Yang Hui:

> This concept is often misinterpreted in the West to mean that China should keep a low profile and bide its time until it is ready to challenge U.S. global predominance. In truth, the concept is most closely associated with diplomatic (not military) strategy and is usually viewed by

Chinese analysts as an admonition for China to remain modest and low-key while building a positive image internationally and achieving specific (albeit limited) gains, in order to avoid suspicions, challenges, or commitments that might undermine Beijing's long-standing emphasis on domestic development.[95]

Swaine is right to argue that observers should see Tao Guang Yang Hui as a defensive rather than offensive strategy. Although the concept is intended to allow China to rise without generating a countervailing balancing coalition, it is still fundamentally about putting off conflict with the United States. First, virtually all Chinese leaders who have elaborated upon it have made clear that it is China's power, implicitly relative to the United States, that sets the conditions for how long Tao Guang Yang Hui should be followed. The empirical record shows that Tao Guang Yang Hui appeared as the American threat grew following the Soviet collapse and that it was officially revised for the first time after the Global Financial Crisis, when unipolarity appeared to Chinese analysts to be on the wane. Second, contrary to Swaine's argument that Tao Guang Yang Hui is a diplomatic principle, Chinese leaders make quite clear that Tao Guang Yang Hui is not merely a "diplomatic guideline" (外交方针) but a much broader "strategic guideline" (战略方针) that sits above all levels of statecraft. Third, a number of China's own prominent think tank scholars and commentators share a more cynical view of Tao Guang Yang Hui than Swaine. For example, Professor Yan Xuetong—one of China's more hawkish and well-connected scholars—parses many of the admonition's phrases and argues that they are fundamentally focused on the United States threat:

> The phrases "undertaking no leadership" and "raising no banner" suggest that China will not challenge American global leadership to avoid a zero sum game between China's national rejuvenation efforts and America's unchallenged global dominance since the end of the Cold War. This will help prevent the United States from focusing on containing the rise of China as a global superpower.[96]

Many Western observers sometimes point to a speech by China's top diplomat Dai Bingguo downplaying the departure from "Tao Guang Yang Hui" in 2010, but Yan disagrees and notes the concept is about the U.S. He openly concedes that Dai's speech and many of the protestations others have made about "Tao Guang Yang Hui's" true meaning are "for the sake of reducing the negative connotation of 'keeping a low profile'" and should not be seen as sincere.[97]

In sum, Tao Guang Yang Hui has been an authoritative organizing principle for China's grand strategy. Its arrival closely followed an increase in China's *perceived threat* from the United States and the country's adherence to it was explicitly justified as conditional on the *perceived relative power gap* with the United States. In authoritative texts, such as the Party newspapers that disseminate ideological doctrine as well as the leader-level speeches that set it, the twenty-four-character admonition has been labeled as a "strategic guideline" (战略方针) and not only "diplomatic guideline" (外交方针), which elevates it above mere policy in Party terminology and gives the phrase a high degree of authority.[98] Finally, in several speeches, the strategy is explained as an effort to reduce the risk of confrontation with the United States and China's own neighbors while simultaneously limiting external pressures on China and expanding China's freedom of maneuver—which is consistent with blunting.

Means—Instruments for Blunting

If Tao Guang Yang Hui is effectively a grand strategy, it should have implications for a variety of instruments of Chinese statecraft. As discussed earlier, Jiang and Hu described the strategy as involving a reduction in external constraints that conforms with blunting.

The trifecta that produced this strategy also produced synchronized, related shifts in China's military, political, and economic behavior.

First, at the military level, the trifecta and the strategic readjustment that followed forced China to change its military strategy to one focused on blunting. In the late 1980s, Chinese leaders had been turning their attention to local wars and territorial disputes—and China began long-term plans for a naval and air structure focused on "sea control" that was designed to hold distant maritime territory. But once the United States became a threat, Beijing jettisoned that strategy in favor of one focused on "sea denial" to prevent the US military from traversing or controlling the waters near China. Deng and Jiang were personally involved in the shift, and in 1993 it was incorporated into China's new 1993 "military strategic guideline." This blunting strategy called for "shashoujian" or "assassin's mace" weapons, defined by China as asymmetric tools against the conventionally superior United States.[99] China made heavy investments in sea denial—it began building the world's largest submarine fleet, largest sea mine arsenal, first ever anti-ship ballistic missile to frustrate US intervention, and even configured virtually every surface combatant for anti-surface warfare at the expense of other missions. All of this was undertaken under the explicit principle of "whatever the enemy is afraid of, we develop that."[100] At the same time, China delayed investments in sea control that would not serve to blunt the United States. It delayed investments in carriers as well as amphibious capabilities, mine countermeasures, anti-submarine warfare, and anti-air warfare. This too was under an official principle—to "catch up in some places but not in others."[101] Critically, these efforts were linked to Tao Guang Yang Hui. Deng himself observed that China should follow "Tao Guang Yang Hui" in weapons production until its power increased. And a decade later, when CMC Vice Chairman Zhang Wannian was confronted with the uncomfortable specter of US war in Kosovo, he reiterated that "what the PLA should do" in response to "the rise of military interventionism" by the United States was to remember that "our approach is Tao Guang Yang Hui."[102] He elaborated, "As a military, this means . . . vigorously developing 'shashoujian' equipment, [and following the principle of] 'whatever the enemy is most afraid of, we develop that.' "[103]

Second, at the political level, the trifecta and China's strategic adjustment led Beijing to reverse its position on joining regional institutions. Memoirs of Chinese ambassadors are explicit on China's need to join institutions to blunt American power in three ways: (1) stalling the institutions so they couldn't become functional; (2) using them to constrain US freedom of maneuver; and (3) using them to reassure neighbors so they wouldn't join a US-led balancing coalition. Beijing feared the transpacific economic organization APEC would become a US platform that would promote Western values damaging to China and could even become an Asian NATO. A similar logic applied to the Association of Southeast Asian Nations Regional Forum (ARF), where top multilateral advisers worried the organization would be used check or contain China.[104] They opposed the institutionalization of both groups on all issues and also tried to reshape some of its norms in ways that would uniquely constrain American military operations. Even so, these efforts were taken consistent with Tao Guang Yang Hui's principle of avoiding claims of leadership [决不当头], which meant China refrained from launching new institutions; moreover, Deng himself had said that China's diplomatic voice would grow louder once Tao Guang Yang Hui was retired.

Finally, the trifecta also shaped Chinese international economic policy. Washington's use of sanctions, its threats to revoke most-favored nation (MFN) status (which would cripple China's economy), and its use of Section 301 trade tariffs against China raised new concerns in Beijing about its vulnerability to US leverage, and blunting these became the focus of Chinese efforts. China not only focused on breaking economic sanctions, it also sought to secure MFN on a permanent basis, or permanent normal trading relations (PNTR). The goal was not to limit China's dependence on the United States but to reduce the discretionary exercise of US economic power. China pushed for PNTR bilaterally and by leveraging negotiations in APEC and WTO as well. It also pushed for WTO membership, hoping it would further tie Washington's hands.

We turn now to each of these instruments to discuss how China's *blunting* efforts across these three domains can be directly traced to the traumatic tri-fecta, how each instrument was adjusted to blunt American power, and how these changes appear to have been synchronized—strongly indicating strategic adjustment by China's leaders.

4

"Grasping the Assassin's Mace"

Implementing Military Blunting

"Whatever the enemy fears most, we develop that."[1]

—Zhang Wannian,
Vice Chairman of the Central Military Commission, 1999

On March 27, 1999, US Air Force Lt. Col Darrell Zelko had just struck a target outside Belgrade as part of a NATO campaign to end Serbia's cleansing of its Kosovar Albanians. As Zelko turned his stealthy F-117A back to Aviano Air Base in northern Italy, he noticed two bright dots rising to meet him through the clouds below. Each dot was a missile traveling at three times the speed of sound, and they had been launched from a Serbian air-defense unit commanded by Zoltan Dani.[2]

Dani's unit was equipped with outdated early 1960s Soviet-era equipment, but he made up for it with innovative tactics. He knew that his unit was extremely vulnerable to US anti-radiation missiles that would home in on his batteries if he left his fire-control radars on for even a second too long—a lesson Iraqi air defense units had failed to learn in the First Gulf War. So Dani trained his unit to activate its fire-control radar in twenty-second bursts, to relocate within ninety minutes to avoid being struck, to create radar decoys to soak up US missiles, to use low-frequency radars to acquire targets, and to engage US aircraft only *after* they completed their ground strike missions. Those tactics had ensured his unit's survival against two dozen NATO missiles during the war, and on that night in September, they also provided an opportunity to make history.[3]

Dani's missiles crippled the Nighthawk, with Zelko ejecting and promptly rescued by US forces. The strike stunned the world: one of the world's stealthiest aircrafts long considered virtually invisible had been downed by one of the world's most dated air defense systems—a system not at all dissimilar from China's own at the time.

Nearly 5,000 miles away, China's military had watched the event with extraordinary interest. Within three days, Zhang Wannian, then vice chairman of the Central Military Commission, raced a rapidly prepared report on the NATO campaign and Serbia's innovative resistance over to President Jiang Zemin. In the report, Zhang noted that "the forces of Yugoslavia have provided a useful reference point for our army on the question of how an inferior equipped force can defeat a superior-equipped force under high-tech conditions."[4] As a sign not only of China's focus on asymmetric weapons but its fundamental concern with blunting US capabilities in particular, Zhang flagged the report as urgent for Jiang and even attached a personal note imploring Jiang to read it.[5] At a high-level meeting not long after, Zhang made clear why studying Serbia was so relevant to defending China, and he then disseminated this message to the entire People's Liberation Army. "NATO airstrikes reflected the characteristics and rules of high-tech weapons," Zhang allowed, but "Serbian resistance . . . gives us a lot of inspiration. We should apply these revelations to preparations for military struggle" with superior adversaries, by which he meant the United States.[6]

Zhang's urgent memo on the "inspiration" Serbia offered in defeating American capabilities came ten years after China—prompted by the fallout from Tiananmen Square and later the Gulf War and Soviet collapse—began looking for a new military strategy that would *blunt* US military power. This chapter explores that effort. It argues that, before the trifecta, Chinese leaders in the late 1980s had been turning their attention to local wars and territorial disputes, and China began long-term plans for a naval and air structure focused on *sea control* that was designed to hold distant maritime territory. But once the United States became a threat, Beijing jettisoned that strategy in favor of one focused on *sea denial* to prevent the US military from traversing or controlling the waters near China. Deng and Jiang were personally involved in the shift, and in 1993 it was incorporated into China's new "military strategic guidelines." This blunting strategy called for "shashoujian" or "assassin's mace" weapons, defined by China as asymmetric tools against the conventionally superior United States.[7] China made heavy investments in sea denial: it began building the world's largest submarine fleet, largest sea mine arsenal, first ever anti-ship ballistic missile (primarily to menace US carriers), and even configured virtually every surface combatant for anti-surface warfare at the expense of other missions—building an asymmetric navy and a complex capable of what many military analysts call "anti-access/area-denial" (A2/AD). All of this was undertaken under the explicit principle of "whatever the enemy is afraid of, we develop that." At the same time, China delayed investments in sea control that would not serve to blunt the United States. It delayed investments in carriers as well as amphibious capabilities, mine countermeasures, anti-submarine warfare, and anti-air warfare. This too was under an official principle—to "catch up in some places but not in others."

Critically, these efforts were linked to Tao Guang Yang Hui. Deng observed China should follow Tao Guang Yang Hui in weapons production until its power increased. And as Zhang Wannian observed the US war in Kosovo, he too reiterated that "what the PLA should do" in response to "the rise of military interventionism" by the United States was to remember that "our approach is Tao Guang Yang Hui." He went on, "As a military, this means . . . vigorously developing 'shashoujian' equipment, [and following the principle of] 'whatever the enemy is most afraid of, we develop that.' "[8]

This chapter proceeds in three parts. First, it lists possible alternative explanations for China's military behavior that are tested against the one proposed here. Second, it uses Chinese memoirs, selected works, essays, and doctrinal sources to demonstrate that China's military strategy after the trifecta was focused on blunting US military power. Third, it analyzes Chinese behavior to likewise demonstrate that a focus on blunting explains China's military investments in this period.

Explaining Military Strategy

We can gain insight into why China made the military investments it did in two ways: (1) by analyzing its decision-making process using authoritative texts; and (2) by analyzing the patterns in China's military investments and activities to test what best explains that behavior.

When we study military investments, there are least four indicators that are important, and variation within them, across them, and between them as well as comparisons with other countries can together be leveraged to dismiss certain theories of Chinese behavior and validate others. These include (1) *acquisition*, or what China acquired and when; (2) *doctrine*, or which sets of institutionalized principles about how to fight China adopted; (3) *force posture*, or how and where China deploys its military; and (4) *training*, or how and for what kinds of conflict China prepares its forces to fight.[9] A focus on these variables, as well as key Chinese texts, can help us test competing theories explaining China's military investments.

What are these competing theories? The first rival explanation is *diffusion*, which suggests that states will emulate the capabilities of the world's strongest states and that China's military would largely copy US force structure and practices.[10] A second explanation is *adoption capacity theory*, which would propose that China cannot copy all US practices because some are too expensive or organizationally complex, so its investments will be shaped by what it can adopt. These two theories focus on what can be supplied to states, but military investments are often just as much about demand, or what the state needs.[11] A third explanation, one that focuses on demand, is that *bureaucratic politics*—internal conflicts in China between Party and military officials, the army and the navy, or surface warfare officers and submariners—explain Beijing's military investments.[12] In contrast, another set of demand-focused theories elevates national interests over parochial ones. As Barnard College professor Kimberly Marten Zisk puts it, militaries "are often concerned not only about their own institutional interests in domestic politics, but also about the protection of state security interests from foreign threats."[13] Applied to China, this approach leads us to a fourth and fifth explanation for China's military investments, both focused on China's perception of the security environment. The fourth theory—one proposed and defended in this chapter—is that China's military investments are best explained by the threat of US military intervention within the region and are intended to *blunt* that threat through anti-access/area-denial capabilities. A fifth theory, proposed by MIT professor Taylor Fravel and Naval Postgraduate School professor Christopher Twomey, is that China's military investments are geared toward a number of local operations focused on Taiwan, the South and East China Seas, and even conflict with Russia, India, and the Korean peninsula. In this view, the region itself is China's primary focus, less so the United States.[14]

This chapter as well as Chapter 8 endorse the fourth and fifth theories and show that the question is not which theory is right but rather *when* each theory is right. The fourth theory, which corresponds to *blunting*, explains Chinese strategy after the trifecta; the fifth theory, which actually aligns with *building*, applies best after the 2008 Global Financial Crisis, when a more confident China overtly pursued capabilities for regional contingencies.

To test these various theories, we now turn to a focus on China's own discourse on its military investments.

Chinese Military Texts

Chinese military memoirs, essays, and doctrinal sources demonstrate that since late 1989, China has identified conflict with the United States as its most significant military challenge.[15] This section (1) establishes that a shift in Chinese strategy followed Tiananmen Square, the Gulf War, and the Soviet collapse; (2) explains the emergence of China's asymmetric blunting strategy focused on the United States by analyzing its discourse on "assassin's mace" or "shashoujian" weapons, a contentious term that is demonstrated here to be a stand-in for asymmetric weapons investments; and (3) briefly considers alternative explanations.

A Shift in Strategy

In the 1980s, the Soviet Union constituted an existential threat to China that occupied the full attention of its defense planners. But by the late 1980s, a gradual decrease in tension led Chinese leaders to turn their attention more concretely to local wars. In 1985, for instance, Deng Xiaoping officially changed China's strategic outlook and declared that there was no longer a threat of imminent ground or nuclear war with the Soviet Union. Following this change in strategic thinking, and as part of a more gradual focus on naval affairs and maritime territorial conflicts, the Chinese navy shifted its strategy in 1986 from "Coastal Defense" to "Offshore Defense."[16]

This emerging trajectory in Chinese security policy was not to last, and the trifecta of Tiananmen Square, the Gulf War, and the Soviet collapse subsequently changed China's security outlook and focused it on the US threat rather than on local (especially maritime) conflicts with neighbors. The memoirs, biographies, selected works, and essays of China's Central Military Commission (CMC) vice chairman—the highest military position in China's system below the General Secretary—provide insight into both *why* and *how* China's military strategy changed. Virtually all CMC vice chairmen attribute the change in China's military strategy to the trifecta.

In 1993, Liu Huaqing—who was then not only China's top military official but also the last military member to serve on the ruling Politburo Standing Committee—published an authoritative essay explaining China's adoption of new Military Strategic Guidelines that year. Consistent with the account above, Liu explicitly enumerated two broad reasons for changing China's military strategy: (1) the Soviet collapse; and (2) the Gulf War. Regarding the first, Liu argued that the "the bipolar structure has come to an end . . . [but] hegemonism and power politics," a reference to the United States in this case, "have yet to step down from the stage of history" and must still be opposed.[17] There would be no peace dividend, because "conflicts and disputes which were covered up during the Cold War have [now] sharpened," a reference to Sino-American disputes over issues like Taiwan that had been somewhat mitigated by the Cold War focus on the Soviet Union. For these reasons, "we cannot say that it is now peacetime so we can let our horses graze in the south mountains, put our swords and guns in the warehouses, and grasp modernization of the military after the economy is developed," Liu argued. Liu's second explicitly enumerated justification for military change was the Gulf War. "We [the central leadership] have attached importance to research in the Gulf War," he wrote. "Limited wars in the last few years, the Gulf War in particular, have shown many distinctive features," and in this regard, he noted, "we should point out that the Gulf War is a special conflict" that required adjusting military strategy.[18] From Beijing's perspective, the Gulf

War was a vision into a frightening future where US high-technology weapons could be wielded against China's outdated forces, and therefore a catalyst for changing strategy, as subsequent sections discuss in greater detail.

Three other CMC vice chairmen—Zhang Zhen, Zhang Wannian, and Chi Haotian—each confirmed that the Soviet collapse, the Gulf War, and the dangers of US hegemonism caused a major change in Chinese military strategy, and they recount this being the subject of several CMC meetings in the early 1990s. Zhang Zhen noted that "the end of the Cold War structure" and "the development of high-tech [weaponry]" were "major changes in the situation and required China's military strategic guidelines to be adjusted accordingly."[19] Zhang Wannian echoed this too, arguing that "the disintegration of the 'bipolar' world structure" and the "new changes in warfare brought by high-tech weaponry" formed a "strategic background against which the CCP Central Committee and the CMC decided to establish new strategic guidelines."[20] Chi Haotian included these factors but also focused on the post-Tiananmen US ideological threat as well as sanctions and containment in a 1991 speech: "Given the stormy and unstable international political environment, under a situation where international *exchange and blockade as well as cooperation and containment coexist*, we need to conscientiously implement the military strategy of this new period."[21] All these generals agreed that despite the end of the Cold War, "new features of hegemony had emerged," and these could also jeopardize China's unification with Taiwan.[22] Outside the military, some of these themes found purchase too. The climate after the trifecta was tense enough that a somewhat outlandish memo written by conservative rabblerouser He Xin—who briefly rose in this moment to become a foreign policy adviser to Premier Li Peng and worked in the office of the Foreign Affairs Leading Small Group—was circulated to the Politburo. It argued that mainland China could be subject to US military strikes and that "isolating China, blockading China, disintegrating it through [instigating] internal disorders, and eventually rendering China innocuous through democratizing it has been and will be a strategic goal that the US will steadfastly continue to implement."[23] The brief rise of its author in policymaking was a sign of the times.

Together, these texts suggest China's military strategy was changing. We turn now to consider what it would soon become.

A Blunting Strategy

In the years after the trifecta, China's strategy cohered into an effort to develop asymmetric weapons to blunt American power. Accordingly, the history of China's strategic adjustment can be recreated through high-level texts and records of these meetings, all of which suggest (1) that China believed it was facing a threat from US high-tech weaponry; and (2) that China needed an asymmetric approach using "shashoujian" or "assassin's mace" weapons to deal with that threat.

This evocative term—"shashoujian"—is sometimes dismissed as mere rhetoric since it also appears in romance or sports columns and therefore seems to have a meaning "somewhat analogous to 'silver bullet' in English idiom."[24] But in historical context, "the term 'shashoujian' originally came from ancient Chinese folk stories, where the hero wielded this magic object to defeat a seemingly overwhelmingly powerful and evil adversary."[25] In its military context in this period, the term indeed meant something specific—it was a synonym for asymmetric weapons and capabilities that could defeat high-technology opponents.

In a speech on military modernization, paramount leader Jiang Zemin said China needed to develop its "own sophisticated 'assassin's mace' weapons equipment aimed *at developed countries* . . . suited to 'winning' as quickly as possible."[26] Similarly, General Fu Quanyou—head of the PLA General Staff Department and a CMC member—wrote that "to defeat a *better equipped enemy* with inferior equipment in the context of high-technology, we should rely upon . . . high-quality shashoujian weapons."[27] More recently, Xi Jinping explicitly defined the term "shashoujian" as asymmetric [非对称] in a speech on technology.[28] And although scholars like former Pentagon official Michael Pillsbury argue the term emerged in the late 1990s, Chinese sources now available demonstrate it—and the asymmetric strategy associated with it—had already emerged by the early 1990s.[29]

The Gulf War, Military Strategy, and Shashoujian

The focus on an asymmetric strategy began shortly after the trifecta. The Gulf War in particular clarified which military technologies were threatening to China and which might be useful against the United States. These lessons were incorporated into China's 1993 Military Strategic Guidelines, and as subsequent sections show, into China's military investments. As a part of this strategy, China endeavored to develop weapons that would allow the "inferior to defeat the superior," constituted "what the enemy fears most," functioned as "trump cards and shrewd chess moves," and were "capable of deterring a powerful enemy." To build these weapons, for which China had to postpone certain military investments in vulnerable carriers and surface vessels, Beijing resolved instead to "catch up in some places, but not others."

At the outset of the Gulf War, Chinese leaders knew that Iraq had equipment similar and in some cases superior to China's own. They expected the Iraqis could wage a form of China's own "People's War under Modern Conditions" that would pull Washington into a long ground war and deliver it a political defeat, in contrast to smoother US interventions in Grenada, Libya, and Panama.[30] When the United States instead prevailed spectacularly in the conflict, a stunned Chinese leadership saw a frightening similarity between Iraq's defeat and China's possible fate in a limited conflict with the United States. In a high-level study session called to explore the Gulf War, Chi Haotian wrote that "the Iraqi forces were not only completely passive in the face of air strikes, on the ground they also lost so quickly and so disastrously," which he admitted was "unexpected."[31] Chinese figures wrote publicly that the Gulf War was an example of US "global hegemonism" and that "the U.S. intended to dominate the world," including China.[32] As Zhang Wannian put it, "after the Gulf War, high technology local war ascended onto the stage, [and] every major country had to adjust its military strategy," including China.[33]

To adjust its military strategy, China launched a series of studies to examine the Gulf War as soon as it ended. In March 1991, the Central Military Commission met to go over the conflict, and Jiang Zemin—then Party General Secretary and CMC Chairman—was directly involved. The participation of China's soon-to-be paramount leader in a study of the Gulf War, especially at the operational level, was remarkable. It suggests that the adjustment of China's military strategy took place at the highest levels possible, and other accounts confirm that Jiang was deeply involved. Chi Haotian's biography notes that Jiang personally "paid great attention to the Gulf War, and instructed the General Staff Department to study the characteristics and laws of warfare, explore new operational patterns, and *put forward corresponding countermeasures*" to cope with the kind of high-tech warfare the United States exhibited at the operational level.[34] Zhang Zhen, who worked closely with Jiang during this period, wrote in his memoirs, "After the outbreak of the Gulf War, [Jiang] was very concerned with the course of the war, in particular the development of modern warfare as manifested by it, and personally participated in a number of military seminars."[35] Jiang even routinely offered "guidance on studying operational issues under high-tech conditions" and on the "preparation for the formulation of military strategic guidelines in the new period."[36]

The General Staff Department also held a Gulf War study session in early 1991, and Chi Haotian's address there indicates the major conclusions of that session. He noted that the Gulf War seemed to reveal US strength and indicated that "the world power balance" was not so favorable.[37] Iraq's defeat meant that China needed to "conscientiously study the lessons and experiences of the Gulf War" and "take from it useful inspiration in order to strengthen China's defense and military construction."[38] This task was urgent, Chi suggested, because China faced a serious threat. Citing the defeat of countries like Argentina and Iraq to Western forces with higher-technology weapons, Chi Haotian related these conflicts directly to what he considered China's own dire situation: "the outcome of these conflicts demonstrates that . . . the weaker countries were subject to control by others, took a beating, suffered humiliation, and even suffered subjugation or destruction."[39] Chi continued, "This is a lesson history has proved countless times, *but bitter reality [i.e., the Gulf War] has once again placed this lesson right in front of us. Connecting this with our own situation, we cannot do without a sense of urgency.*"[40]

To deal with this concerning state of affairs, Chi's speech recommended that China find a way to defeat a stronger opponent under high-tech conditions. Iraq failed to adopt these asymmetric strategies, Chi noted, and "this makes us once again deeply feel that if countries that have inferior weapons want to effectively defeat stronger countries," then they need to plan accordingly. He went on: "The real effective way [to deal with a superior opponent] is still what Chairman Mao said, you fight your way, I fight my way. In other words, you have your advanced technology, I have my own set of inferior equipment to deal with your approach."[41] This old Maoist concept often discussed in concert with "People's War" needed to be repurposed for high-technology conditions and incorporated into China's military guidelines, Chi noted:

> In tactics, including the specific use of the People's War, with respect to using inferior equipment to defeat the enemy's tactics, *we should make great efforts to study and probe.* From our national conditions and military situation, we must create a method with our own characteristics that hides our weaknesses and shows our strengths, limits giving exposure to our weaknesses, [and] slashes at the opponent's weakness. *This is what our usual military guidance needs to conscientiously focus on and study to solve the strategic problem before us.*[42]

The goal, as Chi summarized, was to "develop our high-tech equipment, so in our hands it will ensure that the opponent won't do rash things, and that we won't suffer coercion" from a high-tech adversary (like the United States). Some months after the first meeting of the Gulf War Study group, the General Staff Department released the *Gulf War Study Report* summarizing its findings. According to Chi Haotian, the report contained "extensive and in-depth research on how to use existing equipment in order to deal with the enemy with high-tech advantages," of which of course the United States was the only plausible candidate.[43] Months later, the GSD published a report with recommendations for China's new military strategic guidelines.[44]

As China's strategy began to come into focus in 1991 and 1992, the term "shashoujian" appeared in discussions at the very highest levels of China's political system. According to Zhang Zhen, Deng Xiaoping himself reportedly called for the development of shashoujian weapons in this period within the context of "overcoming the advantages of a superior enemy."[45] In a high-level 1992 speech on China's new Military Strategic Guidelines before both the CMC and the Politburo Standing Committee, Zhang Wannian called for shashoujian weapons to "cope with local wars and armed conflicts under high-tech conditions," a kind of warfare only the United States could wage.[46]

In December 1992, Jiang Zemin actively participated in a "military strategy symposium" with Central Military Commission members for two days to finalize the new military strategic guidelines.[47] Zhang Zhen summarized the discussion on the new strategy in a speech that seemed to reference the US threat. He "traced the history of modern China suffering the invasions of foreign enemies" and linked it to "new features of hegemony [US dominance]," suggesting this be the focus for defense work."[48] The Gulf War showed that "the precision of long-range attack capabilities has obviously been enhanced" and that "long-range precision strike is expected to destroy objectives along the full depth [of the battle space]."[49] At the operational level, he hinted at an asymmetric strategy by arguing that "the strategy and tactics of the People's War need to be innovated" and that in the revised strategy China must "focus on the weaknesses and key points in the enemy's whole system."[50] After a few final meetings of the CMC and reports produced by the GSD, the new guidelines were approved in January 1993, with their core focus being on preparing for "local warfare under high-technology conditions."[51] At long last, China's strategy had been formally adjusted.

The public rollout of these new guidelines in 1993 demonstrated that the asymmetric focus on high-tech opponents like the United States in planning meetings had made it into the final policy. In a long essay explaining these guidelines, Liu Huaqing reiterated the central leadership's conclusions: "our viewpoint is . . . [that] any hi-tech weapon system has its own weaknesses and we can always find ways to overcome it" and that "our military, poorly equipped as they were [in past conflicts], used to triumph over better equipped enemies. This fine tradition will still play a role in future hi-tech wars."[52] In an unmistakable reference to the United States, he wrote, "The modernization of armies in the countries which pursue hegemony is mainly based on the development of long-range offensive weapons and aimed at carrying out global combat operations."[53] Liu was explicit that the Gulf War not only showed the danger of these high-tech weapons, but also how to beat them asymmetrically. And Liu also emphasized the need for a "new" spin on old asymmetric Maoist approaches: "In particular, efforts must be made to study the *new* tactics of using inferior equipment to beat an enemy with superior equipment."[54] Liu worried that "the gap between China and the *advanced standard* in the world will become bigger and bigger" if these asymmetric efforts were not undertaken.[55]

Strategic Tradeoffs and Shashoujian

To ensure that this new strategy was properly implemented, Liu's essay made clear that China would make tradeoffs. He noted that the 1993 Military Strategic Guidelines had determined that land conflicts (e.g., with India, Vietnam, Russia, or newly independent Central Asian states) were not to be the focus of defense investments. Although Liu committed to a 3-million-man army, perhaps to reassure the land forces, other services needed more attention: "priority must be given to the development of the Navy and Air Force and to strengthening the building of technical arms. . . . [W]e must put the modernization of the Navy and Air Force in the priority position."[56] China's major territorial disputes—and its focus on Taiwan—all had maritime components involving the United States, hence the emphasis on the maritime direction. Subsequent documents make the focus on the United States far clearer, and as Zhang Wannian himself stated, the "new strategic guidelines set the strategic direction and the combat opponents" China would face.[57] Once again, context strongly suggests a US focus.

Preparation would be expensive, and Liu's discussion of China's Military Strategic Guidelines emphasized China could not modernize everything: "Since the money for military use is limited . . . the money for purchasing equipment, capital construction . . . is in fact, very small. Under this situation, we must make the best possible use of the limited money."[58] What this would require was a form of prioritization: "We must proceed from our country's conditions and cannot compare everything with advanced international standards." China's paramount leader was involved in these decisions, with generals noting that shashoujian efforts were "under the direct supervision of Jiang Zemin."[59] Jiang Zemin put forward guidelines [方针] for prioritization that were then repeated by senior military officials in many speeches over more than a decade. These included "separate the primary from the secondary, solve things in order of priority" [主次先后、轻重缓急] ,as well as "do some things but not other things, catch up in some places but not others places" [有所为有所不为，有所赶有所不赶].

These phrases were repeatedly and explicitly linked to prioritizing the construction of shashoujian weapons.[60] For example, in a speech before the National Defense Science and Technology Commission, Zhang Wangnian, who helped lead shashoujian efforts argued, "Shashoujian construction requires a lot of funds," which meant that "for those programs involving backwards technology, we must remove them, and we must not allow them to squeeze out our limited funds."[61] He invoked China's guidance that China needed to "catch up in some places and not others" and "do some things and not others" in order to build shashoujian. At a work conference organized to accelerate shashoujian construction, Zhang argued they should be in the "leading position" for modernization over other areas.[62] And in a CMC meeting, Zhang Wannian again echoed Jiang Zemin on these points: "Our funds are limited, our time is constrained, and we cannot do everything. If we do everything, then we will do everything badly, so we must prioritize, distinguish between primary and secondary [investments], and prioritize those that are urgently needed and develop them." In other words, he continued, "The general idea is that what the enemy is afraid of, we develop that."[63]

The Growing Urgency of Shashoujian

In the years after the guidelines were announced, China intensified its focus on asymmetric shashoujian weapons systems at the highest level, particularly given repeated demonstrations of US power.

In a 1994 meeting with senior officials, Zhang Zhen outlined a three-step plan for defeating high-tech adversaries like the United States. First, "in the event of high-tech local wars," he told his audience, "we still have to base [our strategy] on the principle of using inferior equipment to defeat the enemy's superior equipment."[64] He continued, "In waging war under high-tech conditions, we must first master high-tech equipment itself, and split it into two components to study it: it is necessary to understand its strengths and also to understand its weaknesses."[65] Second, with respect to tactics, instead of emulating the enemy, China would adhere to the "you fight your way, I fight my way" line of Mao's military thought modernized for new conditions.[66] Zhang then noted that "the third step, also a key step, is to come up with our own countermeasures, everyone has their strong points and their weak points [寸有所长，尺有所短], *high-tech weapons have limitations*, and we can always find ways to deal with them."[67] Together, the focus on using inferior equipment to defeat superior equipment, to use unique tactics to do so, and to focus on the limitations of high-tech weapons presages China's anti-access strategy. As Zhang Wannian explained, long-range strike was critical, and he stressed the importance of "solving the 'see far, strike far, strike accurately' problem . . . especially to prioritize the development of effective shashoujian.[68]

As tensions with the United States over Taiwan began to intensify, the link between shashoujian and US power was made clearer. In one meeting, Zhang Wannian declared that China needed shashoujian weapons with a "strong deterrent power" by the year 2000 to deal with "the main direction of military struggle," a reference to the Taiwan Strait, which would involve US intervention.[69] At a meeting on research plans for shashoujian weapons in 1999, Zhang again linked them to Taiwan: "President Jiang Zemin has repeatedly emphasized that we should grasp shashoujian, this is the key to . . . *fulfilling unification*. Only after developing our own shashoujian . . . will China have the ability to take the initiative in strategy."[70] Zhang also often stressed their importance for "anti-splittist warfare," another reference to Taiwan.[71] Again, these were seen as asymmetric tools. As Zhang put it in a meeting on weapons development for the 9th Five-Year Plan, "In high technology warfare it is indeed necessary to have an effective 'trick or shrewd chess move' (招), to have a 'shashoujian,' with which to fulfill the requirements of deterring and defeating the enemy."[72]

China's push for this "trick or shrewd chess move" grew more acute with additional demonstrations of US force in the late 1990s. After US strikes on Iraq in 1998, the PLA's General Armament Department expressed concern and declared Beijing needed "to do everything possible as soon as possible to produce shashoujian weapons. Once we have a few shashoujian weapons, only then will our country be able to stand up with a straight spine."[73] After the US campaign in Kosovo in 1999, as the introduction discussed, the PLA focused on how some exchanges showed that "an inferior equipped force can defeat a superior-equipped force under high-tech conditions," with reports sent directly to Jiang Zemin himself.[74] And after the United States accidentally bombed China's embassy in Belgrade in 1999, furious top leaders like Zhang—who believed it "was by no means accidental" but instead "entirely premeditated"—stressed the need to "accelerate the development of shashoujian weapons" at an emergency CMC meeting the next day.[75]

In a July 1999 meeting CMC meeting on Kosovo, Zhang tied all these US demonstrations of force in the 1990s to China's modernization strategy. "The 'Embassy bombing incident' has been a wake-up call for the Chinese military," he declared, "From the Gulf War in 1991 to 'Desert Fox' in 1998 to the Kosovo War in 1999, the PLA . . . has faced a series of major problems."[76] In Zhang's view, every single demonstration of US power projection in the 1990s posed a problem for Chinese security. "The war in Kosovo is an important step in accelerating the implementation of the global strategy by the United States at the turn of the century," he argued in the same speech, "and an important indicator of the new development of U.S. hegemonism."[77] "What is the Chinese People's Liberation Army to do in the face of possible future war threats?" Zhang provided "a loud and clear answer" at the meeting: China should focus on "vigorously producing 'shashoujian' weapons" under the precept that "what the enemy is most afraid of is what we should develop" in order to win "local wars under high-tech conditions."[78] And once again, the focus was on winning these wars against the United States.

Alternative Explanations

Together, several authoritative Chinese military memoirs and selected works make clear that China's military modernization in the 1990s and 2000s was geared toward high-tech war with the United States. They also dismiss alternative explanations for China's behavior. For example, *diffusion* assumes China would emulate leading capabilities and *adoption capacity* that it would do so provided it was not too financially or organizationally complex. But as the texts made clear, Chinese leaders deprioritized many investments—aiming to "catch up in some places but not others," "separate the primary from the secondary," and "do some things but not other things"—in favor of those that would be useful asymmetric tools against the United States. *Bureaucratic politics* likewise cannot explain China's unique focus on asymmetric warfare. The decision to build asymmetric shashoujian weapons was carefully considered and ultimately approved at the highest levels by the Central Military Commission, limiting room for lower-level interests to influence policy, and there appeared to be a strong taboo and even disciplinary action against those engaging in intra-service or inter-service rivalry that detracted from the asymmetric mission. As Zhang Wannian wrote:

> Every department and branch of the military should firmly establish this overall concept [that we should develop what the enemy fears], and go all out to ensure the fulfillment of the goals for new high-tech weapons and equipment. To ensure focus, we must emphasize local compliance with the overall situation, even at the expense of local bureaus. We must resolutely prevent and overcome the decentralization, and cannot unilaterally emphasize number, size, and the "specialness" of the units. We must forbid their taking advantage of the [reform] situation . . . and should make submitting to the overall situation a serious [focus of] discipline.[79]

Finally, the idea that China's military strategy was focused on *regional* neighbors is incorrect. As the preceding discussion showed, China's leaders admittedly focused on local wars, but the opponent was often a described as a "high-technology" opponent or a "superior enemy," one capable of fielding long-range strike and seemingly pursuing hegemony—criteria only the United States fulfilled in this period. It was also US demonstrations of force that were rigorously studied by nervous PLA leaders, who drew explicit connections between the situations of defeated countries and China's own. And every major local conflict—not only the "primary direction" of the Taiwan Strait but also the East China Sea, South China Sea, and Korean peninsula—would likely feature US involvement, which would be the primary impediment to Chinese success. Chinese doctrinal texts, like the *Science of Military Strategy* [战略学], admit this: "Even if the direct [i.e., local] enemy is inferior to us, it is still possible that powerful enemies [i.e., the United States] may intervene. Therefore, strategically, the PLA still should be based on the principle of using inferior weapons to defeat a superior equipped enemy."[80] And while China did face the possibility of land conflicts, primarily with India and Vietnam, the analysis detailed in this section revealed that as early as 1993 Liu Huaqing officially deemphasized those to focus on maritime conflicts—a judgment sustained in subsequent relatively authoritative texts like the 1999 and 2013 *Science of Military Strategy* all the way to President Xi's recent speeches.[81]

Having established China's asymmetric strategy in authoritative military texts, we now turn to explore its practical implementation in military investment.

Denial Platforms: Submarines, Mines, and Missiles

After the trifecta, China overinvested in three capabilities that are useful primarily for denial as part of its blunting strategy: submarines, missiles, and mines. It built the world's largest submarine fleet, the world's largest stockpile of sea mines, and the world's first anti-ship ballistic missile. China's pursuit of these capabilities during the 1990s and early 2000s stands in sharp contrast to its contemporaneous underinvestment in carrier aviation, anti-submarine warfare, anti-air warfare, mine countermeasures, and amphibious warfare, and it is not explainable through any of the theories offered at the chapter's outset, including diffusion-based theories and adoption capacity theories. Moreover, these capabilities do not allow China to control islands or recapture Taiwan, even when viewed as part of a combined operation with China's limited amphibious and sea control capabilities. Again, the best explanation instead is that China focused on those capabilities as part of a blunting grand strategy. They work to asymmetrically deny the United States the ability to operate within the region.

This logic is found in China's pseudo-doctrinal texts. For example, the *2012 Joint Campaign Theory Study Guide* dwells at length on asymmetric strategies, and at one point explicitly advocates the use of missiles, submarines, and mines to create an asymmetric advantage:

> Symmetric advantage occurs when both the enemy and our forces have the same kind of combat capabilities, and when we have the same fundamental quality, so that confronting the enemy takes the form of requiring numerical superiority. With respect to asymmetric advantage . . . If the enemy has combat capabilities that we lack, we must use other means that can defeat the enemy and win in order to create an *asymmetric advantage,* such as having the necessary number of *cruise missiles, submarines, and mines against an aircraft carrier,* which together makes up an asymmetric strike advantage.[82]

In another instance, the authors advocate "using missile assaults, submarine ambushes, and mine blockades against an aircraft carrier battle group in our waters."[83] These three capabilities are invoked against aircraft carriers several times in other doctrinal texts as well, and it is in part for this reason that this case explores the three capabilities discussed earlier, as well as Chinese overinvestment in them. The prioritization of these capabilities during China's blunting strategy should be seen within the context of leader-level discussions of Chinese military strategy where paramount leaders like Jiang Zemin and various vice chairmen of the CMC emphasized the following: developing shashoujian weapons, "developing what the enemy fears," "using the weapons of the weak to defeat a high-technology adversary," and focusing on the "enemy's weak points." Similarly, the relative underinvestment in other capabilities seems related to admonitions to "separate the primary from the secondary" in military modernization, "catch up in some places but not in others," and to "do some things but not all things." We turn now to look at China's investments in each of these asymmetric domains.

Submarines

On April 25, 2003, a group of fishermen out on the Bohai Sea east of Beijing noticed something unusual. Emerging from the water was a thin metal rod glinting in the sun. As they approached it carefully, they realized the rod was in fact a periscope attached to a submarine that appeared to be adrift.[84]

The fishermen quickly radioed Beijing, which promptly investigated. The submarine was China's Ming-class Submarine 361, but since it couldn't be raised over the radio, Chinese sailors towed it back to port and then boarded it. Inside, they found the crew slumped over their stations, apparently having suffocated. Submarine 361 had been listlessly afloat in the Bohai Sea for almost ten days.

A few weeks later in Beijing, a Foreign Ministry spokesperson acknowledged the tragedy and flatly attributed it to "mechanical failure."[85] But some analysts believed the real cause was something more: a botched test of China's long-pursued air-independent propulsion technology that would make its submarines more stealthy against US surface vessels and aircraft carriers.[86] They noted the already cramped vessel had departed with twenty more submariners than typical for its class, including a high-ranking PLAN officer—all of which was unusual and suggested a premature sea trial may have been underway.[87]

Although the tragedy's cause was uncertain to outsiders, the penalties were clear, and heads promptly rolled. PLAN Commander Shi Yunsheng was fired, and four other of the PLAN's most senior officials were dismissed or demoted. Despite this setback, China continued to pour resources into its submarine fleet.

And only three years later, a Chinese Song class submarine—more advanced than the Ming—stunned the world when it surfaced undetected within torpedo range of the carrier USS *Kitty Hawk*.

China's investments in submarines are somewhat puzzling at first glance. Between 1990 and 2015, China undertook a massive modernization effort for its submarines. It retired all 84 of its outdated Romeo submarines and acquired 14 Ming, 12 Russian Kilo, 13 Song, and 12 Yuan-class submarines; it also launched the new Shang SSN—with a total of roughly 70 submarines now in service.[88] When most blue-water navies are organized around carriers, why has China for almost twenty years organized much of its navy around submarines? Why did China decide after the trifecta to build the world's largest submarine fleet and deploy almost all of it close to home?

This chapter's outset offered a few possible explanations, but they fall short. *Diffusion* and *adoption capacity* theories are able to explain acquisition but not overinvestment relative to other militaries. *Bureaucratic* theories might point to a "submariner lobby" in the PLA, but this lobby likely has little influence: few submariners have served on the CMC, none have served as a vice chairman, and only two have ever served as PLAN commander—one for three years and the other, Zhang Lianzhong, for eight (1988–1996). Even so, Zhang was subordinate to CMC Vice Chairman and Politburo Standing Committee member Liu Huaqing, who was personally committed to a carrier-based navy and could overrule Zhang. Finally, explanations that emphasize China's focus on *regional* conflicts are not helpful either. Submarines cannot hold disputed islands in these conflicts, and while they could assist in missions to capture them, China's were not even outfitted to protect its surface ships from rival state's submarines (e.g., Japan's or Vietnam's) or to strike land targets—instead, they were focused on anti-surface warfare.[89] Even if China were focused on its neighbors, why overinvest in submarines while underinvesting in the capabilities needed for control, like aircraft carriers and other surface vessels?

The answers to these questions are intertwined with tragedy of Submarine 361 and the surprise of the *Kitty Hawk* incident: China sought to use submarines to blunt American power. China's focus on submarines came not from bottom-up submariner pressure but a top-down belief that submarines should be prioritized as part of an asymmetric strategy to thwart US carriers and surface vessels in the region. This is clear across several aspects of China's behavior.

First, with respect to *acquisition* of submarines, China overhauled its entire submarine fleet through a series of dramatic decisions undertaken between 1990 and 1995, precisely when concerns over US power projection intensified. In the first few years after the Gulf War, China swiftly decommissioned an astonishing fifty-four of its Romeo class submarines to free up resources for acquiring large numbers of Ming class submarines, the Song class (its first indigenously produced diesel submarine and the first to field the anti-ship cruise missiles needed to deter US vessels), and nuclear attack submarines.[90] The Song class was plagued with problems, so rather than face a reduction in its submarine force, China made the costly decision to purchase twelve Russian Kilo submarines to bridge the production gap.[91] In the following decade, as concerns about American power remained high with repeated US interventions, China acquired a staggering thirty-one new submarines. These enormous expenditures were useful for threatening the US Navy near China but less so for conflicts with neighbors or protecting distant SLOCs. As one senior PLAN strategist writes, citing a US estimate, "China already exceeds [US submarine production] five times over" and the seventy-five or more Chinese submarines in the Pacific will be able to counter a far smaller US force.[92]

The kinds of submarines China built in this period are also revealing. Why did China prioritize diesel submarines with air-independent propulsion (AIP) over nuclear ones?[93] Diesel submarines are quieter than nuclear submarines even though they travel shorter distances. They are also an asymmetric tool and vastly cheaper than the US nuclear submarines and aircraft carriers they threaten. As one PLAN officer noted, "the price of a nuclear submarine can buy several, even more than ten, conventional submarines."[94] For this reason, although China could build more nuclear submarines, it chose not to and opted for a Soviet-style denial-focused navy that mixed diesel and nuclear submarines, in contrast to the all-nuclear submarine focus the US fields.

In this period, China's submarines were equipped for anti-surface warfare useful against the United States rather than other missions against neighbors, like escort, which might require anti-submarine warfare, land-attack capabilities, or nuclear rather than diesel platforms. Since the 1990s, China has focused its submarines on fielding anti-ship cruise missiles in sharp contrast to the US Navy—which until recently did not field an anti-ship cruise missile at all and instead relied on torpedoes against surface vessels. China's emphasis on anti-ship cruise missile offers it both greater range relative to torpedoes (4–10 times more) as well as speed (generally supersonic) in targeting enemy surface vessels. In 1990, none of China's submarines could launch anti-ship cruise missiles; now well more than 64 percent have this capability—virtually every submarine built or acquired since 1994. The US Office of Naval Intelligence argues that China's submarine-launched anti-ship cruise missiles—including the Russian SS-N-27 Sizzler and the indigenous YJ-18—are world-class, while its ASW and land-attack capabilities remain rather poor. All this suggests again that anti-surface warfare is the priority for China's submarines, which in turn suggests a focus on US vessels—notably carriers.[95]

Second, Chinese naval *doctrine* also confirms a focus on submarines as denial tools rather than as assets for escort or sea control, and in this way, it shares features with earlier Soviet doctrine. As Andrew Erickson and Lyle Goldstein note in their review of Chinese texts on submarine warfare, Chinese authors take great inspiration from Soviet submarine doctrine and see their own situation—coping with a superior power-projection navy—as similar to that faced by the Soviets.[96] Chinese doctrinal texts discuss submarines as an asymmetric tool against a powerful country's carrier battle groups, an unmistakable reference to the United States. None of this should be particularly surprising: submarines have been used as asymmetric tools against blue-water navies since the First World War. During the Falkland Islands War, a conflict frequently studied by Chinese strategists looking for ways to cope as an inferior power against the superior United States, the British fleet expended almost all of its anti-submarine warfare munitions on false submarine contacts and failed to sink a single patrolling Argentinian submarine.[97] Moreover, sources that qualify as less official, such as the PLAN journal *Shipborne Weapons*, are explicit about the use of submarines in anti-access/area-denial campaigns, especially involving Taiwan and therefore possible US intervention: "In order to guarantee the required national defense strength and to safeguard the completion of national unification and to prevent 'Taiwan independence,' over the past few years, China has increased indigenous production of new conventional and nuclear submarines."[98] China's conventional submarines would operate closer to home, while its nuclear submarines would attack US supply lines to the Western Pacific.[99]

Third, as discussed previously, China's submarines are *postured* in a way that enables them to focus on conflicts near China's periphery. They are intended to complicate the exercise of American power close to China's shores. And finally, a look at Chinese *training* and exercises involving submarines also indicates a focus on denial operations. In 2006 and 2015, Chinese diesel submarines stalked US aircraft carriers and *surfaced* within torpedo range—risking their own ability to operate undetected and demonstrating China's testing of this capability. In addition, minelaying has been a crucial part of Chinese submarine training programs for more than two decades and a major part of the curriculum for mid-level officers at the Qingdao Submarine Academy. In many cases, these mine-laying operations are not only offensive (against enemy ports) but also defensive (focused on enemy carriers and submarines). Doctrinal texts and other sources make clear that, in attacks on aircraft carriers, mine warfare will play a prominent role.[100]

Mines

At 4:36 A.M. on February 18, 1991, the crew of the USS *Tripoli* was jolted awake. The 18,500-ton amphibious assault ship carrying 600 sailors had just struck an

Iraqi mine in the Persian Gulf. The blast had ripped open a 320 square foot hole fifteen feet below the waterline, and seawater was pouring in.[101]

Two hours later and ten miles away, the USS *Princeton* was rocked by successive explosions. The 9,600-ton guided missile cruiser had just hit two mines in short order, and now it too was taking on water.[102]

Both the USS *Tripoli* and the USS *Princeton* were relatively fortunate: they both suffered no fatalities and managed to stop the flooding before heading to a dock for repairs. But the incident was revealing. These were large and expensive vessels—the *Princeton* alone cost $1 billion—and they had been laid low by Iraqi mines that each cost no more than a few thousand dollars. By some estimates, there were still roughly 1,000 more mines in the northern Gulf, demonstrating the asymmetric advantages of mine warfare against a superior American foe.[103]

China watched these incidents with great interest and invested accordingly. Now, decades later, the Office of Naval Intelligence finds that "China has a robust mining capability," with 50,000 to 100,000 sea mines, as well as a "robust infrastructure for naval mine-related research, development, testing, evaluation, and production."[104] These mines can be deployed on a variety of platforms (submarines, surface vessels, and air-dropped) at several different ranges. In a relatively short period, China has completely modernized its Second World War–era mine arsenal and assembled "a vast mine inventory consisting of a large variety of mine types such as moored, bottom, drifting, rocket-propelled, and intelligent mines."[105] China now fields the world's largest mine arsenal.

There are a few competing explanations for why China has invested so heavily in mines, but most are inadequate. *Diffusion* and *adoption-capacity* theories, which focus on which technologies diffuse and which ones do not, cannot explain overinvestment. *Bureaucratic* theories might attribute overinvestment to powerful bureaucratic forces, but there is no identifiable interest group or coalition for mine warfare powerful enough to affect military policy. Finally, the theory that China was focused on *regional* conflicts with neighbors also cannot explain overinvestment. Mines are a defensive weapon or can be used offensively to block Taiwan's ports, but they cannot alone establish control, and China in any case invested heavily in mines effective against American submarines and aircraft carriers in the deep sea that are qualitatively different from those useful against Taiwan.

The best explanation for China's mine investments is—per China's interest in the Gulf War—that they are part of its effort to asymmetrically blunt US operations in Asia. First, with respect to the *acquisition* of mine warfare capabilities, the concern over US power amplified by the Gulf War provided a catalytic influence. Before the Gulf War, Chinese research proceeded slowly. China fielded its first indigenous sea mine in 1974 but did not field its first minelaying vessel until a decade later in 1988, and that Type 918 minelayer was so slow and detect-able that it had almost no operational survivability.[106] After the Gulf War, China's investments increased and its inventory grew to moored, bottom, drifting, rocket-propelled, and intelligent mines through indigenous development and purchases of Russian mine warfare technology. Investments in deep-sea and rocket mines showed a desire to threaten American carriers far out at sea and SSNs closer to China's coast.[107]

Second, although we lack an authoritative *doctrinal* text on Chinese mine warfare, official PLA writings as well as the writings of secondary authors strongly suggest a focus on the United States, with the Gulf War playing a major role. During the conflict, Chinese authors studied the way Iraqi mines were able to frustrate American power projection, and they discussed sea mines as asymmetric tools. A 1992 article in *Modern Ships* emphasized that mines were a way weak states could repel strong ones and that American mine countermeasure (MCM) capabilities were demonstrated by Iraq to be "rela-tively feeble." Chinese military writers also observed that coalition forces were not able to cope effectively with Iraq's limited mine warfare capabilities: "de-spite deploying 13 vessels from four nations, this force proved insufficient, was plagued by wide discrepancies in the capabilities of each vessel, and made only slow headway [against Iraq's mines]." Roughly a decade later, these conclusions were accepted as conventional wisdom in the Chinese mine war-fare literature. As one piece studying Iraqi mine laying during the Second Gulf War notes: "Everybody knows that during the 1991 Gulf War, Iraqi mines played an important role, mauling [a number of] U.S. Navy warships." This 2004 piece continued to argue that despite advances in American MCM technology, relatively crude and basic mines still could inhibit the power projection capabilities of high-tech US forces. To emphasize the point, the au-thor even quoted a US naval officer in charge of MCM for Operation Iraqi Freedom: "Even in the most optimal sea and combat operations environ-ment, hunting and sweeping mines is slow, causing frustration and danger."[108] Chinese analysts stressed these lessons for US-China conflict, as an article in the *People's Navy* makes clear:

> The U.S. will need to move supplies by sea. But China is not Iraq. China has advanced sea mines. . . . This is a fatal threat to U.S. seaborne trans-port. . . . [T]he moment conflict erupted in the Taiwan Strait, the PLA Navy could deploy mines. U.S. ships that want to conduct ASW [anti-submarine warfare] [would] have to first sweep the area clear. When the U.S. fought in the Gulf War, it took over half a year to sweep all Iraq's sea mines. Therefore, it [would] not be easy for the U.S. military to sweep all the mines that the PLA [might] lay.[109]

Certain Chinese mine warfare capabilities are clearly focused exclusively on frustrating US access. China has invested heavily in fast-rising rocket mines— what it calls a "high-technology sea mine"—that are moored deep in the ocean and rise swiftly to strike their targets.[110] China not only acquired the mines from Russia (the PMK-1 and PMK-2), but Chinese sources suggest China also imported Russian doctrine in using these mines and has focused them, as Russia did, on striking enemy SSNs.[111] The only opponent China faces with SSNs is the United States, and these mines are therefore focused on blunting US capabilities—a point several Chinese authors themselves make explicitly.[112] As one author notes, commenting on Russia's possession of these mines: "These weapons will attack SSNs [i.e., nuclear attack submarines] too rapidly for countermeasures to engage, and are also rated to be highly effective against the mono-hull construction of U.S. submarines."[113] Authoritative texts strongly hint that anti-submarine objectives are a crucial part of mine warfare. For example, the *Campaign Theory Study Guide* calls for "anti-submarine mine zones" and a 2007 textbook in mine-warfare makes repeated reference to their usage against submarines.[114]

Crucially, pseudo-doctrinal writing on Chinese mine warfare generally employs a few set phrases that appear often and strongly suggest a focus on asymmetries relative to a superior opponent. These phrases include that mines are "easy to lay, hard to sweep" [易布难扫], a reference to the asymmetric operational advantage that comes from them, and that "four ounces can move one thousand pounds" [四两可拨千斤], which is a reference to their asymmetric destructive potential.[115] Another routine phrase is that mines are "not attracting attention," with Chinese authors noting that they are not currently focuses of major navies, and explicitly the US Navy.[116] Similarly, Chinese sources routinely write that mines are both "high and low technology" [高低技术], with a typical reference noting that mines in the Gulf War cost as little as $10,000 but did over $96 million in damage to US vessels.[117] In sum, these phrases that appear repeatedly in Chinese texts on mine warfare strongly suggest that it is understood asymmetrically and often focused on the United States.

Third, Chinese mine warfare *training* exercises appear to reflect operations against a high-technology adversary like the United States. Already, China focuses more on training for mine warfare than other navies. As Bernard Cole noted as early as 2001, "PLAN surface combatants are annually required to exercise laying mines, which is not a common practice in most navies," and which further demonstrates that China's investment in mine warfare is more substantial than would be expected under most theories.[118] With respect to submarines, minelaying has been a crucial part of Chinese submarine training programs for more than two decades and a major part of the curriculum for mid-level officers at the Qingdao Submarine Academy. Articles in the *People's*

Navy describe minelaying exercises in great detail and even call minelaying "the most basic requirement of submarine warfare."[119] These exercises emphasize coping with the kinds of anti-submarine capabilities the United States might deploy against minelaying submarines, such as American anti-submarine aircraft and helicopters, anti-submarine minefields, and nuclear submarines. These kinds of capabilities suggest the United States was the focus of China's minelaying efforts.[120] Finally, with respect to aerial platforms, aerial delivery of mines has been a focus of Chinese training efforts since at least 1997, if not earlier. These exercises have also taken place with simulations of sophisticated enemy capabilities not possessed by most Chinese competitors, including advanced electronic warfare capabilities.[121]

Missiles

In 1992, then Central Military Commission vice chairman Chi Haotian—along with much of China's leadership—was furious.[122] Washington had just sold over 100 F-16 fighters to Taiwan and had opted to retain a robust military presence in the region, and China found both developments unnerving. But not long after the sale, Chi noted, the Second Artillery Corps of the PLA came up with a possible solution.

Founded in the late 1960s and personally named by Chinese premier Zhou Enlai—the revolutionary who was once de facto leader of the CCP before being displaced by Mao Zedong during the Long March—the Second Artillery was focused on China's strategic nuclear deterrent for decades. Gradually, however, that was beginning to change. Now, they had a proposal for the Chinese general.

"The Second Artillery Corps leadership," he recounted, "recommended to the Central Military Commission and the General Staff that it build a series of conventional missiles to target enemy airfields, vessels, and infrastructure."[123] This major diversion into conventional warfare was consequential, but Chi Haotian says he "firmly supported this proposal."[124] He then "asked the relevant departments to conduct a serious study immediately, to conduct joint research, and to accelerate the development of conventional missiles" within the Second Artillery.[125] And with that, the program that would eventually produce China's famed "carrier-killer" anti-ship ballistic missiles (ASBMs) was born.

In the years since Chi's meeting with the Second Artillery, China has invested heavily in the ASBM program. In the process, it has innovated a new missile category that has not yet been developed by any state. For that reason, China's ASBM is a case that cannot be explained by *diffusion* or *adoption capacity* theories. A *bureaucratic* account might explain China's investments as the product of advocacy by interest groups like the Second Artillery (now the PLA Rocket Force), which operates these weapons. But despite the Second Artillery's importance for China's nuclear security, it has long been the smallest of China's services and has never had one of its officers serve as a vice chairman of the CMC—which suggests limited influence. Finally, ASBMs are of limited use in *regional* conflicts with China's neighbors, largely because they are designed against aircraft carriers, which China's neighbors generally do not field. India is an exception to this rule, but China's ASBMs likely lack the support to target carriers so far from China's maritime periphery. Even Chinese publications suggest limits to ASBM utility, especially with respect to sea-control operations. As one author notes, ASBMs "cannot replace carriers, submarines, and other traditional naval weapons." They "can be used to destroy enemy forces at sea but not to achieve absolute sea control, let alone to project maritime power."[126] The fact that ASBMs are inadequate for projecting power and achieving sea control means they are of limited utility in campaigns in the Taiwan Strait or the East and South China Seas, unless they are viewed primarily as a means of deterring or responding to US carrier-based intervention. And indeed, China's investment in ASBMs is best explained as part of a grand strategy to blunt American power.

First, with respect to the *acquisition* of ASBMs, China's pursuit of this capability was triggered by anxieties about American power projection. In the period before China regarded the United States as a threat, it did not invest in ASBMs at all. As Andrew Erickson notes, the decision to construct an ASBM was almost certainly made no earlier than 1986. A high-level document written that year by the Second Artillery's chief engineer on anticipated investments to be made over the next fourteen years through to the year 2000 did not once mention ASBMs.[127] Indeed, multiple sources confirm that the Second Artillery lacked any conventional mission at all until roughly 1992, around the time that Chinese military strategy changed in the wake of Tiananmen, the Gulf War, and the Soviet collapse. A semi-official history of the Second Artillery confirms some of these details, suggesting the service's mission changed after the trifecta:

> At the beginning of the 1990s, the Chinese Communist Party Central Committee, the State Council, and the Central Military Commission studied and sized up the situation according to the needs of international military struggle and the development of Chinese weapons and equipment, *scientifically making a strategic decision to speed up the development of new models of Chinese missile weapons.*[128]

It is reasonable to conclude that these new missile weapons may have included a conventional ASBM given the Second Artillery's focus on ballistic missiles, and indeed Chi's biography largely confirms the new focus began in 1992.[129] By the mid-1990s, the ASBM program was apparently well underway, enough for PRC officers to boast about it. As Larry Wortzel notes, "The first time a senior Chinese military officer of the General Staff Department mentioned ballistic missiles attacking carriers was after our two carriers showed up [during the Taiwan Strait Crisis], and he put his arm around my shoulder and said we're going to sink your carriers with ballistic missiles, and we had a long conversation about it. I don't know if they were doing research before that, but . . . the first time it got thrown in my face was 1996."[130] Andrew Erickson documents convincingly that technical work on the ASBM program began accelerating that same year. By 1999, some of the first references to using ASBMs to strike carriers appeared in Chinese pseudo-doctrinal publications. Following the US intervention in Kosovo and the accidental bombing of the Chinese embassy in Belgrade, the Central Military Commission resolved to accelerate development of "assassin's mace" weapons, of which the ASBM was one. Together, this suggests that the main driver of ASBM development has been concerns and anxieties about American power projection—often but not exclusively in Taiwan-related scenarios.

Second, *doctrinal sources* are explicit that ASBMs are useful against developed country militaries with aircraft carriers, which by default must be the United States. *The Science of Second Artillery Campaigns*, a military textbook published in 2004 believed to represent the institutional viewpoint of the Second Artillery, explicitly describes the use of ASBMs against aircraft carriers. It states that ASBMs should be used as an "assassin's mace," and that more specifically, they would be used in "deterring and blocking enemy carrier groups." It lays out some of the requirements of these operations, including the fact that "information on carrier battle groups should be gathered on a real-time basis" because carriers are moving targets. In another section, it states, "when many carrier-borne aircraft are used in continuous air strikes against our coast, in order to halt the powerful air raids, the enemy's core carrier should be struck as with a 'heavy hammer.' "[131] Less official publications are even more explicit that ASBMs are intended to deter the United States. Dong Lu, writing in *Naval and Merchant Ships*, noted that ASBMs were an asymmetric weapon against great powers:

> Since the end of the Cold War, the aircraft carrier has become a symbol of the might of a great power, while the ballistic missile has also become an effective weapon for developing countries around the world to safeguard their own security and challenge great powers. The might of an aircraft carrier is based on the disparity between the comprehensive powers of rich and poor states. The ballistic missile, on the other hand, seeks to exploit the temporal lag in the development of offensive and defensive technologies. . . . ASBMs are undoubtedly an effective means

of deterring military intervention at the present [though perhaps not in the long-term].[132]

Other authors, including senior Second Artillery officers, described ASBMs in similar terms in 2005: "The primary form of future sea combat will be the extensive use of precision-guided ballistic missiles in long range precision attacks. . . . We must view . . . long-range sea-launched precision-guided ballistic missiles as the priority of our weaponry building.[133] These priorities were clearly aimed toward conflict in the East, intended to cope with Chinese technological inferiority and to deter a foreign government from intervention, and therefore could be seen as part of a larger political strategy. As one Chinese strategist argues:

> [ASBMs] provide China with more maneuvering space for military and political strategic operations on its eastern, maritime flank. . . [The creation of a] tactical ballistic missile maritime strike system . . . will establish for China in any high-intensity conflict in its coastal waters an asymmetry, in its favor, in the deliverance of firepower and so will remedy to some extent China's qualitative inferiority in traditional naval platforms. Further, the existence of this asymmetry would set up for both sides a psychological "upper limit" on the scale of the conflict. This would enable both parties to return more easily "to rationality," thereby creating more space for maneuver in the resolution of maritime conflicts.[134]

These views were confirmed at the highest levels. On a visit to the United States in 2009, then Vice Chairman of the Central Military Commission Xu Caihou was asked about China's ASBMs and implicitly linked both ballistic and cruise missiles to deterring US intervention in a Taiwan scenario: "The research and development of weapons and equipment, including that of our cruise missiles and ballistic missiles, some of which were on display on our [October 1, 2009] National Day military parade, is entirely for self-defense . . . and for the minimum requirement of national security. As you also know, China has yet to realize complete unification."[135]

With respect to *training*, there are some indications that the Second Artillery's conventional units trained under the assumption that they would face US interference, strongly suggesting China is focused on contingencies involving the United States. As Christman notes, "One of the most significant advances the Second Artillery Corps has made in preparing its conventional units to deal with a severe threat environment has been establishing an 'opposing force' unit that tests operational units in a wide range of battlefield environments." Christman further notes, "This so-called 'Blue Army' opposing force regiment . . . [is] an effort to replicate potential U.S. counter missile force operations. Various tactics employed by this unit include electronic jamming, computer network operations, virus attacks, firepower attacks, special force operations, electronic deception, and the use of 'logic bombs,'" malicious code that sabotages computer systems.[136] These are conditions that only the United States would likely be able to bring upon China's conventional missile forces, and again suggest a preoccupation with US power.

Aircraft Carriers

On October 25, 1973, the seventy-five-year-old Chinese premier Zhou Enlai was in a meeting with foreign visitors. Zhou was increasingly sickly, but he remained unaware that he was suffering from bladder cancer because Mao had ordered Zhou's doctor—who had made the diagnosis a year earlier—not to tell Zhou or even treat him. Despite his deteriorating health, Zhou kept up a busy schedule. In his meeting that day he turned to China's territorial disputes and the country's need for an aircraft carrier. "I have been engaged in political and military affairs my entire life, and so far, I have not yet seen a Chinese aircraft carrier," he lamented. Zhou strongly believed that China needed one. "Our Nansha and Xisha Islands are occupied by South Vietnam," Zhou argued, "but without an aircraft carrier, China's navy might as well be left to fight with bayonets," exposed and vulnerable to enemy aircraft. His voice rising in emotion, he declared, "I cannot tolerate not having an aircraft carrier!"[137]

From Zhou's remarks to the launch of China's aircraft carrier took forty-one years. And yet, throughout that period, fifteen countries operated aircraft carriers: Argentina, Australia, Brazil, Canada, France, Germany, India, Italy, Japan, the Netherlands, Russia, Spain, Thailand, the United Kingdom, and the United States.[138] The very first carrier, the British Royal Navy's HMS *Furious*, was launched a century before China's in 1917. What took China so long?

Diffusion-based explanations cannot explain why China did not acquire a capability leading states have long had, since it predicts China would acquire one. *Adoption capacity* explanations can do somewhat better because they assume "the high financial and organization requirements for adoption" complicate carrier acquisition.[139] But the evidence suggests this was not the case for China, which could have acquired carriers long before 2012. First, China could probably have constructed its own light and non-nuclear aircraft carrier—admittedly at great cost and difficulty—if it had chosen to make it a priority. As analysts Ian Storey and You Ji note, China was "able to overcome both technical and financial problems in the mid-1960s, the height of the chaotic Cultural Revolution, to develop nuclear weapons; the country's scientific, industrial, and economic bases have been strengthened considerably since then," perhaps to the point where a light carrier would have been possible had it been deemed a strategic necessity by China's leadership.[140] Moreover, even though a carrier program may have consumed a large portion of the navy budget, extra-budgetary financing could have been made available, as it was for the nuclear weapons and nuclear submarine programs.[141] Authoritative Chinese sources confirm this interpretation, and demonstrate carrier acquisition was a question of priorities and not financial or organizational difficulties. In his memoirs, Admiral Liu Huaqing—then commander of the PLAN—recounts his remarks in an important 1987 meeting before the PLA General Staff: "As for whether we were technologically capable of manufacturing aircraft carriers and carrier-based aircraft," he began, "after consulting with leaders and experts from the aviation, shipbuilding, and other relevant industries, [they] said that they believed they were able to fulfill the fundamental requirements."[142] On the separate question of financing, Liu noted that funding could be taken from other programs: "developing aircraft carrier battle groups is a question of how to adjust the trajectory of funding for equipment and would not require a significant increase in equipment expenses."[143] During this period, China was also receiving Western assistance that could benefit a carrier program, including a scrapped carrier from Australia in 1985 and useful technical exchanges—all of which may have helped it build its own in the 1990s.[144]

Second, not only could China have built a carrier, it could have also refurbished or imported a foreign one. Several developing countries have acquired, refurbished, operated, and subsequently maintained light aircraft carriers for decades, including Brazil since 1960, India since 1961, and Thailand since 1996. Even after the Tiananmen Square Massacre and the arms embargo, Western states were willing to help China with its carrier program, with Spain offering to construct a carrier for China, France offering to refurbish one of its older carriers (though both deals fell through), and several European firms signing consulting contracts with Chinese entities that transferred important knowledge or designs. And most important, Russia was willing to continue providing China various blueprints, expertise, technology, and hulls. If Liu Huaqing was right that China could build a carrier in the 1980s, then it should certainly have been able to refurbish a Russian carrier in the 1990s or 2000s—especially with Russian assistance. Within eight years of the Soviet collapse, China had purchased three former Soviet carriers—the *Minsk*, *Kiev*, and *Varyag*—and the *Varyag* apparently came with fully functional engines and blueprints that made renovation feasible.[145] And should renovation have proved difficult, China could have paid Russia to make the carriers operational and provide aircraft as India did for the *Admiral Gorshkov* at a total cost of $2–3 billion.[146] During the 1990s and early 2000s, Russia was already assisting China with other sensitive aspects of its defense modernization. The question thus remains, if China was able to build or refurbish a carrier, why did it delay in acquiring one for decades?

Some might claim that China's delay was the result of *bureaucratic* politics—with submariners or land forces opposed to the resource drain. While some of the most prominent opponents of a carrier program were high-ranking submariners like Wang Shichang, the reality is that the PLAN's senior leadership was clearly interested in aircraft carriers.[147] "Naval brass have always advocated building an aircraft carrier," notes Zheng Min, former head of the Department of Naval Equipment and Technology.[148] Moreover, PLAN deputy commanders in both the 1980s (Zhang Xusan) and the 1990s (He Pengfei) were strong supporters of carrier aviation and backed the decision to covertly acquire the *Varyag*.[149] Most important, Liu Huaqing was a tireless advocate for a Chinese carrier who reportedly studied in the Soviet Union under Admiral Gorshkov, the evangelist for Soviet carrier aviation, and was famous for saying, "if China does not build an aircraft carrier, I will die with my eyelids open" [不搞航空母舰，我死不瞑目].[150] It is highly unlikely that the parochial interests of submariners or land forces could have thwarted the agenda of a powerful carrier advocate like Liu, who commanded the entire navy for much of the 1980s, rose to become the most powerful military officer as CMC vice chairman, joined the Politburo Standing Committee in the 1990s, had close ties to Deng and Jiang, and pushed through major military reforms—including the prioritization of naval and air modernization over land forces.[151] The decision not to develop a carrier was not from low-level bureaucratic politics but from a much higher level of strategic planning, one that likely involved senior leaders like Jiang himself and the broader Party.

Perhaps, some might argue, Chinese officials delayed carrier acquisition because they thought carriers would not be useful in *regional* conflicts with their neighbors. In actuality, Chinese-language sources make plain that the opposite is true: China's government for decades viewed carriers as essential in local contingencies with neighbors, especially for escort and air control purposes. Zhou Enlai had made that clear in 1973, and Liu Huaqing emphasized it repeatedly too at high levels.[152] In November 1986, Liu Huaqing was part of a "naval development strategy study group" that included "military and civilian leaders as well as renowned experts" from all over the government. "From the perspective of what was needed to protect China's maritime rights and interests, recover Nansha and Taiwan, and deal with other strategic circumstances," he notes in his memoir, the members "recommended constructing an aircraft carrier."[153] Liu further noted that, without an aircraft carrier, it would be difficult to secure Chinese interests with surface vessels alone, telling the PLA General Staff in 1987 that: "when thinking about maritime formations, we had only considered destroyers, frigates, and submarines; after further research, we realized that without air cover, there was no way these formations would be able to fight outside the radius of shore-based combat aircraft," and that even *within* the range of shore-based aircraft, air cover would simply not reach quickly enough in times of crisis.[154] The military was convinced carriers were useful not only for conflicts in the distant South China Sea, but also much closer in the Taiwan Strait. Liu wrote that the PLA General Staff looked favorably upon his report and escalated the question of carrier acquisition, all of which suggests that at least as early as 1987, a Chinese focus on narrower local operational contingencies should have included an aircraft carrier. In 1995, Liu in a high-level meeting on aircraft carriers stated that "Defending the South China Sea, peacefully reuniting Taiwan, safeguarding maritime rights and interests—all require aircraft carriers."[155] The fact that China thought carriers would be useful in regional contingencies means that theories of Chinese investment focused on regional considerations cannot account for the delay in building carriers.

The preceding evidence makes clear that a Chinese carrier program was feasible, enjoyed high-level support within the Navy and in the larger military, found support in the late 1980s at the central level, and was believed to be essential in conflicts with neighbors—and yet China did not build them. The reason why is that carriers did not fit into a blunting strategy to asymmetrically weaken the United States.

First, China's *acquisition* process suggests a delay was not incidental but intentional and considered at the very highest levels. Major General Zheng Ming, former head of the PLA Navy Armaments Department, was part of the delegation that was sent to inspect the former Soviet carrier *Varyag* for acquisition as early as 1992. "During the trip [in 1992], we found it was a brand-new ship. Everything was completely new, from the armor plating to other parts, so we suggested [the central government] buy it and bring it home . . . but the central government didn't do it because of the [political] situation at the time."[156] Similarly, in a 2005 interview, former PLAN Deputy Commander Zhang Xusan recalls that, "I certainly advocate having an aircraft carrier soon. . . . When I was [deputy commander of the PLA] Navy I advocated that, and at that time Commander . . . Liu Huaqing advocated it too, but for many reasons it was postponed."[157] Various scholars have concluded from their interviews with interlocutors in Beijing that the Chinese carrier program was delayed or postponed repeatedly in the late 1980s and early 1990s for high-level political reasons, and that Jiang decided to approve national-level preliminary research on a carrier program only in the mid-1990s—and perhaps only as a way of mollifying Liu.[158] You Ji notes that Liu repeatedly lobbied Jiang on behalf of the carrier program, and that Jiang responded carefully since he still relied on Liu for support: "Jiang knew well Liu's personal position on carriers. He continuously agreed to the preliminary carrier research to avoid a direct clash with Liu on carrier affairs [as] . . . a kind of delaying tactic before a final decision to shelve [the carrier]."[159] The situation came to a head when Liu submitted a report on a carrier to the Politburo Standing Committee in May 1995 and proposed purchasing and refitting the *Varyag*. The Standing Committee turned Liu's proposal down and the carrier issue was effectively dead for at least the next eight years.[160] China did not appear to demonstrate interest in the carrier program again until the mid-2000s, and it apparently did not seriously commit resources until after the Global Financial Crisis.

As Liu himself admitted, the decision to construct an aircraft carrier was one that would need to be made at the level of the Central Military Commission and above—a reference, presumably, to the Politburo Standing Committee that had previously turned his proposal down. He situates an aircraft carrier within what might be described as a larger Chinese grand strategy: "The development of a carrier is not just a naval question, instead it is related to such weighty matters as national strategy [国家战略] and defense policy, and it must emerge from accurate determinations of and prudent decision-making concerning the country's comprehensive national strength and the overall national maritime strategy."[161] This indicates that the carrier decision and matters of naval force structure (i.e., carrier-based vs. submarine-based) must have been made at a level that could consider larger grand strategy, not simply military strategy, and these decisions thus provide significant insight into China's strategic aims.

Second, Chinese *doctrine* suggests carriers were not considered useful in operational scenarios involving the United States or consistent with overall Chinese strategic objectives. Authoritative military sources suggest strongly that China saw a carrier as useful in the South China Sea—so much so that, as Tai Ming Cheung writes, "Shortly after the Sino-Vietnamese clash in the Spratlys in March 1988, there were indications that a go-ahead on building a carrier would soon be given."[162] But the traumatic trifecta revealed that the United States was no longer an ally but a plausible opponent with far superior military technology. As China's grand strategy changed to address the threat, its military strategy changed in concert to deemphasize the capabilities needed to make progress against neighbors and to instead emphasize asymmetric weapons less vulnerable and less costly than carriers.

Authors in Chinese military journals have long written of carrier vulnerabilities, informed in part by the lessons of US and Soviet maritime competition. As one military writer argues in the late 1980s: "The US navy's aircraft carrier combat groups are extraordinarily limited in number" and "face a threat from all sorts of [Soviet] guided missile launch platform combat groups."[163] Chinese defense strategists would have been aware of the vulnerability of their own potential carriers as well as of the utility of Soviet anti-access approaches against US carriers. Accordingly, once the United States became the primary strategic threat to China after the trifecta, official assessments of the value of a carrier program would likely have changed.

Chinese military authors have long made arguments consistent with this perspective. Throughout the 1990s and into the present day, many authors and even some pseudo-doctrinal sources have called into question the usefulness of Chinese aircraft carriers in operations against the US Navy. As one official, with admittedly some exaggeration, stated, "even twenty PRC carriers cannot compete with U.S. nuclear carriers."[164] And in an argument that echoes Cold War–era analyses of carrier vulnerabilities, Ye Zicheng—a professor at Beijing University who became a prominent figure in debates over aircraft carriers in the mid-2000s—argued that Chinese carriers would be vulnerable to US missiles. He proposed that "sea power is secondary to land power" and that, as a result, "China should postpone plans to build aircraft carriers." Ye writes that "sea power must obey trends in military technology," and that "with the maturing of precision-guided land/space-based missile technology, the advantage of an aircraft carrier group has been greatly diminished, and it is more likely to become the target of advanced missiles, land-based aircraft, and advanced submarines and destroyers."[165] Some high-speed missiles, Ye notes, will even become "carrier killers." Admittedly, Ye's account is not as authoritative as those of officers within the PLAN, but his profile in military discussions suggests he was channeling widely held views. Indeed, the capabilities outlined by Ye—submarines and carrier-killer missiles—are precisely those which China elevated during this period. China's strategic admonitions not to emulate Western states, to defeat the strong with the weapons of the weak, and to acquire shashoujian weapons all seem to point to a decision to avoid expensive platforms like a carrier that would in any case be inferior to the Western equivalent and to instead focus on different capabilities. Ye argued that funds for a carrier "would be more effectively spent" on "advanced submarines" and "medium- and long-range missile platforms," including "improving missile performance."[166] All of this suggests that there is a consistent discourse in Chinese military and academic writings that argues aircraft carriers would not be effective against the United States; that all carriers are vulnerable to the very trends in military technology that were debuted in the Gulf War; and that China would be better off acquiring those capabilities, rather than an aircraft carrier.

Although we cannot show conclusively that this logic motivated the Central Military Commission or Politburo Standing Committee, this evidence when combined with the textual review of Chinese strategy earlier in the chapter together suggests it likely played a significant factor. Top leaders, including Jiang, would have been familiar with these arguments and the broader operational considerations; indeed, Jiang had taken Deng's advice and immersed himself in defense planning and several all-day CMC meetings as soon as he assumed power. China's leaders were intimately involved in China's decision to build nuclear weapons, satellites, and asymmetric weapons, and carriers are unlikely to have been an exception.

Ultimately, the decision to acquire an aircraft carrier would have meant committing not only to a specific naval force structure, but to a broader military structure that was not suited to blunting. As one PLA textbook makes clear, "whether we should go ahead with a carrier project is not a naval question. It is related to the question of how to adjust our overall force posture and national defense policy."[167] And that is precisely why a carrier would have been an imprudent decision for a grand strategy focused on the United States.

Of course, China eventually did build an aircraft carrier, but only once its perception of American power changed. Until then, as the carrier case and the preceding cases show, China's military was focused on blunting American power. It was the trifecta that initially prompted China to depart from the "sea control" strategy that had been increasingly focused on holding distant maritime territory to a "sea denial strategy" focused on preventing the US military from traversing, controlling, or intervening in the waters near China. And it was the difficulty of that shift that led Beijing to prioritize—to "catch up in some areas and not others" and to commit to the precept that "whatever the enemy fears, we develop that." It put aircraft carriers and other costly and vulnerable vessels on hold, despite having the ability to pursue them, and instead opted to build relatively cheaper asymmetric weapons suitable for an anti-access/area-denial strategy to keep the United States out. In the process, Beijing built the world's largest mine arsenal, the world's first ASBM, and the world's largest submarine fleet to challenge US military power.

That consistency of vision and purpose was not isolated to the military domain. As the next chapter shows, elements of it also guided China's political and diplomatic behavior in China's regional organizations.

5

"Demonstrate Benign Intentions"

Implementing Political Blunting

"An important reason why China now increasingly values multilateral diplomacy is US hegemonic behavior after the Cold War and its super-power position."[1]

—*Peking University Professor Wang Yizhou, 2003*

In October 1993, China's first ambassador to APEC, a new Asian regional organization whose acronym stood for Asia-Pacific Economic Cooperation, was racing to prepare his team for the grouping's first ever leader-level summit. That ambassador, Wang Yusheng, was keenly aware that only a few weeks later, eleven leaders from Asia's largest economies would be gathering in Seattle in the wake of the Cold War and at President Clinton's invitation to discuss the future of the fledgling organization, and with it, Asian order too. For China, the stakes were high.

In his memoirs, Wang Yusheng recounts that his team encountered a major surprise when, just a few weeks before the summit, a Japanese newspaper leaked a report by APEC's US-led Expert Working Group that proposed recommendations for the future of the organization. Wang was entirely blindsided by the report and the recommendations, and he reacted with alarm: "When we saw the report's eye-catching title, 'Towards an Asia Pacific Economic Community,' we cannot help but be surprised," he recounted. "How did this come about? Could this really be? Can we agree with it? What should we do? A series of problems all emerged."[2] The report was an advisory document, but it was still concerning to Wang: "We didn't know if this report was 'consistent' with US President Bill Clinton's Asia-Pacific strategy or 'inconsistent.' There was no way to know, but it was also not necessary to know" since China planned to oppose its recommendations anyway.[3] "At that time," Wang recalled, "I felt the most important thing for us to do was to immediately inform our superiors about the report, think about it seriously, and prepare countermeasures."[4]

For Wang, the report—and its use of the word *Community*—was a call to arms. It was not a benign and innocent decision to insert that word, he thought, but rather another piece of evidence confirming that Washington was deviously maneuvering a US-led organization into position as Asia's most important regional body at China's expense. China therefore needed to stall APEC, and in so doing, blunt US order-building in Asia. Wang worked to downgrade the word *Community*—ensuring APEC would instead refer to Asia-Pacific Economic *Cooperation*—and he made sure that if "community" ever appeared it would be with a lower-case "c" to avoid drawing comparisons to the more institutionalized European Community.

The bizarre fight over the word "community"—and a dozen other issues— was a proxy over how strong APEC should be, and China took it seriously. When an American diplomat teased Wang for his doggedness on this issue in a public address, Wang wrote in his memoirs, "How high-sounding [his words are]. But in fact, they [the Americans] had continuously been trying to make APEC transcend economic issues. . . . Some commentators say that the real intention of these [Americans] is to create a community that they dominate. . . . This claim is not at all unreasonable."[5]

When China succeeded the next year at keeping APEC at a weaker level of institutionalization, Wang was triumphant. "The United States strove to dominate the direction of APEC development from the beginning, and in many ways sought to exert influence and pressure," Wang wrote.[6] "President Clinton led more than two thousand people, divided on ten different planes to attend the meeting, and everywhere inside and outside the meeting there was activity— and yet he still failed."[7] The failure of the United States to secure its objectives was a cause for celebration for China because it meant APEC would remain a "thin" organization, one less suited for US order-building in Asia. And it was a key part of a political blunting strategy that China pursued throughout the region in the aftermath of Tiananmen Square, the Gulf War, and the Soviet collapse.

This chapter explores China's efforts to blunt American power in Asia. It focuses on two puzzling features of China's involvement in regional organizations in this period: (1) why did China suddenly decide to join these organizations in the early 1990s after previously avoiding them; and (2) why did China stall many of the regional organizations it then joined? In answering these questions, it explores China's maneuvering within the leading Asian regional organizations of the time: Asia-Pacific Economic Cooperation (APEC), the Association of Southeast Asian Nations (ASEAN), and the Shanghai Cooperation Organization (SCO).

This chapter argues that China joined and stalled regional organizations to blunt American order-building and create security for itself. Concerned about growing US influence in the region, Beijing undermined the institutionalization of organizations that included the United States like APEC and the ASEAN Regional Forum (ARF) but was more supportive of institutionalization in those that excluded the United States and gave China a major role, like ASEAN Plus Three (APT) and the SCO—both of which it helped launch. By participating in regional organizations, China also hoped to reassure its neighbors and reduce their interest in joining a possible US-led balancing coalition, as well as to use the organization's rules to constrain US power, including its military deployments and economic coercion. This defensive approach to regional organizations, with occasional moments of offensive initiative, persisted until the 2008 Global Financial Crisis pushed China to be even bolder in its political ambition.

Explaining Political Strategy in Regional Organizations

China's participation in Asia's formal multilateral organizations helps us understand Chinese grand strategy.[8] These organizations often require expenditures of time and resources by states and their leaders and are therefore good measures of state preferences and strategies. They can also set norms and rules in the domains that can shape state behavior, making them possible instruments of leading states.

We can assess China's behavior in regional organizations across a few key categories. First, we can look at *membership*, or what kinds of institutions China joins or creates, when it chooses to do so, and whether these institutions are well developed with enforcement and monitoring mechanisms. Second, we can look at *participation*, or what China does within these organizations. This involves a focus on whether China acts to strengthen or weaken the institution's effectiveness, for example, by supporting monitoring mechanisms or undermining the organization's decision-making structure. Third, we can examine an organization's *benefits*, including whether it provides advantages in security competition to China outside of its official, core functions.

After assessing China's behavior, and combining that with a deep dive into texts, we must then try to explain it. This chapter tests two explanations. The first theory is that China is a *sincere participant* in these organizations. China's genuine commitment could evolve from its desire for the material rewards of cooperation and problem solving (liberal explanations) or because it seeks the social rewards of cooperation related to status, image, or identity (social explanations). These two liberal and social explanations can be combined be-cause the implications are generally quite similar: under each theory, China would be genuinely committed to these institutions and to their effectiveness and act accordingly.

The second theory assumes China's involvement in these organizations is not sincere but instrumental and related to *blunting* and *building*. In this view, China's involvement is driven by a grand strategic logic, and multilateral organi-zations do not merely solve problems related to issues like trade or the environ-ment but also serve as instruments through which great powers create order. The same mechanisms—rules, norms, reputation, monitoring, enforcement—that can induce cooperation can also buttress coercive capabilities, consen-sual inducements, and legitimacy claims that together form the core of order. Accordingly, a *blunting* strategy might involve a state joining a rival's organization to undermine it, to repurpose it to constrain the rival's power, or to reassure wary neighbors who might appreciate the apparent show of good faith. In contrast, a *building strategy* might see a state use these organizations—which can span key domains like trade, finance, health, and information—to create forms of control over others. For example, cutting off states from organizational benefits provides coercive leverage; providing organizational benefits creates incentives for com-pliance; and running the organization might improve the legitimacy of one's leadership claims.

If China's organizational involvements are motivated by these grand strategic blunting and building logics, we should expect to see a few patterns that indicate a lack of sincere participation. With respect to *membership*, China might choose to join organizations when the security benefits increase, and it might also build unnecessary parallel institutions rather than sit in institutions that others con-trol. With respect to *participation*, China might be wary of strengthening in-stitutionalization in organizations run by rivals but willing to champion it in organizations Beijing runs. And, with respect to *organizational* benefits, China might emphasize not the problem-solving purpose of the organization but or-thogonal security concerns. Indeed, as this chapter and Chapter 9 show, China's behavior in institutions fits this strategic pattern.

China's Political Texts on Regional Organizations

Chinese texts—such as diplomatic memoirs and essays by key Foreign Ministry officials—reveal that Beijing saw regional organizations as a way to blunt American order-building, reassure neighbors, and complicate US regional in-volvement rather than as forums for genuine problem solving. In making this argument, the section proceeds in two parts. First, it focuses on the impact of the trifecta of the Tiananmen Square massacre, the Gulf War, and the Soviet collapse on Chinese strategy in multilateral organizations. Second, it explains the emergence and content of a strategy to use these organizations to blunt American order.

The Trifecta and Political Strategy

Before the trifecta, and during the Cold War, China rarely engaged in multilateralism—especially at the regional level. Its interactions were limited to the United Nations and organizations like the World Bank, which could provide China technical expertise. But the trifecta forced a reconsideration. As the scholar Kai He argues, "After the collapse of the Soviet Union, China's strategic environment experienced a dramatic change. . . . Given U.S. policies on human rights and Taiwan, the U.S. as the sole superpower posed a very serious challenge to China's internal and external security." American power and China's dependence on "the U.S. market, capital, and technology" prevented Beijing from openly opposing Washington; accordingly, regional organizations became an important part of China's quieter security strategy.[9]

The trifecta led to a comprehensive reevaluation of Chinese grand strategy, as previous chapters discussed, and led to a focus on regional multilateralism. Wang Yusheng, who helped formulate China's first regional multilateral policies, notes that it was "only the end of the Cold War" that gave rise to China's focus on regional institutions, and that was why "around the beginning of the 1990s, China began to take part in some regional mechanisms."[10] He recounts, "After the collapse of the Soviet Union, after the end of the Cold War, China went through several years of 'calm observation' and careful analysis and study." After this study, Wang argues, Chinese leaders determined that "China needed to, and had the capability to, make a certain contribution" to multilateral institutions.[11] The context for these decisions, as Wang notes in his memoir, was the growing US threat:

> The United States made several strategic victories in this period: with respect to military matters, the United States exploited Iraq's military invasion of Kuwait; it flaunted the advantage of a strong dollar; politically, it defeated its enemies—the other superpower, the Soviet Union (or as the United States would put it, "defeated communism"); with respect to economics, it caught the information technology development, and internationally it had a distant lead since Japan—which had once almost caught up with and exceeded the United States—was falling further behind. America's outspoken media threatened that the United States was "the most qualified to lead the world," and that in the 21st

century, "there is nothing but being subordinate to the United States." As leader of the world's only superpower, [President Clinton] needed a "post–Cold War" international order dominated by the United States, and promoted America's values and developmental model.[12]

As Wang repeatedly emphasizes in his memoirs, China believed that a victorious United States sought to dominate Asia and the globe; this required China to join regional multilateral organizations to ensure Washington did not wield them against Beijing or use them to build regional order. Key Foreign Ministry advisers agreed. A report commissioned by China's Ministry of Foreign Affairs and written by Zhang Yunling, a Chinese Academy of Social Science (CASS) scholar who helped shape China's multilateral strategy, begins with the observation: "after the end of the Cold War, China's international environment has undergone tremendous changes" and notes that these changes constituted "an important basis for China to formulate current and future security policies."[13] It then encouraged Beijing to use multilateral instruments as part of this security strategy.

The trifecta raised concerns not only about US order-building, but also that Washington might exploit the "China threat theory"—Beijing's name for supposedly unwarranted wariness of a rising China—and work with Asian states to encircle it. A search of Chinese academic and policy articles reveals that the term "China threat theory" rarely appeared until the trifecta, at which point in a few short years it became extremely important.

Zhang Yunling's memo to the Ministry of Foreign Affairs explicitly articulated the view that US-led encirclement was China's largest post–Cold War threat. He wrote, "In the new [post–Cold War] world pattern, China is a rising power. . . . Of course, the rise in Chinese power will also worry neighboring countries, and even make them fear being threatened [by China], and some countries will try to improve their military and strengthen alliances to cope with the rise in Chinese power."[14] In his memo, Zhang was unambiguous that this encirclement was China's gravest threat. "In the future, the *greatest challenge* to China's security," he argued, "is how to deal with and address the comprehensive changes in its relationships [with neighbors] caused by the rise in its own power." If this challenge were mishandled, Zhang feared that China would "push itself into a circle of hostility" surrounded by unfriendly states. In Zhang's mind, "*the most dangerous situation* is the formation of many countries united together to counter China, to carry out the encirclement and containment of China."[15] And of course, the instigator of such efforts would be the United States, with Zhang fearing the possibility of "the United States, together with its allies, intervening too frequently and too excessively" in China's affairs.[16]

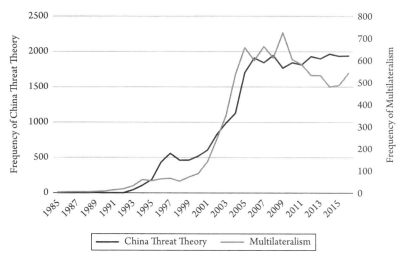

Figure 5.1 Number of Chinese Journal Articles Containing "China Threat Theory" and "Multilateralism," 1985–2016.[196]

These concerns led to a renewed focus on China's region, also known as "peripheral diplomacy" [周边外交]. "In the late 1980s," as one Chinese foreign policy historian notes in a history of this concept, "the disintegration of the Soviet Union, the upheaval in Eastern Europe, the end of the Cold War between the United States and the Soviet Union" led to "a severe situation rarely encountered since the founding of the country." As a result, "China's neighborhood policy was placed in a particularly important position during the 1990s."[17] "Neighborhood policy" became a priority, appearing for the first time ever in a Party Congress political report in 1992—the first Party Congress after the trifecta.[18] And as the preceding graph indicates, the rising focus on the "China threat theory" and neighborhood was accompanied by a focus on "multilateralism" as a solution (Figure 5.1).

A Blunting Strategy

As the preceding section indicated, the trifecta raised two security challenges for China, and a new blunting strategy using multilateral organizations was needed to address them. The first challenge was the threat of US-led encirclement with China's neighbors; the second was an increasingly threatening United States wielding its power and leverage over China. Multilateral institutions were intended to deal with both of these problems, and they were integrated into China's diplomatic layout [外交总体布局], a hierarchy of China's foreign policy focuses. Historically, the focus has been on the great powers first and then the periphery and the developing countries (e.g., "great powers are the key, the periphery is the primary, the developing countries are the foundation"), and China's addition of multilateralism to that formulation indicated its importance in Chinese strategy (e.g., "the multilateral is the important stage").[19] This was a major shift.

First, Chinese scholars and officials explicitly link China's conciliatory multilateralism to its fear of US-led encirclement. Zhang Yunling writes that joining multilateral organizations allowed China to "demonstrate its benign intentions by exercising self-restraint and displaying a willingness to be restrained" and, crucially, that "this idea has led directly to actions such as not devaluing the Renminbi during the 1997 Asian Financial Crisis, joining the TAC-SEA [an ASEAN document], and largely letting ASEAN states dictate the norms regarding the South China Sea dispute."[20] Similarly, a book from the Central Party School Press summarizing China's foreign policy strategy indicates China pursued a policy of self-constraint (自我约束) and "accepting constraint" from others in these bodies (接受约束) to reassure neighbors and confirms that multilateral concessions—like signing an ASEAN South China Sea Code of Conduct—were part of this strategy.[21] In another article, Zhang Yunling makes clear that this "good neighbor policy" was part of a grand strategy to *blunt* American encirclement:

> China has pursued a strategy of maintaining amicable relationships with neighbors (mulin youhao, wending zhoubian) to hedge against downturns in Sino-U.S. relations. Deng Xiaoping and his successors understand clearly that, with more than fifteen countries bordering China, an aggressive posture is simply not in China's interest, no matter how powerful China becomes, because aggression would lead to a counterbalancing alliance of China's neighbors and a distant power (the United States). If, however, China adopts a defensive realist approach, most regional countries would be reluctant to adopt a policy of hard containment, and thus China would likely enjoy a benign regional security environment. To this end, China has made strenuous efforts to improve its relationships with its neighboring countries, sometimes by making significant concessions despite strong domestic opposition.[22]

US scholars like Susan Shirk, who engaged with Chinese diplomats in Track II dialogues in the early 1990s, confirm these views: "Although China has a number of reasons for its more positive attitude toward regional security cooperation, the main one is to reduce regional fears about what the Chinese term 'the so-called China threat.' "[23] Indeed, at the first ARF meeting in 1994, Foreign

Minister Qian Qichen gave an entire series of press interviews to reassure neighbors about China's military threat.[24] Summing up these efforts, prominent Chinese scholar Wu Xinbo notes, "On the security front . . . [China] calculates that by promoting regional cooperation, it can help create a friendlier and more stable security environment around China's periphery, offsetting security pressures emanating from the US pursuit of a hedging strategy vis-à-vis China."[25]

Top political leaders also confirm this focus. At a meeting on peripheral diplomacy in 2001, President Jiang noted that "China is the country with the most neighboring countries in the world" and indicated that, since the Warring States period, "our ancestors have long recognized the importance of dealing [well] with neighboring countries."[26] Jiang then explained China's strategy of reassurance. "China is a big country," he noted, "and it is inevitable that some small countries around us have doubts about us."[27] To dispel them, China "must establish an image of peaceful development and friendly cooperation, as well as patiently and meticulously dispel doubts, and use our own exemplary words and deeds to increase trust so that they gradually realize that the so-called 'China threat' does not exist at all."[28] This also meant prioritizing "long-term interests" over "short-term interests" and temporarily putting aside territorial disputes.[29] Multilateral instruments had a role too. "The role of multilateral diplomacy has become increasingly prominent," Jiang argued, and China needed to give "full play" to regional multilateral initiatives.[30] At the end of the speech, and after hinting at "external plots" to manipulate divisions in Asia, Jiang stressed the degree to which the United States was a major consideration in this strategy: "Here, I want to emphasize one point. The United States is located in the Western Hemisphere. Although it is not our neighbor, it is a key factor affecting the security environment in our country."[31] The purpose of China's peripheral diplomacy, at this stage, was not to build China-led order in the region but to dissuade its neighbors from joining with the United States to encircle China.

Chinese sources suggest this strategy was perceived to have been successful. In a review of Chinese multilateralism in the 1990s, Zhang Yunling noted that "multilateral partnerships established between China and other powers have taken China out of harm's way from potentially hazardous confrontation."[32] "By enabling those countries to understand China better," Zhang asserted, it was possible for China "to lessen their fear of being threatened and hence reduce the possibility of an alliance against China."[33] Indeed, "with multilateral participation and effort," he continued, "China's image as a responsible power will be improved. As countries interact and cooperate with China more, they will worry less about the 'China threat.'"[34] Zhang even borrowed language from military doctrine to make the point, arguing in his memo to the Ministry of Foreign Affairs that multilateralism constitutes an "'active defense' strategy" that "allows China to take the initiative in meeting the challenge of [encirclement]" and "eliminate the possibility of united efforts to counter China."[35] In short, Chinese multilateralism has a powerful *strategic* rationale.

If the first objective of China's institutional strategy was to reduce the risk of a US-led containment coalition, the second objective was clearly to frustrate the exercise of American power. Multilateral institutions offered a way to do this without directly confronting US power. As Zhang Yunling and Tang Shiping argued, China could use institutions "to work with others to restrain US hegemonic behavior" and had elevated certain institutions like the SCO "that are designed to limit US influence."[36] Similarly, Wang Yizhou made the link between multilateralism and American power explicit: "To be clear, an important reason why China now increasingly values multilateral diplomacy is US hegemonic behavior after the Cold War and its superpower position."[37]

These sentiments were found in official texts too. In 1997, the term "multilateralism" was used for the first time in a Party Congress work report when Jiang Zemin said China must "actively participate in multilateral diplomatic activities" and "give full play" to China's role in these bodies.[38] It then appeared in every report after. In the 1997 Ambassadorial Conference address, a kind of speech often used to adjust grand strategy, Jiang reiterated that China must "actively participate in multilateral diplomacy" and linked the trend to multipolarity. "Under the new situation in which the trend of world multipolarity and economic globalization is constantly evolving," he said, "all major countries rely on regional organizations to develop themselves and seek to obtain through multilateral means what they cannot get through bilateral relations. We should pay more attention to this situation and pay attention to making the best use of it to make profits and avoid disadvantages."[39] Gradually, Chinese diplomats and state media reduced calls for multipolarity and "began emphasizing the role of multilateral organizations," and in 2004, Beijing elevated the concept of "cooperation" as one of the three defining principles of China's foreign policy.[40] Jiang Zemin said that, along with the growing strength of developing countries, "a variety of regional, intercontinental and global organizations are unprecedentedly active," and that together "these facts show that the world pattern is accelerating toward multipolarity."[41] Officially, multilateralism began to be seen as an important conduit for multipolarity. In a 2001 address to high-level military leaders, Jiang made this link and argued that participating in institutions could expand China's freedom of maneuver: "We must focus on expanding strategic space and vigorously carrying out multilateral diplomacy. Actively carrying out multilateral diplomacy plays an important role in building the strategic situation for us."[42] After chronicling China's participation in APEC, ARF, and the SCO, among other forums, he noted, "We must profoundly realize that under the conditions of world multipolarization and economic globalization. . . . The use of international mechanisms and regional organizations for multilateral diplomacy has increasingly become an important way for big countries to play their role. We must further strengthen multilateral diplomacy, take the initiative to participate in the transformation and adjustment of the international system, and strive to carry out foreign work at the multilateral level."[43]

Over the following decade, as China's concerns over US power grew following Washington's interventions in Bosnia, Kosovo, Afghanistan, and Iraq, multilateralism became even more critical. Then Vice Foreign Minister Wang Yi gave a 2004 speech entitled "Facilitating the Development of Multilateralism and Promoting World Multipolarization" that implicitly argued that multilateralism could be used to constrain the United States.[44] Top leaders made the link too. In 2006, Hu Jintao declared that China must "strengthen multilateralism and advance the democratization of international relations," reiterating that multilateralism was an important ingredient in multipolarity.[45] Similarly, at the Central Foreign Affairs Work Conference that year, he stated that, "With respect to politics, to promote the building of a harmonious world," China needed to "actively advocate multilateralism, promote the democratization of international relations, and oppose hegemonism and power politics."[46]

In one of Jiang's final addresses, a speech to the Politburo recounting successes over the last decade, Jiang stressed that China had "proposed and implemented strategic thinking stabilizing the periphery" and had "played an important role in multilateral diplomatic organizations."[47] It is notable that Jiang's speech specifically identified APEC, ASEAN, and the SCO as examples of China's strategy; accordingly, these are precisely the three cases to which we now turn.

Asia-Pacific Economic Cooperation (APEC)

"China's experience with regionalism originated with APEC," wrote Chinese scholar Wu Xinbo.[48] Founded in 1989, APEC is a forum for twenty-one Pacific Rim member economies that seeks to promote trade and development assistance. In the wake of the Cold War, and amid growing concerns in Beijing about the power and threat posed by the United States, Beijing began to pursue a blunting strategy through APEC that suggested China's involvement was instrumental and tactical rather than sincere. As China's first APEC diplomat Wang Yusheng makes clear, China feared that the organization—which it perceived as US-led—would ultimately become an instrument of American hegemony in Asia, serving to promote economic liberalization, human rights, and a US-led multilateral security structure. Acting under central-level guidance, Wang sought to stall APEC by opposing its institutionalization and successfully promoting an "APEC Approach" that effectively prohibited institutionalization in the future. Chinese diplomats also worked to wield the organization to inoculate

China against American power (especially economic sanctions), all while simultaneously using the platform APEC provided to reassure China's neighbors that Beijing was not a threat. As a partial consequence, APEC has been ineffective in promoting trade liberalization and generally irrelevant during the Asian Financial Crisis and the 2008 Global Financial Crisis.

Alternative Explanations

What might explain China's participation in APEC? China does not appear to have been a *sincere participant* in the organization. APEC was not particularly "thick." It had only a weak secretariat, avoided trade negotiations, operated on consensus rather than a more efficient set of rules for decision-making, had scant monitoring mechanisms, and did not have binding decisions—and China worked against improvements on each of these items, sometimes standing alone. Perhaps China saw genuine value in APEC as a forum for discussion, consensus, and voluntary commitments, but China worked to dramatically limit what APEC could discuss. Others note that the first APEC summit in 1993 did in fact offer Chinese leader Jiang Zemin the first chance to meet with an American president after Tiananmen, but China's participation continued even after regular presidential interaction was restored. Many argue China saw economic benefits from APEC, but China's economic goals were defensive and oriented toward preventing the region from signing on to an American economic agenda contrary to its interests.[49] Nor did China join and stall APEC out of fear of that Taiwan would use the organization to boost its claims of sovereignty. In his memoirs, China's first APEC ambassador, Wang Yusheng, does not list concerns over Taiwan as a reason for why China joined APEC. Even before China joined, Beijing succeeded in ensuring that Taiwan would be referred to as "Chinese Taipei," that it would never be represented by a president but instead only an economic minister, and that it would be excluded from discussions of security issues since it was not a state.[50] And even after China joined, Wang dismissed Taiwan's efforts to maneuver for sovereignty, noting that the United States and other APEC members largely worked with China to push back on those goals in the 1990s, suggesting these concerns did not animate China's involvement.

Blunting

China's real interest was in blunting American power and reassuring its neighbors, which emerged from its growing perception of American power and threat following the Cold War.

The US Threat

China's involvement in APEC was driven by fears that the institution would become a tool of US hegemony. As scholars like Chien-peng Chung argue, China joined APEC "defensively" to make sure features of Asian order "could not be decided without its participation."[51] Kai He argues that "China used APEC as a diplomatic tool to constrain US influence and resist Western pressures" on economic, security, and political matters.[52] A key priority was to limit US leadership in the Asia-Pacific.

China's concern over APEC was in part a product of post–Cold War anxieties. In his memoirs, Wang Yusheng noted, "The first four years of APEC's start-up phase was a period when the international situation had undergone a historic change" as the post–Cold war dawned.[53] With "APEC as an authoritative official organization in the region," Wang noted, the urgent question for China was "what can it do, and where will it lead us."[54] Wang provided an answer: "The reason why the United States actively promoted the establishment of APEC was to open the Asian markets," at least ostensibly, but "of course, the United States is [also] a superpower, and its goals were not just these [economic goals] and nothing more."[55] Instead, Wang repeatedly argues that APEC was an instrument of American hegemony designed to promote economic and political liberalization, one that could evolve into a US-led "security community." He writes:

> In the face of the post–Cold War world situation, especially the rise of East Asia, the United States has greater strategic considerations and demands. President Clinton, while putting forward the US slogan of economic revitalization, also had a "new Pacificism" slogan, which is [on the surface] "economic globalization." . . . But in reality, *this is precisely "Americanization" or the "American model"*; the *so-called "American values" of popular democracy, freedom, and human rights, among others*; and the establishment of American leadership—at the very least *a "security system" dominated by the United States.*[56]

As Wang's remarks demonstrate, China believed that the United States was pursuing a "new Pacificism" in the wake of the Cold War that would include liberal economics, liberal values, and a US-backed security community—in essence, institutionalized American leadership. These impressions were strengthened by Clinton's own statements in Tokyo, Korea, and at the APEC leaders' meeting in Seattle, in which he announced that the United States sought a "New Pacific Community" and that the American agenda in Asia involved three goals: "working for shared prosperity, for security, and for democracy."[57] APEC was central to these efforts: "In the eyes of the United States, APEC is itself a part of this 'new Pacific-ism,' and it can even become the *starting point* or experimental test for US promotion of 'new Pacific-ism,'" Wang argued, "And of course, the United States would happily proceed accordingly!"[58] China would not stand idly by as Washington rewrote the economic, political, and military rules of Asia through APEC. After the United States sought to elevate APEC at Seattle, Wang observed that "US strategic intent became quite obvious. Its 'community' concept encompasses three pillars: namely economic integration based on trade liberalization; multilateral security mechanisms dominated by the United States; and democratization with American values as the standard."[59] He continued, "The establishment of such a 'community' and its vision, of course . . . is something that *cannot be accepted by China*."[60] And so China sought to prevent the emergence of such a community by weakening APEC itself.

Opposing Institutionalization

China's blunting strategy within APEC proceeded in three ways: it involved a focus on (1) slowing institutionalization; (2) constraining the organization's ability to consider security issues; and (3) pushing back against the institution's economic agenda.

First, with respect to institutionalization, China sought to ensure APEC remained a "thin" organization and to retain Beijing's ability to effectively veto key developments in APEC's consensus-driven decision-making process. Wang argued that, thanks to the emphasis on consensus, any APEC effort "must obtain—or cannot do without—our support." For this reason, the de facto veto "gives us broad freedom of maneuver [广阔的活动天地], and on major issues in the world [discussed at APEC], *we can play to our strengths or impose our unique influence*." China fought hard to ensure that these features remained key parts of APEC, opposing US attempts to institutionalize the organization.

Many of these battles for APEC's institutional future were waged between 1993 and 1995. According to C. Fred Bergstein, who was intimately involved in US policy toward APEC in this period and led APEC's highly influential Expert Working Group, the United States sought to transform the organization "from a purely consultative forum to an action-oriented, substantive group."[61] China prominently opposed these efforts at institutionalization and saw them in hostile terms. As Wang noted in a recent interview, "When China joined APEC, some countries were still driven by Cold War mentality and sought supremacy in the institution," a reference to the United States, "but China called for equal consultation and respect" and pushed back.[62] China's leader Jiang Zemin publicly stated in 1993 that APEC should be a forum and "consultation mechanism" rather than an "institutionalized" organization.[63] In his memoir, Wang notes that

China opposed APEC expanding its mandate beyond economics, being institutionalized, being identified as a "Community," becoming a forum for negotiation, having any non-voluntary commitments, and operating on any principle other than consensus. In 1994, as the introduction discussed, China triumphed against US efforts to define APEC as a "community," with its political leadership directly involved in the effort.[64]

China was successful in these early battles, but it nonetheless remained wary that the tide could turn. As Wang Yusheng noted, "The ghost of 'Community'" and other forms of institutionalization "had [still] been hovering over APEC and had not yet disappeared. In my work, I deeply felt that this was not an illusory shadow but something very real."[65] For that reason, beginning in the late 1990s, China sought to enshrine the anti-institutional approach it had defended in previous years in APEC documents under the phrase "the APEC Approach [APEC 方式]." Wang notes that China's earlier attempts at pushing for a deinstitutionalized approach, using phrases like "big family energy" and "unique approaches," were only "prototypes" for the final "APEC Approach" concept. He recounts that high-level members of the Ministry of Foreign Affairs worked directly on the concept, and that ahead of the 1996 Subic summit, China made inserting the "APEC Approach" into key documents a major priority—with Jiang Zemin involved in promoting this "big Chinese contribution" to APEC.[66] China initially encountered obstacles when, after suggesting the "APEC Approach" would be included in the joint statement, the Philippines, which was hosting the summit and drafting the statement, reversed course and cited American opposition. China's APEC delegation was shocked and threatened what was essentially the nuclear option—to oppose the finding of any consensus on the statement until "the APEC Approach" was included. "How could we let down Chairman Jiang?" Wang asked, "we had no choice but to use our very last move."[67] The gambit worked, and China's success, Wang noted, "declared to [the] world that the 'APEC Approach' was born." The next year, a similarly tough stance helped China elevate the APEC Approach into a core APEC concept, undercutting the organization's institutionalization.[68]

Wang's memoirs also reveal China's fear that APEC might become a security instrument for the United States, and even an Asian NATO. During the Seattle meeting of APEC in 1993, President Clinton had linked APEC to NATO himself in ways that shocked Chinese observers: "We can't imagine now how we could have weathered the Cold War without NATO. In the same way, future generations may look back and say they can't imagine how the Asian-Pacific region could have thrived in such a spirit of harmony without the existence of APEC."[69] When Defense Secretary William Perry argued explicitly for discussing security issues within APEC, China saw it as a step toward an Asian NATO.[70] For China, this was intolerable, and in his memoirs, Wang Yusheng recounts being vigorously opposed to a security role. Observers of various APEC rounds noted that China was more opposed than the others on a security role for APEC, and that "the desire to keep the forum narrowly focused on trade and economic issues [was] acute, at times verging on what to others seems almost paranoiac."[71] Most states, including Southeast Asian ones, eventually supported adding HIV/AIDS, drug trafficking, smuggling, non-traditional security, youth issues, women's issues, and other topics to the APEC agenda. But China took issue with every single one of these topics, even youth issues—fearing that they would provide an opening for the United States to shift APEC's focus. "All of this [focus on noneconomic issues] is actually an attempt to try to change the nature of APEC, and objectively it coincides with the [interests of the] United States," which retained its "determination to eventually establish a 'New Pacific Community' that integrates economic, security, and democracy in the Asia-Pacific region.'" Wang articulates his disappointment that China was isolated on this issue, but in opposing attempts to expand APEC's mandate, Wang was only following the central government's line: "I followed the spirit of domestic instructions, repeatedly did their work, and stressed that APEC must focus on engaging in economic cooperation if it is to maintain its vitality" and avoid "sensitive political and social issues."[72]

Finally, with respect to economics, China opposed allowing the United States to use the organization to set the region's new economic rules, fearing that US-led APEC liberalization could harm China's economy. A key goal was to defeat American rules on market access, investment, and financial sector liberalization—the last of which China did not believe should even be a part of APEC's mandate.[73] China targeted APEC's very capacity to achieve its economic objectives by undermining timelines, monitoring mechanisms, and other coordinating devices. For example, when the United States in 1994 put forward a unified timeline for liberalization, China successfully pushed for a separate developing country timeline. At the 1995 Osaka summit, the United States sought firm commitments and binding decisions for these timelines but China successfully pushed to make them voluntary. And later, when the United States relented and advocated non-binding liberalization standards, China fought these too because in Wang Yusheng's words, "although they are 'non-binding,' [these standards] have political and moral influence, and today's 'non-binding' may become tomorrow's 'binding.'"[74] When some proposed that APEC monitor and compare the voluntary and non-binding movement of members toward liberalization, China opposed a monitoring mechanism. When the United States suggested that economic and technical assistance from developed countries might be linked to voluntary liberalization, China opposed the principle. As this brief review shows, China opposed virtually all major attempts at liberalization, even non-binding timetables, monitoring and comparison mechanisms, and the use of APEC as a negotiation forum—arguing instead it should be focused on discussion.

China's blunting strategy was largely successful, and the United States eventually lost sustained interest in using APEC as a vehicle to promote Asian liberalization—choosing instead to turn to bilateral and later multilateral trade agreements, including the ill-fated Trans-Pacific Partnership.

Security Benefits

China's participation in APEC fit within its larger strategy to blunt American power. It helped deny the United States a platform for promulgating Western economic and political norms, as well as coordinating security or military policy through what it feared might become an Asian NATO, as the previous section mentioned. It also afforded China the opportunity to reassure its neighbors and reduce the likelihood of a countervailing balancing coalition, and ways to weaken US economic leverage over China.

China's APEC strategy was motivated in part by a desire to reassure China's neighbors. As Moore and Yang note in their review of Chinese behavior in the organization, "APEC provides China with an important forum to establish its credentials as a reliable, responsible, cooperative power—especially to its smaller neighbors in the region" and also provides an "opportunity to counteract the 'China threat' argument that has gained currency periodically over the last decade."[75] That geopolitics, and not just economics, was a motivating factor is explicitly confirmed by Wang Yusheng. APEC was useful for improving ties with the very neighbors that could encircle China and the great powers that could assist, most of whom were in APEC: "China can make full use of APEC's activities," Wang noted, "and with respect to politics, APEC can provide the service of helping China advance and build good relations with neighbors." The desire to reassure neighbors was so critical that, in 1993 at the first APEC leader-level meeting, Jiang discussed China's benign intentions at length:

> We never seek hegemony. We keep away from arms races and military blocs and never seek any sphere of influence. We always strive to develop friendly relations and cooperation with our neighbors and all other countries of the world on the basis of the Five Principles of Peaceful Coexistence. . . . A stable, developed and prosperous China will by no means pose a threat to any country."

Along these lines, APEC was a platform for China to make magnanimous concessions to reassure others. When China reduced its import tariff rate from

36 percent to 23 percent in the 1990s, Wang claims that "China chose to declare this initiative in the [APEC] Osaka meeting to demonstrate China's determination to play a role in Asia and to integrate into the international community" and show that China has a "constructive attitude."[76] During the Asian Financial Crisis, President Jiang made speeches at APEC highlighting China's decisions to further cut tariffs, to not devalue its currency, and to provide financial assistance to Asian countries in order to demonstrate, in his words, that "the Chinese government has assumed a highly responsible attitude" even though "China has paid a high price" for these decisions.[77] These policy decisions, especially the decision not to devalue, cost roughly $10 billion but gained China considerable support in Asia. As Wang notes, "Some APEC Asian friends said with emotion that . . . China is a reliable friend in trouble" and others noted that China's policies "won wide praise, increased China's influence in APEC and internationally, and laid a good foundation for China to play the role of a great power with Chinese characteristics in the new century."[78]

And as the next chapter argues in greater detail, China also used APEC to blunt American economic leverage over China. After the Tiananmen Square massacre, the US Congress had repeatedly voted on revoking China's most-favored nation (MFN) status, which would have effectively doubled the price of China's exports and could have done severe damage to its economy.[79] China sought to capture MFN status from APEC. First, it tried to persuade APEC members to adopt a principle of non-discrimination, which would allow China to wrangle MFN from a multilateral process that which had been elusive from the bilateral process with Washington. Second, Beijing understood that accession to the GATT/WTO would render the MFN question moot and blunt US economic leverage, so it supported the principle, as Foreign Minister Qian Qichen put it, that "all APEC members should become GATT members."[80] The United States pushed back on these efforts, and once it accepted China as a WTO member, the issue was moot in any case.

ASEAN-Related Institutions

On a sweltering summer day in Bangkok, Qian Qichen, China's foreign minister, was holding court. Gathered around him was a gaggle of journalists from all over the world who had converged on the Thai capital to cover the first ever meeting of the ASEAN Regional Forum (ARF) in 1994.

A descendent from a prominent scholarly family, Qian Qichen had joined the CCP as a teenager, studied in the Soviet Union, and steadily climbed the ranks of the Ministry of Foreign Affairs across four decades.[81] He was responsible for creating China's system of Foreign Ministry spokespersons—now infamous for its nationalistic bromides and "Wolf Warrior" diplomacy—and had served as its inaugural spokesperson.[82] A decade later, Qian ably steered his country's diplomacy through Tiananmen sanctions and the Soviet collapse, translating Deng's diplomatic guidance at the end of the Cold War into the diplomatic practice of the 1990s. His memoirs detail how he strove to resist American coercion, rehabilitate Beijing, and reassure Asian neighbors. Now, as he addressed the journalists gathered around him, he understood that the ARF provided an opportunity to advance those objectives.

The region was concerned about China's growing military spending, which had increased 34 percent over the preceding year, creating an opening for American coalition-building.[83] So Qian tried to persuade regional states not to worry about China. "There is no big increase of defense expenditures," he said, attributing the increase entirely to inflation.[84] If one compares China's military spending to that of the United States, he argued, "you come to the conclusion that China's military forces are defensive in nature."[85] Qian went on to stress China had no offensive intentions. "In history, China has never invaded any foreign country," he said, overlooking China's invasion of Vietnam fifteen years earlier.[86] Moments later, the Foreign Minister of a country that today has a carrier fleet and overseas bases stressed that Asian states should not worry about China precisely because "China does not have aircraft carriers nor does it have overseas military bases."[87] He ended the point with a rhetorical question, "How can it be possible for the Chinese armed forces to [have an] offensive posture?"[88]

Chinese diplomats continued to emphasize these themes in ASEAN-related forums for years, in addition to looking for ways to complicate US order-building. Over the next decade, Beijing enthusiastically launched additional multilateral organizations with ASEAN support, including ASEAN Plus Three (APT) and the East Asia Summit (EAS), generally undermining those institutions like ARF that featured the United States while seeking to bolster those like APT that did not—all with an eye to reassuring China's neighbors and blunting US power.

Alternative Explanations

Why did Beijing bother joining ASEAN forums at all? These forums have low levels of institutionalization, cannot settle disputes or monitor military buildups, and are unable to substantially reward or punish state behavior. ASEAN states follow the "ASEAN way," which emphasizes "cooperation that is informal, incremental, and consensus-based, and that rests on the basis of non-intervention in states' domestic affairs and avoidance of direct confrontation in the forum's deliberations."[89] Moreover, these organizations generally lack secretariats and all lack mechanisms for mutual assistance from outside attack or formal sanctions against errant members.

Blunting

China's motivation was apparently not driven by a sincere commitment to ASEAN and its processes—which Beijing often stalled; rather, it was driven by a desire to frustrate the US ability to use these organizations to set the terms of regional order.

The US Threat

With the Cold War's conclusion, Asia embarked on regional projects, and China's leadership subsequently "realized that nonparticipation in multilateral security mechanisms was riskier than involvement."[90] Upon the creation of the ARF, as Rosemary Foot observed from her interviews with Chinese interlocutors, some Chinese officials were concerned: "The U.S., it was argued, as sole superpower would . . . seek to dominate the proceedings, perhaps using the body as another venue to marshal collective criticism of China's internal and external behavior."[91] Chinese officials were also concerned that a Western-dominated ARF might form a nascent security grouping that would eventually be part of a containment strategy. Even avid institutionalists like Zhang Yunling argued in reports to the MFA that the ARF was potentially as problematic as US security alliances and missile defense: "Like the strengthening of the US-Japan military alliance, theater missile defense and the ARF both have the real and potential intention to counter China's rising power."[92] Another prominent Chinese observer, Wu Xinbo, argued that the ARF was a larger challenge to China than even APEC because "unlike APEC's original mandate, the ARF is a mechanism aimed at promoting regional security cooperation." He noted that a "principal reason" that China joined the ARF was "that against the background of China's rise and the notion of a 'China threat' in the Asia Pacific, the United States, Japan, and even Southeast Asian countries might employ the ARF to check and contain a stronger China." Wu further explains that "Beijing's concern was not entirely groundless" since "Washington did forge a regional mechanism in the mid-1950s—the Southeast Asian Treaty Organization—to contain China."[93] In light of these fears, as Chien-peng Chung argues in his study of China's institutional involvement, "the PRC's participation in the ARF reflects its desire to monitor and impede a fledgling multilateral security organization for the Asia-Pacific."[94] China feared that the ARF would "link together the separate US military alliances and agreements with Japan, Australia, South Korea, and several Southeast Asians into a network that would ... enable the USA to quickly move to a containment posture if necessary."[95]

Opposing Institutionalization

China feared that the United States and Japan might push the ARF to take positions contrary to China's interests. Beijing therefore sought to "slow down the pace of the ARF and obstruct substantial security cooperation."[96] China chose to pursue a blunting strategy that limited the ARF's effectiveness while at the same time generally supporting institutionalization in ASEAN bodies that did not include the United States, particularly ASEAN Plus Three (APT).

First, China opposed the blueprint adopted by the ARF in 1995 for institutionalizing the organization. That blueprint called for three stages of evolution: Stage 1 involved confidence-building measures (CBMs); Stage 2 would see mechanisms for preventive diplomacy (PD); and Stage 3 called for establishing conflict resolution agreements. China feared this roadmap would allow Washington to more effectively interfere in Taiwan and the South China Sea, so it undermined them.[97] It refused to share much information about its military in the first phase; outright opposed and then weakened PD mechanisms with sovereignty-focused principles in the second phase; and reframed the objective of the third phase from conflict resolution to the almost meaningless "elaboration of approaches to conflicts."[98] Even though a key purpose of the ARF was to discuss the disputes ASEAN states had with China in the South China Sea, Beijing worked to prevent serious discussions.

Second, China opposed ARF's ability to discuss items between ARF sessions, significantly slowing the organization's development.[99] Beijing feared that these intersessional working groups, staffed with government officials, could evolve into structures that would impinge on China's interests. China later gave ground, but moved to weaken their legitimacy by ensuring that (1) they not be called working groups, preferring less formal titles like "Intersessional Support Group"; (2) they not be intergovernmental, but also have academics and others involved; and (3) their scope remain limited. China grew comfortable with these weak institutions but still kept their numbers low and domain restricted, opposing them on the South China Sea.[100]

Third, China opposed strengthening the ARF's ability to act independently or to retain a permanent bureaucracy. It opposed attempts to widen the chair into a council as well as proposals to create a permanent and autonomous ARF secretariat.[101] It also opposed US proposals to allow non-ASEAN states to assume the rotating ARF chairmanship, fearing the United States or Japan might internationalize China's territorial disputes.[102] Because of this, it was not until 2004 that the ARF even established a small "ARF Unit" within the ASEAN Secretariat, after first having established one for the APT, which lacked Western states.

China was ultimately successful in stalling the organization's efforts to be more than a talk shop, and as one observer noted, "China seems very happy to see it remain that way."[103] An ASEAN diplomat concluded, "China still remains the main impediment to the institutional development of the ARF in the eyes of many ARF members."[104]

The strongest evidence that China's institutional involvement was about blunting US power is the fact that Beijing opposed institutionalization in the ARF and APEC, which *included* the United States, but supported it in the APT, which *excluded* the United States. The APT was a successor to the East Asian Economic Group (EAEG), an ill-fated initiative launched by Malaysian Prime Minister Mahathir that self-consciously and rather blatantly excluded Western states. "We call it the ASEAN Plus Three," Mahathir declared, "but we are kidding ourselves. ASEAN Plus Three is, in fact, EAEG." Others like then Chinese Vice President Hu Jintao said as much publicly too.[105]

China, which had previously supported EAEG, was very enthusiastic about APT. Beijing sought to institutionalize it, expand its scope, and make it the heart of Asian regionalism. The double standards between what China supported in APT and opposed in APEC and ARF are remarkable. For example, China opposed discussing security at APEC and stalled those efforts at ARF, but it supported security dialogues at APT, with Chinese Premier Zhu Rongji urging APT to "carry out dialogue and cooperation in political and security fields."[106] China similarly opposed APEC's Expert Working Group and urged its closure, but it backed the creation of a similar East Asian Vision Group in APT.[107] China objected to the word "community" in APEC but it was comfortable when the APT's East Asia Vision Group said it proudly "envisions East Asia moving from a region of nations to a bona fide regional community" and used the term thirty times in its first major report.[108] China opposed Japan's proposal to launch an Asian Monetary Fund during the Asian financial crisis in 1997, but it supported a similar initiative for APT (which later became the APT-led Chiang Mai Initiative) that ensured the achievement would "not directly redound to Japan's leadership role in regional affairs."[109] China was wary of Track II conclaves like the Shangri-La Dialogue and the Council for Security Cooperation in the Asia Pacific (CSCAP), which involved the United States, but it took the lead in launching its own version through APT's Network of East Asian Think Tanks (NEAT) in 2003, which it administered through state institutions.[110] While China continued to stall institutionalization in APEC and ARF, it had extremely ambitious plans for APT. Zhang Yunling, the academic who shaped China's multilateral diplomacy, said China sought a regional parliamentary committee, a defense ministers' meeting, and an East Asian security council—features that, in some cases, China had rejected for the ARF and APEC.[111] China opposed ARF and APEC secretariats and permanent staff, but it successfully launched an APT office within the ASEAN Secretariat well before the longer-running ARF received one.[112]

China's double standards had a purpose. Beijing wanted a thick APT in line with its exclusive, non-Western view of Asian regionalism, and it elevated APT above competing organizations. In 2003, Premier Wen Jiabao said APT should be the "principal channel" for "East Asia cooperation,"[113] while his then Assistant Secretary Cui Tiankai called APT the "major channel" for cooperation along with ASEAN as the "core," pointedly excluding ARF from his list.[114] China supported thicker regionalism as long as it excluded the United States.

In 2004, China became even more ambitious, aiming to spin APT off into a new organization—the East Asian Summit (EAS)—which would become the major regional organization for East Asia. China offered to host the first meeting in Beijing, and in a review of Chinese writings on EAS, Wu Xinbo highlights China's enthusiasm: "From the very beginning, China expected the East Asia Summit to be a major venue in building an East Asian community."[115] As another author notes, "It was China's intention to upgrade the APT to a comprehensive SCO-type EAS that pointedly excludes the United States and other Western countries," a reference to the Shanghai Cooperation Organization— a China-led organization in Central Asia.[116] ASEAN states, Japan, and South Korea went along with the EAS but invited Australia, India, and New Zealand to play a balancing role against China. As Wu notes, "Beijing felt somewhat frustrated" by this, but "what dismayed it even more was the decision that the EAS would be hosted only by ASEAN countries, thus not including China, which was initially enthusiastic about hosting the second meeting." Once the United States was involved, China reversed course and sought to weaken EAS relative to APT.[117] "Under such circumstances," Wu Xinbo noted, "China expects APT to be the main venue for the building of an East Asian community."[118] For example, China fought to remove the term "East Asian community" from the declaration signed at the first EAS summit, though it continued to support the phrase in APT.[119] As an acknowledgment of this small tactical victory, the first East Asia Summit declaration stated that "the East Asian region had already advanced in its efforts to realize an East Asian community *through the ASEAN+3 process*."[120]

Security Benefits

China also used its position within ASEAN-related forums to (1) weaken US influence in Asia; and (2) reassure its neighbors.

First, China sought to promote norms, like its "New Security Concept" that would undermine US alliances after the trifecta. Wu Baiyi, deputy director of research at the China Foundation for International and Strategic Studies, wrote that work on the concept began after "the dissolution of the Soviet Union," when "policy planners and academics began working quietly to amend the country's security strategy." They finally debuted the concept in 1996 unofficially in Track II dialogues.[121] As Chu Shulong argued, key aspects of the concept "denounce the alliance approach" and, at a conference held in Beijing by scholars to discuss it and summarized officially in the Party daily *Renmin Ribao*, participants "identified 'four nos' at the center of the concept: no hegemonism, no power politics, no arms race, and no military alliance."[122] Another *Renmin Ribao* article said the concept stood against Cold War thinking, including alliances, economic sanctions, and arms races.[123] In March 1997, China formally introduced the concept at ASEAN when it hosted and chaired the ARF intersessional working group on CBMs in Beijing; there, it "lambasted bilateral alliances, particularly the US-Japanese alliance, as destabilizing and representative of old-style, Cold War thinking" and put forward several motions that targeted the US military.[124] Then, Foreign Minister Qian Qichen put forward the concept at the 4th ASEAN Regional Forum in July 1997 and several other gatherings. "It has been proved that the security concept and framework of the Cold War era, which were based on military alliances and conducted by increasing arms building, cannot build peace," he argued at ASEAN's thirtieth anniversary. "In the new situation, expanding military blocs and enhancing military alliances are against the current and future historical trend."[125] Similarly, in a 2001 speech discussing the concept, Qian Qichen said "absolute security for oneself through stronger military alliance and intensified arms race is out of tune with the trend of the times."[126] The next year, Beijing submitted a detailed position paper on the concept to ASEAN that included several important elements, arguing that countries:

- should "transcend differences in ideology and social systems" such as China's authoritarian governance;
- should "discard the mentality of Cold War and power politics [*sic*]," a reference to US Cold War–era alliances;
- should hold "mutual briefings on each other's security and defense policies and major operations," a method of securing prior notification for US exercises and curtailing US maritime surveillance;
- should "refrain from interfering in other countries' internal affairs," a reference to US human rights pressure;
- and should "promote the democratization of the international relations," a classic reference to promoting a shift from US hegemony to multipolarity.[127]

Second, China not only criticized alliances, it sought to use ASEAN institutions to frustrate the US military's freedom of maneuver. China proposed requiring prior notification of all joint exercises and allowing observer participation—requirements that effectively only applied to the United States as the main state conducting joint exercises, and succeeded in inserting prior notification into the 2002 Declaration of Conduct of Parties in the South China Sea.[128] China also called for states to cease surveillance of one another, which again principally applied to US maritime surveillance.[129] It used discussions over the South China Sea as "a means to restrict US Naval exercises in the area" by proposing a ban on South China Sea military exercises—targeting recently restarted US-Philippine exercises in particular. China argued that a proposed ASEAN maritime information center be placed in Tianjin, which could have given China influence over information provision.[130] China pressured states not to join Washington's post-9/11 Regional Maritime Security Initiative (RMSI), which involved using US Special Forces, new bases in Malaysia, and high-speed vessels to secure the Malacca Straits from terrorist attack and piracy.[131] Seeing this effort as part of a containment plan, China suggested an alternative eleven-nation joint China-ASEAN patrol to secure the sea lines.[132] China even suggested that "bilateral agreements between ASEAN countries and outside powers," such as alliances with the United States, should *not* supersede multilateral ones made through ASEAN that might limit alliance cooperation or participation in RMSI.[133] Finally, China was the first nuclear state to support ASEAN's interest in nuclear weapons-free zones in Southeast Asia, which if successful, could have complicated US efforts to station strategic nuclear forces or nuclear-equipped vessels and aircraft in the region, thereby limiting US freedom of maneuver without affecting China, which did not deploy such forces abroad.[134]

Finally, China sought to reassure ASEAN states to prevent its encirclement. China's institutional involvements demonstrated Beijing's willingness to work multilaterally rather than bilaterally where it had an advantage and to let ASEAN be in the driver's seat for Asian regionalism, thereby enhancing the credibility of its claims of benign intentions. By 2008, China had a total of forty-six institutionalized mechanisms with ASEAN, compared to America's fifteen.[135] China also made concrete political concessions. In 1995, it accepted that competing claims should be resolved through UNCLOS rather than by force.[136] In 2002, China signed the "Declaration on the Conduct of Parties in the South China Sea" with ASEAN States: it acknowledged (rather than ignored) ASEAN claims; created precedents for multilateral solutions where China's leverage would be weaker; and renounced violence to change the status quo (which it had previously used against Vietnam). In 2003, China also became the first non-ASEAN state to sign the ASEAN Treaty of Cooperation and Amity—effectively the ASEAN Charter, which committed it to non-interference in the affairs of Southeast Asian states. That same year, China signed a "Joint Declaration on a Strategic Partnership." These decisions served "to signal China's commitment to long-term cooperation on regional security issues."[137] China also used ASEAN to provide economic benefits to ASEAN member states. It pursued a concessionary free trade agreement with ASEAN states and expanded loans and investment—all of which reduce security anxieties. At a 2002 APT meeting, China announced debt forgiveness for Vietnam, Laos, Cambodia, and Myanmar. The China-ASEAN FTA included an "early harvest" provision that ensured China cut agricultural tariffs three years before ASEAN states did. China also extended MFN status to new ASEAN states, even though they were not part of the WTO, and gave them five years to reciprocate on their commitments to China.[138] Economic concessions served as costly signals of China's interest in reassurance.[139] In this way, China was able to use the ARF to blunt American order-building in Asia, particularly the possibility of an encircling coalition directed against China.

Shanghai Cooperation Organization (SCO)

On January 18, 2000, Chi Haotian, then a vice chairman of the Central Military Commission, visited Russia to meet with Vladimir Putin. The meeting came at a sensitive time. Less than three weeks earlier, Putin had become acting president following the surprise resignation of President Boris Yeltsin on New Year's Eve.

The meeting gave Chi Haotian an opportunity to assess the young Russian leader, and he judged him to be someone who was "relatively sober and steady, speaks little, but carries a great deal of weight."[140] The meeting apparently went well. After it ended, the Chinese ambassador to Russia turned to Chi Haotian and told him, "Putin rarely smiles, but in his meeting with you, he smiled two times—this is truly rare."[141] Chi Haotian, evidently quite pleased with himself, was delighted to hear it.

One of the key subjects of the meeting between Chi and Putin was the effort by Russia and China to upgrade the Shanghai Five—an annual regional summit among China, Russia, and the three former Soviet republics bordering China first held in 1996—into a formal institution called the Shanghai Cooperation Organization. Chi Haotian's biography recounts that he and Putin had found "consensus" on the need for "opposing hegemonism, safeguarding world peace, opposing human rights interference, opposing missile defense, and other issues"—all clear references to their shared objections to US order.[142] They then agreed on plans to formalize the Shanghai Five defense minister's meeting and schedule it for March. Chi Haotian's biography notes that they made a special point to "hold the first meeting before the NATO leaders summit" that year, perhaps to send a deterrent signal to Western states about NATO expansion, including into Central Asia.[143]

These concerns about the West were not incidental but core to the organization. Following the Soviet collapse and then surging US involvement in the region after 9/11, both Moscow and Beijing feared that the United States might fill the void in Central Asia. As China's State Councilor Dai Bingguo later wrote in his memoirs, China needed to "engage the Shanghai Cooperation Organization" in order to "help change the power imbalance" with the West.[144]

China in particular hoped the SCO would become the paramount organization for regionalism in Central Asia—believing it could blunt American influence there and reassure China's neighbors about Beijing's intentions—and it promptly made the organization a priority. The SCO was named after a Chinese city, its secretariat and staff were located in offices that Beijing donated, its first General Secretary was a Chinese diplomat, and Beijing funded "the lion's share" of its budget from the beginning.[145]

Alternative Explanations

Why was China so dedicated to this organization? Some deny the reason had anything to do with the United States. They argue that, consistent with the SCO's official messaging, the organization's function is to combat what China calls the "three evils"—terrorism, separatism, and religious extremism—in Central Asia. This is important for China's own security.

This conventional explanation is inadequate, as an examination of the SCO Regional Counter Terrorism Structure (RCTS) reveals. RCTS is one of the organization's few permanent bodies and the primary one intended to cope with the "three evils," but it is not taken particularly seriously. China drove the creation of the RCTS, but it and other bodies "remain chronically underfunded and have limited powers to take decisions independently of their member governments."[146] The budget appears to be a paltry $2 million annually, and the staff is only thirty individuals. And as Executive Director of RCTS Zhang Xinfeng admits, of that small staff, "not many people [are] in the office."[147] One analyst calls the budget and personnel numbers "comically low," and "the size of a rounding error in China's estimated $111 billion internal security budget."[148] He notes that a comparable NATO intelligence fusion center has over 200 personnel, showing how unserious RCTS really is.

Given low funding and manpower, RCTS is limited in its functions, and currently it "does not function as a joint analytical environment, collect intelligence, integrate command structures, formulate joint doctrine, identify terrorists, meaningfully interact with other states or regional security organizations, or perform many other tasks one might expect of a security body."[149] When the organization was needed, it was not truly deployed, including during the 2005

Andijan massacre in which Uzbek forces killed hundreds of protesters, Kyrgyz-
Uzbek ethnic cleansing in Kyrgyzstan in 2010, and Tajikistan's decision to shut
down a province and send in troops to suppress a warlord in 2012.[150] For all
these reasons, it is hard to argue the RCTS—and the SCO for that matter—truly
exists to combat the "three evils," especially since China could easily fund the
institution at a higher level or assign more staff if it truly mattered. Why then has
China championed the SCO?

Blunting

China's creation of the SCO—as the meeting between Vladimir Putin and Chi
Haotian suggests—was less about combating the "three evils" and more about
blunting and preempting American power within the region and laying the
foundation for Chinese order-building on China's periphery. All of this flowed
from Beijing's perception of the US threat.

The US Threat

The themes Chi and Putin emphasized with respect to resisting American hegemony appear in virtually every Shanghai Five and SCO statement, the SCO
charter, and in leader-level remarks. Many of these documents and speeches
phrase these goals in terms of promoting "multipolarity" or "democratizing international relations," which are euphemisms for reducing US influence; the texts
often decry—as they put it—US human rights pressure, neo-interventionism,
and missile defense. It was at a 1997 Shanghai Five meeting that China and
Russia signed the "Declaration on a Multipolar World and the Establishment
of a New International Order." The agreement stated that, "in a spirit of partnership, the Parties *shall strive to promote the multipolarization* of the world and
the establishment of a new international order" and that "no country should
seek hegemony, engage in power politics or monopolize international affairs."[151]
These critiques of US hegemony appeared in the Shanghai Five's first declaration
in 1998 and in its annual statements, and Chinese and Russian leaders amplified
them publicly.[152] On the sidelines of the 1999 summit, President Jiang declared
that "hegemony and the politics of force are on the rise, with new forms of so-
called neo-interventionism being resumed."[153] Boris Yeltsin agreed and opposed
"attempts by some states to build a world order that is only suitable for themselves."[154] He then shocked reporters by declaring that he was "really ready for
combat, especially with Westerners," and his Foreign Minister Igor Ivanov confirmed that the United States was a focus of the summit's discussions.[155] When
the SCO finally became institutionalized, its founding charter stated at the

outset that the organization's goals included "developing political multipolarity." These kinds of references to countering US hegemony appear in the vast majority of the organization's statements.[156] And once US power was perceived as declining, the SCO's 2009 statement declared the "tendency towards genuine multipolarity has become irreversible" and that the "role of the regional aspect in the settlement of global problems is on the rise."[157] Regional great powers, in other words, could now push back on Western hegemony and expand their freedom of maneuver.

Supporting Modest Institutionalization

If China's investments in the SCO were largely driven by a desire to blunt US power, then its investments in the organization should have increased as those concerns grew more acute, particularly after 9/11. This is precisely what happened.

Prior to 9/11, China was "quite comfortable and satisfied" with the SCO's pace of institutionalization.[158] After the attacks, "the viability of the SCO was put to a serious test" as the United States became a Central Asian power.[159] The United States invaded and occupied Afghanistan; doubled direct assistance to Central Asian states; increased military assistance several-fold; and spearheaded NATO's "Partnership for Peace" program with the region. To China's horror, Central Asian states, including Russia, actively facilitated the US military presence. Every Central Asian SCO member publicly offered the US military overflight, and most privately extended this overflight to include combat missions.[160] The US military opened bases in Uzbekistan and Kyrgyzstan, gained access to air fields in Tajikistan and Turkmenistan, and was invited to use facilities in Kazakhstan (though the United States declined and received emergency access instead).[161] Russia provided information sharing, accepted US facilities and access in the region, and supplied its own access and logistical support. This "surprised Chinese policymakers and analysts, who complained that the Russian policymakers did not have a correct understanding of the real intention of the United States."[162]

For China, those intentions were dangerous. Luo Gan, a member of the Politburo Standing Committee, fretted that "the US wants to use the war in Afghanistan to have a permanent military force in Central Asia, which will have a big impact on our national security."[163] In a meeting with the Central Military Commission in 2001, Jiang Zemin placed China's fears of the "three evils" on par with concerns over the US role in Central Asia: "After the end of the Cold War, Central Asia saw the emergence of two prominent circumstances. The first was the 'three evils' and the second was the American military presence."[164] China feared a US or NATO presence in each regional state would neutralize the SCO's security role and could grow into something institutionalized, perhaps even an expanded NATO.[165] One Chinese scholar feared that "NATO's eastward expansion may get right up to China's western border."[166] Others feared encirclement, noting that China now faced an American presence in the West in addition to the presence in the East.[167]

China's push for institutionalization was motivated by a desire to keep the organization at the core of Central Asian regionalism by focusing it on terrorism; stave off growing American influence in the region; and prevent its own encirclement. "To avoid the SCO being sidelined by the post-September 11 US military presence in Central Asia," Chung notes, "Beijing pushed hard for the institutionalization of an SCO regional anti-terrorist center [RATS]," which soon became a permanent body, with President Jiang Zemin noting that establishing the center "is the most urgent thing at present."[168] At a prime ministers meeting a few months after September 11, China's Premier Zhu Rongji argued forcefully that the SCO must finish work on a charter and create an anti-terrorism center as soon as possible; in 2003, at the height of America's presence in Central Asia, Hu Jintao declared "institutional building was the top priority of the SCO" and urged the creation of a secretariat— even as he opposed institution-building in organizations involving the United States.[169] These sorts of statements had never been made prior to 9/11. As Song notes, to keep the SCO relevant, "China proved willing to sacrifice short-term interests for long-term ones, and partial interests for overall aims."[170] It offered to move RATS to Uzbekistan, which it feared was drifting toward the United States after declining to participate in some SCO exercises; then, in 2004, it announced nearly $1 billion in loans to SCO member states.[171] Ultimately, China's efforts served to make the SCO relevant to the regional struggle with terrorism, even if the anti-terrorism center never had the resources to accomplish much. Perceptions of rising American power on China's periphery induced China to more eagerly pursue institutionalization. Even so, the SCO remained far less institutionalized than the organizations China would build after the Global Financial Crisis, and once India joined it as a member, it ceased to be as useful.

Security Benefits

If the SCO is too thin to combat the "three evils" or structure regional economic relations, what security benefits could it provide? The SCO provides China a way of (1) reassuring Central Asian states that might have balanced against it; (2) blunting American power; and (3) providing China a platform for order-building in Central Asia.

First, the SCO is meant to reassure Russia and Central Asian states of China's intentions. China understands that Central Asian states see it as an outsider in a place where Russian language and Islamic faith hold influence, and that they fear that China might have territorial designs, support Han emigration, and threaten their domestic industries.[172] From Beijing's perspective, the Soviet collapse created the risk that the United States could exploit these anxieties and tie Central Asian states into a coalition to balance and encircle China. China sought to reassure those states through the SCO structure. By forsaking its bilateral advantage and working in a multilateral setting, China hoped its neighbors would see the SCO as an organization that would help manage China's growing presence. SCO states have opportunities to voice disagreement with Chinese policies, and the organization's consensus-based voting mechanism is designed, as a former general secretary noted, "so no *major country* can outweigh others," including China.[173] In this way, the SCO would demonstrate China had renounced a "divide and conquer" strategy and wished to facilitate informal discussions and resolve problems at the ministerial level in the open, reducing anxieties about China's intentions.[174] Moreover, the SCO provided a platform to announce and implement billions in loans, trade concessions, and military and technical assistance—or to stand with Central Asian states against Western human rights criticisms—all of which served to reassure.

Second, as Yu Bin notes, China has used the SCO to fill Central Asia's political void and sees it "as a platform from which China can deflect, frustrate, and neutralize America's influence" in the region.[175] China has sought to make the SCO the key Central Asian organization while keeping the United States out— it rejected Washington's bid for observer status and prohibited it from viewing military exercises working with the SCO's counterterrorism center—thereby putting itself in prime position to shape the region. It has also used the SCO to deny US access to Central Asian territory and bases. For example, in 2003, the SCO Foreign Ministers meeting discussed how to roll back rising US influence in Central Asia.[176] In 2005, the SCO issued a statement demanding that the United States set a timeline for withdrawing its forces from Central Asia after its summit in Astana, giving cover for member states to make the demand publicly. That same year, China and Russia supported Uzbekistan's decision to expel US forces. In 2007, the SCO's Bishkek Declaration argued against the role of outside powers in security affairs, noting that "stability and security in Central Asia can be ensured primarily by the states of the region based on regional and international organizations already established."[177] Subsequently, Central Asian states evicted what remained of the US presence in 2009 and 2014 respectively.[178]

The SCO has also held more than two dozen military exercises to signal deepening cooperation among its members, demonstrate US regional intervention is unnecessary, and conduct military signaling. The largest of these are

the "Peace Mission" exercises, which involve "tanks, artillery, airborne and amphibious landings, bombers, fighters, warships" and sometimes appear to be "a
demonstration of force" toward the United States.[179] Peace Mission 2005, for
example, appeared to rehearse operations needed to invade Taiwan and "deter or
defeat US military intervention on the island's behalf," and China even proposed
holding it in Zhejiang (a province north of Taiwan) before it was relocated.[180]
The exercise involved China and Russia; was larger than any they held during
the Cold War; featured 10,000 troops, strategic bombers, and 140 warships;
and practiced missions like the neutralization of anti-aircraft defenses, the enforcement of a maritime blockade, and amphibious assault.[181] Other exercises
simulated the defense of an SCO member under attack from an outside power,
quite possibly the United States.[182] Still others, as the chief of Russia's General
Staff said of Peace Mission 2009, would "show the international community that
Russia and China have the necessary resources to ensure stability and security in
the region" without Washington.[183] As one Chinese general who directed Peace
Mission 2014 put it, the exercises were "pushing forward [the] establishment of
a fair and reasonable new international political order."[184]

In addition to pushing the United States out and conducting military
signaling, the SCO also functions as a "latter-day Holy Alliance" to blunt the
spread of Western values and defend the region from democratic revolutions.[185]
Every single Shanghai Five and SCO joint declaration includes rhetorical assaults
on liberal values, usually worded in terms of respecting "non-interference"
and "the diversity of civilizations and cultures" and decrying Western "double
standards" as well as interference "under the pretext of [human rights] protection."[186] The SCO Charter provides support for China's "Five Principles of
Peaceful Coexistence" and urges respect for sovereignty over human rights.[187]
Members receive concrete SCO support when facing Western criticism. The
SCO established an election monitoring program in 2005 (despite the fact
none of its members was a true democracy), which "observed" and "reported"
on elections in Kyrgyzstan, Tajikistan, and Uzbekistan—giving them cover
from Organization for Security and Co-operation in Europe (OSCE) election monitors who found substantial evidence of fraud.[188] When Uzbekistan
massacred hundreds of people following protests in the city of Andijan, the SCO
effectively condoned it as a legitimate act of counterterrorism.[189] "A significant
achievement of the SCO," notes former Chinese Ambassador Wang Yusheng, "is
that the member states successfully defended themselves against the 'color revolution' incited by the neo-conservative idealists of the United States."[190]

Third, the SCO is a tool for Chinese order-building. Indeed, joint statements
speak openly of "tapping the SCO['s] growing potential and international prestige" for international and regional aims.[191] The SCO is a platform for China
to offer consensual bargains to the region, including loans, trade concessions,

investment, military and technical assistance, and political cover, providing an alternative to US order and Russian efforts too.[192] China has used it to propose an SCO Development Bank and natural gas consortium, all of which would benefit Beijing and help it shape the region.[193] The SCO also offers Beijing a way to build support for its positions and norms globally.[194] The SCO has criticized US military interventions in Serbia, Kosovo, Libya, Iraq, and Afghanistan.[195] SCO statements have repeatedly been used to support Chinese positions and assail US positions on a wide variety of issues that have little or only modest relevance to most SCO members, including: (1) the South China Sea; (2) Taiwan independence; (3) the Korean peninsula; (4) US missile defense; (4) UN Security Council expansion; (5) outer space militarization; and (6) Internet sovereignty. China also used the SCO to put a cooperative and multilateral sheen on China's Belt and Road Initiative (BRI). For example, the 2016 statement commits members to supporting multilateral transportation projects, and the organization itself has become a vehicle for agreements promoting BRI regionally.

The SCO was an effort for China to use what many consider liberal instruments of order-building, such as multilateral institutions, to advance goals that were fundamentally related to China's power and to China's strategic interests. This kind of "strategic liberalism" was not restricted only to the institutional realm but was also a feature of the economic one. As the next chapter shows, China saw economic instruments as ways to constrain US power over China and to cultivate the "wealth and power" that had been the focus of Chinese nationalists for generations. And that same lesson would hold true into the future, not only when China sought to *blunt* American power, but also when it sought to build its own.

6

"Permanent Normal Trading Relations"

Implementing Economic Blunting

"The question of most-favored nation status between China and the United States is a central issue that will determine the rotation of world history."[1]

—He Xin, former adviser to Jiang Zemin and Li Peng, 1993

On a cold and windy afternoon in January 1979, China's vice premier Deng Xiaoping landed at Andrews Air Force Base. This was a historic moment. Deng's visit marked the very first time a leader of the People's Republic of China had ever visited the United States. Dressed in black, the seventy-five-year-old revolutionary descended the stairs to light applause, pausing to smile and wave at the small crowd as he made his way to Vice President Walter Mondale, who waited on the tarmac to greet him.[2] Only weeks earlier, Deng had achieved political normalization with the United States. Now his aim was the economic equivalent.

The next day, Deng met with President Jimmy Carter at the White House, the first in a whirlwind of talks that would last over two days. The two leaders eventually turned to discuss economic ties. Deng wanted access to American markets, capital, and technology to fuel China's economic development. To achieve it, however, China would first need to sign an agreement for most-favored nation (MFN) trade status with the United States.[3] At the time, MFN status was restricted by the Jackson-Vanik Amendment, which stated that communist or non-market states could only receive MFN if they allowed freedom of emigration, a determination that was subject to a congressional vote each year.[4] A decade later, Deng's decision to open fire on student protesters in Tiananmen Square would make those once pro-forma annual votes extremely controversial, and throughout the 1990s they posed a nearly existential threat to a Chinese economy still dependent on US openness. But back in the late 1970s, Deng and Carter's meeting was taking place in a far less contentious era: indeed, if MFN was a source of tension in 1989, it was apparently a source of humor in 1979. As the two leaders discussed MFN's emigration requirements, Deng reportedly joked to Carter, "We'll qualify right now. If you want us to send you 10 million Chinese tomorrow, we'll be glad to do it." Carter responded good-naturedly, "I'll reciprocate by sending you 10,000 news correspondents." "No," Deng replied, "this might prevent normalization from going forward."[5]

Deng's visit was a success, and the next year, he secured MFN status. Throughout the 1980s, China's MFN status sailed through annual votes in Congress each year without the slightest bit of controversy. China grew rapidly, but it also became increasingly dependent on US markets, capital, and technology—as well as access to US-run global institutions.[6] Despite occasional US-China tensions over Taiwan, Beijing was relatively unconcerned about the strategic implications of its growing dependence on the United States given the shared cooperation against the Soviet threat. In a period when *permanent* MFN could plausibly have been achieved, limiting US leverage over China and freeing China from annual votes on its trade status, Beijing never bothered to seek it.

It took the Tiananmen Square Massacre, and then the follow-on shock of the collapse of the Soviet bloc, to refocus China's mind not only on obtaining US access—but on keeping it. China's perception of American threat rose, and Beijing watched as Washington exploited its economic leverage over China for political aims, including through the use of sanctions, the threatened revocation of MFN status, the use of Section 301 trade tariffs, and the cancellation of science and technology cooperation. China's strategy changed in response, and Beijing sought not to eliminate its dependence on the United States but rather to *blunt* American efforts to manipulate that dependence in ways that would harm China.

Concerns over US sanctions, influence over science and technology cooperation, and control of critical commodities were part of this blunting strategy. But China's laser-like focus on permanent MFN status was unquestionably its core component, and it is the primary consideration of this chapter. MFN was about more than trade or the continued access to capital and technology it helped sustain. For China's leaders, annual MFN review was a political tool of the United States, and securing permanent MFN would grant China freedom of maneuver. China's leaders pursued permanent MFN through bilateral negotiations as well as through multilateral processes like APEC and accession into the GATT/WTO. They worked for eight years, as Qian Qichen notes, to rename permanent MFN as "permanent normal trading relations" (PNTR), a term they believed would seem less generous to China.[7] They were even willing to make enormous economic concessions, risk the country's political stability and the Party's hold on power, and blow up a bilateral US-China WTO agreement to achieve it. The fight over MFN was a more than decade-long struggle and a core part of a larger focus on tying US hands and reducing Washington's discretionary use of economic power against Beijing. We turn now to explore those efforts in greater detail.

Explaining Economic Behavior

This chapter seeks to explain China's international economic policy through a focus on texts and behavior, and it tests its proposed explanation—that grand strategic considerations informed that policy—against alternative explanations. This book considers two alternative explanations for international economic behavior: that it can be explained by (1) whether officials are motivated by possible *economic benefits* to the country at large, whether in absolute and aggregate terms or as part of a broader state-directed developmental strategy; or by (2) rewards certain key *interest groups* that are powerful and well connected receive, irrespective of the national consequences. These theories and the models that flow from them have their place in explaining economic behavior, but they suffer drawbacks in explaining China's behavior: they inadequately consider security considerations in international economic policy and they discount the ways Leninist party-states like China that are often relatively independent from society, particularly compared to democratic governments, might sometimes be less susceptible to vested interests. Accordingly, this chapter holds that many major international economic decisions can be informed by grand strategic considerations and serve as parts of *blunting* strategies designed to reduce a hegemon's economic leverage over a rising state as well as *building* strategies that seek to increase a rising state's leverage over others. This leverage can be *relational*, which stresses manipulating interdependence between states; *structural*, which focuses on shaping the systems and frameworks within which global economic activity takes place; or *domestic*, which focuses on reshaping a state's internal politics and preferences.

The chapter shows that China's efforts in this period were primarily driven by grand strategic considerations. They were part of a *blunting* strategy that sought to minimize American economic power and leverage over China—relational, structural, and domestic—all while ensuring Beijing could continue to access American markets, capital, and technology. Accordingly, it focuses *not* on every economic initiative China undertook during this period, but instead how it structured its international economic relations to achieve its goals.

Chinese Economic Texts

The Trifecta and Economic Strategy

Before the trifecta of Tiananmen Square, the Gulf War, and the Soviet collapse, the 1980s was a good decade for China's economy. Beginning in the late 1970s, Deng Xiaoping had moved China away from Maoist autarky and joined the international capitalist trading system, not simply for prosperity but also to achieve security. "If China wants to withstand the pressure of hegemonism and power politics," Deng argued, "it is crucial for us to achieve rapid economic growth and to carry out our development strategy."[8] This strategy, often referred to as "reform and opening," was inaugurated in 1978 at the historic 3rd Plenum of the 11th Central Committee and launched the country on what the Party called "a new Long March to make China a modern, *powerful* socialist country."[9]

The reform package was inextricably tied to the international economy. China sought new markets for Chinese goods, and it sought to produce those goods by attracting foreign capital through special economic zones, joint ventures, and reforms to the rule of law. Technology transfer was also a critical focus of these efforts. At the 3rd Plenum, Deng elevated the "four modernizations"—a concept that focused on modernizing agriculture, industry, defense, and science and technology. "The crux of the four modernizations," Deng declared earlier that year, "is the mastery of modern science and technology. Without that it is impossible to build modern agriculture, modern industry, or national defense."[10] Accordingly, the reformist five-year plans covering 1981–1990—China's sixth and seventh respectively—both dedicated billions of dollars to importing foreign technology to modernize China. In his 1979 visit, Deng criticized US export controls and made signing the Science and Technology Agreement between the United States and China a priority; "almost every U.S. technical agency began to develop constructive relations with its Chinese counterpart" soon after and for the remainder of the next decade.[11]

China's economic strategy could not be achieved without US support. China needed access to US markets, capital, and technology—as well as the international economic system Washington established. And to secure it, it needed MFN status. MFN was primarily about ensuring that Chinese goods had access to the market, but it was also clearly tied to capital and technology. Access to the US market would make it worthwhile for foreign investors to put their capital in China; moreover, the exports themselves would help finance China's imports of technology. As Deng put it during his White House visit, "we have to take care of letting Chinese goods into the U.S. market because somebody has raised the issue of how the Chinese are going to pay for all of this" foreign technology; similarly, at a press gathering that same day, he said that if "the U.S. provides capital and technology, we can use our products and compensatory trade to repay it."[12] For that reason, securing MFN status was a priority for Deng in his 1979 visit, and he met several US congressional delegations in the following months to lobby for it. In those meetings, he stressed that although "there are many things to do" in the relationship spanning "politics, culture, trade and other fields . . . some of these things are more urgent, such as addressing MFN."[13]

From 1980 on, bilateral economic ties were strong. US investment and technology flowed to China, and Chinese exports largely flowed to the United States. China's MFN status was approved annually without event, and disputes over a variety of issues—intellectual property rights, prison labor, human rights, Taiwan—did not jeopardize the trading relationship.[14] Beijing was focused on the economic benefits of trade and relatively unconcerned that Washington would ruthlessly exploit China's dependence on the US for markets, capital, and technology. It was even content to let Congress vote annually on its MFN status for a decade, apparently unconcerned that it could be used as a subject of leverage by the United States.

All this changed after Tiananmen—especially when the United States proved willing to use economic leverage against China. China's perception of American threat rose, and Chinese leaders saw the United States move to sanction China and enlist Europe and Japan in the cause. Beijing was now acutely aware of its dependence on the United States, but its leaders hoped that US strategic ties with China would lead to an eventual reset.[15] Deng put forward a four-part "package deal" to move past Tiananmen that mixed human rights concessions, sanctions relief, some cooperative economic initiatives, and a US visit by Jiang Zemin. In December 1989, Scowcroft visited China and suggested the "package deal" might work, and Beijing's leaders felt confident that the crisis might be resolved.[16]

That confidence was premature, and another shock soon arrived: the collapse of the communist world and the Soviet Union. Qian Qichen, who was directly involved in these negotiations, argued that the communist collapse in Eastern Europe and Central Asia, as well as the weakening of the Soviet Union, completed the change in China's view of the United States that had begun with Tiananmen, and vice versa:

> After Scowcroft returned to the United States, there were signs of improvement in Sino-American relations, but just at this moment dramatic changes took place in Eastern Europe. The Romanian government was rocked by domestic unrest. The ruling Romanian Communist Party was overthrown overnight and its leader, Nicolae Ceausescu, was executed on December 25. The political changes in Eastern Europe brought about changes in the international situation. The United States

began to assess the general situation of the world and was no longer so eager to improve relations with China. Thus Sino-American relations backpedaled to where they had been before China's package solution was proposed. The package solution was put aside. . . . *The historic changes in Eastern Europe, plus the political turmoil in the Soviet Union, dramatically altered the strategic foundation for Sino-American cooperation.* Believing that they no longer needed China's cooperation, some people in the United States began to talk about how to "restrain China."[17]

Then, at a high-level Party meeting held on June 15, these views were essentially ratified. Li Peng summarized the meeting consensus, which was that the United States was using sanctions as a tool to undermine the Party's leadership. "The central government analyzed the international situation and believed that the United States, after the changes in Eastern Europe and the Soviet Union, *was attempting to use pressure to cause our country to change*," he wrote in his diary.[18]

In the years that followed, Beijing saw the United States use its coercive economic leverage across four categories: (1) sanctions; (2) MFN status; (3) Section 301 investigations; and (4) technology transfer. These four areas of tension led to a reassessment of China's economic dependence, which in turn triggered a focus on blunting American economic leverage.

The first domain was sanctions, which fast became the priority in China's foreign policy, crowding out other issues. Sanctions were the focus of Brent Scowcroft's secret visit to Beijing, President Bush's private letter to Deng, Deng's response to Bush, virtually every subsequent high-level exchange over the next two years, and the overwhelming focus for the country's top diplomats.[19] Qian Qichen described the international sanctions and isolation following Tiananmen Square as "the most difficult time" during his ten years as foreign minister and—in contrast to Deng's bravado about how the sanctions would only marginally affect China—admitted that "the pressure of isolation was extremely great."[20] Accordingly, his memoirs devote an entire chapter entitled "Withstanding International Pressure" to this period where he makes clear their central place in Chinese foreign policy. Premier Li Peng wrote that the sanctions on China seemed to him almost as significant as the Soviet Union's withdrawal of experts in the 1960s and "affected China's economic development, causing the speed to slow down."[21] In 1990, he attended a high-level meeting "regarding how to break the sanctions," which determined that China "must find some breakthroughs [with other countries]" to escape the sanctions.[22] Qian Qichen worked to implement that approach, and he recounts that he attempted to secure sanctions relief by promising to release the dissident Fang Lizhi; playing the Soviet card; identifying "Japan as a weak link in the united front of Western countries" and the "best target" for getting sanctions relief; exploiting European fears "that they might lose market share in China" and conveying them to the United States and Japan to break unity; and encouraging developing countries to "break the sanctions" as well.[23] These coordinated moves worked: they defeated the international pressure for sanctions in large part by leveraging China's market and playing other parties against each other. Even so, the fear of US economic leverage would remain.

A second major source of US relational leverage over China was even more consequential than sanctions: the rising threat that the United States might cancel China's MFN status. Just as securing MFN had been a principal preoccupation in 1979, ending the annual review of MFN would become a critical objective after Tiananmen. There were only two efforts to revoke China's MFN waiver throughout the 1980s, and those "resolutions of disapproval" promptly went nowhere; after Tiananmen, resolutions of disapproval were introduced every year to effectively remove China's MFN status until it was made permanent in 2002. China's strategy to secure permanent MFN status began immediately. For example, on March 27, 1990, Li Peng hosted a high-level meeting to discuss MFN treatment. At the meeting, the Ministry of Economic Affairs and Trade [经贸部] presented figures suggesting revocation would affect $10 billion worth of trade, or more than half the trade volume and significantly more than half of China's exports. Other estimates were more dire, suggesting not only that a majority of China's exports would be affected, but that the actual volume shipped to the United States would fall by even more than half. Li Peng said at the meeting that he hoped China's strategic position vis-à-vis the Soviets as well as its market size might eventually soften Washington.[24] But by 1991, with the Soviet Union increasingly out of the picture, Li was less positive: "The United States may cancel its MFN status for China," he wrote; "the pressure we face is increasing, there is danger, and while we should work hard and strive to maintain the status quo, we should also plan for the worst."[25] For example, in interviews with Chinese business leaders around the country, Li Peng asked them "what impact MFN cancellation would have" and found, perhaps unsurprisingly, that "the impact was great. First, the [export] market would be lost, and second, the confidence of foreign investors would fall."[26] Some resolutions of disapproval passed Congress with congressional majorities, and while they were ultimately vetoed by the president, one only narrowly escaped a Congressional override of that veto which would have devastated China's economy (the House overrode the veto comfortably; the Senate failed by six votes).[27] MFN was thus an enormous risk for China.

The third sign for China in this period that the United States might wield its economic leverage against it was the initiation of Section 301 investigations by the US Trade Representative (USTR) office. In April 1991, USTR classified

China as a "target priority foreign country" and launched a six-month investigation that would trigger sanctions if China was not providing adequate intellectual property (IP) protection. Beijing quickly published new copyright laws, and eventually an agreement was reached after Washington threatened tariffs on $700 million of goods—or nearly 5 percent of China's exports.[28] A number of additional investigations and sanctions threatened to follow in the future, and Beijing hoped that joining a multilateralized rules-based trading order would reduce US discretion on these issues—an assumption that proved largely accurate until the election of Donald Trump.

The fourth concerning development was the immediate blow Tiananmen dealt to China's science and technology modernization. China's five-year plans, its four modernizations, and its "863 Program" for high-tech R&D all assumed billions in technology imports from the United States and continued people-to-people scientific exchanges, all buttressed by broader umbrella agreements between the two countries. After Tiananmen, the United States put in place new export controls on certain high-tech goods and allowed the Science and Technology agreement to lapse; similarly, organizations like the National Science Foundation and the National Academy of Sciences suspended cooperation as well as visits and programs with China. Although cooperation resumed subsequently, the restrictions reminded China's leaders of their country's dependence on US scientific expertise, and that the possibility of losing the US export market would complicate their ability to afford technology imports.[29]

Together, these four forms of American economic leverage rattled Beijing's leaders and kept them fully on the defensive from 1989 onward. That led to a new blunting strategy.

A Blunting Strategy

After the Soviet collapse and the exercise of US economic statecraft against China, it became critical for China to maintain access to the United States while blunting US ability to curtail that access. China's pursuit of permanent MFN status as well as WTO accession were meant to tie American hands with respect to economic leverage, particularly trade sanctions, tariffs, Section 301 investigations, and technology restrictions.

China's awareness of its economic vulnerability made its way into the speeches that set Chinese grand strategy, including the Ambassadorial Conference addresses in which Chinese leaders acknowledged both the US threat and Chinese economic dependence on the United States. During the 8th Ambassadorial Conference, Jiang declared that "economic security is increasing as a proportion" of international strategy.[30] He declared the United States to be

China's "main diplomatic adversary," and in the very same paragraph stressed China's economic vulnerability: "Whether Sino-U.S. relations can be stabilized often affects everything. The United States is still our principal export market and an important source for our imported capital, technology, and advanced management experience. Protecting and developing Sino-U.S. relations is of strategic importance to China."[31]

These remarks effectively ruled out an overtly confrontational strategy to reduce US leverage and made the case for a quieter *blunting* approach. Part of this blunting approach would be to flaunt China's market. As Jiang furthered argued in his 1993 speech, "U.S. policy towards China has always been two-sided," and on the one hand it uses issues like trade to "pressure China" and is "domineering in its dealings with our country"; "on the other hand, the United States out of consideration for its . . . fundamental economic interests will have to focus on our country's vast market."[32] Like Deng after Tiananmen, Jiang tried to use China's economic market to dissuade the United States from wielding its relational economic leverage over Beijing. For example, in 1993, Jiang told Clinton the following:

> The development of China's economy is beneficial to the development of the United States and other countries in the world. China's vast market has great potential, and we welcome the US business community to expand investment and strengthen economic and trade exchanges with China. *Adopting a containment policy against China and resorting to economic "sanctions" will harm the interests of the United States itself.*[33]

Concerns about interdependence were present in subsequent high-level foreign policy addresses. For example, in his next Ambassadorial Conference address in 1999, Jiang further stressed the importance of balancing interdependence and globalization. China "must make full use of the various favorable conditions and opportunities brought about by economic globalization," he noted. But "at the same time," he argued, "we must maintain a clear understanding of the risks brought about by economic globalization." This in turn required Beijing to "safeguard China's economic security" by "enhancing the ability to resist and resolve" foreign pressure and "adhering to the principle of independence [独立自主]."[34]

Even after China secured PNTR and WTO accession—a case discussed in greater detail subsequently—fears of American economic power remained. At the 2003 Ambassadorial Conference, Hu noted that "the task of developing countries to develop their economies and maintain economic security is even more arduous."[35] As he told the assembled foreign policy apparatus, "It is necessary to see that even as China's development and growth continues to improve its international status, we must also see that our country still faces the pressure of developed capitalist countries' economic and technological strength . . . [and] we must also see the grim reality that Western hostile forces are still implementing Westernization and splittist political plots against China."[36] He hoped that "multipolarization will further promote the diversification of economic power," creating space for China.[37] Even so, as Wen Jiabao noted in preparatory documents for the 16th Party Congress that took place not long after PNTR and China's accession to the World Trade Organization (WTO), the relationship was finally moving in a direction favorable to China: "From the perspective of economic and trade relations, the interdependence between China and the United States has been accepted by the two governments."[38]

Hu Jintao shared Jiang Zemin's concern about US economic leverage and broadened it from markets, capital, and technology to resources and trade flows. Shortly after taking power, Hu gave an important speech identifying the "Malacca Dilemma"—China's reliance on the Strait of Malacca—and stating that some great powers, such as the United States, sought to control that chokepoint and the resources upon which China's surging economy increasingly depended. Hu saw American ill intentions throughout the global economy: "China's overseas oil and gas resource development, its cross-border mergers and acquisitions, and its importation of advanced technology have been continuously suffering from interference. This is because of the willful instigation and malicious sensationalization of some people," presumably Americans, though Hu allowed that "in some cases there is an actual conflict of interests" rather than political maneuvering.[39] Hu's answer was to formulate "a new energy security concept" that entailed considering the "diplomatic, security, and economic risk" and supporting state-owned enterprises in their "overseas energy development" and their purchase of other commodities.[40] As a consequence, China began to pursue trade with more developing countries and to take equity stakes in commodity projects across Latin America, Africa, and Central Asia under what Hu called the "going out" policy. While these techniques may have been slightly different from those pursued under Jiang, the essential pressure was the same—to reduce China's dependence on those flows that might be subject to foreign, particularly US, economic pressure. China began to take equity positions in mines and oil fields around the world, fearing that reliance on markets alone would not provide adequate security—though securing these would also require military investments that were to come a few short years later.

Hu remained convinced that economics was about more than absolute gains or serving vested interests but about strategic objectives too. As he declared at the 2006 Central Foreign Affairs Work Forum, "Economic and technological cooperation must be carried out from the consideration of the country's overall diplomatic situation and long-term interests" not merely its economic ones.[41] At the 2006 Central Foreign Affairs Work Forum, Hu noted that economic leverage in great power politics was taking many forms: "Great powers are paying attention to the use of trade, energy, resources, finance, and other economic means to carry out political operations, which makes the political and economic strategy more closely related.[42] Accordingly, "Security issues such as energy, finance, information, and transportation channels have become increasingly prominent."[43] In this way, the same concerns about US influence over the global economy that emerged after 1989 remained acute even decades after, though the bilateral economic relationship nonetheless remained the central preoccupation. Even so, the core concern of this period, and the one with the highest stakes for China, was the question of MFN status and the closely related question of WTO accession.

Permanent Normal Trading Relations and WTO Accession

In 1992, with the fate of China's MFN status left in the hands of Congress, American business swung into action. That year, the American Chamber of Commerce in China (AmCham) launched a new program—DC Doorknock— regularly sending large delegations of business leaders to key federal agencies, members of Congress, and others across Washington to make the case for freer trade with China. The goals were simple: to first prevent Congress from revoking China's MFN status, and then over time, to make China's MFN status permanent and secure China's admission to the WTO.

AmCham and its allies were ultimately successful. Years later when Chinese officials spoke at AmCham banquets, they often expressed their gratitude effusively. "I still remember the days when we were fighting for MFN and later PNTR," recalled China's WTO ambassador Sun Zhenyu. "AmCham, every year at this time, organized a doorknock team to visit Washington and lobby senators and congressmen." China sent its own teams too, Sun remembered, and "your doorknock team and ours were on airplanes at the same time and knocking on the same doors." At another banquet, then Chinese commerce minister Bo Xilai (later imprisoned for corruption amid a power struggle) also expressed his thanks. "You helped us with permanent normal trade relations (PNTR) and with our accession to the WTO," he said, and "we Chinese people always remember in our hearts the good things our friends have done."[44]

"The good things" that flowed from permanent MFN and WTO accession were incredibly consequential. Beijing had feared that the loss of MFN would prompt an immediate tariff increase on 95 percent of Chinese exports to the United States and double their cost—crippling China's economy. For that reason, it saw permanent MFN status as the critical international economic priority after the Cold War, and it viewed WTO negotiations as one way to achieve them. China was willing to pay absolute economic costs and risk domestic political instability to free itself from annual votes on MFN.

China's willingness to make these concessions stands in contrast to the US view of MFN status, which was that it was a minor concession that China already had in de facto terms. The differing views of MFN's importance in part created the bargaining space that made possible an agreement and China's eventual WTO accession.

Alternative Explanations

There are two plausible alternative explanations for China's pursuit of permanent MFN status, also known as permanent normal trade relations (PNTR), as well as its pursuit of membership in the WTO and its predecessor organization, the General Agreement on Tariffs and Trade (GATT). The first is that China pursued these two objectives because it was motivated by the absolute economic benefits of joining; the second explanation is that it was motivated by the narrower preferences of specific interest groups.

The first alternative explanation has some merit. Jiang Zemin generally agreed that MFN status and WTO membership would strengthen the country's economy in the long run, even if joining the latter created significant adjustment costs.[45] But even so, strategic motivations played an enormous and likely decisive role, with China willing to make significant economic concessions for permanent MFN status—in effect trading away some of the benefits of protectionism for the security and strategic benefits that a deal would bring by reducing the risk of US economic coercion. This was intentional: as Jiang Zemin stated time and again, and as will be discussed in greater detail subsequently, the WTO was to be viewed first as a political issue and then as an economic issue.

The second alternative explanation for China's pursuit of MFN and WTO membership is that it was the product of interest group politics. But there are reasons to be skeptical of interest group explanations. One is that the negotiations over permanent MFN status and WTO accession were deliberately insulated from public pressure. As Joseph Fewsmith argues, Jiang Zemin was directly involved—limiting scope for pushback—and he gave immense authority to the agreement's negotiators, notably Zhu Rongji and Long Yongtu, empowering them to make necessary concessions at the expense of interest groups.[46] Indeed, the Party made clear that "industry arguments needed to be framed in terms of national interest."[47]

The other reason to be skeptical of interest group arguments is that, to the extent groups were a factor at all, they were a factor *against* China's pursuit of MFN and WTO accession, with many opposed to the economic concessions China would need to make in that pursuit. As then US ambassador Li Zhaoxing argued in his memoirs, "within the country [China] there was controversy about China's accession to the WTO. Some fragile industries, such as agriculture and textiles, would be relatively hard hit. Some experts worry that 20 million textile workers and hundreds of millions of farmers will be affected."[48] Powerful figures were concerned about these concessions too. China's number two ranking official, Li Peng, reportedly favored domestic protection and sought to undermine his rival Zhu Rongji, who was leading the negotiations. Opposition became more pronounced when the USTR leaked the draft agreement between the United States and China in April 1999 before any agreement was finalized, which humiliated Zhu Rongji, a development that was promptly followed by the accidental US bombing of China's Belgrade embassy, which inflamed public opinion. Yet, at the moment where domestic forces against China's concessions were strongest, they accomplished virtually nothing—only delaying the agreement rather than altering its substance. Li Peng's memoirs recount that as early as August 23, 1999, the central government met and agreed to relaunch the negotiations and began a discussion on strategy the very next week.[49] The final agreement signed between the United States and China was virtually identical to that negotiated in April 1999 before the leak of the draft text and before the NATO bombing. Even Li Peng—in a meeting condemning Zhu Rongji at a time of his rival's greatest weakness—notably did *not* attack him for making overly generous concessions.[50] Together, this demonstrates that the central leadership had sufficient autonomy from society and its various interest groups to push through an agreement.

The debate over permanent MFN and WTO accession was less over *whether* China should pursue it and more over *what* concessions it should offer, with even skeptics like Li Peng arguing that China could carefully roll back some concessions after the fact. In a high-level meeting with Jiang and other senior officials on August 30, 1999, Li argued that "joining the WTO has its advantages and disadvantages, the advantages outweigh the disadvantages, and some provisions that are disadvantageous can still be addressed through the law in the implementation [phase]."[51] After the United States and China signed a bilateral accession agreement in November, he continued to promote these views. At the Central Economic Work Conference held on November 15 in part to educate ministerial and provincial officials on China's accession, Li Peng said "the drawbacks can be overcome through domestic protection and through increased competitiveness."[52] And Li Peng even pushed back in some meetings on protectionist sentiments, such as in a meeting with the NPC Standing

Committee, which would pass the legislation harmonizing China's laws with WTO requirements: "Allowing a company's foreign shares to reach 49 percent is not the same as saying that the [entire] industry allows foreign capital to stand at 49 percent."[53] In short, protectionist impulses were channeled by one of its leading proponents into how WTO rules were implemented—not what rules were agreed to—another piece of evidence that interest group explanations may not have been determinative.

Grand Strategic Explanations

China's pursuit of MFN was motivated by powerful strategic logic. First, this section demonstrates that Chinese leaders saw MFN as a strategic rather than purely economic issue. Second, it explores how China pursued MFN, including through APEC and the WTO.

First, China initially did not see MFN or membership in GATT as a strategic issue. It had obtained MFN from the United States in 1979 and seen it renewed annually without any controversy.[54] But as discussed previously, the trifecta changed everything. Before Tiananmen, China had been on the verge of striking a deal with the United States on GATT membership that might have addressed MFN, which was relatively uncontroversial at the time. After all, other communist states had been allowed into GATT and been extended MFN, and China was a partner against the Soviet Union. As Gilbert Donahue, chief for external economic affairs at the Beijing embassy, recounts: "USTR was ready to enter what I might call the final stage of negotiations to bring about Chinese participation in the GATT. . . . They were just ready to send a delegation in late June to wrap this up."[55] But after Tiananmen that same June, Mark E. Mohr, deputy director of the US Consulate in Shanghai's Political Section at the time, noted, "The Congress, the media, and public opinion . . . felt we should be doing more to punish China for shooting the students, especially in the economic area. A consensus therefore built up to abolish most-favored-nation (MFN) trade status with China."[56]

The significance of this development was not lost on China's leadership, and they knew it would have profound consequences for China's future. He Xin, a conservative rabblerouser who rose to become a prominent foreign policy adviser to Jiang Zemin and Li Peng in this period, said in 1993 that the stakes were enormous: "The issue of MFN status between China and the United States is a central issue that will determine the rotation of world history."[57] Chinese leaders clearly understood the MFN question in post–Cold War terms and as part of a potential strategy of containment that emerged after Tiananmen Square and the Soviet collapse. Two prominent foreign ministers—Qian Qichen, who concurrently served as vice premier and a Politburo member during the MFN debates, and Li Zhaoxing, who served as ambassador to the United States during the final push for permanent MFN status—argue in their memoirs that they believed many who were "hostile to China" in the United States saw MFN and human rights as key instruments of containment.[58] In his memoirs, Foreign Minister Li Zhaoxing is explicit that MFN was an instrument of containment that had arisen because of the new strategic environment:

> After the disintegration of the Soviet Union, some members of the US Congress acting out of ideological bias used MFN as a weapon to counter China. From 1990 to 2000 . . . the US Congress would debate whether to grant China's MFN status for more than two months, but what was discussed was not whether China allows freedom-of-emigration; instead it was human rights, religion, family planning, Taiwan, Tibet, nuclear non-proliferation, trade deficits, labor reform products, and other irrelevant questions. In actuality this [MFN status] has actually become an important means for the US Congress . . . to coerce and put pressure on [要挟] China.[59]

After the Cold War ended, he continues, "No matter what problems surfaced in the two country's relationship, they would all be reflected in the U.S. Congressional debate on China's MFN status." This was a form of enduring leverage because "China had to beg the United States. China must be obedient, otherwise it will be punished by the United States Congress." China saw MFN as a form of constraining relational economic power over China that needed to be blunted. As Li puts it: "Why did the United States use MFN status to criticize China and coerce China? If this is not hegemonism then what is?"[60] Zhu Rongji, China's premier and the leader of the negotiating process, saw the United States as wielding its economic relational leverage to bully China through MFN. "China has made 9 years of efforts for 're-entry.' During this period, although the United States also claimed to support China's 're-entry,' it actually used its status as a great power to repeatedly obstruct the negotiation process, and it put forward various harsh and unrealistic demands."[61] In a major 2002 address delivered to all high-level Party insiders after China finally succeeded in securing MFN and joining the WTO, Jiang put the success in security terms: "We have finally defeated the unreasonable demands of the United States and some other Western countries and safeguarded China's fundamental interests and national security."[62] The speech focused on the importance of MFN in the larger struggle for power, and it was notable that Jiang emphasized it as a win for national security—which stresses its strategic implications.

Chinese officials pursued MFN at great economic and domestic-political costs because they believed it would secure China the kind of autonomy from

American relational leverage that would be key to the country's future. As even one skeptic of economic liberalization, Li Peng, argued at the 1999 Central Economic Work Forum held in November, an agreement with the United States would ensure that "China has more room for maneuver on the international stage."[63] WTO negotiations could be used to secure MFN, and for his part, President Jiang repeatedly stated that the WTO accession should be seen primarily as a political issue and not an economic issue. Indeed, Li Peng recounts at an important central government meeting convened on August 30, 1999, especially to discuss WTO negotiations one week after a decision was made to reopen negotiations, "Jiang Zemin emphasized that the WTO is a political issue, and it is not a generic technical business issue. . . . Everyone agreed with Jiang's point that joining the WTO is not merely an economic issue but a political one."[64] An important element of this was to reduce US leverage and thereby stabilize relations with Washington. As Zhu Rongji put it in one interview, "The reason why we made such a big concession is to take into account the overall situation of the friendly and cooperative relations between China and the United States and to build a constructive strategic partnership based on the goals set by President Jiang Zemin and President Clinton."[65]

China was determined to bear great risks in tying Washington's hands. Beijing understood that WTO membership could increase domestic instability and undermine the Party's hold on power, a fact that suggests strategic motivations when combined with Jiang's argument that WTO accession be seen as a political issue first and an economic issue second. For example, in an April 2000 speech on Party building, Hu Jintao argued, "Following the expansion of opening up, the development of internet culture, *and especially China's accession to the WTO,* bourgeoisie ideological infiltration and the challenge of cultural erosion caused by various decadent ideologies . . . will become more important . . . and be a major test for us for a long time."[66] Indeed, these were precisely the forces that Western elites had hoped would change China through MFN and WTO accession. Jiang Zemin echoed this language in a speech on November 28, 2000, at the Central Economic Work Conference. He stated that "the transformation of the economic system" and the process of "opening up" further would "inevitably have a profound impact on people's ideas and concepts, and will inevitably bring about the mutual penetration of various ideologies and cultures." Moreover, "after joining the WTO, we will face new challenges in the entry of Western cultural products. We must, with regard to ideological content and expression, enhance the competitiveness of China's cultural products."[67] On February 25, 2002, at a major event organized by the Central Committee and involving all provincial and ministerial-level leading cadres, several high-ranking senior officials spoke, including Jiang. The purpose of the address was to essentially set the line on China's WTO membership and educate all the leaders on how WTO membership fit into China's international political strategy as well as to discuss its economic advantages and the reforms it would require. In a blistering speech, Jiang made clear that the US strategy in allowing MFN and WTO accession was to weaken China domestically:

> The United States finally reached an agreement with us not because of sudden good intentions and benevolence. On the one hand, our strength lays bare before them, so if they didn't let us join that won't be good for them. On the other hand, they had their own strategic considerations, and we must not be naive. Promoting the so-called political liberalization through the implementation of economic liberalization is an important strategic tool for certain political forces in the West to implement Westernization and splittist political plots in socialist countries. The United States and China have reached a bilateral agreement on China's accession to the WTO, and this is closely linked to its [American] global strategy. On this point, Clinton had been quite clear. In a statement to the Congress on the issue of granting China's permanent MFN status, he said, "Joining the WTO will bring an information revolution to millions of Chinese people in a way the government cannot control. It will accelerate the collapse of Chinese state-owned enterprises. This process will make the government further from people's lives and promote social and political changes in China." With regard to this [intention], we must keep a clear head, clearly see the essence, avoid the danger through precaution and preparedness [做到有备无患], work hard to fulfill our strategic intentions, and promote China's economic development.

China's willingness to incur serious domestic risk in favor of MFN and WTO membership is further evidence that strategic, not merely economic, motivations may have played an important role.

This leads to a second point: how then did China ultimately achieve MFN? As a sign of how all-consuming the issue was, top Chinese officials made MFN a priority even when it was outside of their formal purview. For example, when Clinton sought to link annual MFN renewal to human rights, Liu Huaqing—then a Standing Committee member as well as vice chairman of the CMC—spoke with the US secretary of the navy, as well as then former Secretary of Defense Dick Cheney, and told them that "the issue of MFN status cannot be linked to human rights. If the United States cancels MFN status for China, it will be very disadvantageous to the United States and other countries and regions, and the loss incurred by the United States may be even greater."[68]

China pursued two approaches to secure permanent MFN status, seeking to leverage negotiations first in APEC and then in the WTO to resolve the MFN issue. As an account from the time put it, "[China's] trading future, indeed rests on the . . . continued MFN access to markets in the United States. China needs the certainty and protection that might be expected from the GATT and APEC frameworks for free trade. Otherwise, it will continue to be at risk of discriminatory barriers, sanctions, and retaliatory action by the United States on any number of grounds, including human rights."[69]

Economic Blunting through APEC

China used APEC to blunt American relational leverage over it. As China's first APEC ambassador Wang Yusheng argues, "APEC would allow us to carry out the necessary struggles and go after advantages while avoiding disadvantages."[70] One of these struggles was over Washington's ability to limit Beijing's access to the US market. Through APEC, China sought to push "regional trade rules that would prevent the Americans from holding its [China's] trade status hostage to its human rights and arms sales record."[71] As Thomas Moore and Dixia Yang argue, "From the start, Chinese officials have hoped that APEC could become a multilateral forum within which Beijing would be able to protect itself from threats such as the imposition of unilateral trade sanctions by the U.S."[72] China has used two tactics in pursuit of this goal.

The first tactic was to ensure that APEC accepted the principle of non-discrimination in trade, which it saw as a shortcut to the "unconditional application of most favored nation trade status among APEC members."[73] A review of its negotiating positions revealed that "China has sought to achieve multilaterally a policy objective—permanent MFN status from the United States—it has not been able to achieve bilaterally."[74] APEC ambassador Wang Yusheng conceded in his memoirs that "the principle of non-discrimination was actually a matter between China and the United States," but he also noted that multilateralizing it was useful because "other members [of APEC] sympathized with and supported us to varying degrees." "Therefore," he continues, "we have always stressed that this is not just a difference between China and the United States, it is a problem for all of APEC, it includes the United States and China and all the APEC members and they must work together to solve it."[75] Wang recalled that China tried to make the US liberalization agenda contingent on first accepting an APEC principle of non-discrimination: "We emphasized that non-discriminatory treatment should be given to APEC members first, which is the basis for APEC's trade and investment liberalization."[76] The United States opposed this effort.

China's second tactic was to use APEC to gain admission directly to the GATT/WTO, which would effectively grant China MFN and weaken US economic leverage over China. China supported the principle that, as Foreign Minister Qian Qichen put it, "all APEC members should become GATT members."[77] China threatened to hold the US liberalization agenda hostage to GATT/WTO accession. The point was explicitly made by Trade Minister Wu Yi in a conference with reporters:

> We have indeed asked the APEC forum to give sincere support to China's bid to rejoin the GATT. . . . If China is out of the GATT . . . not only will this daunt the universality of the global multilateral trade system, *even China's thorough implementation of the plan of trade liberalization in the APEC region will be affected.* So long as China's GATT contracting party status is not resumed, it would be very difficult for China to commit itself to the implementation of the Uruguay Round agreements, and the *implementation of the APEC regional trade liberalization program would be affected adversely.*[78]

If China could not get direct entry into the GATT/WTO, it hoped to at least lower the bar to entry by encouraging APEC members to support the principle that those APEC states designated as "developing countries" should also be designated as such within the GATT/WTO. This approach was designed to counter the American position that a country as large as China needed to be held to developed country—not developing country—standards. By leveraging "developing country" status in APEC to secure it in the GATT/WTO, China hoped to lower the bar to joining and hasten its entry. As Trade Minister Wu Yi argued, "The United States has already consented to [a separate timetable for developing countries in APEC]. . . . We wish the United States would apply the same principle to the talks on China's 'GATT reentry' so that the talks can make progress as soon as possible."[79]

China's APEC efforts suggest Beijing's preoccupation with MFN and US economic leverage. But it was ultimately the WTO negotiation process that offered Beijing the leverage it needed to draw out US concessions on MFN.

Economic Blunting through the WTO

China's negotiations with the United States over WTO entry were not fundamentally about the WTO—both parties understood them as in actuality being negotiations about whether or not China would receive MFN status.

Indeed, China did not actually need US approval to join the WTO; instead, it only needed two-thirds of the WTO members to support China's membership, and it was on track to secure that membership despite possible US opposition. Negotiator Long Yongtu argues that securing MFN was a "core interest" of the negotiations and stated his belief that WTO accession would resolve the issue. "High-level leaders asked me more than once whether the United States would cancel the annual review of China's Most Favored Nation status after China's entry into the WTO," he stated in one interview recounting the WTO negotiation process.[80] In another interview, he stated, "the WTO can help resolve China's increasing trade frictions with developed countries and *free China from the threat of revocation of most-favored-nation status*."[81]

How did the WTO accession process provide China leverage in the MFN negotiation? The answer comes down to its unique particularities. WTO membership requires parties to have unconditional MFN status; if China joined the WTO without securing unconditional MFN status from the United States, the United States would have to invoke the "non-applicability clause," which would have the effect of ensuring that the WTO rules that the United States and China had agreed to would be "non-applicable" in the bilateral trading relationship. In effect, this meant that US firms would suffer significantly in the China market as rival European or Japanese firms benefited from WTO terms with China that American companies would not be able to access. In essence, under non-applicability, China would not necessarily be any worse off than it otherwise had been—especially if Washington still granted it annual MFN status—but the United States could be considerably worse off relative to its competitors. Chinese senior leadership was keenly aware of this leverage and used it to secure MFN. As then US Ambassador Li Zhaoxing noted:

> According to the WTO regulations, members should give each other unconditional MFN status. After China's accession to the WTO, the US Trade Act of 1974 would conflict with this regulation. The United States faced a choice: either grant China permanent MFN status so that the United States could benefit from China's WTO accession; or invoke the non-applicability clause to hand over the opportunities brought about by China's open market to other countries.[82]

Accordingly, China knew that the more WTO accession agreements it was able to sign with major economies, the greater the pressure it would create for the United States to provide MFN status. Indeed, as Li Peng noted in a May 2000 meeting on the various accession agreements, "An agreement with the EU can promote the United States to adopt permanent normal trade relations with China (PNTR)."[83] In addition, China's leaders suggested that they would fully reverse many if not all the concessions made in exchange for MFN on agriculture, automobiles, foreign investment caps, and anti-dumping measures

if the United States did not grant PNTR. For example, in a high-level economic planning meeting between Li Peng and Zhu Rongji on June 30, 1999,
the question of how to sequence China's concessions surfaced. Li Peng argued
that, "After joining the WTO, there should be a total restriction on the foreign
banks' operation of RMB, [and investment in] insurance and telecommunications. He [Zhu Rongji] agreed to legislate this after the WTO. He said that
joining the WTO has already been negotiated, and China and the United States
have resumed permanent normal trade relations. I said that if the US Congress
obstructs the approval of the restoration of normal trade relations between
China and the United States, the Standing Committee of the National People's
Congress of China will veto [liberalization legislation] accordingly."[84] In essence, China's concessions in the bilateral WTO negotiation process would
be reversed entirely, disadvantaging US firms relative to other states while
leaving China's firms scarcely any worse off. This kind of hardball approach
was consistent in China's negotiating strategy, and visits to foreign countries
to sign accession agreements and discuss trade made it all the more credible.
For example, after discussing trade on a six-country tour including economic
heavyweights like the United Kingdom, France, and Saudi Arabia in November
1999, Jiang reiterated the policy that "If the US Congress does not pass China's
normal trade relations status, the agreement between China and the United
States [on WTO accession] should be considered invalid" and all concessions
would be revoked.[85]

From the US perspective, China's focus on MFN provided a useful opportunity. Indeed, many Americans did not think that the extension of MFN status
to China had any real economic consequences for Washington or substantial
economic benefit for China. Writing in *The New York Times,* Paul Krugman
declared, "You could argue that the question whether to grant China 'permanent normal trade relations,' or PNTR, is mainly a procedural issue. The United
States won't be reducing any existing trade barriers; all the concessions in terms
of opening market will come from the Chinese side."[86] Clinton made these same
points in a speech the very same day he submitted legislation to grant China
permanent normal trading relations: "The W.T.O. agreement will move China
in the right direction. It will advance the goals America has worked for in China
for the past three decades. Economically, this agreement is the equivalent of a
one-way street. It requires China to open its markets—with a fifth of the world's
population, potentially the biggest markets in the world—to both our products
and services in unprecedented new ways. All we do is to agree to maintain the
present access which China enjoys."[87]

The negotiating process over a bilateral WTO accession agreement was full
of difficulties, but China's teams retained a laser-like focus on MFN throughout
it. In an economic meeting following the negotiation's breakdown in 1999 and

Washington's decision to leak China's concessions to the general public, Li Peng met with senior officials on China's response. As he recounts:

> On April 8, the US unilaterally published the negotiation's draft joint declaration manuscript and a list of American terms, and said that an agreement had already been reached [on these points]. The Chinese side put out a statement in response and denied an agreement had been reached. But this list had already been widely spread. At the time, 95% of the clauses and content that had been agreed upon were consistent with the list that the United States had published, and China had only added a number of protective clauses. What was unclear was whether the annual review of trade with China would or would not end at this point and whether the United States so-called "most-favored-nation status" would or would not be included in the agreement. Therefore, I added two items to the document: the United States must give China permanent normal trading status, and cannot continue to examine and approve whether or not China will get MFN status annually; secondly, it must pass certain laws to ensure the correct implementation of the WTO provisions and to guarantee China's role in opening to the outside world.

In essence, despite the opportunity to attack his rival Zhu Rongji for making enormous concessions—many of which had galvanized the opponents—Li Peng remained focused on the question of MFN. That was the essential focus of these negotiations and the main way of neutralizing American relational leverage over China. Zhu's concessions were essentially the price of securing such an important strategic instrument.

As these high-level statements suggest, China saw the concessions it made in the bilateral accession agreement with the United States as primarily being about MFN, not the WTO. After the agreement was signed, and with the US Congress then debating whether to make China's MFN status permanent, Zhu Rongji explicitly linked that agreement to MFN: "There's nothing I can do. We have made the biggest concessions [in the accession agreement], and we are now watching to see what they do."[88] Those concessions were justified not because they would ensure diplomatic support that China did not require to join the WTO, but because Beijing saw the WTO as a forcing mechanism to reduce US economic leverage over China.

China's concessions were largely a product of its weakness and dependence on the capitalist West to propel its development forward. By the early 2000s, it was clear that China had played its weak hand well in the negotiations over PNTR and WTO. China had bought itself stable market access abroad, which in turn made multinational companies more willing to invest in and export from China—setting off a virtuous cycle of explosive growth in China while accelerating deindustrialization and increasing unemployment in the industrialized world. Just as critically, PNTR and WTO helped Beijing bind American economic coercion for two decades, until the Trump administration broke some of those self-imposed constraints in 2018 and pursued a trade war with China. By then, of course, China's economy was no longer quite so weak: an economy that had been only 10 percent the size of the American economy at the time of WTO accession was now 70 percent the size of the American economy at the dawn of the trade war. That enormous change in China's relative strength would inevitably upend virtually every aspect of China's grand strategy, and as the following chapters demonstrate, that strategic shift began years earlier with the Global Financial Crisis.

PART II

"ACTIVELY ACCOMPLISHING SOMETHING"

Building as China's Second Displacement Strategy
(2009–2016)

"A Change in the Balance of Power"

The Financial Crisis and the Dawn of Building

"In the past we had to keep a low profile [Tao Guang Yang Hui] because we were weak while other states were strong.... Now, with 'Striving for Achievement,' we are indicating to neighboring countries that we are strong and you are weak. This is a change at a very fundamental level."[1]
—*Yan Xuetong, Dean of Tsinghua University's Institute of International Relations, 2013*

Hundreds of Chinese diplomats and foreign policy officials stood in a row. They were all dressed the same—white shirts, black pants, no jacket, and no necktie—and their unusually informal attire contrasted with the significance of the historic occasion. For decades, China's Party leaders had met with the assembled foreign policy apparatus in "ambassadorial conferences" that were usually held every five to six years. Now, in a drab conference room, China's foreign policy apparatus was gathering for the eleventh such occasion in the history of the People's Republic of China—and this time, it was occurring in the midst of a Global Financial Crisis that had shaken the global economy and laid bare the weaknesses of US power.

After the outbreak of the crisis, and in the run-up to the conference, China's think tank scholars were writing that the power gap between China and the United States had narrowed. They began advocating for China to revise or jettison its "hiding and biding" grand strategy.[2] And now their unofficial judgments were about to be made official.

Hu Jintao, the famously reserved Chinese president, smiled and shook hands as he made his way down the lines of assembled diplomats. And then, following remarks from a few functionaries, he began his address. In typical Party fashion, Hu's language was subtle and obscured in Party jargon even as he upended Chinese grand strategy. There had been "a major change in the balance of international forces," he observed in a reference to the financial crisis. The "prospects for multipolarity were now more obvious" too.[3]

These were not trivial declarations. Concepts like "international balance of power" [国际力量对比] and "multipolarity" [多极化] are euphemisms for the decline of American power rather than general statements on the balance of power among the world's leading states. The Party's discourse on them is a good indicator of where it thinks China stands relative to the United States, and it is telling that these concepts are also at the core of Party discussions of grand strategy. As this chapter demonstrates, China's leaders have made clear that their adherence to "hiding capabilities and biding time" was never permanent but instead contingent on the "international balance of power." So while Hu may have sounded rather dryly formulaic when he told China's foreign policy apparatus that "adhering to 'hide and bide' [韬光养晦] is a strategic decision made by the center based on comprehensively analyzing the entire international balance of power," this was in fact a revealing statement.[4] If China's strategy was dependent on the "international balance of power," and if—as Hu had declared—the "international balance of power had changed," then it meant China's grand strategy needed revision.

In his address, Hu then proposed precisely such a revision. He declared that China needed to modify Deng's "hiding capabilities and biding time" by more "Actively Accomplishing Something" [积极有所作为].[5] This seemingly mundane semantic shift—the addition of the word "actively" to one part of Deng's doctrine—was momentous. Deng's guiding doctrine and the larger twenty-four-character phrase in which it was embedded had been consensus for nearly twenty years. Hu had now modified it. That move at such a high-profile forum was a major sign that China was changing its grand strategy. China was no longer interested only in blunting American power. Hu's invocation of "Actively Accomplishing Something," and Xi's spin on the concept with "Striving for Achievement" [奋发有为], indicated a shift to building regional order within Asia.

As the next three chapters show, after this speech, China's behavior changed in ways that corresponded to this strategic shift. At the military level (Chapter 8), the Global Financial Crisis accelerated China's shift away from a singular focus on blunting American power through sea denial, which had emphasized mines, missiles, and submarines. China would instead focus on building regional order through sea control and amphibious capabilities, which emphasized aircraft carriers, more capable surface vessels, amphibious units, overseas facilities, and a variety of capabilities it had once neglected. These capabilities would help China assemble military leverage over its neighbors, seize or hold distant islands and waters, safeguard sea lines of communication, intervene in the affairs of its neighbors, or provide public security goods. At the political level (Chapter 9), the Global Financial Crisis pushed China to depart from a strategy focused on joining and stalling regional organizations to blunt US political influence and to instead pursue a building strategy that saw it launch its own. China spearheaded the launch of the Asian Infrastructure Investment Bank (AIIB) in the economic domain and the elevation and institutionalization of the previously obscure Conference on Interaction and Confidence-Building Measures in Asia (CICA) in the security domain—hoping both would help it build regional order in line with its preferences. At the economic level (Chapter 10), the Global Financial Crisis helped Beijing depart from the defensive economic statecraft characteristic of blunting American economic leverage and instead pursue offensive economic statecraft that would allow China to build its own coercive and consensual economic capacities over others. At the core of this effort was China's Belt and Road Initiative (BRI), its robust use of economic statecraft against its neighbors, and its attempts to gain greater financial influence. None of these activities would have been justifiable under the doctrine of Tao Guang Yang Hui.

This chapter discusses the departure from Tao Guang Yang Hui in Party documents toward a strategy of *building*. The discussion is structured in four parts. Through a review of Party texts, it shows (1) a decrease in Beijing's *perceived relative power gap* with the United States following the Global Financial Crisis; (2) a change in Beijing's grand strategic ends, which shifted from a focus on the United States to a more specific focus on regional order-building through "peripheral diplomacy" and the construction of a "Community of Common Destiny"; (3) a departure from Deng's strategic guideline of "Hide and Bide" to "Actively Accomplishing Something" and its successor concepts; and (4) a shift in grand strategic means from those suitable to blunting to those suitable for building strategies.

A Shift in Perceived US Power—The Multipolarity Discourse

After the 2008 Global Financial Crisis, Chinese views of American power shifted profoundly, and that shift is reflected in China's discourse on multipolarity (多极化) and the "international balance of forces" (国际力量对比). "Multipolarity" is a term originally from the international relations literature that refers to an international system characterized by several great powers. But for China, the term has a long history. During the Cold War, "multipolarity" appeared occasionally and referred to the dilution of American and Soviet power; after the Soviet collapse, the term became a euphemism for the dilution of American power—and it exploded in use.

To make that case, this section draws from a review of nearly every reference to multipolarity in Party Congress reports, the speeches of leaders as contained within their selected works, and in the three-volume compilations of CCP documents published between Party Congresses. It also finds a clear trend: in the early 1990s China feared multipolarity was far off but that, beginning in 2007–2008, it felt it was truly emerging. This in turn called for a new strategy.

The Multipolarity Discourse

China's discourse on multipolarity took off in the post–Cold War era, and the term was less frequently included in Party texts before it. For example, virtually no Party Congress report before the Cold War's conclusion referenced multipolarity, but after the trifecta of Tiananmen, the Gulf War, and the Soviet collapse, *every* single report included it—often at the report's outset and in its foreign policy section, suggesting the term's importance to strategy. And while multipolarity almost never appeared in the selected works of China's post-reform Cold War leaders (e.g., Hu Yaobang, Zhao Ziyang), it appears in the post–Cold War portions of Deng's selected works and then 77 times and 72 times in Jiang and Hu's selected works. Similarly, while the term appeared only about 1,000 times in Chinese journal articles during the 1980s, it appeared nearly 13,000 times in the 1990s and roughly 46,000 times from 2000 to 2010.[6]

The fact that China's focus on multipolarity emerged after the trifecta strongly suggests that for the last three decades it has been a proxy for diluting US power, but viewing multipolarity in these terms can be controversial. Some dismiss it as a rhetorical device calling for reduced superpower influence, but they overlook the fact that the Party defines it as a serious analytical judgment. Others believe multipolarity indicates a desire by China to be one among many poles, but they take the concept too literally. As Iain Johnston has noted, "if one asks Chinese strategists if support for multipolarity means support for a rise in the relative power and strategic independence of Japan or nuclear weapons development in India, for instance, the response is often a negative or an ambivalent one."[7] Instead, as we will see, discourses on multipolarity have often focused on assessments of the US willingness to use military force, the impact of US economic crises on US power, US export performance, the US domestic situation, US science and technology innovation, and a variety of other specific factors—all of which reveal that the core input in judgments of multipolarity are US-related.[8]

Still others ask whether multipolarity even matters for Chinese strategy. In 2003, leading China scholars observed that "the multipolarity discourse plays an ambiguous role in China's foreign policy process" and it is "unclear whether the multipolarity discourse informs leadership decisions, reflects leadership preferences, or is the manifestation of a deeply ingrained victimization view of China's relationship to the world."[9] But if the term were unimportant, why would it appear in every Party Congress Political Report dating back to 1992, in nearly all leader-level foreign affairs speeches, and in addresses at plenums, Central Economic Work Conferences, Politburo meetings, conclaves of provincial Party secretaries and ministers, and commemorations of major Party anniversaries?

Chinese leaders in fact give us an answer, and they are clear that multipolarity is a high-level Party judgment that directly impacts strategy. For example, in an address to the CMC, Jiang Zemin declared multipolarity the first of "four important factors" that he considers when surveying world politics.[10] At the 1999 Central Economic Work Conference, he stressed that the assessment of the "the multipolarization pattern" is "an important judgment made by the Party Central Committee."[11] This judgment mattered for the work of all cadres: "Comrades of the whole party, especially the party's senior cadres, must open their eyes .. and have comprehensive and accurate understanding of the background, pattern, and general trends of the world's politics and economy," he argued, "Only by understanding the general trend of the world can we make the overall situation of the country better and concentrate on managing our own affairs."[12] Similarly, at the 2006 Central Foreign Affairs Work Conference, Jiang's successor Hu Jintao discussed multipolarity in great detail as one of the "basic judgments on the international situation in the new century" made by the "central Party and state" (中央).[13] These remarks demonstrate why speeches often begin with or feature prominent discussions of multipolarity—it is viewed as central to China's strategic decision-making.

How then does multipolarity shape strategy? Both Jiang and Hu tell us that multipolarity, and its sister concept the "international balance of forces" [国际力量对比], are critical inputs in China's grand strategy that reflect China's relative power. For example, at the 9th Foreign Ambassadorial Conference in 1998, Jiang made the link explicitly: "We should hide our capabilities and bide our time [韬光养晦], draw in our claws, preserve ourselves, and consciously plan our development. Our country's situation and the international balance of power determine that we must do this."[14] Hu Jintao also stressed this linkage. At a 2003 diplomatic symposium, Hu argued, "The more multipolarity develops, the greater our freedom of maneuver."[15] He also stressed that China followed Tao Guang Yang Hui because of its limited power: "Comprehensively taking into consideration our country's current situation and the development of the trends in the international balance of power (国际力量对比), this [Tao Guang Yang Hui] is a strategic guideline that should be adhered to for a long time."[16] Later, he reiterated that Chinese diplomatic choices were "based on changes in the international balance of power (力量对比) and the needs of our country's development and security."[17] In the 2009 address that officially modified Tao Guang Yang Hui for the first time, Hu stated, "Adherence to Tao Guang Yang Hui is strategic decision made by the central government from *comprehensively analyzing the entire international balance of power* (力量对比)."[18]

Together, these leader-level statements in authoritative foreign policy speeches suggest that the Party (1) observes the international structure; (2) makes judgments about the trends in multipolarity and the "international balance of forces"; and (3) modifies strategy according to these trends. We now turn to consider how these important judgments have changed over time—and how they ushered in a new era in Chinese grand strategy.

Multipolarity over Time

After the Cold War, China believed multipolarity would come but that its arrival would be tortuous given enduring US power. For example, the 1992 Party Congress Political Report was the first to mention multipolarization, and it argued that "the bipolar structure has come to an end . . . and the world is moving towards multipolarization" but that "the formation of a new structure will be long and complex," indicating confidence that American power would remain high.[19]

Six years later, at the 9th Ambassadorial Conference in 1998, this judgment still stood. Jiang argued that "world was accelerating towards multipolarity, but we must fully recognize that the present balance of just about every kind of power is very unbalanced. The United States is trying to build a unipolar world and it dominates world affairs."[20] American power was still too great. "Although it is constrained by a variety of parties," Jiang noted, "for a long time, the United States will maintain significant advantages in politics, economy, science and technology, and military affairs."[21] He then focused closely on US economic power: "In recent years, the United States' economic strength has not only not declined but has been revived, regaining the world's position as the largest exporter and most competitive economy."[22]

Jiang continued to stress these themes at the next year's Central Economic Work Forum, where he discussed Washington's intervention in Kosovo. Although multipolarity would one day come, "the final formation of the multipolarization pattern will be a long-term process full of complex struggles," he argued; "this is an important judgment made by the party Central Committee."[23] Jiang elaborated on multipolarity and the "international balance of power," revealing that US power drove that judgment. "The current balance of international power is seriously out of balance. The economic, military, and scientific and technological strength of the United States is obviously better than that of other countries.

It is the superpower of the world today."[24] The US willingness to use force was part of this assessment. "The United States is stepping up its implementation of its global strategy, advocating 'new interventionism,' introducing a new 'gunboat policy,' interfering in other countries' internal affairs, and even using force."[25] Even American domestic elements factored into Jiang's analysis of American power, and he noted "there have been many internal conflicts in the United States" that could complicate its autonomy.[26]

Public and private speeches sometimes diverged in their assessments of the United States. In the year 2000, Jiang declared in international addresses before the United Nations that "the trend towards multipolarity is developing rapidly," but in virtually every speech behind closed doors addressed to Party leadership, he was not so confident.[27] That same year in a speech on party-building, Jiang argued that "the final formation of a multipolar structure will undergo a long and arduous process."[28] Similarly, in an address to the CCP Central Committee that year, he declared the "final formation will experience a long-term development process."[29] In an address to the 5th Plenary of the 15th Central Committee—an important Party speech used to set lines—he continued this language and said "the international pattern is generally oriented towards multipolarity, but it will not be easy and there will be struggles and twists and turns."[30] Similar language was used in Jiang's speeches before an enlarged CMC, where he declared that there was a "serious imbalance in the balance of world military forces," referencing the US success in harnessing new military technologies as part of what many called the Revolution in Military Affairs.[31] When Jiang went to the SCO in 2001, he would say that multipolarity was deepening or accelerating.[32] But in key Party addresses—his address on the eightieth anniversary of the founding of the Communist Party that year, his 2002 Party Congress Political Report—he said that multipolarity was "developing in twists and turns."[33] This was not a sign of confidence.

The judgment that multipolarity was still far away spanned administrations. When Hu Jintao took office and delivered an important address to a 2003 diplomatic symposium, he retained Jiang's language, declaring that hegemony and unilateralism (both US-led) ensured that "the multipolarization of the world will be a tortuous and complicated process" and that the global "balance of power is seriously out of balance," and he directly concluded that as a result China needed to adhere to Tao Guang Yang Hui.[34] The language continued into 2004, where in another major Party speech, this time before the CCP CCDI, Hu repeated that "multipolarity was developing in twists and turns," demonstrating that assessments of multipolarity carried across administrations.[35] Even in 2005, in a meeting with all senior provincial and ministry Party secretaries, Hu reflected on both the slow emergence of multipolarity and the imbalanced "international balance of forces" as well: "The global situation is in an important period of transition to multipolarity. . . . As the imbalance of world power cannot be fundamentally changed in the short term, the development of the trend of multi-polarization in the world will not be easy."[36] Like Jiang, even as he held this line in internal Party meetings, in visits to the United Nations, the United Kingdom, and Saudi Arabia *that very same year*, Hu told his hosts that the "trend towards multipolarity was deepening," evidence that international addresses are more bullish than internal Party ones on multipolarity.[37] Indeed, the very next year, at the seminal 2006 Central Foreign Affairs Work Conference—which had previously been held only twice in the entire CCP's history—Hu reiterated the more cautious language that "multipolarity is developing amid twists and turns," and that "the trend of multipolarization is continuing to develop, but unipolar or multipolar struggles are still profoundly complex," thereby contextualizing and limiting some of the more positive phrases he had previously used and continuing to suggest multipolarity would be difficult to achieve.[38] As the preceding record shows, at least when authoritative Party Congress Political reports, leader-level foreign policy addresses, and leader-level Party addresses are considered, there is a clear belief after the end of the Cold War that multipolarity was distant throughout the period in which China pursued blunting—a sign that perceptions of American relative power were high.

In the run-up to the Global Financial Crisis, and especially in its aftermath, these views changed dramatically and align with China's shift to a building strategy. A few months into the early stages of the financial crisis in 2007, and following US setbacks in Iraq, President Hu in his 2007 Political Report to the 17th Party Congress declared that "progress towards a multipolar world was irreversible" and that "the international balance of power is changing in favor of the maintenance of peace."[39] This was language far more positive than that in any previous address, and similar language about multipolarity's irreversibility appeared in his address to the CMC that year as well.[40] Even though language on the irreversibility of multipolarity had been used at least once before, the departure from stating that multipolarity was proceeding amid "twists and turns"—language that had been used for six years—suggested that China felt confident about the trendline toward multipolarity, even if it did not quite have a sense of the pace of the transition. And even though the looming economic crisis also affected China, leaders in Beijing saw it as delegitimizing the once formidable model of American financial capitalism and asymmetrically weakening the United States. As Dai Bingguo put it in his memoirs, in December 2008 it was clear that "the United States had fallen into the most serious financial crisis since the Great Depression of the 1930s; at the same time, China's economy continued to maintain strong growth."[41]

The Party gained consensus on the pace of multipolarity after the crisis went global in 2008. By then, language on multipolarity and the international balance of forces was dramatically more triumphant than ever before. In his 2009 11th Ambassadorial Conference Address, the first such address since the crisis, Hu used the opportunity to explore these themes in great detail. He declared that there had been "a major change in the balance of international power," a reference to the financial crisis, and that "prospects for multipolarity were now more obvious."[42] Moreover, Hu linked China's own economy to the onset of multipolarity, declaring that "China's development must inevitably influence the comparison of international forces."[43] As a result of the Global Financial Crisis, the world and peripheral security situation was more complicated and China faced challenges from the West, but overall, "the opportunity is greater than the challenge," Hu concluded.[44] The opportunity came from his assessment that "external conditions for China's development have further increased," that the "overall strategic environment continues to improve," that "our country's ability to maintain sovereignty and security continues to increase," that "our country's influence on the periphery has been further expanded," and that "China's soft power has further risen."[45] Importantly, it was in this speech that Hu outlined a revision to Tao Guang Yang Hui. He made clear that while "adhering to Tao Guang Yang Hui is strategic decision made by the central government and based from comprehensively analyzing the entire international balance of power," it was also clear that there had been "a major change in the international balance of power" upon which those decisions are based had changed, and therefore clear that China's grand strategy needed revision.

The next year, in his 2010 address to the Central Economic Work Forum, Hu continued these themes, declaring that "multipolarity was deepening" and that "the international balance of power is changing rapidly."[46] That same year, he delivered his 5th Plenary Address to the CCP Central Committee, stating not only that "multipolarity was deepening" but also that, "from an international point of view, although the international financial crisis has had a large impact on the global economy. . . . China's international influence and international status have been significantly improved."[47] Hu's 2012 Political Report to the 18th Party Congress two years later maintained this language, holding that "multipolarity was developing deeply" and that "the balance of international forces was tipping in favor of the maintenance of world peace."[48] Together, these statements represent a departure from years of more cautious estimates delivered to Party members.

These judgments were largely upheld by Hu's successor, President Xi. In his 2014 address to the Central Affairs Work Forum, Xi stated that "the onward advance of multipolarity in the world will not change" and that "the world today is a world of change. . . . It is a world of deep adjustments in the international system and international order. It is a world with profound changes in international balance of forces conducive to peace and development."[49]

Ends—Prioritizing Peripheral Diplomacy

On March 16, 2013, Chinese diplomat Wang Yi was formally promoted to minister of foreign affairs.[50] The urbane but fierce defender of Chinese interests was sometimes known as a "silver fox" for both his "looks and his diplomatic wiles," but he was also brilliant and diligent.[51] After graduating high school during the Cultural Revolution, Wang Yi was sent to labor on a farm in northeast China for eight long years. A former classmate of his recalls that Wang Yi "did not waste his time" but engrossed himself in literature and history entirely at his own direction.[52] When the Cultural Revolution ended, Wang Yi's diligence paid off, and he earned a spot at Beijing International Studies University, where he dedicated himself to Japanese language studies.

Soon after graduating, Wang Yi embarked on a career in the Ministry of Foreign Affairs (MFA) and married into diplomatic royalty. His new father-in-law, Qian Jiadong, had been part of China's delegation to the Geneva conference in the 1950s (the country's first major diplomatic outing), principal foreign affairs secretary for Premier and MFA founder Zhou Enlai in the 1960s and 1970s, and later a UN ambassador in the 1980s. A fluent Japanese speaker, Wang Yi began his career in Japan and then rose up the ranks of the MFA as a Japan and Asia expert. He was wily too. During discussions over North Korea, Wang Yi knew Washington wanted a trilateral involving China and North Korea, while Pyongyang wanted a bilateral with only the United States. Wang Yi's solution was simple, if unconventional. He organized a banquet involving all three countries, excused himself to go to the restroom halfway through, and ordered his staff to file out surreptitiously, thereby turning the trilateral into a bilateral—to Pyongyang's delight and Washington's chagrin.[53]

In light of Wang Yi's skills, his ascent through the MFA was not unexpected. But for some observers, his elevation to the top post of foreign minister was still a bit surprising. China's previous two foreign ministers—Li Zhaoxing and Yang Jiechi—had essentially been America hands who had served long stints in the United States, and their prominence was seen as a sign that the United States remained what China called the "key" in its foreign policy hierarchy. The promotion of an Asia expert like Wang Yi was seen—right or wrong—as a sign that China's neighborhood was now at least as important if not more important than managing ties with Washington.

The precise logic behind high-level Chinese promotions like Wang Yi's remains impenetrable for most foreign observers, and it is important not to overread them. But it is also worth noting that Wang Yi's elevation did come at a time when—as China's perception of American power fell after the Global Financial Crisis—Chinese leaders began to adjust the ends of the country's strategy away from a narrow focus on blunting American power toward a broader focus on building regional order. This effort was broadly subsumed under concepts like "Peripheral Diplomacy" [周边外交], a term that refers to diplomacy in China's neighborhood (i.e., its "periphery") and a policy with roots in the Asian Financial Crisis of the late 1990s. In the past, China saw its periphery as a source of threat, fearing that the United States would organize a balancing coalition within it to challenge China.[54] Now, after the Global Financial Crisis, China saw the periphery not only as a place to push back on the "China threat theory" but as a site for a more affirmative and less defensive Chinese strategy. Over time, concepts like a "Community of Common Destiny" would serve as a declaration of China's interest in building order within the region. Asia hands like Wang Yi would be all the more critical in carrying it out.

Chinese texts show that the country's focus on more assertive order-building in the periphery indeed emerged after the Global Financial Crisis, with the goal elevated as the top strategic direction in Chinese foreign policy behavior.[55] Hu Jintao began that elevation in his 11th Ambassadorial Conference address in 2009—the one in which he also departed from Tao Guang Yang Hui. Hu noted that peripheral diplomacy was "an important external condition" for the new focus on "'accomplishing something' internationally."[56] China now needed to focus not only on "stabilizing" the periphery but also on "developing" it.[57] Hu indicated that due to the Global Financial Crisis, "our country's influence on peripheral affairs has been further expanded," and wielding that influence well would require planning.[58] "From a comprehensive perspective, we need to strengthen our strategic planning for the periphery," Hu declared, and he noted for the first time in any official Party document that the principle of "be good with neighbors, do good with neighbors"—which had first been articulated by Jiang—was now considered a "peripheral diplomatic guideline," elevating it as a policy goal.[59]

Two years after Hu's landmark speech, China outlined the concept of a "Community of Common Destiny" in a White Paper that focused on China's foreign policy. The discussion of the term provided insight into what China's order-building would mean in practice. China's preference was for an Asia where others were dependent on China economically and divorced from US alliances militarily, and the concept was defined in such terms. On the economic and institutional side, China said the "Community of Common Destiny" was a state of being "interconnected" and "intertwined"; on the security side, it defined it as being against the "Cold War mentality," which generally refers to the United States and its Asian alliances.[60] The phrase then reappeared in Hu's 2012 18th Party Congress Political Report.[61] In some early cases, the term was initially applied to Taiwan, but the context indicates a similar logic: in both cases, China could constrain the agency of others by enmeshing it within China's economy and separating it from the United States.

Xi Jinping took power after that address, and over the next year, he continued the elevation of "peripheral diplomacy." In a June 2013 speech and later in an important essay released shortly after in the *People's Daily*, Xi's Foreign Minister Wang Yi stated that "peripheral diplomacy was the priority direction" [周边方向] for Chinese foreign policy, language that had previously never been used.[62] He declared that China would provide "public goods," and he outlined a program for greater Chinese focus on the region in arenas spanning from economic cooperation to multilateral institutions to regional hotspots and military affairs. These inducements were conditional, Wang Yi noted in his essay: "For those neighboring and developing countries that *have long been friendly to China* and have arduous tasks for their own development," China would "better consider their interests."

The next month, President Xi held an unprecedented Work Forum (座谈) on Peripheral Diplomacy and used it to elevate the concept and link it formally with the "Community of Common Destiny," the clearest expression of China's new focus on building regional order. Xi even titled the meeting "Let the Sense of the Community of Common Destiny Take Deep Root in Neighboring Countries," making clear that China's end goal for peripheral diplomacy was for its neighbors to subscribe to Beijing's "Community of Common Destiny."[63] The meeting marked China's first major foreign policy work forum since Hu Jintao's 2006 Work Conference (会议), and it also marked China's first ever work forum on the subject of peripheral diplomacy. It was clearly intended to coordinate grand strategy in the periphery: it included all the major foreign policy actors and every member of the Politburo Standing Committee, and the official *Xinhua* readout declared that "the main task of this conference" was "to determine the strategic objectives, guidelines, and overall layout of diplomatic work for peripheral countries for the next five to ten years, and to clarify the thinking and implementation plans for resolving the major problems and issues facing neighboring country diplomacy."[64]

Xi stressed that his focus on the periphery was a continuation of past policy and was linked to the "diplomatic political guidelines" made at the 18th Party Congress under the Hu administration. The effort had long been centrally coordinated. "The CCP Central Committee," he noted, "had actively defined, planned, and carried out a series of major diplomatic initiatives for peripheral countries."[65] Like Hu before him, Xi also stated that China's "be good to neighbors and do good with neighbors" principle was a "fundamental peripheral diplomatic guideline." But Xi also went much further than any other leader by stressing that "China's diplomacy in this area [i.e., the periphery] is driven by and must serve the Two Centenary Goals and our national rejuvenation," another sign of the shift in the focus of peripheral diplomacy from combating the China threat theory to order-building, as well as its importance to China's grand strategic focus.[66] In a powerful sign that the region was now the focus of China's grand strategy, Xi offered an alternative to "hide and bide" that built on Hu's "Actively Accomplishing Something." This phrase, "Striving for Achievement," was explicitly linked to "promoting peripheral diplomacy."[67]

Xi also made clear what this meant in practice: China would "take actions that will win us support and friendship" and "in response, we hope that neighboring countries will be well inclined towards us, and we hope that China will have a stronger affinity with them, and that our appeal and our influence will grow."[68] The hope for greater influence within the region, and the coordinated strategy to achieve it, is explicit in these documents and represents a marked contrast from the previous era's focus on blunting US power and ad hoc gestures of reassurance. Here now was a comprehensive regional program. As one *People's Daily* online article noted shortly after Xi's landmark 2013 meeting, "the conference raised peripheral diplomacy to the level of national rejuvenation in its importance."[69] It further noted that "the high specificity of the meeting" on peripheral diplomacy was "extremely rare."[70] Another *People's Daily* article called peripheral diplomacy a Chinese "grand strategy."[71] Months later, in a review of some of that year's developments, Wang Yi wrote, "China has broken new ground in its neighborhood diplomacy" and "has given greater importance to neighborhood diplomacy in its overall diplomatic agenda."[72] As evidence of the elevation of peripheral diplomacy, he cited that Xi Jinping and Li Keqiang's first visits overseas after taking office were to neighboring countries, that they had met the heads of twenty-one neighboring countries in less than a year, that Xi had participated in regional organizations, and that the Party had "held the first conference on neighborhood diplomacy since the founding of the PRC."[73] Peripheral diplomacy was indeed the "priority direction."

The next year, China held the 2014 Central Foreign Affairs Work Forum meeting, a meeting held only four times in history and generally during periods of transition. This meeting was more general than the 2013 Work Forum on Peripheral Diplomacy; the fact that the neighborhood was once again the focus is quite revealing. At this meeting, Xi elevated the periphery over other focuses for Chinese strategy. In most Party addresses on foreign policy, when Chinese leaders discuss areas of focus, they have always listed them hierarchically with great powers coming first as the "key," the periphery coming second as the "priority," and the developing world coming third. Xi's important speech changed the order, putting the periphery first for the first time ever, a subtle but highly significant change in the formulaic templates of many of these addresses.[74] The official readout of Xi's speech declared his desire to "turn China's neighborhood areas into a community of common destiny," and a detailed write-up had him stressing that China must "forge a peripheral Community of Common Destiny."[75] This ordering was repeated in some subsequent addresses, such as Li Keqiang's 2014 Work of the Government Report—another critical policy setting address.[76] In it, Li Keqiang stated that "the diplomatic work in the periphery has entered a new phase." Although this ordering of peripheral diplomacy over priorities is not consistently applied in all speeches, it nonetheless continues in many, and even if the phrase "peripheral diplomacy" is not used, the "Community of Common Destiny" framework often gets pride of place relative to other concepts. For example, in Xi's 19th Party Congress address, the foreign policy section of the speech was even titled after the concept and its discussion of the "Community of Common Destiny" came before a discussion of great power relations, which again suggests a shift on the ends of Chinese grand strategy to a focus on the periphery. Similarly, Yang Jiechi has sometimes put peripheral diplomacy ahead of the great powers.[77]

Party texts also make clear that this focus on China's neighborhood would be buttressed by a series of economic, institutional, and security initiatives that would help change the region's view of China. Indeed, these steps would, in Xi's words, "interpret the Chinese Dream from the perspective of our neighbors" and would even "let a sense of common destiny take root," one based on the understanding and acceptance of China's centrality to the region's affairs.[78] As a part of these efforts, the Community of Common Destiny became a mainstay of Xi's speeches abroad, especially at each of China's major economic, institutional, and security initiatives. For example, in his 2013 speech to the Indonesian Parliament that famously announced the BRI, Xi Jinping mentioned the phrase five times.[79] Then, in his 2013 speech announcing the AIIB, the concept was brought up again.[80] In 2014, at his speech assuming chairmanship of CICA, he brought up the term while putting forward a New Asian Security Concept that was both part of the "Community of Common Destiny" and also critical of US alliances.[81] Xi even made the "Community of Common Destiny" the main theme of the 2015 Boao Forum.[82] China's 2017 White Paper on Asian Security Cooperation acknowledged that "Chinese leaders have repeatedly elaborated on the concept of a community of common destiny on many different occasions" and went on to note that "China is working to construct a community of common destiny . . . in Asia and the Asia-Pacific area as a whole."[83] In each of these speeches, Xi situated infrastructure investments, new financial instruments, and new security institutions respectively as efforts promoting this concept, demonstrating a regional focus that differs dramatically from the previous focus on the United States.

Peripheral Diplomacy and China's Global Rise

Leading Chinese foreign policy commentators observed that peripheral diplomacy and order-building through a "Community of Common Destiny" had been elevated over a focus on the United States. They also believed consolidating regional hegemony under the banner of "Community of Common Destiny" was essential to China's ultimate global rise. Liu Zhenmin, vice foreign minister for foreign affairs, pulled these themes together succinctly in an essay he wrote in 2014. "For China to realize its dream of national rejuvenation, it first needs to acquire identification and support from other Asian countries and to tie the dream of the Chinese people with those of the Asian nations."[84]

In a piece published on the *People's Daily* website, Professor Jin Canrong of Renmin University said he had observed a major strategic shift: "We often say that 'the great powers are the key [关键], and the periphery is the priority [首要].'[85] Although the 'key' and 'priority' are important in diplomatic positioning, in the practice of diplomacy, peripheral diplomacy often ranks second in the encounter with great power relations. However, in this conference, China has released to the outside world that in the future diplomatic practice, 'periphery' and 'great power' are equally important."[86] Building was at least as important a strategy now as blunting.

Meanwhile, others like Yan Xuetong saw the US focus and the peripheral focus not at parity, but with the latter eclipsing the former.[87] "The significance of China's peripheral or neighboring countries to its rise is growing more important than the significance of the United States," he noted, which meant that China was elevating the periphery over its past focus on dealing with US pressures.[88] "The nature of a country's rise is to catch up with the most powerful country in the world, and the more powerful country can only be an obstacle to the rising country and cannot become its supporter, and this has created a structural contradiction between the United States and China." Because of this, he argued, "China had long believed that as long relations with the United States are handled well, China could reduce U.S. restraints on China's rise . . and therefore the United States should be regarded as the 'highest priority' [重中之中]." This view, which resembles a blunting strategy, eventually gave way to building, and Yan argued for putting the periphery above the United States: "For the rise of China, it is more important to strive for the support of many neighboring countries than to reduce the prevention efforts of the United States," and China could emphasize projects like the BRI, which Yan said was part of the "strategy for consolidating the rise of our country" and the "foundation for establishing a Community of Common Destiny" at the regional level. Indeed, "The rise of great powers is a process in which a country first becomes a regional power and only then can become a global one," and China's elevation of "neighboring countries as the top priority of diplomacy will help prevent the danger of running before you can walk" and focus China on Asia instead of dragging China into quagmires outside of its region.

Others also echo these views. Xu Jin and Du Zheyuan from the Chinese Academy of Social Sciences note, "The importance that China places on its relations with its neighbors will surpass that accorded to China-US ties. The Working Conference illustrated that neighboring states will become the priority focus of Chinese diplomacy."[89] They go on to argue that "the Chinese government realizes that for a state to rise, it must first rise in the region to which it belongs. If it cannot establish a favorable regional order, building good relations with a distant country will be of limited use."[90] When Xi Jinping states that peripheral diplomacy is necessary for national rejuvenation, these scholars believe that he is essentially saying that it is necessary to become a global superpower: "The so-called great rejuvenation of the Chinese nation is actually the equivalent of becoming a superpower. The term is by no means a new one, but China has been quiet about the extent to which it will accomplish such rejuvenation."[91]

Similarly, Chen Xulong, who leads the international and strategic studies department at the China Institute of International Studies, wrote that "a good periphery is vital for China to be a global power . . . and will serve as a springboard for China to go global." The emphasis on it marked a departure from the past: "China will not be able to make progress in tackling these challenges [in the periphery] just by keeping a low profile [Tao Guang Yang Hui]. Instead, it must take initiative in creating a favorable periphery."[92] Professor Wang Yizhou from Peking University made the same point. "It is obvious that China's new thinking about periphery diplomacy demonstrates its shifting position away from a passive, disadvantageous diplomacy of the past era," Wang argued, and movement toward "leadership in shaping the security structure in Asia." The evidence was in official formulations. "New wording alerts all concerned to this major shift" in China's foreign policy, Wang argued.[93]

As this section's review makes clear, since the Global Financial Crisis, China has dramatically increased its emphasis on the periphery and the creation of a regional "Community of Common Destiny" as a strategic focus, and considerable textual evidence suggests this focus has even superseded China's blunting strategy centered on the United States. This shift was accompanied by a formal revision in China's main strategic guideline, and we turn now to examine that shift.

Ways—Departing from Deng

On July 23, 2010, Yang Jiechi was in Hanoi for a meeting of the ASEAN Regional Forum. The first foreign minister born after the founding of the People's Republic of China in 1949, Yang was an exemplar of the newly professionalized Chinese diplomatic corps. After the Cultural Revolution, which saw Yang sent to toil at the Pujiang Electricity Meter Factory, he landed a rare spot as a trainee at the MFA in 1972.[94] There, he focused on studying English, and five years later, the twenty-seven-year-old Yang was assigned to serve as translator and host to future president George H. W. Bush on a sixteen-day tour of Tibet. "Yang was with us the whole time," recalled James Lilley, a member of the delegation and later ambassador to China; "we hit it off with him right away."[95] Yang befriended the Bush clan, launching an unlikely decades-spanning friendship that both Bush and Beijing at times deployed at sensitive moments in US-China relations—one that also catapulted Yang's career forward. During his time as host to the Bush clan, Yang was even given an affectionate nickname by the future president's entourage. "We nicknamed him 'Tiger' because he was, in fact, just the opposite," Lilley recalled, "kind and decent."[96]

That affable and charming side of Yang's personality, however, seemingly disappeared at the 2010 ASEAN Regional Forum after Secretary of State Hillary Clinton criticized China's South China Sea claims. Yang stormed out of the meeting for an hour. When he returned, he delivered a thirty-minute rebuttal in which, according to US and Asian accounts, he accused the United States of anti-China plotting, questioned Vietnam's socialist credentials, and threatened Singapore. Then he delivered a famous line that seemed to capture China's new diplomacy: "China is a big country and other countries are small countries, and that's just a fact."[97]

Yang's tone shocked many in the region. Yang was an experienced diplomat with a light touch even in tense moments, and China was a great power that had long used the ARF to reassure others and not reproach them. The marked shift in both Yang's demeanor and in China's regional policy hardly seemed accidental. And indeed, it was not. Both coincided with a shift in China's strategic guidelines—one that, in the wake of the Global Financial Crisis, moved China away from "hiding capabilities and biding time" to "actively accomplishing something," with China now laying the foundations for regional order-building.

For decades, in speeches by Deng, Jiang, and Hu, China's adherence to "hiding capabilities and biding time," or Tao Guang Yang Hui, was explicitly linked to perceptions of China's relative power. That linkage means that when China's perception of power changes, so too would its commitment to Tao Guang Yang Hui.

As this chapter's introduction outlined, China's departure from Tao Guang Yang Hui began nearly a year after the Global Financial Crisis in Hu Jintao's speech to the 11th Ambassadorial Conference. There, in language strikingly different from past ambassadorial addresses—and after announcing favorable trends in the progression of multipolarity and the international balance of power—he announced a revision in Chinese grand strategy. In his speech, Hu offered a new Chinese doctrine, which was to "uphold Tao Guang Yang Hui, and *Actively* Accomplish Something."[98] At first blush, this might appear to be continuity with past policy. But Hu's formulation had departed from Deng's by adding the word "actively," and he then proceeded to elevate the adjusted term to a "strategic guideline." This decision, announced at a major foreign policy conclave, meant that the inclusion of the word "actively" was not a rhetorical twist but a fundamental shift in strategy, though one taken with fidelity and deference to Deng's original formulations. This may appear subtle, but two Chinese scholars—Chen Dingding of Jinan University and Wang Jianwei of the University of Macao—argue that "the significance cannot be underestimated. According to scholars and officials who are familiar with the top decision-making processes, to 'proactively get some things done' [i.e., Actively Accomplish Something] is the emphasis of the new strategy."[99] And that emphasis likely shaped Yang's behavior at the ARF.

The relationship between "Tao Guang Yang Hui" and "Accomplishing Something" is at first not evident to casual observers, in part because it is rooted in Chinese Communist Party ideological jargon. But once that jargon is properly understood, Hu's call to "Actively Accomplish Something" is revealed as far more than a minor semantic shift. Deng's initial formulation of "Tao Guang Yang Hui" had not been explicitly rooted in Marxist dialects—that is, the strategy was posited in its own terms as a standalone approach for Chinese behavior. But in speeches in 1995 and 1998 by Jiang, Tao Guang Yang Hui was put in an explicitly dialectical relationship with the term "Accomplishing Something," which was itself already part of Deng's original admonition.[100] This formulation was echoed by former Foreign Minister Li Zhaoxing, who stated in his memoirs that " 'Tao Guang Yang Hui' and 'Accomplishing Something' have a dialectical relationship."[101]

What does this mean? In Marxist theory, a dialectical relationship is generally one between two opposing concepts or forces. For example, up and down are opposites, but because one cannot exist without the other, they constitute a dialectical unity. Despite this unity, the two sides of a dialectical relationship are not necessarily balanced (which would result in stasis) and one side may be stronger than the other. From this perspective, putting "Tao Guang Yang Hui" in a dialectical relationship with "Accomplishing Something" is profoundly important ideologically and means that these two concepts were viewed essentially as opposites. And while China could not "one-sidedly stress one of these concepts" to the complete absence of the other, as Li Zhaoxing had cautioned, it could nonetheless emphasize one half of this dialectic. Indeed, in Jiang's 1995 speech, which referred to Deng's precept as "Tao Guang Yang Hui, Accomplishing Something," he argued essentially that China should follow Tao Guang Yang Hui but accomplish things where possible, stressing the first half of the formulation.[102] "We have the conditions to 'Accomplish Something,'" Jiang noted, "but when I say 'Accomplish Something' here I mean that only those things that we must do or that we can do are the things that we should do, and we must not try to do everything. We cannot go beyond our reality in trying to do things" on the international stage.[103]

In understanding which side of the dialectic to stress, Jiang clarified in a later speech, the "key is grasping the [international] structure," which in the Party refers to multipolarity and the international balance of power.[104] When that structure changed, China would stress a different part of the dialectic. Indeed, when President Hu then emphasized "*Actively* Accomplishing Something" in 2009 after the Global Financial Crisis and revised the nearly twenty-year-old guideline, the addition of the word "actively" suggested that it was time to emphasize one aspect of the dialectical relationship—the accomplishment part—and that in turn called for an increasingly assertive foreign policy. In that same speech, Hu stated that Tao Guang Yang Hui and "Actively Accomplishing Something" were "part of a dialectical unity" but also that "they are not opposed [对立]," which seems paradoxical since dialectics are based on oppositional relationships.[105] Hu was not saying these concepts were not opposites but rather that they were not part of an "oppositional unity" [对立统一], a key concept in dialects. The meaning of these phrases and their important distinctions are spelled out authoritatively in the *Dictionary of Philosophical Concepts* published by the Party Education Press, which goes into detail on Chinese Communist Party dialectics.[106] An "oppositional unity" is a clear-cut pair of mutually exclusive opposites; in contrast, a "dialectical unity" is a less concrete and more abstract pair of opposites with some possibility of overlap. To translate this into concrete terms, Hu's claim that Tao Guang Yang Hui and "Actively Accomplishing Something" are a "dialectical unity" and not an "oppositional unity" is a statement that these two concepts are not in a binary relationship but have a spectrum between them. In other words, even as China pursued "Actively Accomplishing Something," Hu is saying that it could nonetheless retain some aspects of its opposite concept, "Tao Guang Yang Hui." Hu's subsequent elaboration that Tao Guang Yang is not so extreme as to "unduly humble one's self and exercise complete passivity" and Actively Accomplishing Something is not so extreme as to "arrogantly show one's abilities or to do everything and stop at nothing" serves to accentuate the point.[107] In moving toward Actively Accomplishing Something, Hu noted, China is more actively "using our country's growing overall national strength and international influence to better safeguard our country's interests" and moving away from Tao Guang Yang Hui, which by contrast Hu saw as a strategy for China to "avoid becoming the focus of major international conflicts and to avoid falling into the whirlpool of conflict and confrontation so as to minimize the external pressures and resistance to China's development."[108] From the Cold War to the Global Financial Crisis, China stressed the self-restraining Tao Guang Yang Hui part of the dialectic and sought to blunt "external pressure." After the Cold War, China stressed the more proactive "Actively Accomplishing Something" part of the dialectic and sought to become more assertive, especially within the region.

Hu's 2009 language about "Actively Accomplishing Something" stands in stark contrast to the more passive language in his 2006 address that featured an extended section encouraging China to avoid "speaking too much" and taking leadership.[109] Instead, Hu argues in 2009 that "China must proceed from a strategic height" and "strive for greater action in international affairs," including "assuming international responsibilities and obligations that are compatible with China's national strength and status and giving play to China's unique constructive role," though concern about a U.S.-China so-called "G-2" or major international responsibilities still remained.[110]

The departure from Deng that was marked by Hu's 2009 speech was made even more explicit under Xi Jinping. In an important 2013 address laying out China's new "Great Power Diplomacy" [大国外交], Wang Yi appeared to explicitly reject Tao Guang Yang Hui in favor of "Actively Accomplishing Something." "Today, China is already standing under the world's limelight," Wang argued, drawing a contrast in his terminology with Deng's suggestion to "hide the light" under Tao Guang Yang Hui. Wang declared that, accordingly, China would pursue a "more proactive diplomacy" that involved undertaking new responsibilities.[111] Indeed, Wang Yi used the phrase proactive, active, or actively at least thirteen times in the speech, establishing a clear link to Hu's "Actively Accomplish Something" and demonstrating consistency across administrations.[112] For his part, Xi has not mentioned Tao Guang Yang Hui at all in any of his Party speeches—the first paramount leader since Mao to never use the phrase. And at his 2013 meeting on peripheral diplomacy, Xi appeared to convert Hu's "Actively Accomplish Something" into his signature phrase "Striving for Achievement" [奋发有为], marking the first time the phrase appeared in foreign policy. "We must *strive for achievement* in promoting peripheral diplomacy," Xi declared, "we must work hard for a good periphery for our country's development, and we must make sure our country's development brings benefits to peripheral countries and achieves shared development."[113] The driving focus of China's new assertiveness, Xi made clear, was to exercise greater influence and foster greater connectivity within China's region.

Underpinning this stark contrast with the previous era is a shift in China's sense of self. The "Striving for Achievement" framework is closely related to the Party's concept of "great power diplomacy" [大国外交], which has changed as China views itself as more powerful. This concept referred initially to China's relations with other powers, but Wang Yi's 2013 speech "Exploring Great Power Diplomacy with Chinese Characteristics" demonstrated that China is itself now the great power and needs a diplomacy commensurate with its new status. This view was then legitimized by President Xi Jinping, who echoed the same sentiment in his 2014 Central Foreign Affairs Work Conference: "*China must have its own great power diplomacy . . .* we must enrich and develop the concept of our external work so that it has distinctive Chinese characteristics, Chinese style, and China's dignified bearing."[114] Indeed, as Yan Xuetong notes, "the term of 'major country' [i.e., great power] no longer refers to foreign powers but 'to China itself.' "[115] And as Xu Jin and Du Zheyuan write, "Guiding other states will replace the policy of 'never taking the lead,' which is a policy suitable for weak states, or a policy that signals weakness. . . . China needs to be more assertive and proactive, to take a stand more often, and to take on greater responsibility."[116]

In sum, Tao Guang Yang Hui was the *way* for China to achieve the *end* of a reduced risk of US-led containment. After the Global Financial Crisis, this strategy was no longer seen as necessary; instead, "Actively Accomplishing Something" and "Striving for Achievement" became the *way* for China to achieve the *end* of greater regional influence through a strategy that openly seeks to bind China's neighbors to it more tightly, offer an alternative to US balancing and alliances, and pursue China's regional and territorial interests more forcefully. As with the shift in ends and ways, the new strategy also entailed a marked shift in means.

Means—Instruments for Building

As the preceding sections make clear, China's new strategy was not abstract, and high-level speeches make clear how the strategy would be translated into specific instruments of statecraft. In Hu's important 2009 11th Ambassadorial Conference speech, he elaborated on what "Actively Accomplish Something" and China's new assertiveness meant in concrete terms. Fundamentally, it meant significant and coordinated changes in China's political, economic, and military behavior, all with an eye toward proactively reshaping the region. With respect to China's political behavior, Hu declared that China "must *more actively* participate in the formulation of international rules" and institutions, anticipating the eventual creation of AIIB and leadership of CICA.[117] On economic issues, he declared China "must *more actively* promote the reform of the international economic and financial system" and proposed robust infrastructure investment as a part of this.[118] "In particular," and anticipating the later BRI, Hu declared that "we must actively participate in and vigorously promote the construction of surrounding highways, railways, communications, and energy channels in the periphery to form a network of interconnected and interoperable infrastructure around China."[119] And on militarized territorial disputes, Hu declared that China "must *more actively* promote the resolution of international and regional hot-spots related to China's core interests . . . strengthen our strategic planning, *make more offensive moves* [先手棋], and actively guide the situation to develop in a favorable direction."[120] This assertive language essentially called for taking the initiative and resolving disputes on China's terms and was a sharp departure from Hu's language at the 2006 Foreign Affairs Work Forum, where he declared in a discussion of China's core interests that "for issues that do not impede the overall situation, we must embody mutual understanding and mutual accommodation so that we can concentrate our efforts on safeguarding and developing longer-term and more important national interests."[121] "More active" involvement would require different military capabilities, especially those oriented toward sea control and amphibious operations rather than the sea denial of blunting.

Xi's efforts to elevate Peripheral Diplomacy and create a "Community of Common Destiny" essentially build on the foundation Hu laid in in his 2009 speech.

First, on institutional and economic issues, Xi has been clear in multiple speeches that major Chinese leadership efforts, like the BRI and the AIIB, are part of his strategy for creating a "Community of Common Destiny" and are core parts of "peripheral diplomacy," which in turn is necessary for national rejuvenation. His speeches at the Indonesian Parliament and in Kazakhstan announcing BRI, and his speeches before APEC announcing AIIB, all make this linkage clear. As discussed earlier, Xi made the theme of the entire 2015 Boao Forum "Asia's New Future: Towards a Community of Common Destiny" and mentioned these same instruments as essential. And at the 2017 BRI Forum, Xi was explicit on these linkages, stating that all parties to BRI would "continue to move closer toward a Community of Common Destiny for mankind. This is what I had in mind when I first put forward the Belt and Road Initiative. It is also the ultimate goal of this initiative."[122] In short, these are the economic and institutional means at the heart of China's grand strategy to build regional order.

In contrast to public speeches, Xi's Party speeches have been more explicit about how these instruments will boost China's regional influence, particularly his address to the 2013 Work Forum on Peripheral Diplomacy that presaged the maturation of AIIB, BRI, and other major regional initiatives.[123] In that address, and on the economic side, Xi proposed offering public goods and facilitating mutual interdependence, both of which would "create a closer network of common interests, and better integrate China's interests with [neighbors], so that they can benefit from China's development."[124] He explained precisely how China would do this. "We must make every effort to achieve mutually beneficial reciprocity," Xi declared, "We have to make overall plans for the use of our resources . . . [and] take advantage of our comparative strengths, accurately identify strategic points of convergence for mutually beneficial cooperation with neighbors, and take an active part in regional economic cooperation."[125] In practical terms, he stated, "we should work with our neighbors to speed up connection of infrastructure between China and our neighboring countries" and explicitly listed the BRI and AIIB as tools to do so.[126] In addition, Xi wanted to "accelerate the implementation of the strategy of free trade zones" and to put "our neighboring countries as the base," another sign of the elevation of the periphery.[127] New investment as well as active interlinkage between Chinese border regions and neighbors was also essential. The overall objective, Xi stated, was "to create a new pattern of regional economic integration," one that he declared multiple times would be linked closely to China.[128] Left unstated was that the active cultivation of this kind of asymmetric interdependence would give China great freedom of maneuver and potentially constrain its neighbors as well.

Second, on security issues, Xi appears to see multilateral organizations as a means to create the "Community of Common Destiny" with a diminished role for US alliances. In his 2013 Peripheral Diplomacy Work Forum address, Xi declared boldly that "a new outlook on security is required" for Asia and that, to provide it, China "must develop a comprehensive security strategy with neighboring countries."[129] Similarly, at the institutional level, Xi was clear that goals for regional influence would require Beijing to "actively participate in regional and sub-regional security initiatives."[130] These remarks anticipated China's high-profile efforts to use its chairmanship of CICA to put forward its own pan-Asian vision of Asian security architecture, where Xi urged Asian states to create a Community of Common Destiny and put at its center a detailed New Asian Security Concept of "common, comprehensive, cooperative, and sustainable security." As Chapter 9 discusses, that four-pronged concept explicitly called external alliances into question and suggested Asian states were responsible for Asia's affairs.[131] For example, Xi's address at the "Community of Common Destiny"-themed 2015 Boao Forum stated unequivocally that "to build a community of common destiny, we need to pursue common, comprehensive, cooperative and sustainable security. . . . As people of all countries share common destiny and become increasingly interdependent . . . the Cold War mentality should truly be discarded and new security concepts be nurtured as we explore a path for Asia that ensures security for all, by all and of all."[132] And in a section of the 19th Party Congress Political Report discussing the Community of

Common Destiny, Xi declared that achieving it would require "common, comprehensive, cooperative, and sustainable security," and he called for all states to "resolutely reject the Cold War mentality and power politics, and take a new approach to developing state-to-state relations with communication, not confrontation, and with partnership, not alliance."[133] Multilateral organizations, then, are seen as a critical instrument for rewriting regional norms on Asian security, enhancing China's leadership, and reducing the US role. Speaking broadly about the power of these norms, Xi suggested in his 2013 Work Forum on Peripheral Diplomacy address that "we must embrace and practice these ideas, so that they will become the shared beliefs and norms of conduct for the whole region."[134]

Military instruments were a tool for achieving greater regional influence, including through intensified security ties with neighbors, influence on resolving territorial disputes, and the provision of public security goods. Regarding ties with neighbors, Xi's calls for a "Community of Common Destiny" often stress the importance of China expanding security cooperation with Asian neighbors. In a 2013 address, Wang Yi linked "cooperation in traditional and non-traditional security fields" and expanded "defense and security exchanges with neighbors" as part of this effort.[135] With respect to public security goods, China's rhetoric in CICA is clear that China views itself as a future public security provider. China's anti-piracy missions are an element of this, but so too are more ambitious future plans. For example, Chinese Defense Minister Wei Fenghe announced that China was "ready to provide security guarantees for the One Belt, One Road project," a sign that the Community of Common Destiny may involve the provision of public security goods by the Chinese military.[136] Finally, China has toughened its position on territorial disputes after the 2008 Global Financial Crisis beginning with Hu's own 11th Ambassadorial Conference Address. That strong rhetoric has continued into the present, with Xi Jinping promising in his 2017 address to the NPC that "not one inch" of territory would be separated from China.[137]

In sum, statements by Hu and Xi—as well as their various ministers—strongly suggest that political, economic, and military tools were coordinated together to advance China's peripheral diplomacy and its "Community of Common Destiny." Hu's decision to emphasize "Actively Accomplishing Something" over "Tao Guang Yang Hui" in 2009 reshaped Chinese grand strategy and was the driver behind the "new assertiveness" so many detected in China's post–Global Financial Crisis conduct. Some of the most tangible manifestations of this new strategy were in the military domain as China began to build carrier battlegroups, amphibious vessels, and overseas facilities—a development we now turn to in the next chapter.

"Make More Offensive Moves"

Implementing Military Building

"In 2009, China put forward the idea and plan for building aircraft carriers. This indicates China has entered the historical era of building itself into a maritime great power."[1]

—*China's State Oceanic Administration, 2010*

For much of his life, the "father of China's Navy" had never seen the sea. Liu Huaqing grew up in the mountains, fought with the Communists at the age of fourteen, went on the Long March, and served with distinction as an officer in the People's Liberation Army. It was not until February 1952, when the thirty-six-year-old Liu was summoned to Beijing and informed to his apparent surprise that he would be made deputy political commissar of the newly created Dalian Naval Academy, that he forged what he called his "indissoluble bond with the sea."[2]

At the time, the PLA had virtually no navy. It had been focused on guerrilla warfare for decades, so when Liu reported to the academy, he soon found out most of the cadets and staff had never spent much time on the open ocean. Only a small handful had been allowed field training, and that was on a rented merchant boat propelled by sails, to the amusement of both the students and staff. Liu made it a priority to improve the school's field training: the next year, he set out with the trainees for a few weeks on an actual naval vessel—ironically, a decommissioned American Navy ship built before the Second World War. "This was the first time in my life I'd gone to sea," Liu wrote in his memoirs, and it went far from smoothly. "Old sailors and students accustomed to sea life don't fall seasick easily," Liu recounted, "but although I was a veteran soldier, I was hardly a veteran sailor." The father of the Chinese Navy, along with most of his trainees, spent much of the journey vomiting.[3]

Decades later, China's Navy is modern, professional, and capable. It has moved from its early reliance on sailboats and decommissioned US vessels to now rival the United States within the Indo-Pacific in quantitative and increasingly qualitative terms, a credit to Liu's dedication and leadership. Liu's brief stint at Dalian had set him up for a long career focused on naval affairs, and not long after his fateful sea outing, Liu left China to study at the Soviet Union's Voroshilov Naval Academy for four years to get the training so few in China had. He then rose rapidly to become the longest-serving commander of the People's Liberation Army Navy, the vice chairman of China's Central Military Commission, and then a member of China's ruling Politburo Standing Committee.

Liu's great dream was a carrier-centric navy focused on sea control to safeguard China's overseas interests. His legacy when he retired, however, was a submarine-centric navy focused on *sea denial* to prevent US military intervention in the waters near China. Liu's push for aircraft carriers had been repeatedly overruled, as Chapter 4 discussed, because Chinese leaders were focused on blunting the American military threat, and that mission was better accomplished with asymmetric weapons like submarines than more vulnerable assets like carriers—which might even frighten China's neighbors and push them toward the United States. Liu dutifully oversaw the construction of that asymmetric navy, but he nonetheless resolved that "if China does not build an aircraft carrier, I will die with my eyelids open [不搞航空母舰，我死不瞑目]."[4] Liu died in 2011, one year before China launched its first aircraft carrier. But by then, the reorientation of China'sNavy he had long hoped for toward sea control, the blue-water, and aircraft carriers was already underway.

This chapter discusses that reorientation.[5] It argues that when the Global Financial Crisis struck and reduced China's assessment of US power, Chinese grand strategy shifted. A focus on blunting American power gave way to one focused on building the foundations for China-led order within Asia. The military component of this grand strategy was critical. Chinese writers knew that the mines, missiles, and submarines so useful in denying US operations or intervention as part of China's *blunting* strategy were less useful for a strategy to *build* order by assembling enduring military leverage over China's neighbors. These kinds of assets could not on their own seize or hold distant islands or waters, safeguard sea lines of communication, allow China to intervene in the affairs of its neighbors, or provide public security goods. For that, China needed a different force structure, one better suited for sea control, amphibious warfare, and power projection. China's leaders, as Liu's own writings suggest, had long wanted such a structure but had felt constrained in pursuing it, and had largely postponed those plans by making minimal, unthreatening investments in such a force structure. The crisis largely lifted those constraints, and China emerged from it more confident in itself, less impressed with US power and resolve, and more convinced that the 1990s-era fears that its frightened neighbors would encircle China were a product of past circumstances and not the emerging reality before them. And so, shortly after the crisis, China significantly stepped up investments in constructing aircraft carriers, more capable surface vessels, amphibious warfare capabilities, and even overseas bases—all while building facilities in the South China Sea and increasing its territorial assertiveness.

To make this argument, this chapter follows an approach discussed in Chapter 4 and analyzes authoritative Chinese texts and four key dimensions of China's behavior. These dimensions include what China acquired and when (acquisition); how China thinks it might fight (doctrine); how and where China deploys its military (force posture); and how China prepares to fight (training). A focus on texts and these key dimensions of behavior can help us test competing theories explaining China's military investments and behavior.

As this chapter demonstrates, the best explanation for China's military behavior after the Global Financial Crisis is that Beijing sought capabilities to more effectively deal with its neighbors in the Indo-Pacific so it could create the military foundations for regional hegemony—all as part of a broader post-crisis grand strategy to *build* regional order.

Other prevailing explanations that assume China would emulate the capabilities of others under most circumstances (diffusion, adoption capacity), or that powerful vested interests shaped China's behavior (bureaucratic politics), or that it was focused primarily on the US threat (blunting) fail to adequately explain the shift in its behavior. As we will see, none of these explanations can account for why China waited to acquire capabilities it could have acquired sooner, nor can China's concern over the US threat explain why it pursued capabilities that would be uniquely vulnerable to the US military. The best explanation for China's investments in carriers, more capable surface vessels, and overseas facilities is that these capabilities were part of an effort at building order across the region.

Chinese Military Texts

Chinese authoritative and pseudo-authoritative texts demonstrate shifts in Chinese military strategy after the Global Financial Crisis. Admittedly, there are limitations to this approach: many of the materials available for the 1980s or 1990s are not available for the last decade, and while the memoirs and selected works of several Central Military Commission (CMC) vice chairmen whose terms ended as late as 2002 are available, not a single volume is available for any who served after that period. Those sources that do exist—primarily speeches by senior leaders and White Papers—suggest that the Global Financial Crisis was followed by a decision by Beijing to pursue a *building* strategy. This would lead it to invest in capabilities that would enable it not merely to blunt American power but to project power, launch amphibious invasions, intervene in the Indo-Pacific to protect overseas interests, and provide what it called "public security goods."

A Shift in Strategy

After the Global Financial Crisis, it appears that top Chinese leadership decided to reorient Chinese grand strategy toward *building* order in China's periphery, especially by expanding its regional influence and securing China's sovereignty and overseas interests. Signs of that shift were occasionally detectable even earlier, for example, when Hu Jintao told the PLA to prepare for "New Historic Missions" including greater overseas involvement, but texts and behavior alike show a more significant movement in this direction was initiated by the Global Financial Crisis. In general, Chinese sources emphasize two reasons for a shift in strategy: (1) a desire to better protect China's maritime rights and interests; and (2) a desire to protect China's expanding overseas interests, particularly in the Indo-Pacific.

First, in President Hu's 2009 Ambassadorial Conference address—which linked China's strategic adjustment to the Global Financial Crisis—this military shift is clear. It was in that speech that Hu revised Tao Guang Yang Hui by encouraging "Actively Accomplish Something," and he made clear that some of the areas of greater activism would be territorial: China "must *more actively* promote the resolution of international and regional hot-spots related to China's core interests, and regarding the issues concerning our core interests, we must strengthen our strategic planning, *make more offensive moves* [先手棋], and actively guide the situation to develop in a favorable direction."[6] This assertive language essentially called for taking the initiative and resolving disputes on China's terms. In contrast, at the 2006 Central Foreign Affairs Work Forum, Hu had softer language on core interests: "for issues that do not impede the overall situation, we must embody mutual understanding and mutual accommodation so that we can concentrate our efforts on safeguarding and developing longer-term and more important national interests."[7] In an articulation of the new approach in 2010, as the last chapter outlined, Foreign Minister Yang Jiechi told Southeast Asian states concerned about its claims in the South China Sea that "China is a big country and other countries are small countries, and that's just a fact."[8]

Hu's focus on proactively resolving China's territorial disputes and securing its overseas interests was further emphasized by President Xi, who, like Hu, suggested a subtle shift away from peace and development. In a 2013 Politburo

Study Session on the concept of "Peace and Development," Xi Jinping declared in stark language that "We love peace and adhere to the path of peaceful development but we cannot give up our country's legitimate rights and interests, and we cannot sacrifice the core interests of the country."[9] Xi repeated this same language verbatim at another Politburo Study Session that year in a session on "the construction of maritime power" in reference to China's maritime sovereignty.[10] China needed to "prepare to deal with various complex situations," he said of various territorial disputes, and it would be "necessary to coordinate maintaining stability with safeguarding rights," that is, to strengthen the protection of China's sovereignty short of war.[11] In particular, "China needed to make sure that the protection of maritime rights and interests was matched with the enhancement of China's comprehensive national strength."[12] As China got stronger—as it had after the Global Financial Crisis—Beijing would take a correspondingly firmer line on territorial disputes. In 2014, when Foreign Minister Wang Yi was asked about China's new assertiveness, he answered, "We will never bully smaller countries, yet we will never accept unreasonable demands from smaller countries. On issues of territory and sovereignty, China's position is firm and clear."[13]

Second, China's focus was not only on territorial disputes but increasingly on overseas interests, particularly the resource flows across the Indo-Pacific on which China's economy depended. The 2008 Defense White Paper was the first to note that "struggles for strategic resources," an oblique reference to oil, were intensifying and that the PLAN needed to develop the ability to operate in "distant waters" [远海].[14] Then, beginning in 2009, Hu elevated a focus on these "overseas interests" in his 2009 Ambassadorial Conference address. While Hu had also mentioned these in his 2004 Ambassadorial Conference address, the attention they received in 2009 was far more significant and indicated an elevation of their importance and linked their protection with growing Chinese strength. He specifically mentioned overseas interests at the beginning of his speech, noting that as China grew more powerful, it would have more overseas interests, and that "the greater the expansion of overseas interests" the more "pressure and resistance" China would face."[15] In a departure from previous addresses, he listed "persisting in safeguarding China's overseas interests and strengthening the capacity building of rights protection" as an enumerated task for China's foreign policy and devoted an entire section of his speech to it. For the first time in any major speech, Hu declared that "overseas interests have become an important part of China's national interests."[16]

This perspective was sustained in the transition to Xi's administration. In 2012, China's Defense White Paper began by explicitly stressing the importance of China's overseas economic interests in a way previous papers had never before. The 2013 White Paper was the first with its own subsection on "protecting overseas interests,"[17] which it defined as "overseas energy resources" as well as "strategic sea lines of communication." The paper noted that these interests were becoming "increasingly prominent" in China's security situation and that "the security risks to China's overseas interests are on the rise." Xi Jinping often stressed these themes too, including in a 2014 speech: "The maritime channel is China's main channel for foreign trade and energy imports. Safeguarding the freedom and safety of maritime navigation is of vital importance to China."[18] Then, the 2015 White Paper listed "safeguarding the security of China's overseas interests" as one of the eight "strategic tasks" of the military. China previously used "comprehensive tasks" [总任务] and "comprehensive goals" [总目标] to indicate its objectives, so the identification of overseas interests as a "strategic task" was important.[19] The White Paper defined overseas interests as "energy and resources, strategic sea lines of communication (SLOCs), as well as institutions, personnel and assets abroad." It also listed specific threats to the "security of overseas interests," which included "international and regional turmoil, terrorism, piracy, serious natural disasters and epidemics." The paper also stressed how serious these threats were, finding that the vulnerability of China's overseas interests "has become an imminent issue."

As China's strength grew relative to the United States, it became possible and even increasingly important for China to attend to its territorial and overseas interests. To accomplish this goal, China needed to lay the foundations for a wider range of military missions that would help it *build* regional order.

A Building Strategy

As part of China's *building* strategy after the Global Financial Crisis, Beijing began to emphasize the importance of maritime power. China's past force structure largely optimized for *blunting* American power would be inadequate to hold or seize the islands and waters China claimed, to intervene overseas to protect Chinese interests, to police the SLOCs upon which China depended, or to provide the region public security goods that would burnish China's leadership credentials.

As the subsequent cases illustrate, Chinese political and military texts have for decades made clear what capabilities China believed were necessary for securing its regional interests—that is, what instruments were needed for its *building* strategy. These doctrinal texts, as well as speeches from top leaders ranging from Zhou Enlai to Liu Huaqing, all make clear that aircraft carriers as well as surface vessels capable of anti-submarine warfare (ASW), anti-air warfare (AAW), mine countermeasures (MCM), and amphibious warfare (AMW) would all be essential in contingencies involving the East and South China Seas, the Taiwan Strait, the Korean Peninsula, and the protection of overseas Chinese interests and resource flows.[20] In other words, as the cases demonstrate, the decision to focus on such capabilities was not the result of changing beliefs about their efficacy or changing financial situations, but primarily about changed political circumstances and the new strategy they produced.

After the Global Financial Crisis, China stressed that to achieve its maritime security interests, it needed to increase its investments in sea control platforms—especially in blue-water capabilities that it had deliberately neglected. In short, a different kind of naval investment was needed for a *building* strategy. The State Oceanic Administration, which plays an important role in developing civilian and military components of China's maritime strategy, indicated that a strategic shift occurred around this time. While China had set ambitious goals in 2003 for building maritime power and encouraged the PLAN to take "new historic missions" abroad in 2004, it was only in 2009 that they began to execute them. As the report notes, "In 2009, China put forward an idea and plan for building aircraft carriers. This indicates China has entered the historical era of building itself into a maritime great power." It went on to argue, "The period 2010–2020 is a key historical stage for achieving this strategic mission, and the goal is to strive to become a medium-sized maritime great power [中等海洋强国] during this period."[21]

A few years later, China's 2012 Defense White Paper was the first to argue that "China is a major maritime as well as land country," emphasizing a renewed focus on regional maritime challenges and a continued reorientation of the PLA in that direction. It argued that China needed to acquire "blue-water capabilities," consistent with a *building* strategy and a reversal from its past deprioritization of carriers and blue-water surface vessels during its *blunting* phase. It stated that "securing the country's peaceful development" was a "sacred mission," an objective that required a more active role in the Indo-Pacific. That same year, in Hu's 18th Party Congress Work Report, he declared for the first time in such an address that China's leadership needed to "build China into a maritime great power" [海洋强国] and "resolutely safeguard China's maritime rights and interests."[22] China's blue-water focus was official.

That focus was also accentuated in subsequent documents. For example, Xi's 2013 Politburo Study Session on building Chinese "maritime power" was convened to discuss China's maritime strategy and included senior officials from the State Oceanic Administration's Institute of Ocean Development Strategy who were responsible for developing it. In his address to the Politburo, Xi stressed that the focus on improving China's maritime power was part of a broader plan dating back to Hu Jintao: "The 18th Party Congress put forward an important plan for building China into a maritime great power. The implementation of this important plan is of great and far-reaching significance . . . for safeguarding national sovereignty, security, and development interests" and "for achieving the great rejuvenation of the Chinese nation." Xi said that Beijing must "promote building China into a maritime great power to continuously realize new achievements." Unsurprisingly, Xi repeatedly stressed the need to "improve China's ability to protect its maritime rights and interests."[23] Premier Li Keqiang made the same point in his Report on the Work of the Government the next year, adding that "the seas are our valuable national territory."[24] Some time later, in a visit to a major shipbuilder, Xi stressed, "The marine industry is related to the survival and development of the nation, it is related to the rise and fall of the country. It meets the requirements of building maritime power."[25]

China's Defense White Papers continued to highlight this new strategy. China's 2015 Defense White Paper stated that "the traditional mentality that land outweighs sea must be abandoned, and great importance has to be attached to managing the seas and oceans and protecting maritime rights and interests." It also noted that "it is necessary for China to develop a modern maritime military force structure commensurate with its national security and development interests" and to "safeguard its national sovereignty and maritime rights and interests, protect the security of strategic SLOCs and overseas interests." In short, China would need to build itself into a maritime power.

This objective had direct operational implications and constituted a fundamentally different military with substantially different requirements, the White Paper noted:

> In line with the strategic requirement of offshore waters defense and open seas protection, the PLA Navy (PLAN) will gradually shift its focus from "offshore waters defense" to the combination of "offshore waters defense" with "open seas protection," and build a combined, multi-functional, and efficient marine combat force structure. The PLAN will enhance its capabilities for strategic deterrence and counterattack, maritime maneuvers, joint operations at sea, comprehensive defense and comprehensive support.

An official commentary by one of the drafters of the White Paper elaborated on this point: "The key to safeguarding the safety of overseas interests is achieved through . . . international peacekeeping, offshore escort, joint anti-terrorism, joint military exercises, overseas evacuation, and international rescue operations."[26] China would need to invest more in power projection platforms like aircraft carriers and surface vessels to realize this vision, and that is indeed what we see in the cases discussed in this chapter.

Aircraft Carriers

It seems preposterous that a basketball player who spent twelve years playing for the Guangzhou Military Region's team would be at the center of China's efforts to obtain an aircraft carrier. But Xu Zengping, the man now called a "national hero" and a "red capitalist" by many, was the critical middleman in an effort by PLA officials to purchase the *Varyag*—an incomplete hull from the Soviet Union's most advanced operational carrier class that had been left languishing in a Ukrainian shipyard. Over the last decade, Xu has gradually revealed his role in an acquisition that gave China its first aircraft carrier, the *Liaoning*, as well as the critical blueprints for more carriers that followed.

Xu joined the PLA in 1971 and left to go into business in the 1980s, founded a trading company that he claims made him wealthy, and then moved to Hong Kong with his wife—a basketball player on China's national team who once played alongside Yao Ming's mother.[27] Roughly a decade later, Xu encountered PLAN Vice Admiral He Pengfei, who wanted Xu to serve as the military's intermediary in the *Varyag* purchase and met with him personally over a dozen times. "I was totally convinced and moved by him when he held my hand and said: 'Please do me a favor—go and buy [the carrier] and bring it back for our country and our army,'" Xu later recounted in an interview with the journalist Minnie Chan.[28] PLA intelligence chief Major General Ji Shengde—who later tried to steer hundreds of thousands of dollars to US political candidates in the late 1990s—was the "real boss" in the effort, according to Xu. He "personally endorsed my planning and gave me a lot of support and professional advice."[29] In March 1997, Xu signed on to the effort.

To avoid Western opposition to the purchase—and given China's own reluctance to depart from the "hiding capabilities and biding time" guideline with a flashy *public* carrier acquisition that could frighten others—Xu and his colleagues knew they had to deceive the world about Xu's wealth, intentions, and government connections. Ironically, they did so with Chinese government support. Almost immediately after signing on, Xu got to work cultivating an image as an outlandish tycoon who wanted to use the carrier to build a floating casino in Macao. In June that year, his company sponsored a famous publicity stunt to mark the handover of Hong Kong to China, which saw Taiwanese daredevil Blackie Ko drive a car over the Hukou Waterfall on the Yellow River.[30] Then, in August, Xu set up a Macao shell company, the Agência Turistica e Diversões Chong Lot, and spent nearly $1 million acquiring documents from Macao that would authorize a floating casino.[31] Next, Xu bought one of the most expensive villas in Hong Kong for almost $30 million. "In the very beginning, I needed to try every means to let the outside world believe the deal was just a pure personal investment," Xu recounted, "The most simple way was to buy the most luxurious home in the city because Western countries didn't believe Beijing would give me money to buy a villa."[32] The purchase of the villa was part of an elaborate deception, so Xu posed for magazine spreads that featured him well dressed and in stylish thick-framed glasses reclining next to his wife in a gilded and garish luxury interior.[33] Xu also noted that funds flowed into his effort from a variety of murky sources. For example, he sold "equity positions" in one of his shell companies to a Chinese SOE for $30 million, and acknowledged later that "All the transfers were done in an accounting firm in Beijing, not in Hong Kong or Macao, because we couldn't let the outside world know there was a state-owned company involved in the deal."[34] He also received funds from China's state-owned Huaxia Bank.[35] And some wealthy Hong Kong individuals also helped capitalize the effort, with one providing some $30 million to him that year "without any guarantee" requested.[36] Xu used the funds to set up an office in Kiev, and quite tellingly, one in Beijing too. He hired roughly a dozen shipbuilding and naval experts to help with the deal, including Xiao Yun—then the deputy head of the PLAN air force's armament department—who retired as a civilian so he could lead Xu's Beijing office.[37] Former CMC officials served as intermediaries between Xu and the PLA to ensure some plausible deniability.[38]

After putting together a cover story, financing, and offices, Xu went to Kiev. From October 1997 to March 1998, Xu worked hard to close the deal. One winter day, he was even allowed to stroll atop the desolate, rusted, and incongruously snow-covered carrier deck. Xu wore a white button-down shirt and a formal brown vest—and somewhat discordantly—a billowy bright yellow ski jacket from The North Face with matching pants. "It was the first time I had ever been on a carrier and I was overwhelmed [by its size]."[39] Over the following months, Xu paid millions in bribes and kept the Ukrainian sellers liquored up in the evenings. "I felt that I was soaking in liquor back then," Xu remembers, "In the critical four days, I brought them more than 50 bottles [of Erguotou, a 100-proof Chinese liquor]. But I still felt I had the energy to do it and was always able to keep a sober mind because my drinking was goal-directed; the Ukrainians were drinking to get drunk."[40] A deal was struck to sell the carrier for $20 million, but Xu wanted more than the carrier itself, he also wanted the blueprints and the engines—which were of course hard to justify given his nominal plans for a floating casino. "The blueprints were more precious than the aircraft carrier," he told himself at the time, "and they must be bought together."[41] Eventually, the Ukrainian side relented and offered up the forty-five tons worth of documents that later proved invaluable in China's refit of the *Varyag* and in the construction of its own carriers. As for the engines, which were far more advanced than anything China could manufacture, both sides of the deal suggested publicly that they had already been removed. As Xu put it, "the engine removal [reports] were all cover stories to confuse the Western countries."[42] The engines were in actuality still on the ship, Xu recounted, and they were "brand new and carefully grease-sealed" and now powered China's first carrier.[43] With the deal completed, Xu's next task was transporting the carrier to the Dalian shipyards—a process that took four years given delays in obtaining transit permissions from Turkey to cross out of the Black Sea through the Bosporus. This time, public Chinese government intervention was necessary. Jiang Zemin visited Ankara in April 2000, promised market access for Turkish goods, and then agreed to some twenty safety conditions and a $1 billion insurance guarantee to secure the vessel's passage.[44] In March 2002, the *Varyag*'s long voyage out of Ukraine ended in Dalian.

But then an even longer voyage started. It would be seven long years before serious work would even *begin* on the *Varyag* to turn it into an operational aircraft carrier. All of China's clever deceptions, careful planning, diplomatic maneuvering, and staggering expenditures (over $120 million spent on the acquisition in total) ended anticlimactically in a long period of waiting. The carrier acquisition was an investment in a future blue-water force. But for China, still wary of antagonizing the United States and its neighbors, that future had not yet arrived.

After the *Varyag* docked in Dalian, Jiang and Hu both reportedly visited it the next year. But in lieu of authorizing a major refit of the carrier that would make it operational, they instead merely supported a series of studies on refurbishing that took place from 2004 to 2005.[45] When the final studies were completed, the CMC signed off on them and the *Varyag* was then towed into a berth in the Dalian Shipyard, where it was cleaned, repainted, sprayed with anti-corrosion coating, and then underwent basic repair to preserve the hull.[46] The work ended in December 2005, and *Varyag* was then promptly left alone for the next several years—or what some Chinese sources call "three years of stillness"—and no major work was done.[47] Some reports suggest work may have been done on the carrier's interior, but China was not ready to incur the political and strategic costs of a carrier program, so any major refurbishment that would be detectable by foreign governments could not take place. Indeed, as late as 2008, a spokesman for China's Commission on Science, Technology, and Industry for National Defense (COSTIND) told the public that major construction had not begun.[48]

It was not until after the Global Financial Crisis that work on the carrier began in earnest.[49] This was part of an official adjustment of China's grand strategy according to the State Oceanic Administration, which was charged with developing its maritime component. Their 2010 report made the shift clear: "In 2009, China put forward an idea and plan for building aircraft carriers. These indicate China has entered the historical era of building itself into a maritime great power."[50] Some accounts based on interviews with Chinese military sources indicate that

China's carrier program was approved at an expanded meeting of the Politburo in April 2009, and that the decision was previously fraught because of fears "that it would fan concerns in neighboring nations about the Chinese military threat."[51] A month after this rumored Politburo meeting, in May 2009, the carrier was towed into a new berth, the project was given a new director (Yang Lei), an agreement was signed with the Dalian Shipyards, the carrier's original Soviet pennant and ship's name were finally removed, and major work began shortly thereafter.[52] The refit took roughly fifteen months from 2009 until late 2011.[53]

Around this same time, China began planning construction of its own indigenous carrier (Type 002) based on the *Varyag*'s blueprints—possibly as early as 2009. Planning began in 2013, construction in March 2015, and sea trials in 2018.[54] A third Chinese carrier (Type 003) has been under construction since 2015 and is expected to have a flattop rather than a ramp as well as an electromagnetic catapult.[55] Additional carriers in this Type 003 line are expected, based on the informal assessments of PLAN officials. Finally, a fourth nuclear-powered carrier class (Type 004) has been under development, with plans accidentally leaked by the China Shipbuilding Industry Corporation (CSIC).[56] In sum, the acquisition timeline shows the post-crisis shift to a carrier-based navy was rapid, with China promptly ending decades of constraints on its carrier program and working so furiously that within a decade it had two completed carriers, one near completion, one more under construction, and nuclear-powered carriers in planning.

This raises an important puzzle: why did China essentially launch its carrier program in 2009? As Chapter 4 demonstrated, the answer has less to do with China's ability to build and acquire carriers than one might suspect, nor was the delay about bureaucratic resistance since top officials within the military and on the Politburo Standing Committee supported the program. None of these can explain China's shift on carriers in 2009.

Others suggest that China's pursuit of a blue-water navy was motivated by nationalism or perhaps changing views on carrier utility, but both explanations are inadequate for the same reason—China has long seen carriers as essential to regional contingencies. If status were the driving motivator and not China's strategic interests, then the Party could have pursued a barely functional show carrier and refurbished it for military service (like Brazil and Thailand) when its legitimacy was most in doubt after Tiananmen Square. It consciously did not do so then, refusing to even purchase the *Varyag* because of the political risk, and three other carriers it purchased (the HMS *Melbourne*, the *Minsk*, and the *Kiev*) were either scrapped or converted into parks and hotels rather than entered into service.[57] Since then, China's carrier ambitions have gone far beyond what status might require: Beijing is building four to six carriers, attendant carrier battle groups, replenishment infrastructure, and overseas facilities—all of which permanently alters China's force structure.

The most defensible explanation for this course of action is also the simplest: Beijing has understood for more than fifty years that a carrier and blue-water PLAN would help it accomplish strategic goals, particularly in its home region. As early as 1970, Xiao Jingguang, the first commander of the PLAN, had said, "the Chinese Navy needs aircraft carriers: if a fleet is active in the open sea without an aircraft carrier, there is no air supremacy, and without air supremacy, there is no victory."[58] In 1973, Chinese Premier Zhou Enlai linked carriers to China's maritime sovereignty: "Our Nansha and Xisha Islands are occupied by the Republic of Vietnam (South Vietnam); without an aircraft carrier, we cannot put China's Navy at risk [by] fighting," as China's Navy would be left "to fight just with bayonets."[59] Senior PLAN officials continued to hold this view years later. In November 1986, Liu Huaqing was part of a "naval development strategy study group" that included "military and civilian leaders as well as renowned experts" from all over the government. "From the perspective of what was needed to protect China's maritime rights and interests, recover Nansha and Taiwan, and deal with other strategic circumstances," he noted in his memoir, the members "recommended constructing an aircraft carrier."[60] Liu further argued that, without an aircraft carrier, it would be difficult to secure Chinese interests with surface vessels alone. The next year, he told the PLA General Staff, "when thinking about maritime formations, we had only considered destroyers, frigates, and submarines; after further research, we realized that without air cover, there was no way these formations would be able to fight outside the radius of shore-based combat aircraft," and that even *within* the range of shore-based aircraft (e.g., a Taiwan scenario), air cover would simply not reach quickly enough in times of crisis.[61] Liu wrote that the PLA General Staff generally agreed with his report and escalated the question of carrier acquisition, all of which suggests that at least as early as 1987, a Chinese focus on narrower local operational contingencies stressed the need for an aircraft carrier. This perspective persisted after the Cold War too. In 1995, Liu in a high-level meeting on aircraft carriers stated, "Defending the South China Sea, peacefully reuniting with Taiwan, safeguarding maritime rights and interests—all require aircraft carriers."[62] As China's dependence on overseas resource and commodity flows increased in the early 1990s, the need for carriers that could venture into the Indian Ocean increased too.

If the change in China's carrier ambitions was not the result of changes in China's capabilities, bureaucratic politics, status anxieties, or assessments of carrier utility, then what was it? The answer lies in China's grand strategy. Although Beijing understood that carriers would be useful against neighbors in local conflicts and in exercising sea control, these goals did not fit into China's *blunting* strategy. Beijing authorized studies and planning for a future carrier force but waited to launch the program until the timing was right. After the 2008 Global Financial Crisis, the timing had improved markedly, and China now focused on "actively accomplishing something" rather than merely "hiding capabilities and biding time." Accordingly, China began to openly build the foundations for regional hegemony, which meant prioritizing conflicts with neighbors and being able to exercise sea control, pursue amphibious landings, and patrol SLOCs. In pursuit of these capabilities, Beijing was no longer as concerned about the costs of alarming its neighbors or the United States. For these reasons, a larger carrier-based navy was a strategic objective whose time had come.

The most persuasive objection to this argument is that China's plans for a carrier were proceeding according to a fixed modernization timeline that was largely divorced from grand strategy. From this perspective, the decision to launch a carrier program in 2009 was a product of chance that had nothing to do with the Global Financial Crisis or the shift in grand strategy; carrier construction is complex and requires a long lead time, and a program is unlikely to launch in 2009 in response to an event that occurred in 2008.

This is a powerful argument, but it is not necessarily true. For example, even as China kept a low profile in the 1990s and early 2000s, it was ensuring its carrier program would have a running start once the decision to proceed was made. To that end, China's leaders commissioned research on carrier aviation, invested in relevant carrier technologies, launched a state-backed effort to acquire the *Varyag*, intervened politically to bring it through the Bosporus, authorized study of its blueprints, prepared a plan to upgrade the *Varyag*, and even began a few training programs for future carrier aviation. This preparation meant that China could promptly launch the program once the strategic conditions were favorable. Moreover, most preparatory steps China took were taken quietly, and there was a clear and firm limit to what China was willing to authorize. Before the Global Financial Crisis, Beijing had stopped far short of taking more explicit steps that could alienate others: it did not move the carrier into a new (and visible) berth for major refurbishment, give the *Varyag* a PLAN designation, or even commit to one (let alone four) carriers. All those steps would have to be taken if China were to launch a blue-water fleet, but because China refused to take them, its carrier program was stalled.

That delay in carrier development was not set according to some technocratic modernization timeline, but was instead likely political and shaped largely by grand strategic considerations for a few reasons. First, as Chapter 4 and this case study have indicated, Party elites feared alienating China's neighbors and the United States and repeatedly delayed the program in the past at the highest levels, with Jiang Zemin pushing back against a full carrier program and authorizing only preliminary research. Second, if China were preparing a carrier according to a fixed modernization timeline, it seems difficult to dismiss as mere coincidence the fact that the timeline for launching the carrier program happened to fall on 2009—the year China revised its grand strategy—and not some other year. Moreover, the aggressive refurbishment and construction timeline established in 2009 came after years of relative quiet, suggesting again that China was not following a preset, fixed timeline. Third, China did not just begin refurbishing the *Varyag* in 2009, it began openly pushing more carriers too, which again suggests carrier modernization was not proceeding according to a set timeline but was shaped by strategic adjustment. Fourth, as discussed previously, authoritative documents from the State Oceanic Administration indicate that 2009 was a key year when China's political leadership made major decisions about the carrier program, and other sources suggest that the program was authorized by the Politburo in 2009.

In sum, China avoided building an aircraft carrier despite its manifest ability and strategic interests in doing so because it was pursuing a *blunting* strategy and knew carriers would send the wrong signal to the United States and to China's neighbors—all while remaining extremely vulnerable to attack. After the 2008 Global Financial Crisis, China began to emphasize *building* regional order. It no longer felt the need to constrain itself for fear of rattling Washington or the wider region. The capabilities that carriers were known for were now fully in line with China's own strategic objectives, which leaned increasingly toward enforcing maritime sovereignty and cultivating the ability to intervene regionally. And so, China entered the ranks of carrier-fielding great powers.

Surface Vessels

China's strategic adjustment after the Global Financial Crisis did not involve only a new focus on aircraft carriers—it also involved wider changes to its surface fleet. Beijing understood that capabilities like amphibious warfare (AMW), anti-submarine warfare (ASW), anti-air warfare (AAW), and mine countermeasures (MCM) made possible the kinds of missions China wanted to accomplish as part of a strategy to *build* regional order. But for decades, these capabilities were not a priority: Beijing instead prioritized anti-surface warfare (ASuW). This raises a puzzle: why did China systematically prioritize ASuW capabilities over other major capabilities among its surface combatants for two decades, and why did it then change course after 2008? This section argues that China's shift from a *blunting* to a *building* grand strategy accounts for the changes in its surface fleet. It explores the shift across China's (1) main surface combatants; (2) MCM vessels; and (3) AMW investments.

Main Surface Combatants

As one review notes, in the 1990s and 2000s China's main surface combatants were "carrying very capable anti-ship missiles" even as many continued to have "limited AAW and ASW capabilities."[63] Time and again, China deliberately upgraded anti-surface capabilities useful for *blunting* American power while delaying investment in anti-air and anti-submarine capabilities needed for the kinds of sea control, SLOC protection, or amphibious missions needed for *building* regional order—even though it could have pursued them. It was not until it shifted to a *building* grand strategy that this state of affairs changed.

Skeptics might disagree that shifts in grand strategy explain these decisions and point to *adoption capacity* explanations instead. They would argue that overinvestment in anti-surface warfare and underinvestment in anti-air and anti-submarine warfare was due simply to the fact that the latter capabilities are more financially or organizationally challenging. But the picture is more complex upon further analysis. Indeed, China did not invest in anti-surface warfare simply because it was easier or cheaper; rather, it thought it was necessary. Chinese analysts have long written of Soviet strategies to use missile saturation attacks against US carriers: "should [US carriers] simultaneously face a threat from all sorts of guided missile launch platform combat groups, their operational response can only be to make greatest use of their own technical superiority to . . . destroy the enemy one by one," which would fail.[64] Similarly, a book on cruise missiles published by China's Academy of Military Science explicitly noted that "an aircraft carrier . . . will undoubtedly be the main target in future sea battles" and the focus of cruise missile strikes.[65] Chinese sources suggest that if missiles are employed in a saturation attack, a US carrier battle group would likely be unable to reverse these unfavorable ratios.[66] Accordingly, one authoritative US estimate counted China fielding seven times as many of these missiles as the US Navy within the region.[67]

The focus on anti-surface warfare was apparent in China's surface vessel *acquisition* decisions. China's first post–Cold War destroyers, the *Luhu* class, had vastly better anti-surface weaponry than their predecessors (the capable YJ-83) but nonetheless retained their significantly outdated anti-submarine mortars and anti-air systems (the HQ-7).[68] In 1997, China introduced the *Luhai*, which was stealthier and had better propulsion but which retained the anti-aircraft weaponry of its predecessor, had only modestly improved anti-submarine weaponry (torpedoes and helicopters, which were too limited in number), and possessed no advances in detection capabilities. Most tellingly, China then acquired four *Sovremenny* class destroyers from Russia, which were outfitted for anti-surface warfare with Sunburn/Moskit missiles considered "more capable than any antiship cruise missile in the US inventory" and designed for use against US carrier battle groups.[69] And yet, these new vessels also featured anti-submarine capabilities similar to China's own and only modestly superior anti-air weapons that were essentially "point defense weapons" with a 15 nautical mile range.[70] China then began experimenting with new destroyer models, including the *Luzhou, Luyang I,* and early *Luyang II* classes all commissioned between 2004 and 2007, which generally employed poor anti-submarine technology and point defenses for anti-air warfare. China's frigate modernization followed a similar path, and quite tellingly, China also invested in vast numbers of small missile boats that utterly lacked survivability, could field eight impressive YJ-83 anti-ship cruise missiles, and had no meaningful anti-air warfare and anti-submarine warfare capabilities. For decades, as the Office of Naval Intelligence noted, anti-surface warfare continued to be the PLAN's "core strength."[71]

China had the ability to acquire anti-air and anti-submarine capabilities had they been a priority. For example, with respect to air defense, China's *Luda, Luhu, Luhai, Sovremenny,* and *Luzhou* classes all fielded relatively poor point-defense systems despite the possibility of importing superior Russian systems. It was only with the Type-52 *Luyang* DDGs in 2007, and only one variant of it in particular (the Type-52C), that China put a leading air-defense system, the HHQ-9, on a naval vessel.[72] Similarly, with respect to anti-submarine warfare, China continued to field anti-submarine mortars into the 2010s, even though torpedoes were more effective and relatively inexpensive. It was not until 1997 that China finally built a vessel capable of fielding ASW torpedoes and not until 2005 that it had a towed sonar array.[73] In contrast, India had fielded ASW torpedoes since the 1980s (on its *Rajput* destroyers and *Abhay* corvettes) and towed sonar arrays since the 1990s (on its *Delhi* destroyers and *Brahmaputra* frigates)—suggesting China could have done so too. More broadly, China never seriously attempted to purchase Russia's *Udaloy* class destroyers, which had advanced anti-submarine and anti-air capabilities and were intended to complement the anti-surface warfare capabilities of the *Sovremennyy* class destroyers Beijing did purchase from Moscow.

All this appears to have changed after China shifted to a *building* strategy. In 2012, for example, China dramatically improved its AAW and ASW capabilities for the first time, with its advanced model of the Luyang-II. With respect to AAW, these boasted an "Aegis-like" system and marked "the first Chinese warships capable of the area AAW mission vital to defending the *Liaoning*."[74] Interestingly, this class of vessel was last manufactured in 2005; then, after a hiatus, roughly four were made between 2010 and 2012 for the apparent purpose of carrier escort. When this model was finalized, China began building the Luyang-III, all of which are equipped with these advanced ASW and AAW capabilities. What is impressive about them, however, is not only the fact that their advanced capabilities finally show a PLAN that is embracing missions beyond anti-surface warfare, but also that it is doing so on a large scale. Indeed, serial construction began well after the Global Financial Crisis, and an astounding number of twenty are planned, with the first commissioned in 2014. This scale of production constitutes perhaps the clearest sign of China's new military strategy. The successor to the Luyang-III, the Type 055 Renhai destroyer, saw simultaneous construction on six vessels begin in 2014. The construction of nearly thirty advanced destroyers with more sophisticated ASW and AAW capabilities is significant, and while some of these lines began before the Global Financial Crisis, production schedules strongly suggest expansion afterward; moreover, the largest lines accounting for twenty-six destroyers all appear to have begun a few years after the strategic shift precipitated by the Global Financial Crisis.

Mine Countermeasures

In any operation in which China expects to project naval power or engage in amphibious operations, mine countermeasures (MCM) will be an important capability, and a large number of minesweepers a military necessity. This is something Chinese military texts have long understood. The 2006 edition of the *Science of Military Strategy* was explicit that China would need to clear sea mines near the landing zone in any amphibious operation.[75] Similarly, the 2012 edition of the *Joint Campaign Theory Study Guide* argued that countermine efforts are needed in campaigns involving islands.[76] The fact that China nonetheless went almost two full decades after the end of the Cold War before investing significantly in these capabilities is important and puzzling. It indicates that these missions were not priorities when China was pursuing a grand strategy to *blunt* American power. Conversely, the fact that China began investing in MCM after the Global Financial Crisis revealed its growing interest in the kinds of operations needed to *build* regional order.

Throughout the 1990s and 2000s, China's investments in MCM were surprisingly limited. As Bernard Cole noted in 2010, while China had made a significant investment in offensive mine warfare (as Chapter 4 discussed), the PLAN had "not made a concomitant investment in the mine-hunting and-clearing mission."[77] For decades, China had only a small number of 1950s-era mine-clearing vessels, including some twenty-seven Soviet-designed T-43/Type 010 ocean-going minesweepers and eight coastal ones, and most of these vessels were antiquated and ineffective, with an estimated 75 percent placed in reserve.[78] It was not until 2007—almost twenty-five years after its first MCM vessel—that China finally introduced a new minesweeper design that could provide both mine-sweeping and mine-hunting capabilities (the *Wochi* class) and replace China's aging T-43 fleet.[79] By then, Russia had already introduced nearly ten new classes to succeed the versions it had sold to China.

Contrary to *adoption capacity* theories, China's limited MCM capabilities were due not to cost or organizational complexity but to choice. Minesweepers are admittedly expensive weapons relative to their tonnage because of their passive countermeasures—including wood and fiberglass hulls and special-ized propellers that lower magnetic, pressure, and acoustic signatures that could trigger mines. Even so, they are still far less expensive than major surface combatants. With respect to organizational challenges, minesweeping opera-tions have been undertaken by China and developing navies since the 1950s. While MCM has progressed since then—and now involves using ship sonar (or helicopters) to identify mines and projectiles, divers, and remote-controlled methods to destroy them—they are not especially complex. Many developing countries, including Indonesia, Pakistan, Saudi Arabia, and Turkey, have en-gaged in such operations since the 1990s. Ultimately, China did not need to rely on outdated 1950s-era minesweepers for more than two decades and could have built its own or acquired one of Russia's upgraded models. And indeed, China's approach changed once it shifted to a grand strategy focused on *building* regional order. After building a new class of MCM vessel in the mid-2000s in limited numbers, China then built no other minesweepers until apparently restarting production lines after the Global Financial Crisis. Since then it has built several advanced MCM vessels. As the Office of Naval Intelligence puts it, Chinese *ac-quisition* and *training* have both changed to reflect an emerging focus on these capabilities:

> China has also invested heavily in improving its mine countermeasure (MCM) capabilities. A number of advanced, dedicated MCM vessels have joined the fleet in recent years, including the capable WOCHI-class mine-hunting ships (MHS) and new WOZANG-class minehunters acting as mother-ships to the remote-controllable WONANG-class inshore minesweepers (MSI). China is improving its mine-hunting capabilities with improved SONARs and mine neutralization vehicles. Chinese warfare exercises have routinely included both mining and mine countermeasure events.[80]

China's new focus on MCM is in sharp contrast to its past neglect of this capa-bility and strong evidence of a change in Chinese strategy.

Amphibious Warfare

China has always believed amphibious warfare (AMW) capabilities would be necessary for operations in East and South China Seas or the Taiwan Strait, as well as for other missions essential to *building* regional order. But for decades it made investments far beneath its abilities in both. As Beijing pursued a grand strategy to *blunt* American power, more offensive AMW capabilities were not a priority; when China shifted to a strategy intended to *build* regional order after the Global Financial Crisis, AMW became a priority.

With respect to AMW, from its founding until 2010, the PLAN had not "constructed a large amphibious force" despite the ability to invest more in these capabilities.[81] From the late 1980s onward, China made only halfhearted efforts to improve its amphibious capabilities. By 2000, the majority of its vessels were still incapable of open-ocean navigation and, of the roughly fifty-five medium to large amphibious vessels it possessed, many were over forty years old and in reserve.[82] In the mid-1990s and early 2000s, China began constructing more landing and supply ships to replace its outdated vessels, including the *Yuting-I* and *Yuting-II* LSTs, *Yunshu* class LSMs, and the *Yubei* class LCUs. These efforts are revealing because, as Bernard Cole noted, they were "directed at modernizing the amphibious force, but not at significantly expanding its capacity," with the PLAN "still limited to transporting approximately one mechanized division of fully equipped troops"—virtually unchanged from the year 2000.[83] It was not until the construction of the *Yuzhao* class LPDs in 2006 that China began to acquire significant sealift capacity, though in the decade since China has acquired only four of these vessels. Even then, these LPDs are "relatively lightly armed, with just a single 76-mm gun and four 30-mm CIWS," suggesting their real value may not be in AMW but in conducting military operations other than war, such as disaster relief.[84] In addition to vessels, marines are also an important component of China's amphibious capabilities. Although China created a marine brigade in 1979 and a second one in 1998, with a total marine strength of somewhere around 10,000–12,000 active-duty soldiers, it did not expand their numbers in this period.[85]

China's delayed investments in amphibious capabilities cannot be explained by *adoption capacity* theories that indicate the cost or organizational complexity of these vessels prevented it from acquiring them. Indeed, several developing countries of varying technical abilities have built or acquired these vessels, including Algeria, Brazil, Chile, India, Indonesia, Peru, the Philippines, Singapore, and South Korea. China's shipbuilding industry was certainly capable of building LPDs well before 2007. And with respect to marines, it is clear that standing up or expanding a marine corps is neither particularly costly nor operationally difficult. Several other countries, including

Brazil (15,000 marines), Colombia (24,000), South Korea (30,000), and Thailand (20,000), have all had marines for decades, and China too has its own limited force of 10,000 marines that it could have expanded. Indeed, decades earlier in the 1950s, when an invasion of Taiwan seemed plausible, China had nearly 100,000 marines before eliminating the marine corps in 1957 when US intervention undercut these plans.[86] China's relatively low and delayed investment in marines and amphibious capabilities was not about cost or complexity but strategy—these capabilities were simply not necessary for *blunting* American power.

As China shifted to pursue a strategy for *building* regional order, it began major investments in transport craft and amphibious infantry that dramatically boosted its lift capacity. China has dramatically increased its number of Type 071 landing platform docks from only one in 2007 to seven by 2020. While the production of these vessels began before the Global Financial Crisis, China appears to have expanded its production line. And it was after the Global Financial Crisis that China launched production of three enormous Type 075 landing helicopter docks, each of which displaces nearly twice as much as the Type 071 LPD, is far better armed, and has substantially greater capacity—including the ability to accommodate thirty helicopters. Together, these ten large amphibious transport vessels will give China amphibious assault capabilities second only to the United States, and they were all nonexistent ten years ago. In addition, China has significantly increased the number of its medium-sized landing vessels; after building nine in the 2000s, it then stopped production until after the Global Financial Crisis, when it restarted and nearly doubled its production by 2016, with more planned. Aside from vessels, China also dramatically expanded its marine corps following the Global Financial Crisis after keeping its numbers stable at no more than 12,000 for several decades. It doubled the number of marines in 2017 and then announced plans to increase the number tenfold above their previous level to at least 100,000.[87] This is a large number, especially since the entire PLAN only has about 235,000 personnel, making the creation of the marine corps a service-transforming decision. As former Navy Commissar Liu Xiaojiang stated, the massive increase indicated a focus on "possible war with Taiwan, maritime defense in the East and South China seas" and new missions across the Indo-Pacific to "the country's maritime lifelines, as well as offshore supply depots like in Djibouti and the Gwadar port in Pakistan."[88] In other words, it was consistent with a *building* strategy focused on securing China's overseas interests, especially in Asia.

Overseas Facilities and Interventions

Over the last few years, the Chinese public has time and again returned a series of movies based on virtually the same conceit to the top of the box office.
These movies—including *Wolf Warrior* and its sequel *Wolf Warrior 2*, *Operation
Mekong*, and *Operation Red Sea*—feature Chinese military forces swinging into
action outside China's borders to rescue overseas Chinese citizens, protect
Chinese investments, and provide international public goods. China's military
provides these movies with some funding, assistance with action set pieces,
and—critically—inspiration too. These films draw their plots from the Chinese
military's first forays into protecting its overseas interests, including the evacuation of Chinese citizens from Libya and Yemen, its anti-piracy efforts, as
well as China's extradition of a drug kingpin who killed a dozen Chinese citizens in 2011. In *Operation Red Sea*, for example, a Chinese Gulf of Aden task
force rescues kidnapped Chinese citizens, stops a nuclear proliferation ring, and
sails home triumphantly. On the way back, it encounters American vessels in
the South China Sea and orders them to vacate. As the credits roll, a Chinese J-
15 takes off from an aircraft carrier—the former *Varyag*—and heads toward the
interloping American ships.

The public's unflagging interest in these kinds of movies—two of them were
among the three highest-grossing movies ever in China—reflects both the
causes and consequences of China's quest to become a "maritime great power."
A rough overview of China's greater activism throughout the Indo-Pacific,
whether in counter-piracy missions or on territorial disputes, can be instructive.
On December 26, 2008, China began dispatching anti-piracy naval task forces
to the Gulf of Aden—with "31 escort fleets, 100 ships, 67 shipboard helicopters
and more than 26,000 soldiers" dispatched within the first ten years.[89] From
that point forward, its military began regularly using a number of regional
ports in the Indo-Pacific for replenishment and resupply. In 2011, China sent
warships to support the evacuation of 30,000 citizens from Libya. That same
year, after thirteen Chinese merchant sailors were killed along the Mekong,
Beijing worked to extradite six suspected foreigners to face consequences in
China; launched the first ever extraterritorial joint patrols of the Mekong with
Myanmar, Thailand, and Laos; and even considered a drone strike on an overseas drug lord.[90] In 2013, China declared an Air Defense Identification Zone
over the East China Sea. In early 2014, China opened negotiations for its first
official overseas base in Djibouti under a "security and defense strategic partnership" that it signed with the country.[91] That same year, it began building and
then militarizing artificial islands in the South China Sea, a significant departure
from its previous approach, and constructed airfields, docks, and facilities on

them. That move came alongside several precedent-breaking provocations into Japanese-administered waters in the East China Sea. In 2015, China evacuated roughly a thousand citizens from Yemen and then used military helicopters to evacuate over a hundred citizens from Nepal. Together, these actions show that China was far more willing to act as a "maritime great power" across the Indo-Pacific than it had previously been willing to do, which is consistent with the shift to a *building* grand strategy.[92]

China's pursuit of this strategy has required not only a navy capable of power projection, amphibious operations, sea control, and SLOC patrols—which China dutifully built—it has also required a departure from two of China's Deng-era commitments that were once firmaments of a grand strategy of *blunting*: (1) avoiding overseas interventions; and (2) avoiding overseas bases. Beginning after the Global Financial Crisis, the call to break from these practices grew much louder.

First, with respect to the norm against overseas intervention, General Chen Zhou, a former author of many of China's Defense White Papers, has argued in favor of its relaxation. Writing a year after the crisis, Chen observed that "whether or not a country can effectively protect its overseas interests . . . is also a very sensitive point because it involves the sovereign interests" of others. Chen goes on to note that, "historically, before World War I, the international community generally recognized the legitimacy of using force to protect the lives and property of a country's overseas citizens," but that because of China's "relatively weak national power," he observed, "we completely equated this view with aggression and interference." Of course, the situation had since changed, and he remarked that with "the growth of our comprehensive national power, we must protect the safety of our energy resources and transportation passages and protect the legal rights and interests of Chinese nationals . . . and we must treat this as an important aspect of national security." Intervention in these cases "is the right and the power of the state, as well as its responsibility and obligation." The reason this was not a hypocritical retreat from past principle, Chen argued, was because China was different from the West. China followed the "five principles of peaceful coexistence," while the West had secured its interests "through wars and unequal treaties." As a result, "our interests enjoy true legality and legitimacy," and the use of force abroad to protect Chinese interests was therefore justifiable.[93] Chen's tortured logic nonetheless put an intellectual sheen on breaking from the principle of non-interference.

Second, to support its overseas presence and secure China's interests, including the Belt and Road, China has had to break from another principle: avoiding overseas facilities. For decades China had promised, not to "station any troops or set up any military bases in any foreign country," language that was even included in several of its official Defense White Papers.[94] Given China's past commitments to never establish an overseas "military base" [军事基地], the PLA has used other terms to describe the facilities it hopes to establish, including "strategic strong points" [海外军事基地], "maritime stations" [海上驿站], "support bases" [保障基地], or simply "facilities" [设施], among other euphemisms. After the Global Financial Crisis, commentary increasingly began to stress the importance of these facilities and eventually migrated into authoritative documents. Deputy Chief of the Joint Staff Department Admiral Sun Jianguo wrote in *Qiushi* that the 18th Party Congress in 2012 has instructed China to "steadily promote the construction of overseas bases," a process that was likely underway earlier.[95] Moreover, the 2013 *Science of Military Strategy* argued:

> We must build strategic strong points that rely on the mainland, radiate out into the periphery, and go into the two oceans [i.e., Pacific and Indian Oceans], providing support for overseas military operations or serving as a forward base for the deployment of military forces overseas, as well as exerting political and military influence in relevant regions.[96]

This language makes clear that these facilities are part of a grand strategy of *building* regional order. The next year, Liu Cigui, the former director of the State Oceanic Administration that devises China's maritime strategy, wrote that "sea stations" [海上驿站] and connectivity were the first priority for developing the maritime security component of the Belt and Road. "We must grab hold [抓住] of the key channels, key nodes, and key projects" and "build maritime public service facilities with countries along the route," he wrote. "The security of sea lanes is the key to sustaining the stable development of the Maritime Silk Road, and ports and docks are the highest priority for securing the sea lanes."[97] These ports must "not only have the function of cargo handling, but must also provide replenishment and logistics services, and *most importantly*, ensure the safety of the surrounding waterways."[98] Liu's "sea stations" could be "built separately from the host country, jointly with China and other countries, or could involve leasing currently existing ports as a base of operations." And Liu was not alone in these views. General Chen Zhou, author of several of China's Defense White Papers, wrote, "We should expand the sphere of maritime activity, strive to demonstrate our presence in some critical strategic regions, use diplomatic and economic means to establish strategic supporting points, and make use of berthing points and supply points to which we legally get access from relevant countries in the relevant sea areas."[99] Less authoritative sources are even more candid.[100] Professor Liang Fang at the National Defense University argued that securing the Belt and Road had two requirements.[101] First, it required a more robust overseas presence that sustained "offshore mobile warfare forces with the aircraft carrier formation as the core." Second, China also needed to "establish an overseas military presence system." Liang Fan argued that "From a strategic point of view, we should choose to establish overseas strategic presence in areas of great interest and concentration." These need not be bases, they could be "temporary berths and replenishment points for our naval vessels," such as dual-use commercial ports.

The focus on these kinds of overseas facilities likely guided several of China's key maritime decisions, particularly with respect to overseas port investment. In 2014, experts from China's Naval Research Institute—the PLA Navy's research institute for strategy and doctrine—listed seven locations for a future military base: the Bay of Bengal, Myanmar, Pakistan (Gwadar), Djibouti, Seychelles, Sri Lanka (Hambantota), and Tanzania (Dar es Salaam).[102] And as the Naval War College's Conor Kennedy finds in a review of Chinese sources, a large number of Chinese port projects have been referred to as potential "strategic strongpoints." China's current base in Djibouti is referred to in this way, as are the possible future facilities in Pakistan (Gwadar) and Sri Lanka (Hambantota). China's investments in several regional ports are made cautiously and with an eye toward their future potential for military access. Indeed, PLA authors refer to the need for planning for numerous bases or "points," but only letting some of them "bloom" at first.[103] For example, China has invested heavily in Gwadar's port— which Pakistan's navy currently uses—as well as its airport. PLA authors openly write that Gwadar could become a long-term rest and replenishment point for PLAN task forces or even a site for a future support base like the one currently in Djibouti. Its military potential is to some degree a foregone conclusion, and according to some PLA officers, "The food is already on the plate; we'll eat it whenever we want to."[104] Meanwhile, Pakistan's Karachi port is already used by the PLAN for replenishment. When China launched its *building* strategy, it became more essential: the port saw only five PLAN visits before 2008 and seventeen visits after it.[105] China invested heavily in Sri Lanka's Hambantota port, previously docked a submarine and warship at its Columbo port, requested more such privileges unsuccessfully, and even sought military access when it took over Hambantota after Sri Lanka was unable to cover the loans that built it.[106] Other projects across the region in Myanmar, Bangladesh, the Maldives, and the east coast of Africa are undoubtedly seen in similar terms—and essential to China's regional order-building.

These projects, together with the PLA's growing focus on carriers and advanced surface vessels, demonstrate that China's military was leaving behind its focus on *blunting* American power and embarking on *building* the military forms of control need to sustain regional order. This new imperative—to make "more offensive moves," as Hu Jintao put it in 2009—would not be confined only to the military domain. As the next chapter discusses, China's greater assertiveness would also become a defining feature of Asia's regional organizations.

9

"Establish Regional Architecture"

Implementing Political Building

"In the final analysis, it is for the people of Asia to run the affairs of Asia,
solve the problems of Asia, and uphold the security of Asia."
—*Xi Jinping, 2014*

In October 2014, Chinese President Xi Jinping flew to Astana, the capital city
of Kazakhstan. What followed was a bit of a paradox—a historic moment at an
otherwise obscure organization.

The Conference on Interaction and Confidence Building-Measures (CICA)
in Asia has one of the longest titles of any multilateral body, but the extra words
in its name in no way compensate for its lack of apparent purpose. The institution was initially proposed and led by Kazakh President Nursultan Nazarbayev
in a 1992 speech. It then took roughly a decade to finally come into existence
after a series of informal meetings and aborted statements. For most of its history, the organization in both informal and formal incarnations had been led by
Kazakhstan and then for four years by Turkey (2010–2014). Now, it would be
led by China.

China's eventual chairmanship of CICA was not an accident of the calendar
but a conscious courtship that began as early as 2012. Where others saw an obscure and powerless entity, China saw an opportunity. Beijing had been looking
for ways to build security architecture in Asia that reflected its preferences, but it
was stymied in ASEAN-led forums and by US alliances. Here now was an organization that included most of Eurasia's states, avoided ASEAN centrality, and,
most importantly, did not contain the United States and Japan. It was a relatively simple matter to lead the organization, and now China could elevate it.
CICA, it hoped, would be a platform for promoting norms that would undermine US alliances and for setting a Chinese vision for regional architecture that
the United States and Japan could not torpedo. As one Chinese think tank put

it, "CICA is capable of providing a solid institutional foundation for charting the shortest path toward an Asian security architecture," one that reflected China's priorities.[1] And so, in his first ever address as leader of CICA, Xi announced a "New Asian Security Concept"—upgraded from a version offered in the 1990s—that attacked US alliances. In the most famous section, Xi declared that "it is for the people of Asia to run the affairs of Asia, solve the problems of Asia, and uphold the security of Asia." There was, in other words, no need for the United States and no need for its alliances.

These words were so shocking that some China analysts in the West dismissed the speech as an aberration—the unvetted product of a few unskilled Chinese diplomats.[2] But they were wrong to be so dismissive, in part because these were long-standing aims amplified by the Global Financial Crisis. Leaked Chinese preparatory documents for past CICA meetings improperly posted to obscure corners of the CICA website make clear that China advocated these themes after the crisis within the organization. These documents and their attendant PowerPoint slides pushed for Asia's transition from "closed bilateral military alliances" with the United States to a "new architecture" free of them. Over time, what was once said behind closed doors was increasingly stated openly. In 2012, China's deputy foreign minister wanted a joint Russian and Chinese proposal critical of US alliances to be the foundation for CICA's approach to Asia's security architecture, and he proposed that others conform to this exclusive vision: "We suggest elaborating *rules of behavior* for all Asian countries in the sphere of security on the basis of the Chinese-Russian initiative," he declared.[3]

Xi's 2014 speech and his leadership of CICA was the culmination of this multiyear focus on building Chinese order in Asia set off by the Global Financial Crisis. When Xi declared "Asia for the Asians," it was thus clearly no fluke, and Chinese diplomats kept saying it at CICA years after his 2014 address. With China now running CICA, it finally had a chance to instantiate its exclusive vision of regional order.

This chapter discusses that effort to *build* regional order through Asian organizations. It answers two puzzles: (1) Why did China create costly new forums and elevate previously obscure ones when there were existing, more mature institutions ready to be used?; and (2) Why did China, which had previously resisted institutionalizing Asian organizations, now readily support institutionalization? The answers to both questions are related to the change in China's grand strategy after the Global Financial Crisis. Beijing wanted new forums that it could lead, and it supported institutionalization because it served Chinese order-building and because the United States was not involved. Gone was the nervousness and timidity with which Beijing reacted to APEC or the ARF for fear of US-led encirclement. Now, China would build its own forums, and these would be consistent with its vision. Building order would require "forms of control" that could regulate the behavior of its neighbors, and multilateral organizations could provide opportunities for coercion (particularly economic), consent (through public goods or beneficial bargains), as well as legitimacy (through claiming leadership and setting norms). China's efforts spanned a number of organizations, and not all were successful, but two in particular warrant attention: CICA and the Asian Infrastructure Investment Bank (AIIB). If CICA was the security component of China's multilateral order building in Asia, then AIIB was the economic component. While AIIB is by far the more significant of the two organizations, the two taken together demonstrate China's preferences and the scope of its strategic ambitions. Together, in the minds of Chinese strategists at the time, these two organizations offered a path to building Asian order on China's terms.

China's Political Texts

China's writing on international institutions shifted after the Global Financial Crisis. Although we lack access to some of the core internal diplomatic texts of the last decade, speeches by Presidents Hu and Xi reveal China's shift away from using regional organizations to blunt American power or reassure wary neighbors and toward a desire to set the terms for regional order in Asia. Both leaders elevated China's focus on its neighboring region—that is, its "peripheral diplomacy"—and they saw multilateral organizations as tools to build a "community of common destiny" in Asia that would reflect China's interests.

The Global Financial Crisis and Political Strategy

In the very speech that outlined China's post–Global Financial Crisis strategic shift, Hu called for a strengthened focus on "peripheral diplomacy." The character of this focus was qualitatively different from what it had been in the past.

As past chapters have demonstrated, China's interest in "peripheral diplomacy" involving its neighborhood increased after the trifecta as well as the 1997 Asian Financial Crisis, which offered China a chance to earn some goodwill with economic concessions.[4] That focus remained in the following period, but it was generally motivated by defensive concerns related to *blunting* US coalition-building or encirclement. Indeed, in those years, Chinese officials stressed concerns about encirclement and wary neighbors who believed in the "China threat theory," and these concerns shaped China's participation in international institutions.

After the Global Financial Crisis, that fear had diminished, and the purpose of "peripheral diplomacy" had begun to change. In his address, Hu instead sounded surprisingly confident. He emphasized that China had reduced its external pressure and would have greater freedom of maneuver in the region. Indeed, after the crisis, he declared, the "overall strategic environment continues to improve" and "our country's influence on the periphery has been further expanded."[5] A good example of this diminished concern for neighboring opposition was in his language on territorial disputes. In contrast to his dramatically more conciliatory 2006 Central Foreign Affairs Work Forum address, Hu in 2009 reversed his emphasis on shelving conflicts, Instead, he said, "We must correctly grasp the relationship between safeguarding rights and maintaining stability, and properly handle disputes over maritime rights, territories, and cross-border rivers between China and neighboring countries. We must resolutely fight against the violations of China's rights and interests by the countries concerned and defend our core interests."[6] This kind of language had in rare cases appeared in other addresses, but it was usually tempered. Instead, Hu's 2009 address argued further that China needed to "make offensive moves" on territorial issues. This bullish new line suggested that a fundamental impetus behind China's previous multilateral policy was changing and that China now wanted to more actively reshape the region. And so China's regional multilateralism would need to change too.

In his 2009 address, Hu acknowledged this shift and argued that diplomacy needed a post-crisis adjustment that would make it more assertive. "Diplomatic work should adapt to changes in the global structure and advance in all directions and multiple levels," he put it.[7] This adjustment called for "more actively developing multilateral diplomacy," and Hu stated that China "must actively participate in multilateral affairs and make full use of multilateral diplomatic means and multilateral mechanisms to safeguard our national interests." Indeed, he argued multilateral diplomacy is "unprecedentedly lively and important."[8] Moreover, and especially with respect to peripheral diplomacy, Hu argued that "it is necessary to vigorously strengthen the pragmatic cooperation in the areas of security, economy, and cultural affairs" within multilateral bodies and to "actively promote regional cooperation in East Asia."[9] These statements, coming as they did in a speech that modified China's diplomacy in response to the crisis, suggested greater multilateral activism was a direct consequence and critical to China's regional aims.

After Hu's speech, "peripheral diplomacy" with China's neighbors continued to see elevation in Chinese grand strategy as part of efforts to create a "Community of a Common Destiny," which became a stand-in for Chinese order-building—and multilateral institutions played a critical role. In 2011, China first released a White Paper that advocated for a "Community of Common Destiny."[10] Two years later, in 2013, Chinese Foreign Minister Wang Yi declared "peripheral diplomacy" with China's neighbors was the "priority direction" for Chinese foreign policy, and Xi then held an unprecedented Work Forum on Peripheral Diplomacy—the first meeting of that magnitude convened on foreign policy since 2006 and the first ever on peripheral diplomacy. There, Xi linked China's diplomacy directly to the ultimate goal of "national rejuvenation" and declared Beijing's objective as the realization of a regional "Community of Common Destiny," an indication of the seriousness of China's order-building ambitions. The next year, at the 2014 Central Foreign Affairs Work Conference, Xi modified the "diplomatic layout" for the first time and elevated peripheral diplomacy over a focus on great powers like the United States.

Multilateral bodies were platforms to realize the "Community of Common Destiny," and Xi relentlessly elevated the concept at regional gatherings. In case any doubt remained about whether China was directing its energies to build a "Community of Common Destiny," China's 2017 White Paper on Asian Security Cooperation made it clear: "Chinese leaders have repeatedly elaborated on the concept of a community of common destiny on many different occasions. China is working to construct a community of common destiny . . . in Asia and the Asia-Pacific area as a whole."[11] These sources all strongly suggest the emergence of regional order-building as a major focus if not the central priority of Chinese grand strategy, and indeed, China began to stress its interest in shaping regional architecture, as the discourse on AIIB and CICA in the case studies outlined in this chapter will make clearer.

A Building Strategy

As Chapter 4 has already documented, the Global Financial Crisis sharply revised China's assessment of US power and brought about a regional strategy that was focused more intensely on shaping—rather than protecting China from—the periphery. In the 1990s and early 2000s, China's "peripheral diplomacy" sought to address the "China threat theory." Now, reassurance was less a priority than building the foundation for regional order.

Multilateral institutions would play a role in China's greater regional activism, especially in emerging discourse on shaping regional architecture. They would allow China to build the foundations for order—coercion, consent, and legitimacy—and that approach is reflected in some of the discourse on institutions.

All three of these forms of control swirl together in China's discourse, including in Hu's 2009 address, China's 2011 White Paper, and the 18th Party Congress—among others, which together set the contours for a new strategy by China to shape Asia's regional security and economic multilateral structure.

In his 2009 Ambassadorial Conference address, President Hu advocated efforts to integrate regional economies into China's: "We must focus on deepening regional cooperation in Asia, paying attention to promoting the integration of regional and sub-regional cooperation with China's domestic regional development strategy."[12] This idea was emphasized at the 18th Party Congress, where President Hu stressed multilateral and regional as well as sub-regional initiatives—together with a greater focus on infrastructure: "We should make overall plans for bilateral, multilateral, regional, and sub-regional opening up and cooperation, accelerate implementation of the strategy of building free trade areas, and promote infrastructure connectivity with our neighboring countries."[13] In this way, institutions—like the AIIB—would be used to provide economic public goods, and China's status as the beneficent economic partner integrated with its smaller neighbors would provide a degree of legitimacy. And in all these addresses, Hu stressed "actively" participating in multilateral affairs, a reference to his reminder that China now needed to not only "Hide and Bide" but also "Actively Accomplish Something." What China sought from these efforts was something like deference, and the 2011 White Paper noted, countries in the region "should . . . be open-minded to other [i.e., Chinese] proposals for regional cooperation" while making clear that China would "be bold in opening new ground" within the region.

Under Hu's successor, Xi Jinping, China's interest in using multilateral institutions to shape Asia grew more apparent and explicit, but in many ways followed the form outlined initially by Hu. Many important policies on assuming leadership over CICA and launching AIIB that occurred under Xi were likely first set in Hu's administration, demonstrating strategic continuity. Most of Xi's major addresses on regional affairs—to APEC in 2013, to the Peripheral Diplomacy Work Forum in 2013, to the Central Foreign Affairs Work Forum in 2014, to CICA in 2014, to the Boao Forum in 2015, to the BRI Forum in 2017 and 2019, among others—are explicit about China's desire to shape Asia's regional economic and security architecture.

The "forms of control"—coercion, consent, and legitimacy—so critical to order-building make appearance in Xi's multilateral discourses, with a particular focus on mutually beneficial bargains and new public goods. For example, in his 2013 speech announcing the launch of AIIB and his 2014 speech assuming the chairmanship of CICA, Xi claimed leadership for China and explicitly offered economic and security public goods, respectively. His AIIB address made clear that "The nations of the Asia Pacific region are a big family, and China is one of the members. China cannot develop in isolation from the Asia Pacific region while the Asia Pacific region cannot prosper without China."[14] It also stated that China's economy "delivers tangible benefits to Asia" and was responsible for 50 percent of Asia's growth. Similarly, China's 2017 White Paper on Asia-Pacific

Security Cooperation noted that Beijing would provide public goods: "China will shoulder greater responsibilities for regional and global security, and provide more public security services to the Asia-Pacific region and the world at large."[15] China's discourses on securing the Belt and Road, discussed in the previous chapter, echo this interest.

At the same time, China has sought to constrain its neighbors' security partnerships more proactively. This was clearest at CICA, where Xi declared Asia needed to "establish a new regional security architecture" in opposition to US alliances. In that gathering and at subsequent ones, Xi has put forward a concept of "common, comprehensive, cooperative, and sustainable security in Asia," within which the words "common" and "cooperative" were tied to efforts to weaken alliances. And China's own behavior—including punishing countries like South Korea for deploying US missile defenses—indicates that these anti-alliance norms are sometimes accompanied by bilateral punishments. Chinese think tank scholars regularly make these linkages clear, and multilateral organizations allow opportunities to elevate the linkage into a regional norm.

Together, these efforts to create a "Community of Common Destiny" in Asia have been a major focus of China's regional diplomacy for roughly a decade. We now turn to two key examples of this conduct, China's construction of AIIB and its activism within CICA.

Asian Infrastructure Investment Bank

On January 16, 2016, the Asian Infrastructure Investment Bank (AIIB) was declared "open for business," and a gray-haired enthusiast for English literature, Jin Liqun, was elected its first president.[16] Jin, an experienced financial official, had stewarded the bank's tortuous evolution from a concept Xi Jinping announced in 2013 to the multilateral development bank (MDB) that had thrown open its doors in 2016. Now he would lead the bank he had helped build.

Jin grew up in an educated but poor family with what was then an unusual passion for English literature. When he was sent to labor in the countryside for a decade during the Cultural Revolution, he spent three-quarters of his meager annual salary and what little time he had after a day's work in the field continuing that pursuit.[17] "I was outfitted with a worn-out Remington typewriter and a copy of Webster," he said later, as well as a radio he kept tuned to the BBC that gave his English a trace of the "standard BBC accent of the 1970s."[18] When the Cultural Revolution abated, the twenty-nine-year-old autodidact won a seat at the Beijing Institute of Foreign Languages, excelled in graduate work, and was offered a faculty position. "An academic life that I had so coveted was just beginning to unfold," recalled Jin.[19]

It was not to be. That same year, China joined the World Bank, and English-speakers were needed to staff its new office in Washington. His advisrs encouraged him to go, and Jin switched careers from English to banking. He spent a dozen years at the World Bank and then the Asian Development Bank, rising to become its first Chinese vice president, and developed a résumé and Rolodex in multilateral finance no other Chinese official could match. When China decided to build its own development bank, Jin was the logical choice.

Jin is not so dissimilar from the bank he helped found. Both are outwardly cosmopolitan. Jin's bookshelves are filled with Shakespeare and Faulkner, and his bank's membership is filled with American allies and partners. Both are inflected with Western influence. Jin gracefully navigates international business norms and the bank styles itself in international rules and structures. And both, despite all this, are still firmly rooted in China.

Jin is a proud Party member. He tells interviewers that, although he was born two months before the CCP took national power, they controlled his province of Jiangsu at the time. "I was born under a red flag," he hastens to point out.[20] Jin is sometimes publicly skeptical of America's continued global leadership. "History has never set any precedent that an empire is capable of governing the world forever," he wrote in a recent essay on China's rise and American order.[21] And he sees the bank he leads—where China is founder, largest shareholder, chief political patron, and host to its headquarters—as less international than one might think despite its global trappings. "I would hope a Chinese can succeed me" in leading the bank, he states clearly.[22]

China's launch of this institution was a notable departure from its previous opposition to institutionalization within ASEAN, the ARF, and even the SCO discussed previously. It "marks China's emergence as an institution-builder" and signifies the shift from regional blunting to building in Chinese grand strategy.[23] But while Jin carried out this shift, he did not cause it. That came from a level above.

China's decision to launch AIIB emerged from the 2008 Global Financial Crisis. Its initial preferences for the bank suggest it sought a tool that it could singularly dominate and use to advance both its political goals and its new Belt and Road Initiative. Over time, China struck a bargain with member states: it gave up some political control and voice to those who joined; in return, those states signed on to the initiative and legitimized Chinese power and leadership. Like other MDBs built by other great powers, the AIIB serves the order-building aims of its patron. It (1) strengthens China's coercive capacity; (2) provides a foundation for securing consent through public goods provision and bargains; and (3) legitimizes Chinese power.

Alternative Explanations

Why did China create AIIB? Some argue that AIIB was created to help China export its surplus industrial capacity by providing foreign governments funds for infrastructure projects that would in turn employ Chinese firms and workers. But China's surplus capacity vastly exceeds what AIIB could finance, with the excess in steel alone roughly $60 billion annually, three times what the AIIB might hope to lend in a given year.[24] AIIB President Jin Liqun concedes this, arguing that "with the size of China's economy," AIIB could not absorb the excess.[25] Others argue that China's decision to form AIIB is motivated by a sincere desire to address Asia's infrastructure gap. But even the bank's ambitious plans for $10–$20 billion in annual lending would scarcely dent the $800 billion that the Asian Development Bank estimates the region needs each year for infrastructure.[26] AIIB is smaller than the World Bank and the Asian Development Bank, and China could easily use its own development banks, the China Development Bank (CDB) and the Export-Import Bank of China (CEB). These banks are far larger than the World Bank, lend more to the developing world than the World Bank does in some years, and do not "limit China's freedom of action" by placing its lending under the "formal governance strictures and external oversight associated with a multilateral body."[27] This then provides a puzzle: why has China chosen to build an institution that might limit its freedom of action, and what then is its purpose?

The answer is related to the fundamental reasons states create MDBs in the first place. As Dani Rodrik argues, MDBs should be unnecessary in a world where bilateral aid and well-developed international capital markets exist. The reason these banks exist, he argues, is to signal good investment climates through their loan commitments and to divorce that signal as well as the loans themselves from a given state's political interests.[28] But this function could be served by one bank, notes Christopher Kilby, so why does the world have so many overlapping *regional* MDBs?[29] The reason for this redundancy is not economic, but related in part to the political interests of great powers. And it is this political logic that explains why China created AIIB.

Great powers use MDBs for order-building. The founders give up some of their control to entice smaller states to join them; those smaller states in turn legitimize the founding state's power and its new institution, which can be wielded for political purposes. For example, during the Cold War, Washington created the Inter-American Development Bank (IADB) to help combat the spread of communism, controlled the bank in part through threats to withhold funding, and ensured that the bank generally did not lend to communist states.[30] Similarly, Japan has "systematic influence over the distribution of ADB funds," with one study finding that when Japan was lobbying for a UN Security Council seat it increased loan disbursements to Asian states that might be able to support it.[31] More generally, banks set the rules and norms of regional order through loan conditionality and signaling; similarly, bank reports, indices, convening power, and loans are often intertwined with questions related to human rights, government transparency, indigenous rights, environmental considerations, the role of SOEs, and a host of other matters that are fundamentally political in nature. Indeed, China itself has previously objected to the inclusion of human rights and other liberal values in World Bank reports and disbursements. From a historical perspective, it should be unsurprising that China's interest in AIIB is as much about order as it is about development gains.

Building

China's pursuit of AIIB (1) began after the Global Financial Crisis; (2) involved uncharacteristic investments in its institutionalization; and (3) provided China order-building benefits. Here, we turn to each of these three key points.

The Post-Crisis Opportunity

China's interest in creating AIIB emerged from the 2008 Global Financial Crisis. The first proposal for AIIB was issued in 2009 at the Boao Forum, a Chinese-founded forum that Beijing has often used to test major new initiatives, such as "Peaceful Rise" (和平崛起) in 2003. The proposal was made by a top think tank—the China Center for International Economic Exchanges (CCIEE)—which proposed an "Asia Infrastructure Investment Bank" as well as an "Asia Agriculture Investment Bank" at the gathering.[32] This proposal was authoritative: the think tank that released it has strong connections to China's leadership, is located "only a few hundred meters" from the Zhongnanhai leadership compound, and was run by former Vice Premier Zeng Peiyan.[33] CCIEE was expressly created by the State Council after the financial crisis, and its first major set of initiatives was to study policy responses to it. It even held a major conference on the subject attended by both Premier Wen Jiabao and then Executive Vice Premier Li Keqiang. Prominent board members at the time had foreign policy backgrounds, including former Foreign Minister Tang Jiaxuan and former Director of the Foreign Affairs Office of the CCP Central Committee Liu Huaqiu. In addition, CCIEE's AIIB proposal was likely related to work at the

Central Policy Research Office, and the official who proposed AIIB at the 2009 Boao Forum, Zheng Xinli, had only months prior served as deputy director of the Central Policy Research Office (CPRO).[34] That institution, which is highly authoritative, was behind much of the CCP's guiding ideology and long-term policy, and it seems that the concept for the bank may well have originated there—suggesting its centrality to the Party's strategic planning. Taken together, the fact that a well-connected think tank like CCIEE created to recommend policy adjustment after the Global Financial Crisis would send a recent CPRO deputy director to propose AIIB—and to do so at a Chinese forum often used to test major Chinese concepts—strongly suggests that China's leadership was thinking about launching a Chinese development bank not long after the crisis itself.

After proposing AIIB at Boao, Zheng Xinli and other staff members at CCIEE continued to send reports to senior leadership on AIIB, though the bank was not launched for years in part because, in Zheng's words, "I think in the first few years the situation and the conditions were not mature." Zheng noted that it was only at the 18th Party Congress that "the conditions were mature, and also that President Xi made the decision there."[35] Zheng also clarifies that the leadership's rationale behind AIIB was threefold: (1) Asia needed infrastructure spending that could not be met by the World Bank or ADB; (2) China needed to find something to do with its foreign reserves; and (3) China had an opportunity to develop relations with its neighbors through economic infrastructure support that would connect these economies to China. When Xi Jinping surprised his Indonesian hosts in 2013 by announcing the bank, Zheng Xinli accompanied him on the journey.[36] For his service in AIIB's creation, Zheng has been referred to in state media as the "father of AIIB."[37] AIIB soon became a focus of interagency Chinese efforts. As Jin Liqun notes, "The Chinese governmental institutions, the minister of finance, foreign affairs, the central bank and others, are involved in conceptualizing this new bank" and in deliberations "over the architect[ure] of this new bank [sic]."[38]

Other figures closely connected with the bank also link its establishment to the financial crisis. In an essay on the future of the Bretton Woods system, Jin Liqun strongly suggested that the bank's origins were in the perceived decline of the United States after the Global Financial Crisis. "From day one, the function and sustainability of the Bretton Woods system were contingent on the power of the US," he notes. But now, the United States is less able to reform and uphold the system and "risks forfeiting its international relevance while stuck in its domestic political quagmire."[39] He concludes with an extended mediation on US decline:

Ever since Edward Gibbon's magnum opus, the monumental *The Decline and Fall of the Roman Empire*, was produced, the phrase "decline and fall" has been applied to the saga of defunct empires in history, and indiscriminately to some nations that have lost much of their former luminous energy in recent history. While a power's "decline" seems to be the process, "fall" is not necessarily the inevitable denouement. In some cases, it is not true that a nation has suffered a straightforward decline or fall; it is just the consequence of the constant shift in the balance of power between nations. The new powers will perhaps nudge the big ones to indicate their need for a bit more elbow room. . . . To some people who prefer status quo, they should perhaps savor the thought-provoking quote from the movie *The Leopard*—the words of an aristocrat when social change is looming large—"If we want things to stay as they are, things will have to change."[40]

Jin's excerpted quote links China's constructive impulses to America's perceived decline. Those constructive impulses were also highlighted by China's top leadership, who linked AIIB to China's growing confidence, its leadership ambitions, and public goods provision. During his speech inaugurating AIIB, Xi declared that the "initiative to establish the AIIB is a constructive move" intended to "enable China to undertake more international obligations" and to "provide more international public goods."[41] He also stated that "China welcomes all countries to ride on its development." Similarly, AIIB President Jin Liqun declared that "now that China is more developed and thus, can afford to provide financial resources to other developing countries in Asia, it is our turn to do something for the rest of Asia. . . . It's our turn to contribute."[42] Indeed, "father of AIIB" Zheng Xinli remarked that the reasons for founding AIIB were to benefit China's neighbors and to link them to China's economy: "China as a large Asian country has to help its neighboring countries so that they can get on the wagon of our development. Once the infrastructure foundation is in place, we can begin to exchange with them, we can transform the resource advantages of those countries into economic advantages, and we can meet our natural resource and agricultural needs."[43] Together, these statements suggest that AIIB is seen as an agent of public goods provision, one that will tie neighboring economies to China's own economic engine, and thereby help constitute regional order. As Chan concludes, "In short, the AIIB has been founded to serve a grand strategy of China's regional order-building."[44]

Supporting Deep Institutionalization

China's negotiation over AIIB's institutionalization also provides insight into its institutional preferences. As a development bank, AIIB is one of China's deepest institutions, with a secretariat, charter, staff, regular meetings, obligations, and monitoring provisions. But when China first announced the bank in 2014, it appeared to envision a Chinese-dominated tool of economic statecraft rather than a high-standards development bank. At the institutional level, China initially sought (1) a narrower *membership* excluding extra-regional states; (2) a *veto* with China holding half the bank's shares; (3) a strong bank *staff* with weak external supervision; and (4) its *mission* as advancing the Belt and Road Initiative (BRI). This bank would be China-dominated with few rules restricting Beijing's political use of it. But Western and Asian states, in contrast, preferred the Bank "be commercially-oriented, have rules-based lending practices, be transparent in its operations, and uphold existing best practices through environmental and social safeguards."[45] The struggle between these two impulses shaped the institutionalization of the bank in four key areas: membership, the veto, staff, and mission. The resultant bargain saw China make concessions and other states legitimize China's power.

First, with respect to *membership*, China initially assumed few would join the bank and was prepared to dominate it. AIIB President Jin Liqun indirectly quoted Xi Jinping's guidance on this point: "Even if we end up having only one country, only China, [a] one man band running this institution, we would do it."[46] When China began soliciting participants to join the bank in October 2013, it excluded rivals, likely fearing their ability to shape the process against China's interests. Seven months into the process, the Japanese and Indian governments admitted that China had not even approached them about the bank, let alone invited them to join it, with India's finance minister conceding, "The Chinese have yet to speak to us or discuss it with us. What I know is what I read from the newspaper."[47] In the first round of multilateral discussions about AIIB held on the sidelines of a May 2014 ADB meeting in Kazakhstan, Beijing invited a number of Asian states, though "India, Japan, and the US were not approached."[48] China also excluded extra-regional countries from negotiations on the memorandum of understanding (MOU) that began AIIB's institutionalization in October 2014, with Finance Minister Lou Jiwei declaring that China followed the "principle" of "regional countries prior to non-regional countries."[49] After excluding India from the initial invitation and the first AIIB preparatory meeting in March 2014, China reversed course and invited India to join in July 2014.[50] The first MOU signed three months later saw twenty-one Asian countries sign on.[51] For some time after, extra-regional states remained unwelcome, with Lou stating in a speech to the National People's Congress that "prospective founding membership is open to countries from the region first and applications from countries outside the region are not considered for now."[52] Gradually it changed course when it saw the benefit of their participation, and the United Kingdom joined AIIB in March 2015, with others soon following.[53]

Second, China worked to maintain a powerful *veto* within the organization. When China first launched AIIB, it proposed a $50 billion bank with the overwhelming majority of the capital coming from China itself, providing a comfortable margin for veto power. Foreign funds were sought, but to Jin Liqun, they were not essential because "if the worst comes to the worst, we have a huge Chinese market to tap" for financing.[54] Asian states took issue with China's domination of the bank's financing and the resultant allocation of vote shares, so in June 2014, China doubled the bank's registered capital from $50 billion to $100 billion and indicated it would commit half that amount and gain half the votes.[55] As more countries expressed interest in the bank, China reduced its capital share and its voting powers, ultimately declaring it would not pursue a formal veto in March 2015 and that the bank would instead operate on consensus.[56] China eventually reversed course and pursued an informal veto, with its vote share of 26.06 percent sufficient to block bank decisions that required a three-quarters majority. China's reversal occurred *after* the bank's membership expanded and, according to one former Chinese Academy of Social Sciences (CASS) researcher, "reflects the concern within China over losing control of the bank to Western countries if China does not have the veto."[57] To protect that influence, China capped extra-regional vote shares at 25 percent of the bank's total; the remaining 75 percent would be held by Asians, and China was of course the dominant Asian economy. China's AIIB vote share (26 percent) exceeds the US share in the World Bank (15.02 percent) and the Japanese share in the ADB (12.84 percent); and AIIB has the largest gap between the first- and second-highest vote shares (China's 26 percent vs. India's 8 percent) and capital shares (China's 31 percent and India's 9 percent) of any MDB.[58] Moreover, because so many decisions require a three-quarters majority, China's informal veto is more powerful than "that enjoyed by major shareholders in other MDBs."[59] According to the 2015 Articles of Agreement, China's veto effectively covers any change in the bank's capital, a member's capital subscription, the board, the president, and Articles of Agreement, as well as more mundane matters.[60] Ultimately, China's position in the bank is safe. As Bin Gu, a professor at Beijing Foreign Studies University Law School, argues, countries that "missed the chance to be founding members" are unlikely to have significant influence if they join now "since only a small unallocated capital stock is available for subscription by new members."[61] China can also veto any threats to its veto (e.g., a capital increase for the bank); and if it narrowly lost the veto, it retains a coalition of states that would nonetheless vote with it.

A third major area of institutionalization was AIIB's *personnel and oversight.* Most multinational development banks have a resident board of directors that acts as an oversight and a check on political manipulation.[62] China, however, initially resisted including one and instead proposed a vague "technical panel" fill the role; it then compromised and agreed to a *non-resident,* unpaid twelve-member board as new member states joined.[63] Banks are often able to retain considerable discretion even with resident boards, slow-walking shareholder initiatives or undercutting board instructions.[64] China's decision to choose a weaker, unpaid, non-resident board suggests the bank's decisions will reflect the preferences of its president and senior management, which are largely selected by China. In a departure from other MDBs, AIIB's Operational Policy on Financing suggests that the non-resident board will delegate powers directly to the bank president—a marked departure from other models.[65]

Fourth, AIIB's was initially intended as a Chinese tool to support BRI. A month after AIIB's MOU was signed, Xi Jinping said in an interview that "China's inception and joint establishment of the AIIB with some countries is aimed at providing financial support for infrastructure development in countries along the 'One Belt, One Road' and promoting economic cooperation."[66] These sentiments were amplified by readouts of Leading Small Group meetings that said the "primary task" of AIIB was to provide capital for BRI and by NPC statements that explained that AIIB was "created for the better implementation of 'One Belt, One Road.' "[67] It was not until mid-2016, after facing criticism from European and Asian states alike, that Beijing finally put some official distance between BRI and AIIB. During a meeting with business leaders, Jin Liqun declared that AIIB "would finance infrastructure projects in all emerging market economies even though they don't belong to the Belt and Road Initiative.' "[68] And yet, all thirteen of AIIB's 2016 projects were nonetheless part of Belt and Road. As a former CASS researcher put it, "During the process of pushing forward the establishment of the AIIB and the One Belt, One Road Initiative, Chinese policy makers appeared to unexpectedly be faced with a situation in which the two needed to be distanced from one another to a certain extent. . . . To announce 'the AIIB is not exclusively for the One Belt, One Road Initiative' constitutes a clever approach in this regard."[69]

In sum, China supported an institutionalized AIIB—one with far clearer rules and decision-making processes than its previous involvements in APEC and ARF—because it was ready to build order. It initially planned to use the bank to more effectively pursue its interests; but by the time it was launched, China had compromised to address member concerns about AIIB serving as a Chinese instrument, which in turn legitimized Beijing's leadership credentials. As President Xi Jinping said at his speech inaugurating AIIB, China wanted the bank to be a "rule-based and high-standard institution in all aspects involving its governance structure, operation policy, safeguards and procurement policy, and human resources management."[70] What is striking about this bargain is how China "successfully satisfied these concerns [of member states] without forgoing significant control over the bank."[71] The bank is based in China; China is the largest funder; China retains a veto over all decisions; the non-resident board is a weak check; and the staff is largely composed of Chinese nationals—with the bank's executive director a former deputy finance minister for the Chinese government.[72]

Building Order

AIIB offers several benefits for China's order-building strategy. It (1) provides China coercive ability to constrain its neighbors; (2) helps China set rules and strike consensual bargains; and (3) provides China legitimacy.

First, AIIB institutionalizes China's coercive capacity, providing it some plausible deniability when it is exercised and reducing some of the friction otherwise generated by its nakedly unilateral use. China's control over AIIB's membership, veto, and bank staff—and the relative autonomy of the staff and president over loan disbursements—creates the possibility for economic statecraft. And if AIIB adopts some forms of conditionality, either explicit or implicit, that involve criteria in line with China's own political or economic preferences, it would constrain autonomy for Asia's developing states and increase the likelihood that they might align their foreign policies more closely to China's in order to access capital. Indeed, some Chinese officials and scholars privately suggest that countries with disputes with China will be less likely to access funds from AIIB.[73] Others have observed the dichotomy between a growing "economic dependence on China and a security reliance on the United States" and argued that economic inducements will enhance China's freedom of maneuver.[74]

China has previously wielded its influence in multilateral organizations against others. For example, it refused to approve the ADB's multilateral development plan for India because some funds would be used in Arunachal Pradesh, which China claims.[75] AIIB also offers opportunities for giving others important roles within Chinese order. Already, the decisions regarding which countries hold AIIB vice presidencies is assumed to be linked to China's political interests. South Korea was promised one of AIIB's vice presidencies because of its early support for AIIB, but it lost that slot to France in a decision linked to Seoul's deployment of US missile defense systems."[76] China privately offered Australia a senior role in AIIB if it signed the October 2014 MOU, but then retracted that offer when Australia's hesitance was perceived as flowing from US and Japanese pressure.[77] And even when AIIB is not used in this way, it can still help build economic flows that would tie Asian neighbors to China's own economy and create coercive capacity in the future. Writing on these motivations, Fudan University Professor and former Chinese diplomat Ren Xiao argues that "geo-economics and geopolitics are constantly working" together, that "it is not true that China is simply altruistic," and that through AIIB China believes it can "win friends and influence in the region" and "make nearby countries more attractive as suppliers to Chinese manufacturers and as consumers of Chinese-made goods."[78] Finally, the rules and standard-setting power AIIB generates can affect the fates of Asian economies. Australian officials were concerned that AIIB's draft guidelines did not seem to reference coal technology, and requirements regulating who might participate in lucrative infrastructure projects also offer China constraining power over its neighbors.[79] Just as Japan and the United States used development banks to advance political goals, so too can China.

Second, AIIB provides a foundation not only for coercion but for consensual order-building. As discussed previously, top Chinese leaders have repeatedly framed AIIB as part of China's effort to provide public goods. For example, in March 2016, Foreign Minister Wang Yi told journalists that AIIB "shows that China is transitioning rapidly from a participant in the international system to a provider of public goods." China's regional efforts were "an open initiative, not the Monroe Doctrine or some expansionism" and that the bank demonstrated that "China has the confidence to find a path to great-power status different from the one followed by traditional powers. It is going to be different in that China will not play the bully."[80] When Xi announced AIIB, he did it in Indonesia and stressed that Beijing "would give priority to ASEAN countries' needs."[81] In public speeches, AIIB is often described as a way to allow other states to better benefit from China's rise, including through the BRI. In addition, AIIB also offers an opportunity to shape the content of Asian order.

Third, AIIB provides China legitimacy. As Chapter 5 showed, China has been sensitive to *who* leads Asian order-building, and it has undermined efforts by the United States through APEC and Japan through ASEAN to claim that mantle.[82] AIIB was its bid for leadership, and by offering some political influence in the bank to member states it in turn got them to effectively legitimize its leadership claims. The focus on *China's* leadership is key. As Jin Liqun argued: "What the world and Asia lack is not money [for infrastructure] but motivation and leadership," and China could provide it through AIIB. Similarly, as one scholar from the government-affiliated China Foundation for International Studies argued, "The ADB is mainly led by Japan, and the World Bank is mainly led by America, and so the AIIB is mainly led by China."[83] Ren Xiao argues AIIB marked China's "push for a regional institution within which it would be dominant."[84] This is why, in contrast to past efforts, China did not choose to work with others to make AIIB an outgrowth of ASEAN+3 or any other institutional forum. And to elevate AIIB, Chinese officials have sometimes criticized other institutions harshly. Finance Minister Lou Jiwei declared that the ADB's "current capacity is really insufficient" and that China has superior experience, arguing that the domestic "China Development Bank has been doing commercial loans and its business is far bigger than the ADB and World Bank combined—and that happened in less than 20 years."[85] Lou has also criticized the ADB for being too bureaucratic.[86] Jin Liqun called its governance system a "disaster."[87] Similar criticisms have been made of the World Bank as well.

AIIB, like other MDBs, also helps its founder legitimize the norms and principles it supports. For example, the World Bank and IMF have allowed Washington to push economic norms in line with its interests, and the World Bank's Ease of Doing Business indicator has even reshaped the policies and domestic politics of developing states. Similarly, Wang Jisi has been clear that AIIB is part of an attempt at ensuring that global economic governance conforms more closely to Chinese norms and values than Western ones.[88] In his speech introducing AIIB at the Boao Forum, the then expected head of the institution, Jin Liqun, argued in favor of China's development experience and AIIB's ability to help others emulate it: "China's development methodology is logical. China's experience can be transplanted to any other country. If China can make it, there is no reason why another country cannot."[89] Other officials, like Lou Jiwei, have criticized the West as a model: "I've said many times that I don't acknowledge best practice. Who is best? . . . We need to consider their [developing countries'] needs and sometimes the West puts forward some rules that we don't think are optimal . . . we don't see the existing system as being the best."[90] It is likely that as AIIB grows, it will help normalize China's view on limiting the role of political, human rights–related, and good governance standards in lending. In this way, the AIIB can chip away at the legitimacy of the liberal values that undergird much of the West's political power and influence—and that pose a threat to China's own stability.

CICA

The Conference on Interaction and Confidence Building-Measures in Asia (CICA) was proposed in 1992, held its first major meeting in 1999, and then held leader-level meetings every four years beginning in 2002. Long led by Kazakhstan, with Turkey taking over the rotational chair in 2010, the organization had little profile, few relationships with existing organizations, little great power interest, and slow and generally empty institutionalization. All of this changed in 2014 when China assumed leadership of the organization and promptly set about elevating it as a vehicle to either create or debate a new Asian security structure. And yet, China's investments in the organization are rather puzzling.

Alternative Explanations

China's decision to assume leadership over CICA is puzzling because the otherwise obscure organization has virtually no purpose or meaningful capabilities. CICA is nominally intended to sponsor confidence-building measures (CBMs) spanning military-political issues; terrorism; and economic, environmental, and human dimensions.[91] In practice, these CBMs are toothless and consist of action plans without actions. States are asked to undertake them on a voluntary basis, and in general the vast majority of these consist of prosaic items like mutual military visits, exchanges of military CVs, regulatory harmonization on trade or immigration, as well as information exchange.[92] The organization has extremely low levels of institutionalization. CICA admits that its secretariat plays a largely logistical role: it provides only "administrative, organizational, and technical support for meetings and other activities of the CICA," and it lacks monitoring mechanisms—with information on CBM implementation provided on a voluntary basis.[93] As a result of these weaknesses, CICA generally fails to fulfill its stated functions relative to other groups. Despite its focus on CBMs, unlike ASEAN and the ARF, CICA did not have any affirmative agenda for preventive diplomacy or conflict prevention until 2014. And while CBMs in Europe during the Cold War and among Shanghai Cooperation Organization (SCO) participants placed sharp limits on activities and positioning of military personnel, nothing in the CICA approaches this level of constraint. While the organization at times claims to focus on counterterrorism, it lacks any coordinating capacity to address it similar to the SCO's. At best, CICA has been a talk shop, and it struggles even there: it holds leader-level summits once every four years, in contrast to APEC, ARC, and the SCO, which host such meetings annually. Why then did China invest in it and seek to lead it?

Building

China's decision to invest in CICA despite these challenges was motivated not by the organization's present capabilities but by its future potential. China viewed CICA as a template for creating a pan-Asian security framework that would exist outside of the US-led alliance system and the ASEAN-dominated multilateral forums of Southeast Asia, and one that would be characterized by Chinese influence.

The Post-Crisis Opportunity

China has long been involved in CICA, but after the Global Financial Crisis, it began to use the organization to advance its own vision for Asia's security architecture—one that targeted the United States. As the chapter's introduction noted, the process started in the run-up to the first post-crisis CICA summit in 2010. China and Russia had just signed the "Joint Russian-Chinese Initiative on Strengthening Security in the Asia Pacific Region," and they pushed CICA to adopt it at the 2010 Summit and subsequent Special Working Group meetings as a foundation for a "future regional architecture." Joint Sino-Russian English-language preparatory documents and presentation materials—likely prepared by China rather than Russia given the use of Chinese-style notation for quotations—reveal that the initiative targeted US alliances and was directly linked to the new political circumstances produced by the Global Financial Crisis.[94] "The global financial and economic crisis has accelerated a whole series of trends that . . . shift the balance of forces in global politics and economics, entailing a profound transformation of the entire system of international relations," begins one document. "The crisis has highlighted that . . . new economic powers and centers of political influence are on the rise. The gravity center of political activity is likewise shifting towards the Asia-Pacific," it continues. "Under the impact of global transformations a process of *reshaping the regional architecture has started in the Asia-Pacific*."[95] The document then criticizes the US-based regional architecture:

> It is increasingly obvious that the existing security architecture in the Asia Pacific region which is based upon non-transparent military alliances does not correspond to the modern realities of the multipolar world as well as to the nature and scale of multiplying threats and challenges the region is facing. The region still lacks a well-structured system of institutions and legal instruments able to guarantee peace and stability at this vast area. These factors highlight the urgency of elaboration of additional measures to strengthen security in the region.[96]

Instead of the U.S. approach, "the future regional architecture should be open, transparent and equal," the document argued, and "it should be based on the non-bloc principle." The document noted that this "is exactly what the leaders of Russia and China" agreed to "during the Russian Chinese summit in September last year in Beijing."[97] In short, in the wake of the Global Financial Crisis, the time had come for an Asian architecture based on a Sino-Russian regional framework opposed to US alliances, and CICA was the vehicle to build that architecture.

The links between the Global Financial Crisis and China's efforts were broadcast in high-level CICA speeches by Chinese diplomats. In 2010, State Councilor Dai Binguo argued, "with an eye towards the *post-financial-crisis era*, CICA members should increase trust and coordination and unswervingly pursue" a new Asian security architecture.[98] Indeed, the period after the Global Financial Crisis was a new era because the crisis had changed everything. Dai argued that the crisis revealed that the "trend towards multi-polarity had never been so clear," and the call for "greater democracy in international relations had never been so strong." "The days are gone," Dai declared, "when one or two, or a handful of countries dominated world affairs." In this post–financial crisis era, CICA would be a tool: "to create a good regional environment, it is important to make full use of CICA and other regional mechanisms of multilateral exchanges and cooperation."[99] At the next major CICA meeting in 2012, Deputy Foreign Minister Chen Guoping continued this line of argumentation and introduced what would become a new signature concept, declaring that interdependence had produced a "community of common destiny." Chen went further than Dai, and he proposed a path forward based on Sino-Russian regional security framework proposed earlier, indicating it should apply to the behavior of all Asian countries.[100] Two years later, Xi Jinping raised the Sino-Russian initiative at the 2014 CICA Summit, arguing it "had played an important role in strengthening and maintaining peace and stability in the Asia-Pacific region."[101]

China could only do so much from the sidelines. To promote these views, it needed some degree of control over CICA. For most of its history, the organization had been led by Kazakhstan and then for four years by Turkey (2010–2014), and although plans for a rotational chairmanship had been discussed, there was as yet no settled order of succession. China's eventual chairmanship of CICA was something it actively engineered, and it began at least as early as 2012. Indeed, the first public reference to China's pursuit of the CICA chairmanship was at the 2012 CICA Summit, when Deputy Foreign Minister Chen Guoping not only suggested a new regional architecture but, in the very same speech, declared that "we have already applied for Chairmanship for the period 2014–2016" and asked for the "support of other Member States."[102] Despite these efforts, the 2012 Joint Statement makes no reference to any consensus behind a Chinese chairmanship.

China's campaign received a substantial boost in 2013 when President Xi Jinping visited Astana to meet with Kazakh President Nazarbayev. In a readout of their private discussions, China's Foreign Ministry noted that CICA had been a topic of discussion and that "the Kazakh side supports China for holding CICA's rotating presidency from 2014 to 2016 and supports China for hosting the CICA Summit in 2014."[103] Both governments released a joint statement formalizing these points and endorsing institutionalization, declaring "both sides will continue to develop and strengthen CICA processes."[104] With the statement released, China had essentially secured leadership of the organization for a two-year term; roughly halfway through that first term, it secured a term extension to 2018—even though past CICA statements suggested chairs would serve only one two-year term.[105]

Supporting Deep Institutionalization

Once China had gained leadership in CICA, it enthusiastically pushed to institutionalize the organization. As Chen Guoping stated on the twentieth anniversary of CICA in 2012, "China supports CICA's development into a formal international organization" from a loose forum.[106] With these ambitions in mind, President Xi in his 2014 Summit speech articulated a broad vision for CICA's future: "China proposes that we make CICA a security dialogue and cooperation platform that covers the whole of Asia and, on that basis, explore the establishment of a regional security cooperation architecture."[107] To that end, China worked to improve CICA's institutionalization in three main ways—all of which was a dramatic departure from its opposition to institutionalizing in APEC and ARF.

First, ever since its 2002 launch, CICA had held either a summit or a ministerial level meeting every two years with a Special Working Group or Senior Officials Conference held in between, making it far less institutionalized than ARF, APEC, or EAS, which hold annual leader-level summits. For that reason, Xi argued for more regular high-level meetings: "China believes that it is advisable to increase the frequency of CICA foreign ministers' meetings and even possibly summits in light of the changing situation, so as to strengthen the political guidance of CICA and chart a blueprint for its development."[108] China has made modest progress in these efforts by pushing forward an additional ministerial in 2017 and by encouraging CICA states to meet together on the sidelines of the UN General Assembly.[109] Official CICA Think Tank Forum documents written by the Shanghai Institute for International Studies suggest even broader plans, including regular meetings of defense ministers and public security ministers, among others.[110] These measures would bring CICA's institutionalization closer to the levels of ASEAN-related forums.

Second, China sought to improve the capacity of the secretariat, including for monitoring and supervisory purposes that would better enable it to encourage the implementation of confidence-building measures. As Xi argued in 2014, "China proposes that we enhance the capacity and institutional building of CICA, support improving the functions of the CICA secretariat, [and] establish . . . a task force for supervising the implementation of confidence building measures in various areas within the CICA framework." This was a dramatic departure from China's participation in APEC and ARF, which saw Beijing oppose monitoring for such measures. Think Tank Forum documents go even further, suggesting China's preferences are for more funding for the secretariat, more personnel, and an explicit "mandate to monitor the implementation of CBMs," as well as "crisis management and emergency response mechanisms."[111]

Third, China hoped to expand CICA exchanges across multiple domains, with President Xi urging the creation of "a defense consultation mechanism of member states" and "counter-terrorism, business, tourism, environmental protection, culture, and people-to-people exchanges."[112] Indeed, within a year China had launched a variety of new CICA initiatives, including a CICA Youth Council, a Business Council, a Non-Governmental Forum, and Think Tank Forum—almost all coordinated with Chinese funds and support. In addition, China plans to host a regular CICA Dialogue on Asian Awareness. Before these initiatives, CICA had been a rather thin organization; these efforts set a precedent for CICA's expanded functionality that China has continued to push.

Building Order

CICA provides a number of concrete benefits to China as it seeks to assert its own vision of Asia's regional security architecture. It helps China build a regional order in Asia by (1) providing China with the means to constrain its neighbors; (2) promoting the consensual foundations and content of China-led order; and (3) promoting Chinese leadership and legitimacy.

First, China has attempted to use CICA to constrain the ability of its neighboring states to cooperate with the United States, in part by promoting norms that would stigmatize alliances or possibly even security cooperation with the United States. As the chapter introduction discussed, China used CICA for this purpose as early as 2010, when China and Russia pushed a regional security architecture at a CICA summit that was explicitly anti-alliance. China continued to push this joint initiative with Russia in 2011, 2012, and 2014 CICA meetings.[113] The ultimate goal was to constrain the security behavior of regional states, as Deputy Foreign Minister Chen Guoping made clear in 2012, when he proposed the Sino-Russian initiative as the basis for Asian rules of behavior.[114] In 2014, these ideas were front and center in Xi's address. His claim that "one cannot live in the 21st century with the outdated [zero sum] thinking from the age of the Cold War" is a criticism of US security architecture. Similarly, his declaration that "to beef up and entrench a military alliance targeted at a third party is not conducive to maintaining common security" is an argument against greater security cooperation between the United States and Asian states wary of China's rise.[115] His most controversial "Asia for Asians" remark flowed naturally from these sentiments. In 2017, Chinese diplomat Wang Tong addressed the 2017 CICA Ministerial and, in language nearly identical to Xi's, declared, "The Chinese side believes that the issue of Asian security can be resolved only by the Asian countries themselves and their peoples, who also have the opportunity and the desire to resolve these issues."[116]

Second, China has used CICA to position itself as an economic and security public goods provider that embeds neighboring economies in a mutually interdependent "community of common destiny," one where, in Xi's words, China's rise "delivers tangible benefits to Asia."[117] Key Chinese concepts like "community of common destiny" and "New Asian Security Concept" simultaneously emphasize China's centrality to Asia's economic interdependence while also criticizing US alliances, and by doing both, they mark an evolution from the earlier concepts China had long ago promoted in ASEAN. China intends for these concepts to be at the center of Asia's security architecture. As CICA's Executive Director Gong Jianwei argues, "While CICA has been moving towards achieving this aim [of establishing a security architecture] at a steady pace, President Xi Jinping has sought to accelerate the pace by proposing a New Asian Security Concept."[118] Indeed, the New Asian Security Concept, which Xi introduced as the foundation for Asia's new security structure at the 2014 CICA Summit, entails "common, comprehensive, cooperative, and sustainable security."[119] In his speech, Xi carefully explains each element of the concept, and China's 2017 White Paper on Asia-Pacific Security Cooperation elaborates on these elements: (1) "Common security" refers to the "community of common destiny" and also involves explicit criticism of alliances because they provide security for some states but not others;[120] (2) "comprehensive security" refers to traditional and non-traditional security threats and is relatively uncontroversial; (3) "cooperative security" references efforts by Asians to cooperate together to resolve problems through "dialogue and in-depth communication" and implicitly critiques external involvement in issues like China's territorial disputes;[121] and (4) "sustainable security" argues that Asian countries "need to focus on both development and security to realize durable security." CICA Think Tank Forum documents explain that this is a reference to Asia's "dual track," which sees China provide development and the US provide security, and the caveat that development is needed to achieve security is meant to elevate China's role in the "dual track" over the US role.

When these four are put together, the concept defines regional security as consisting of a "community of common destiny" whose members benefit from Chinese development, avoid alliances, do not involve outside states in disputes, and prioritize China's development benefits over external security guarantees. This concept has become foundational for CICA and has appeared in every CICA joint statement. Indeed, in 2017, Wang Yi declared triumphantly that "since China's assumption of the CICA chairmanship, the common, comprehensive, cooperative and sustainable Asian Security Concept it proposed has won wide recognition."[122] CICA's executive director stated that "it is our earnest hope that all the member states will work together to adopt and implement the new security concept with a view to achieving the ultimate objective of CICA" and that China's aim was "to make the concept a reality and create a better security architecture in Asia."[123] CICA's official Think Tank reports are more forthcoming about the concept's ultimate purpose as an alternative to US-led order: "The differences over Asian security architectures are widening. The China-proposed and CICA-adopted New Asian Security Concept calls for a common, comprehensive, cooperative, and sustainable one. [In contrast,] the United States still clings to the military alliance and bloc security."[124]

A crucial final component of the New Asian Security Concept is its linkage to the BRI, which provides the kinds of public goods that underwrite the "community of common destiny." Given BRI's importance to China's order-building, China has worked to ensure that BRI is endorsed by CICA, giving it greater legitimacy and putting it at the center of Asian security order. CICA's executive director linked BRI directly to CICA: "China's Belt and Road initiative is another important step in promoting regional cooperation *in the true spirit of CICA.*"[125] Foreign Minister Wang Yi tied all these concepts together, combining both development and security into an integrative regional vision:

> In the future, we should use the [New] Asian Security Concept to lead in the promotion and establishment of a framework for Asian regional security cooperation; we should combine the CICA [New Asian Security] Concept with the Silk Road spirit, and use the framework of CICA to explore how the development strategies of Asian countries can be integrated with the construction of the "Belt and Road." We should probe into CICA's integrative properties to create a community of common destiny.[126]

Third, CICA helps China claim leadership over the debate on Asian regionalism. China's 2017 White Paper on Asia-Pacific Security Cooperation noted three paths to Asian regionalism: "In this region there are [1] ASEAN-led security cooperation mechanisms and [2] platforms such as the SCO and CICA, as well as [3] military alliances formed in history."[127] China preferred the second path, and CICA has allowed it to bypass ASEAN leadership and US and Japanese interference. As Ma Chunshan notes, CICA is the only pan-Asian "platform for international cooperation that does not include the United States and its important Asian ally, Japan, as members," thereby allowing China to shape it as it sees fit.[128]

Moreover, CICA is quite useful for the effort to shape the debate on regionalism. Its large membership allows it to credibly claim to be a forum that is representative of Asia—a point China repeatedly calls attention to. While Chinese addresses at CICA from 2002 through 2012 generally described CICA only as an "important organization," once it took over the organization in 2014, it used explicitly comparative language elevating CICA over alternative groupings.[129] "CICA is the largest and most representative regional security forum with the largest number of participants," Xi Jinping argued at the 2014 CICA Summit. CICA "is the only structure of its kind" in Asia, Executive Director Gong Jianwei declared.[130] Wang Yi said in 2016 that CICA was "Asia's largest and most representative security forum." In remarks for CICA's twenty-fifth anniversary the next year, he said it had "grown into the most representative security forum with the biggest coverage and largest number of members in Asia."[131] The purpose of these statements was to suggest CICA had a greater claim to serve as a foundation for establishing an Asian security architecture than other efforts. Indeed, Chinese think tank reports posted on the government's CICA website not only repeatedly articulate this point, they also point out a possible end stage for CICA is to become an Asian version of the OSCE, or what they might call an OSCA (Organization for Security and Co-operation in Asia). One report by the Shanghai Institute for International Studies, which was given pride of place on the website, argues that, because of its representativeness, "CICA is capable of providing a solid institutional foundation for and charting the shortest path toward an Asian security architecture."[132] Another report notes, "If CICA's potential and advantages can be fully tapped to propel its transformation and development into an OSCA, the future establishment of the new Asian security architecture will benefit greatly."[133] This is in part because CICA can play a consolidating role. As Vice Minister Chen Guoping noted in a speech before the CICA Senior Officials Committee, "Sub-regional security cooperation has been thriving in Asia, but cooperation mechanisms are fragmented and overlapping in function. It is imperative to integrate all the resources, build a broader and effective cooperation platform, and put in place a new architecture for regional security cooperation. In this process, CICA may play a central role by leveraging its strength in large geographical scope, inclusiveness, and confidence building measures."[134]

Finally, China has also sought to use CICA to build a common identity that China could lead. It has sought to do this in part by sponsoring a CICA NGO Forum and a CICA Think Tank Forum.[135] Just as similar efforts around APEC and ASEAN were central to the debates on Asian regionalism in the 1990s, China hoped that CICA could be central to those debates beginning in 2014. As Wang Yi explained in 2016, these forums are meant to "encourage all parties to explore a new Asian security architecture at the track II and non-governmental level"

and thereby "build consensus for CICA's future development and transformation."[136] Similarly, Xi Jinping has said these forums will "lay a solid social foundation for spreading the CICA concept of security, increasing CICA's influence,
and promoting regional security governance."[137] And, of course, China largely
leads these processes. One goal in these efforts is to contrast Asian countries
with Western ones. Indeed, the CICA Think Tank Forum reports and remarks
by Chinese officials suggest the belief that "the shortage of a common 'Asian
awareness' or a common Asian identity has further complicated the prospect of
establishing an overarching security mechanism" in Asia.[138] Another Think Tank
Forum report argues that "fostering a pan-Asian sense of shared destiny through
substantive inter-civilizational dialogues and closer economic cooperation"
should be a major Chinese goal.[139] To this end, President Xi Jinping urged the
creation of a regular CICA Dialogue on Asian Civilizations in 2014, and China
succeeded in pulling it together in 2018. Although such maneuvers are unlikely
to overcome internal Asian divisions, China clearly sees them as a way to gradually bind the region together under China's leadership.

Asian regional institutions can on their own only go so far in securing such
an objective. Beyond them, the other way China might bind the region together is through economic statecraft and the forms of control—both coercive
and consensual—that flow from it. As the next chapter demonstrates, economic instruments are rather like multilateral institutions in at least one critical respect: both are ostensibly liberal element of statecraft, and both can be
repurposed for more nakedly political goals like building regional order.

"Aboard Our Development Train"

Implementing Economic Building

"We must actively participate in and vigorously promote the construction of surrounding highways, railways, communications, and energy channels in the neighboring region to form a network of interconnected and interoperable infrastructure around China."[1]

—*Hu Jintao in 2009, four years before the launch of the Belt and Road*
Initiative

In 2012, Professor Wang Jisi—the dean of Peking University's School of International Relations—published an influential article in the nationalist tabloid the *Global Times*. Wang Jisi was a well-connected figure, once an informal adviser to China's paramount leader Hu Jintao, and his article was provocative. To the east, China faced security challenges: maritime disputes, island chains, wary neighbors, and the US Navy. "Marching westward" over the land, Wang noted, provided an attractive alternative.[2]

"Unlike East Asia, there is no U.S.-led regional military alliance among the countries to the west, and there is no possibility that one will arise," Wang argued.[3] Instead, China had abundant resources and a continental vacuum in that direction, as well as the surplus capacity and dollar reserves to fill it with pipelines, railways, highways, and even overland Internet infrastructure that would reduce China's dependence on the sea and bind the region tighter to China. This was a form of order-building, and although the ideas Wang outlined had been articulated by others—including Hu Jintao, who had called for a similar network of infrastructure around China years earlier—they appeared to find purchase. Many Chinese elites say that Wang's essay caught the attention of the country's leadership and helped shape the continental components of the Belt and Road Initiative (BRI) that Xi would launch the next year. Perhaps, but a similar focus on building infrastructure had been announced years earlier by Hu Jintao in the very speech he used to revise China's grand strategy after the Global Financial Crisis.[4] Regardless of whether Wang helped catalyze a new initiative or instead helped validate an existing one, the policy trajectory was increasingly clear: China would use economic power and infrastructure spending for geostrategic purposes, including to build order.

Wang had encouraged a rising China to march westward to avoid a hostile east. But about a century earlier, a rising Germany had decided to march eastward to avoid a hostile west. Germany's leadership had sought to construct a 1,000-mile railway from Berlin all the way to Baghdad and onward to the Persian Gulf. For Germany, this "Berlin-Baghdad railway" would not only bypass the preeminent British navy, it would also spread German influence deeper into the Middle East, open up the Ottoman Empire as an export market and source for raw materials, and offer Germany a way to protect its overseas possessions in Africa. Germany's grand infrastructure ambitions then were hardly unique: Britain had built the Suez Canal, the United States had built the Panama Canal, and the Japanese had hoped to build their own canal across Thailand's "Isthmus of Kra" to bypass British control over Singapore and the Malacca Strait. All understood that geography could reshape geopolitics.

Germany's project, which saw significant progress but fell short of completion due to the First World War, could have revolutionized Eurasia's strategic geography. But where that program failed, China's Belt and Road has continued onward. More broadly, China's use of economic instruments to build order, like Germany's, was hardly limited to infrastructure financing. Just as a rising Germany was concerned about British control over finance and sought ways to reduce it, a rising China has long been concerned about American dollar dominance and sought to circumvent it as well—both to *blunt* American power and to *build* China's own financial advantages.

China's effort in infrastructure and finance are not motivated primarily by absolute economic benefits or the demands of China's interest groups but by a desire to cultivate economic leverage. That leverage can take many forms, as Chapter 6 discussed. Economic leverage can be *relational*, which involves manipulating the interdependence between states (e.g., a bilateral trade agreement). It can be *structural*, which involves shaping the systems and frameworks within which global economic activity takes place (e.g., control over currency). And it can be *domestic*, which involves reshaping a state's internal politics and preferences (e.g., elite capture).

This chapter explores China's effort to *build* these forms of leverage. It shows that China's Belt and Road and its financial statecraft were precipitated in large part by the Global Financial Crisis, which led Beijing to feel more assertive about using economic tools to build order. We turn now to China's changing discourse on economics before analyzing its economic behavior.

Chinese Economic Texts

For years, China's economic efforts were focused on *blunting* American economic leverage and ensuring China had access to markets, technology, and capital to continue its development. In the post-crisis era, Chinese texts show its economic strategy shifted in two major ways. First, China focused intently on the economic component of "peripheral diplomacy," which in practical terms took the form of Chinese-led order-building through the cultivation of relational, structural, and domestic-political economic leverage over Chinese neighbors. The main instruments for creating this leverage were massive infrastructure investments as well as concessionary trade and trade sanctions. The second track focused on greater activism in global finance, an area of serious and growing vulnerability to the United States. There, China's new approach focused on building alternatives to US financial architecture. Just as in the blunting period, not all of China's economic activity in the building period had exclusively strategic motivations, but economic tools were clearly a part of its larger strategy.

A Second Shift in Strategy

Before the Global Financial Crisis, even as late as 2006, China's focus was different. When China took stock of its foreign policy assumptions during that year's Central Foreign Affairs Work Conference, the dominant focus of its grand strategy was explicitly on Tao Guang Yang Hui (i.e., hiding and biding) and *blunting* the foreign pressure China faced.[5] Only two years later, however, the 2008 Global Financial Crisis caused a much bigger shift. China's assessment of the relative power gap with the United States fell significantly, and President Hu then officially revised Tao Guang Yang Hui by stressing "Actively Accomplishing Something" in his 2009 address.[6] In the process, Hu jettisoned the extensive rhetoric from his 2006 address on the importance of avoiding "speaking too much" and claiming leadership.[7]

In the post-crisis era, China's economic approach changed, with Beijing exhibiting a greater focus on order-building in its neighborhood. Indeed, in his 2009 address resetting Chinese grand strategy, Hu called for greater "peripheral diplomacy" and stressed that China now faced reduced external pressure and would have greater freedom of maneuver in the region.[8] After the crisis, he declared, the "overall strategic environment continues to improve" and "our country's influence on the periphery has been further expanded."[9] This created the opportunity for more proactive economic behavior, and Hu therefore stated that "we must strengthen economic diplomacy."[10] His speech made clear that this focus on economic diplomacy would take place both within the periphery as well as with respect to the international financial system.

Chinese leaders stressed these themes in subsequent years. As Chapter 7 discussed, "peripheral diplomacy" continued to see elevation in Chinese grand strategy after Hu's speech under the rubric of a "Community of a Common Destiny." In 2011, China released a White Paper advocating for a "Community of Common Destiny" in Asia, a concept that soon became shorthand for Chinese order-building in Asia.[11] Two years later, in 2013, Chinese Foreign Minister Wang Yi declared the periphery a "priority direction" for Chinese foreign policy, ostensibly above other focuses like the great powers, and linked it directly to the concept of a "Community of Common Destiny" for the first time.[12] That same year, President Xi held an unprecedented Work Forum on Peripheral Diplomacy—the first meeting of that magnitude convened on foreign policy since 2006 and the first ever on peripheral diplomacy. In his address, he made clear peripheral diplomacy's central importance in Chinese foreign policy, deemed it necessary for national rejuvenation, and declared its purpose as the realization of a regional "Community of Common Destiny."[13] Academic and think tank commentary picked up on the trend, with Yan Xuetong writing that "the significance of China's peripheral or neighboring countries to its rise is growing more important than the significance of the United States," which meant that China was elevating the periphery over its past focus on dealing with US pressures.[14] The next year, at the 2014 Central Foreign Affairs Work Conference—a major foreign policy gathering previously held only four times in Party history and usually only at moments of great transition—Xi appeared to elevate peripheral diplomacy over a focus on great powers like the United States.[15] That same language was then repeated again in the 2014 Government Work Report, suggesting its formalization.[16] Xi even made the "Community of Common Destiny" the main theme of the 2015 Boao Forum, and China's 2017 White Paper on Asian Security Cooperation states that "Chinese leaders have repeatedly elaborated on the concept of a community of common destiny on many different occasions. China is working to construct a community of common destiny . . . in Asia and the Asia-Pacific area as a whole."[17] These sources all strongly suggest the emergence of regional order-building as a major focus, if not the central priority, of Chinese grand strategy.

In addition to the growing focus on the periphery, China also began to become far more active in pushing for international monetary reform. As the case study on financial alternatives discusses in greater detail, from 2008 onward, Chinese officials took the unprecedented step of routinely calling for monetary diversification and a weakening of the dollar's role as reserve currency. These statements were made not only by the head of the People's Bank of China, but also by President Hu and other senior leaders at top economic forums including the G20. This strategy was explicitly outlined in Hu's own 2009 speech and has remained a feature of Chinese policy since.

A Building Strategy

China's efforts to build regional order emerged under the rubric of Hu's call to "Actively Accomplish Something." Hu declared that China "must *more actively* participate in the formulation of international rules" and institutions, anticipating the eventual creation of the Asian Infrastructure Investment Bank (AIIB) and leadership of CICA.[18] On financial issues, he declared China "must *more actively* promote the reform of the international economic and financial system," which that year led to new efforts to promote monetary diversification away from the dollar as well as parallel financial structures, a project that Hu stated would need to be undertaken "through coordination and cooperation with developing countries."[19] Finally, he proposed robust infrastructure investment as a part of China's economic strategy. Anticipating the BRI, Hu declared that "we must actively participate in and vigorously promote the construction of surrounding highways, railways, communications, and energy channels in the periphery to form a network of interconnected and interoperable infrastructure around China."[20] In short, trade, infrastructure, and monetary diversification were all core elements of China's more active economic strategy as early as 2009.

The link between China's regional economic efforts and its building was made clear in speeches by Hu as well as by Xi. Hu's 2009 address stressed that "operating in a good periphery is an important external condition for China," and it suggested concessionary economic arrangements—and "in particular" infrastructure agreements—were a part of peripheral diplomacy.[21] China would need to "adhere to the peripheral diplomacy policy of being a good neighbor and partner, strengthen strategic planning for the periphery as a whole, strengthen mutual trust and promote cooperation."[22] This could be accomplished in part by creating greater complementarities between China's economy and that of its neighbors. Indeed, Hu called for China to "strengthen the common interests of our country and peripheral countries . . . we must focus on deepening regional cooperation in Asia, paying attention to promoting the integration of regional and sub-regional cooperation with China's domestic regional development strategy," thereby linking China's economy with that of its neighbors.[23] Hu also stressed, "we must participate more actively in the formulation of international rules, actively promote the reform of the international economic and financial system, [and] more actively safeguard the interests of the vast number of developing countries."[24]

Many of these themes were stressed in subsequent years. China's 2011 White Paper, which first introduced the concept of a Community of Common Destiny, stressed the importance of "mutual dependence" as well as "intertwined" and "interconnected" interests, which in practical terms effectively would mean asymmetric dependence on China given its size.[25] The White Paper also called for regional cooperation along the lines proposed by Hu and more fully implemented under Xi. For its periphery, China advocated "increased trade" and said it would "promote regional economic integration," taking care to remind its neighbors that "China's prosperity, development, and long-term stability represent an opportunity rather than a threat to its neighbors."[26] All of this anticipated the announcement of BRI four years later, as well as China's concessionary trade agreements.

Under President Xi, these efforts were discussed more explicitly. On the economic side, in his 2013 Work Forum on Peripheral Diplomacy, Xi proposed offering public goods and facilitating mutual interdependence, both of which would "create a closer network of common interests, and better integrate China's interests with [neighbors], so that they can benefit from China's development."[27] He explained precisely how China would do this. "We must make every effort to achieve mutually beneficial reciprocity," Xi declared. "We have to make overall plans for the use of our resources . . . [and] take advantage of our comparative strengths, accurately identify strategic points of convergence for mutually beneficial cooperation with neighbors, and take an active part in regional economic cooperation."[28] In practical terms, he stated, "we should work with our neighbors to speed up connection of infrastructure between China and our neighboring countries" and explicitly listed the BRI and AIIB as tools to do so.[29] In addition, Xi wanted to "accelerate the implementation of the strategy of free trade zones" and to put "our neighboring countries as the base," another sign of the elevation of the periphery.[30] New investment as well as active interlinkage between Chinese border regions and neighbors was also essential. The overall objective, Xi stated, was "to create a new pattern of regional economic integration," one that he stated multiple times would be linked closely to China.[31] Left unstated was that the active cultivation of this kind of asymmetric interdependence would give China great freedom of maneuver and potentially constrain its neighbors as well. But at the 2017 BRI Forum, Xi was clear that these efforts fit under his work to create a Community of Common Destiny. All parties to BRI, he argued, would "continue to move closer toward a community of common destiny for mankind. This is what I had in mind when I first put forward the Belt and Road Initiative. It is also the ultimate goal of this initiative."[32] China was enjoying "rapid growth," he said in another speech, and would therefore "open our arms to the people of other countries and welcome them aboard the express train of China's development."[33] In short, these are the economic and institu-tional means at the heart of China's grand strategy to build regional order.

Infrastructure Investment and BRI

Infrastructure investment not only facilitates trade and connectivity, it also offers the opportunity to practice "economic power projection"—and through it, an opportunity to reshape the strategic geography of great power competi-tion. Like past great powers, Beijing has used infrastructure investment as a tool to build order, and the most visible example of this pursuit is China's BRI as well as the financial institutions that support it.

Alternative Explanations

Although this section argues that many BRI projects have strategic motivations, there are several alternative explanations common in the BRI literature.

First, some believe that the BRI is primarily driven by China's pursuit of ab-solute economic benefits. Most of the projects, however, are loss-making, which raises some doubts about this explanation. For example, an analysis shows BRI's port projects, which constitute an "easy case" for evaluating profitability since maritime trade dramatically exceeds overland trade, are generally struggling. An analysis of their finances by the think tank C4ADS finds that "several marked examples of unprofitability—suggest that Beijing is actively seeking to leverage the geopolitical capacity of its port projects."[34] For example, China's $8 billion investment in a Malaysian port near the Malacca Strait is evaluated as com-pletely redundant by the World Bank given that nearby existing ports remain under capacity. China's Hambanatota port in Sri Lanka has lost hundreds of millions of dollars since it opened and has virtually no real cargo traffic (its traffic is one-hundredth the amount of its neighboring port in Columbo), but China has nonetheless assumed the liabilities and taken a ninety-nine-year lease of the port.[35] China's construction of the Gwadar port in Pakistan is similarly unprofit-able but sees continued Chinese investment, and China has undertaken a forty-year lease and assumed its liabilities as well. There is no economic rationale for these investments, but as we will see, there is evidence of strategic motivations.

Second, some account for the poor finances of the projects by suggesting that they may be serve the interests of powerful vested interest groups. In par-ticular, BRI is seen as a way to support China's domestic economy by creating opportunities for its connected industries to be involved in infrastructure projects overseas. This explanation also has problems. As David Dollar notes,

BRI will struggle to absorb China's surplus capacity even under the most optimistic circumstances. "In steel alone," he notes, "China would need $60 billion per year of extra demand to absorb excess capacity. This figure excludes excess capacity in cement, construction, and heavy machinery." He concludes that BRI and the projects it supports are "much too small to make any dent in China's excess capacity problem—even if it were the sole supplier for these projects, which it won't be."[36] Moreover, a growing percentage of China's loans will not be paid back. This has already been the case in Sri Lanka and may well prove the case in countries like the Maldives, where roughly 20 percent of the budget is spent on servicing Chinese debt. Lending capital at a loss makes no economic sense, but if the result is a strategic asset, it does make strategic sense.

Third, some argue that the BRI is neither economic nor strategic but motivated in large part by status—they see it as a vanity project for Xi Jinping. But the timeline does not support this account. Many of the major projects (e.g., Gwadar, Hambanatota, and several rail and gas projects across Central Asia) not only preceded Xi and his BRI but were also explicitly described in strategic terms in Chinese government discourses, as we will see.

Fourth, a number of critics argue that BRI is largely meaningless. They argue that if everything China does is now folded by the government under BRI—from a Polar Silk Road to vaguely conceived BRI space roads—then the term means nothing. This criticism is entirely warranted, but even if the brand is at times empty many of the projects are quite real. A narrow focus on the BRI brand alone obscures the way infrastructure both within and outside the program creates enduring economic leverage. If BRI is taken to mean those key projects in the Indo-Pacific that China has pursued for years—which were of course the original focus of the initiative—then there is little question that many of the marquee projects are motivated by strategic designs.

Grand Strategic Explanations

Understood in these narrower terms, the BRI is at least as much—and likely much more—a strategic initiative than an economic or domestic-political one, and it creates multiple forms of relational, structural, and domestic-political leverage essential to order-building. We now consider each of these three.

Relational Leverage

First, BRI creates several important forms of relational leverage. It creates financial leverage over those that accept loans from Beijing, such as Sri Lanka and the Maldives, who are then unable to pay them back. In the case of the Maldives, as discussed earlier, some 20 percent of the country's budget now pays off interest on Chinese loans. In Sri Lanka, annual loan repayments—most of which are to China—now equal nearly the entirety of Sri Lanka's government revenue.[37] Interest rates are also exorbitant, running nearly 6 percent for Hambanatota expansion versus roughly half a percent for Japanese infrastructure loans.[38] Countries that cannot afford to repay China have on occasion taken additional loans from separate Beijing banks, deepening the cycle of indebtedness.[39]

BRI also creates the possibility of asymmetric trade interdependence, especially as increased connectivity effectively increases bilateral trade between China and its neighbors and creates dependence on China. Putting China at the center of Asian economies is explicitly the point. In his address to the 2013 Work Forum on Peripheral Diplomacy that preceded the maturation of BRI, Xi discussed how infrastructure investment and AIIB would "speed up the connection of infrastructure between China and our neighboring countries" and "create a closer network of common interests, and better integrate China's interests with [neighbors], so that they can benefit from China's development."[40] In 2017, Xi explicitly listed BRI as part of his effort to create a "Community of Common Destiny" in Asia, and several speeches make clear that interdependence and intertwined economies with China are key criteria for such a community. Many of these same points were made by a variety of top officials, including the Zheng Xinli, the high-level Central Party Research Office figure who proposed AIIB, suggesting their centrality to BRI.[41] In non-official sources, a variety of scholars have hoped that this kind of interdependence would constrain China's neighbors.

Finally, aside from relational leverage through finance and trade, BRI creates leverage over maintenance given that many Chinese projects will require Chinese engineers for upkeep, especially since Chinese state firms dominate many of these markets, ranging from hydroelectric power to high-speed rail.[42]

Structural Level

At the structural level, BRI allows Beijing to create connectivity that essentially excludes other countries. One form of this is through commercial ports, which in some ways constitute the new choke points of maritime trade, and a growing number are operated or leased by Chinese state companies—which can offer important economic leverage over the structure of Asian trade. For example, China's port project in Colombo, Sri Lanka, may well create an "artificial choke point" that is effectively under Chinese control. Nearly 30 percent of India's future maritime trade is likely to come through Colombo, where large container ships have their cargo placed on smaller ships that then enter India's ports.[43] That artificial choke point is in fact 85 percent controlled by the China Merchants

Holding Corporation (CMH)—which also now manages the Hambanatota port—and is of course itself controlled by the Chinese government.[44] China's investment in the port doesn't seem to be producing economic benefits. In fact, the Colombo port is actually making significant losses and is not expected to break even for at least ten years. The financial situation is so poor that Aiken Spence, a private firm that was the major private sector partner with CMH—and that unlike the Chinese government, is actually profit-seeking—felt compelled to sell its stake in the project.[45] Given the dire financial prospects for the project, perhaps a strategic motivation explains China's steadfast dedication to such an economically questionable venture. Similarly, CMH had begun preliminary construction of a massive $11 billion port in Bagamoyo, Tanzania—which will soon be the largest port in all of Africa. It will be connected by Chinese-built rail to various land-locked resource-supplying states such as the Democratic Republic of the Congo, Zambia, Rwanda, Malawi, Burundi, and Uganda.[46] These states will be dependent on the Bagamoyo port to access international markets, which is likely to be managed by CMH, creating a Chinese-owned choke point to the western Indo-Pacific.

In addition, the possibility that Beijing will export not only its engineering standards on traditional infrastructure like rail lines but also new high-tech infrastructure supporting the Internet or 5G creates path dependence in connectivity—that is, it could make it far easier for Beijing to lock in its ties with Asian states and far harder for those states to diversify toward Western countries. One could imagine, for example, that future American-made autonomous vehicles could be unable to connect to Chinese wireless networks in BRI countries.[47]

Domestic Leverage

Finally, at the domestic-political level, the BRI creates clear opportunities to bribe powerful constituencies in recipient countries, altering their politics. Indeed, China has used its state-owned enterprises (SOEs) that are involved in these projects expressly for that purpose. The *New York Times* confirmed that "during the 2015 Sri Lankan elections, large payments from the Chinese port construction fund flowed directly to campaign aides and activities for Mr. Rajapaksa."[48] Indeed, the funds were disbursed directly from the Chinese SOE contracted to build the port (China Harbor) from its account at Standard Chartered directly to affiliates of then Prime Minister Rajapaksa—including roughly $3.7 million less than ten days before the election. Similar reports suggest Chinese companies including China Harbor, but also the China Communications Construction Company, have bribed high-level officials in Bangladesh and the Philippines.[49]

Admittedly, the preceding forms of leverage exist regardless of whether Beijing intended them or not, but some of the evidence suggests that in many cases these were intentionally acquired and economically unwise—thereby strongly suggesting that infrastructure is an important part of China's larger grand strategy.

Military Significance

Some BRI projects clearly have military significance, providing opportunities for overseas facilities, as Chapter 8 and Chapter 12 discuss in greater detail. If Beijing is to build order in the Indo-Pacific, it needs the ability to ensure its military can project power over its vast distances. Beijing's port projects offer it the ability to resupply across the Indo-Pacific, thereby not only assuring China it can secure its resource flows from possible American or Indian intervention but also providing it the ability—if necessary—to intervene abroad. Accordingly, port projects were the priority in some leaked BRI planning documents, in which the Chinese government insisted on "accelerating the development of the Maritime Silk Road construction plan"[50] with "port construction as the priority."[51]

More concretely, top Chinese military officials have privately told foreign delegations that these port projects are built as dual-use because China expects it will use them in the future for military purposes—and China's first overseas military base in Djibouti along with its militarized island-building in the South China Sea, both of which ran against prior promises Beijing had made about bases and militarization, provide important context for these comments.[52] Government officials in both Pakistan and Sri Lanka who negotiated with China over port access noted that strategic and intelligence interests were part of the discussion. When Sri Lanka essentially sold its port to China, government officials from China refused to consider any option short of Chinese equity, indicating to Sri Lankan officials that a takeover had long been a preference of theirs. Chinese officials also left open questions about whether China's military could use the facility—it was only Indian intervention that allowed a clause to be inserted that required China to request Sri Lanka permission before using the port for military purposes.[53]

Finally, a number of quasi-official sources have discussed these port projects as long-term military investments. Zhou Bo, a fellow with China's Academy of Military Science, concedes that "access, rather than bases, is what the Chinese Navy is really interested in in the Indian Ocean."[54] Access of course still facilitates the goal of projecting power through these important waters; it just does so with a lighter footprint. As Zhou Bo and others admit, a key component of achieving access is through the use of such port projects. Xu Guangyu, a former vice president of the PLA Defense Institute, noted that China's commercial port projects in places such as Tanzania have military purposes. He argues that "as China's Navy travels farther and farther, it needs to establish a supply base to support the fleet . . . this is a normal need, but foreign countries aren't accustomed to China going into the blue-water."[55] The president of the Macau Military Institute argued that such ports have "potential military uses" but that China will not allow warships to dock there until some time has passed after the port's construction, and even then, will likely use the ports only when necessary to avoid fanning the flames of the "China threat theory."[56]

BRI is complex, and no one explanation can account for every single Chinese economic investment abroad. What this section suggests, however, is that China is not dissimilar from other great powers that came before it: it too is using infrastructure in certain key cases to enhance its relational, structural, and domestic-political leverage as well as to gain military access to the waters upon which it is dependent. All of this was largely unthinkable when China was merely pursuing the *blunting* of American power, and it is strong evidence of China's move to a focus on *building* regional order.

Building Financial Alternatives

Encouraged in part by the 2008 Global Financial Crisis, China invested in a number of parallel institutions to give it structural power over global finance. Financial power comes from a currency's centrality to global finance, and in the American case, it comes from the dollar's hegemony, which allows the United States to "turn banks and financial institutions into instruments of policy, even if they are based outside the United States."[57] American financial hegemony serves as both an example of how China can build order as well as a threat that China must blunt.

The 2008 Global Financial Crisis, and the perceived decline in the prestige of the American economic model, precipitated a coordinated Chinese effort to gradually *build* sources of structural power over the global economy while *blunting* American financial power. China's efforts were spread across three broad arenas. First, China sought to gradually weaken the dollar while promoting its own currency; second, it pursued alternatives to the SWIFT interbank payments system to weaken Western leverage and give China control over renminbi payments; third, it sought to promote alternatives to the "big three" sovereign credit rating agencies located in the United States whose ratings shape capital markets and can affect the fates of countries and companies. While some might argue that China's efforts were driven by the pursuit of absolute economic benefits or the power of interest group lobbies, as the analysis in this section will demonstrate, this was not the case; instead, the best explanation for China's push in global finance remains a grand strategic one. American structural power could not be bypassed without leaving the system, which would be economic suicide, or building a parallel set of infrastructure—accordingly, China chose the latter option.

Dollar Diversification and Renminbi Promotion

After the Global Financial Crisis, China began to call for a diversified international monetary system with a reduced role for the dollar and for alternatives like the IMF's special drawing rights (SDR) as well as the renminbi (RMB). Might this have been motivated by economic pursuits or interest group power? Hongying Wang answers no, noting that China's position "can't be neatly explained in terms of its economic interest."[58] A substantial decline in the value of the dollar would damage China's export-driven economy and reduce the value of China's enormous holdings of dollar-denominated assets.

Wang instead argues that national identity concerns explain China's policy, but there is evidence against this account. In internal documents, including speeches to the Central Economic Work Forum, Hu Jintao's call for a reduced role for the dollar is not accompanied by any chest-beating nationalist rhetoric about China's status, nor are his statements at the G20. Moreover, in his criticisms of the dollar, Hu did not generally call even for the RMB internationalization that a more nationalist leader might seek as a sign of status.

Instead, China's actions reveal intense and long-standing hopes for an international economic architecture in which the dollar is only one among many reserve currencies, and it is reasonable to see China's advocacy for the renminbi in such terms as well. Beijing has increasingly turned to renminbi internationalization as an instrument to not only hasten diversification, but also build the foundation for China's own structural power across Asia.

The 2008 Global Financial Crisis marked the start of this effort. After the crisis, China's leadership increasingly called into question the dollar's reserve currency status. Of course, various Chinese officials had for decades criticized the international economic order as unfair and called for its reform, and leading central bank officials had at times been critical of the "irrational" monetary system and urged greater monetary surveillance of advanced economies.[59] In this sense, the 2008 Global Financial Crisis marked a shift less in China's preferences and more in its confidence that it could reshape the international economic architecture around it. Accordingly, as Gregory Chin notes, after the crisis "China's leaders elevated financial and monetary policy, and monetary diplomacy, to a top priority."[60] The same year the crisis broke out, China's Central Economic Work Conference [中央经济工作] set a Party line on monetary policy and promptly concluded that "international monetary diversification will advance, but the status of the US dollar as the main international currency has not fundamentally changed."[61] In other words, it would take concerted effort to promote diversification.

An important symbol and proponent of this effort was President Hu Jintao, who quickly "became the lead spokesperson on China's global monetary thinking." This marked a shift from the pre-crisis decade when China's monetary statecraft was largely "the preserve of senior technocrats from the central bank, and to a lesser extent, the finance ministry."[62] At the G20 meeting in 2008, the first convened to coordinate a response to the crisis, President Hu called on the leaders of each country to "improve the international currency system and steadily promote the diversification of the international monetary system [国际货币体系多元化].[63] These views were expressed in a far more operational form in a 2009 essay by then Governor of the People's Bank of China Zhou Xiaochuan, who specifically advocated for SDR as an alternative to the dollar-based system. In a provocative essay entitled "Reform of the International Monetary System" timed for impact just before the 2009 London G20 summit, Zhou argued that the use of the US dollar as the reserve currency "is a rare special case in history" and that "the crisis again calls for creative reform of the existing international monetary system." Although Zhou only implicitly referenced the dollar, Hu was far more direct about his intentions to diversify away from it at the 2009 Central Economic Work Conference held shortly after Zhou's essay was published: "Since the international financial crisis, the international community has generally recognized a major reason for the imbalance in the world economy and for the international financial crisis is the inherent drawback associated with a US dollar-dominated international monetary and financial system."[64] For that reason, "promoting the diversification and rationalization of the international monetary system" was essential to reform. Hu was explicit that weakening the centrality of the dollar was a key goal, but that it would not be quick. "At the same time," Hu continued, "we must see that the dominant position of the US dollar is determined by US economic strength and comprehensive national power, and for a long period of time it would be relatively difficult to fundamentally change it." China's strategy would be prolonged: "We must adhere to the principles of comprehensiveness, balance, gradualism, and effectiveness in promoting the reform of the international monetary system."[65] For the next several years, at major multilateral economic gatherings—including most G20 summits, BRICS summits, and the G8 + G5 summit—President Hu or top Chinese officials continued to call for reserve diversification, SDR, and monetary reform.[66] Many G7 countries, including the United Kingdom, Canada, and Japan, all defended the dollar and questioned the "appropriateness" of China's focus on it.[67] But China continued to push, in part because, as the President of China's Export-Import

Bank Li Ruogu noted, the dollar's power was dangerous to China: "the US used this method [manipulation of the dollar] to topple Japan's economy, and it wants to use this method to curb China's development."[68] China needed to blunt and bypass this US power, and "only by eliminating the US dollar's monopolistic position," he noted, would it be possible to reform the international monetary system.[69]

Not only has Beijing sought to promote international monetary diversification through its quixotic quest for SDR adoption and through informal agreements on central bank reserve diversification away from dollars and into other currencies, it has also carefully sought to promote and internationalize the renminbi—especially within Asia and with its commodity-suppliers. These initiatives bring some economic benefits to China, but they may also reflect Beijing's desire to build structural power by increasing the use of the RMB in international transactions. As Jonathan Kirchner argues, summarizing his own scholarship on attempts by great powers to promote their currency, "States that pursue leadership of regional (or global) monetary orders are almost always motivated by political concerns—in particular, the desire to gain enhanced influence over other states."[70] He notes that France sought to establish a frank area to exclude Germany in the 1860s; that Nazi Germany and imperial Japan extended their currencies in the twentieth century to gain structural power; and that the United States did this as well following the Second World War.

Like so many of China's efforts to reshape the global economic order, China's promotion of the renminbi also began after the 2008 Global Financial Crisis. Conventional wisdom holds that a currency's role in the international system depends on the capital account convertibility of the country issuing it, the currency's usage in denominating and settling cross-border trade and financial transactions, and the currency's proportion in central bank reserves, and China increased its efforts in all three areas after 2008 to varying degrees.[71] China has taken extremely modest steps toward capital account convertibility—that is, allowing its currency to be exchanged for other currencies through normal market mechanisms—and attempted to promote the renminbi as a reserve currency.

Ultimately, however, where China has been most active is in promoting the renminbi's use in international trade, especially through signing several dozen swap agreements of different varieties that facilitate the use of its currency overseas. By 2015, trade settlement in RMB reached $1.1 trillion—30 percent of China's total trade—from virtually zero in 2000.[72] If this percentage increases, it partly reduces China's vulnerability to US structural power because China will increasingly be able to settle trade in its own currency. At the same time, however, the development should not be overstated. The fact that China uses RMB in settling its own trade does not mean the RMB is becoming a widely accepted medium for international transactions, which limits China's own ability to exercise structural power over others. Data from SWIFT suggests that the RMB accounts for only between 1 and 2 percent of all international payments, and while SWIFT data is not reflective of all transactions worldwide (especially those denominated in RMB), it nonetheless provides a useful estimate.[73]

If the RMB has so far failed to gain a global position, it may still achieve a regional one. By 2015, the RMB constituted 30 percent of all transactions between China and Asian states, which made it the main currency in regional trade with China—outstripping the dollar, the yen, and the euro.[74] In the next decade, if that proportion continues to rise, China may enjoy a renminbi zone within Asia that allows it to wield structural power over its neighbors. Indeed, as Kirshner argues, the renminbi is not likely to overtake the dollar in the near future globally, but China's centrality to Asia's economy and supply chains makes it likely that it will eventually become the dominant currency in the region.[75] He further argues that China may be taking a different path to regional internationalization, one that involves creating infrastructure for the renminbi, promoting its use in transactions, and encouraging central banks to hold it as a reserve currency—all while retaining some capital controls and regulation.[76] China's swap agreements help advance this goal, as does China's promotion of renminbi-denominated bonds that can be purchased by foreign central banks, which creates a deeper and more liquid pool of renminbi assets others might invest in—a key reason for dollar dominance.

If much of Asia becomes an effective renminbi zone in the next decade or more, then some of the instruments of American financial power could be wielded by China against its neighbors. Those neighbors would need access to the renminbi system, payments infrastructure like CIPS and CNAPS, and Chinese banks—all of which China can control. An era of Chinese financial statecraft and sanctions within Asia, though perhaps not globally, may not be so distant, and may in turn lay the foundation for a sphere of influence within Asia. In this way, a Chinese financial zone in Asia would be layered over the US financial order worldwide.

SWIFT

SWIFT is a standard-setting and messaging institution with a network that makes cross-border financial payments possible, thereby constituting the substructure of global finance. The organization, known as the Society for World Interbank Financial Telecommunication, was founded in 1973 when 239 banks from fifteen different countries created unified messaging standards, a messaging platform, and a network to route messages.[77] According to the organization, SWIFT became the nodal financial messaging system with "the connection of the first central banks in 1983," which "reinforced SWIFT's position as the common link between all parties in the financial industry."[78] SWIFT promptly replaced Telex, a slow and error-prone patchwork manual system with conflicting standards that effectively required banks to work in several contradictory formats to make payments. Today, SWIFT spans 200 countries and more than 10,000 institutions, it facilitates 15 million messages daily, and is the essential infrastructure that makes international payments possible. Importantly, SWIFT is a messaging service and does not engage in clearing and settling, so no money flows through it—only messages that make money transfers possible. Clearance and settling often occur through US services like Fedwire (which makes payments between bank accounts at the Federal Reserve) and CHIPS (which is privately owned and engages in "netting" to capture the total differences in transactions between two banks in a given day), as well as a variety of other services.

Because SWIFT is an institution essentially intended to solve a coordination problem—the need for a universal and consistent messaging language to send money from one bank to another—there is little to no reason why any state would develop alternative standards and infrastructure once the coordination problem had been solved. The current system is economically vastly more attractive to an alternative because of network effects that make it far more liquid and fast-acting. In contrast, an alternative system would be more costly, and no specific constituency would benefit from the added difficulty of using it. In essence, there is no meaningful economic or interest group rationale for China to create its own alternative to SWIFT's messaging apparatus. As this chapter later explains, a strategic rationale makes the most sense.

Perhaps the best explanation for China's investment in SWIFT alternatives is that it provides reduced vulnerability to US financial power. Although SWIFT is a messaging service and does not engage in clearing and settling, if a bank is cut off from the network, it is essentially cut off from the global financial system and from much of the clearing and settling infrastructure that exists. In this way, control over SWIFT offers considerable structural power.

That structural power has already been wielded against others. While the organization sees itself as apolitical, it is nonetheless required to comply with the laws of Belgium, the European Union, and—through the threat of secondary sanctions—the United States as well. In 2012, the United States and Europe used their influence over the organization to force it to delink Iranian banks from SWIFT networks, which marked the first time in SWIFT's history that the institution had cut off an entire country from access to the company's network.[79] Iran had relied on SWIFT for two million cross-border payments annually—a volume that could not be replaced by another messaging network—and loss of access made payment for Iranian oil impossible, devastated Iran's economy, and prevented the government from accessing substantial amounts of its own foreign reserves that it had invested abroad.[80] A few years later, in 2017, SWIFT access was denied to North Korean banks.[81]

SWIFT's structural power has even been threatened against great powers like Russia after its invasion of Crimea. The threat was concerning enough that then Russian Prime Minister Medvedev discussed it publicly and threatened that Russia's "reaction will be without limit."[82] Russian Central Bank Governor Elvira Nabiullina then began preparing a Russian alternative to SWIFT as early as 2014. In a meeting with Putin, she stated that "there were threats that we can be disconnected from SWIFT. We have finished working on our own payment system, and if something happens, all operations in SWIFT format will work inside the country. We have created an alternative."[83] Russia has sought to popularize its alternative system within the Eurasian Union and discussed it with Iran, and though it is imperfect, it demonstrates that great powers are actively searching for ways to bypass US influence over SWIFT for strategic reasons.[84]

The United States has threatened to wield SWIFT against China. Washington already sanctioned at least one Chinese bank involved in trade with North Korea, and then Treasury Secretary Mnuchin threatened that "If China doesn't follow these sanctions [on North Korea], we will put additional sanctions on them and prevent them from accessing the US and international dollar system." Similarly, members of Congress have suggested cutting off some of China's largest banks from the global financial system.[85] China indeed has reasons to fear SWIFT termination, and like Russia, appears to be acting on them.

The People's Bank of China—with approval from the Chinese government—began developing its own alternative to SWIFT for financial messaging and interbank payments as early as 2013, roughly one year after the West cut off Iran.[86] This system, known as the China International Payments System (CIPS), would not only insulate China from financial pressure but also increase its own autonomy, giving it sovereign control over all information that passes through its network, the power to help others bypass sanctions, and the ability to one day cut others off from China's system. Moreover, the ambition for CIPS exceeds that for SWIFT: the former would not only be a messaging service like SWIFT but will also provide clearance and settlement—that is, full integration of the payments process. Unlike Russian elites, China's elites have been far less obvious in telegraphing their system's possibility as a rival to SWIFT; nevertheless, its strategic potential is real, if still somewhat distant.

Skeptics would point out that China's pursuit of CIPS has some genuine economic motivations as well. First, CIPS is an improvement on the previous system of cross-border RMB payments. Before CIPS, China's domestic interbank clearing and settlement system, the China National Advanced Payment System (CNAPS), could not support international payments; instead, cross-border transactions would take place through designated offshore yuan clearing banks or correspondent banks in China. Moreover, CIPS for the moment is primarily concerned with clearing and settling. Indeed, CIPS and SWIFT signed a 2016 agreement that provided CIPS access to the SWIFT messaging system. From that perspective, a charitable observer might conclude that CIPS does not appear to be an alternative to SWIFT financial infrastructure but a complementary appendage.

Neither of these arguments dismisses the strategic logic underlying CIPS. First, if China had purely economic and technical motivations for launching CIPS, it may have been more economical to simply reform the existing CNAPS system so it could communicate with SWIFT. Other countries with domestic interbank payments systems that similarly do not communicate with SWIFT have often modified those systems to allow communication. This suggests economic motivations may not have been the leading factors in the establishment of CIPS.

Second, the fact that CIPS has signed an agreement for access to the SWIFT network, and the fact that it uses SWIFT messaging standards, does not reduce its viability as a strategic alternative to SWIFT because CIPS is building the capability to process messages outside of the SWIFT network. Indeed, just as SWIFT requires banks to purchase costly technology connecting them to the network, so does CIPS—which allows it to exist in parallel to SWIFT's technology.[87] And as CIPS continues to develop, the goal is in many ways to operate independently from SWIFT. As an individual with knowledge of the People's Bank of China's plans for CIPS told the *Financial Times*, "In the future CIPS will move in the direction of using its own dedicated [communications] line. At that point it can totally replace SWIFT" for interbank messaging involving renminbi.[88] Indeed, as Eswar Prasad argues, "CIPS has been designed as a system that could eventually also serve as a conduit for interbank communications concerning international RMB transactions that operates independently of SWIFT. This would make it not only a funds transfer system, but also a communication system, reducing the SWIFT's grip on interbank communications related to cross-border financial flows. China's government is astute enough not to challenge SWIFT until the CIPS has matured, but no doubt one day the challenge will come."[89] The collaboration between SWIFT and CIPS helps the latter mature, providing China with market share and expertise as it builds a parallel system. It also gives SWIFT continued relevance, and indeed, employees at SWIFT have been concerned that "Chinese authorities were considering replacing SWIFT with an indigenous network built to rival, if not exceed, SWIFT's own."[90] SWIFT's China head, Daphne Wang, apparently tried to persuade CIPS not to invest in alternative messaging but to focus on clearance: "We do not do clearing, as in CIPS's case. When we talked to CIPS, we said: 'Why build your highway [i.e., messaging platform] if the highway exists already? As of now it's as if you are selling a car [i.e., clearance and settling] but nobody can drive it on the highway that's already built.' "[91] Despite SWIFT's attempt to disincentivize the creation of an alternative highway, China's desire to develop it remains. As one person involved with CIPS noted, the system was launched without all these features but there was "ambition" for more: "[CIPS] doesn't include a lot of things [yet], but there is pressure for delivery."[92] Eventually, the system is intended to "allow offshore banks to participate, enabling offshore-to-offshore renminbi payments as well as those in and out of China."[93] This would make CIPS a wholly independent financial infrastructure and provide any two parties anywhere in the world a method for messaging, clearance, and settlement entirely free from US review, which would seriously undermine US financial power worldwide.

Third, even when CIPS does not act in parallel to SWIFT, its connection to and through SWIFT still provides useful influence. Before CIPS, SWIFT was already operating in China for more than thirty years and was connected to 400 Chinese financial institutions and corporate treasuries.[94] Now, all SWIFT messages to China must be routed through CIPS. As one payments expert notes, "CIPS is trying to be the middleman between SWIFT and CNAPS," which would give China's central bank an ability to determine who has access to China's financial system.[95] This provides a central control point over transactions in renminbi and boosts China's structural power.

For now, CIPS is not a meaningful alternative to the SWIFT system. It may bolster China's structural power by making it much easier for China to cut off other institutions or countries from China's financial system, but it is not yet ready to serve as an alternative messaging system for cross-border payments outside of China. Even so, that day will come. Other great powers like Russia are already investing in such systems, and China—which also faces the threat of Western financial sanctions—has ample reason to continue developing CIPS into an alternative that can bypass American structural power over international payments in the coming decade. As one columnist observes, "A return to a pre-SWIFT world, in which banks were forced to send and accept transaction information in a multitude of formats, isn't unimaginable," and it demonstrates the way in which China's strategic anxieties will intertwine with its rise to fragment the sub-structure of global finance.[96]

Credit Rating Agencies

Credit rating agencies help provide investors information on the risks of various kinds of debt, and their ratings can significantly alter the fortunes of companies and countries. The market for international credit ratings is largely dominated by the "big three" US firms—Standard and Poor's, Moody's, and Fitch Group—which together have a global market share of more than 90 percent. The dominance of these three firms is in part a function of American structural power—the centrality of the dollar, the importance of New York financial institutions, and the ability of the Securities and Exchange Commission to determine who can issue ratings.

There are reasonable economic motivations for China to create an alternative credit rating agency. At the national level, China may be concerned that the "big three" do not accurately rate China's sovereign or corporate debt; at the local level, specific Chinese state-owned enterprises may feel that they would stand to benefit from a friendlier rater. At least initially, it is unlikely a Chinese credit rating agency would win business abroad given presumed state connections and a lack of experience; for that reason, it will require costly subsidies and state support. If the Chinese state is propping up China's main external credit rating agency, that does not deny economic motivations, but it also raises the possibility of political ones, as we will see.

After the 2008 Global Financial Crisis, the "big three" were seen as vulnerable given their mistaken appraisal of the assets that set off the crisis. For their part, many European leaders blamed them as biased and political for having touched off and then intensified the Eurozone debt crisis, especially following their downgrade of Greek debt to junk status in 2010, and some leaders encouraged (unsuccessfully) the creation of an alternative European credit rating agency.[97] The fact that even American allies sought alternatives to the influence of the "big three"—which have retained more than 76 percent market share within Europe even after the crisis—should make it relatively uncontroversial that China might act according to similar motivations.[98]

As with Europe, China's interest in alternative agencies was precipitated by the Global Financial Crisis that tarnished the "big three" while also revealing their ability to shape capital flows. Although Washington lacks the ability to directly control these credit raters or manipulate their ratings, China views them as tools of direct or indirect American power corrupted by political bias. At the 2010 G20 summit in Toronto, President Hu Jintao called for the countries to "develop an objective, fair, reasonable, and uniformed method and standard for sovereign credit rating," demonstrating that the issue had received top-level political attention. Only a month later, seemingly in coordination with Hu's call, Dagong Global Credit Rating—China's largest credit rating agency—launched its own sovereign credit ratings for the first time. For years following the crisis, China's government has continued to formally attack the credit rating agencies. Finance Minister Lou Jiwei declared that "there's bias" in the ratings of the "big three," while the Finance Ministry issued a statement calling a Moody's downgrade of China's credit "the wrong decision" in 2017.[99]

Dagong is the lead instrument in China's effort to influence the global ratings system and the country's only major Chinese-owned credit rating agency. China's only other large credit rating agencies—China Lianhe Credit Rating and China Chengxin International—are joint ventures between private Chinese entities and different members of the "big three." Dagong's public documents, as well as the statements by its founder Guan Jianzhong—essentially the face of credit rating in China—indicate both a view that credit ratings are strategic instruments and that the United States' domination of them is harmful to China's political interests. As Guan wrote in 2012, "US dominated ratings serve the global strategy of the United States" and "the existing international rating pattern will restrict the rise of China." Guan and others argue that rating agencies exercise "rating discourse power" that enables them to shape the global economy. If the United States controls this "rating discourse power," then China "will lose financial sovereignty." Worse, the "rating discourse power can be manipulated . . . in an effort to erode the social basis of the ruling party." In contrast, the 2008 Global Financial Crisis offered "a great historical opportunity for China to strive for international rating discourse power."[100] China's ratings, even if they do not gain overwhelming market share, could nonetheless pressure the "big three" to adjust their ratings and "converge" toward China's, an outcome Guan welcomes.[101]

Accordingly, in the midst of the of the Global Financial Crisis in 2008, Dagong began to float proposals for a "Universal Credit Rating Group" (UCRG), which was finally launched in June 2013 when Dagong partnered with a Russian firm and smaller American rater. The new initiative's mission was to compete with the "big three," and it purported to be a private, collaborative, and apolitical venture. These claims proved false when the CEO of that initiative, Richard Hainsworth, stepped down and later admitted that the effort was essentially financed and supported by the Chinese government.[102] Hainsworth claimed that the Russian and US partners provided little capital, that the venture was primarily controlled by Dagong, that virtually every major expenditure was subject to a vote by Dagong's board, and that the Chinese government was likely bankrolling not only UCRG but even Dagong. In this light, Dagong's collaboration with foreign raters appeared to be a fig leaf to boost the legitimacy of its revisionist undertaking. Hainsworth further argued that UCRG's true purpose appeared political rather than commercial—to both reduce the legitimacy of Western ratings and to put forward a Chinese alternative, though spending on the latter objective was inadequate. Dagong hired a number of senior Western officials on behalf of UCRG to criticize US ratings, including former French Prime Minister Dominique de Villepin, who traveled the world attacking Western agencies in ideological terms and drew a "straight line from the Opium Wars, the British Raj, and the European colonial powers' grab for Africa to current forms of Western privilege, including its control of credit ratings."[103] Eventually, despite its ideological bent and alleged Chinese-backing, UCRG sputtered and was shut down.

The failure of UCRG did not mark the end of China's ambition to reshape global credit ratings. Instead, China appears to have increased its support for Dagong to go global, and the firm has opened up offices around the world and overtly stated its interest in competing with the "big three." Dagong is clearly carrying on the mission that UCRG was to have undertaken and has retained many of the same international advisors to give it legitimacy.[104] Although Dagong claims to be fully private, Hainsworth suggested the company was funded by Beijing; moreover, its CEO and founder, Guan Jianzhong, was a government official immediately before he launched Dagong. Not only did he apparently continue to be employed by China's State Council for years while running Dagong, his firm so directly implicates the interests of SOEs that it is genuinely hard to believe it is free from state influence.[105] Even so, Beijing clearly seeks to maintain some plausible distance from Dagong to enhance its legitimacy. Indeed, Chinese officials have privately opposed efforts to create a BRICS credit rating agency precisely because they believe that "a government-backed credit rating agency will not have any credibility" in challenging the "big three."[106] Despite the fact that Dagong is formally a private and apolitical entity, its rankings have also given rise to claims of political bias. Dagong raised eyebrows when it rated the Chinese Railway Ministry's debt higher than China's sovereign debt, as well as when it rated Russia and Botswana's debt higher than US debt. In a discussion of its methodology, Dagong includes ideological Party phrases and claims to use Marxian "dialectical materialism" as part of its evaluative approach.[107] The firm is usually eager to downgrade the United States, as its own website boasts: "Dagong is the first agency in the world to study American credit rating theories and methodologies and reveal their shortcomings. It is also the first agency to downgrade the US credit rating."[108]

China's efforts to influence global credit ratings, while clearly motivated by the Global Financial Crisis, remain somewhat modest. Its goal appears to be to gradually gain market share, not displace the "big three," especially since a higher market share may be sufficient to bring about convergence. Moreover, China has allowed the "big three" into China, a policy ostensibly intended to help promote foreign investment as China's government pursues deleveraging. This is a positive step, but one possibly consistent with the goal of influencing global credit ratings: as American credit rating agencies gain access to China's lucrative domestic market, they may find it more challenging to negatively rate politically sensitive Chinese entities or the government's sovereign debt.

Together, China's focus on monetary diversification and its construction of an alternative payments substructure through CIPS and an alternative credits rating agency through Dagong reveal a long-standing interest in weakening and bypassing the US dollar's constraining effects on China—one that will, if successful, transform the global economic architecture into one of financial multipolarity.

These are efforts befitting a great power that seeks to dominate its own region and to contest the influence of the reigning hegemon, and they were motivated in large part by China's confidence in the aftermath of the Global Financial Crisis as well as its continuing concern over US influence. When combined with China's interest in infrastructure financing via the Belt and Road Initiative and its growing comfort with economic sanctions, the overall picture is one of a rising power that is increasingly risen—and willing to use economic tools to build order at home at first, and now increasingly, globally. As the next chapter shows, these ambitions are not confined only to the region. Beijing now seeks to take *blunting* and *building* worldwide, and in the process, gradually elevate China and displace the United States from global order.

PART III

"GREAT CHANGES UNSEEN IN A CENTURY"

Global Expansion as China's Third Displacement Strategy (2017 and Beyond)

11

"Toward the World's Center Stage"

American Decline and China's Global Ambition

"The Western-centered world order dominated by the US has made great contributions to human progress and economic growth. But those contributions lie in the past."[1]

—Fu Ying, 2016

"The world is undergoing great changes unseen in a century, but time and momentum are on our side. This is where our force and vigor reside, and it is also where our determination and confidence reside."[2]

—Xi Jinping, 2021

On October 18, 2017, General Secretary Xi Jinping strode out into the Great Hall of the People to the applause of 2,280 party leaders all clapping in rhythm to the entry music. The occasion was the Chinese Communist Party's 19th Party Congress. Held once every five years, the Party Congress is China's most authoritative institution, and the General Secretary's speech is always the Party's most significant event—one that sets the line on new Party policy.

The Congress started with the usual pageantry, but was perhaps less polished than one might expect. While American political figures rely on teleprompters to make their oratory seem effortless, Premier Li Keqiang stood to speak with papers in hand. He looked down, then up, and then back down again as he announced the opening of the Congress, called for a minute of silence for the Party's revolutionary martyrs, and then summoned the audience to stand and sing the national anthem—all before finally turning the floor over to Xi.

Xi looked stern as he approached the lectern. He wore a black suit, a maroon tie, and an entirely unnecessary red nametag affixed to his jacket pocket spelling out his name for the attendees, who of course already knew it. He too had no teleprompter, only a thick stack of papers sitting atop the lectern. He would dutifully read aloud each one in the course of what proved to be a marathon three-and-a-half-hour, 30,000-word speech.

Xi's speech requires stamina, but more for the guests than the speaker. The Party Congress address is generally a tedious affair, and past general secretaries kept their addresses shorter, with Hu Jintao sticking to ninety minutes while Jiang sometimes read for only fifteen, submitting the rest into the written record. For Xi, the decision to read the entire text was a kind of power move that forced all senior officials to remain at attention, but he was only somewhat successful in securing that deference.[3] While lesser functionaries dared not show any distraction, Jiang yawned widely throughout and then fell asleep on the stage while Hu visibly pointed to his wristwatch after Xi's speech concluded.

Xi's jargon-filled speech, despite its stale delivery and incredible length, was nonetheless one of the most consequential addresses in recent decades, particularly with respect to China's position in the world. The speech announced a "new era," put forward timetables for China's rejuvenation in 2049, promised greater Chinese activism in global governance, called for a "world-class" military, committed China to becoming a "global leader in innovation," and declared that China would "become a leading country in comprehensive national strength and international influence."[4] Xi was launching a new era in Chinese foreign engagement, one that went beyond the focus on *blunting* and *building* in Asia and was now increasingly global. As he put it memorably in his address, this "new era" would be one that "that sees China moving closer toward the world's center stage."[5]

Like other changes in China's grand strategy, this shift toward greater global ambition was driven by what Beijing saw as the West's irreversible decay and decline. In 2016, a year before Xi's Party Congress address, the United Kingdom voted to leave the European Union and Donald Trump was elected president of the United States. From China's perspective—which is highly sensitive to changes in perceptions of American power—these two events were shocking. The world's most powerful democracies were withdrawing from the international order they had helped erect, creating what China's leadership and foreign policy elite has called a "period of historical opportunity" [历史机遇期] to expand the country's strategic focus from Asia to the wider globe and its governance systems.

In the run-up to these events, high-level Chinese officials had already been speaking more boldly about China's ambitions. Fu Ying, chair of the foreign affairs committee of China's National People's Congress and a former senior diplomat, wrote in early 2016, "The Western-centered world order dominated by the US has made great contributions to human progress and economic growth. But those contributions lie in the past." The title of her piece captured the point succinctly: "The US World Order Is a Suit That No Longer Fits."[6] After the events of 2016, frustration with the order was turning to a sense of opportunity for the Chinese leadership. As the deputy director of an influential think tank connected to the Ministry of State Security put it, "US withdrawal has led to greater confidence in and respect for China's role, enabling China to move closer to the center of the world stage through participating in global governance and expanding its clout and voice in the world."[7]

The next year, Yang Jiechi—the "America handler" who as a twenty-seven-year-old tour guide charmed the Bush family and decades later was now a Politburo member directing the Party's Central Foreign Affairs Commission—wrote derisively of the West in the *People's Daily*. "Western Centralism, where the international landscape is dominated by the West and the concept of international relations is mainly oriented toward Western values, is hard to sustain," he declared. This was because "Western governance concepts, systems and models have become increasingly difficult to adapt to the new international structure and the trend of the times" and "even the big Western powers are confronted with poor governance and piles of questions." Now was the time for "a new concept of global governance," he argued.[8]

At the same time, the election of Donald Trump posed undeniable challenges to Beijing too. Steadily increasing tensions, together with President Trump's decision to launch a trade war against China and a new bipartisan turn against the past policy of engagement, made clear that the bilateral relationship was entering uncharted waters. The two-pronged conclusion that the United States was in retreat globally but at the same time was waking up to the China challenge bilaterally convinced Beijing that it no longer needed to restrain its global ambitions and now had an opportunity—if not an imperative—to pursue them. By 2017, Xi Jinping declined to simply modify Deng's admonition to "hide capabilities and bide time," as Hu had. He went a step further. In a 2017 address to the National Security Work Forum, he appeared to retire it completely, suggesting that it was time to "leave behind" the era of "hiding capabilities and biding time" according to authoritative commentaries on his remarks.[9]

Just as "hiding capabilities and biding time" or "actively accomplishing something" served as the guidelines [方针] for grand strategies of blunting American order and building Chinese order in Asia, a new concept would be needed to organize strategy in Xi's "new era" focused on increasingly global ambitions. The key successor concept, offered shortly before President Trump's inauguration, is what the CCP has termed the "great changes unseen in a century." Not long after Xi's Party Congress address, this phrase began appearing in dozens of speeches by Xi Jinping and his foreign policy team, was placed at the start of China's foreign policy and defense White Papers, and became the overwhelming focus of its foreign policy academics. Xi Jinping had made its importance to strategy abundantly clear. "I often say that leading cadres must keep two overall situations in mind," he noted in a recent speech, "one is the great rejuvenation of the Chinese nation and the other is the great changes unseen in a century. *This is the basic starting point of our planning work.*"[10]

As the introductory chapter noted, the phrase has a history. It was in 1872 that the Qing Dynasty general Li Hongzhang lamented the predations of Western powers with a famous phrase: the world was experiencing "great changes unseen in 3,000 years." That sweeping declaration, a reminder to China's nationalists of the country's own humiliations, has been repurposed by President Xi since 2017 to inaugurate the new phase in China's post–Cold War grand strategy. If Li's line marks the highpoint of China's humiliation, then Xi's marks an occasion for its rejuvenation. If Li's evokes tragedy, then Xi's evokes opportunity. But both capture something essential: the idea that world order is once again at stake because of unprecedented geopolitical and technological shifts, and that this requires strategic adjustment.

This chapter and the one that succeeds it discuss China's global *expansion*. They follow the structure of previous chapters that outlined Chinese grand strategies of *blunting* and *building*. This chapter focuses on how China's perception of accelerating American decline following Brexit, Trump, and the coronavirus pandemic of 2020 led to strategic adjustment. This chapter then explores the end goals of this new global phase of Chinese grand strategy, which appear to be to catch up and surpass the United States in a competition for global leadership. The next chapter explores the political, economic, and military ways and means China has wielded to achieve these objectives. It demonstrates that China is now consciously targeting the underpinnings of what it considers to be US hegemony, hoping to blunt American global order while building the foundations for China's own order. Together, this chapter and the next one paint a picture of what Chinese order might look like globally.

That Chinese order involves seizing the opportunities of the "great changes unseen in a century" and displacing the United States as the world's leading state. To do so, Beijing would seek to weaken the forms of control supporting American global order while strengthening those forms of control supporting a Chinese alternative. Politically, Beijing would project leadership over global governance and international institutions, advance autocratic norms at the expense of liberal ones, and split American alliances in Europe and Asia. Economically, it would weaken the financial advantages that underwrite US hegemony and seize the commanding heights of the "fourth industrial revolution" from artificial intelligence to quantum computing while the United States deindustrializes. Militarily, the PLA would field a world-class force with bases around the world that could defend China's interests in most regions and even in new domains. Taken together, China would erect a "zone of super-ordinate influence" in its home region and "partial hegemony" across the developing countries tied to its Belt and Road Initiative—and perhaps parts of the developed world too, a vision some Chinese popular writers describe using Mao's revolutionary guidance to "surround the cities from the countryside" [农村包围城市].[11]

The fact that aspects of China's global ambitions and strategy are visible in high-level speeches is strong evidence that China's ambitions are not limited to Taiwan or to dominating the Indo-Pacific. The "struggle for mastery," once confined to Asia, is now over the global order and its future.

"Great Changes Unseen in a Century"

The concept "great changes unseen in a century" is critical to understanding China's global grand strategy, and it implies a belief that the United States has entered a decline so pronounced that its status as the sole superpower is now in doubt. The term's formal elevation in 2017 was evidence that China was adjusting its grand strategy in response.

The concept first emerged from conversations about Western decline after the Global Financial Crisis. One of its first usages was in a 2009 essay titled "The Financial Crisis and American Economic Hegemony" written by Yuan Peng—an authoritative figure who led the US Institute at the Ministry of State's Security's think tank CICIR and now leads the entire think tank. Yuan Peng observed that the United States "for the first time in the history of its hegemony" was suffering from a series of grave challenges, that these were producing "great changes unseen in a century," and that those great changes in turn were "impacting the US-led political and economic order."[12] But while

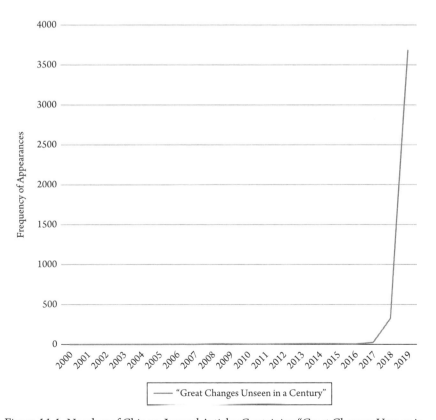

Figure 11.1 Number of Chinese Journal Articles Containing "Great Changes Unseen in a Century," from 2000–2019.

the United States was in decline, Chinese commentators believed it would still remain the sole superpower, and for that reason the phrase appeared only a handful of times subsequently—perhaps most notably in a 2012 interview by the rising-star Chinese diplomat Le Yucheng, who was later one of the brains behind China's Belt and Road. Although these references showed the phrase had entered official consciousness, it had not yet gained the Party's imprimatur, and with the United States still seemingly formidable, it largely disappeared from official discourses.

All that changed in 2017, when the phrase rose rapidly to a central position in official and semi-official discourses in the immediate aftermath of Brexit and Trump's election. Those events suggested to Beijing that Western influence was waning and that the status of the United States as the world's sole superpower was at risk, and the term's sudden emergence that year indicated that a broader strategic adjustment was underway.

The process began only a week before President Trump's inauguration, when State Councilor Yang Jiechi debuted the phrase in a 2017 essay posted to the Ministry of Foreign Affairs website expounding on the foreign affairs component of the newly developed and soon-to-be-ratified "Xi Jinping Thought." Yang linked the concept to assessments of the United States. "The current international situation is undergoing great changes that have not been encountered since the end of the Cold War—or even a century—and all kinds of chaos has emerged," Yang noted. "The impact of changes on the political situation in some countries [i.e., the United Kingdom and the United States] and on the international situation deserves attention."[13] International structure was now changing, and the "great changes" underway presaged a major strategic shift.

The next month, only weeks after President Trump's inauguration, the shift began. President Xi made it clear that China's perception of American power was changing in a 2017 address to China's National Security Work Forum, a high-level meeting convened to discuss foreign affairs. Xi declared that he perceived "great changes" and "deep adjustments" to both "the international system and international order."[14] "This was a world of *profound changes* in the international balance of forces," he argued, using a euphemism for US decline and the very concept to which Chinese leaders anchor the country's grand strategy.[15] These themes were sharpened in an official commentary on his speech written for Party cadres.[16] "Although Western regimes appear to be in power," it noted, "their willingness and ability to intervene in world affairs is declining. The United States may no longer want to be a provider of global security and public goods, and instead pursue a unilateral and even nationalist foreign policy."[17] Underlying Xi's speech and the commentary was a belief that Brexit and Trump had revealed Western democracy was weakening and the United States and its order were in decline. This kind of language also appeared in Xi's 19th Party Congress Report that fall, which argued that "changes in the global governance system and the international order are speeding up" and that "the balance of relevant international forces is becoming more balanced," another reference to the critical variable on which China's grand strategy appears to turn.[18] As we will see subsequently, many of the key themes of China's new global grand strategy to reach "the world's center stage"—namely, its interest in global governance, technology leadership, and a global military profile—emerged in this speech.

A month after that major address, Xi attended the 2017 Ambassadorial Conference.[19] These gatherings, which involve the entire foreign policy apparatus and all of China's overseas ambassadors, have historically been used to adjust China's strategy, and this speech did the same. In it, Xi finally debuted the very concept that Yang Jiechi had subtly introduced after Trump's election. "Looking at the world today," he declared, "we are facing great changes unseen in a century."[20] This marked a major shift in China's view of the United States and China's own grand strategy, and the speech exuded a sense of confidence. "The great rejuvenation of the Chinese nation has shown unprecedented bright prospects," Xi noted, and as long as China stayed the course, "it will increasingly approach the center of the world stage."[21] In some areas, Xi's speech subtly intensified language from the Party Congress address. "The international structure [国际格局] has become increasingly balanced, and this general international trend has become irreversible"—phrases stronger than he or his predecessors had used and a sign that strategy was changing.[22]

What did this mean? At his 2018 Central Foreign Affairs Work Conference, only the sixth ever held in China's history, Xi explained: "At present, China is in the best development period since modern times, and the world is in a state of great changes not seen in one hundred years, and these two [trends] are simultaneously interwoven and mutually interacting." To Xi, China's global rise and the apparent decline of the West were trends that reinforced each other.

Xi's language on American decline amid the "great changes unseen in a century" was often oblique, but top Chinese scholars and semi-official commentaries were far more candid. They indicated that the key "great change" was unquestionably the decline of the United States and the West relative to China. Critically, these sources followed Xi's lead and explicitly linked the "great change" with the same variable that shaped decades of China's own grand strategy: the international balance of forces. As the famous Chinese international relations scholar Zhu Feng wrote, "the 'great change' in 'great changes unseen in a century' is an acceleration in the redistribution of power among nations within the international structure."[23] A commentary posted online at the *Study Times* argued that "the essence of the great changes is that the power balance among major international actors has undergone major changes" that "triggered a major reshuffle of the international structure and a major adjustment to international order."[24]

Zhang Yuyan, a member of the National Committee of the Chinese People's Political Consultative Conference, wrote, "the most critical variable of the great changes unseen in a century lies in the international balance of power among the major countries."[25] Writing more expansively, Duqing Hao from the Central Party School argued that all "the great changes in world history" have included "major changes in the international balance of power among the major international actors."[26]

But what was the cause of this change in power? These scholars argue it was not only China's rise but also the West's fall, which was made clear by a new trifecta of shocking and discontinuous events that began with Brexit and Trump's election and was capped off by the West's disastrous response to COVID-19. In an essay on the "great changes," Wu Xinbo argues that the United States was "spiritually exhausted, physically weak, and could no longer carry the world."[27] Zhu Feng from Nanjing University argued that, as "Western countries experience serious domestic contradictions" due to populism, "the East rises and the West falls."[28] Central Party School figures like Luo Jianbo tasked in part with standardizing and disseminating Party concepts wrote that the "great changes unseen in a century" were a "grand strategic judgment" and noted that they marked the end of the "Atlantic era" in global politics.[29] Gao Zugui, a dean at the Central Party School and deputy director of its Institute for International Strategy, proclaimed, "The willingness, determination, and ability of the United States to control the regional and international situation alone have declined significantly."[30]

Behind these bold pronouncements stood thousands of papers on Western decline from China's top academics. The papers showcase China's own biases, including a tendency to focus on the "base structure" of the economy which flows from Marxist theory, to see diversity as weakness given China's relative homogeneity, and to see information flows as dangerous given China's own illiberalism. Most papers tell a similar if simplistic causal story: the West's forty-year experiment with "neoliberal" economic policies exacerbated economic inequality and ethnic strife, which in turn produced populist waves that paralyzed the state—all amplified by a freewheeling Western information environment. These are not the views of a handful of obscure experts, but so common as to be consensus. Xi Jinping may never tell this story in public, but it is undoubtedly one he and his fellow Party elites believe about the United States—and it is why they are now emboldened.

A brief tour of China's discourse on American decline can be instructive. The story often begins with economic inequality. After the 1970s, writes Deputy Dean at Beijing Foreign Studies University Xie Tao, "neoliberalism was in the dominant position" and governments put "economic freedom first, advocated tax cuts, and paid less attention to social inequality."[31] Jin Canrong, a well-known professor and dean at Renmin University, argued this "neoliberalism" wave began with the "Thatcher Revolution in 1979 and the Reagan Revolution in 1980" and led to "a division between the rich and poor."[32] The economic structure changed too. Nie Wenjuan, deputy director of the Institute of International Relations at China Foreign Affairs University, argued that, "With its democratic society, the US is unable to prevent financial capitalism from swelling, or to take dramatic action against vested interests," which causes stagnation and inequality.[33] Wu Baiyi, an America Institute director at the Chinese Academy of Social Sciences, emphasized these forces "hollowed out" the US economy, with success in the technology and financial services industries coming at the expense of exports and traditional industry.[34]

From China's perspective, when the 2008 Global Financial Crisis hit, the bill for these trends came due, and populism and ethnic strife increased over the next several years, paralyzing Western states. As one paper from the MFA-connected think tank China Institute for International Studies (CIIS) argued, "the populism that is now emerging in Europe and America reflects the intensification of the contradiction between the middle and lower classes vs. the upper classes" that the Global Financial Crisis produced.[35] Ideological extremism also intensified. As Jin Canrong argued, "in the field of ideas, the trend of extremist ideas has continued to expand," with "populism and racism becoming more open and influential."[36] Zhu Feng similarly argued that "white nationalism in the United States and Europe is becoming increasingly active."[37] Technology amplified all these trends. An authoritative commentary on Xi's 2017 National Security Work Forum cited Western reports to argue that "the most basic pillars of the Western world order are weakening. In the 'post-truth' era, 'liberal democracies' are vulnerable to misinformation."[38] The "information explosion" was causing "social tearing," noted one Chinese Academy of Social Science (CASS) scholar, all amplified by algorithms, targeted advertising, and disinformation that "accelerate the spread of global populism/nationalism" and cause "serious polarization."[39] Jin Canrong argued that the culmination of these trends was illiberalism and dysfunction: "the polarization of the rich and the poor leads to widespread dissatisfaction in the lower and middle classes. The dissatisfaction in the lower and middle classes will surely brew populist politics on the left and right. Populist politics will inevitably be used by strong men. This is an inevitable result."[40] Chinese scholars point to the Tea Party movement in 2009, Occupy Wall Street in 2011, and particularly Brexit and Trump in 2016 as evidence of populism's hold.[41]

When the West struggled to handle COVID-19 in 2020, these diagnoses were seen to have been vindicated. Xi Jinping declared that year that "this new coronavirus epidemic" was "a big test for the governance system and governance capabilities" worldwide.[42] Virtually all Chinese writers on the subject believed

China had passed the test and the West had largely failed it. One article published on the Ministry of Finance and Commerce website argued, "the epidemic shows that the United States and Western countries are increasingly unable to carry out institutional reforms and adjustments, and are caught in a political stalemate from which they cannot be extricated."[43] Similarly, the editor of a major CASS journal on American studies argued, "The shortcomings of the US federal government's bureaucratization and 'small government' tendency over the past half century have been very evident in this major public health crisis response," and that dysfunction would reproduce "political radicalization."[44] A professor at the Central Party School noted, with apparent pleasure, that COVID-19 would bolster Western nationalism and further damage the liberal order. "Before the COVID-19 outbreak, nationalism had become a trend [supporting China's] rejuvenation. The Trump administration and Brexit delivered star performances," he argued, and COVID-19 would "further strengthen" these in ways that benefited China.[45] According to Wu Baiyi, the economic calamity, social unrest, and poor COVID-19 response meant that "the country that has bragged about being 'a light on a hill' has sunk into sustained social unrest. . . . Chaos and division are suffocating the people."[46] Accordingly, a former vice president of the Central Party School argued, the pandemic would "certainly promote the further development of great changes unseen in a century."[47] Yuan Peng argued that America's poor response to COVID-19 "is a blow to America's soft and hard power, and America's international influence has suffered a serious decline."[48]

Many see this Western institutional decline as largely intractable and believe that the West is unlikely to resolve it promptly. A focus on "so-called 'post-materialist values,'" noted Xie Tao, had produced a politics that is "more about self-expression and a demand for respect rather than traditional economic redistribution," complicating efforts to address the structural roots of inequality. Similarly, a professor at Beijing Foreign Studies University argued the "absorption of these two forces [left-wing and right-wing populism] by the US political system may not be solved by a single election vote."[49] Some believe dysfunction will prove long-term. "The cognitive roots of populism will exist for a long time," speculated a paper published by the MFA-connected CIIS.[50] Xie Tao believed this populist phase "may continue for some time—ten or twenty years."[51] And partisan dysfunction was likely to accompany populism. As Jin Canrong put it in an article posted to the Ministry of Defense website, "the contradictions between the two parties in the United States are also very deep."[52] Indeed, Nie Wenjuan, a professor at China Foreign Affairs University, argued that "the pandemic has added urgency [for reform], but American politicians appear not to have found the answers." Even with a change in administration, she argued, the United States was likely to engage in only "tinkering" around its structural problems.[53] Wu Baiyi argued that the United States faced a great "American disease" that he likened to the "Dutch disease" and "Latin American disease" used to describe other dysfunctional states. Observers could no longer "cherish fantasies about the US capacity for self-rectification": the economic pie was shrinking, "general manufacturing" had "withered," good jobs were rarer, exports were falling, and the economy was tilted toward technology and financial services—all of which increased inequality while "narrowing channels for upward mobility."[54] Political institutions were failing too: "No matter whether the public support for a certain bill is 30 percent or 100 percent, it has no influence on whether it passes or fails" because of polarization, so no progress is made on the sources of US dysfunction. He argued this created "a vicious circle" where "wide gaps in American society keep widening, the room for institutional compromise keeps shrinking and national decision-making drifts further and further away from the 'people first' principle."[55]

One of the "megatrends" that emerged from this state of affairs, noted Jin Canrong, was the end of the United States as the sole superpower. Instead, he argued that "the world structure is changing from one superpower, many great powers to two superpowers, many great powers."[56] This was a *major* declaration, since China had for decades perceived a world in which the United States was the sole superpower as a key factor shaping its grand strategy. Not only had that now changed, but it seemed just as plausible to elites that given their confidence in American decline, the world could eventually return to "one superpower, many great powers"—this time with China as the sole superpower. There are many who see the ends of its global grand strategy in such terms.

Ends—Achieving National Rejuvenation

The end goal of China's global grand strategy is to achieve national rejuvenation by 2049. From Beijing's perspective, the essential task over the next three decades is to seize the opportunities of the "great changes unseen in a century" to surpass the United States globally all while avoiding the growing risk of a United States unwilling to gracefully accept its decline. The period of the "great changes" is one that Beijing indicates is full of both great opportunities and risks, but China's leaders believe the former outweigh the latter. This is why they maintain that China remains in a period of "strategic" or "historical" opportunities for achieving rejuvenation.

The link between the "great changes" and rejuvenation is clear in authoritative speeches. "The world is facing great changes unseen in a century . . . which brings great opportunities for the great rejuvenation of the Chinese nation," Xi and his fellow leaders declared in 2018.[57] "The world today is undergoing great changes unseen in a century, and the realization of the great rejuvenation of the

Chinese nation is at a critical period," he said in a 2019 address.[58] That same year, he told the Central Party School, "The world today is in a state of changes unseen in a century. The great struggle, great project, great cause, and great dream of our party are in full swing," referencing rejuvenation. This understanding is widespread. In a summary of academic writing on the concept, one scholar from CASS argued that, "on the whole, it is generally believed that the 'great changes unseen in a century' is an important historic opportunity for the great rejuvenation of the Chinese nation."[59]

If the "great changes" mark an opportunity to seize rejuvenation, what then does rejuvenation mean? Although it is controversial in Western circles to suggest the goal of this concept is to displace the United States as the world's leading state by 2049, this is now often implicit and sometimes explicit in discussions of rejuvenation and the "great changes." For example, even Zhang Yunling—a senior Chinese academic and sometime adviser to the Ministry of Foreign Affairs who generally advocates a liberal foreign policy—links rejuvenation to surpassing the United States in an essay on the concept. "In history, China was the country with the strongest comprehensive power in the world," he notes; "it is expected that by the middle of the 21st century, that is, in 2050, China will be able to rank first in the world in terms of comprehensive strength and complete the great goal of the rejuvenation of the Chinese nation."[60] In another essay, he writes, "the greatest change in the last century was the continuous improvement of American power, from surpassing Britain, defeating Germany and Japan, the disintegration of the Soviet Union, and becoming the only superpower." But now, "in the first half of the 21st century," he continued, "the greatest change is most likely to be that China's comprehensive strength surpasses the United States. . . . This is undoubtedly the most important change in the power structure since Western industrialization."[61]

Similarly, an authoritative Xinhua editorial published during the Chinese Communist Party's 19th Party Congress declared, "By 2050, two centuries after the Opium Wars, which plunged the 'Middle Kingdom' into a period of hurt and shame, China is set to regain its might and re-ascend to the top of the world."[62] An article published on the website of the Central Party School's journal *Study Times* under a pseudonym makes clear that the "great changes" are about the changing international "power balance," with the author writing in sweeping terms about how "the United States gradually replaced Britain as the leader of the Western camp and the leader of world order" on its path to "world domination," suggesting the changes brewing now between the United States and China are of equal historical significance.[63] In an essay commissioned by the central government, CASS Deputy Director of the Belt and Road Research Center Ren Jingjing argues, "China will become a high-income country around 2021; by 2030, China's GDP may significantly exceed the United States; by 2035, China's high-tech R&D expenditure may exceed the United States; by 2050, China's military expenditure may exceed that of the United States."[64] This statement aligns China's desire to surpass the United States with the official timeline for rejuvenation, both of which focus on the Party's centenary in 2049. "If China develops smoothly," Ren continues, "China's strength in all aspects will continue to approach or even surpass the United States in the next 30 years."[65] In fact, the "the trend of the 'great changes' depends on the next 30 years," which Ren argues constitute "a transitional period."[66] Party officials appear to share this assessment that the next three decades—and the next decade in particular—are at the core of seizing the opportunities posed by the "great changes unseen in a century." As Xi himself argued, "The next ten years will be a decade of accelerated evolution of the international structure and balance of power [国际力量对比]," and "the next ten years will [also] be a decade of profound remodeling of the global governance system."[67]

These "great changes" involve risk and reward, and in the very speech debuting the "great changes" concept, Xi described this transitional period as one of "unprecedented opportunities and unprecedented challenges."[68] He has stressed these themes on multiple occasions. "We are facing rare historical opportunities and a series of challenges," he noted in a speech on the "great changes" and national rejuvenation.[69] "Crises and opportunities coexist in the great changes," he and other Party leaders noted at the 2018 Central Economic Work Forum.[70]

What exactly are these opportunities and challenges? China's 2019 White Paper "China and the World in the New Era" provides an answer. It features a detailed section on the "great changes," which is divided into opportunities and challenges.[71] And it, together with scholarly commentary, strongly suggests that the opportunity comes from US withdrawal and decline; the risk, however, comes from greater US resistance to China's rise as its own decline becomes obvious.

First, the White Paper stated clearly that "these great changes expedite the arrival of new opportunities" and that "the greatest change of the 'changes unseen in a century' is precisely *China's rise* . . . which fundamentally changes the international power balance." It argued that, "Since the First Industrial Revolution, international politics and the economic system have been dominated by Western powers." This was no longer the case, the White Paper noted, including a graph depicting the decreasing global share of "developed country" GDP. As a result, "in the world today, multipolarity is accelerating, modern development models are increasingly diverse, and . . . no single country or bloc of countries can exercise dominance in world affairs alone." All these trends produced China's "opportunities," an interpretation that other commentaries largely echoed. For example, in a October 2018 interview, Yan Xuetong declared, "I think this is the best period of strategic opportunity for China since the end of the Cold War."[72]

Explaining his logic, Yan argued, "Trump has ruined the US-led alliance system and improved China's international environment. . . . In a strategic sense, China's international environment is much better than before Trump came to power."[73] He put the situation in historical context: "In short, compared with the Korean War in the 1950s, the Vietnam War in the 1960s, and international sanctions in the 1990s, China's current international difficulties are very small, and the gap between China and the United States is much smaller than before."[74] His overall point: "What matters most now is how China should take advantage of this strategic opportunity.[75] Others had a similar perspective. Wu Xinbo notes that the Trump administration had been "constantly retreating" internationally, from "the withdrawal from TPP, the Paris Agreement on climate change, UNESCO, the Universal Postal Union, the termination of the JCPOA with Iran, the threat of withdrawal from the WTO, slamming NATO and even the UN, withdrawing from the INF treaty, announcing the withdrawal of troops from Syria, etc. It seems that the United States cannot help but give up its position in the post-war order." "De-Americanization," Wu Xinbo argued, "objectively creates a window of opportunity for various regions and countries to reposition themselves and solve various historical problems." When the United States declines, the "delegation of its powers and loosening of its restrictions" can also bring people unexpected strategic dividends and benefits."[76]

Second, the White Paper also pointed to challenges, namely risks, emanating from the United States. "The Cold War mentality of encirclement, constraint, confrontation, and threat is resurfacing," it argued. "Some Western countries are facing serious difficulties in governance, populism is widespread, and attacks on globalization are intensifying." Xi Jinping implied this when he said in a 2019 speech: "the world today is undergoing great changes unseen in a century, and the realization of the great rejuvenation of the Chinese nation is at a critical stage. *The closer the goal is, the more complicated the situation and the more arduous the task*."[77]

Scholarly commentaries echo these themes more explicitly. The main challenge to rejuvenation is the United States, argues a dean at the Central Party School writing in the institution's Central Party and Government Cadre Forum: "For China, the great changes bring both challenges and opportunities. The challenge mainly comes from the strategic game of great powers. The United States has regarded China as a strategic competitor, and the overall strength of the United States is still stronger than that of China. In this case, whether it can cope with the strategic competitive pressure of the United States is a severe test for China."[78] Most see a declining United States lashing out, sometimes self-destructively, at an ascendant China. Ren Jingjing from CASS argues, "The United States is the biggest constraint on China's road to its rise and national rejuvenation" and seeks to "remove China from the global value chain" to undermine it.[79] Zhu Feng, who often cautions a more restrained foreign policy, worries that triumphalism in China's discourse—particularly the discourse on "great changes unseen in a century"—will prematurely trigger Western anxieties. "The more China's rise sees forward momentum, the more Western countries will worry about losing their power advantages, and strong and powerful containment of and checks and balances on China will become more obvious. The discussion of 'great changes' cannot indulgently focus only on the redistribution of power in the international system, it also needs to avoid becoming a new target for the West to attack China."[80] By late 2019, it was clear the United States was the core obstacle. For example, a piece written by a scholar at the Shanghai Institute of International Studies on the "great changes" argues, "The United States and other Western countries openly regard China as their main competitor," though "the leading position of Western civilization in global politics, economy, military, and ideology has entered a relatively weak cycle," in part due to populism, offering a potential reprieve.[81]

China's strategists would prefer the United States graciously accept its decline. A dean at the Central Party School writing in the institution's Central Party and Government Cadre Forum argued: "In the great changes, the most uncertain factor is the Western powers, especially the only superpower, the United States. Whether the United States can judge the current situation, follow the trend, respond rationally to the great changes, and realize the decline of hegemony in an elegant and decent way is an important factor that determines the process of the great changes." Even if it did not, US resistance "can only delay the progress of the great changes but could not determine their direction."[82] In the long run, US decline was inevitable.

How then to weigh the balance between opportunities and risks? In general, the opportunities were greater. A dean at the Central Party School writing in the institution's Central Party and Government Cadre Forum: "The opportunities brought about by the great changes should be more worthy of attention [than risks]. General Secretary Xi Jinping's discussion of major changes is usually linked to the assertion that China is still in a period of important strategic opportunities."[83] China would have to strive vigorously to achieve rejuvenation by 2049. As Xi put it in a 2017 address, "The great rejuvenation of the Chinese nation cannot be achieved with great ease or simply playing drums and gongs [敲锣打鼓]. A great struggle must be waged to realize this great dream. . . . The various struggles we face are not short-term but long-term, and they will accompany us throughout the process of fulfilling our second centenary goal [of rejuvenation]."[84] As a 2021 speech made clear, he was confident in the future. "The world is undergoing great changes unseen in a century, *but time and momentum are on our side.* This is where our force and vigor reside, and it is also where our determination and confidence reside."[85]

In short, China would need an approach integrating political, economic, and military means to achieve these lofty goals and displace the United States from global order. That strategy, as the next chapter demonstrates in great detail, would involve putting forward global institutions at the political level, seizing the "fourth industrial revolution" at the economic level, and securing increasingly global capabilities at the military level—all to apply the *blunting* and *building* strategies long underway within Asia to the wider world.

"Standing Tall and Seeing Far"

The Ways and Means of China's Global Expansion

"For our friends, we have fine wine, but for our enemies, we have
shotguns."[1]

—*China's Ambassador to Sweden Gui Congyou, 2019*

On November 30, 2019, China's Ambassador to Sweden Gui Congyou sat down
for an interview with Swedish public radio. The interview did not go well.

Ties between China and Sweden were strained at the time, though by most
accounts they should not have been. Sweden was a country with a long history
of neutrality and non-alignment dating back to the Napoleonic Wars. During
the Second World War, Sweden let the Germans use the country's railways while
providing the Allies intelligence and occasional military access; during the Cold
War, Sweden was quietly aligned with the West but stridently neutral in public.
For Beijing, Sweden's instincts for non-alignment made it an attractive partner,
and Chinese sources frequently said so.[2] The two should have gotten along even
at a time of rising US-China tension, and Gui's interview should have gone better.

But Gui's interview came at a difficult moment. A rupture in bilateral ties had
opened when Beijing, despite having had rather warm relations with Sweden
for years, sent its agents to kidnap a Swedish citizen and bookseller named Gui
Minhai who was living in Thailand. Gui published critical books on the Chinese
elite, so China had him renditioned, forced him to give a televised confession,
and then after two years of detaining him sentenced him to another ten years in
prison.

Sweden is of course a liberal society with a free press, and the kidnapping of
a Swedish citizen was not a story its media could ignore. But for Beijing, the independent Swedish civil society groups that reported on Gui Minhai's capture
and advocated for his release were intolerable despite the Swedish government's
comparatively more restrained public line. And it was in the context of this civil

society activism that Ambassador Gui decided to clarify the stakes if Sweden continued to make trouble over the kidnapping of its own citizen. "For our friends, we have fine wine," Gui said, "but for our enemies, we have shotguns" [朋友来了有好酒,坏人来了有猎枪].[3]

Gui's impolitic threat was an example of what many call China's "Wolf Warrior" diplomacy—a sharper, nationalistic tone that is at times self-defeating. It also proved a sign of things to come. Almost exactly one year later, China sent a list of fourteen grievances to Australia that supposedly justified its economic punishment of the country. Taken together, the grievances formed a rough blue-print for Chinese order. Australia was ostensibly to reduce its foreign investment screening, tolerate Huawei, roll back counter foreign interference legislation, open up its visa policy, cease its human rights criticism, change its South China Sea stance, stop publicly attributing cyber-attacks to China, allow Australian states to join China's Belt and Road Initiative, and constrain the independent actions of its think tanks, media, and local officials that China found distasteful.[4] Otherwise, it would face even greater economic punishment.

Gui's line, and China's letter to Australia, captured an evolving state of af-fairs: China would increasingly exercise its "forms of control" over countries like Sweden and Australia—with punishments for those who displeased China and inducements for those who sided with it. The great power behavior China some-times deployed in its immediate neighborhood was becoming more common outside it. Now, as Beijing pursues a more ambitious grand strategy, it is taking those forms of control—coercive capability, consensual inducements, and its pursuit of legitimacy—global.

This chapter looks at how it seeks to do so. It examines the "ways and means" of China's global grand strategy, discussing in concrete terms how it is building forms of control globally while weakening those of the United States. It examines this effort across three domains of statecraft, describing how Beijing has put for-ward global institutions and illiberal norms at the political level, sought to seize the "fourth industrial revolution" and weaken US financial power at the eco-nomic level, and increasingly acquired global capabilities and new facilities at the military level—all as part of a broader effort to achieve its nationalistic vision of rejuvenation and to displace US order.

Ways and Means—A Global Grand Strategy

Some Western observers have speculated that China has two paths to shaping global order—a regional path that requires "establishing dominance in the Western Pacific and then expanding outward from there" and a global one that involves "outflanking the US" and "building up economic and political power around the world."[5] For China, the regional strategy has been pursued more assertively since 2008 as China sought to lay the foundations for regional hegemony, and it is ongoing. What has change since 2016 is the dawn of a new, more global focus, one that contests global order more broadly.

China's new global efforts began with an open break from Deng Xiaoping. An authoritative commentary on Xi's 2017 National Security Work Forum paraphrased a key portion of Deng's remarks and suggested they were outdated: "At this moment, our diplomatic strategy must keep pace with the times and step out of the stage of 'hiding our capabilities and biding our time.'"[6] In his important 2018 Central Foreign Affairs Work Conference address, Xi seemed to question whether Deng's guidance still held today when he argued that "the so-called correct view of our role is to not only calmly analyze various international phenomena," which Deng had famously advocated as part of his "hide and bide" dictum, "but also to put ourselves in [it], look at the issues between China and the world, understand clearly our status and role in the evolution of the international structure, and scientifically formulate our country's foreign policy."[7] China, he argued, needed to "fundamentally strengthen strategic self-confidence." As he argued in an important meeting commemorating BRI's fifth anniversary, "the world today is in a period of great development, great changes, and major adjustments. We need to have a strategic vision and establish a global perspective. We must have both a sense of risk and a sense of historical opportunity and grasp the course of these changes not seen in one hundred years."[8]

What does China's order-building at the global level look like in concrete terms? Beijing's strategy is evolving, but Chinese sources and behavior help us sketch out its emerging contours. At its center is the amorphous concept of a "community of shared future for mankind," which countless officials have said is central to national rejuvenation. While early formulations of this concept were regional, it has clearly gone global, appearing in every major foreign policy address and more than twenty-two times in China's 2019 White Paper as an example of "Chinese wisdom and strength for solving world problems."[9] The concept involves China "providing public goods . . . to establish itself as a great power," note two CASS scholars, themes that China's White Paper also emphasizes.[10] It is "the most important goal of the 21st century for China to achieve national rejuvenation and build a modern powerful country," argues Zhang Yunling.[11] And it is a foundation for a loose political bloc, notes Yuan Peng, who warns that if the United States seeks to break the world into "two economic groups," then China "will turn its hand to 'One Belt One Road' and the community of common destiny" to construct its own coalition of support "revolving around China."[12] Ultimately, the concept appears to be a stand-in for global Chinese hierarchical order that secures deference to Beijing's prerogatives through a mix of coercion, consensual tools like public goods, and rightful legitimacy. It resembles what some might call a kind of "partial hegemony," one that is not necessarily geo-graphically bound but rests on a complex web of different instruments of state-craft all radiating outward from China around the world.

China's emerging global strategy to achieve this kind of order has three broad prongs, according to Party documents and relevant commentaries. We turn now to explore each of these prongs in detail.

Political Ways and Means—Claiming Global Leadership

At the political level, China once sought to blunt regional institutions operated by others and to build regional institutions that it controlled. Now, as Party texts and China's own behavior indicate, its efforts are focused on *global* governance and order as well as on more vigorously promoting the legitimacy of its own system. A review of China's major foreign policy documents and speeches makes this focus clear.

The more global focus first appeared Yang Jiechi's 2017 essay, which, not coin-cidentally, also first introduced the "great changes unseen in a century" and was published a week before Trump's inauguration. Yang listed several "main points" for China's new "great power diplomacy," all of which were global: "proposing the China dream and giving it profound world significance," "advocating the cre-ation of a community of common destiny for mankind," "building a global part-nership network," striving to "contribute Chinese wisdom to the improvement of global governance," and promoting the Belt and Road. In an apparent shift from past language, Yang's essay explicitly stressed Chinese leadership by arguing that "participating in and *leading* global governance" would be a "pioneer direction" for Chinese diplomacy and that China would "actively *lead* international eco-nomic cooperation" too. Yang's was a more self-consciously global agenda than in the past, and he declared it would "surpass the traditional Western theory of international relations based on zero-sum games and power politics" and would give Chinese diplomacy "the moral high ground."[13]

Xi's high-level foreign policy addresses amplified these themes. For example, in his 2017 address to the China National Security Work Forum, Xi went be-yond the more general, rhetorical language previously used to describe China's ambitions for international order: "It is necessary [for China] to *guide* the in-ternational community to jointly shape a more just and reasonable new in-ternational order," he declared.[14] An authoritative commentary on his speech went further and advocated that China become a "benefactor and leader of the international system." It also declared that "the world needs a new order," that "China is qualified to be a leader," and that "we have the qualifications and capability to be the guide of the international order and international security."[15] Xi's 19th Party Congress address a month later continued these themes, with Xi announcing a "new era that will see China move closer to the world's center stage," that would see it far more active in global governance (a contrast to Hu's address five years earlier). And at his 2017 Ambassadorial Conference a few months later, Xi argued that China needed to "establish a broader global vision and greater strategic ambitions" and listed the same global tasks Yang Jiechi had included in his essay earlier that year.[16]

Then, at the 2018 Central Foreign Affairs Work Conference address, Xi not only repeated Yang's list of global tasks (which he declared essential to rejuvenation) but also evoked Yang's language on leadership. Where Xi's predecessors might have called for China to "actively participate" in global governance reforms, Xi said China should "*lead* the reform of the global governance system."[17] In a commentary on this important address, State Councilor Wang Yi stressed that a "key word" for China is "leadership" and that "the leadership trend reflects China's concern for the common good of humanity."[18] "At present, the reform of the international system is facing a critical moment," he declared. "Faced with the disagreement, disillusionment, and disquiet among some countries," China was "standing tall and seeing far" as it built a global "community of common destiny," moved to "actively lead the reform of the global governance system," and served as "a source of stability amid the world's chaos," a reference to the United States.[19] Similarly, China's 2019 White Paper declared China would "lead and promote an open global economy" and, again, "lead the reform of the global governance system."[20]

Academic and think tank commentary was far more explicit about the political elements of China's grand strategy and believed that US withdrawal created an opportunity. A dean at the Central Party School writing for cadres argued, "in the past, Western countries have always been the key players and played a central role in global governance. However, at present, the United States, which is the leader of the Western world, has lost its impetus to promote global governance, and even frequently 'backed out.' This is a new situation unseen in a century."[21] As a result, noted a pseudonymous commentary by the *Study Times*, "the transition from the old order to the new one, and the breaking of the system in this transition period, provides an important opportunity for China to cultivate and expand its power in the international system."[22] The stakes were high, noted Yuang Guangbin: "the current world order has entered a 'no man's land,' and we don't know where to go. Whoever gets out of the 'no man's land' first can lead the world."[23] Most, like Jin Canrong, believed China could fill the void: "we are interested in global governance. China is a country with strong administrative capabilities. We participate in global governance, and we may be better at solving problems than the West."[24] After all, "faced with so many global issues, whoever responds well will have more voice and higher international popularity in the future."[25] And as two CASS scholars noted, beyond popularity or leadership or solving transnationalproblems, there was a chance to build order. "This [global governance] is not only about meeting various global challenges, but also about setting rules and directions for the international order and the international system," they argued, and about "the long-term institutional arrangements" in the world as well as "status and roles in the system." The core order-building concept for China was clear too. "The goal is to build a community of common destiny," they noted, which involves China "providing public goods . . . to es-tablish itself as a great power," all of which "provides an important foundation for maintaining China's period of strategic opportunity."[26] Legitimacy would un-derwrite these objectives. As one CASS scholar argued in a state-commissioned report, "In the final analysis, the rise of a great power is a cultural phenomenon. It must be accepted by the international community, be accommodated by the international system, rely on the international system, and be recognized by in-ternational norms."[27]

China's greater interest in shaping global political order and building a "com-munity of common destiny for mankind" has manifested itself across a broad range of efforts. These broadly help China build the foundations of hegemonic order—coercion, consent, and legitimacy—and take place across a variety of arenas: (1) the UN system; (2) global regional organizations; (3) new coalitions; and (4) exports of certain governance practices.

First, China's interest in "leading the reform of the global governance system" runs through the United Nations because—as its own 2019 White Paper makes clear—"the UN is at the core of the global governance system."[28] Influence in the UN allows China to build some coercive and consensual leverage as well as legitimacy—allowing it to displace liberal values as the global default and to elevate, legitimize, and globalize Chinese principles and programs.[29] Chinese government documents brag that Beijing's "global community of shared future and the Belt and Road Initiative . . . have been written into many UN resolutions and . . . won extensive recognition and a warm response from the international community."[30] In pursuing UN influence, Beijing has seized on US inattention and worked diligently to place its officials in the top leadership spots of four of fifteen UN specialized agencies—more than any other state—including the UN Industrial Development Organization (IDO), the International Civil Aviation Organization (ICAO), the International Telecommunication Union (ITU), and the Food and Agriculture Organization (FAO). Moreover, China previously led the WHO and INTERPOL, presently leads the UN Department of Economic and Social Affairs (DESA), and narrowly missed out on leading the World Intellectual Property Organization (WIPO) in 2020. In the FAO election, for example, Beijing threatened exports from Argentina, Brazil, and Uruguay to earn support for its candidate while forgiving the debt of Cameroon so it would withdraw its competing candidate.[31] Since 2016, it has intensified efforts to wield this influence to embed its programs and principles in UN architecture. The UN's highest leadership has repeatedly praised the Belt and Road Initiative (BRI); BRI has been inserted into the critical Sustainable Development Goals; BRI and the Community of Common Destiny have appeared in UN resolutions; and a wide range of UN bodies—such as UNICEF, UNESCO, UNHCR, and DESA—have either endorsed BRI or funded and collaborated with it.[32] In other cases, China has used its leverage in the ICAO and the WHO to marginalize Taiwan. It successfully de-platformed some NGOs critical of Beijing's human rights record and platformed its own "government-organized" NGOs (i.e., GONGOs) that follow Beijing's lead on key issues. And its top officials, like former DESA head Wu Hongbo, have been unapologetic about putting national over international obligations: "as a Chinese-national international civil servant, I don't yield in matters concerning China's national sovereignty or security interests and resolutely defend the interests of my country."[33] He once boasted of using UN security to "drive out" a Uyghur activist that he declared was not part of an "approved NGO" and had been the subject of an INTERPOL "red notice"—factors for which Beijing was itself responsible, and a useful case study in China's efforts to "deliberalize" UN architecture.

Second, outside the UN system and apart from its regional involvements in Asia, China has also set up a hub-and-spokes arrangement with virtually every world region. The most significant of these include the Forum on China-Africa Cooperation (FOCAC); the China-Arab States Cooperation Forum (CACF); the China-Central and Eastern European Countries (CEEC, or "17+1"); and the China and the Community of Latin American States (China-CELAC). These bodies cover 125 countries and channel relations between China and each region in a bilateral way rather than fostering multilateral engagement among the plurality of actors involved.[34] Though these bodies were established before the more global turn in Chinese strategy, they are likely to become more central to Chinese global order-building and have recently been the focus of greater attention—with more meetings, activities, and institutionalization undertaken since 2016.[35] On the consensual side, Beijing uses these organizations as platforms for regional engagement and "public goods" provision, including to announce tens of billions in loans or aid, infrastructure spending, or COVID support. Each regularly involves "Action Plans" or "Development Plans" that set the agenda for China's beneficent interaction with the region. And each includes a wide range of "sub-forums" involving think tanks, young political leaders, political parties, parliaments, media, businesses, culture, science, the environment, and other domains that not only build ties but (particularly in media and technology) share Chinese practices, standards, training, and other technocratic governance guidance. Finally, with respect to questions of legitimacy, these organizations have been used to challenge liberal norms and build support for Chinese preferences: most have statements supporting global regime "diversity," progress toward multipolarity, resistance to human rights "interference," and critiques of US policy—all while supporting Chinese positions on issues as varied as Taiwan, Tibet, and Hong Kong.[36] For example, a special June 2020 FOCAC meeting on COVID-19 released a statement including language supporting African states pursuing "development paths suited to their national conditions" in addition to supporting "China's efforts to safeguard national security in Hong Kong in accordance with the law."[37]

Third, in recent years, China assembled coalitions of like-minded countries to support its authoritarian domestic policies that could, in the future, become more operational and active. For example, in 2019 and 2020 liberal democracies organized some twenty states to sign three separate statements and letters critical of China's policies in Xinjiang and then Hong Kong. In response, China organized more than fifty states to sign three separate letters that supported China's "remarkable achievements in the field of human rights" and expressed "'firm opposition' to relevant countries' practice of politicizing human rights issues."[38] In all three cases, a comparison of the letters' signatories reveals geographic and ideological differences between the two groups, with BRI signatories and many of China's trading partners signing onto its letters, and liberal democracies and European states composing a bulk of the other camp. Beijing's objective is to globalize China's approach to human rights. As the *People's Daily* put it, with fifty countries supporting China and only twenty critical of China, it was clear that Washington was standing "on the opposite side of international society."[39] These loose coalitions could collaborate on other normative issues in the future.

Finally, due to the trifecta of Brexit, Trump, and COVID-19, China has more enthusiastically promoted its model and values—both defensively to push back on Western liberalism and offensively to build the normative foundations of hegemony. The phrase "China solution" [中国方案], which was debuted in 2013 in high-level speeches, has surged since Brexit and Trump's election, with the number of journal articles discussing it increasing fourteen-fold from 337 articles in 2015 to 4,845 in 2017.[40] Xi even declared in his 19th Party Congress address that China "offers a new option for other countries and nations who want to speed up their development while preserving their independence," language that was then repeated in China's 2019 White Paper, which also stated *five* times that Beijing should share "Chinese wisdom and strength" with the world.[41] That document also argued that "some Western countries are facing serious difficulties in governance" and struggling with populism; that "some countries blindly copied or were forced to adopt the Western model," and that these countries then "fell into social unrest, economic crisis, governance paralysis, and even endless civil war."[42] Other sources, such as an official commentary printed in the *People's Daily* under the name "Declaration" or [宣言] contrasted the "rule of China" favorably with the Western-induced "chaos of the world."[43] Academic commentators have gone even further. "Any country regarded as a great power must have had an important influence and made important contributions to the historical process of humanity," noted one CASS scholar. He argued that Britain, the Soviet Union, and the United States all shared their model and it was China's time to share something too.[44] Others said the West should study China. "The pandemic has profoundly shaken the US sense of superiority in values, culture and systems since the Enlightenment," argued a typical passage authored by Nie Wenjuan, a professor at China Foreign Affairs University. "From the depth of their hearts, Americans confront the reality that the beacon of freedom has to learn from the authoritarian government of communist China in some respects."[45] Countless others have made similar arguments over the last four years, arguing even that China's "development concept" is more exportable than Western liberalism and can better deal with "extremism, terrorism, and populism."[46]

What might this look like in practice? Just as the United States does not export its specific institutions but instead broad liberal principles, China does not export "socialism with Chinese characteristics" but instead broad, illiberal, and tech-enabled solutions to twenty-first-century governance challenges. These include information management, terrorism, crime, and pandemic response—problems Chinese scholars claim the West cannot address given its dysfunction and "absolutism" on liberal values.[47] To solve these challenges, China exports surveillance and censorship equipment, and engages on standards, training, and governance mechanisms through a variety of channels such astelecommunications assistance, regulatory consultations, and media trainings. Chinese firms have actively assisted the Ugandan and Zambian governments in compromising the private information of dissidents; helped Ecuador build an extensive surveillance system; and are so involved in Ethiopia's telecom network that NGO workers believe they must self-censor to avoid monitoring and arrest.[48] These practices, iterated across dozens of countries, embed illiberal norms in governance across Asia, Africa, and Latin America. Beijing claims it is only providing an answer to how technology and governance should interact, one consistent with its own illiberal systems, while the West is silent on this key twenty-first-century question. And while China's model is not yet neatly packaged in a coherent ideology, as the West organizes democratic coalitions to control the substructure of the global system (technology, trade, finance, etc.), China may feel compelled to export its system, intervene for ideological reasons, and engage in its own coalition-building—amplifying ideological competition. Such an outcome should not be surprising. Ideology has suffused great power politics for centuries, whether Catholic and

Protestant states, republican governments and monarchies, communist states and capitalist ones, and of course democracies and authoritarian regimes.

Economic Ways and Means—Technology and Finance

With respect to economic instruments, Beijing now sees technology as central to its ambitions to displace American order. A key component of China's "great changes unseen in a century" is the belief that the world is experiencing a new wave of technological innovation sometimes referred to as the "Fourth Industrial Revolution" that offers an opportunity for China to overtake the West. This term, originally developed at the World Economic Forum in 2015, has now been adopted by Beijing and generally refers to a wide range of technologies: artificial intelligence (AI), quantum computing, smart manufacturing, biotechnology, and even sovereign digital currencies, among many others. Beijing believes that technology's intersection with supply chains, trade patterns, financial power, and information flows has the potential to reshape order alongside traditional economic instruments more central to past eras of Chinese grand strategy. For that reason, economic instruments—and technology in particular—are increasingly at the center of the US-China contest over global order.

Most references to the "great changes unseen in a century" evoke the idea that waves of technological transformation have occasionally reshaped history. As Xi Jinping argued in a 2018 speech, "From the mechanization of the first industrial revolution in the 18th century, to the electrification of the second industrial revolution in the 19th century, to the informatization of the third industrial revolution in the 20th century," each round of "disruptive technological innovation" has reshaped the world.[49] Now, China was facing a fourth industrial revolution, and over the next decade, it had an opportunity to seize technology leadership. "The next ten years will be a key decade . . . for the world economy," Xi argued. "A new round of technological revolution and industrial change, such as in artificial intelligence, big data, quantum information, and biotechnology, are gathering strength" and bringing "earth-shaking changes" while offering an "important opportunity to promote leapfrog development," bypassing legacy systems and overtaking competitors.[50]

Technology leadership could help China realize the potential of the "great changes unseen in a century." Indeed, most Chinese commentators have argued that the last three revolutions caused a "divergence" that allowed some countries to become geopolitical leaders and left others as geopolitical laggards. Beijing missed out on these revolutions, but now it hopes to ride the fourth industrial revolution to global leadership. In a passage typical of writing on the subject, two CASS scholars made this argument explicitly. "China did not participate in the steam engine and mechanical revolutions of the 18th century or the power and transportation revolution of the 19th century; China partially participated in the electrical and information revolution of the 20th century." This time would be different, they argued, "in the current brewing of artificial intelligence, Internet of Things, energy Internet, biotechnology, China is 'overtaking by curve.'"[51] This seemingly inscrutable phrase—overtaking by curve—is rooted in some of the post-2009 debates about US power after the Global Financial Crisis, with "overtaking by curve" a reference to sprinting ahead as a competitor slows down or mishandles a turn around a racetrack and "overtaking by lane change" a reference to innovating new methods to surpass a rival.

Chinese discourses on China's grand strategy under the "great changes" often reinforce this technological and materialist view of power transition. For example, a typical and authoritative commentary on the subject posted online at the *Study Times* roughly two months after Xi's 2018 address on the Fourth Industrial Revolution is clear on the geopolitical stakes of these technological changes. "The driving force for the great changes is the decisive role of productivity," it argued.[52] "Britain seized the opportunity of the first industrial revolution" provided by coal and steam technology and "established an empire on which the sun never set."[53] Afterward, "the United States seized the dominant power of advanced productivity from Great Britain" by dominating the second industrial revolution of electrification and promptly "jumped into position as the world's number one industrial power, laying a solid foundation for establishing global hegemony."[54] Then, "the third industrial revolution originated in the United States," and by seizing this digital revolution, the United States boosted its "comprehensive strength" and extended American hegemony.[55] The arrival of the Fourth Industrial Revolution now offers an opportunity to make up for lost time. For decades, China's leaders have long employed phrases like "catch up and surpass" [赶超] to describe their technological ambitions, with the United States and the West seen as the critical benchmark.[56] But now, Beijing believes that the goal of "surpassing" the West is not simply rhetorical but actually achievable. As China's 2019 White Paper puts it, "China is catching up and getting ahead."[57]

The "key" to stealing the march on these new waves of industrial revolution was a country's "institutional advantages," the *Study Times* commentary noted. "Britain replaced Spanish hegemony because the capitalist system was far superior to the feudal system that bound farmers to the land. The great changes a hundred years ago stemmed from the establishment of a more thorough democratic republican system in the United States, which created a modern market system and a standardized large industrial production system [e.g., assembly lines] that were significantly different from the United Kingdom."[58] But now, the US system was seeing challenges. "The combined effects of governance dilemmas inside and outside the West have become more apparent . . . the century-old neoliberal development standard and the Western-centered international hierarchical structure have been gradually broken," it noted.[59] China's system looked better by comparison: "in the face of great changes, contradictions within the Western camp and contradictions among various political forces and social trends in some major powers are developing. There is a strong contrast between the rule of China and the chaos in the world . . . [and] the emergence of a new round of scientific and technological revolution and industrial transformation is conducive to China's institutional advantages and to achieving 'overtaking by curve.'"[60] China had an opportunity given its supposedly superior system to follow in the footsteps of Britain and the United States, seize a new industrial revolution, and become the world's leading state.

These sentiments appear to be shared by most prominent Chinese international relations scholars and experts who argue that the relationship between technology and power is at the core of the "great changes unseen in a century." As Jin Canrong argues, "In the next decade . . . the competition for the Fourth Industrial Revolution will begin between China and the United States."[61] Jin Canrong sees this as a groundbreaking development: "This is a major change that has not occurred in the past 500 years. In the past 500 years, the industrial revolution has all involved the West, and this time the industrial revolution will involve both East and West. This is an opportunity for China and a huge challenge for the United States."[62] Others share this perspective. Technology is in reality geopolitics, argues prominent Nanjing University scholar Zhu Feng: "Scientific and technological capabilities have become an important indicator of a country's comprehensive strength, and it has also become the main battlefield for great power competition."[63] China's tech industry has become a source of tension," notes Zhang Yuyan. "Power politics mainly refers to any means among the great powers of the century to suppress their opponents, even at the expense of their own interests. The deep-seated reason for the change in the world today comes down to one thing: China's rapid entry into the high-tech industry."[64] Yan Xuetong sees a bipolar world emerging with technology at the center of competition. "The core of the bipolar US-China strategic competition is over the competitive advantage of technological innovation," he argues; "it is inevitable to adopt the strategy of technological decoupling to obtain technological advantage."[65] Yuan Peng argues that conflicts over "high tech are increasingly becoming the core disputes in international politics."[66]

China is pursuing a robust, state-backed effort to dominate these technologies and to use them to erode various American advantages.

First, China has taken a page from American history and used the state to make enormous investments in basic science research that the market may otherwise shun. The National Science Foundation estimates that China's total R&D spending is roughly equivalent to US spending, even though China's economy is smaller.[67] And in the technologies central to the Fourth Industrial Revolution, China may well spend more. For example, China spends at least ten times more than the United States does in quantum computing.[68] Similarly, in artificial intelligence, China spends at least as much as the United States and likely more, according to estimates from Georgetown's Center for Security and Emerging Technology.[69]

Second, China believes its institutions are better designed to mobilize the state, society, and market to wield industrial policy to achieve the country's technological ambitions, particularly compared to the more polarized and short-term US political system.[70] Beijing has identified specific industrial policies meant to support China's efforts to secure the commanding heights of the Fourth Industrial Revolution, with over 100 Science and Technology plans and over $1 trillion spent toward this purpose.[71] Key efforts include Made in China 2025, which targets ten high-tech industries, seeks to indigenize key technologies in them, and sets market share targets for foreign and domestic markets—all backed by tens of billions in state subsidies, technology transfer, market access restrictions, state-backed acquisitions, and other instruments.[72] While Beijing formally deemphasized the initiative in its official discourses following backlash from the United States and Europe, the core of the initiative remains very much alive. And since 2016, Beijing has launched several similar and heavily resourced programs, including a plan to become a world leader in AI by 2030, a plan to dominate standard-setting by 2035, and a plan to invest $1.4 trillion in five years to build 5G networks across China.[73]

Third, Chinese sources see their role in supply chains as an enormous advantage worth preserving as technology competition intensifies. Even as countries around the world sought to diversify away from China following COVID-19, President Xi declared that protecting China's role in global supply chains was one of his top national priorities. These chains are one reason some scholars like Jin Canrong argue that "China has a greater chance of winning" the Fourth Industrial Revolution.[74] Although the United States does have "the best innovation capabilities," he argues, the country now "has a major problem, which is the hollowing out of its industrial base."[75] This means it "cannot turn technology into a product acceptable to the market" without China's factories. "China has just about every industry" and its "manufacturing industry will account for more than 50 percent of the world's total by 2030."[76] The country's superior numbers of engineers, its ability to reverse-engineer, and its factories' centrality to global technology are "China's real advantage in long-term industrial competition."[77]

China should press this advantage. "Regardless of how the United States feels," he argues, "China . . . must work hard to seize the Fourth Industrial Revolution" and become the "leader" of it.[78] For now, China is retaining its hold on global supply chains despite foreign pressure. The European Chamber of Commerce in China found that only about 11 percent of its members were considering relocation out of China in 2020; similarly, the president of AmCham China noted that the majority of the group's members are not planning on exiting China.[79] For these firms, the rationale goes beyond cost alone. As the Paulson Institute scholar Damien Ma argues, it is hard for Americans to quit Amazon because it is the "everything store," and it is hard for manufacturers to quit China because it is the "make everything country."[80]

Fourth, China is increasingly focused on setting standards in technical bodies relative to the United States. China's objectives include promoting its industries, earning lucrative royalties when its patents are used, and embedding its values and governance approaches in the architecture of technology. Even before its 2035 Standards Plan was announced, China had already grown influential in key bodies like the Third Generation Partnership Project (3GPP) and the International Telecommunication Union (ITU), and in some cases sought to shift standard-setting discussions to bodies where its influence was greater. With respect to governance, Chinese companies like ZTE have proposed standards for streetlight architecture that would allow video monitoring capabilities to be built in, for facial recognition that would require specific and extraneous demographic and biometric data to be stored, and for a new Internet architecture that would advantage monitoring, censorship, and control.[81] Beijing's success in these bodies is in part a product of its successful investments in next-generation technologies like 5G but also the more "hands-on" approach the Party appears to take relative to the more industry-led and "hands-off" approach that the United States takes. Although many standard-setting bodies are primarily composed of companies that are supposed to vote based on their own interests, at least in China's case, companies like Lenovo that initially voted to endorse approaches backed by US companies were criticized by nationalists for doing so and pressured to instead endorse approaches backed by major Chinese companies like Huawei. As Lenovo's leadership team noted in an apologetic message posted online, "We all unanimously believe that Chinese companies should unite and should not allow outsiders to play them against each other."[82] If China's efforts continue to be successful, Beijing may be able to lock in its approaches and extend its lead in certain key global technologies to the detriment of universal values and US interests.

Technology also intersects with other more conventional goals of Chinese economic statecraft. For example, China has largely struggled to reduce its vulnerability to the dollar, but it clearly hopes that with the issuance of its own digital currency it might ride a disruptive wave of financial innovation to blunt US financial advantages and build its own at a global level. Chinese officials have long been worried about the possibility that Facebook's plan for a digital currency, Libra, would constitute the kind of epochal transformation that would once again bolster the US dollar system. Wang Xin, director of the People's Bank of China's research bureau, stated that "if the digital currency [Libra] is closely associated with the U.S. dollar . . . there would be in essence one boss, that is the U.S. dollar and the United States," which would have geopolitical consequences.[83] That concern led the People's Bank of China to accelerate plans for its own digital sovereign currency, with hopes that it could help China reduce its reliance on the dollar and leapfrog ahead of enduring US advantages.

Finally, the coercive and consensual foundations of order-building very much remain a focus for Beijing. On the coercive side, over the last few years, China's economic statecraft has become increasingly global, and it has expanded in both frequency and scope. Countries on virtually every continent—as wide-ranging as Brazil and the Czech Republic—have been threatened if they do not accede to China's preferences not only over once familiar sovereignty issues but even on other questions too.[84] This is not unusual behavior for a great power, but it does indicate a departure from past eras when China was more focused on consensual elements of order-building rather than punitive ones—particularly in the developing world it sees as its natural base. Moreover, Beijing has encouraged boycotts of various companies for perceived slights, most famously in the US National Basketball Association because one team manager posted a tweet in support of Hong Kong protesters. Of course, consensual elements of China's order-building also remain and have been globalized too. Providing global "public goods" is now an official and high-level part of Chinese foreign policy, given its own special section in China's 2019 White Paper. To that end, China has continued to globalize its Belt and Road, which now boasts at least 138 countries.[85] And China's efforts to use aid and assistance to win favor have evolved, particularly following COVID-19 and Beijing's pandemic diplomacy involving vaccines, masks, and other health goods.

Military Ways and Means—Going Global

If China's military strategy once prioritized blunting American power and then building Chinese power within the Indo-Pacific, the third phase of its grand strategy suggests a more global turn, with China's military increasingly looking beyond its home region.

This argument can be controversial. Some skeptics note that contingencies involving Taiwan and the South and East China Seas will continue to hold

China's military attention. While that is certainly true, it does not therefore follow that Beijing will refrain from pursuing a more global expeditionary capability. Others note that China is unlikely to adopt the same complex network of far-flung bases and global capabilities that the United States has retained. This is it overlooks the fact that China may be able to engage in operations outside the Indo-Pacific without precisely replicating America's complex and costly global footprint. Indeed, the United States did not adopt Britain's network of coaling stations and continental-sized colonies; similarly, China may not adopt the American reliance on allies and large numbers of overseas bases—pursuing its own hybrid path instead.

The most authoritative Chinese sources are often circumspect about the country's global ambitions, but the indications of a more global focus are there, particularly after 2016, and they can be found in three broad areas related to (1) China's desire for a world-class army; (2) its discussion of the military's role in China's global objectives; and (3) its discussion of its overseas interests.

First, Xi's 19th Party Congress address declared on multiple occasions that it was Beijing's "goal" in the "new era" to ensure that "by the middle of the twenty-first century, the PLA is fully transformed into a world-class military"—language that then reappeared in China's 2019 Defense White Paper.[86] Given the overall tone of that address, which was clearly global in scope and declared China would "move closer to the world's center stage" and "become a global leader in terms of composite national strength and international influence," it is reasonable to interpret the phrase "world-class army" in global terms. Some scholars who resist such an interpretation and suggest the phrase is a "force development concept" nonetheless acknowledge, in a review of commentaries on the subject, "certainly, some degree of power projection is implied by using the United States, Russia, France and others as examples of world-class militaries. All of these armed forces can project and sustain at least some combat power beyond their home regions of the world."[87] As a result, "China's global military presence outside of East Asia will grow in the coming decade," though, compared to the robust US military presence, it is likely to remain "relatively modest" for now given the challenges of power projection.[88]

Second, authoritative texts suggest China's military will be used to support policy priorities that are deemed critical to rejuvenation and that are fundamentally global in nature, including the "community of common destiny for mankind" and the Belt and Road—indicating a more global military is desirable. For example, China's 2019 White Paper titled "China and the World in the New Era" explicitly says, "The Chinese army faithfully carries out [践行] the concept of a *global* community of common destiny." It also argues that "China is moving closer to the center of the world stage, and the international community expects more international public security goods from the Chinese military."[89]

The 2019 Defense White Paper released the same year goes into far more detail on these global themes, and unlike past Defense White Papers, even has a lengthy section entitled "Actively Contributing to Building a Community with a Shared Future for Mankind"—with subsections for UN involvements, global security partnerships, and public security goods provision. It also indicates that China's military will "stand ready to provide strong strategic support for the realization of the Chinese Dream of national rejuvenation, and to make new and greater contributions to the building of a community with a shared future for mankind."[90] "China's national defense in the new era" has "global significance," it argues, and will "actively participate in the reform of the global security governance system."[91] These texts thus clearly situate the PLA within the more global turn in China's grand strategy.

Third, authoritative texts indicate China needs a global military to secure specific, concrete objectives related to the country's overseas interests. As Chapter 9 discussed, although Chinese leaders had talked about the country's Malacca Dilemma years earlier, China began more prominently emphasizing the protection of its broader overseas interest [海外利益] in Hu's 2009 speech at the 11th Ambassadorial Conference. That shift has grown more pronounced and even more global after 2016, with specific emphasis on the overseas capabilities needed to secure those interests. Authoritative documents have defined China's overseas interests as including Chinese citizens and personnel, institutions, organizations, assets, overseas energy and resources, sea lines of communication (SLOCs), and even the Belt and Road.[92] Protecting these interests is a truly global task. Before COVID-19, for example, China's own statistics indicated that 120 million Chinese citizens traveled abroad annually, millions lived overseas, and 30,000 businesses were registered abroad too.[93] One estimate finds that "about one-sixth of all Chinese laborers (16 percent) and just over one-fifth of China's FDI stock (21 percent) are in countries that the World Bank has ranked in the bottom quartile of its instability index, suffering from the most serious instability problems."[94] Accordingly, a growing number of China's citizens have been killed or kidnapped in countries including Afghanistan, Iraq, Pakistan, Nigeria, Ethiopia, Niger, Congo, Syria, and Laos, among others.[95] Resource flows too are insecure. China surpassed the United States as the world's largest importer in 2017; that year, more than two-thirds of its oil and 40 percent of its natural gas were imported—much which came overseas and through key chokepoints.[96] More than 90 percent of China's imports of commodities like iron, coal, and copper—and roughly the same amount of its foreign trade—are also conducted by sea.[97] Even so, at least as late as 2016, authoritative Chinese speeches make clear that Beijing did not believe it had made sufficient progress in securing these global interests. As then Foreign Minister Wang Yi noted in a speech at CSIS, an important "task of China's diplomacy is to effectively protect China's ever-growing overseas interests," but "to be honest, we don't have the resources and capability to do that."[98] Perhaps because of that inadequacy, President Xi Jinping's 19th Party Congress work report the next year and the associated commentary around it called for investment in a more global Chinese force. Xi's 19th Party Congress work report does not mention overseas interests explicitly, but it advocates "stepping up efforts to build China into a strong maritime country," in addition to stressing movement toward "the world's center stage" and a "world-class military."[99] Moreover, the 2019 White Paper that followed it listed "protecting overseas interests" as one of nine key tasks for the Chinese military, along with "supporting the sustainable development of the country."[100] That paper also restored a dedicated section on China's overseas interests that had been subsumed into other sections in the previous White Paper. Importantly, it also listed what China needed to secure them: "to address deficiencies in overseas operations and support, the PLA builds far seas forces, develops overseas logistical facilities, and enhances capabilities in accomplishing diversified military tasks." This language is notable—the previous White Paper had mentioned a "gradual shift" to "far seas" protection, but this paper was far more definitive and the first to mention overseas facilities as necessities.[101] The 2019 White Paper also specified the kinds of missions that China was undertaking to protect overseas interests: "The PLA conducts vessel protection operations, maintains the security of strategic SLOCs, and carries out overseas evacuation and maritime rights protection operations."[102] Once again, these missions require a global footprint.

China's behavior is consistent with this growing focus on a global posture, even if its evolving approach is dramatically lighter than the US alternative. China has previously laid the groundwork for military priorities years before actually pursuing them openly: indeed, China's carrier research goes back decades but Beijing did not launch the program officially until after the Global Financial Crisis despite having had the capacity to do so sooner. Similarly, China had thought and planned for overseas facilities for years before it opened its first in Djibouti in 2017—the product of negotiations that began three or four years earlier. And as Chapter 9 discussed, China has treated some of its BRI port projects as speculative investments that could one day be upgraded into military access or even basing—an interpretation privately confirmed by some Chinese military officials and even by the former head of the State Oceanic Administration, which helps shape China's maritime strategy. Indeed, since 2016, China's officials have become more open about its efforts to acquire overseas facilities. For example, in 2016 Foreign Minister Wang Yi said of China's overseas ambitions, "we are trying to build some necessary infrastructure and logistical capacities in regions with a concentration of Chinese interests. This is not just reasonable and logical, but also consistent with international practice."[103] In 2019, the political commissar of China's Djibouti base, Li Chunpeng, said, the Chinese Navy's "support for far sea escort missions will gradually shift from a model based on supply ships supplemented by foreign ports to one that is based on overseas bases supplemented by foreign ports and domestic supports."[104] As late as 2014, China was denying the possibility of overseas military deployments without a UN Security Council mandate; now, "the focus is no longer on denying that China is pursuing a [global expeditionary] capability but on defining the practical conditions that would lead to an overseas operation."[105]

China's post-2016 activity appears to support these statements. In 2017, the same year China opened its facility in Djibouti, some accounts indicate that its negotiations for a ninety-nine-year lease on Sri Lanka's Hambantota port also included questions related to military access.[106] In 2016 and 2017, a Chinese firm acquired a fifty-year lease over the island of Feydhoo Finolhu in the Maldives, paying only $4 million for it, and then began land reclamation.[107] Around this same time, there is evidence China established an outpost in Tajikistan too. In 2018, a Chinese firm sought to fund and construct three airports in Greenland, a long-standing focus of its Arctic ambitions that came after an attempt to purchase an abandoned former US military base there.[108] In 2019, China negotiated a lease on a Cambodian naval facility and began construction on ports and airfields that could accommodate Chinese military vessels, and though these projects were nominally civilian, there were indications of discussions of military access between the two governments.[109] That same year, a Chinese conglomerate leased an entire island in the Solomon Islands, though the decision was temporarily reversed.[110] Admittedly, some of the details in these cases are difficult to corroborate, but the balance of evidence—particularly when juxtaposed with Chinese statements and Beijing's willingness to break its pledge never to station forces overseas—suggests a growing interest in global facilities.

The other key source of evidence comes from China's investments, which demonstrate a growing focus on expeditionary capabilities. For example, since 2016, the PLA has expanded its marine corps from 10,000 to more than 30,000, and there are some suggestions these forces are intended for missions outside the Taiwan scenario while, by contrast, army expeditionary forces are reserved for Taiwan. Some reports indicate that the PLA Marine Corps has also diversified its training beyond the South China Sea–like contingencies to include different kinds of terrain, climate, and geography, suggesting a wider mission set.[111] More broadly, over the last few years it has become clear that China might pursue nuclear-powered carriers needed to project power globally. While there are reports the program may have been temporarily postponed due to technical challenges, even so, China is continuing with plans for at least a four-carrier navy.[112] To support extra-regional operations, China has increased investments in "underway replenishment ships, air to air refueling capability, ship tenders, and increasing the number of PLAN ships with satellite communications" also critical for a global reach.[113] In some cases, China's global ambitions are truly broad. Xi Jinping has declared the poles, space, and the deep sea the "new strategic frontiers," and Beijing is increasingly investing military capabilities to secure them. For example, in 2018, Beijing announced a tender for nuclear-powered icebreakers—an expensive investment that comes after additional investments in icebreakers, and a powerful indication that a global PLA will seek to operate in the Arctic and Antarctic too.[114]

China's global military posture may not resemble the American variant. Beijing may lack alliance networks and bases with tens of thousands of soldiers and eschew costly interventions. It is more likely to opt for dual-use facilities, rotational access, and a lighter footprint—at least for now—when its military still faces difficulties in challenging the United States outside of the Indo-Pacific. This approach has drawbacks, but it might allow Beijing to better secure its interests, provide public security goods, and in some cases, position itself as a leader.

These military priorities, when combined with China's political and economic ones, reveal a desire to shape global order in the twenty-first century that may prove as consequential as the way that the United States reshaped the twentieth. That desire faces significant challenges, many of which Chinese sources too often discount but that Washington and its allies and partners should not dismiss. We now turn to the question of how the United States might respond to China's global ambitions and activism.

An Asymmetric Strategy for US-China Competition

"The United States has to be as good as or better than its opponent in the effectiveness with which resources are used, now that [they] are spending comparable resources."
—*Andrew Marshall, Director of the Office of Net Assessment, 1973*

In mid-1973, China's cosmopolitan premier, Zhou Enlai, met with an American delegation. Zhou was one of modern China's founding fathers, the organizer of the Long March, and the mentor to later reformers like Deng Xiaoping. Upon meeting the American delegation, Zhou called the youngest American member to step forward. He then asked a question. "Do you think China will ever become an aggressive or expansionist power?" The meeting followed on the heels of a historic rapprochement between Beijing and Washington, and the young, optimistic American responded, "No." But the Premier shot back immediately: "Don't count on that. It is possible. But if China were to embark on such a path, you must oppose it." Stopping for emphasis, he then exclaimed, "And you must tell those Chinese that Zhou Enlai told you to do so!"[1]

Zhou Enlai may have encouraged others to check the more harmful aspects of Chinese expansion, but he did not explain how to do so. That is the task of this chapter, which seeks to put forward an asymmetric approach for competing with China. That is no easy task. Within Asia, China accounts for more than half of the region's military spending and more than half of its economic activity. And with respect to the United States, China is the first US competitor to surpass 60 percent of US GDP—and when one accounts for purchasing power, it is already 25 percent larger than the American economy.

Owing in part to these trends, China has become bolder over the last decade and broken several of the commitments it kept when it was weaker. Since 2016, as the last two chapters demonstrated, it has grown increasingly assertive in its home region and worldwide. A partial list of these activities paints a striking picture: China has opened concentration camps in Xinjiang; violated its international commitment to Hong Kong's autonomy; killed twenty Indian soldiers in the first use of deadly force on the Sino-Indian border in decades; placed missiles on South China Sea islands despite promising not to do so; sent a list of fourteen grievances to Australia under penalty of further economic punishment; kidnapped European citizens from third countries; and threatened or deployed economic coercion against dozens of states around the world, including the Czech Republic and historically neutral Sweden.

While it is clear today that China has so far not followed in the bloody footsteps of the last century's rising powers, the fact that even Zhou Enlai did not take his country's moderation for granted provides a cautionary note. Rising powers throughout history have tended to abrogate old commitments and sometimes use violence as they blunt the orders of others and build their own. Previous chapters have shown that top Chinese officials now self-consciously advertise not merely regional but truly global Chinese ambitions. Beijing's ultimate objective is to displace the US order globally in order to emerge as the world's dominant state by 2049. While some remain skeptical that China has these ambitions, the same nationalist Party that sat uneasily within the Soviet order is unlikely to willingly defer to an American order in perpetuity. And in any case, as this book has argued, it has already worked to challenge that order for decades.

In light of intensifying US-China competition, this chapter assesses competing visions of long-term US strategy toward China. In doing so, it undertakes three lines of inquiry.

First, it analyzes the nature of US-China competition. As Chapter 1 established, US-China competition is primarily over regional and global order as well as the "forms of control"—coercive capability, consensual inducements, and legitimacy—that sustain one's position within that order.

Second, it explores two broad categories of strategic approaches: (1) strategies that seek to accommodate or reassure China, perhaps through a grand bargain or through "cooperation spirals"; and then (2) strategies that seek to change China whether through "peaceful evolution" or subversion. It engages in a comparative assessment of the relative efficacy of these strategies, finding both strategies face significant obstacles.

Third, this chapter advocates for a strategy focused on *blunting* Chinese power and order and *building* the foundations for US power and order. In many places, and particularly with respect to blunting, this strategy is intended to be asymmetric and draws partly from China's own grand strategy in the 1990s and early 2000s. The United States cannot compete with China symmetrically—that is, dollar-for-dollar, ship-for-ship, or loan-for-loan—in part because of China's sheer relative size. Asymmetric approaches to *blunting* seek to frustrate the effects—and, in some cases, the sources—of Chinese power and influence at lower cost than China expends in generating them. The *building* component of this strategy is more symmetric, but it generally seeks to invest in the foundations for US order, particularly when the coercive, consensual, or legitimacy benefits dramatically exceed the cost of investment and in virtually all cases where doing do so is cheaper than China's own efforts to blunt US order. This strategic approach would seek to compete with China not through internal change or efforts at reassurance but by limiting China's ability to convert its power into regional and global order. In this effort, the United States has certain advantages that flow from the ability of its open system to attract resources and talent, its network of alliances that China cannot yet split or replicate, and its geographic distance from rival great powers. Even so, its advantages are not inexhaustible, and the United States must compete cost-effectively.

In the very same year Zhou Enlai met with his American delegation, Andrew Marshall—who would later lead the Pentagon's Office of Net Assessment for decades and was already on track to become one of America's most influential strategists—was grappling with a problem not dissimilar from that the United States faces today. His report, entitled *Long-Term Competition with the Soviets: A Framework for Strategic Analysis*, circulated around the Pentagon that year. Marshall noted that to compete effectively with rising Soviet spending, "the United States has to be as good as or better than its opponent in the effectiveness with which resources are used now that the Soviets are spending comparable resources."[2] The key was to take actions that imposed a cost on the opponent greater than the cost of the action itself, which in turn required identifying areas of American and adversary advantage and disadvantage. Despite China's own significant challenges and weaknesses, sheer size suggests it is likely that Beijing—unlike the Soviets—could eventually generate and spend *more* resources on competition than the United States, which is presently encountering substantial domestic headwinds. This requires that the questions of symmetric and asymmetric competition—once felt acutely by past generations of strategists—be restored in discussions of how to compete with China across military, political, economic, and other domains.

The Nature of the Competition

As US-China competition intensified over the last few years, a number of policymakers and scholars have frequently returned to the same question, "What is this competition over?" For China, and for most objective observers, the stakes of the competition have long been clear. US-China competition is primarily a competition over who will lead regional and global order and what kind of order they might create from that position of leadership. In many places, but not all, it is a zero-sum game because it is over a positional good—that is, one's role within a hierarchy. In other places, there may be room for mutual adjustment, particularly over the kind of order that results, as well as collaboration on transnational issues. We now turn to the question of order, peacetime competition, and the stakes of the present contest.

Defining Order

As the first chapter discussed, although international relations scholars have generally assumed the world to be anarchic, the reality is that it has often been hierarchic, with some states exercising authority over other states.[3] In a hegemonic order, the preeminent state "mobilizes its leadership" atop the hierarchy to structure relations between states and within them.[4] Hegemonic orders involve what Robert Gilpin called some "form of control" by a dominant state to regulate its subordinates, and that control often involves a mixture of coercive capability (to force compliance), consensual inducements (to incentivize it), and legitimacy (to rightfully command it).[5]

Coercion emerges from the threat of punishment, including military strength or structural control over nodes in the system like currency, trade, and technology. Consensual inducements involve incentivized cooperation through mutually beneficial bargains or enticements, such as security guarantees, public or private goods provision, or even elite capture. Finally, legitimacy is the capability to command simply by virtue of the dominant state's identity or ideology, which constitutes a kind of authority. For example, the Vatican was once able to command states over which it exercised little material power simply due to its theological role. Together, coercive capacity, consensual inducements, and legitimacy secure the deference of states within order.

Defining Peacetime Competition

The peacetime competition between the United States and China is over regional and global order and the forms of control that underpin both. How then will a US-China competition over order unfold, and how might the US-led order change? Most analysts assume that hegemonic orders change through massive great power war. American order, for example, emerged from the aftermath of the Second World War. But for the United States and China, great power war is less likely than in the past given the nuclear revolution, and that has led some to prematurely assume that US order is fundamentally stable.

Nothing in the preceding discussion of order, however, requires that order change only through war; in fact, order can also change through peacetime competition. An order weakens when the preceding forms of control—coercion, consent, and legitimacy—are undermined; conversely, an order strengthens when these same forms of control are bolstered. From this perspective, order transition can occur even absent war. These transitions can occur gradually through incremental evolution or suddenly, as the Soviet Union's collapse demonstrates, but they need not require great power war or even a great power competitor.[6] Prominent Chinese scholars speculating on order transition understand this as fact, with Yuan Peng—the head of the Ministry of State Security's think tank—arguing that the pandemic may play the same role in order transition as a great power war.

What then does peacetime competition over order look like? As the preceding chapters have noted, and as Chapter 1 discussed in greater detail, if a hegemon's position in the order emerges from "forms of control" like coercion, consent, and legitimacy, then competition over order revolves around efforts to strengthen and weaken these forms of control. Accordingly, this book has focused on two broad strategies generally pursued in sequence that rising states like China can use to peacefully displace hegemonic powers like the United States short of war.

The first of these is to *blunt* the hegemon's exercise of its forms of control, particularly those that are extended over the rising state; after all, no rising state can displace the hegemon if it remains largely at the hegemon's mercy. The second is to *build* leverage or forms of control over others, as well as the foundations for consensual bargains and legitimacy; indeed, no rising state can become a hegemon if it cannot constrain the autonomy of others or entice them with consensual bargains and legitimacy to ensure they follow the rising state's preferences. Blunting generally precedes building, and both are generally pursued at the regional level before the global level. China, as this book has demonstrated, has used these two strategies as a means of ascent—challenging US order at the regional and global level while laying the foundation for its own.

This chapter builds on that foundation to argue that established powers can use these strategies too. The United States, for example, can also blunt a Chinese order while building or rebuilding its own.

Defining the Stakes

What are the stakes of a competition over order? The United States often inadequately examines the foundations of its own order. Instead of studying the foundations of hegemony, many Americans take features of the international system as granted rather than as products of American power. For example, the presumption that states should generally be democratic, and that they should not engage in genocide, nuclear proliferation, territorial conquest, biological weapons usage, or nakedly illiberal behavior (versus illiberal behavior at least wrapped notionally in a cloak of legitimacy) is a product of the costs generated for engaging in that behavior by US order, even if Washington's own adherence to or defense of these norms is imperfect. The deference the United States receives from its allies and partners in many cases is also a product of order, as is the relatively uncontroversial acceptance of American overseas bases or of the dollar as reserve currency. This is a fact illiberal states like China, which have written for decades about the liberal bias of the international system and the foundational aspects of American hegemony, cannot afford to forget. China does not simply bemoan the international system's presumptions of American structural advantages but interrogates them, asks why they are the way they are, and seeks to reshape the system more to its liking by constructing its own order.

This book has speculated on what Chinese order might look like. At the regional level, where China already accounts for more than half of Asian GDP and half of all Asian military spending, a sphere of influence may be likely absent an external balancer. A fully realized Chinese order might eventually involve the withdrawal of US forces from Japan and Korea, the end of American alliances, pushing the US Navy from the Western Pacific, deference from China's regional neighbors, unification with Taiwan, and the resolution of territorial disputes in the East and South China Seas. Chinese order would likely be more coercive than the present order, consensual in ways that primarily benefit connected elites even at the expense of voting publics, and considered legitimate mostly to those few who directly benefit. China would deploy this order in ways that damage liberal values, with authoritarian winds blowing stronger across the region. Order abroad is often a reflection of order at home, and China's order-building would be distinctly illiberal relative to US order-building.

At the global level, as the last two chapters demonstrated, Chinese order would involve seizing the opportunities of the "great changes unseen in a century" and displacing the United States as the world's leading state. This would require successfully managing the principal risk flowing from the "great changes"— Washington's unwillingness to gracefully accept decline—by weakening the forms of control supporting American global order while strengthening those forms of control supporting a Chinese alternative. Politically, Beijing would project leadership over global governance and international institutions, advance autocratic norms at the expense of liberal ones, and split American alliances in Europe and Asia. Economically, it would weaken the financial advantages that underwrite US hegemony and seize the commanding heights of the "fourth industrial revolution" from artificial intelligence to quantum computing, with the United States declining "into a deindustrialized, English-speaking version of a Latin American republic, specializing in commodities, real estate, tourism, and perhaps transnational tax evasion."[7] Militarily, the PLA would field a world-class force with bases around the world that could defend China's interests in most regions and even in new domains like space, the poles, and the deep sea. Taken together, China would erect a "zone of super-ordinate influence" in its home region and "partial hegemony" across the developing countries tied to its Belt and Road Initiative (BRI) that might eventually expand to the developed world too—a vision some Chinese popular writers describe using Mao's revolutionary guidance to "surround the cities from the countryside" [农村包围城市].[8]

Neither of these orders is to America's interests, nor are they beneficial to its allies and partners. We now turn to an analysis of two broad strategies for addressing China's rise—accommodating China and changing China—and consider their shortcomings.

Accommodating China

A number of analysts have put forward the idea that accommodation might mellow Chinese power and reduce tension. Accommodationist perspectives can be grouped into a few broad categories: (1) full unilateral territorial accommodation; (2) a "maximalist" grand bargain; (3) a much more careful, "minimalist" grand bargain that phases in mutual accommodation; and (4) tactical or operational reassurance at the political and military level.

The first of these options, unilateral accommodation, attempts to mellow Chinese power by offering China a sphere of influence for nothing in return. Even most proponents of accommodation believe unilateral concessions could be counterproductive: "China appears too likely to misinterpret such a large change in U.S. policy which could fuel Chinese overconfidence and intensify challenges to U.S. interests," writes one grand bargain advocate.[9]

Unlike the previous option, the second and third options—maximalist and minimalist grand bargains, respectively—are not unilateral but true "bargains" in which US concessions are tied to some concessions from China. The "maximalist" advocates of grand bargains encourage ending US alliances, pulling the US military out of the Western Pacific, and granting China a sphere of influence in exchange for concessions from Beijing on a variety of issues—though Washington might have to allow China to settle territorial disputes on its terms and annex Taiwan to get them. But once again, even most proponents of restraint, such as Barry Posen, do not support such an approach because it requires sweeping and irreversible US concessions for speculative promises and is ultimately unenforceable.[10] Similarly, a Quincy Institute report that calls for a less confrontational line with Beijing nonetheless opposes "completely withdrawing U.S. forces from East Asia and allowing China to establish an exclusive sphere of influence in East Asia."[11]

The third and fourth options—a minimalist grand bargain and some kind of strategic reassurance—are the strongest and most defensible of the options, and they are worthy of extended consideration.

A "Minimalist" Phased Grand Bargain

A "minimalist" and phased grand bargain would ostensibly trade away less to Beijing than unilateral concessions or a "maximalist grand bargain" by attempting to preserve US alliances and presence in Asia and offer Beijing what it wants most—Taiwan. Prominent proponents like Charles Glaser argue that the United States should "negotiate a grand bargain that ends its commitment to defend Taiwan against Chinese aggression."[12] Others with this perspective include the Naval War College's Lyle Goldstein, who claims "one significant reason (among many) that U.S.-China relations have reached a new nadir, not seen since perhaps the 1950s, is due to emergent tensions around Taiwan" and he urges a "sound policy of military disengagement from the Taiwan issue" involving phased concessions.[13] Peter Beinart similarly argues that "if China renounces the use of force, the United States should support its reunification with Taiwan along the principle of 'one country, two systems' " because the US commitment to Taiwan is "insolvent."[14] Former ambassador Chas Freeman makes a similar argument, and like Beinart, suggests Beijing would be generally respectful of Taiwan's autonomy.[15] Bruce Gilley suggests such respect is less critical and encourages the United States to accede to the Finlandization of Taiwan.[16]

A US-China grand bargain over Taiwan would supposedly reduce US rivalry through the following logic: "satisfy" China if it has limited aims, remove the most likely path to conflict, and—given how grand and costly a concession on Taiwan might be—"signal that U.S. goals in the region are limited" and thereby change Beijing's beliefs about US intentions.[17] Another proponent notes that a grand bargain could even change China's internal politics because it would "undermine hardline militarists who use the Taiwan issue to stoke nationalist flames to sideline pro-Western technocrats."[18] In short, a bargain would supposedly eliminate significant US-China security competition through a mixture of concession and changed beliefs. The bargain would also provide a series of additional benefits. It would avoid a "multi-trillion-dollar arms race," freeing up resources for domestic renewal or possibly other domains of competition with China.[19] And it would seemingly elicit a range of valuable concessions.

Proponents of such a bargain list several possible concessions that could be part of a bargain: the forgiveness of US debt; a promise not to militarize Taiwan and to respect its political freedoms; the peaceful resolution of the South and East China Seas disputes; acceptance of the US military role in Asia; the end of significant support for Iran, North Korea, and Pakistan; and a less contentious relationship globally.

A "minimalist" grand bargain over Taiwan is likely to fail. In particular, while this limited approach is intended to preserve the US position in Asia, it could eventually collapse into the first and second enumerated options—that is, produce an effective US exit from Asia. While beliefs about the importance of US credibility may at times be exaggerated, a decision by Washington to voluntarily terminate its commitment to Taiwan will startle US allies in the region like Japan, South Korea, and Australia and may even induce bandwagoning behavior if they believe balancing is futile, undermining the US regional position. More broadly, given that China would likely annex Taiwan following such a bargain and gain the geostrategic advantages that the island brings, US commitments in the East China Sea and in the South China Sea would be rendered far less credible and quite possibly entirely indefensible, frustrating even a US "deterrence by denial" strategy that seeks not overmatch or primacy but only to complicate Chinese adventurism. The United States would also have no guarantee that China would adhere to most commitments that Washington would request, including tolerance of a US regional military role, peaceful resolution of disputes, and commitments not to militarize Taiwan or to guarantee its political freedoms. A grand bargain would not function like a contract in a court of law, and there would be no judge to enforce China's commitments.

To maximize the odds that China honors its commitment in the bargain, some might suggest a phased approach—that is, "a path that divides the grand bargain into smaller, more attainable increments," allowing the United States the opportunity to reverse course on a grand bargain if it is clear Beijing will not comply with its terms.[20] For example, Lyle Goldstein suggests that the United States reduce forces in Guam, close the AIT military office, and halt arms sales in exchange for China's decision to pull missiles back from East China, allow Taiwan more international presence, and restrict the PLA's development of amphibious capabilities. Each of these steps taken one at a time would ultimately lead to China's absorption (perhaps within a confederation) of Taiwan.[21] While a phased approach to Taiwan may at first glance seem workable, it would be extremely unstable in practice. Whatever sequence of concessions the two sides put forward, the negotiations over them would occur with the expectation that an eventual abrogation of the US commitment to Taiwan is possible for the right series of concessions and assurances. Simply by signaling this, the United States would be making an enormous concession at the outset of negotiations and inviting Beijing to test its commitment. It simply would not be credible for the United States to declare that it would be willing to withdraw from its costly commitment to Taiwan for some negotiated "price," but at the same time, still remain willing to fight an even costlier war if that "price" were not sufficiently to its liking. A phased approach would therefore offer no great protection against China breaking the agreement and would likely even increase instability.

Strategic Reassurance and "Cooperation Spirals"

Some observers, most notably Mike O'Hanlon, Jim Steinberg, and Lyle Goldstein, have laid out detailed step-by-step efforts for mutual reassurance, generally with respect to regional security issues. As O'Hanlon and Steinberg argue, the purpose of strategic reassurance is to "give credibility to each side's profession of good intentions by reducing as much as possible the ambiguity and uncertainty associated with unilateral security policies."[22] In this view, the United States and China should exercise voluntary restraint—which involves forgoing some technologies, postures, or doctrines that might threaten the other side—and this restraint would then be reciprocated by each side and reinforced through other interactions. These efforts are sustained by transparency and information-sharing, which reduces the risk of misunderstanding and resilience. Steps on each side could also be implemented successively to allow for adjustment if one side cheats.

Many of the efforts at reassurance explored by the O'Hanlon, Steinberg, Goldstein, and others are worth considering and are quite clever, and the overall idea of pursuing "cooperation spirals" is sound and could conceivably have worked at the highpoint of American hegemony in the early 2000s. In many cases, however, these efforts face obstacles. First, efforts that are explicitly or implicitly part of negotiations to reduce US defense commitments to allies and partners may be destabilizing. As discussed previously, reassurance in those cases actually undermines US resolve prematurely by demonstrating that Washington is willing to limit or end its defense commitments for a hypothetical Chinese concession, which could invite a test before the negotiation sequence is completed or if the negotiations stall.

Second, the prospects for what Lyle Goldstein calls "cooperation spirals" to emerge—where one set of reassurances begets another and so on—should not be discounted, but in many cases the jump within them from low-level concessions (e.g., a reduction in the number of marines in Okinawa) to a higher-level of mutual concessions seems extremely challenging. As all authors agree, reassurance is hardest precisely where it is needed most. It is unlikely, as some propose, that the United States could safely "restrain modernization and deployment" of long-range precision strike systems and that China might reciprocally "limit development and deployment of anti-ship ballistic missiles."[23] Moreover, successful efforts at cooperation spirals in one domain might be undermined by action or disagreement in another. Some authors suggest that certain concessions could produce long-term restraint on Chinese force structure (e.g., reducing China's interest in building a blue-water navy), but many of the examples of hypothetical restraint are now moot, and China's interests in pursuing military modernization are grounded in more than one regional contingency, making its resolution inadequate on the most vital questions.

Third, accommodation from a position of strength is different from accommodation from a position of weakness. In many cases, the writers assume that the United States will reassure China by accommodating it from a position of strength. As Goldstein writes, "the United States is in a very strong, almost unassailable strategic position. It has the strength to make judicious and reasonable compromises for the sake of peace."[24] Even when this was written, this assessment seemed strained; now, years later, it no longer holds. As Chapter 11 demonstrated, China perceives the United States as in irreversible decline. It would therefore likely see US efforts at reassurance as acquiescence to China's new status, which could make it less likely to reciprocate or more likely to engage in provocations. In contrast, had the US made efforts toward some cooperation spirals in the early 2000s when China perceived the American position as truly unassailable, the two sides may have had more success in achieving sustainable outcomes. If trend lines continue to move against the United States, these kinds of efforts are unlikely to be successful.

Fourth, China has repeatedly reneged on its various tactical concessions or returned accommodation by others with eventual hostility or more expansive claims. This suggests that Beijing focuses more on interests and power than the question of whether its commitments remain credible—complicating efforts at "cooperation spirals" or grand bargains. When India recognized the CCP's control over China and accepted its claims of sovereignty over Tibet—a complicated concession for the Indian government to make at the time—the gesture did not preclude China's decision to initiate a conflict over the Sino-Indian border a few years later, nor did it stop Beijing from believing that New Delhi was too closely aligned to Washington and too expansionist. Other efforts at reassurance, including US efforts after the Global Financial Crisis to delay arms sales to Taiwan, a somewhat concessionary joint statement on China's "core interests," and a willingness to temporarily put aside human rights disputes, did not preclude a more assertive turn in Chinese foreign policy—instead, it may have encouraged it. Chinese suggestions that it would not build an aircraft carrier later proved unfounded; its promise not to build overseas bases were likewise belied by its acquisition of a facility in Djibouti (and plans for facilities elsewhere); its promises not to militarize the South China Sea were contradicted just months after they were made; and its agreement on cyber issues in 2015 later collapsed.

Moreover, on territorial matters, China's claims have sometimes expanded. With India, China's previous claim to Tawang eventually expanded in the mid-1980s to include all of Arunachal Pradesh.[25] With Japan, some nationalists—with implicit support from the government—have suggested China should control not only the Senkaku/Diaoyu islands but also the Japanese island of Okinawa and the entire Ryukyu island chain.[26] With Russia, major state media figures and even Chinese diplomats attacked the Russian government in 2020 for posting a video marking the founding of Vladivostok, noting it was originally a Chinese city, though official sources fell short of a call for retaking it.[27] On Hong Kong, the record is particularly poor, with Beijing prematurely terminating its promise to maintain the city's autonomy. Some scholars like Peter Beinart have recently argued that the United States should request that Beijing "commit publicly not to station troops or Communist Party officials in Taiwan, and to let Taiwan manage its domestic political affairs," arguing that "the best precedent" for why China would honor such a commitment was its treatment of Hong Kong; Chas Freeman in 2011 similarly pointed to Hong Kong as a sign that China might offer Taiwan autonomy.[28] These hopeful predictions have been largely proven false by the end of "one country, two systems" in 2020. Together, Beijing's behavior bodes ill for both a grand bargain and for efforts to achieve sustainable cooperative spirals.

The Challenge of Reassurance

Calls for grand bargains and cooperation spirals generally rest on the notion that China could be reassured but tend to discount the ways that the CCP's Leninist worldview makes such reassurance exceedingly difficult. That difficulty increased dramatically after the traumatic Tiananmen Square Massacre and the collapse of the Soviet Union, which left the Party fearing for its own continued existence. After this period, China's elites have repeatedly seen the West as seeking to undermine the Party's hold on power. As China integrated into the global economy, that process brought with it some liberal ideas, empowered certain social classes, and generally amplified the Party's fears that it could lose its hold on power.

As Chapter 2 and 3 demonstrated, before the Tiananmen Square Massacre, China saw the United States as a quasi-ally. After it, Deng Xiaoping made clear that China believed that the United States sought the Party's overthrow. Deng declared that there was now "no doubt that the imperialists want socialist countries to change their nature. The problem now is not whether the banner of the Soviet Union will fall—there is bound to be unrest there—but whether the banner of China will fall."[29] "The United States has coined an expression: waging a world war without gunsmoke," he argued, "We should be on guard against this. Capitalists want to defeat socialists in the long run. In the past they used weapons, atomic bombs and hydrogen bombs, but they were opposed by the peoples of the world. So now they are trying peaceful evolution."[30]

His successors held the same views. Beginning in the early 1990s, Jiang's administration put forward the concept of the "five poisons" that threatened Party rule, with pro-democracy activism listed among them, and promoted efforts to prevent "spiritual pollution" from liberal values by strengthening what came to known as "patriotic education." He also used high-level foreign policy addresses—the Ambassadorial Conferences held once every five or six years and often used to announce adjustments in Chinese grand strategy—to reiterate the US ideological threat. "The U.S. policy on China has always been two-sided. The peaceful evolution of our country is a long-term strategic goal for some in the United States," Jiang argued, further adding that the United States was China's chief "adversary."[31] His successor, Hu Jintao, also called the United States China's chief adversary.[32] Many members of his Standing Committee went further in leaked documents, convinced that the United States sought to contain China because it feared its long-term power.[33]

Under Xi Jinping, Beijing has continued to promote these ideological lines. Xi has repeatedly stressed the importance of ideological rectitude and warned of liberalization. The famous leaked "Document Nine" directive—which also reflects much open Party literature on the West—is explicit about the threat of "peaceful evolution" and ideological subversion. As the dean of the School of Marxism at Tianjin University, Yan Xiaofeng, argues: "Ideology is about national political security. The collapse of a regime often starts in the field of ideology. When the ideological defense line is broken, other defense lines are difficult to defend."[34] This is why, in October 2013, the PLA released a popular documentary, *Silent Contest*, intended for military indoctrination that argued that Washington sought to use liberal values to undermine the CCP and China's national rejuvenation. This sentiment not only finds expression in the hawkish corners of Chinese officialdom, it even finds expression among those retired diplomats who often serve as the reassuring face of Chinese diplomacy in the United States. An unlikely admission by Fu Ying, a former Chinese diplomat who now serves in this role, is that, "From the Chinese perspective, the U.S. has never given up its intent to overthrow the socialist system led by the Communist Party of China."[35]

Perhaps the strongest evidence that credibly reassuring China is exceedingly difficult is the persistence of China's existential threat perception even as the United States pursued a largely benign and welcoming policy toward China under the policy of engagement. For decades, successive US presidents publicly welcomed a stronger China. At the economic and technological levels, they kept US universities open to Chinese students, permitted technology transfer to China, allowed US capital to flow to China, supported US industry's relocation to China, and worked to facilitate China's entrance into the WTO—granting China permanent normal trading relations and voluntarily reducing US economic leverage over the country. At the political level, they welcomed China into regional and global institutions led by the United States. At the military level, they sought risk reduction and crisis management mechanisms with China's military, implicitly opposed Taiwan's independence, and remained formally neutral on the sovereignty claims of those states involved in territorial disputes with China. Throughout this time, the most accommodating in American history, top Chinese officials nonetheless continued to write in Party texts that they believed the United States was pursuing a strategy of "peaceful evolution" and containment. In fact, Chinese leader Jiang Zemin gave a major but private speech after China's WTO accession to all of China's provincial Party secretaries and government ministers on how the United States sought to use China's WTO accession to undermine the CCP.[36] Hu Jintao also echoed this argument in high-level speeches.[37] What many in the United States saw as a kind of concession to China was openly viewed by Party elites as a tactic intended to "peacefully evolve" its very system of government. If reassurance was challenging then, it is likely even harder now.

Changing China

A series of policy prescriptions fall into the broad category of seeking to change China, that is, removing or softening the internal structures that supposedly make China a competitor. Efforts that sought to "peacefully evolve" China in a more liberal direction or support supposedly liberal factions have not been successful and are now especially unlikely to succeed; conversely, efforts to subvert or overthrow the Party discount its strength and the challenges of engineering China's politics. Both efforts, each backed by widely opposed parts of the policy debate, ultimately flow from a similar set of strained and idealistic assumptions about Washington's ability to influence the politics of a powerful, sovereign country.

Peaceful Evolution

Efforts to shape China's internal politics in positive directions are unlikely to succeed. China already believes that the United States seeks its peaceful evolution, which means that strategies that seek to liberalize parts of China's society through engagement—while at one time theoretically promising—have always run into eventual Party repression. In the 1990s and 2000s, China did in fact have a marginally more open Internet, more freedom for academics, some tolerance for human rights lawyers, and a willingness to consider some marginal distance between the Party and state. But the moment the Party ascertained that these developments were a threat to its power, it reversed course—a process that began in the mid-2000s and has intensified with every passing year since.

Similarly, arguments that the United States should support "pro-reform" Party members were untenable in the past, when even powerful ostensible reformers remained committed to the Party and suspicious of the United States. Western observers often have a poor record of identifying potential allies. Western journalists like Nicholas Kristof argued: "The new paramount leader, Xi Jinping, will spearhead a resurgence of economic reform, and probably some political easing as well. Mao's body will be hauled out of Tiananmen Square on his watch, and Liu Xiaobo, the Nobel Peace Prize–winning writer, will be released from prison."[38] Every one of these predictions proved incorrect. Writing in 2014, Lyle Goldstein claimed that Xi was not particularly illiberal or even nationalist: "Rather, Xi is an engineer whose family suffered terribly during the mass hysteria and radicalism of the Cultural Revolution. He has few connections with the military, and he lived briefly in Iowa. Betraying his rather liberal and even pro-Western worldview, he has sent his only child to be educated at Harvard."[39] This too has been proven incorrect. Supposed liberal reformers like Zhu Rongji, Li Ruihuan, and Wang Qishan, among others, have likewise been unable or unwilling to advocate the reformist political cause. In the present, it is highly unlikely reformers exist at the highest levels or would be able to seriously shape Xi Jinping's choices.

The argument that the United States should adopt conciliatory policies to avoid amplifying hardliners or nationalists is equally flawed. While US-China dynamics may affect Chinese nationalism, the far greater variable explaining the strength of nationalist ideology is domestic. Given the Party's control of the information system, and its decades-long pursuit of "patriotic education," there is no reason to believe that the United States can shape China's domestic information environment or that US policies will have any great impact on the public as a whole.

Finally, efforts to empower certain groups in China believed to play a role in liberalizing processes—lawyers, university professors, NGOs, and the private sector—should continue, but are unlikely to succeed given the more than decade-long crackdown on these efforts and China's increasingly repressive climate.

Subversion and Overthrow

Efforts to subvert China's government are particularly dangerous and unlikely to succeed. First, efforts to overthrow the CCP would produce all-out confrontation that could transform the competition from one that is over order to one that is fundamentally existential. It is likely that this effort would dramatically increase the risk of war, eliminate almost any prospect for cooperation on shared threats like climate change, and likely invite significant reciprocal Chinese interference in American electoral politics. China has considered but largely refrained from significant election interference in the United States—forgoing the kind of campaign it has deployed in Taiwan's elections—and has instead confined its efforts to more conventional information influence campaigns that support or punish institutions and individuals for their positions on China and seek to gain influence in US traditional and new media.

Second, efforts to overthrow the CCP would likely fail, given the Party's resilience, or produce results that Washington could not shape. China is not ripe for a bottom-up color revolution, and the prospects for one have declined as the government's digital authoritarianism has reduced the cost for the state to monitor or punish dissidents. Political polling is extremely complicated in China, but there is some social science evidence showing a lack of widespread discontent with the Party's leadership.[40] Moreover, the government's effort to paint itself as a superior model to the West within China has likely succeeded, particularly post-COVID-19. China is likely not as sclerotic and incompetent as the Soviet Union, and the United States is not as attractive within China as it was in the 1980s and 1990s.

Elites are likely less satisfied with Xi than the public, but China is not ripe for an elite revolt either. As the former Central Party School professor and now dissident Cai Xia has made clear, Xi is closely monitoring the country's high-level cadres to prevent collective action against him. As she argued, "The advanced surveillance technology is not only utilized in monitoring Xinjiang and Tibet, but it is also applied to monitor CCP members as well as mid- and high-level officials," and "normal socialization" among Party cadres is often prohibited.[41] It is unlikely that the United States can dramatically stimulate collective action against the Party at the elite level given the Party's surveillance apparatus and control over information flows. None of this is to say that China's system is perfectly stable at the elite level, and it is likely that the peaceful transition of power between Xi Jinping and some future leader could be fraught with tension, as autocratic transitions often are. Even so, it is difficult to imagine how the United States can exacerbate tensions within the elite of a political system that is opaque and tightly surveilled and that Washington cannot easily understand.

Moreover, as strategists Hal Brands and Zack Cooper note, US sanctions have failed to topple weaker and less entrenched regimes. And even in the event of success, "the collapse of Communist Party rule could lead to the rise of a radical nationalist military clique just as easily as it could the emergence of a stable democracy."[42]

An Asymmetric Strategy

If efforts to accommodate China or change China are unlikely to succeed, then the most logical remaining alternative is a strategy of competition. This is a broad category, and there are several different works that propose a more competitive strategy generally consistent with the approach offered here.[43] Most of these works share a common logic, and this section seeks to add to it by stressing two features. First, it demonstrates that a truly competitive strategy with China cannot be entirely symmetric. US efforts should often be asymmetric and seek to blunt Chinese order-building at a cost lower than the one China incurs to advance it. Second, this section argues that any competitive strategy should begin with the understanding that US-China competition is predominantly over regional and global order as well as the "forms of control" that underpin it. Accordingly, a competitive strategy will involve not only efforts to blunt Chinese order, but also efforts to rebuild the foundations of US order. Some of these efforts will be symmetric, but others will be lower cost than China's blunting efforts; if undertaken in concert with others, the burden of shoring up order become more diffuse.

Why Strategy Must Be Asymmetric

The United States will be unable to compete with China symmetrically—that is, dollar-for-dollar, ship-for-ship, or loan-for-loan—in part because of China's sheer relative size. For more than a century, no US adversary or coalition of adversaries reached 60 percent of US GDP. Neither Wilhelmine Germany during the First World War, the combined might of Imperial Japan and Nazi Germany during the Second World War, nor the Soviet Union at the height of its economic power ever crossed this threshold.[44] And yet, this is a milestone that China itself quietly reached as early as 2014. China is also on track to surpass the United States in economic size. When one adjusts for the relative price of goods (i.e., purchasing power parity), China's economy is already 25 percent larger than the US economy.[45] In nominal terms, it is expected to catch up to the United States in 2028 given the impact of the coronavirus, which led the US

economy to shrink 8 percent in one year while China's grew 1–2 percent.[46] It is
clear, then, that China is the most powerful competitor that the United States
has faced in the last century, and that it will be able to summon more resources
in the competition than previous US rivals.

Both the United States and China have various advantages in mobilizing
resources for strategic competition. China's system affords it significant influence over the economy through state-owned enterprises and the penetration
of major private companies that in reality often act as national champions. In
contrast, the United States has far less control over its economic base and resources, and its public debt levels are already high—now exceeding the size of
the entire US economy for the first time since World War II due to the 2020
pandemic. While interest payments remain relatively low because of the dollar's
status and the desire for safe assets, they could eventually rise. And when those
payments are combined with mandatory non-discretionary spending, a large
and growing share of GDP that is difficult to adjust through public policy, the
fiscal space for strategic competition shrinks further. It is true that China faces
disadvantages—a demographic slowdown, the middle-income trap, high levels
of public debt, a problematic financial system—and that the openness of the US
system buttresses the dollar's dominance and enables Washington to raise significant resources in debt markets. But overall, while the United States remains
a large, young, and growing country, it is still a smaller one than China, and one
that faces democratic limits on resource mobilization for long-term competition as well as significant fiscal headwinds. No US strategy that ignores these
realities will be sustainable, and therefore the starting point for any strategy must
be asymmetric.

What might be the strengths the United States could leverage? American
democracy—and the order it has produced—provide competitive strengths relative to its authoritarian competitor. Conventional wisdom sees authoritarian
states as unconstrained by institutional checks or public opinion and therefore able to act covertly, decisively, and ruthlessly, often mobilizing enormous
resources and charting long-term strategies. But that provides risks as well.
Autocracies can move rapidly in the right direction or equally rapidly in a disastrous one, all without the mediating effect of public debate and consent.

In contrast, American openness and rule of law produce more constant
advantages. They offer allies and even adversaries voice opportunities within the
order, broadcast American intentions and ambitions, and are often combined
with global goods provision—thereby making US hegemony less threatening
and more acceptable. Critically, these advantages also ensure that the country
can attract the allies, immigrants, and capital that underpin liberal order, technological innovation, military power, and dollar dominance. These are the

foundations of American order, and they provide a unique advantage relative to China. Building and rebuilding them must remain a priority.

Ends, Ways, and Means

What should be the *ends* of US strategy? Washington must recognize that it is fundamentally in a competition over regional and global order, as well as the various "forms of control" that sustain it. At the regional level, the United States has historically sought to prevent the emergence of a hegemon in maritime and continental Eurasia.[47] This is one goal that must once again drive US China policy because China's grand strategy and its aspirations for global leadership ultimately run through Asia—making the Indo-Pacific the most efficient region within which to concentrate US efforts. Second, at the global level, Washington should similarly seek to undermine Beijing's efforts to displace the United States from order globally while reinforcing the foundational elements of American order—particularly its alliances, financial power, military power, technology leadership, role in global institutions, and influence over information flows, among others. All these objectives also require maintaining some space for transnational cooperation.

What are the *ways* in which the United States should achieve these ends, especially given that Washington faces significant domestic political and economic headwinds and a rival whose own economy by some measures has already exceeded the American one in size? If we accept that the United States and China are competing over order, then strategies for competition should begin with an analysis of how order functions. As discussed previously, order consists of "forms of control" used by a dominant state to regulate subordinate states within a hierarchy, and those forms involve a mixture of coercion (to force compliance), consent (to incentivize it), and legitimacy (to rightfully command it)—with liberal orders generally relying more on consent and legitimacy and illiberal ones often relying more on coercion. Accordingly, competition over order is about *blunting* an opponent's "forms of control" and *building* one's own forms of control. In competition with China, these strategies—blunting and building—should not be implemented in a symmetric way that puts forward an American initiative to match up against each Chinese economic, military, or political initiative. Instead, the objective would be to compete judiciously, prioritizing certain countries, regions, and sub-structures within the international system. Ironically, China's own experience as a weaker state in the 1990s shows that an asymmetric approach can be quite effective in blunting a rival's hegemonic ambitions—and this approach will be even more effective when wielded by a still quite powerful United States. Building order is extremely difficult, and frustrating the effort to build order is far less challenging. The logic of such an approach is relatively straight-forward: to undermine China's hegemonic ambitions at a lower cost than what China incurs in trying to advance them. Similarly, with respect to building, the goal is to rebuild US order—including its forms of control over China—in most cases and particularly when these efforts are lower-cost than China's blunting efforts.

It is worth pausing to note that forms of control have upstream and down-stream components. For example, when the United States wields financial state-craft, that exercise has an "upstream" source (American dollar dominance) from which flows the "downstream" effect (the punished state faces financial stress). China could seek to blunt American financial power by focusing on that "up-stream" source by working to make the dollar less dominant or by targeting the "downstream" effect by providing financial support to the sanctioned state. When blunting asymmetrically, it can sometimes be cheaper to target forms of control downstream; when building or safeguarding one's own forms of control, it may be more valuable to prioritize a competitor's challenge to the upstream sources of that leverage rather than the varouis challenges to the downstream effects of that leverage.

This leads to a final set of questions: what are the *means* by which an asym-metric blunting and building strategy might be implemented? In broad terms, the "forms of control" upon which order rests are multifaceted—including var-ious military, political, and economic components. A grand strategy to blunt or build order should be integrated and coordinated across these multiple means of statecraft, and it should also address narrower domains within them, including competition in technology, finance, supply chains, information, ideology, and other domains.

The succeeding two sections lay out a few notional prescriptions that might compromise such a strategy. But before delving deeply into competition, it is also worth considering the question of cooperation. China is the necessary partner for the United States on virtually every transnational challenge from nonproliferation to climate change. As Chapter 3 demonstrated, Chinese leaders have sometimes recognized that Washington's desire to cooperate on these issues provides leverage for Beijing, and they have therefore linked prog-ress on shared global interests to concessions in the US-China bilateral rela-tionship. In the period ahead, the United States will need to delink the two and hold fast to the rule that there will be two tracks in US-China ties: one focused on cooperation and one on competition. Such a principle may seem far-fetched, but it is worth noting that the United States and Soviet Union man-aged to collaborate in a far more existential competition than this one on a host of issues ranging from ozone to polio vaccination to space. Washington and

Beijing can do so too, but that will require American leaders to shed their perception that they are eager suitors and recognize that Beijing too has much to gain from working together.

We now turn to the competitive track in the bilateral relationship, focusing on blunting and building strategies.

Blunting Chinese Order

A strategy of blunting Chinese order focuses on the main "forms of control" China is constructing at the regional and global level and then seeks to address them asymmetrically. In general, US strategy should be to undermine China's order-building at the regional level in part by blunting the exercise of Chinese power as well as by empowering states that might otherwise fall within Chinese order so that they retain some agency from Beijing. At the global level, a similar strategy will also be useful, but US efforts will also have to extend to competition over the substructure of the global system, including domains like finance, technology, information, and multilateral institutions. In general, the United States is advantaged in its blunting strategy by the fact that order is generally easier to undermine than it is to create and sustain.

China's order-building rests on military, economic, and political foundations. With respect to the military foundations, China has for the last decade increasingly pursued a navy capable of amphibious operations, sea control, and distant blue-water missions. This kind of navy—which is increasingly going global as China pursues myriad overseas facilities—helps China build order by providing military leverage over other states as well as the ability to seize or hold distant islands and waters, safeguard sea lines of communication, offer public security goods, and intervene in the affairs of others. At the economic level, China has sought to build order through infrastructure spending (with the BRI a prime example), as well as coercive economic statecraft. It is also pursuing leadership over global technology's so-called fourth industrial revolution, hoping to achieve what Xi Jinping has repeatedly stressed as leapfrog development over Western competitors. Finally, at the political level, China has sought to erect institutions that serve its interests and shape global information flows in ways that reinforce its narratives—building, it hopes, foundations that either legitimize Chinese power or at the least reduce the reputational harm of some of China's illiberal practices.

The succeeding recommendations offer thoughts on how best to undermine China's order-building at relatively low cost—and often take a page directly from China's own asymmetric strategic playbook during the 1990s and 2000s.

Military Blunting

- *Invest in Asymmetric Denial Weapons*: After the Gulf War, China began to pursue cheaper, asymmetric weapons to challenge expensive US power projection platforms. China's efforts, sometimes referred to as "anti-access/area-denial," involve using "a series of interrelated missile, sensor, guidance, and other technologies designed to deny freedom of movement" to the United States in East Asia.[48] The United States is increasingly open to drawing from China's approach and pursuing these same kinds of denial capabilities, thereby complicating China freedom of movement—an approach some refer to as pursuing "deterrence by denial" or achieving a kind of "No Man's Sea" where no actor can successfully control waters or islands or launch amphibious operations in the First Island Chain.[49] The United States has the technical proficiency to develop these capabilities, and there is already consensus on the rough outlines of this approach: long-range precision strike, unmanned carrier-based strike aircraft, unmanned underwater vehicles, submarines with large missile payloads, high-speed strike weapons, and mine warfare, among others, would be key priorities. These capabilities would be less vulnerable to China's own anti-access/area denial suite and would also complicate China's amphibious operations across the Taiwan Strait or East and South China Seas at lower cost than the pricey assets upon which China would rely to mount them.

- *Help Allies and Partners Develop Anti-Access/Area-Denial Capabilities*: The United States should also develop ally and partner anti-access/area-denial weapons to deter Chinese assertiveness. These efforts might focus on Taiwan, Japan, Vietnam, the Philippines, Indonesia, Malaysia, and India—all of which could benefit from wielding the same capabilities that China has used to deter US naval intervention and which cost less than China's investments in amphibious operations or sea control. Although these capabilities may be low-cost, neighboring countries will be unlikely to adopt them quickly without US assistance. Washington will need to help them come up with new operational concepts apart "from traditional maneuver and territorial defense" that might focus on "area denial, long-range fires, cyberattacks, electronic warfare, and mobile defenses in depth."[50] US efforts might involve joint wargaming, exercises, and concept development; assisting in the development and exercise of command, control, communications, intelligence, surveillance, and reconnaissance (C4ISR) capabilities for targeting in contested environments; and support for the acquisition of mines, mobile air and missile defenses, ground-launched anti-ship cruise missiles, submarines, and unmanned surface and undersea vessels. These efforts put China on the wrong end of cost ratios and warfare trends—thereby complicating China's costly investments in military coercion and power projection.

- *Undermine China's Costly Efforts to Establish Overseas Bases*: The United States can undermine China's efforts to establish overseas bases and logistical facilities at lower marginal cost than China's efforts to acquire them. This too can involve borrowing from elements of China's strategy. Just as Beijing used regional institutions to set norms or raise concerns over US activities and basing, so too can Washington do so for possible Chinese facilities in Cambodia or other regions. And Washington should also alert countries that are considering hosting Chinese facilities, particularly in Asia, that those bases could become targets. Often, US policymakers and diplomats are reluctant to state what should be obvious—that strikes on US forces emanating from an overseas Chinese base will put those facilities at risk. Finally, the United States can work with allies and partners to make side payments or infrastructure payments to discourage these countries from hosting Chinese facilities. While the total sum of this compensation may exceed China's investment, the fact it comes from a consortium of allies and partners—perhaps as infrastructure spending—makes this an asymmetric opportunity.

Economic Blunting

- *Call for Multilateralizing and Institutionalizing BRI to Frustrate China's Political Arm-Twisting*: Just as China institutionalized its trade with Washington to prevent overt economic coercion, multilateralization and institutionalization can limit Beijing's ability to dictate terms to other states at lower cost than competing loan-for-loan. The danger of BRI is its opacity and the leverage it generates. Conversely, promoting the multilateralization of BRI and engaging in co-investment on BRI projects in exchange for equity or adherence to high standards and key reporting requirements could forestall unfortunate outcomes, provide regional states a voice in these transactions, bring transparency, and complicate Beijing's political arm-twisting. For example, when Sri Lanka was unable to pay back $1 billion in loans to China for the Hambantota port project—a relatively modest sum given the geopolitical stakes—Chinese state-owned enterprises took a ninety-nine-year lease over the port. That kind of outcome might have been prevented if other states had equity in the project or veto rights over that decision. Moreover, if China refuses to work with others to multilateralize BRI projects, it would further damage BRI's credibility and strengthen the US argument that China's ultimate aims are often political. Finally, better infrastructure helps Asian states become manufacturing powers in their own right and makes possible the relocation of supply chains from China to other developing countries.

- *Provide Training to Assist Partners in Assessing Chinese Financing*: In the developing world, many states have little experience in due diligence for major infrastructure projects, which can put them in a poor position when negotiating with Chinese entities over loans and investments. The United States should advance efforts to train personnel in foreign governments on how to navigate some of these engagements, avoid common pitfalls, and understand some of the security implications at stake. It should retain a team of specialists—economists, diplomats, and especially lawyers and development experts—that can be dispatched abroad to "scrutinize contracts, flag bad deals, and empower the country to push for better terms with Chinese agencies and companies."[51]

- *Use the Information Space to Counter China's Political Corruption Abroad*: As part of the Belt and Road Initiative, Chinese state-owned enterprises and investment vehicles have struck corrupt deals with politically influential actors in third countries, such as Malaysia, Djibouti, Cambodia, Sri Lanka, the Maldives, Ecuador, Equatorial Guinea, the Solomon Islands, and several more—sometimes receiving resources or military access in exchange.[52] Because Chinese political influence is in many cases sustained by corrupt compacts between foreign leaders and Chinese firms, media reporting is sometimes a low-cost way to undermine China's budding political influence in those states. Revelations about Chinese corruption have undermined projects and the relationships China has attempted to cultivate, including in Sri Lanka, Malaysia, and the Maldives, among other countries. Relatively modest efforts by the United States to reveal this corruption can make an outsized impact on dramatically more costly BRI projects. The United States should empower or finance local journalism abroad, ideally through third-party nonprofit entities to preserve independence, thereby providing alternatives in the world's "media deserts." Efforts to ensure social media and Internet access in these countries, expand the reach of Voice of America and Radio Free Asia, fund access to Western wire services (as the United States has done in the Pacific Islands), and assist in the development of restrictions on Chinese investment in foreign media can make a difference.

- *Provide Select Alternative Financing with Allies and Partners*: The United States cannot and should not provide a counter to every project Beijing chooses to support. Working with allies and partners, the United States should fund alternatives to those projects that have the greatest strategic potential (e.g., dual-use port projects, undersea cables, airfields) or work to multilateralize Chinese funding to ensure the United States has a seat at the table.

- *Counter Chinese Technology Acquisition and Theft*: China has sought to "catch up and surpass" the West in technology, and while some of this effort is driven by domestic investment and research, a significant portion also seeks to exploit the openness of US financial markets, universities, and companies to accelerate China's technological programs. While many argue that the United States need only "run faster" in the race with China, doing so provides few benefits if China takes shortcuts to the finish line. First, with respect to finance, the United States has taken steps to limit predatory investment into its companies. These steps can be expanded beyond the Committee on Foreign Investment in the United States (CFIUS) process, which is still voluntary, and should include more ambitious efforts at corporate transparency that complicate the use of pass-throughs and shell companies by foreign actors. Second, with respect to universities, the United States will need to restrict access to Chinese nationals associated with universities with close PLA ties while taking pains to continue attracting and retaining the best Chinese researchers—the majority of whom wish to stay in the United States. This will also require vastly expanding Department of Justice resources, closing Chinese-language skill gaps in the FBI, greater technical knowledge for investigators, enhanced visa screening, better exploitation of open sources, and—critically—far greater collaboration between government, university, and business on espionage risks. Finally, the United States needs greater institutional resources to institute more nimble and effective export controls in advanced industries to prohibit US companies from, in effect, surrendering American technology for short-term quarterly returns. It should also deploy sanctions against companies benefiting from technology theft.

Political Blunting

- *Join Chinese-Led Multilateral Processes to Shape and Sometimes Stall Their Development*: China once challenged costly US efforts to set rules through multilateral organizations like APEC and ARF with a simple seat at the table, which allowed it to shape or stall those efforts. Similarly, Washington should join Chinese-led institutions, improving them or—failing that—stalling them at a lower cost than China's efforts to build them. Within Asia, these efforts might focus on the Asia Infrastructure Investment Bank (AIIB) and the Conference on Interaction and Confidence-Building Measures in Asia (CICA), both of which Beijing has used to set economic and security norms across Asia. If the United States is unable to join, or if in some cases Congress refuses to authorize funding for US participation, then the United States could join in an advisory or observer role or encourage its allies and partners to join (e.g., Japan has not joined either institution).

- *Elevate Alternatives to China-Led Multilateral Bodies*: Efforts to strengthen regional multilateral bodies, including various Association of Southeast Asian Nation (ASEAN) forums and the East Asia Summit, reduce the likelihood that Chinese-led alternatives become focal and give Asian states a larger role in the future of their region. The United States should regularly participate in these bodies at the highest level to ensure that they—and not China-led alternatives—remain at the center of Asian regional efforts.

- *Contest Chinese Influence in the UN System and Global Bodies*: China's interest in "leading the reform of the global governance system" runs through the United Nations because—as its own 2019 White Paper on its diplomacy makes clear—"the UN is at the core of the global governance system." Influence in the UN enables China to build some coercive and consensual leverage as well as legitimacy—allowing it to displace liberal values as the global default and to elevate, legitimize, and globalize Chinese principles and programs. Top UN officials from China openly admit that, although international civil servants are not supposed to have any national loyalty, they nonetheless prioritize Chinese interests on issues as varied as human rights and sovereignty.[53] China currently leads four of fifteen UN special agencies, far more than any other state, due in large part to over a decade of US inattention and neglect. China's leadership is a product of a conscious strategy to cultivate influence within the UN system through both elections and staff appointments. In the Food and Agriculture Organization election, for example, Beijing threatened exports from Argentina, Brazil, and Uruguay to earn support for its candidate while forgiving the debt of Cameroon so it would withdraw its competing candidate.[54] While an American candidate may not always prevail in an election, the United States can often play a spoiler role when Beijing puts up its preferred candidate and steer the election toward a friendly alternative without incurring great cost. For example, in 2020, US efforts helped dissuade votes for China's candidate—previously the frontrunner—for the World Intellectual Property Organization (WIPO).

- *Promote Legal Standards That Undermine China's Global Information Influence Efforts*: To win what its Propaganda Department officials define as a struggle for "discourse power" against Western "discourse hegemony," China has invested heavily in efforts to pressure different nodes in the *information supply chain* that runs from people (content creators) to institutions (media organizations) to platforms (social media) to information consumers. The United States can push back on these efforts asymmetrically. For example, China uses relatively open libel laws in Taiwan and Australia to harass critical journalists and scholars, but simple regulatory reforms could put an end to the practice. China is using investment, advertisement, co-production, and paid inserts to shape media organizations from Latin America to Europe and Asia. Helping countries adopt regulations on Chinese investment, foreign agent registration, and foreign advertising can address these influence channels. Finally, senior Chinese propaganda officials have written that platforms were the "lifeblood" of information flows, and that "whoever owns the platforms will seize the initiative in propagating views and in dominating public opinion."[55] Just as the United States would have concerns over Russian ownership of Facebook, so too must it be equally concerned about China's ownership of major platforms like TikTok because they offer enormous opportunities for manipulation of information flows and domestic politics. Accordingly, encouraging restrictions on autocracy-owned social media apps like TikTok—including forced divestiture or de facto bans— are inexpensive and necessary to blunt Chinese efforts in the information space.

Building American Order

Blunting Chinese order building at low cost may work in many domains, but it is not sustainable without efforts to simultaneously reinvest in the foundations of American order. China too has pursued a blunting strategy that targets American advantages at the regional and global level, and it requires a US effort to recommit to those advantages.

Within the military domain, China's pursuit of so-called anti-access/area-denial capabilities blunts US intervention in Asia and undermines a major source of American regional influence and leverage. At the economic level, China's use of economic statecraft—both through the Belt and Road Initiative and through economic coercion—blunts relative US economic leverage. Beijing is also targeting the foundations of US financial power with a new digital sovereign currency, as well as the foundations of US technology dominance with aggressive industrial policy. Finally, at the political level, China is increasingly gaining influence over global bodies in ways that leave them either dysfunctional or in some cases instruments of Beijing's foreign policy, blunting the advantages that the United States had generated within them.

For the United States, building order is more costly than blunting it, so aspects of this strategy will be more symmetrical than the efforts outlined in the previous section; nonetheless, judicious investment in key foundations of US strength— and coordination with allies where possible to diffuse the costs of order-building and maintenance—can ensure resources are used more conservatively.

Military Building

- *Build Resilience to Chinese Anti-Access/Area-Denial Efforts*: China has pursued efforts to blunt American military power in the Western Pacific. For example, China's air-launched cruise missiles and ground-launched ballistic missiles can strike bases as far away as Guam, crippling runways, destroying fuel facilities, and disabling aircraft on the tarmac. In response, the United States should make a number of investments—many of which are well understood but have lacked adequate resourcing—to build resilience against China's denial capabilities. These include hardening critical facilities; burying fuel or information infrastructure deep underground; acquiring capabilities for rapid movement between bases or across the first and second island chains; expanding runways and improving runaway repair capabilities; significantly expanding stockpiles of critical munitions; and increasing the use of camouflage, concealment, and deception; among other methods.

- *Build a Diverse US Posture in the Indo-Pacific*: US military bases in Asia are increasingly vulnerable to disabling missile attacks. Resilience requires a more dispersed posture across the region, as well as a demonstrated capability to rapidly move forces across it. Distributing US assets across a number of bases in different countries and outlying islands would not solve this problem entirely, but it would mitigate some of the danger posed by consolidating US forces in a few locations. Presently, and as a legacy of the Cold War, the United States posture in Asia is overweighted toward Northeast Asia and underweighted with respect to Southeast Asia, the Indian Ocean, the Pacific Islands, and Oceania. Some of these steps are already underway, but more could be taken—including facilities in Palau and Yap among other locations. Moreover, US force posture should not involve only permanent bases but should increasingly include a variety of access and status of forces agreements that can also be useful in diversifying military posture to "low-cost, small footprint" facilities while providing the United States the ability to respond nimbly to faraway regional crises. Finally, a more diversified force posture will facilitate US access in humanitarian assistance and disaster relief, afford more opportunities for military diplomacy from India to Vietnam and the Pacific Islands, and provide some insurance from political risk.

- *Build Resilient Information Infrastructure*: US military operations in Asia and worldwide are especially dependent on resilient information flows for command, control, communications, intelligence, surveillance, and reconnaissance (C4ISR).. For example, precision-guided munitions will be far less effective in striking their targets without access to information. Much of this information architecture was established in an era that presumed opponents would not be able to effectively challenge it, and it now needs to be rebuilt to address the challenge posed by China. In many cases, this may mean investing in alternatives to space assets for communication or positioning, navigation, and timing; innovative ISR systems that mass sensors and collaborate in contested environments; improvements in artificial intelligence and autonomy that reduce dependence on information flows; continued innovation in electronic warfare; and training to operate in environments where C4ISR may be degraded.[56] Some analysts suggest that "improving the resilience of U.S. C4ISR architecture in the face of attack might be the single most effective step the United States can take to strengthen its conventional deterrent."[57]

Economic Building

- *Maintain Dollar Dominance amid Challenges from China and New Technology*: The dollar's status as the reserve currency is the backbone of US global hegemony, and it makes it easier for the United States to finance deficit spending, monitor cross-border financial transactions, and implement financial sanctions. The United States might constitute only a quarter of global GDP, but the dollar is 60 percent of global reserve currencies—an advantage amplified by the fact that the United States is open, retains deep and liquid financial markets, and possesses a large and diversified economy. The dollar's success has brought complications: the United States suffers from a dollar-driven variant of "Dutch Disease," where reliance on a particular export can cause deindustrialization if institutions cannot properly manage the windfall. In this respect the United States is "the Saudi Arabia of money," with much of its manufacturing capacity atrophying while its assets skyrocket in price.[58] Currency has driven Dutch Disease in other countries in the past—colonial Spain benefited from a windfall of gold from the Americas, for example—but the end of that gold supply brought a disastrous geopolitical fall. Although the dollar's position is strong, two trends now threaten it, and relatedly, US hegemony. The first is the overuse of financial sanctions, which has already driven some allies and adversaries to unite in (so far unsuccessful) efforts to bypass the dollar system. Second, and more important, China is rolling out a digital RMB to compete with the US dollar that completely bypasses US payments infrastructure. Chinese officials have long worried about the potential of a US-led digital currency that would bolster the US dollar system, and so they have raced for first-mover advantage. Wang Xin, director of the People's Bank of China's research bureau, stated that "if the digital currency is closely associated with the U.S. dollar . . . there would be in essence one boss, that is the U.S. dollar and the United States," which would have geopolitical consequences.[59] The United States should carefully study and then consider rolling out a digital currency that preserves its financial advantages and brings about precisely the world Wang Xin was concerned about—a digital currency that complements and is anchored to the US dollar system. Finally, as Mike O'Hanlon notes, maintaining these strengths provides a nonkinetic and nonlethal way of deterring or responding to small Chinese territorial provocations.[60]

- *Bring Existing Institutions into Global Infrastructure Investment and Build New Ones to Extend US Economic Influence*: Washington should strongly push existing development institutions, especially the World Bank, to play a higher-profile role in global infrastructure investment despite reluctance to do so. At the same time, the United States should consider new vehicles for supporting global infrastructure, particularly in the low-cost and high-impact digital realm. For example, because China's investments in information infrastructure are heavily subsidized and often lack competitors, the United States could create a digital development bank with allies and partners to compete for those projects, which may induce developing countries to pick infrastructure providers and operators more in line with liberal or democratic values.

- *Create an Entity to Audit the US Supply Chain*: China has demonstrated a willingness to use its nodal position in modern supply chains as leverage against other countries. The United States presently has a poor understanding of these connections. Indeed, the pandemic has revealed that no government agency was aware of how dependent the United States was on China for medicine, and similar dependencies from rare earths to microelectronics persist. To secure itself and position its allies and partners to resist China's coercive economic diplomacy, the United States should launch a permanent effort institutionalized in a federal government agency and bolstered through mandatory reporting requirements to audit supply chains across most industries. The office would also run stress tests of the US supply chain.[61]

- *Reinvest in the Talent Base for US Innovation*: American innovativeness has several foundations, many of which are presently eroding. The United States needs to attract and retain the world's best talent in STEM. In fields like electrical engineering, roughly 80 percent of graduate students are foreign nationals, the vast majority prefer to stay in the United States, and most of them do so when provided the opportunity.[62] Similar data holds for other fields. To sustain this advantage, the United States should raise H1-B visa caps for STEM fields and grant green cards to postgraduate STEM degree holders, among other reforms.[63]

- *Reinvest in Basic Science Research for US Innovation*: As a percentage of GDP, the US federal government spends only 0.61 percent of GDP on R&D—a percentage that is one of the lowest in seventy years, lower than ten other science powers, and lower even than pre-Sputnik funding, with half of this limited amount going to life sciences alone.[64] Business contributes to US R&D spending, but mostly in applied research, while basic research generally comes from the federal government and has historically formed the foundation for major breakthroughs—including radar, computing, and nuclear power.[65] For example, Congress spent $3 billion in the 1980s to map the human genome when industry was reluctant to do so; this in turn helped create the genomics industry that employs 280,000 people in the United States and generates taxes of $6 billion annually.[66] Increasing such spending, and diversifying it beyond life sciences, should be a priority.

- *Reform Financial Markets and Tax Policy to Incentivize Longer-Term Corporate Planning*: The shareholder revolution of the 1980s helped usher in a focus on returns on capital at the expense of longer-term planning. Most shares of stock are held for less than a year now, compared to eight years in the 1950s; CEO tenure is now near a historic low of roughly five years; and the pressure to generate financial returns often disincentivizes manufacturing relative to other more lucrative business activities—and sometimes even encourages companies to transfer technology to China for short-term payoffs. Efforts to adjust the institutionalized "short-termism" of US capital markets are supported by some prominent executives, like JPMorgan Chase CEO Jaimie Dimon and Berkshire Hathaway CEO Warren Buffet. Efforts could include new benchmark metrics that include longer timeframes, as well as tax policy that encourages holding equity positions for longer periods, among others.[67]

- *Build a Competitive Industrial Policy Architecture to Sustain Key US Industries and Innovation*: To compete with Chinese industrial policy approaches in advanced industries, the United States may need to adopt its own industrial policy. Doing so will require more than subsidies: it will require strategies to educate and attract talent in key fields; to incentivize foreign manufacturers and US companies alike to return to the United States through a mixture of credits and localization requirements; to use state power to restructure supply chains; to break up monopolies that reduce innovation and are so large they reduce US economic resilience; and to provide a degree of protection against unfair competing trade practices. These approaches should seek to support industries rather than individual firms. This is particularly critical at the technology frontier, where firms frequently must make bets about the progress of future technology that may or may not be valid (e.g., investment in super-computing vs. personal computing). When only one state champion exists in a given industry, the price of making the wrong bet can be devastating for the wider economy and for the country's technological leadership. In contrast, when there are multiple companies operating in a critical industry, the odds that one will make the right bet and sustain the country's leadership in that industry are far greater. When market structure sometimes complicates efforts at ensuring competition, Congress can assist weaker competitors, a policy approach it has used in the past to ensure a competitive defense industrial base.[68] Then, as now, competition between leading firms in these essential industries is more likely to produce lower prices, higher-quality products, industrial resilience, and greater innovation—advantaging the United States relative to outright mercantilist competitors with one leading state champion.

- *Build an Allied Ecosystem for Research and Development*: Basic science research is already an international endeavor, and US-China scientific cooperation is increasingly common. But while the United States and China spend roughly equivalent amounts on R&D presently, the combined total spent by Japan, Germany, South Korea, India, France, and the United Kingdom exceeds the United States and China respectively. Congress should relax some of the people-to-people impediments to greater allied and partner collaboration (e.g., visa policies) while also encouraging basic science research organizations to engage more with allies and partners. Greater diffusion across allied and partner channels could help sharpen the American technological edge, allowing the country to benefit from others. Moreover, formal partnerships could involve efforts to "set standards and values around sharing data, transparency, reproducibility and research integrity," as Georgetown's Center for Strategic and Emerging Technology argues.[69]

- *Build the Capacity for Greater State Involvement and Coordination in Nominally Commercial Standard-Setting Bodies*: While many standard-setting bodies are composed of companies rather than countries, China's top-down effort to shape standards requires a response from the US government. This is particularly urgent during times when standard-setting processes might be inaugurating new paradigms in critical industries, including telecommunications (e.g., the Open Radio Access Network concept) and the Internet of Things, that could long shape the future. First, Congress could support establishment of interagency working groups on standards that could coordinate internally. For example, White House Office of Science and Technology Policy could establish an interagency working group on technology standards that brings together the Departments of State, Commerce, Justice, and Defense as well as the US intelligence community—and that also consults with US industry.[70] Second, to build coalitions among different companies and countries, Congress could support the establishment of offices within the Departments of Commerce and State to coordinate US approaches with like-minded stakeholders.[71]

Political Building

- *Build Democratic or Allied Coalitions for Governance Issues from Technology to Trade and Supply Chains to Standards*: Over the last three years, a series of great and middle powers have proposed organizing democratic coalitions to push back on China's efforts to stall or impose its preferences in more inclusive global forums. These coalitions—such as the "D10" proposed by the United Kingdom for 5G, which would include G7 countries as well as Australia, India, and South Korea—would be liberal in composition and would work to organize elements of the international system around liberal states, thereby serving as a form of order-building. The United States should support these approaches, using them to pressure formal organizations, or when necessary, to organize alternative rules. These coalitions, which might proliferate across issue areas, would effectively function as "cartels" that provide "club goods" for their members but few benefits for those who choose to stay outside of the group. For example, allied coalitional approaches on trade modeled after TPP or TTIP might bypass the WTO, where China has influence. A democratic cartel could also set up standard-setting bodies reserved for states within the coalition, bypassing global bodies like the International Telecommunications Union that include China and ensuring liberal protections are built into Internet architecture. Entire industries—or even supply chains—might be organized around these democratic or allied coalitions, particularly in the very sectors China hopes to climb. Chinese authors are worried about these approaches and understand that autocratic states have less wealth, less technological influence, and more dependence on the formal equality of global institutions to shape international outcomes. For its part, this kind of inclusive order-building is asymmetric—it costs the United States little, particularly when middle powers propose it, but imposes significant costs on China's recalcitrance in other forums.

As this book has demonstrated, China seeks to displace the United States not only from regional but also global leadership and may be able to devote more resources to that task than the United States can devote to preserving its own order. Even those skeptical of the idea that China has global ambitions must concede that the CCP's nationalist and Leninist foundations make it difficult to dismiss the possibility outright. Party rhetoric on rejuvenation strongly indicates that the goal of displacing the United States is implicit in China's present thinking and that Beijing is unlikely to permanently accept junior status in a US-led order, particularly one with a liberal character threatening to China's Leninist governance.

Against this state of affairs, strategies seeking to accommodate or change China are unlikely to produce favorable outcomes. Instead, in the competition for regional and global order, the United States will need to *blunt* China's "forms of control" while *building* or rebuilding the foundations of its own. In most cases, this effort can be asymmetric, particularly with respect to blunting since undermining an order can be less expensive than constructing it. With respect to rebuilding the foundations of its own order, the United States has several advantages, and particularly benefits from its network of alliances that can help it diffuse the costs of order-building. This competitive approach cannot be guaranteed to change Chinese strategy, but it may be able to limit some elements of Chinese power and influence, achieving a "mellowing" of Chinese power less through an internal change of China's politics or an effort to reassure Beijing than through external constraint on China's ability to convert the sources of its power into political order.

Conclusion

"The United States is unlikely to decline so long as its public is periodically convinced that it is about to decline."[1]
—*Political scientist Samuel Huntington, 1988*

On November 28, 1970, Chief of Naval Operations Admiral Elmo Zumwalt and
National Security Advisor Henry Kissinger sat together on a special military
train. The two were headed together to Philadelphia for the Army-Navy football
game. It was to be a relaxed outing, and yet six years later, their conversation that
day would be litigated in the national press at the height of a presidential primary
campaign.

Both men, roughly the same age but of vastly different backgrounds, had
arrived at the apex of their relative fields at the same time, with Zumwalt the
youngest ever chief of naval operations and Kissinger one of the youngest national security advisors. Both had grown up professionally with America's emergence as the world's leading state. And both had formative experiences in the
Second World War, where they rose to positions of leadership at young ages—
experiences that pushed them toward national security careers neither had initially considered.

In the Pacific, the twenty-five-year-old Lieutenant Elmo Zumwalt had become the "prize crew captain" of a captured 1,200-ton Japanese river gunboat.
He and his seventeen American sailors took the captured ship and its 190-
person Japanese crew to Shanghai, where they entered the Yangtze as the first
American-flagged vessel in years, captured Japanese docks, and made contact
with American guerrilla forces—an experience that pushed Zumwalt to give
up his dream of being a country doctor.[2] Kissinger, who had once harbored his
own dreams of being an accountant, was not a naval officer like Zumwalt but
a drafted army private. Placed in charge of a regimental Counter-Intelligence
Corps (CIC) team, the German-speaking Kissinger excelled at identifying and
arresting former Nazis and at breaking up Gestapo sleeper cells ordered to sabotage American forces in occupied Germany. For his work, he was promoted to

sergeant, then awarded a Bronze Star, then promoted to staff sergeant, and then nominated to become "chief investigator for the CIC in the European Theatre."[3]

Those formative experiences for both men came at a time of American ascent. But in the train car twenty-five years later, their conversation turned to America's decline from those heady postwar days, and they fretted over Soviet superiority in the military balance. Zumwalt recounted that Kissinger believed that the "U.S. has passed its historic high point like so many earlier civilizations" and that Americans "lack the stamina to stay the course against the Russians who are 'Sparta to our Athens.'"[4] In light of these trends, Kissinger said his job was "to persuade the Russians to give us the best deal we can get, recognizing that the historical forces favor them."[5] Zumwalt disagreed, but found himself shaken by the logic of Kissinger's argument.

Six years later, that conversation became national news. Zumwalt had published the conversation in his memoirs; then Ronald Reagan had quoted the conversation as ammunition against President Gerald Ford in a presidential debate; and, finally, Kissinger denied the quote vociferously: "I am going to nominate the good Admiral for the Pulitzer Prize for fiction," he said.[6] While Zumwalt certainly had reason to exaggerate—he was running for Senate in Virginia—Kissinger had in fact openly written about American decline in the 1960s and spoken of it frequently in interviews with the press throughout the 1970s. His gloominess about the US position relative to the Soviet Union had long been well known.[7]

That gloominess is now back among many in American strategic circles, and the conversation between Zumwalt and Kissinger fifty years ago could just as easily have happened today. Then, as now, the United States was facing enormous domestic strains while a rising power loomed over the horizon. And then, as now, some believed that US policy should be less provocative and competitive, reflect the fact that "historical forces" were supposedly arrayed against the country, and seek the best deal possible with an ascendant rival. A refashioned version of Kissinger's argument today might point out that China dominates global manufacturing, increasingly rivals the United States in high-technology, boasts an economy larger than the American one in purchasing power terms, fields the world's largest navy, and has weathered a once-in-a-century pandemic better than most others—the only great power to avoid recession in 2020. The United States, by contrast, seems to many in Beijing and even in Washington hopelessly divided and gridlocked, with its governance and institutions deteriorating. As of this book's publication, it confronts a years-long pandemic, industrial erosion, burgeoning debt, a wounded democracy, and a diminished global reputation. Might Kissinger's pessimism be warranted?[8]

A descent into fatalism is likely premature. American declinism is a tradition with a rich but often inaccurate history, and there have been four declinist waves

in the last century. In each of them, the country displayed what the political scientist Samuel Huntington once called "an unusual capacity for self-correction,"
with declinists ironically playing "an indispensable role in preventing what they
are predicting."[9]

The first wave of American declinism began during the Great Depression in
the 1930s. Kissinger and many others may have seen the postwar period as the
American high point, but the economic calamity only years before—from which
Germany and Japan seemed to emerge more swiftly than the United States—
had stirred American doubts about the country's system of self-governance. The
United States rebounded through innovative New Deal programs that President
Franklin Delano Roosevelt used to reshape the US economy, and by the postwar
era, an America that seemed down and out was back in prime position. Then, in
1957, the Soviet Union launched its Sputnik satellite, provoking a second wave of
declinist handwringing. But the muscle memory of the New Deal remained: the
United States built federally supported institutions for research and education
that made the country a technological leader for decades.

Declinism crested in a long, third wave in the 1960s and 1970s that tested
the faith of Kissinger, Zumwalt, and countless others in the country's resilience.
The United States went through social unrest and political assassinations; the
collapse of Bretton Woods and the arrival of stagflation; the impeachment of
President Richard Nixon and the fall of Saigon—all set against the backdrop of
Soviet advancement. But eventually even these developments brought adjustment and renewal. Social unrest propelled civil rights reforms, impeachment
reaffirmed the rule of law, Bretton Woods' collapse brought eventual dollar dominance, defeat in Vietnam ended the draft, and the Soviet Union's Afghan invasion hastened its collapse.

A fourth declinist wave marked by industrial erosion, trade deficits, and rising
inequality rattled American leaders in the 1980s and early 1990s, prompting
Senator Paul Tsongas of Massachusetts to declare that "the Cold War is over, and
Japan and Germany won." But despite those pressures, the United States success-
fully harnessed the information technology revolution. Less than a decade after
Tsongas's comment, the United States was heralded as an unrivaled superpower.

The United States is now in its fifth wave of declinism—one that began
with the global financial crisis in 2008 and accelerated through Trump's norm-
breaking presidency, the COVID-19 pandemic, and the storming of the US
Capitol by extremists. All of this has been set against China's continued rise.
And as this book has demonstrated, China has had a grand strategy to displace
American order and build its own order at both the regional and global level. It
now seeks to be the world's leading state.

Despite their popularity in Beijing, narratives on American decline are
often incomplete. Declinists point to forces—such as inequality, polarization,

disinformation, and deindustrialization—that are real and formidable in the United States, but they forget these same forces are also global in nature rather than uniquely American. At the same time, they overlook US advantages over China, which has a fast-aging population, enormous debt, slowing growth, and a currency still far from rivaling the dollar. In contrast, the United States still retains enviable advantages: a young population, financial dominance, abundant resources, peaceful borders, strong alliances, and an innovative economy. Moreover, it is hardly incidental that throughout most of China's four-decade rise, the United States has consistently held a quarter of the world's GDP.[10]

Declinists also underestimate the power of the United States' appeal. American openness attracts the allies that sustain the global liberal order, the immigrants who fuel American growth, and the capital that sustains dollar dominance. US soft power flows from the country's open society and civic creed, not from the state. The protests that followed the killing of George Floyd, which China saw incorrectly as a sign of decline, instead reflected a public struggle to realize the founding values of the United States—values whose appeal was so universal that the struggle for them captivated global audiences and inspired marches abroad. The United States attracts more criticism than other great powers "precisely because it holds itself to a higher standard," argues the South Africa–based journalist Dele Olojode. "Nobody holds China to that kind of standard."[11]

For the United States, decline is less a condition than a choice. The downward path runs through the country's polarized political system. The path away from decline, meanwhile, may run through a rare area susceptible to bipartisan consensus: the need for the United States to rise to the China challenge.

As this book has shown, this challenge is in most respects not a choice. China's scale and its increasingly global ambitions are geopolitical facts, and the country seeks to set the terms for the twenty-first century in the same way that the United States set them for the twentieth. The last chapter discussed a policy response to China's ambitions, one that strengthens the "forms of control" upon which American order depends while undermining those that Chinese order will soon require. The United States can and should avoid competing dollar-for-dollar, ship-for-ship, or loan-for-loan, and could instead adopt an asymmetric approach that blunts Chinese advances at lower cost than China expends in generating them, all while reinvesting in the sources of American order and power.

The imperative for reinvestment is particularly urgent. Meeting the China challenge will require the kinds of reinvestments in American competitiveness and innovation that are also critical to domestic renewal and working-class prosperity. Policymakers can link these two agendas, not to amplify American anxieties but to make clear that accomplishing the country's most important domestic tasks will also have salutary effects abroad. At the same time, policymakers must resist the common declinist tendency to see US competitors as ten feet tall and instead calibrate a response that spurs innovation without stoking fear and prejudice. The arrival of an external competitor has often pushed the United States to become its best self; handled judiciously, it can once again. During the Cold War, US politicians endeavored to leave foreign policy differences "at the water's edge." In this time of partisan gridlock, domestic consensus may once again begin beyond America's shores.

With a constructive China policy that strengthens the United States at home and makes it more competitive abroad, American leaders can begin to reverse the impression of US decline. But they cannot stop there. They must also find affirmative ways to rebuild the solidarity and civic identity that make democracy work. An effort to stress a shared liberal nationalism, or what the historian Jill Lepore calls a "New Americanism," has been part of our civic culture and can be again.[12]

As a presidential candidate sixty years ago, when Americans were still reeling from the Sputnik shock, John F. Kennedy addressed a municipal auditorium in Canton, Ohio. The country faced serious crises, and Kennedy enumerated them: low wages, high housing costs, a growing risk of conflict, the gradual shrinkage of industry, and the rise of a new rival that appeared to be on the march while the United States stood still. "What we have to overcome," Kennedy said then, is "that psychological feeling in the world that the United States has reached maturity, that maybe our high noon has passed, maybe our brightest days were earlier, and that now we are going into the long, slow afternoon. . . . I don't hold that view at all, and neither do the people of this country."[13]

APPENDIX

This book draws from an original and fully digitized database of authoritative Chinese-language Communist Party documents personally excavated over several years from libraries; bookstores in Taiwan, Hong Kong, and mainland China; and Chinese e-commerce sites.

Gathering these sources has proved challenging in the Xi Jinping era. In China, many archives are closed or restricted; similarly, bookstores that once sold a wide array of Party or military material have, in some cases, reduced what they are willing to sell to foreigners. In the United States, a handful of libraries boast impressive Chinese collection, but significant amounts of Chinese material remain unavailable.

Given these limitations, building the database from which this book draws has required eclectic approaches. Indeed, some texts used were circulating in Taiwan or Hong Kong; other cited works had been spirited out and sold to a few US libraries in enormous caches; a few were provided by generous scholars; and a surprising number were inadvertently posted online to Chinese government sites.

The largest source of the book's material comes from the official publications of the Communist Party presses, many of which receive little attention. Older volumes of these publications are quite useful and help establish longitudinal changes in policy but can be challenging to find in bookstores. These materials can also be difficult to purchase online given limitations placed on foreign account access, sales to foreigners—and of course, e-commerce scams. To gather more material, I opted to work with a local intermediary better known for sourcing fashion products. This allowed for faster sourcing of open source material and allowed me to piece together a rich, fully digitized collection of Party texts.

This textual approach to Chinese grand strategy relies on establishing a hierarchy of open source and classified Chinese sources in order of authoritativeness and drawing from them accordingly. The most authoritative of these are leader-level memoirs, doctrinal texts, archival sources, official speeches, classified materials, and essays by senior leaders. They better reflect Party thinking than more frequently cited but often less reliable sources like Chinese journal articles and think tank reports. It is worth briefly considering them here.

Leader-Level Speeches

Party and leader-level documents can be ranked in order of authoritativeness based in part on their audience and purpose.

The first category are *leader-level Party addresses* that are intended to set the line, guideline, and policy on major issues before key Party institutions. The most authoritative of these are Party Congress Reports, which are delivered by the General Secretary at the Party Congress, which is itself held every five years. This gathering is the most important within the Communist Party, and the 30,000-word Political Reports delivered there set the line on all major policy issues, including foreign policy. The speeches often begin with a quick but telling survey of the Party consensus on international trends. Of lesser but similar importance are those addresses by top leaders to major Party institutions below the Party Congress, such as those to the two hundred or so members of the Central Committee. These occur annually and are known as plenums.

Following major addresses to Party institutions come *major foreign policy addresses*, the second category of authoritative leader-level documents useful for research into grand strategy. These addresses can be to either Party or state institutions. They include the Ambassadorial Conferences, which are held on average every six or so years; the Central Foreign Affairs Work Conferences, which have only been held a handful of times (1976, 1991, 2006, 2014, and 2018); and major foreign policy conclaves and symposiums, such as the Peripheral Work Conference held in 2013. Because these kinds of speeches are made infrequently and are often made in front of much of the foreign policy apparatus, they are particularly important, and a review of them shows that they are often used to announce shifts in foreign policy or to grapple with new or changing circumstances. The judgments in these speeches are often explicitly rooted in Party consensus at the level of the Central Committee, Politburo, or even Politburo Standing Committee. Another category of foreign policy speeches are those regularly made by leaders to key institutions such as the Central Military Commission or the Ministry of Foreign Affairs, often to crystalize or convey a Party consensus.

A final category of leader-level speeches are those made to non-foreign policy bodies, both Party and state. To a surprising degree, many of these kinds of speeches discuss foreign policy in some detail and can be seen as attempts to disseminate or reinforce the Party consensus on international politics and Chinese strategy.

External-Facing Foreign Policy Sources

The preceding speeches are generally for internal audiences and rarely released to the public unless in the form of compendiums of a leader's major works, though they are sometimes summarized online. In contrast, the government publishes a number of leader-level addresses or ministry white papers that are intended for external audiences around the world. These can include speeches to the United Nations or in neighboring capitals as well as important papers released by state ministries. Although these are authoritative because they are released by high-level Chinese institutions after close consideration and deliberation, they are also undoubtedly intended to shape external views. For that reason, they can be useful in some cases, but they are not necessarily the best indicator of Chinese internal thinking. For example, in my comprehensive review of speeches by Presidents Jiang and Hu, I consistently found—often in the same year and sometimes even in the same month—more confident assessments that the world was moving toward multipolarity before external audiences and far more restrained assessments before internal audiences. Even so, these are among the most useful documents that we have for gauging Chinese strategy.

Party Media

The CCP often uses authoritative Party media to disseminate its judgments on key issues. These include daily newspapers such as the Party newspaper *Renmin Ribao* as well as prominent Party magazines such as *Qiushi* and *Xuexi Shibao*. These venues are not only used to highlight Party views, they are also used to provide lengthy commentaries on important leader-level addresses and even used at times to give voice to Party debates. For that reason, it is of particular importance to pay attention to the author or pseudonym and publication date of articles.

Functional Sources

As discussed previously, a wide variety of authoritative documents are released by ministries, the military, and their associated publishing houses. These as well as memoirs or selected works of top officials and ministry or service newspapers can be useful in understanding the guidelines or policies for key state organs.

With respect to military matters, the book consults Chinese-language doctrinal texts from the 1980s onward with an eye toward tracing changes in military doctrine. It also consults memoirs, essay compilations, records of daily activities, and official biographies of all vice-chairman of the Central Military Commission from the 1980s onward that have been published—including those of Ye Jianying, Liu Huaqing, Zhang Zhen, Zhang Wannian, and Chi Haotian. In addition, the book references valuable leader-level compendiums on military matters that have been published for Deng Xiaoping, Jiang Zemin, Hu Jintao, and Xi Jinping. Finally, several pseudo-doctrinal publications as well as histories from the Academy of Military Sciences, the National Defense University, other military think tanks, and a variety of military-affiliated presses are also cited.

With respect to international political decisions, particularly in international institutions, this book draws from published memoirs, essay compilations, and documents from foreign affairs ministers and relevant state councilors with responsibility for foreign affairs, including Wu Xueqian, Qian Qichen, Tang Jiaxuan, Li Zhaoxing, Dai Bingguo, Yang Jiechi, and Wang Yi, among others. The book also draws carefully from the views of other less senior diplomats and officials closely involved with these institutions as well as academics who are known to have shaped Chinese foreign policy, especially with respect to international institutions, such as Zhang Yunling, Qing Yaqing, and Wang Yizhou. In addition, the statements and publications of various international organizations are particularly useful.

Third, with respect to Chinese international economic behavior, this dissertation relies on works by Zhu Rongji and Li Peng to recreate some aspects of economic decision-making. It also draws from works by a wide variety of other officials, including those within the Ministry of Finance and Commerce (MOFCOM) and the People's Bank of China (PBOC), as well as leader-level and diplomatic accounts and speeches.

Think Tank Commentary

A number of professors, research scholars, former officials, and think tank analysts are also regularly cited by scholars of Chinese foreign policy. In most cases, these sources are not authoritative or representative of Party views.

Even so, there are ways such sources can be used fruitfully under certain conditions. First, prominent Chinese think tank and academic officials serve or previously served as informal foreign policy advisors, and their views can therefore provide some context for decisions that were made. Some scholars have been asked to work on major projects for the Politburo, which convenes a "study session" every month on major issues of Party interest. Academics may spend months if not years preparing for these sessions, and following their presentations, are sometimes given tasks to continue their research (e.g., the rising power [大国崛起] series). These writings may not be authoritative statements of Party consensus, but they suggest areas of Party interest or concern. Second, many think tank and academic officials are connected to Party research priorities. Several work at university centers funded to focus on specific functional or regional topics while others work at think tanks associated with certain ministries. More broadly, most ministries publish a wide range of journals and books under ministry-linked presses, and these can provide context on present policy and rationales for past policy. Third, think tank and academic sources can sometimes provide insight into interesting debates within the foreign policy apparatus. They can be representative of various strains of elite foreign policy opinion (e.g., Wang Jisi, Zhang Yunling).

Together, these documents help capture how the Party thinks as well as how that thinking has changed over time.

NOTES

Introduction

1. Harold James, *Krupp: A History of the Legendary British Firm* (Princeton: Princeton University Press, 2012), 51.
2. For this memo, see Li Hongzhang [李鸿章], "Memo on Not Abandoning the Manufacture of Ships [筹议制造轮船未可裁撤折]," in *The Complete Works of Li Wenzhong* [李文忠公全集], vol. 19, 1872, 45. Li Hongzhang was also called Li Wenzhong.
3. Xi Jinping [习近平], "Xi Jinping Delivered an Important Speech at the Opening Ceremony of the Seminar on Learning and Implementing the Spirit of the Fifth Plenary Session of the 19th Central Committee of the Party [习近平在省部级主要领导干部学习贯彻党的十九届五中全会精神专题研讨班开班式上发表重要讲话]," *Xinhua* [新华], January 11, 2021.
4. Evan Osnos, "The Future of America's Contest with China," *The New Yorker*, January 13, 2020, https://www.newyorker.com/magazine/2020/01/13/the-future-of-americas-contest-with-china.
5. For example, John Lewis Gaddis, *Strategies of Containment: A Critical Appraisal of American National Security Policy during the Cold War* (Oxford: Oxford University Press, 2005).
6. Robert E. Kelly, "What Would Chinese Hegemony Look Like?," *The Diplomat*, February 10, 2014, https://thediplomat.com/2014/02/what-would-chinese-hegemony-look-like/; Nadège Rolland, "China's Vision for a New World Order" (Washington, DC: The National Bureau of Asian Research, 2020), https://www.nbr.org/publication/chinas-vision-for-a-new-world-order/.
7. See Yuan Peng [袁鹏], "The Coronavirus Pandemic and the Great Changes Unseen in a Century [新冠疫情与百年变局]," *Contemporary International Relations* [现代国际关系], no. 5 (June 2020): 1–6, by the head of the leading Ministry of State Security think tank.
8. Michael Lind, "The China Question," *Tablet*, May 19, 2020, https://www.tabletmag.com/sections/news/articles/china-strategy-trade-lind.
9. Graham Allison and Robert Blackwill, "Interview: Lee Kuan Yew on the Future of U.S.-China Relations," *The Atlantic*, March 5, 2013, https://www.theatlantic.com/china/archive/2013/03/interview-lee-kuan-yew-on-the-future-of-us-china-relations/273657/.
10. Andrew F. Krepinevich, "Preserving the Balance: A U.S. Eurasia Defense Strategy" (Washington, DC: Center for Strategic and Budgetary Assessments, January 19, 2017), https://csbaonline.org/uploads/documents/Preserving_the_Balance_%2819Jan17%29HANDOUTS.pdf.
11. "GDP, (US$)," World Bank, 2019, https://data.worldbank.org/indicator/ny.gdp.mktp.cd.
12. Angela Stanzel et al., "Grand Designs: Does China Have a 'Grand Strategy'" (European Council on Foreign Relations, October 18, 2017), https://www.ecfr.eu/publications/summary/grands_designs_does_china_have_a_grand_strategy#.

13. Susan Shirk, "Course Correction: Toward an Effective and Sustainable China Policy" (National Press Club, Washington, DC, February 12, 2019), https://asiasociety.org/center-us-china-relations/events/course-correction-toward-effective-and-sustainable-china-policy.

14. Quoted in Robert Sutter, *Chinese Foreign Relations: Power and Policy since the Cold War*, 3rd ed. (Lanham, MD: Rowman & Littlefield, 2012), 9–10. See also Wang Jisi, "China's Search for a Grand Strategy: A Rising Great Power Finds Its Way," *Foreign Affairs* 90, no. 2 (2011): 68–79.

15. Jeffrey A. Bader, "How Xi Jinping Sees the World, and Why" (Washington, DC: Brookings Institution, 2016), https://www.brookings.edu/wp-content/uploads/2016/07/xi_jinping_worldview_bader-1.pdf.

16. Michael Swaine, "The U.S. Can't Afford to Demonize China," *Foreign Policy*, June 29, 2018, https://foreignpolicy.com/2018/06/29/the-u-s-cant-afford-to-demonize-china/.

17. Jamie Tarabay, "CIA Official: China Wants to Replace US as World Superpower," CNN, July 21, 2018, https://www.cnn.com/2018/07/20/politics/china-cold-war-us-superpower-influence/index.html. Daniel Coates, "Annual Threat Assessment," § Senate Select Committee on Intelligence (2019), https://www.dni.gov/files/documents/Newsroom/Testimonies/2019-01-29-ATA-Opening-Statement_Final.pdf.

18. Alastair Iain Johnston, "Shaky Foundations: The 'Intellectual Architecture' of Trump's China Policy," *Survival* 61, no. 2 (2019): 189–202; Jude Blanchette, "The Devil Is in the Footnotes: On Reading Michael Pillsbury's The Hundred-Year Marathon" (La Jolla, CA: UC San Diego 21st Century China Program, 2018), https://china.ucsd.edu/_files/The-Hundred-Year-Marathon.pdf.

19. Jonathan Ward, *China's Vision of Victory* (Washington, DC: Atlas Publishing and Media Company, 2019); Martin Jacques, *When China Rules the World: The Rise of the Middle Kingdom and the End of the Western World* (New York: Penguin, 2012).

20. Sulmaan Wasif Khan, *Haunted by Chaos: China's Grand Strategy from Mao Zedong to Xi Jinping* (Cambridge, MA: Harvard University Press, 2018); Andrew Scobell et al., *China's Grand Strategy Trends, Trajectories, and Long-Term Competition* (Arlington, VA: RAND Corporation, 2020).

21. See Avery Goldstein, *Rising to the Challenge China's Grand Strategy and International Security* (Stanford, CA: Stanford University Press, 2005); Aaron L. Friedberg, *A Contest for Supremacy: China, America, and the Struggle for Mastery in Asia* (New York: W. W. Norton, 2012); David Shambaugh, *China Goes Global: The Partial Power* (Oxford: Oxford University Press, 2013); Ashley J. Tellis, "Pursuing Global Reach: China's Not So Long March toward Preeminence," in *Strategic Asia 2019: China's Expanding Strategic Ambitions Paperback*, eds. Ashley J. Tellis, Alison Szalwinski, and Michael Wills (Washington, DC: National Bureau of Asian Research, 2019), 3–46.

22. For the full text, as well as the responses to it within the British Foreign Office, see Eyre Crowe, "Memorandum on the Present State of British Relations with France and Germany," in *British Documents on the Origins of the War, 1898–1914*, eds. G. P. Gooch and Harold Temperley (London: His Majesty's Stationary Office, 1926), 397–420.

23. Ibid., 417.

24. Ibid., 415.

25. Ibid., 415.

26. Ibid., 414.

27. Ibid., 414.

28. Interview.

29. Robert Jervis, *Perception and Misperception in International Politics* (Princeton: Princeton University Press, 1976).

Chapter 1

1. "Mike Wallace Interview with Henry Kissinger," Harry Ransom Center at the University of Texas at Austin, July 13, 1958, https://hrc.contentdm.oclc.org/digital/collection/p15878coll90/id/67/.

2. Quoted in Beatrice Heuser, *The Evolution of Strategy: Thinking War from Antiquity to the Present* (Cambridge: Cambridge University Press, 2010), 4.

3. Hal Brands, *What Good Is Grand Strategy?: Power and Purpose in American Statecraft from Harry S. Truman to George W. Bush* (Ithaca, NY: Cornell University Press, 2014), vii. The question of how Chinese sources define grand strategy is important, but since this book uses grand strategy as an analytic concept, differences in the term's meaning across culture are less relevant. The question is whether this kind of phenomenon, which this book calls grand strategy, exists in China's case—not what this term might mean in other cultures. While the *association* of the term "grand strategy" with this phenomenon might have originated from the Western strategic canon, the phenomenon exists regardless of cultural context and need not be considered "Western."

4. Barry R. Posen, *Restraint: A New Foundation for U.S. Grand Strategy* (Ithaca, NY: Cornell University Press, 2014), 1.

5. For example, when grand strategy was first introduced in the nineteenth century, it was a military shorthand for Napoleonic generalship. By the late nineteenth century, rising interdependence and transoceanic trade led maritime strategists like Alfred Thayer Mahan and Julian Corbett to push open the concept to include economic means. After the First World War, scholars like John Fuller and Basil Liddell Hart included even more means of statecraft while broadening the ends to include not only victory in war but also success in peacetime competition. Finally, after the Second World War, scholars like Edward Meade Earle wove these strands together and helped set the modern definition of grand strategy used in this book.

6. For the full text, as well as the responses to it within the British Foreign Office, see Eyre Crowe, "Memorandum on the Present State of British Relations with France and Germany," in *British Documents on the Origins of the War, 1898–1914*, eds. G. P. Gooch and Harold Temperley (London: His Majesty's Stationary Office, 1926), 397–420.

7. Brands, *What Good Is Grand Strategy?*, 6.

8. Daniel Drezner, "Does Obama Have a Grand Strategy?: Why We Need Doctrines in Uncertain Times," *Foreign Affairs* 90, no. 4 (2011): 59.

9. David A. Welch, *Painful Choices: A Theory of Foreign Policy Change* (Princeton: Princeton University Press, 2005), 37.

10. Ibid., 31–33.

11. Michael A. Glosny, "The Grand Strategies of Rising Powers: Reassurance, Coercion, and Balancing Responses" (PhD diss., Massachusetts Institute of Technology, 2012), 27.

12. This book's focus on the politics of hegemonic orders, and particularly on how rising powers might contest it, places it within what John Ikenberry and Dan Nexon term the "third wave" in studies of hegemonic order.

13. Kenneth Waltz, *Theory of International Politics*, (Long Grove, IL: Waveland Press, 2010 [1979]); David Lake, *Hierarchy in International Relations* (Ithaca, NY: Cornell University Press, 2009).

14. John G. Ikenberry, *Liberal Leviathan: The Origins, Crisis, and Transformation of the American World Order* (Princeton: Princeton University Press, 2011), 13. See also Kyle Lascurettes, *Orders of Exclusion: Great Powers and the Strategic Sources of Foundational Rules in International Relations* (Oxford: Oxford University Press, 2020).

15. Paul Musgrave and Dan Nexon, "Defending Hierarchy from the Moon to the Indian Ocean: Symbolic Capital and Political Dominance in Early Modern China and the Cold War," *International Organization* 73, no. 3 (2018): 531–626; Alex D. Barder, "International Hierarchy," in *Oxford Research Encyclopedia of International Studies* (Oxford: Oxford University Press, 2015).

16. Robert Gilpin, *War and Change in World Politics* (Cambridge: Cambridge University Press, 1981), 26. This approach is also similar to the way that Robert Cox discusses hegemony, as involving economic, military, and political dominance backed by an ideology that secures a "measure of consent" from other states and publics. See Robert W. Cox, "Gramsci, Hegemony, and International Relations: An Essay in Method," *Millennium: Journal of International Studies* 12, no. 2 (1983): 162–75. Others also emphasize the ideological content of order. See, for example, Bentley B. Allan, Srdjan Vucetic, and Ted Hopf, "The Distribution of Identity and the Future of International Order: China's Hegemonic Prospects," *International Organization* 72, no. 4 (2018): 839–69.

17. Gilpin, who focuses on great power wars, also allows that evolution in order can take place gradually.

18. Other recent works that discussing rising power and established power strategies and interactions include Joshua R. Itzkowitz Shifrinson, *Rising Titans, Falling Giants: How Great Powers Exploit Power Shifts* (Ithaca, NY: Cornell University Press, 2018); and David M. Edelstein, *Over the Horizon: Time, Uncertainty, and the Rise of Great Powers* (Ithaca, NY: Cornell University Press, 2017).

19. John Mearsheimer, *The Tragedy of Great Power Politics* (New York: Norton, 2001).

20. Gilpin calls this an "international system," but he acknowledges that in the modern world this system is global. See Chapter 1 of Gilpin, *War and Change in World Politics*.

21. Threat perceptions can be amplified by ideological divides. China finds the United States more threatening than it otherwise might precisely because the United States is a liberal power whose values, by the Party's own admission, threaten its hold on power. These dynamics can be found throughout history. Mark Haas, *The Ideological Origins of Great Power Politics, 1789–1989* (Ithaca, NY: Cornell University Press, 2005).

22. James C. Scott, *Weapons of the Weak: Everyday Forms of Peasant Resistance* (New Haven: Yale University Press, 1987).

Chapter 2

1. Zhao Ziyang, *Prisoner of the State: The Secret Journal of Premier Zhao Ziyang*, eds. Adi Ignatius, Bao Pu, and Renee Chiang (New York: Simon & Schuster, 2010), 252.

2. Ibid.

3. Ibid., 252.

4. Ibid., 252.

5. Orville Schell and John Delury, *Wealth and Power: China's Long March to the Twenty-First Century* (New York: Random House, 2013), 263.

6. Alexander Pantsov and Stephen I. Levine, *Deng Xiaoping: A Revolutionary Life* (Oxford: Oxford University Press, 2015), 56.

7. Lucian Pye, "An Introductory Profile: Deng Xiaoping and China's Political Culture," *The China Quarterly*, no. 135 (1993): 432.

8. "Resolution of the 19th National Congress of the Communist Party of China on the 'Articles of Association of the Communist Party of China (Amendment)' [中国共产党第十九次全国代表大会关于《中国共产党章程（修正案）》的决议]," *Xinhua* [新华网], October 24, 2017, http://www.xinhuanet.com/politics/19cpcnc/2017-10/24/c_1121850042.htm..

9. Richard McGregor, *The Party* (New York: HarperCollins, 2010), 18.

10. Ibid.

11. David L. Shambaugh, *China's Communist Party: Atrophy and Adaptation* (Berkeley: University of California Press, 2008), 1.

12. Zheng Wang, "Not Rising, But Rejuvenating: The 'Chinese Dream,'" *The Diplomat*, February 5, 2013, https://thediplomat.com/2013/02/chinese-dream-draft/.

13. Schell and Delury, *Wealth and Power*, 15.

14. Ezra Vogel, *Deng Xiaoping and the Transformation of China* (Cambridge: Harvard University Press, 2011), 17.

15. Schell and Delury, *Wealth and Power*, 263.

16. Jonathan Spence, *Mao Zedong: A Life* (New York: Penguin Books, 2006), 9.

17. Schell and Delury, *Wealth and Power*, 262.

18. Vogel, *Deng Xiaoping and the Transformation of China*, 11–12.

19. Jiang himself admits this in his 15th Party Congress address, Jiang Zemin [江泽民], *Jiang Zemin Selected Works* [江泽民文选], vol. 2 [第二卷] (Beijing: People's Press [人民出版社], 2006), 2. The Party sometimes translates both 振兴 and 复兴 as "rejuvenation."

20. Deng Xiaoping [邓小平], *Collection of Deng Xiaoping's Military Writings* [邓小平军事文集], vol. 1 (Beijing: Military Science Press [军事科学出版社], 2004), 83; Zheng Wang, "The Chinese Dream from Mao to Xi," *The Diplomat*, September 20, 2013, https://thediplomat.com/2013/09/the-chinese-dream-from-mao-to-xi/. Interestingly, Jiang Zemin personally inscribed the cover for Deng's military writings.

21. Jiang Zemin [江泽民], *Jiang Zemin Selected Works* [江泽民文选], vol. 1 [第一卷] (Beijing: People's Press [人民出版社}, 2006), 37.

22. See Hu Yaobang [胡耀邦], "Create a New Situation in All Fields of Socialist Modernization [全面开创社会主义现代化建设的新局]," in Literature Research Office of the Chinese Communist Party Central Committee [中共中央文献研究室], *Selection of Important Documents since the 12th Party Congress* [十二大以来重要文献选编], vol. 1 (Beijing: Central Party Literature Press [中央文献出版社], 1986), 6–62.

23. See Zhao Ziyang [赵紫阳], "Advance along the Road of Socialism with Chinese Characteristics [沿着有中国特色的社会主义道路前进]," in Literature Research Office of the Chinese Communist Party Central Committee [中共中央文献研究室], *Selection of Important Documents since the 13th Party Congress* [十三大以来重要文献选编], vol. 1 (Beijing: People's Publishing House [人民出版社], 1991), 4–61.

24. For Jiang's 14th Party Congress Address, see Jiang Zemin [江泽民], "Accelerating the Reform, the Opening to the Outside World and the Drive for Modernization, so as to Achieve Greater Successes in Building Socialism with Chinese Characteristics [加快改革开放和现代化建设步伐 夺取有中国特色社会主义事业的更大胜利]," in Literature Research Office of the Chinese Communist Party Central Committee [中共中央文献研究室], *Selection of Important Documents since the 14th Party Congress* [十四大以来重要文献选编], vol. 1 (Beijing: People's Publishing House [人民出版社], 1996), 1–47. For the 15th Party Congress address, see Jiang Zemin [江泽民], "Hold High the Great Banner of Deng Xiaoping Theory for an All-round Advancement of the Cause of Building Socialism with Chinese Characteristics' into the 21st Century [高举邓小平理论伟大旗帜，把建设有中国特色社会主义事业全面推向二十一世纪]," in Literature Research Office of the Chinese Communist Party Central Committee [中共中央文献研究室], *Selection of Important Documents since the 15th Party Congress* [十五大以来重要文献选编], vol. 1 (Beijing: People's Publishing House [人民出版社], 2000), 1–51. For the 16th Party Congress address, see Jiang Zemin [江泽民], "Build a Well-off Society in an All-round Way and Create a New Situation in Building Socialism with Chinese Characteristics [全面建设小康社会，开创中国特色社会主义事业新局面]," in Literature Research Office of the Chinese Communist Party Central Committee [中共中央文献研究室], *Selection of Important Documents since the 16th Party Congress* [十六大以来重要文献选编], vol. 1 (Beijing: Central Party Literature Press [中央文献出版社], 2005), 1–44.

25. For the 17th Party Congress report, see Hu Jintao [胡锦涛], "Hold High the Great Banner of Socialism with Chinese Characteristics and Strive for New Victories in Building a Moderately Prosperous Society in All Respects [高举中国特色社会主义伟大旗帜 为夺取全面建设小康社会新胜利而奋斗]," in Literature Research Office of the Chinese Communist Party Central Committee [中共中央文献研究室], *Selection of Important Documents since the 17th Party Congress* [十七大以来重要文献选编], vol. 1 (Beijing: Central Party Literature Press [中央文献出版社], 2009), 1–44. For the 18th Party Congress report, see Hu Jintao [胡锦涛], "Firmly March on the Path of Socialism with Chinese Characteristics and Strive to Complete the Building of a Moderately Prosperous Society in All Respects [坚定不移沿着中国特色社会主义道路前进 为全面建成小康社会而奋斗]," in Literature Research Office of the Chinese Communist Party Central Committee [中共中央文献研究室], *Selection of Important Documents since the 18th Party Congress* [十八大以来重要文献选编], vol. 1 (Beijing: Central Party Literature Press [中央文献出版社], 2014), 1–43.

26. Xi Jinping [习近平], "Secure a Decisive Victory in Building a Moderately Prosperous Society in All Respects and Strive for the Great Success of Socialism with Chinese Characteristics for a New Era" [决胜全面建成小康社会 夺取新时代中国特色社会主义伟大胜利], 19th Party Congress Political Report (Beijing, October 18, 2017).

27. Hu Jintao [胡锦涛], *Hu Jintao Selected Works* [胡锦涛文选] , vol. 1 [第一卷] (Beijing: People's Press [人民出版社], 2016), 364, 556.

28. Ibid., vol. 1 [第一卷], 149.

29. Ibid., vol. 1 [第一卷], 149.

30. This focus is apparent in the Zhao Yang's 13th Party Congress address and in Jiang Zemin's 14th Party Congress address, for example.

31. This gathering is different from a Party Congress and infrequently held. *Deng Xiaoping Selected Works* [邓小平文选], 2nd ed., vol. 3 [第三卷] (Beijing: People's Press [人民出版社], 1993), 143.

32. Jiang Zemin [江泽民], *Jiang Zemin Selected Works* [江泽民文选], vol. 3 [第三卷] (Beijing: People's Press [人民出版社}, 2006), 308.

33. Ibid., vol. 3 [第三卷], 299.

34. *Deng Xiaoping Selected Works* [邓小平文选], vol. 3 [第三卷], 204–6.

35. Jiang Zemin [江泽民], *Jiang Zemin Selected Works* [江泽民文选], 2006, vol. 3 [第三卷], 127.

36. Ibid., vol. 2 [第二卷], 63. See also Jiang's 15th Party Congress address.

37. Ibid., vol. 3 [第三卷], 399.

38. Hu Jintao [胡锦涛], *Hu Jintao Selected Works* [胡锦涛文选], vol. 3 [第三卷] (Beijing: People's Press [人民出版社], 2016), , 560–61.

39. Ibid., vol. 3 [第三卷], 659.

40. Xi Jinping [习近平], "Secure a Decisive Victory in Building a Moderately Prosperous Society in All Respects and Strive for the Great Success of Socialism with Chinese Characteristics for a New Era [决胜全面建成小康社会 夺取新时代中国特色社会主义伟大胜利]."

41. Franz Schurmann, *Ideology and Organization in Communist China* (Berkeley: University of California Press, 1966), 22–26, 122.

42. Vladimir Lenin, "A Letter to a Comrade on Our Organisational Tasks, 1902," in *Lenin Collected Works*, vol. 6 (Moscow: Progress Publishers, 1964), 231–52.

43. McGregor, *The Party*, 12.

44. Ibid., 9.

45. Kinling Lo, "The Military Unit That Connects China's Secret 'Red Phone' Calls," *South China Morning Post*, July 21, 2017, https://www.scmp.com/news/china/diplomacy-defence/article/2103499/call-duty-military-unit-connects-chinas-secret-red.

46. McGregor, *The Party*, 9.

47. Christopher K. Johnson and Scott Kennedy, "Xi's Signature Governance Innovation: The Rise of Leading Small Groups," CSIS, October 17, 2017, https://www.csis.org/analysis/xis-signature-governance-innovation-rise-leading-small-groups; David M. Lampton, "Xi Jinping and the National Security Commission: Policy Coordination and Political Power" 24, no. 95 (2015): 772.

48. For more on the reform of this structure, see Nis Grünberg and Katja Drinhausen, "The Party Leads on Everything China's Changing Governance in Xi Jinping's New Era" (Mercator Institute for China Studies, September 24, 2019), https://www.merics.org/de/china-monitor/the-party-leads-on-everything.

49. Alice Miller, "More Already on the Central Committee's Leading Small Groups," *China Leadership Monitor*, no. 4 (2014): 4, https://www.hoover.org/research/more-already-central-committees-leading-small-groups.

50. Ibid.; Johnson and Kennedy, "Xi's Signature Governance Innovation"; Grünberg and Drinhausen, "The Party Leads on Everything China's Changing Governance in Xi Jinping's New Era"; Scott Kennedy and Chris Johnson, https://www.csis.org/analysis/xis-signature-governance-innovation-rise-leading-small-groups.

51. Lampton, "Xi Jinping and the National Security Commission," 767.

52. Wen-Hsuan Tsai and Wang Zhou, "Integrated Fragmentation and the Role of Leading Small Groups in Chinese Politics," *The China Journal* 82 (2019): 22.

53. Ibid., 4.

54. Ibid.; Kjeld Erik Brødsgaard, ed., "'Fragmented Authoritarianism' or 'Integrated Fragmentation'?," in *Chinese Politics as Fragmented Authoritarianism* (New York: Routledge, 2017), 38–55.

55. Suisheng Zhao, "China's Foreign Policy Making Process: Players and Institutions," in *China and the World*, ed. David Shambaugh (Oxford: Oxford University Press, 2020), 94.

56. Li Yuan, "Coronavirus Crisis Shows China's Governance Failure," *New York Times*, February 4, 2020, https://www.nytimes.com/2020/02/04/business/china-coronavirus-government.html?action=click&module=Top%20Stories&pgtype=Homepage.

57. Quoted in Jerry F. Hough and Merle Fainsod, *How the Soviet Union Is Governed* (Cambridge, MA: Harvard University Press, 1979), 19.

58. See Shambaugh, *China's Communist Party*, 141–43.

59. Yun Sun, "Chinese Public Opinion: Shaping China's Foreign Policy, or Shaped by It?," Brookings Institution, December 13, 2011, https://www.brookings.edu/opinions/chinese-public-opinion-shaping-chinas-foreign-policy-or-shaped-by-it/.

60. Andrew Chubb, "Assessing Public Opinion's Influence on Foreign Policy: The Case of China's Assertive Maritime Behavior," *Asian Security* 2 (2018): 159–79.

61. Jessica Chen Weiss, *Powerful Patriots: Nationalist Protest in China's Foreign Relations* (Oxford: Oxford University Press, 2014).

62. Joseph Fewsmith and Stanley Rosen, "The Domestic Context of Chinese Foreign Policy: Does 'Public Opinion' Matter," in *The Making of Chinese Foreign and Security Policy, 1978–2000*, ed. David M. Lampton (Stanford: Stanford University Press, 2001), 151–90; Peter Gries, "Nationalism, Social Influences, and Chinese Foreign Policy," in *China and the World*, ed. David Shambaugh (Oxford: Oxford University Press, 2020), 63–84.

63. Thomas J. Christensen, "More Actors, Less Coordination?: New Challenges for the Leaders of a Rising China," in *China's Foreign Policy: Who Makes It, and How Is It Made?*, ed. Gilbert Rozman (New York: Palgrave, 2011), 21–37; Linda Jakobson and Dean Knox, "New Foreign Policy Actors in China," SIPRI Policy Paper (Stockholm: Stockholm International Peace Research Institute, 2010).

64. Shambaugh, *China's Communist Party*; Minxin Pei, *China's Crony Capitalism* (Cambridge, MA: Harvard University Press, 2016).

65. Zhao, "China's Foreign Policy Making Process," 105–6.

66. Zhao Ziyang's Collected Works Editing Team [赵紫阳文集编辑组], *The Collected Works of Zhao Ziyang 1980--1989* [赵紫阳文集 1980-1989], vol. 3 (Hong Kong: The Chinese University Press [香港中文大学], 2016), 218..

67. Ibid., vol. 3, 218.

68. Jiang Zemin [江泽民], *Jiang Zemin Selected Works* [江泽民文选], vol. 1 [第一卷], 315.

69. Ibid., vol. 1 [第一卷], 315.

70. Ibid., vol. 1 [第一卷], 315.

71. Hu Jintao [胡锦涛], *Hu Jintao Selected Works* [胡锦涛文选], vol. 2 [第二卷] (Beijing: People's Press [人民出版社], 2016), 98–99 .

72. Ibid., vol. 2 [第二卷], 98–99.

73. Xi Jinping [习近平], *Xi Jinping: The Governance of China* [习近平谈治国理政], vol. 1 (Beijing: Foreign Language Press [外文出版社], 2014), 299.

74. Xi Jinping [习近平], *Xi Jinping: The Governance of China, Volume 2* [习近平谈治国理政], vol. Volume 2 [第二卷] (Beijing: Foreign Language Press [外文出版社], 2014), 444.

75. Yang Jiechi [杨洁篪], "Chinese Diplomatic Theory and Innovation in Practice in the New Situation [新形势下中国外交理论和实践创新]," *Qiushi* [求是] 2013, no. 16 (August 16, 2013), http://www.qstheory.cn/zxdk/2013/201316/201308/t20130813_259197.htm.

76. Xi Jinping [习近平], "Xi Urges Breaking New Ground in Major Country Diplomacy with Chinese Characteristics [努力开创中国特色大国外交新局面]," *Xinhua* [新华网], June 22, 2018, http://www.xinhuanet.com/politics/2018-06/23/c_1123025806.htm.

77. Ibid.

78. Ibid.

79. Ibid.

80. Ibid.

81. Ibid.

82. Richard Baum, *China Watcher: Confessions of a Peking Tom* (Seattle: University of Washington Press, 2014), 235.

83. Ibid.

84. Simon Leys, "The Art of Interpreting Nonexistent Inscriptions Written in Invisible Ink on a Blank Page," *New York of Review Books*, October 11, 1990, https://www.nybooks.com/articles/1990/10/11/the-art-of-interpreting-nonexistent-inscriptions-w/.

85. Alice Miller, "Valedictory: Analyzing the Chinese Leadership in an Era of Sex, Money, and Power," *China Leadership Monitor*, no. 57 (2018), https://www.hoover.org/sites/default/files/research/docs/clm57-am-final.pdf.

86. Geremie R. Barmé, "The China Expert and the Ten Commandements," *China Heritage*, January 5, 2018, http://chinaheritage.net/journal/the-china-expert-and-the-ten-commandments/.

87. Ibid., 16.

88. Samuel Wade, "On US-China Trade Tensions," *China Digital Times*, June 29, 2018, https://chinadigitaltimes.net/2018/06/minitrue-on-u-s-china-trade-tensions/.

Chapter 3

1. *Deng Xiaoping Selected Works* [邓小平文选], 2nd ed., vol. 3 [第三卷] (Beijing: People's Press [人民出版社], 1993), 344–46.

2. This account is contained in numerous open sources spanning 1980 to 2000. See Philip Taubman, "US and Peking Join in Tracking Missiles," *New York Times*, June 18, 1981, https://www.nytimes.com/1981/06/18/world/us-and-peking-join-in-tracking-missiles-in-soviet.html; John C. K. Daly, "US, China—Intel's Odd Couple," *UPI*, February 24, 2001, https://www.upi.com/Archives/2001/02/24/Feature-US-China-intels-odd-couple/6536982990800/.

3. Charles Hopper, "Going Nowhere Slowly: US-China Military Relations 1994–2001" (Cambridge, MA: Weatherhead Center for International Affairs, July 7, 2006), 5, https://scholarsprogram.wcfia.harvard.edu/files/fellows/files/hooper.pdf.

4. "Claims China Using HMAS Melbourne for Study," *The Age*, March 8, 2002, https://www.theage.com.au/world/claims-china-using-hmas-melbourne-for-study-20020308-gdu178.html; Sebastien Roblin, "Meet the Australian Aircraft Carrier That Jump-Started China's Own Carrier Quest," *The National Interest*, December 10, 2018, https://nationalinterest.org/blog/buzz/meet-australian-aircraft-carrier-jump-started-chinas-own-carrier-quest-38387.

5. *Deng Xiaoping Selected Works* [邓小平文选], vol. 3 [第三卷], 127–28.

6. This full phrase often appears as 冷静观察，站稳脚跟，沉着应付，韬光养晦，善于守拙，绝不当头, though it is sometimes modified. Early references to it appear in Deng's September 1989 comments to central government in *Deng Xiaoping Selected Works* [邓小平文选], vol. 3 [第三卷], 321. One of his first official uses of "Tao Guang Yang Hui" was in Leng Rong [冷溶] and Wang Zuoling [汪作玲], eds., *Deng Xiaoping Nianpu* [邓小平年谱], vol. 2 (Beijing: China Central Document Press [中央文献出版社], 2006), 1346. The phrase was also cited and attributed to Deng in a major report by former foreign minister Tang Jiaxuan. See Tang Jiaxuan [唐家璇], "The Glorious Course of China's Cross-Century Diplomacy [中国跨世纪外交的光辉历程]," Foreign Ministry of the People's Republic of China [中华人民共和国外交部], October 17, 2020, https://www.fmprc.gov.cn/web/ziliao_674904/zt_674979/ywzt_675099/zt2002_675989/2319_676055/t10827.shtml.

7. George H. W. Bush and Brent Scowcroft, *A World Transformed: The Collapse of the Soviet Empire, The Unification of Germany, Tiananmen Square, The Gulf War* (New York: Knopf, 1998), 195–96.

8. Ibid.

9. These documents are available at the George H. W. Bush Presidential Library and Museum and were provided to ChinaFile by George Washington University professor David Shambaugh. "U.S.-China Diplomacy after Tiananmen: Documents from the George H. W. Bush Presidential Library," ChinaFile, July 8, 2019, https://www.chinafile.com/conversation/other-tiananmen-papers.

10. Ibid.

11. Ibid.

12. Ibid.

13. Ibid.

14. "Brent Scowcroft Oral History Part I—Transcript," University of Virginia Miller Center, November 12, 1999, https://millercenter.org/the-presidency/presidential-oral-histories/brent-scowcroft-oral-history-part-i.

15. Bush and Scowcroft, *A World Transformed*, 204.

16. Ibid., 178.

17. Ibid., 179.

18. Ibid., 179.

19. Ibid., 180.
20. *Deng Xiaoping Selected Works* [邓小平文选], vol. 3 [第三卷], 294.
21. Hu Yaobang, "Report to the 12th National Congress of the Communist Party of China: Create a New Situation in All Fields of Socialist Modernization," *Beijing Review*, April 12, 2011, http://www.bjreview.com/90th/2011-04/12/content_357550_9.htm.
22. See *The Science of Military Strategy* [战略学] (Beijing: Academy of Military Science Press [军事科学出版社], 1987); Taylor Fravel, "The Evolution of China's Military Strategy: Comparing the 1987 and 1999 Editions of Zhanluexue," in *China's Revolution in Doctrinal Affairs: Emerging Trends in the Operational Art of the Chinese People's Liberation Army*, eds. James Mulvenon and David Finkelstein (Alexandria, VA: Center for Naval Analyses, 2005), 79–99.
23. *Deng Xiaoping Selected Works* [邓小平文选], vol. 3 [第三卷], 168.
24. Ibid., vol. 3 [第三卷], 320.
25. Ibid., vol. 3 [第三卷], 325.
26. Ibid., vol. 3 [第三卷], 325–26.
27. Ibid., vol. 3 [第三卷], 331.
28. Ibid., vol. 3 [第三卷], 344.
29. Ibid., vol. 3 [第三卷], 348.
30. Ibid., vol. 3 [第三卷], 348.
31. Harlan W. Jencks, "Chinese Evaluations of 'Desert Storm': Implications for PRC Security," *Journal of East Asian Affairs* 6, no. 2 (1992): 454.
32. Ibid.
33. David L. Shambaugh, *China's Communist Party: Atrophy and Adaptation* (Berkeley: University of California Press, 2008).
34. Gao Yu [高瑜], "Xi Jinping the Man [男儿习近平]," DW.com, January 26, 2013, https://www.dw.com/zh/男儿习近平/a-16549520. https://www.dw.com/zh/%E7%94%B7%E5%84%BF%E4%B9%A0%E8%BF%91%E5%B9%B3/a-16549520.
35. J. D. Frodsham, *The Collected Poems of Li He* (New York: Penguin, 2017). The introduction contains a compilation of biographical details.
36. Ibid.
37. Jiang Zemin [江泽民], *Jiang Zemin Selected Works* [江泽民文选], vol. 2 [第二卷] (Beijing: People's Press [人民出版社], 2006), 452.
38. The term 对手 connotes an adversarial, oppositional, or rivalrous relationship in contrast a more neutral term like interlocutor.
39. For Jiang's 8th Ambassadorial Conference address, see Jiang Zemin [江泽民], *Jiang Zemin Selected Works* [江泽民文选], vol. 1 [第一卷] (Beijing: People's Press [人民出版社}, 2006), 311–17.
40. Ibid., vol. 1 [第一卷], 312.
41. Ibid., vol. 1 [第一卷], 312.
42. Ibid., vol. 1 [第一卷], 312.
43. Ibid., vol. 1 [第一卷], 312.
44. Ibid., Jiang Zemin [江泽民], *Jiang Zemin Selected Works* [江泽民文选], 2006, vol. 2 [第二卷], 197.
45. Ibid., vol. 2 [第二卷], 197.
46. Ibid., vol. 2 [第二卷], 198.
47. Ibid., vol. 2 [第二卷], 202–3.
48. Ibid., vol. 2 [第二卷], 203.
49. Ibid., vol. 2 [第二卷], 203.
50. Ibid., vol. 2 [第二卷], 196.
51. Ibid., vol. 2 [第二卷], 451.
52. Ibid., vol. 2 [第二卷], 451.
53. Ibid., vol. 2 [第二卷], 452.
54. Ibid., vol. 2 [第二卷], 452.
55. Ibid., vol. 2 [第一卷], 353.
56. Hu Jintao [胡锦涛], *Hu Jintao Selected Works* [胡锦涛文选], vol. 2 [第二卷] (Beijing: People's Press [人民出版社], 2016), 91.

57. Andrew Nathan and Bruce Gilley, *China's New Rulers: The Secret Files* (New York: New York Review of Books, 2002), 207–9.

58. Zong Hairen [宗海仁], *China's New Leaders: The Fourth Generation* [中國掌權者: 第四代] (New York: Mirror Books [明鏡出版社], 2002), 76–78.

59. Ibid., [宗海仁], 76–78.

60. Ibid., [宗海仁], 168. For a good translation for many of the quotes in Zong Hairen's compilation of leaked documents, see Nathan and Gilley, *China's New Rulers*, 207–9.

61. Zong Hairen [宗海仁], *China's New Leaders: The Fourth Generation* [中國掌權者: 第四代], 322–26.

62. Ibid., [宗海仁], 125.

63. Hu Jintao [胡锦涛], *Hu Jintao Selected Works* [胡锦涛文选], vol. 2 [第二卷], 503–4.

64. Ibid., vol. 2 [第二卷], 509.

65. Paul A. Cohen, *Speaking to History: The Story of King Goujian in Twentieth-Century China* (Berkeley: University of California Press, 2010).

66. Ibid.

67. Ibid.

68. Ibid.

69. "冷静观察，站稳脚跟，沉着应付，韬光养晦，善于守拙，绝不当头."

70. Xiao Feng [肖枫], "Is Comrade Deng Xiaoping's 'Tao Guang Yang Hui' Thinking an 'Expedient Measure'? [邓小平同志的'韬光养晦'思想是'权宜之计'吗?]," *Beijing Daily* [北京日报], April 6, 2010, http://dangshi.people.com.cn/GB/138903/141370/11297254.html; Zhang Xiangyi [张湘忆], "Observe Calmly, Calmly Cope with the Situation, Tao Guang Yang Hui, Do Not Take Leadership, Accomplish Something" [冷静观察、沉着应付、韬光养晦、决不当头、有所作为], *People's Daily Online* [人民网], October 28, 2012, http://theory.people.com.cn/n/2012/1028/c350803-19412863.html.

71. Zhu Weilie [朱威烈], "Tao Guang Yang Hui: A Commonsense Concept in the Global Cultural Mainstream [韬光养晦 : 世界主流文明的共有观念]," *People's Daily Online* [人民网], April 28, 2011, http://world.people.com.cn/GB/12439957.html. Zhu Weilie is a professor at Shanghai International Studies University.

72. For example, see Liu Huaqing [刘华清], *Memoirs of Liu Huaqing* [刘华清回忆录] (Beijing: Revolutionary Army Press [解放军出版社], 2004), 601.

73. *Deng Xiaoping Selected Works* [邓小平文选], vol. 3 [第三卷], 321.

74. Chen Dingding and Wang Jianwei, "Lying Low No More?: China's New Thinking on the Tao Guang Yang Hui Strategy," *China: An International Journal* 9, no. 2 (September 2011): 197.

75. Leng Rong [冷溶] and Wang Zuoling [汪作玲], *Deng Xiaoping Nianpu* [邓小平年谱], vol. 2, 1346.

76. Jiang Zemin [江泽民], "Jiang Zemin Discusses Opposing Peaceful Evolution [江泽民论反和平演变]," http://www.360doc.com/content/09/0203/23/97184_2452974.shtml. I was given this document, but it can be accessed at this link too.

77. Ibid.

78. Jiang Zemin [江泽民], *Jiang Zemin on Socialism with Chinese Characteristics (Special Excerpts)* 江泽民论有中国特色社会主义 【专题摘编】 (Beijing: 中央文献出版社, 2002), 529–30.

79. Ibid., 529–30.

80. Jiang Zemin [江泽民], *Jiang Zemin Selected Works* [江泽民文选], 2006, vol. 1 [第一卷], 289.

81. Ibid., vol. 1 [第一卷], 315.

82. Ibid., vol. 2 [第二卷], 202. Emphasis added.

83. Hu Jintao [胡锦涛], *Hu Jintao Selected Works* [胡锦涛文选], vol. 2 [第二卷], 97. Emphasis added.

84. Ibid., vol. 2 [第二卷], 97.

85. Ibid., vol. 2 [第二卷], 97.

86. Ibid., vol. 2 [第二卷], 97.

87. Ibid., vol. 2 [第二卷], 97. Emphasis added.

88. Zong Hairen [宗海仁], *China's New Leaders: The Fourth Generation* [中國掌權者: 第四代], 78.

89. Hu Jintao [胡锦涛], *Hu Jintao Selected Works* [胡锦涛文选], vol. 2 [第二卷], 518.

90. Ibid., vol. 2 [第二卷], 518.
91. Ibid., vol. 2 [第二卷], 518. Emphasis added.
92. Ibid., vol. 2 [第二卷], 510.
93. Ibid., vol. 2 [第二卷], 519.
94. Yang Wenchang, "My Views about 'Tao Guang Yang Hui,'" *Foreign Affairs Journal*, no. 102 (2011); Yang Wenchang, "Diplomatic Words of Wisdom," *China Daily*, October 29, 2011, http://usa.chinadaily.com.cn/opinion/2011-10/29/content_13999715.htm.
95. Michael D. Swaine, "Perceptions of an Assertive China," *China Leadership Monitor*, no. 32 (2010): 7.
96. Yan Xuetong, "From Keeping a Low Profile to Striving for Achievement," *Chinese Journal of International Politics* 7, no. 2 (2014): 155–56.
97. Ibid., 156.
98. For example, even Central Party textbooks refer to the concept this way. See Zhang Xiangyi [张湘忆], "Observe Calmly, Calmly Cope with the Situation, Tao Guang Yang Hui, Do Not Take Leadership, Accomplish Something [冷静观察、沉着应付、韬光养晦、决不当头、有所作为]."
99. This phrase is discussed in greater detail in Chapter 4.
100. This phrase is discussed in greater detail in Chapter 4.
101. This phrase is discussed in greater detail in Chapter 4.
102. Zhang Wannian Writing Group[张万年写作组], *Biography of Zhang Wannian* [张万年传], vol. 2 [下] (Beijing: Revolutionary Army Press [解放军出版社], 2011), 419.
103. Ibid., vol. 2 [下], 419.
104. See Chapter 5 for a discussion of these concerns.

Chapter 4

1. Zhang Wannian Writing Group [张万年写作组], *Biography of Zhang Wannian* [张万年传], vol. 2 [下] (Beijing: Revolutionary Army Press [解放军出版社], 2011), 419.
2. Darrell Whitcomb, "The Night They Saved Vega 31," *Air Force Magazine*, December 1, 2006, https://www.airforcemag.com/article/1206vega/.
3. For a cursory summary of these events and tactics, see Paul F. Crickmore, *Lockheed F-117 Nighthawk Stealth Fighter* (Oxford: Osprey, 2014), 56–58.
4. Zhang Wannian Writing Group [张万年写作组], *Biography of Zhang Wannian* [张万年传], vol. 2 [下], 415.
5. Ibid., vol. 2 [下], 415.
6. Ibid., vol. 2 [下], 417–18.
7. For Western literature on this concept, see Michael Pillsbury, *China Debates the Future Security Environment* (Washington, DC: National Defense University Press, 2000); Jason Bruzdzinski, "Demystifying Shashoujian: China's 'Assassin's Mace' Concept," in *Civil-Military Change in China: Elites, Institutions, and Ideas after the 16th Party Congress*, eds. Andrew Scobell and Larry Wortzel (Carlisle: US Army War College, 2004), 309–64; Alastair Iain Johnston, "Toward Contextualizing the Concept of Shashoujian (Assassin's Mace)" (Unpublished Manuscript, August 2002). This chapter takes a slightly different approach on elements of the term in light of newer sources.
8. Zhang Wannian Writing Group, *Biography of Zhang Wannian*, vol. 2 [下], 419.
9. Barry R. Posen, "Military Doctrine and the Management of Uncertainty," *Journal of Strategic Studies* 39, no. 2 (2016): 159.
10. Kenneth Waltz, *Theory of International Politics* (Long Grove: Waveland Press, 2010 [1979]), 127.
11. João Resende-Santos, *Neorealism, States, and the Modern Mass Army* (New York: Cambridge University Press, 2007).
12. See Chapter 2 of Barry R. Posen, *The Sources of Military Doctrine: France, Britain, and Germany between the World Wars* (Ithaca, NY: Cornell University Press, 1984).
13. Kimberly Marten Zisk, *Engaging the Enemy* (Princeton: Princeton University Press, 1993), 3.

14. Taylor Fravel and Christopher P. Twomey, "Projecting Strategy: The Myth of Chinese Counter-Intervention," *Washington Quarterly* 37, no. 4 (2015): 171–87.

15. For a precinct work on the implications and limitations of these trends in a conflict over Taiwan, see Richard C. Bush and Michael E. O'Hanlon, *A War Like No Other: The Truth about China's Challenge to America* (New York: John Wiley & Sons, 2007).

16. There are several excellent Western studies on China's doctrinal shifts, particularly on the evolution from the focus on "local wars" to the focus on "local wars under high-tech conditions" and ultimately to "local wars under high-tech informatized conditions." The definitive study is Taylor Fravel, *Active Defense: China's Military Strategy since 1949* (Princeton: Princeton University Press, 2019). See also Dennis J. Blasko, "China's Evolving Approach to Strategic Deterrence," in *China's Evolving Military Strategy*, ed. Joe McReynolds (Washington, DC: Brookings Institution Press, 2018), 335–55; You Ji, *China's Military Transformation* (Malden, MA: Polity, 2016); Dennis J. Blasko, *The Chinese Army Today: Tradition and Transformation for the 21st Century* (New York: Routledge, 2006); Paul Godwin, "Change and Continuity in Chinese Military Doctrine: 1949–1999," in *Chinese Warfighting: The PLA Experience since 1949*, eds. David M. Finkelstein, Mark A. Ryan, and Michael A. McDevitt (Armonk: M.E. Sharpe, 2003), 23–55; and Ellis Joffe, *The Chinese Army after Mao* (Cambridge, MA: Harvard University Press, 1987).

17. Liu Huaqing [刘华清], "Unswervingly Advance along the Road of Building a Modern Army with Chinese Characteristics [坚定不移地沿着建设有中国特色现代化军队的道路前进]," *PLA Daily [解放军报]*, August 6, 1993.

18. Ibid.

19. Zhang Zhen [张震], *Memoirs of Zhang Zhen [张震回忆录]*, vol. 2 (下) (Beijing: Liberation Army Press [解放军出版社], 2004), 359, 361.

20. Zhang Wannian Writing Group [张万年写作组], *Biography of Zhang Wannian [张万年传]*, vol. 2, [下], 60.

21. Chi Haotian Writing Group [迟浩田写作组], *Biography of Chi Haotian [迟浩田传]* (Beijing: Liberation Army Press [解放军出版社], 2009), 352–354. Emphasis added.

22. Zhang Zhen [张震], *Memoirs of Zhang Zhen [张震回忆录]*, vol. 2 (下), 361; Group [张万年写作组], *Biography of Zhang Wannian [张万年传]*, vol. 2, [下], vol. 2, 59.

23. A full version appears in "中华复兴与世界未来." Major excerpts are included in the Willy Wo-Lap Lam, "American Ties Are in the Firing Line," *South China Morning Post*, February 27, 1991. A significantly edited version of the memo appears in He Xin [何新], *Selected Works of Hexin on Political Economy [何新政治经济论文集]* (Beijing: Heilong Jiang Education Publishing House [黑龙江教育出版社], 1995), 403–6. See also Haarlan W. Jencks, "Chinese Evaluations of 'Desert Storm': Implications for PRC Security," *Journal of East Asian Affairs* 6, no. 2 (1992): 455–56; and Lam, "American Ties Are in the Firing Line."

24. Johnston, "Toward Contextualizing the Concept of Shashoujian (Assassin's Mace)."

25. Ibid.

26. Cited in Andrew S. Erickson, *Chinese Anti-Ship Ballistic Missile (ASBM) Development: Drivers, Trajectories, and Strategic Implications* (Washington, DC: Jamestown Foundation, 2013), 36. Emphasis added.

27. Cited in Bruzdzinski, "Demystifying Shashoujian," 324. Emphasis added.

28. Xi Jinping [习近平], "The Full Text of Xi Jinping's Speech at the Forum on Cybersecurity and Informatization Work-Xinhuanet [习近平在网信工作座谈会上的讲话全文发表-新华网]," April 25, 2016, http://www.xinhuanet.com//politics/2016-04/25/c_1118731175.htm.

29. Pillsbury, *China Debates the Future Security Environment*; Johnston, "Toward Contextualizing the Concept of Shashoujian (Assassin's Mace)."

30. These sources are summarized in Jencks, "Chinese Evaluations of 'Desert Storm,'" 454. Other excellent surveys of the Gulf War's impact around found in Fravel, *Active Defense*; Pillsbury, *China Debates the Future Security Environment*; Ellis Joffe, "China after the Gulf War" (Kaohsiung: Sun Yatsen Center for Policy Studies, May 1991); David Shambaugh, *Modernizing China's Military* (Berkeley: University of California Press, 2003); Godwin, "Change and Continuity in Chinese Military Doctrine"; and Blasko, *The Chinese Army Today*. One excellent volume explores how China studied other's conflicts: Andrew Scobell, David Lai, and Roy Kamphausen, eds.,

Chinese Lessons from Other People's Wars (Carlisle, PA: Strategic Studies Institute, 2011). The *China Quarterly*'s special 1996 issue has several works that touch on these themes. See David Shambaugh, "China's Military in Transition: Politics, Professionalism, Procurement and Power Projection," *China Quarterly*, no. 146 (1996): 265–98.

31. Chi Haotian [迟浩田], *Chi Haotian Military Writings* [迟浩田军事文选] (Beijing: Liberation Army Press [解放军出版社], 2009), 282.

32. Jencks, "Chinese Evaluations of 'Desert Storm,'" 454.

33. Zhang Wannian Writing Group [张万年写作组], *Biography of Zhang Wannian* [张万年传], vol. 2, [下], 59.

34. Chi Haotian Writing Group [迟浩田写作组], *Biography of Chi Haotian* [迟浩田传], 326. Emphasis added.

35. Zhang Zhen [张震], *Memoirs of Zhang Zhen* [张震回忆录], vol. 2, 361.

36. Ibid.

37. Chi Haotian [迟浩田], *Chi Haotian Military Writings* [迟浩田军事文选], 282.

38. Ibid., 282.

39. Ibid., 283. Emphasis added.

40. Ibid., 283. Emphasis added.

41. Ibid., 287.

42. Ibid., 287. Emphasis added.

43. Ibid., 326.

44. Ibid., 327.

45. Zhang Zhen, *Memoirs of Zhang Zhen*, vol. 2, (下), 394.

46. Zhang Wannian Writing Group [张万年写作组], *Biography of Zhang Wannian* [张万年传], vol. 2, [下], 63.

47. Chi Haotian Writing Group [迟浩田写作组], *Biography of Chi Haotian* [迟浩田传], 327; Zhang Zhen [张震], *Memoirs of Zhang Zhen* [张震回忆录], vol. 2, (下), 361.

48. Zhang Zhen [张震], *Memoirs of Zhang Zhen* [张震回忆录], vol. 2, (下), 362.

49. Ibid., vol. 2 (下), 364.

50. Ibid., vol. 2 (下), 364.

51. Ibid., vol. 2 (下), 364–65.

52. Liu Huaqing [刘华清], "Unswervingly Advance along the Road of Building a Modern Army with Chinese Characteristics [坚定不移地沿着建设有中国特色现代化军队的道路前进]."

53. Ibid.

54. Ibid. Emphasis added.

55. Ibid. Emphasis added.

56. Ibid.

57. Zhang Wannian Writing Group [张万年写作组], *Biography of Zhang Wannian* [张万年传], vol. 2, [下],165–67. Emphasis added.

58. Liu Huaqing [刘华清], "Unswervingly Advance along the Road of Building a Modern Army with Chinese Characteristics." [坚定不移地沿着建设有中国特色现代化军队的道路前进]."

59. Zhang Wannian Writing Group [张万年写作组], *Biography of Zhang Wannian* [张万年传], vol. 2 [下], 164. Jiang Zemin [江泽民], *Jiang Zemin Selected Works* [江泽民文选], vol. 2 [第二卷] (Beijing: People's Press [人民出版社], 2006), 85, 161, 544.

60. Zhang Wannian Writing Group [张万年写作组], *Biography of Zhang Wannian* [张万年传], vol. 2, [下], 169–71.

61. Ibid., vol. 2 [下], 165–67.

62. Ibid., vol. 2 [下], 170–71.

63. Zhang Wannian [张万年], *Zhang Wannian Military Writings* [张万年军事文选] (Beijing: Liberation Army Press [解放军出版社], 2008), 732.

64. Zhang Zhen [张震], *Memoirs of Zhang Zhen* [张震回忆录], vol. 2 (下), 390.

65. Ibid., vol. 2 (下), 390.

66. Ibid., vol. 2 (下), 391–93.

67. Ibid., vol. 2 (下), 391–93.

68. Zhang Wannian Writing Group [张万年写作组], *Biography of Zhang Wannian*, [张万年传], vol. 2 [下],165.

69. Ibid., vol. 2 [下], 82.
70. Ibid., vol. 2 [下], 169–70.
71. Ibid., vol. 2 [下], 170.
72. Ibid., vol. 2 [下], 81.
73. Ibid., vol. 2 [下], 169.
74. Ibid., vol. 2 [下], 415.
75. Ibid., vol. 2 [下], 415–17.
76. Ibid., vol. 2 [下], 420.
77. Ibid., vol. 2 [下], 419.
78. Ibid., vol. 2 [下], 419.
79. Zhang Wannian [张万年], *Zhang Wannian Military Writings [张万年军事文选]*, 732.
80. The 2001 and English-translated 2005 version of the *Science of Military Strategy*, which are identical, include this language. Similar language is found in other versions. See Peng Guangqian [彭光谦] and Yao Youzhi [姚有志], *The Science of Military Strategy [战略学]* (Beijing: Military Science Press [军事科学出版社], 2005), 451.
81. "Establishing Party Command Capable of Creating a Style of a Victorious Army [建设一支听党指挥能打胜仗作风优良的人民军队]," *People's Daily Online [人民网]*, July 14, 2014, http://opinion.people.com.cn/n/2014/0714/c1003-25279852.html. This source was initially quoted in Timothy Heath and Andrew S. Erickson, "Is China Pursuing Counter-Intervention?," *Washington Quarterly* 38, no. 3 (2015): 149. See also Wang Wenrong [王文荣], *The Science of Military Strategy [战略学]* (Beijing: National Defense University Press [国防大学出版社], 1999), 308; Shou Xiaosong [寿晓松], *The Science of Military Strategy [战略学]* (Beijing: Military Science Press [军事科学出版社], 2013), 100.
82. Li Yousheng [李有升], *Joint Campaign Studies Guidebook [联合战役学教程]* (Beijing: Academy of Military Science [军事科学院], 2012), 199. Emphasis added
83. Li Yousheng [李有升], *Joint Campaign Studies Guidebook*, 269.
84. James Mulvenon, "The Crucible of Tragedy: SARS, the Ming 361 Accident, and Chinese Party-Army Relations," *China Leadership Monitor*, no. 8 (October 30, 2003): 1–12.
85. "Foreign Ministry Spokesperson's Answers to Journalists' Questions at the Press Conference on May 8, 2003 [2003年5月8日外交部发言人在记者招待会上答记者问]," Foreign Ministry of the People's Republic of China [中华人民共和国外交部], May 8, 2003, https://www.fmprc.gov.cn/web/fyrbt_673021/dhdw_673027/t24552.shtml.
86. Harvey B. Stockwin, "No Glasnost Yet for the Victims of Submarine 361," *Jamestown China Brief* 3, no. 12 (June 17, 2003), https://jamestown.org/program/no-glasnost-yet-for-the-victims-of-submarine-361/.
87. Sebastien Roblin, "In 2003, a Chinese Submarine Was Lost at Sea," *The National Interest*, March 25, 2018, https://nationalinterest.org/blog/the-buzz/2003-chinese-submarine-was-lost-sea-how-the-crew-died-25072.
88. Yves-Heng Lim, *China's Naval Power: An Offensive Realist Approach* (Burlington: Ashgate, 2014), 90; "The PLA Navy: New Capabilities and Missions for the 21st Century" (Washington, DC: Office of Naval Intelligence, 2015). See also Stephen Saunders, *Jane's Fighting Ships 2015–2016* (Couldson: IHS Jane's, 2015).
89. "The PLA Navy."
90. Lim, *China's Naval Power*, 90; Liu Huaqing [刘华清], *Memoirs of Liu Huaqing [刘华清回忆录]* (Beijing: Revolutionary Army Press [解放军出版社], 2004), 477.
91. Lim, *China's Naval Power*, 90.
92. Andrew S. Erickson and Lyle J. Goldstein, "China's Future Nuclear Submarine Force: Insights from Chinese Writings," in *China's Future Nuclear Submarine Force*, eds. Andrew S. Erickson et al. (Annapolis, MD: Naval Institute Press, 2007), 199.
93. William S. Murray, "An Overview of the PLAN Submarine Force," in *China's Future Nuclear Submarine Force*, eds. Andrew S. Erickson et al. (Annapolis, MD: Naval Institute Press, 2007), 59.
94. Erickson and Goldstein, "China's Future Nuclear Submarine Force," 191.
95. "The PLA Navy," 19.
96. Erickson and Goldstein, "China's Future Nuclear Submarine Force," 188–91.
97. Murray, "An Overview of the PLAN Submarine Force," 65.

98. Erickson and Goldstein, "China's Future Nuclear Submarine Force," 192.

99. Ibid.

100. Andrew S. Erickson, Lyle J. Goldstein, and William S. Murray, *Chinese Mine Warfare: A PLA Navy "Assassin's Mace" Capability* (Newport, RI: Naval War College Press, 2009), 9.

101. R. W. Apple, "War in the Gulf: The Overview; 2 U.S. Ships Badly Damaged by Iraqi Mines in Persian Gulf," *New York Times*, February 19, 1991, https://www.nytimes.com/1991/02/19/world/war-gulf-overview-2-us-ships-badly-damaged-iraqi-mines-persian-gulf.html.

102. Richard Pyle, "Two Navy Ships Strike Mines in Persian Gulf, 7 Injured," *Associated Press*, February 18, 1991, https://apnews.com/article/f9c1f4aa006d0436adeaadf100fa6640.

103. Rod Thornton, *Asymmetric Warfare: Threat and Response in the 21st Century* (New York: Wiley, 2007), 117.

104. "The PLA Navy," 24.

105. Ibid.

106. Erickson, Goldstein, and Murray, *Chinese Mine Warfare*, 9.

107. "The PLA Navy," 24; Erickson, Goldstein, and Murray, *Chinese Mine Warfare*, 44.

108. Erickson, Goldstein, and Murray, *Chinese Mine Warfare*, 3–5.

109. Quoted in ibid., 5.

110. Ibid., 20.

111. Ibid., 21.

112. Ibid., 21.

113. Quoted in ibid., 44.

114. Ibid., 44.

115. Ibid., 41.

116. Ibid., 41.

117. Ibid., 43.

118. Bernard D. Cole, *The Great Wall at Sea: China's Navy Enters the Twenty-First Century* (Annapolis, MD: Naval Institute Press, 2001), 156.

119. Erickson, Goldstein, and Murray, *Chinese Mine Warfare*, 33.

120. Ibid., 33–34.

121. Ibid., 33–34.

122. Chi Haotian Writing Group [迟浩田写作组], *Biography of Chi Haotian* [迟浩田传], 357.

123. Ibid.

124. Ibid.

125. Ibid.

126. Erickson, *Chinese Anti-Ship Ballistic Missile (ASBM) Development*, 71.

127. Ibid., 50.

128. "The 'Long Sword' Owes Its Sharpness to the Whetstone—A Witness's Account of the Build-Up of the Two Capabilities of a Certain New Type of Missile," in *Glorious Era: Reflecting on the Second Artillery's Development and Advances during the Period of Reform and Opening* [辉煌年代回顾在改革开放中发展前进的第二炮兵] (Beijing: CCP Central Committee Literature Publishing House [中央文献出版社], 2008), 681–82. Emphasis added.

129. Chi Haotian Writing Group [迟浩田写作组], *Biography of Chi Haotian* [迟浩田传], 357.

130. Erickson, *Chinese Anti-Ship Ballistic Missile (ASBM) Development*, 31.

131. Yu Jixun [于际训], *The Science of Second Artillery Campaigns* [第二炮兵战役学] (Beijing: Liberation Army Press [解放军出版社], 2004).

132. Quoted in Erickson, *Chinese Anti-Ship Ballistic Missile (ASBM) Development*, 27.

133. Quoted in ibid., 70.

134. Quoted in ibid., 70.

135. Ibid., 29–30.

136. Ron Christman, "Conventional Missions for China's Second Artillery Corps," *Comparative Strategy* 30, no. 3 (2011): 211–12, 216–20. See also endnote 91.

137. This quote appears in multiple accounts. See Andrew Erickson, "China's Ministry of National Defense: 1st Aircraft Carrier 'Liaoning' Handed Over to PLA Navy," September 25, 2012, https://www.andrewerickson.com/2012/09/chinas-ministry-of-national-defense-1st-aircraft-carrier-liaoning-handed-over-to-pla-navy/; Huang Jingjing, "Chinese

Public Eagerly Awaits Commissioning of Second Aircraft Carrier," *Global Times*, April 6, 2016, https://www.globaltimes.cn/content/977459.shtml.

138. Michael Horowitz, *The Diffusion of Military Power* (Princeton: Princeton University Press, 2010), 68.

139. Ibid., 65.

140. Ian Storey and You Ji, "China's Aircraft Carrier Ambitions: Seeking Truth from Rumors," *Naval War College Review* 57, no. 1 (2004): 90.

141. Tai Ming Cheung, *Growth of Chinese Naval Power* (Singapore: Institute of Southeast Asian Studies, 1990), 27. See also John Wilson Lewis and Xue Litai, *China Builds the Bomb* (Stanford, CA: Stanford University Press, 1988).

142. Liu Huaqing [刘华清], *Memoirs of Liu Huaqing* [刘华清回忆录], 480.

143. Ibid.

144. Storey and You Ji, "China's Aircraft Carrier Ambitions," 79.

145. Minnie Chan, "Mission Impossible: How One Man Bought China Its First Aircraft Carrier," *South China Morning Post*, January 18, 2015, http://www.scmp.com/news/china/article/1681710/sea-trials-how-one-man-bought-china-its-aircraft-carrier.

146. "Gorshkov Deal Finalised at USD 2.3 Billion," *The Hindu*, March 10, 2010, http://www.thehindu.com/news/national/gorshkov-deal-finalised-at-usd-23-billion/article228791.ece.

147. Zheng Dao, "Voyage of the Varyag," *Caixin*, July 27, 2011, http://english.caixin.com/2011-07-27/100284342.html?p2.

148. Ibid.

149. Minnie Chan, "PLA Brass 'Defied Beijing' over Plan to Buy China's First Aircraft Carrier Liaoning," *South China Morning Post*, April 29, 2015, https://www.scmp.com/news/china/diplomacy-defence/article/1779721/pla-brass-defied-beijing-over-plan-buy-aircraft-carrier.

150. See Liu Huaqing's obituary in *Xinhua*, "Liu Huaqing, Father of the Modern Navy [现代海军之父刘华清]," *Xinhua*, January 15, 2011, http://news.xinhuanet.com/mil/2011-01/15/c_12983881.htm.

151. You Ji, "The Supreme Leader and the Military," in *The Nature of Chinese Politics*, ed. Jonathan Unger (New York: M. E. Sharpe, 2002), 195.

152. This quote appears in multiple accounts. See Erickson, "China's Ministry of National Defense"; Huang Jingjing, "Chinese Public Eagerly Awaits Commissioning of Second Aircraft Carrier."

153. Liu Huaqing [刘华清], *Memoirs of Liu Huaqing* [刘华清回忆录], 478.

154. Ibid., 479–80.

155. *Liu Huaqing Chronicles* [刘华清年谱] *1916–2011*, vol. 3 [下卷] (Beijing: Liberation Army Press [解放军出版社], 2016), 1195.

156. Minnie Chan, "The Inside Story of the Liaoning: How Xu Zengping Sealed the Deal for China's First Aircraft Carrier," *South China Morning Post*, January 19, 2015, https://www.scmp.com/news/china/article/1681755/how-xu-zengping-became-middleman-chinas-deal-buy-liaoning. Parentheticals are in the original.

157. Andrew S. Erickson and Andrew R. Wilson, "China's Aircraft Carrier Dilemma," *Naval War College Review* 59, no. 4 (2006): 19.

158. You Ji, "The Supreme Leader and the Military"; You Ji, *China's Military Transformation*, 194–95; Robert S. Ross, "China's Naval Nationalism Sources, Prospects, and the U.S. Response," *International Security* 34, no. 2 (2009): 46–81.

159. You Ji, *China's Military Transformation*, 195.

160. "The Significance of the Varyag Aircraft Carrier to China's National Strategy Is Something That Cannot Be Purchased with Money [瓦良格号航母对中国意义国家战略金钱买不来]," *Sina.com* [新浪财经], March 24, 2015, http://mil.news.sina.com.cn/2015-03-24/1058825518.html; *Liu Huaqing Chronicles* [刘华清年谱] *1916-2011*, vol. 3 [下卷] (Beijing: Liberation Army Press [解放军出版社], 2016), 1195.

161. Liu Huaqing [刘华清], *Memoirs of Liu Huaqing* [刘华清回忆录], 480.

162. Tai Ming Cheung, *Growth of Chinese Naval Power*, 27.

163. Tai Ming Cheung, *Growth of Chinese Naval Power*, 40.

164. Erickson and Wilson, "China's Aircraft Carrier Dilemma," 27.

165. Ye Zicheng [叶自成], "China's Sea Power Must Be Subordinate to Its Land Power [中国海权须从属于陆权]," *International Herald Leader* [国际先驱导报], March 2, 2007, http://news.xinhuanet.com/herald/2007-03/02/content_5790944.htm.

166. Ye Zicheng mentions a number of platforms, all of which could be used for denial purposes. His blog is no longer available, but excerpts can be found here: Christopher Griffin and Joseph Lin, "Fighting Words," American Enterprise Institute, April 27, 2007, http://www.aei.org/publication/fighting-words-3/print/; Ye Zicheng 叶自成, "China's Sea Power Must Be Subordinate to Its Land Power [中国海权须从属于陆权]."

167. Quoted in You Ji, *China's Military Transformation*, 195.

Chapter 5

1. Wang Yizhou [王逸舟], *Global Politics and Chinese Diplomacy* [全球政治和中国外交] (Beijing: World Knowledge Press [世界知识出版社], 2003), 274.

2. Wang Yusheng [王嵎生], *Personally Experiencing APEC: A Chinese Official's Observations and Experiences* [亲历APEC: 一个中国高官的体察- 王嵎生] (Beijing: World Knowledge Press [世界知识出版社], 2000), 36.

3. Ibid., 36.

4. Ibid., 36.

5. Ibid., 168.

6. Ibid., 62.

7. Ibid., 62.

8. There is a rich literature on China's institutional participation. See Scott L. Kastner, Margaret M. Pearson, and Chad Rector, *China's Strategic Multilateralism: Investing in Global Governance* (Cambridge: Cambridge University Press, 2018); Hoo Tiang Boon, *China's Global Identity: Considering the Responsibilities of Great Power* (Washington, DC: Georgetown University Press, 2018); David Shambaugh, *China Goes Global: The Partial Power* (Oxford: Oxford University Press, 2013); Marc Lanteigne, *China and International Institutions: Alternate Paths to Global Power* (New York: Routledge, 2005); and Elizabeth Economy and Michael Oksenberg, *China Joins the World: Progress and Prospects* (New York: Council on Foreign Relations Press, 1999).

9. Kai He, *Institutional Balancing in the Asia Pacific: Economic Interdependence and China's Rise* (New York: Routledge, 2009), 36.

10. Wu Jiao, "The Multilateral Path," *China Daily*, June 1, 2011, http://www.chinadaily.com.cn/china/cd30thanniversary/2011-06/01/content_12620510.htm.

11. Ibid.

12. Wang Yusheng [王嵎生], *Personally Experiencing APEC: A Chinese Official's Observations and Experiences* [亲历APEC: 一个中国高官的体察- 王嵎生], 30.

13. I have a version of this report, but it is not public. It is, however, very similar to an article Zhang Yunling published in a Chinese journal. So that others may reference this material, I cite the Chinese journal article here in lieu of the report. Zhang Yunling [张蕴岭], "The Comprehensive Security Concept and Reflecting on China's Security [综合安全观及对我国安全的思考]," *Contemporary Asia-Pacific* [当代亚太], no. 1 (2000): 4–16.

14. Ibid., 9.

15. Ibid., 11.

16. Ibid., 9.

17. Shi Yuanhua [石源华], "On the Historical Evolution of the Zhoubian Waijiao Policy of New China [论新中国周边外交政策的历史演变]," *Contemporary China History Studies* [当代中国史研究] 7, no. 5 (2000): 47.

18. See Jiang's 14th Party Congress speech in Jiang Zemin [江泽民], "Accelerating the Reform, the Opening to the Outside World and the Drive for Modernization, so as to Achieve Greater Successes in Building Socialism with Chinese Characteristics [加快改革开放和现代化建设步伐 夺取有中国特色社会主义事业的更大胜利]," 14th Party Congress Political Report (Beijing, October 12, 1992).

19. Hu Jintao [胡锦涛], *Hu Jintao Selected Works* [胡锦涛文选], vol. 2 [第二卷] (Beijing: People's Press [人民出版社], 2016), 508.

20. Zhang Yunling and Tang Shiping, "China's Regional Strategy," in *Power Shift: China and Asia's New Dynamics*, ed. David L. Shambaugh (Berkeley: University of California Press, 2005), 52.

21. 在和平,发展,合作的旗帜下: 中国战略机遇期的对外战略纵论 252, Quoted in Suisheng Zhao, "China and East Asian Regional Cooperation: Institution-Building Efforts, Strategic Calculations, and Preference for Informal Approach," in *China and East Asian Strategic Dynamics: The Shaping of a New Regional Order*, eds. Mingjiang Li and Dongmin Lee (Rowman & Littlefield, 2011), 152.

22. Zhang Yunling and Tang Shiping, "China's Regional Strategy," 50.

23. Susan Shirk, "Chinese Views on Asia-Pacific Regional Security Cooperation," *NBR Analysis* 5, no. 5 (1994): 8.

24. Nayan Chanda, "Gentle Giant," *Far Eastern Economic Review*, August 4, 1994.

25. Wu Xinbo, "Chinese Perspectives on Building an East Asian Community in the Twenty-First Century," in *Asia's New Multilateralism: Cooperation, Competition, and the Search for Community*, eds. Michael J. Green and Bates Gill (New York: Columbia University Press, 2009), 59.

26. Jiang Zemin [江泽民], *Jiang Zemin Selected Works* [江泽民文选], vol. 3 [第三卷] (Beijing: People's Press [人民出版社], 2006), 314–15.

27. Jiang Zemin [江泽民], *Jiang Zemin Selected Works*, vol. 3 [第三卷], 314–15.

28. Ibid., vol. 3 [第三卷], 314–15.

29. Ibid., vol. 3 [第三卷], 314–15.

30. Ibid., vol. 3 [第三卷], 317.

31. Ibid., vol. 3 [第三卷], 313, 318.

32. Zhang Yunling, *Rising China and World Order* (New York: World Scientific, 2010), 8.

33. Ibid., 8.

34. Ibid., 19.

35. Zhang Yunling [张蕴岭], "The Comprehensive Security Concept and Reflecting on China's Security [综合安全观及对我国安全的思考]," 11.

36. Zhang Yunling and Tang Shiping, "China's Regional Strategy," 54, 56.

37. Wang Yizhou [王逸舟], *Global Politics and Chinese Diplomacy* [全球政治和中国外交], 274.

38. Jiang Zemin [江泽民], "Hold High the Great Banner of Deng Xiaoping Theory for an All-Round Advancement of the Cause of Building Socialism with Chinese Characteristics into the 21st Century [高举邓小平理论伟大旗帜，把建设有中国特色社会主义事业全面推向二十一世纪]," 15th Party Congress Political Report (Beijing, September 12, 1997).

39. Jiang Zemin [江泽民], *Jiang Zemin Selected Works* [江泽民文选], vol. 2 [第二卷] (Beijing: People's Press [人民出版社}, 2006), 205–6.

40. This shift is clear in comparing the 2000 and 2002 Chinese National Defense White Papers. See also Evan S. Medeiros, *China's International Behavior: Activism, Opportunism, and Diversification* (Santa Monica, CA: RAND, 2009), 169.

41. Jiang Zemin [江泽民], *Jiang Zemin Selected Works* [江泽民文选], 2006, vol. 2 [第二卷], 195.

42. Ibid., vol. 3 [第三卷], 355.

43. Ibid., vol. 3 [第三卷], 355.

44. Wang Yi, "Facilitating the Development of Multilateralism and Promoting World Multi-Polarization," Foreign Ministry of the People's Republic of China, August 20, 2004, https://www.fmprc.gov.cn/mfa_eng/wjb_663304/zzjg_663340/gjs_665170/gjzzyhy_665174/2616_665220/2617_665222/t151077.shtml.

45. Hu Jintao [胡锦涛], *Hu Jintao Selected Works* [胡锦涛文选] , vol. 2 [第二卷], 445.

46. Ibid., vol. 2 [第二卷], 516.

47. Jiang Zemin [江泽民], *Jiang Zemin Selected Works* [江泽民文选], 2006, vol. 2 [第二卷], 546–47.

48. Wu Xinbo, "Chinese Perspectives on Building an East Asian Community in the Twenty-First Century," 56.

49. Chien-peng Chung, *China's Multilateral Co-Operation in Asia and the Pacific: Institutionalizing Beijing's "Good Neighbour Policy"* (New York: Routledge, 2010), 30.

50. Ibid., 37.

51. Ibid., 15.

52. He, *Institutional Balancing in the Asia Pacific*, 33.

53. Wang Yusheng [王嵎生], *Personally Experiencing APEC: A Chinese Official's Observations and Experiences* [亲历APEC: 一个中国高官的体察- 王嵎生], 29.

54. Ibid., 29.

55. Ibid., 4.

56. Ibid., 4–5.

57. William J. Clinton, "Remarks to the Seattle APEC Host Committee" (Seattle, November 19, 1993), http://www.presidency.ucsb.edu/ws/?pid=46137.

58. Wang Yusheng, *Personally Experiencing APEC*, [王嵎生], *Personally Experiencing APEC: A Chinese Official's Observations and Experiences* [亲历APEC: 一个中国高官的体察- 王嵎生], 5.

59. Ibid., 37. Emphasis added.

60. Ibid., 37. Emphasis added.

61. David E. Sanger, "Clinton's Goals for Pacific Trade Are Seen as a Hard Sell at Summit," *New York Times*, November 14, 1993.

62. Wu Jiao, "The Multilateral Path."

63. "Speech by President Jiang Zemin at the Informal APEC Leadership Conference, November 20, 1993," China Ministry of Foreign Affairs, http://www.fmprc.gov.cn/eng/wjdt/zyjh/t24903.htm.

64. Wang Yusheng, *Personally Experiencing APEC*, [王嵎生], *Personally Experiencing APEC: A Chinese Official's Observations and Experiences* [亲历APEC: 一个中国高官的体察-王嵎生], 166–67.

65. Ibid., 167.

66. Ibid., 103–6.

67. Ibid., 102–3.

68. Ibid., 116.

69. Clinton, "Remarks to the Seattle APEC Host Committee."

70. He, *Institutional Balancing in the Asia Pacific*, 70.

71. Frank Langdon and Brian L. Job, "APEC beyond Economics: The Politics of APEC" (University of Notre Dame, October 1997), 14, https://kellogg.nd.edu/sites/default/files/old_files/documents/243_0.pdf.

72. Wang Yusheng, *Personally Experiencing APEC*, [王嵎生], *Personally Experiencing APEC: A Chinese Official's Observations and Experiences* [亲历APEC: 一个中国高官的体察-王嵎生], 114–15.

73. Thomas G. Moore and Dixia Yang, "China, APEC, and Economic Regionalism in the Asia-Pacific," *Journal of East Asian Affairs* 13, no. 2 (1999): 402.

74. Wang Yusheng, *Personally Experiencing APEC*, [王嵎生], *Personally Experiencing APEC: A Chinese Official's Observations and Experiences* [亲历APEC: 一个中国高官的体察-王嵎生], 63.

75. Moore and Yang, "China, APEC, and Economic Regionalism in the Asia-Pacific," 390.

76. Wang Yusheng, *Personally Experiencing APEC*, [王嵎生], *Personally Experiencing APEC: A Chinese Official's Observations and Experiences* [亲历APEC: 一个中国高官的体察-王嵎生], 84.

77. For example, see Jiang Zemin, "Speech by President Jiang Zemin at the Sixth APEC Informal Leadership Meeting," Ministry of Foreign Affairs of the People's Republic of China, November 15, 2000, https://www.fmprc.gov.cn/mfa_eng/wjb_663304/zzjg_663340/gjs_665170/gjzzyhy_665174/2604_665196/2606_665200/t15276.shtml.

78. Wang Yusheng, *Personally Experiencing APEC*, [王嵎生], *Personally Experiencing APEC: A Chinese Official's Observations and Experiences* [亲历APEC: 一个中国高官的体察-王嵎生], 156.

79. "Tiananmen: Another Bump in China's Road to WTO Accession," Association for Diplomatic Studies and Training, 2016, https://adst.org/2016/04/tiananmen-another-bump-in-chinas-road-to-wto-accession/.

80. Quoted in Moore and Yang, "China, APEC, and Economic Regionalism in the Asia-Pacific," 394.

81. Chris Buckley, "Qian Qichen, Pragmatic Chinese Envoy, Dies at 89," *New York Times*, May 11, 2017, http://www.nytimes.com/2017/05/11/world/asia/qian-qichen-dead-china-foreign-minister.html.

82. "Qian Qichen," *People's Daily*, n.d., http://en.people.cn/data/people/qianqichen.shtml.

83. Chanda, "Gentle Giant."

84. Ibid.

85. Ibid.

86. Ibid.

87. Ibid.

88. Ibid.

89. Chien-peng Chung, "China's Policies towards the SCO and ARF: Implications for the Asia-Pacific Region," in *Rise of China: Beijing's Strategies and Implications for the Asia-Pacific*, eds. Xinhuang Xiao and Zhengyi Lin (New York: Routledge, 2009), 170.

90. Bates Gill, *Rising Star: China's New Security Diplomacy* (Washington, DC: Brookings, 2007), 32.

91. Rosemary Foot, "China in the ASEAN Regional Forum: Organizational Processes and Domestic Modes of Thought," *Asian Survey* 38, no. 5 (1998): 426.

92. Zhang Yunling [张蕴岭], "The Comprehensive Security Concept and Reflecting on China's Security [综合安全观及对我国安全的思考]," 11.

93. Wu Xinbo, "Chinese Perspectives on Building an East Asian Community in the Twenty-First Century," 56.

94. Chung, *China's Multilateral Co-Operation in Asia and the Pacific*, 51.

95. Ibid.

96. He, *Institutional Balancing in the Asia Pacific*, 36.

97. Ibid.

98. See Foot, "China in the ASEAN Regional Forum," 432; Alastair Iain Johnston, *Social States: China in International Institutions, 1980–2000* (Princeton: Princeton University Press, 2008), 185–86; He, *Institutional Balancing in the Asia Pacific*, 37; Chung, *China's Multilateral Co-Operation in Asia and the Pacific*, 45.

99. Johnston, *Social States*, 183.

100. Chung, *China's Multilateral Co-Operation in Asia and the Pacific*, 52.

101. Ibid.

102. Ibid.

103. Ibid.

104. Takeshi Yuzawa, "The Fallacy of Socialization?: Rethinking the ASEAN Way of Institution-Building," in *ASEAN and the Institutionalization of East Asia*, ed. Ralf Emmers (New York: Routledge, 2012), 79.

105. "Hu Jintao: Jointly Writing a New Chapter of Peace and Development in Asia [胡锦涛：共同谱写亚洲和平与发展的新篇章]," *People's Daily Online* [人民网], April 25, 2002, http://www.people.com.cn/GB/shizheng/252/7944/7952/20020425/716986.html; Lyall Breckon, "Former Tigers," *Comparative Connections* 4, no. 2 (2002), http://cc.csis.org/2002/07/former-tigers-dragons-spell/.Hu.

106. Zhu Rongji, "Address by Premier Zhu Rongji of the People's Republic of China at the Third ASEAN+3 Informal Summit" (Manila, November 28, 1999), http://asean.org/?static_post=address-by-premier-zhu-rongji-of-the-people-s-republic-of-china-at-the-third-asean3-informal-summit-28-november-1999. Zhu Rongji, "Strengthening East Asian Cooperation and Promoting Common Development—Statement by Premier Zhu Rongji of China at the 5th 10+3 Summit" (Bandar Seri Begawan, November 5, 2001), http://www.fmprc.gov.cn/mfa_eng/wjb_663304/zzjg_663340/gjs_665170/gjzzyhy_665174/2616_665220/2618_665224/t15364.shtml.

107. Chung, *China's Multilateral Co-Operation in Asia and the Pacific*, 74.

108. "Towards an East Asian Community Region of Peace, Prosperity and Progress" (East Asian Vision Group, ASEAN Plus Three, October 31, 2001), 14, https://www.asean.org/wp-content/uploads/images/archive/pdf/east_asia_vision.pdf.

109. Robert Sutter, *China's Rise in Asia: Promises and Perils* (New York: Rowman & Littlefield, 2005), 82.

110. Brendan Taylor, "China's 'Unofficial' Diplomacy," in *China's "New" Diplomacy: Tactical or Fundamental Change?*, eds. Pauline Kerr, Stuart Harris, and Qin Yaqing (New York: Palgrave, 2008), 204–5.

111. He, *Institutional Balancing in the Asia Pacific*, 44.

112. Vinod K. Aggarwal, ed., *Asia's New Institutional Architecture: Evolving Structures for Managing Trade, Financial, and Security Relations* (Springer, 2008), 79.

113. Wen Jiabao, "Speech by Premier Wen Jiabao of the People's Republic of China at the Seventh China-ASEAN Summit" (Bali, October 13, 2003).

114. Cui Tiankai, "Speech of Assistant Foreign Minister Cui Tiankai at the Opening Ceremony of the East Asia Investment Forum" (Weihai, August 1, 2006), http://www.fmprc.gov.cn/mfa_eng/wjdt_665385/zyjh_665391/t265874.shtml.

115. Wu Xinbo, "Chinese Perspectives on Building an East Asian Community in the Twenty-First Century," 60.

116. He, *Institutional Balancing in the Asia PacificI*, 44.

117. Ibid., 45.

118. Wu Xinbo, "Chinese Perspectives on Building an East Asian Community in the Twenty-First Century," 60.

119. Ibid.

120. "Chairman's Statement of the First East Asia Summit Kuala Lumpur" (East Asia Summit, Kuala Lumpur, 2005), http://asean.org/?static_post=chairman-s-statement-of-the-first-east-asia-summit-kuala-lumpur-14-december-2005-2.

121. Wu Baiyi, "The Chinese Security Concept and Its Historical Evolution," *Journal of Contemporary China* 27, no. 10 (2001): 278.

122. Chu Shulong, "China and the U.S.-Japan and U.S.-Korea Alliances in a Changing Northeast Asia" (Stanford, CA: Shorenstein APARC, 1999), 10, https://fsi.stanford.edu/sites/default/files/Chu_Shulong.pdf.

123. Quoted in ibid.

124. Foot, "China in the ASEAN Regional Forum," 435; Chu Shulong, "China and the U.S.-Japan and U.S.-Korea Alliances in a Changing Northeast Asia," 8.

125. Chu Shulong, "China and the U.S.-Japan and U.S.-Korea Alliances in a Changing Northeast Asia," 6.

126. Qian Qichen, "Speech by Vice-Premier Qian Qichen at the Asia Society" (New York, March 20, 2001), http://wcm.fmprc.gov.cn/pub/eng/wjdt/zyjh/t25010.htm.

127. "China's Position Paper on the New Security Concept," Ministry of Foreign Affairs of the People's Republic of China, 2002, https://www.fmprc.gov.cn/ce/ceun/eng/xw/t27742.htm.

128. Lyall Breckon, "China Caps a Year of Gains," *Comparative Connections* 4, no. 4 (2002), http://cc.pacforum.org/2003/01/china-caps-year-gains/.

129. Johnston, *Social States*, 189.

130. Ibid., 189.

131. Ibid., 189.

132. Ibid., 136–37.

133. Yahuda, "China's Multilateralism and Regional Order."

134. Gill, *Rising Star*, 100.

135. Lijun Shen, "China and ASEAN in Asian Regional Integration," in *China and the New International Order*, eds. Gungwu Wang and Yongnian Zheng (New York: Routledge, 2008), 257.

136. Foot, "China in the ASEAN Regional Forum," 431.

137. Medeiros, *China's International Behavior*, 129–31.

138. Alice D. Ba, "Who's Socializing Whom?: Complex Engagement in Sino-ASEAN Relations," *Pacific Review* 19, no. 2 (2006): 172.

139. Chung, *China's Multilateral Co-Operation in Asia and the Pacific*, 73–74.

140. Chi Haotian Writing Group [迟浩田写作组], *Biography of Chi Haotian* [迟浩田传] (Beijing: Liberation Army Press [解放军出版社], 2009), 407.

141. Ibid.

142. Ibid.

143. Ibid.
144. Dai Bingguo [戴秉国], *Strategic Dialogues: Dai Binguo's Memoirs* [战略对话：戴秉国回忆录] (People's Press [人民出版社], 2016), 194.
145. Jianwei Wang, "China and SCO: Toward a New Type of Interstate Relation," in *China Turns to Multilateralism: Foreign Policy and Regional Security*, eds. Guoguang Wu and Helen Lansdowne (New York: Routledge, 2008), 104–15.
146. Richard Weitz, "The Shanghai Cooperation Organization (SCO): Rebirth and Regeneration?," Center for Security Studies, October 10, 2014, https://www.ethz.ch/content/specialinterest/gess/cis/center-for-securities-studies/en/services/digital-library/articles/article.html/184270.
147. Thomas Wallace, "China and the Regional Counter-Terrorism Structure: An Organizational Analysis," *Asian Security* 10, no. 3 (2014): 205.
148. Ibid., 205–6.
149. Ibid., 200.
150. Ibid., 210.
151. "Russian-Chinese Joint Declaration on a Multipolar World and the Establishment of a New International Order," April 23, 1997, http://www.un.org/documents/ga/docs/52/plenary/a52-153.htm. Emphasis added.
152. "Joint Declaration by the Participants in the Almaty Meeting," July 3, 1998, http://repository.un.org/bitstream/handle/11176/177192/A_52_978-EN.pdf?sequence=3&isAllowed=y.
153. Michael Walker, "Russia and China Plug a 'Multipolar Order,'" *The Straits Times*, September 1, 1999.
154. Ibid.
155. Ibid.
156. See the SCO Charter and the 2001, 2002, 2003, 2006, 2009, 2011, 2012 declarations, all of which contain this language. Other declarations convey similar ideas in slightly different terms.
157. "Yekaterinburg Declaration, 2009," June 16, 2009.
158. Wang, "China and SCO," 110.
159. Ibid.
160. Olga Oliker and David A. Shlapak, *U.S. Interests in Central Asia: Policy Priorities and Military Roles* (Arlington, VA: RAND, 2005), 12.
161. Ibid., 11–16.
162. Weiqing Song, *China's Approach to Central Asia: The Shanghai Co-Operation Organisation* (New York: Routledge, 2016), 75.
163. Andrew Nathan and Bruce Gilley, *China's New Rulers: The Secret Files* (New York: New York Review of Books, 2002), 209.
164. Jiang Zemin [江泽民], *Jiang Zemin Selected Works* [江泽民文选], 2006, vol. 3 [第三卷], 355.
165. Wang, "China and SCO," 110.
166. Liwei Zhuang, "Zhongguo Guoji Zhanlue Zhongde Dongmeng Keti [The ASEAN Issue in China's International Strategy]," *Dangdai Yatai [Contemporary Asia-Pacific]*, no. 6 (2003): 22. Zhang is a professor at Jinan University.
167. Zhuang, "Zhongguo Guoji Zhanlue Zhongde Dongmeng Keti," 22.
168. Chung, "China's Policies towards the SCO and ARF," 178.
169. Wang, "China and SCO," 111.
170. Weiqing Song, "Feeling Safe, Being Strong: China's Strategy of Soft Balancing through the Shanghai Cooperation Organization," *International Politics* 50, no. 5 (2013): 678.
171. Song, "Feeling Safe, Being Strong," 678–79.
172. Anna Mateeva and Antonio Giustozzi, "The SCO: A Regional Organization in the Making" (LSE Crisis States Research Centre, 2008), 11.
173. Wang, "China and SCO," 118.
174. Mateeva and Giustozzi, "The SCO," 7.
175. Yu Bin, "Living with Russia in the Post 9/11 World," in *Multidimensional Diplomacy of Contemporary China*, eds. Simon Shen and Jean-Marc Blanchard (Lanham, MD: Lexington Books, 2009), 193.

176. "Central Asia Report: September 12, 2003," *Radio Free Europe*, September 12, 2003, https://www.rferl.org/a/1342224.html.

177. "Bishkek Declaration, 2007," August 16, 2007.

178. Yu Bin, "China-Russia Relations: The New World Order According to Moscow and Beijing," *CSIS Comparative Connections*, no. 3 (2005); Adrian Blomfield, "Russia Accuses Kyrgyzstan of Treachery over US Military Base," *The Telegraph*, June 24, 2009, http://www.telegraph.co.uk/news/worldnews/asia/kyrgyzstan/5624355/Russia-accuses-Kyrgystan-of-treachery-over-US-military-base.html.

179. Marcel de Haas, "War Games of the Shanghai Cooperation Organization and the Collective Security Treaty Organization: Drills on the Move!," *Journal of Slavic Military Studies* 29, no. 3 (2016): 387–88.

180. Richard Weitz, *Parsing Chinese-Russian Military Exercises* (Carlisle, PA: Strategic Studies Institute, 2015), 6.

181. Ibid., 5–6.

182. Bin, "Living with Russia in the Post 9/11 World"; Wang, "China and SCO," 110.

183. Weitz, *Parsing Chinese-Russian Military Exercises*, 46.

184. Ibid., 45.

185. Stewart M. Patrick, "The SCO at 10: Growing, but Not into a Giant," Council on Foreign Relations, June 14, 2011, https://www.cfr.org/blog/sco-10-growing-not-giant.

186. See, for example, the SCO's 2002 and 2005 joint statements.

187. "Charter of the Shanghai Cooperation Organization" (Shanghai Cooperation Organization, June 7, 2002), http://eng.sectsco.org/load/203013/.

188. Sean Roberts, "Prepared Testimony on the SCO and Its Impact on U.S. Interests in Asia," § Commission on Security and Cooperation in Europe (2006).

189. Chung, "China's Policies towards the SCO and ARF," 178.

190. Wang Yusheng [王嵎生], "SCO Shows the Shanghai Spirit," *China Daily*, September 12, 2013.

191. "Yekaterinburg Declaration, 2009."

192. Weitz, "The Shanghai Cooperation Organization (SCO)."

193. Robert Sutter, *Chinese Foreign Relations: Power and Policy since the Cold War* (Lanham, MD: Rowman & Littlefield, 2009), 265; Mateeva and Giustozzi, "The SCO," 5.

194. Gill, *Rising Star*, 39.

195. For example, "Astana Declaration, 2011" (Shanghai Cooperation Organization, June 15, 2011).

196. This search was conducted in CNKI's Full Text Journal Database using the term "中国威胁论" for China Threat Theory and "多边主义" for multilateralism.

Chapter 6

1. He Xin [何新], *Selected Works of Hexin on Political Economy* [何新政治经济论文集] (Beijing: Heilong Jiang Education Publishing House [黑龙江教育出版社], 1995), 17.

2. For a video recording of the arrival, see "War and Peace in the Nuclear Age; Haves and Have-Nots; Deng Xiaoping Arrives at Andrews AFB," OpenVault from GBH Archives, July 29, 1979, http://openvault.wgbh.org/catalog/V_7F39E138353E4AB0997C4B85BAB58307.

3. "Document 209—Memorandum of Conversation, President's Meeting with Vice Premier Deng," *Foreign Relations of the United States, 1977–1980, Volume XIII, China*, January 31, 1979, https://history.state.gov/historicaldocuments/frus1977-80v13/d209.

4. Vladimir N. Pregelj, "Most-Favored-Nation Status of the People's Republic of China," CRS Report for Congress (Congressional Research Service, n.d.), 1–3.

5. Don Oberdorfer, "Trade Benefits for China Are Approved by Carter," *Washington Post*, October 24, 1979, https://www.washingtonpost.com/archive/politics/1979/10/24/trade-benefits-for-china-are-approved-by-carter/febc46f2-2d39-430b-975f-6c121bf4fb42/?noredirect=on&utm_term=.e1efd858846c; Jimmy Carter, *Public Papers of the Presidents of the United States: Jimmy Carter, 1979* (Washington, DC: US Government Printing Office, 1981), 359. Note that *Foreign Relations of the United States* offers a summary—not a transcript—of these remarks. For that reason, I've used Carter's recollection.

6. Harold K. Jacobson and Michel Oksenberg, *China's Participation in the IMF, the World Bank, and GATT* (Ann Arbor: University of Michigan Press, 1990).

7. Qian Qichen, *Ten Episodes in China's Diplomacy* (New York: HarperCollins, 2006), 299.

8. Deng Xiaoping, "The International Situation and Economic Problems: March 3, 1990," in *Selected Works of Deng Xiaoping* (Beijing: Renmin Press, 1993), 227. Excerpt from a talk with senior CCP members.

9. "Communiqué of the 3rd Plenary Session of the 11th Central Committee of the Chinese Communist Party [中国共产党第十一届中央委员会第三次全体会议公报]," Digital Library of the Past Party Congresses of the Communist Party of China [中国共产党历次代表大会数据库], December 22, 1978, http://cpc.people.com.cn/GB/64162/64168/64563/65371/4441902.html. Emphasis added.

10. Laurence A. Schneider, "Science, Technology and China's Four Modernizations," *Technology in Society* 3, no. 3 (1981): 291–303.

11. Richard P. Suttmeier, "Scientific Cooperation and Conflict Management in U.S.-China Relations from 1978 to the Present," *Annals New York Academy of Sciences* 866 (1998): 137–64; "Document 209—Memorandum of Conversation, President's Meeting with Vice Premier Deng."

12. "Document 209—Memorandum of Conversation, President's Meeting with Vice Premier Deng"; Leng Rong [冷溶] and Wang Zuoling [汪作玲], eds., *Deng Xiaoping Nianpu* [邓小平年谱], vol. 1 (Beijing: China Central Document Press [中央文献出版社], 2006), 498.

13. Deng Xiaoping [邓小平], *Collection of Deng Xiaoping's Military Writings* [邓小平军事文集], vol. 1 (Beijing: Military Science Press [军事科学出版社], 2004), 498.

14. Yangmin Wang, "The Politics of U.S.-China Economic Relations: MFN, Constructive Engagement, and the Trade Issue Proper," *Asian Survey* 33, no. 5 (1993): 442.

15. Li Peng [李鹏], *Peace and Development Cooperation: Li Peng Foreign Policy Diary* [和平发展合作李鹏外事日记], vol. 1 (Beijing: Xinhua Publishing House [新华出版社], 2008), 397.

16. Qian Qichen, *Ten Episodes in China's Diplomacy*, 142–43.

17. Ibid., 143–44. Emphasis added.

18. Li Peng [李鹏], *Peace and Development Cooperation*: Li Peng Foreign Policy Diary [和平发展合作 李鹏外事日记], 2008, vol. 1, 215. Emphasis added.

19. See, for example, Qian Qichen, *Ten Episodes in China's Diplomacy*, 133–39.

20. Ibid., 127.

21. Li Peng [李鹏], *Peace and Development Cooperation*: Li Peng Foreign Policy Diary [和平发展合作 李鹏外事日记], 2008, vol. 1 [上], 209–10.

22. Ibid., vol. 1 [上], 215.

23. Qian Qichen, *Ten Episodes in China's Diplomacy*, 140, 144, 150, 153, 156.

24. <<<REFO:BK>>>Li Peng [李鹏], Peace and Development Cooperation: Li Peng Foreign Policy Diary [和平发展合作 李鹏外事日记], 2008, 397.

25. Ibid., vol. 1 [上], 399.

26. Li Peng [李鹏], *Market and Regulation: Li Peng Economic Diary* [市场与调控:李鹏经济日记], vol. 2 (Beijing: Xinhua Publishing House [新华出版社], 2007), 926.

27. Vladimir N. Pregelj, "The Jackson-Vanik Amendment: A Survey" (Washington, DC: Congressional Research Service, August 1, 2005), 11. The vote tallies were 357–61 in the House; 60–38 in the Senate. Jim Mann, "Senate Fails to Override China Policy Veto," *Los Angeles Times*, March 19, 1992, http://articles.latimes.com/1992-03-19/news/mn-5919_1_china-policy.

28. Wang, "The Politics of U.S.-China Economic Relations," 449.

29. Suttmeier, "Scientific Cooperation and Conflict Management in U.S.-China Relations from 1978 to the Present."

30. Jiang Zemin [江泽民], *Jiang Zemin Selected Works* [江泽民文选], vol. 1 [第一卷] (Beijing: People's Press [人民出版社], 2006), 311.

31. Ibid., vol. 1 [第一卷], 312.

32. Ibid., vol. 1 [第一卷], 312.

33. Ibid., vol. 1 [第一卷], 332.

34. Ibid., vol. 2 [第二卷], 201.

35. Hu Jintao [胡锦涛], *Hu Jintao Selected Works* [胡锦涛文选], vol. 2 [第二卷] (Beijing: People's Press [人民出版社], 2016), 90.

36. Ibid., vol. 2 [第二卷], 91.

37. Ibid., vol. 2 [第二卷], 94.

38. Zong Hairen [宗海仁], *China's New Leaders: The Fourth Generation* [中國掌權者: 第四代] (New York: Mirror Books [明鏡出版社], 2002), 167.

39. Hu Jintao [胡锦涛], *Hu Jintao Selected Works* [胡锦涛文选], vol. 2 [第二卷], 513.

40. Ibid., vol. 2 [第二卷], 514.

41. Ibid., vol. 2 [第二卷], 513–14.

42. Ibid., vol. 2 [第二卷], 504–5.

43. Ibid., vol. 2 [第二卷], 506.

44. Graham Norris, "AmCham China Legacy: Furthering US-China Relations," American Chamber of Commerce China, May 26, 2016, https://web.archive.org/web/20160803020436/https://www.amchamchina.org/news/amcham-china-legacymoving-us-cn-relations-forward; Dai Yan, "Minister Urges Stronger Sino-US Trade," *China Daily*, December 10, 2005, http://www.chinadaily.com.cn/english/doc/2005-12/10/content_502259.htm.

45. Jiang Zemin [江泽民], *Jiang Zemin Selected Works* [江泽民文选], 2006, vol. 2 [第二卷], 442–60.

46. Joseph Fewsmith, "China and the WTO: The Politics behind the Agreement," *NBR Analysis* 10, no. 5 (December 1, 1999), https://www.iatp.org/sites/default/files/China_and_the_WTO_The_Politics_Behind_the_Agre.htm; Joseph Fewsmith and Stanley Rosen, "The Domestic Context of Chinese Foreign Policy: Does 'Public Opinion' Matter," in *The Making of Chinese Foreign and Security Policy, 1978–2000*, ed. David M. Lampton (Stanford, CA: Stanford University Press, 2001), 151–90.

47. Pearson, "The Case of China's Accession to the GATT/WTO," 357–62.

48. Li Zhaoxing [李肇星], *Shuo Bu Jin De Wai Jiao* [说不尽的外交] (Beijing: CITIC Publishing House [中信出版社], 2014), 51.

49. Li Peng [李鹏], *Market and Regulation: Li Peng Economic Diary* [市场与调控: 李鹏经济日记], vol. 3 (Beijing: Xinhua Publishing House [新华出版社], 2007), 1534.

50. For an extremely useful overview of the domestic politics of the negotiation, see Fewsmith, "China and the WTO: The Politics Behind the Agreement."

51. Li Peng, Market and Regulation: Li Peng Economic Diary [市场与调控: 李鹏经济日记], 2007, vol. 3, 1536.

52. Ibid., vol. 3, 1546.

53. Ibid., vol. 3, 1579.

54. Jayetta Z. Hecker, "China Trade: WTO Membership and Most-Favored-Nation Status," Pub. L. No. GAO/T-NSIAD-98-209, § Subcommittee on Trade, Committee on Ways and Means, House of Representatives (1998), 14.

55. "Tiananmen: Another Bump in China's Road to WTO Accession," Association for Diplomatic Studies and Training, 2016, https://adst.org/2016/04/tiananmen-another-bump-in-chinas-road-to-wto-accession/.

56. "Tiananmen: Another Bump in China's Road to WTO Accession."

57. He Xin [何新], *Selected Works of Hexin on Political Economy* [何新政治经济论文集], 17.

58. Li Zhaoxing [李肇星], *Shuo Bu Jin De Wai Jiao* [说不尽的外交], 34–35; Qian Qichen, *Ten Episodes in China's Diplomacy*, 314–15.

59. Li Zhaoxing [李肇星], *Shuo Bu Jin De Wai Jiao* [说不尽的外交], 47.

60. Ibid., 47–48.

61. Zhu Rongji [朱镕基], *Zhu Rongji Meets the Press* [朱镕基答记者问] (Beijing: People's Press [人民出版社], 2009), 93.

62. Jiang Zemin [江泽民], *Jiang Zemin Selected Works* [江泽民文选], vol. 3 [第三卷] (Beijing: People's Press [人民出版社], 2006), 448–49.

63. Li Peng [李鹏], *Market and Regulation: Li Peng Economic Diary* [市场与调控: 李鹏经济日记], 2007, vol. 3, 1546.

64. Li Peng [李鹏], *Peace and Development Cooperation*: Li Peng Foreign Policy Diary [和平发展合作李鹏外事日记], vol. 2 (Beijing: Xinhua Publishing House [新华出版社], 2008), 802–3.

65. Zhu Rongji [朱镕基], *Zhu Rongji Meets the Press* [朱镕基答记者问], 101–13.

66. For the whole speech, see Literature Research Office of the Chinese Communist Party Central Committee [中共中央文献研究室], *Selection of Important Documents since the 15th Party Congress* [十五大以来重要文献选编], vol. 2 (Beijing: People's Publishing House [人民出版社], 2001), 1205–27. Emphasis added.

67. Ibid., Literature Research Office of the Chinese Communist Party Central Committee [中共中央文献研究室], vol. 2, 1461–75.

68. Liu Huaqing [刘华清], *Memoirs of Liu Huaqing* [刘华清回忆录] (Beijing: Revolutionary Army Press [解放军出版社], 2004), 702–5.

69. Gary Klintworth, "China's Evolving Relationship with APEC," *International Journal* 50, no. 3 (1995): 497.

70. Wang Yusheng [王嵎生], *Personally Experiencing APEC: A Chinese Official's Observations and Experiences* [亲历APEC: 一个中国高官的体察- 王嵎生] (Beijing: World Knowledge Press [世界知识出版社], 2000), 14–15.

71. David E. Sanger, "Clinton's Goals for Pacific Trade Are Seen as a Hard Sell at Summit," *New York Times*, November 14, 1993.

72. Thomas G. Moore and Dixia Yang, "China, APEC, and Economic Regionalism in the Asia-Pacific," *Journal of East Asian Affairs* 13, no. 2 (1999): 386.

73. Ibid., 394.

74. Ibid., 394.

75. Wang Yusheng [王嵎生], *Personally Experiencing APEC: A Chinese Official's Observations and Experiences* [亲历APEC: 一个中国高官的体察- 王嵎生], 70.

76. Ibid., Wang Yusheng [王嵎生], 70.

77. Quoted in Moore and Yang, "China, APEC, and Economic Regionalism in the Asia-Pacific," 394.

78. Quoted in ibid., 396.

79. Ibid., 394.

80. Zhang Bin, "Core Interests: A WTO Memoir by China Chief Negotiator Long Yongtu," *China Pictorial* [人民画报], 2002, http://www.chinapictorial.com.cn/en/features/txt/2011-11/01/content_402102.htm.

81. "Long Yongtu(龙永图): China's Chief Negotiator," CCTV.com, March 19, 2012, https://web.archive.org/web/20130119080612/http://english.cntv.cn/program/upclose/20120319/118542.shtml.

82. Li Zhaoxing [李肇星], *Shuo Bu Jin De Wai Jiao* [说不尽的外交], 49–50.

83. Li Peng [李鹏], *Market and Regulation*: Li Peng Economic Diary [市场与调控: 李鹏经济日记], 2007, vol. 3, 1585.

84. Ibid., vol. 3, 1529.

85. Li Peng [李鹏], *Peace and Development Cooperation*: Li Peng Foreign Policy Diary [和平发展合作 李鹏外事日记], 2008, vol. 2, 803.

86. Paul Krugman, "Reckonings: A Symbol Issue," *New York Times*, May 10, 2000, https://www.nytimes.com/2000/05/10/opinion/reckonings-a-symbol-issue.html.

87. Sanger, "Clinton's Goals for Pacific Trade Are Seen as a Hard Sell at Summit."

88. Zhu Rongji [朱镕基], *Zhu Rongji Meets the Press* [朱镕基答记者问], 391.

Chapter 7

1. Yan Xuetong [阎学通], "From Tao Guang Yang Hui to Striving for Achievement: China's Rise Is Unstoppable [从韬光养晦到奋发有为，中国崛起势不可挡]," *People's Daily China Economic Weekly* [人民日报中国经济周刊], November 11, 2013, http://www.ceweekly.cn/2013/1111/68562.shtml.

2. Interviews, Beijing, Kunming, Chengdu, 2011–2012.

3. Hu Jintao [胡锦涛], *Hu Jintao Selected Works* [胡锦涛文选], vol. 3 [第三卷] (Beijing: People's Press [人民出版社], 2016), 234.

4. Ibid., vol. 3 [第三卷], 236.
5. Ibid., vol. 3 [第三卷], 234–46.
6. From CNKI text search.
7. Alastair Iain Johnston, "Is China a Status Quo Power?," *International Security* 27, no. 4 (2003): 5–56.
8. For example, see Jiang's 1998 9th Ambassadorial Conference Address, Jiang Zemin [江泽民], *Jiang Zemin Selected Works [江泽民文选]*, vol. 2 [第二卷] (Beijing: People's Press [人民出版社], 2006), 195–206. See also his 1999 address to the Central Economic Work Forum, Jiang Zemin [江泽民], vol. 2 [第二卷], 421–49.
9. Johnston, "Is China a Status Quo Power?," 30.
10. Jiang Zemin [江泽民], *Jiang Zemin Selected Works* [江泽民文选], 2006, vol. 2 [第二卷], 170.
11. Ibid., vol. 2 [第二卷], 422.
12. Ibid., vol. 2 [第二卷], 421.
13. Hu Jintao [胡锦涛], *Hu Jintao Selected Works* [胡锦涛文选], vol. 2 [第二卷] (Beijing: People's Press [人民出版社], 2016), 503–4.
14. Jiang Zemin [江泽民], Jiang Zemin Selected Works [江泽民文选], 2006, vol. 2 [第二卷], 202.
15. Hu Jintao [胡锦涛], Hu Jintao Selected Works [胡锦涛文选], 2016, vol. 2 [第二卷], 93.
16. Ibid., vol. 2 [第二卷], 92. Emphasis added.
17. Ibid., vol. 2 [第二卷], 93.
18. Ibid., vol. 3 [第三卷], 236. Emphasis added.
19. Jiang Zemin [江泽民], "Accelerating the Reform, the Opening to the Outside World and the Drive for Modernization, so as to Achieve Greater Successes in Building Socialism With Chinese Characteristics [加快改革开放和现代化建设步伐 夺取有中国特色社会主义事业的更大胜利]," 14th Party Congress Political Report (Beijing, October 12, 1992).
20. Zemin [江泽民], Jiang Zemin Selected Works [江泽民文选], 2006, vol. 2 [第二卷], 195–96.
21. Ibid., vol. 2 [第二卷], 195–96.
22. Ibid., vol. 2 [第二卷], 195–96.
23. Ibid., vol. 2 [第二卷], 422.
24. Ibid., vol. 2 [第二卷], 422–23.
25. Ibid., vol. 2 [第二卷], 422–23.
26. Ibid., vol. 2 [第二卷], 422–23.
27. Ibid., vol. 3 [第三卷], 107.
28. Ibid., vol. 3 [第三卷], 7.
29. Ibid., vol. 2 [第二卷], 545.
30. Ibid., vol. 3 [第三卷], 125.
31. Ibid., vol. 3 [第三卷], 160.
32. Ibid., vol. 3 [第三卷], 258.
33. Ibid., vol. 3 [第三卷], 297; Jiang Zemin [江泽民], "Build a Well-off Society in an All-Round Way and Create a New Situation in Building Socialism with Chinese Characteristics [全面建设小康社会，开创中国特色社会主义事业新局面]," 16th Party Congress Political Report (Beijing, November 28, 2002).
34. Hu Jintao [胡锦涛], *Hu Jintao Selected Works* [胡锦涛文选], 2016, vol. 2 [第二卷], 236.
35. Ibid., vol. 2 [第二卷], 152.
36. Ibid., vol. 2 [第二卷], 276.
37. Ibid., vol. 2 [第二卷], 352, 380, 444.
38. Ibid., vol. 2 [第二卷], 503–4.
39. Hu Jintao [胡锦涛], "Hold High the Great Banner of Socialism with Chinese Characteristics and Strive for New Victories in Building a Moderately Prosperous Society in All Respects [高举中国特色社会主义伟大旗帜 为夺取全面建设小康社会新胜利而奋斗]," 17th Party Congress Political Report (Beijing, October 15, 2007).
40. Hu Jintao [胡锦涛], *Hu Jintao Selected Works* [胡锦涛文选], 2016, vol. 3 [第三卷], 35.
41. Dai Bingguo [戴秉国], *Strategic Dialogues: Dai Binguo's Memoirs [战略对话：戴秉国回忆录]* (People's Press [人民出版社], 2016), 143.

42. Hu Jintao [胡锦涛], Hu Jintao Selected Works [胡锦涛文选], 2016, vol. 3 [第三卷], 234.

43. Ibid., vol. 3 [第三卷], 236.

44. Ibid., vol. 3 [第三卷], 234.

45. Ibid., vol. 3 [第三卷], 234.

46. Ibid., vol. 3 [第三卷], 457–58.

47. Ibid., vol. 3 [第三卷], 437.

48. Hu Jintao [胡锦涛], "Firmly March on the Path of Socialism with Chinese Characteristics and Strive to Complete the Building of a Moderately Prosperous Society in All Respects [坚定不移沿着中国特色社会主义道路前进 为全面建成小康社会而奋斗]," 18th Party Congress Political Report (Beijing, November 8, 2012).

49. Xi Jinping [习近平], *Xi Jinping: The Governance of China* [习近平谈治国理政], vol. 2 [第二卷] (Beijing: Foreign Language Press [外文出版社], 2014), 442.

50. Peter Ford, "The New Face of Chinese Diplomacy: Who Is Wang Yi," *Christian Science Monitor*, March 18, 2013, https://www.csmonitor.com/World/Asia-Pacific/2013/0318/The-new-face-of-Chinese-diplomacy-Who-is-Wang-Yi.

51. Christian Shepherd, "China Makes 'Silver Fox' Top Diplomat, Promoted to State Councilor," *Reuters*, March 18, 2018, https://www.reuters.com/article/us-china-parliament-diplomacy/china-makes-silver-fox-top-diplomat-promoted-to-state-councilor-idUSKBN1GV044.

52. Ford, "The New Face of Chinese Diplomacy."

53. Ibid.

54. Avery Goldstein, "The Diplomatic Face of China's Grand Strategy: A Rising Power's Emerging Choice," *The China Quarterly*, no. 168 (2001): 835–64; David Shambaugh, ed., *Power Shift: China and Asia's New Dynamics* (Berkeley: University of California Press, 2005); David Shambaugh, "China Engages Asia: Reshaping the Regional Order," *International Security* 29, no. 3 (2004): 64–99.

55. The most cogent expression of this argument can be found in Timothy Heath, "China's Big Diplomacy Shift," *The Diplomat*, December 22, 2014, https://thediplomat.com/2014/12/chinas-big-diplomacy-shift/.

56. Hu Jintao, *Hu Jintao Selected Works* [胡锦涛文选], 2016, vol. 3 [第三卷], 241.

57. Ibid., vol. 3 [第三卷], 241.

58. Ibid., vol. 3 [第三卷], 234.

59. Ibid., vol. 3 [第三卷], 241.

60. "China's Peaceful Development" (Beijing: Information Office of the State Council, September 2011), http://english.gov.cn/archive/white_paper/2014/09/09/content_281474986284646.htm.

61. Hu Jintao [胡锦涛], "Firmly March on the Path of Socialism with Chinese Characteristics and Strive to Complete the Building of a Moderately Prosperous Society in All Respects [坚定不移沿着中国特色社会主义道路前进 为全面建成小康社会而奋斗]."

62. This could plausibly be translated as "a priority direction," but the language clearly indicates centrality based on its usage in other contexts. See Wang Yi [王毅], "Speech by Minister Wang Yi at the Luncheon of the Second World Peace Forum [王毅部长在第二届世界和平论坛午餐会上的演讲]," Foreign Ministry of the People's Republic of China [中华人民共和国外交部], June 27, 2013, https://www.fmprc.gov.cn/web/wjbxw_673089/zyjh_673099/t1053901.shtml. See also Wang Yi [王毅], "Insist on Correct View of Righteousness and Benefits, Actively Play the Role of Responsible Great Powers: Deeply Comprehend the Spirit of Comrade Xi Jinping's Important Speech on Diplomatic Work [人民日报：坚持正确义利观 积极发挥负责任大国作用: 深刻领会习近平同志关于外交工作的重要讲话精神]," *People's Daily Online* [人民网], September 10, 2013, http://opinion.people.com.cn/n/2013/0910/c1003-22862978.html.

63. "Xi Jinping: Let the Sense of a Community of Common Destiny Take Root in Peripheral Countries [习近平：让命运共同体意识在周边国家落地生根]," *Xinhua* [新华网], October 25, 2013, http://www.xinhuanet.com/politics/2013-10/25/c_117878944.htm.

64. Ibid.

65. Xi Jinping, *Xi Jinping: The Governance of China*, vol. 1, 296.

66. Ibid., vol. 1, 297.

67. Ibid., vol. 1, 296.

68. Ibid., vol. 1, 297.

69. "China's Peripheral Diplomacy: Advancing Grand Strategy [中国周边外交：推进大战略]," *Renmin Wang [人民网]*, October 28, 2013, http://theory.people.com.cn/n/2013/1028/c136457-23344720.html.

70. Ibid.

71. Ibid.

72. Wang Yi, "Embark on a New Journey of China's Diplomacy," http://www.fmprc.gov.cn/mfa_eng/wjb_663304/wjbz_663308/2461_663310/t1109943.shtml.

73. Ibid.

74. This prioritization is clear in the online English readout and the official printed version. "The Central Conference on Work Relating to Foreign Affairs Was Held in Beijing," Ministry of Foreign Affairs of the People's Republic of China, November 29, 2014, http://www.fmprc.gov.cn/mfa_eng/zxxx_662805/t1215680.shtml; Xi Jinping [习近平], Xi Jinping: The Governance of China, Volume 2 [习近平谈治国理政], vol. 2 [第二卷], 444.

75. "The Central Conference on Work Relating to Foreign Affairs Was Held in Beijing"; <<<REFO:BK>>>Xi Jinping [习近平], Xi Jinping: The Governance of China, Volume 2 [习近平谈治国理政], vol. 2 [第二卷], 444.

76. Li Keqiang, "Full Text: Report on the Work of the Government (2014)," http://english.gov.cn/archive/publications/2014/08/23/content_281474982987826.htm.

77. Yang Jiechi [杨洁篪], "Continue to Create New Prospects for Foreign Work Under the Guidance of General Secretary Xi Jinping's Diplomatic Thoughts [在习近平总书记外交思想指引下不断开创对外工作新局面]," Foreign Ministry of the People's Republic of China [中华人民共和国外交部], January 14, 2017, https://www.fmprc.gov.cn/ce/ceus/chn/zgyw/t1430589.htm.

78. <<<REFO:BK>>>Xi Jinping [习近平], Xi Jinping: The Governance of China [习近平谈治国理政], vol. 1, 296–99.

79. Note, the full text of this speech is not in Xi Jinping's *Governance of China*. It can be found in Xi Jinping, "Speech by Chinese President Xi Jinping to Indonesian Parliament" (Jakarta, October 2, 2013), http://www.asean-china-center.org/english/2013-10/03/c_133062675.htm.

80. Ibid.

81. Xi Jinping, "New Asian Security Concept for New Progress in Security Cooperation" (4th Summit of the Conference on Interaction and Confidence Building Measures in Asia, Shanghai, May 21, 2014), http://www.s-cica.org/page.php?page_id=711&lang=1.

82. Xi Jinping, "Towards a Community of Common Destiny and a New Future for Asia" (Boao Forum for Asia, Boao, March 28, 2015), http://www.fmprc.gov.cn/mfa_eng/wjdt_665385/zyjh_665391/t1250690.shtml.

83. "China's White Paper on Asia-Pacific Security Cooperation Policies [中国的亚太安全合作政策白皮书] (Beijing: State Council Information Office [国务院新闻办公室]," January 2017), http://www.scio.gov.cn/zfbps/32832/Document/1539907/1539907.htm.

84. Liu Zhenmin, "Insisting on Win-Win Cooperation and Forging the Asian Community of Common Destiny," *China International Studies* 45, no. 5 (2014), http://www.ciis.org.cn/english/2014-06/17/content_6987936.htm.

85. Ling Chen [凌陈], "The Highest Level Sets Out a 'Top-Level Design' for Speeding Up the Upgrade of China's Peripheral Diplomacy [最高层着手'顶层设计' 中国周边外交提速升级]," *Renmin Wang [人民网]*, October 27, 2013, http://politics.people.com.cn/n/2013/1027/c1001-23339772.html.

86. "China's Peripheral Diplomacy: Advancing Grand Strategy [中国周边外交：推进大战略]."

87. Yan Xuetong [阎学通], "Yan Xuetong: The Overall 'Periphery' Is More Important than the United States [阎学通：整体的'周边'比美国更重要]," *Global Times [环球时报]*, January 13, 2015, http://opinion.huanqiu.com/1152/2015-01/5392162.html.

88. Ibid.

89. Xu Jin and Du Zheyuan, "The Dominant Thinking Sets in Chinese Foreign Policy Research: A Criticism," *Chinese Journal of International Politics* 8, no. 3 (April 13, 2015): 277.

90. Ibid.

91. Ibid.

92. Chen Xulong, "Xi Jinping Opens a New Era of China's Periphery Diplomacy," *China-US Focus*, November 9, 2013, https://www.chinausfocus.com/foreign-policy/xin-jinping-opens-a-new-era-of-chinas-periphery-diplomacy.

93. Wang Yizhou, "China's New Foreign Policy: Transformations and Challenges Reflected in Changing Discourse," *The Asan Forum* 6, no. 3 (March 21, 2014), http://www.theasanforum.org/chinas-new-foreign-policy-transformations-and-challenges-reflected-in-changing-discourse/.

94. Yi Wang, "Yang Jiechi: Xi Jinping's Top Diplomat Back in His Element," *China Brief* 17, no. 16 (2017), https://jamestown.org/program/yang-jiechi-xis-top-diplomat-back-element/.

95. Jim Mann, "China's Tiger Is a Pussycat to Bushes," *Los Angeles Times*, December 20, 2000, https://www.latimes.com/archives/la-xpm-2000-dec-20-mn-2466-story.html.

96. James R. Lilley and Jeffrey Lilley, *China Hands: Nine Decades of Adventure, Espionage, and Diplomacy in Asia* (New York: Public Affairs, 2005).

97. John Pomfret, "U.S. Takes a Tougher Tone with China," *Washington Post*, July 30, 2010, https://www.washingtonpost.com/wp-dyn/content/article/2010/07/29/AR2010072906416.html.

98. Hu Jintao [胡锦涛], *Hu Jintao Selected Works* [胡锦涛文选], 2016, vol. 3 [第三卷], 234–46.

99. Chen Dingding and Wang Jianwei, "Lying Low No More?: China's New Thinking on the Tao Guang Yang Hui Strategy," *China: An International Journal* 9, no. 2 (September 2011): 212.

100. For the 1995 address, see Jiang Zemin [江泽民], *Jiang Zemin on Socialism with Chinese Characteristics (Special Excerpts)* [江泽民论有中国特色社会主义 【专题摘编】] (Beijing: 中央文献出版社, 2002), 529–30. For the 1998 address, see Jiang Zemin, *Jiang Zemin Selected Works*, vol. 2 [第二卷], 202.

101. Li Zhaoxing [李肇星], *Shuo Bu Jin De Wai Jiao* [说不尽的外交] (Beijing: CITIC Publishing House [中信出版社], 2014), 295–96.

102. Jiang Zemin [江泽民], *Jiang Zemin on Socialism with Chinese Characteristics (Special Excerpts)* 江泽民论有中国特色社会主义 【专题摘编】, 529–30.

103. Ibid.

104. <<<REFO:BK>>>Jiang Zemin [江泽民], Jiang Zemin Selected Works [江泽民文选], 2006, vol. 2, [第二卷], 202.

105. Hu Jintao [胡锦涛], *Hu Jintao Selected Works* [胡锦涛文选], 2016, vol. 2 [第二卷], 236.

106. Li Zongyang [李宗阳] and Tu Yinsen [涂荫森], *A Dictionary of Philosophical Concepts* [哲学概念辨析辞典] (Beijing: Central Party School Press [中共中央党校出版社], 1993), 94.

107. Hu Jintao [胡锦涛], *Hu Jintao Selected Works* [胡锦涛文选], 2016, vol. 2 [第二卷], 236.

108. Ibid., vol. 2 [第二卷], 236.

109. Ibid., vol. 2 [第二卷], 518.

110. Ibid., vol. 3 [第三卷], 237.

111. Wang Yi, "Exploring the Path of Major-Country Diplomacy with Chinese Characteristics" (Beijing, June 27, 2013), http://www.fmprc.gov.cn/mfa_eng/wjb_663304/wjbz_663308/2461_663310/t1053908.shtml.

112. Bonnie S. Glaser and Alison Szalwinski, "Major Country Diplomacy with Chinese Characteristics," *China Brief* 13, no. 16 (August 9, 2013), https://jamestown.org/program/major-country-diplomacy-with-chinese-characteristics/.

113. Xi Jinping [习近平], *Xi Jinping: The Governance of China* [习近平谈治国理政], vol. 1, 296.

114. Ibid., vol. 2 [第二卷], 443. Emphasis added.

115. Yan Xuetong [阎学通], "From Keeping a Low Profile to Striving for Achievement," *Chinese Journal of International Politics* 7, no. 2 (April 22, 2014): 168.

116. Xu Jin and Du Zheyuan, "The Dominant Thinking Sets in Chinese Foreign Policy Research," 277.

117. Hu Jintao [胡锦涛], Hu Jintao Selected Works [胡锦涛文选], 2016, vol. 3 [第三卷], 237.

118. Ibid., vol. 3 [第三卷], 237.

119. Ibid., vol. 3 [第三卷], 241.
120. Ibid., vol. 3 [第三卷], 236–37. Emphasis added.
121. Ibid., vol. 2 [第二卷], 519.
122. Xi Jinping [习近平], "Chairman Xi Jinping's Opening Remarks at the Roundtable Summit of the 'Belt and Road' International Cooperation Summit Forum [习近平主席在'一带一路'国际合作高峰论坛圆桌峰会上的开幕辞]," Ministry of Commerce of the People's Republic of China, May 15, 2017, http://www.mofcom.gov.cn/article/i/jyjl/l/201705/20170502576387.shtml.
123. Xi Jinping [习近平], Xi Jinping: The Governance of China [习近平谈治国理政], vol. 1, 296–99.
124. Ibid., vol. 1, 296–99.
125. Ibid., vol. 1, 296–99.
126. Ibid., vol. 1, 296–99.
127. Ibid., vol. 1, 296–99.
128. Ibid., vol. 1, 296–99.
129. Ibid., vol. 1, 296–99.
130. Ibid., vol. 1, 296–99.
131. See Chapter 9 for an in-depth discussion.
132. Xi Jinping, "Towards a Community of Common Destiny and a New Future for Asia."
133. Xi Jinping [习近平], "Secure a Decisive Victory in Building a Moderately Prosperous Society in All Respects and Strive for the Great Success of Socialism with Chinese Characteristics for a New Era [决胜全面建成小康社会 夺取新时代中国特色社会主义伟大胜利]," 19th Party Congress Political Report (Beijing, October 18, 2017).
134. Xi Jinping, Xi Jinping: The Governance of China, vol. Xi Jinping [习近平], Xi Jinping: The Governance of China [习近平谈治国理政], vol. 1, 297–98.
135. Wang Yi, "Exploring the Path of Major-Country Diplomacy with Chinese Characteristics."
136. "China Desires Consolidated Ties with Pakistan," Dawn, April 20, 2018, https://www.dawn.com/news/1402694/china-desires-consolidated-ties-with-pakistan.
137. Xi Jinping [习近平], "Speech at the First Meeting of the 13th National People's Congress [在第十三届全国人民代表大会第一次会议上的讲话]" (2018 National People's Congress [全国人民代表大会], Beijing, March 20, 2018), http://www.xinhuanet.com/politics/2018lh/2018-03/20/c_1122566452.htm.

Chapter 8

1. Research Group of the Institute of Ocean Development Strategy, State Oceanic Administration [国家海洋局海洋发展战略研究所课题组], China's Ocean Development Report 2010 [2010中国海洋发展报告] (Beijing: China Ocean Press [海洋出版社], 2010), 482.
2. Liu Huaqing [刘华清], Memoirs of Liu Huaqing [刘华清回忆录] (Beijing: Revolutionary Army Press [解放军出版社], 2004), 252.
3. Ibid., 261–65.
4. See Liu Huaqing's obituary in Xinhua, "Liu Huaqing, Father of the Modern Navy [现代海军之父刘华清]," Xinhua, January 15, 2011, http://news.xinhuanet.com/mil/2011-01/15/c_12983881.htm.
5. Some of the key works on China's navy include, among others, Michael McDevitt, China as a Twenty-First-Century Naval Power: Theory Practice and Implications (Annapolis, MD: Naval Institute Press, 2020); Bernard D. Cole, The Great Wall at Sea: China's Navy in the Twenty-First Century, 2nd ed. (Annapolis, MD: Naval Institute Press, 2010); Yves-Heng Lim, China's Naval Power: An Offensive Realist Approach (Burlington, VT: Ashgate, 2014).
6. Hu Jintao [胡锦涛], Hu Jintao Selected Works [胡锦涛文选], vol. 3 [第三卷] (Beijing: People's Press [人民出版社], 2016), 236–37. Emphasis added.
7. Ibid., vol. 2 [第二卷], 519.
8. John Pomfret, "U.S. Takes a Tougher Tone with China," Washington Post, July 30, 2010, https://www.washingtonpost.com/wp-dyn/content/article/2010/07/29/AR2010072906416.html.

9. Central Party History and Literature Research Institute of the Chinese Communist Party [中共中央党史和文献研究院], ed., *Excerpts from Xi Jinping's Statements on the Concept of Comprehensive National Security Concept* [习近平关于总体国家安全观论述摘编] (Beijing: Central Party Literature Press [中央文献出版社], 2018), 259.

10. "Xi Jinping: Caring More about the Ocean, Understanding the Ocean, Planning and Controlling the Ocean, and Promoting the Construction of a Maritime Great Power and Constantly Acquiring New Achievements[习近平：进一步关心海洋认识海洋经略海洋推动海洋强国建设不断取得新成就]," *Renmin Wang* [人民网], August 1, 2013, http://cpc.people.com.cn/n/2013/0801/c64094-22402107.html.

11. Ibid.

12. Ibid.

13. "Foreign Minister Wang Yi Meets the Press," Foreign Ministry of the People's Republic of China [中华人民共和国外交部], March 8, 2014, https://www.fmprc.gov.cn/mfa_eng/wjb_663304/wjbz_663308/2461_663310/t1135385.shtml.

14. Information Office of the State Council, "China's National Defense in 2008," January 2009, http://english.gov.cn/official/2009-01/20/content_1210227_3.htm.

15. Hu Jintao [胡锦涛], *Hu Jintao Selected Works* [胡锦涛文选], 2016, vol. 3 [第三卷], 235.

16. Ibid., vol. 3 [第三卷], 243–44.

17. "The Diversified Employment of China's Armed Forces, 2013" (Information Office of the State Council, April 2013), http://eng.mod.gov.cn/TopNews/2013-04/16/content_4442750.htm.

18. "Xi Jinping: Join Hands to Pursue the Development Dream of China and Australia and Achieve Regional Prosperity and Stability [习近平：携手追寻中澳发展梦想 并肩实现地区繁荣稳定]," *Renmin Wang* [人民网], October 18, 2014, http://cpc.people.com.cn/n/2014/1118/c64094-26043313.html.

19. Pan Shanju [潘珊菊], "Released White Paper on China's Military Strategy Is the First to Put Forward 'Overseas Interests Area' [中国军事战略白皮书发布 首提"海外利益攸关区"]," *Jinghua Times* [京华时报], May 27, 2015, http://res.cssn.cn/dybg/gqdy_zz/201505/t20150527_2011778_1.shtml.

20. In particular, see the discussion of aircraft carriers and surface vessels later in this chapter.

21. Research Group of the Institute of Ocean Development Strategy, State Oceanic Administration [国家海洋局海洋发展战略研究所课题组], *China's Ocean Development Report 2010* [2010中国海洋发展报告], 482.

22. Hu Jintao [胡锦涛], "Firmly March on the Path of Socialism with Chinese Characteristics and Strive to Complete the Building of a Moderately Prosperous Society in All Respects [坚定不移沿着中国特色社会主义道路前进 为全面建成小康社会而奋斗]," 18th Party Congress Political Report (Beijing, November 8, 2012).

23. "Xi Jinping: Caring More about the Ocean, Understanding the Ocean, Planning and Controlling the Ocean, and Promoting the Construction of a Maritime Great Power and Constantly Acquiring New Achievements[习近平：进一步关心海洋认识海洋经略海洋推动海洋强国建设不断取得新成就]."

24. Literature Research Office of the Chinese Communist Party Central Committee [中共中央文献研究室], *Selection of Important Documents since the 18th Party Congress* [十八大以来重要文献选编], vol. 1 (Beijing: Central Party Literature Press [中央文献出版社], 2014), 844.

25. "Xi Jinping: Deeply Implementing the Innovation-Driven Development Strategy to Add Momentum to the Revitalization of the Old Industrial Base [习近平：深入实施创新驱动发展战略 为振兴老工业基地增添原动力]," *Renmin Wang* [人民网], September 2, 2013, http://cpc.people.com.cn/n/2013/0902/c64094-22768582.html.

26. Yu Miao [于淼], "Author of the Military Strategy White Paper: The First Time 'Overseas Interest Area' Was Put Forward [军事战略白皮书作者澎湃撰文：首提'海外利益攸关区']," *The Paper*, May 26, 2015, https://www.thepaper.cn/newsDetail_forward_1335188.

27. Minnie Chan, "The Xu Family: From Basketball to the Aircraft Carrier," *South China Morning Post*, January 19, 2015, https://www.scmp.com/news/china/article/1681753/xu-family-basketball-aircraft-carrier-business.

28. Minnie Chan, "'Unlucky Guy' Tasked with Buying China's Aircraft Carrier: Xu Zengping," *South China Morning Post*, April 29, 2015, https://www.scmp.com/news/china/diplomacy-defence/article/1779703/unlucky-guy-tasked-buying-chinas-aircraft-carrier-xu.

29. Ibid.

30. Zhang Tong [张彤], "Shandong Native Xu Zengping Bought the Varyag [山东人徐增平买回'瓦良格']," *Jinan Times [济南时报]*, September 30, 2011, http://jinantimes.com.cn/index.php?m=content&c=index&a=show&catid=8&id=14936; "Taiwan Stuntman Jumps China Waterfall," CNN World News, June 1, 1997, http://www.cnn.com/WORLD/9706/01/china.jump/.

31. Minnie Chan, "The Inside Story of the Liaoning: How Xu Zengping Sealed the Deal for China's First Aircraft Carrier," *South China Morning Post*, January 19, 2015, https://www.scmp.com/news/china/article/1681755/how-xu-zengping-became-middleman-chinas-deal-buy-liaoning.

32. Minnie Chan, "How a Luxury Hong Kong Home Was Used as Cover in Deal for China's First Aircraft Carrier," *South China Morning Post*, August 19, 2017, https://www.scmp.com/news/china/diplomacy-defence/article/2107370/how-hong-kong-luxury-home-was-used-cover-deal-chinas.

33. Ibid.

34. Ibid.

35. Yu Wei [余 玮], "Through Twists and Turns, from the 'Varyag' to the Birth of China's First Aircraft Carrier [历经周折 从"瓦良格"号到中国首艘航母诞生始末]," *Party History [党史]*, November 23, 2012, http://dangshi.people.com.cn/n/2012/1123/c85037-19679177-1.html.

36. Chan, "The Inside Story of the Liaoning."

37. Chan, "'Unlucky Guy' Tasked with Buying China's Aircraft Carrier."

38. Ibid.

39. Chan, "The Inside Story of the Liaoning."

40. Ibid.

41. "How the 'Varyag' Came to China ['瓦良格'号如何来到中国]," *Chinese Community Party News [中国共产党新闻网]*, January 22, 2015, http://cpc.people.com.cn/n/2015/0122/c87228-26427625.html.

42. Chan, "How a Luxury Hong Kong Home Was Used as Cover in Deal for China's First Aircraft Carrier."

43. Minnie Chan, "Mission Impossible: How One Man Bought China Its First Aircraft Carrier," *South China Morning Post*, January 18, 2015, http://www.scmp.com/news/china/article/1681710/sea-trials-how-one-man-bought-china-its-aircraft-carrier.

44. Zhang Tong [张彤], "Shandong Native Xu Zengping Bought the Varyag [山东人徐增平买回'瓦良格']"; Minnie Chan, "Mission Impossible II: The Battle to Get China's Aircraft Carrier Home," *South China Morning Post*, January 20, 2015, https://www.scmp.com/news/china/article/1682731/mission-impossible-ii-battle-get-chinas-aircraft-carrier-home.

45. Yu Wei [余 玮], "Through Twists and Turns, from the 'Varyag' to the Birth of China's First Aircraft Carrier [历经周折 从"瓦良格"号到中国首艘航母诞生始末]."

46. "The Significance of the Varyag Aircraft Carrier to China's National Strategy Is Something That Cannot Be Purchased with Money [瓦良格号航母对中国意义 国家战略金钱买不来]," *Sina.com [新浪财经]*, March 24, 2015, http://mil.news.sina.com.cn/2015-03-24/1058825518.html.

47. Xiong Songce [熊崧策], "The 'Varyag' That Came All This Distance [不远万里来到中国的'瓦良格'号]," *Science and Technology Review [科技导报]* 30, no. 5 (2012): 15–17. This refers sometimes to the period 2002–2005 or also 2005–2008. Activity taken in 2005 mainly kept the hull usable.

48. "China Announced That It Has the Technology to Manufacture Modern Aircraft Carriers [中國宣布已擁有制造现代航母的技術]," *Radio Free Asia*, August 25, 2008, https://www.rfa.org/cantonese/news/china_millitary-08252008112237.html.

49. Yu Wei [余 玮], "Through Twists and Turns, from the 'Varyag' to the Birth of China's First Aircraft Carrier [历经周折 从"瓦良格"号到中国首艘航母诞生始末]."

50. Research Group of the Institute of Ocean Development Strategy, State Oceanic Administration [国家海洋局海洋发展战略研究所课题组], *China's Ocean Development Report 2010* [2010中国海洋发展报告], 482.

51. Kenji Minemura, "Beijing Admits It Is Building an Aircraft Carrier," *Asahi Shimbun*, December 17, 2010.

52. Yang Lei was interviewed by the Changsha Evening News on Hunan Satellite TV, and transcripts are available on several sites. See Xiao Yonggen [肖永根], *Yang Lei: I Supervised and Built an Aircraft Carrier for My Homeland* [杨雷：我为祖国监造航母], Absolute Loyalty [绝对忠诚] (Hunan [湖南]: Hunan Satellite TV [湖南卫视], 2014), http://tv.81.cn/2014/2014-08/01/content_6075529.htm; Yu Wei [余 玮], "Through Twists and Turns, from the 'Varyag' to the Birth of China's First Aircraft Carrier [历经周折 从"瓦良格"号到中国首艘航母诞生始末]."

53. Chang Xuemei [常雪梅] and Cheng Hongyi [程宏毅], "Our Military's Aircraft Carrier Construction: 30 Months of Work Completed in 15 Months [我军航母建设：15月完成30月工作量 1个部门15人牺牲]," *People's Daily Online* [人民网], June 1, 2013, http://cpc.people.com.cn/n/2013/0601/c87228-21699891.html.

54. "China Launches Second Aircraft Carrier," *Xinhua*, April 26, 2017, http://www.xinhuanet.com/english/2017-04/26/c_136237552.htm.

55. Liu Zhen, "Three Catapult Launchers Spotted in Image of China's New Aircraft Carrier," *South China Morning Post*, June 20, 2018, https://www.scmp.com/news/china/diplomacy-defence/article/2151703/chinas-newest-aircraft-carrier-likely-have-catapult.

56. Liu Zhen, "China Aims for Nuclear-Powered Aircraft Carrier by 2025," *South China Morning Post*, February 28, 2018, https://www.scmp.com/news/china/diplomacy-defence/article/2135151/china-aims-nuclear-powered-aircraft-carrier-2025; Jeffrey Lin and Peter W. Swinger, "A Chinese Shipbuilder Accidentally Revealed Its Major Navy Plans," *Popular Science*, March 15, 2018, https://www.popsci.com/china-nuclear-submarine-aircraft-carrier-leak/.

57. Chan, "How a Luxury Hong Kong Home Was Used as Cover in Deal for China's First Aircraft Carrier."

58. Yu Wei [余 玮], "Through Twists and Turns, from the 'Varyag' to the Birth of China's First Aircraft Carrier [历经周折 从"瓦良格"号到中国首艘航母诞生始末]."

59. This quote appears in multiple accounts. See Andrew Erickson, "China's Ministry of National Defense: 1st Aircraft Carrier 'Liaoning' Handed Over to PLA Navy," September 25, 2012, https://www.andrewerickson.com/2012/09/chinas-ministry-of-national-defense-1st-aircraft-carrier-liaoning-handed-over-to-pla-navy/; Huang Jingjing, "Chinese Public Eagerly Awaits Commissioning of Second Aircraft Carrier," *Global Times*, April 6, 2016, https://www.globaltimes.cn/content/977459.shtml.

60. Liu Huaqing [刘华清], *Memoirs of Liu Huaqing* [刘华清回忆录], 478.

61. Ibid., 479–80.

62. *Liu Huaqing Chronicles* [刘华清年谱] *1916–2011*, vol. 3 [下卷] (Beijing: Liberation Army Press [解放军出版社], 2016), 1195.

63. Lim, *China's Naval Power*, 74.

64. See Tai Ming Cheung, *Growth of Chinese Naval Power* (Singapore: Institute of Southeast Asian Studies, 1990), 40.

65. Quoted in Dennis M. Gormley, Andrew S. Erickson, and Jingdong Yuan, *A Low-Visibility Force Multiplier: Assessing China's Cruise Missile Ambitions* (Washington, DC: NDU Press, 2014), 62.

66. Ibid., 79.

67. Ibid., 79.

68. Lim, *China's Naval Power*, 76.

69. Roger Cliff, *China's Military Power: Assessing Current and Future Capabilities* (New York: Cambridge University Press, 2015), 64.

70. Bernard D. Cole, *The Great Wall at Sea: China's Navy Enters the Twenty-First Century* (Annapolis, MD: Naval Institute Press, 2001), 99.

71. "The PLA Navy: New Capabilities and Missions for the 21st Century" (Washington, DC: Office of Naval Intelligence, 2015), 16.

72. Cole, *The Great Wall at Sea*, 102.

73. The Luda refits of the late 1980s may have provided some vessels this capability, but it was entirely useless because the sonar was scarcely able to operate given the noise.

74. Bernard D. Cole, "China's Carrier: The Basics," *USNI News*, November 27, 2012, https://news.usni.org/2012/11/27/chinas-carrier-basics.

75. *The Science of Campaigns [战役学]* (Beijing: National Defense University Press [国防大学出版社], 2006), 316–30.

76. Li Yousheng [李有升], *Joint Campaign Studies Guidebook [联合战役学教程]* (Beijing: Academy of Military Science [军事科学院], 2012), 259.

77. Cole, *The Great Wall at Sea*, 105.

78. Ibid., 102; Lim, *China's Naval Power*, 93.

79. "Jane's World Navies" (IHS Jane's, May 19, 2015).

80. "The PLA Navy: New Capabilities and Missions for the 21st Century," 24.

81. Cole, *The Great Wall at Sea*, 106.

82. You Ji, *Armed Forces of China* (Singapore: Allen & Unwin, 1999), 194.

83. Cole, *The Great Wall at Sea*, 106.

84. Ibid., 106–7.

85. "Jane's World Navies."

86. Tai Ming Cheung, *Growth of Chinese Naval Power*, 30–32; You Ji, *Armed Forces of China*, 193–94.

87. Minnie Chan, "As Overseas Ambitions Expand, China Plans 400 Per Cent Increase to Marine Corps Numbers, Sources Say," *South China Morning Post*, March 13, 2017, https://www.scmp.com/news/china/diplomacy-defence/article/2078245/overseas-ambitions-expand-china-plans-400pc-increase.

88. Ibid.

89. Guo Yuandan, "Chinese Navy Sees Broadened Horizon, Enhanced Ability through 10-Year Escort Missions," *Global Times*, December 30, 2018, https://www.globaltimes.cn/content/1134066.shtml.

90. Shaio H. Zerba, "China's Libya Evacuation Operation: A New Diplomatic Imperative—Overseas Citizen Protection," *Journal of Contemporary China* 23, no. 90 (2014): 1092–1112; Ernest Kao, "China Considered Drone Strike on Foreign Soil in Hunt for Drug Lord," *South China Morning Post*, February 19, 2013, https://www.scmp.com/news/china/article/1153901/drone-strike-was-option-hunt-mekong-drug-lord-says-top-narc.

91. "Djibouti and China Sign a Security and Defense Agreement," *All Africa*, February 27, 2014, https://allafrica.com/stories/201402280055.html.

92. During its blunting phase, China resorted to force in three instances. In 1988, Chinese and Vietnamese forces clashed over control of the Johnson South Reef in the South China Sea; in 1994 it seized Mischief Reef from the Philippines, and in 1995–1996, it launched missiles into the waters of Taiwan. Since then, China has actually been far less willing to use deadly force, with the prominent exception of a 2020 border clash with Indian troops that left roughly twenty Indian soldiers dead. But after the Global Financial Crisis, it demonstrated greater willingness to do so.

93. This quote and translation is provided in full in Murray Scott Tanner and Peter W. Mackenzie, "China's Emerging National Security Interests and Their Impact on the People's Liberation Army" (Arlington, VA: Center for Naval Analyses, 2015), 85–86.

94. For example, see 1995, 1998, 2000 China Defense White Papers.

95. Sun Jianguo [孙建国], "Contributing Chinese Wisdom to Leading World Peaceful Development and Win-Win Cooperation—Deepen Study of Chairman Xi Jinping's Thoughts on the Mankind's Common Destiny [为引领世界和平发展合作共赢贡献中国智慧:深入学习习近平主席人类命运共同体重要思想]," *Qiushi [求是]*, August 2016, http://web.archive.org/web/20160601120417/http://www.qstheory.cn/dukan/qs/2016-04/15/c_1118595597.htm.

96. Shou Xiaosong [寿晓松], *The Science of Military Strategy [战略学]* (Beijing: Military Science Press [军事科学出版社], 2013).

97. Li Cigui [刘赐贵], "Some Thinking on Developing Maritime Cooperative Partnership to Promote the Construction of the Twenty-First Century Maritime Silk Road

[发展海洋合作伙伴关系 推进21 世纪海上丝绸之路建设的若干思考]," *Guoji Went Yanjiu [国际问题研究]*, April 2014, http://intl.cssn.cn/zzx/gjzzx_zzx/201408/t20140819_1297241.shtml.

98. Ibid.

99. Tanner and Mackenzie, "China's Emerging National Security Interests and Their Impact on the People's Liberation Army," 87.

100. Conor Kennedy, "Strategic Strong Points and Chinese Naval Strategy," *Jamestown China Brief*, March 22, 2019, https://jamestown.org/program/strategic-strong-points-and-chinese-naval-strategy/.

101. Liang Fang (梁芳), "What Are the Risks to the 'Maritime Silk Road' Sea Lanes? [今日'海上丝绸之路'通道风险有多大？]," *Defense Reference [国防参考]*, March 13, 2015, http://www.globalview.cn/html/strategy/info_1707.html.

102. See Li Jian, Chen Wenwen, and Jin Chang, "Overall Situation of Sea Power in the Indian Ocean and the Expansion in the Indian Ocean of Chinese Seapower [印度洋海权格局与中国海权的印度洋扩展]," *Pacific Journal [太平洋学报]* 22, no. 5 (2014): 74–75. Quoted in Erica Downs, Jeffrey Becker, and Patrick deGategno, "China's Military Support Facility in Djibouti: The Economic and Security Dimensions of China's First Overseas Base" (Arlington, VA: Center for Naval Analyses, 2017), 40.

103. Kennedy, "Strategic Strong Points and Chinese Naval Strategy."

104. Peter A. Dutton, Isaac B. Kardon, and Conor M. Kennedy, "China Maritime Report No. 6: Djibouti: China's First Overseas Strategic Strongpoint" (Newport, RI: US Naval War College China Maritime Studies Institute, April 1, 2020), 50–51, https://digital-commons.usnwc.edu/cgi/viewcontent.cgi?article=1005&context=cmsi-maritime-reports.

105. Isaac B Kardon, Conor M. Kennedy, and Peter A. Dutton, "China Maritime Report No. 7: Gwadar: China's Potential Strategic Strongpoint in Pakistan" (Newport, RI: US Naval War College China Maritime Studies Institute, August 1, 2020), https://digital-commons.usnwc.edu/cgi/viewcontent.cgi?article=1005&context=cmsi-maritime-reports.

106. Shihar Aneez and Ranga Sirilal, "Chinese Submarine Docks in Sri Lanka Despite Indian Concerns," *Reuters*, November 2, 2014, https://www.reuters.com/article/sri-lanka-china-submarine/chinese-submarine-docks-in-sri-lanka-despite-indian-concerns-idINKBN0IM0LU20141102; Shihar Aneez and Ranga Sirilal, "Sri Lanka Rejects Chinese Request for Submarine Visit: Sources," *Reuters*, May 11, 2017, https://www.reuters.com/article/us-sri-lanka-china-submarine/sri-lanka-rejects-chinese-request-for-submarine-visit-sources-idUSKBN1871P9; Maria Abi-Habib, "How China Got Sri Lanka to Cough Up a Port," *New York Times*, June 25, 2018, https://www.nytimes.com/2018/06/25/world/asia/china-sri-lanka-port.html.

Chapter 9

1. "CICA at 25: Review and Outlook" (Shanghai: Second Conference of the CICA Non-governmental Forum, June 2017), http://www.cica-china.org/eng/xjzs/sa/.

2. Linda Jakobson, "Reflections from China on Xi Jinping's 'Asia for Asians,'" *Asian Politics and Policy* 8, no. 1 (2016): 219–23.

3. "Statement by H.E. Mr. Chen Guoping at CICA Meeting of Ministers of Foreign Affairs" (CICA Meeting of Ministers of Foreign Affairs, Ankara, 2012), http://www.s-cica.org/page.php?page_id=605&lang=1. Emphasis added.

4. Evan Medeiros and Taylor Fravel, "China's New Diplomacy," *Foreign Affairs* 82, no. 6 (2003): 22–35.

5. Hu Jintao [胡锦涛], *Hu Jintao Selected Works [胡锦涛文选]*, vol. 3 [第三卷] (Beijing: People's Press [人民出版社], 2016), 234.

6. Ibid., vol. 3 [第三卷], 239–40.

7. Ibid., vol. 3 [第三卷], 240.

8. Ibid., vol. 3 [第三卷], 242.

9. Ibid., vol. 3 [第三卷], 241.

10. "China's Peaceful Development" (Beijing: Information Office of the State Council, September 2011), http://english.gov.cn/archive/white_paper/2014/09/09/content_281474986284646.htm.

11. "China's White Paper on Asia-Pacific Security Cooperation Policies [中国的亚太安全合作政策白皮书]" (Beijing: State Council Information Office [国务院新闻办公室], January 2017), http://www.scio.gov.cn/zfbps/32832/Document/1539907/1539907.htm.

12. Hu Jintao [胡锦涛], *Hu Jintao Selected Works* [胡锦涛文选], vol. 3 [第三卷], 241.

13. Hu Jintao [胡锦涛], "Firmly March on the Path of Socialism with Chinese Characteristics and Strive to Complete the Building of a Moderately Prosperous Society in All Respects [坚定不移沿着中国特色社会主义道路前进 为全面建成小康社会而奋斗]," 18th Party Congress Political Report (Beijing, November 8, 2012).

14. Xi Jinping [习近平], *Xi Jinping: The Governance of China [习近平谈治国理政]*, vol. 1 (Beijing: Foreign Language Press [外文出版社], 2014), 343–52.

15. Ibid., vol. 1, 353–59.

16. "The AIIB Was Declared Open for Business on January 16, 2016, and Mr. Jin Liqun Was Elected as the Bank's First President," Asia Infrastructure Investment Bank, February 2, 2016, https://www.aiib.org/en/news-events/news/2016/The-AIIB-was-declared-open-for-business-on-January-16-2016-and-Mr-Jin-Liqun-was-elected-as-the-Banks-first-President.html.

17. Jamil Anderlini, "Lunch with the FT: Jin Liqun," *Financial Times*, April 21, 2016, https://www.ft.com/content/0564ce1e-06e3-11e6-a70d-4e39ac32c284.

18. Brian Bremmer and Miao Han, "China's Answer to the World Bank Wants Green, Clean Asian Infrastructure," *Bloomberg*, April 8, 2018, https://www.bloomberg.com/features/2018-asian-infrastructure-investment-bank-jin-liqun-interview/; Anderlini, "Lunch with the FT."

19. Bremmer and Han, "China's Answer to the World Bank Wants Green, Clean Asian Infrastructure."

20. Jane Perlez, "A Banker Inspired by Western Novelists Seeks to Build Asia," *New York Times*, January 13, 2017, https://www.nytimes.com/2017/01/13/world/asia/china-aiib-jin-liqun.html.

21. Ibid.; Jin Liqun, "Bretton Woods: The System and the Institution," in *Bretton Woods: The Next Seventy Years*, ed. Marc Uzan (New York: Reinventing Breton Woods Committee, 2015), 211–16.

22. Perlez, "A Banker Inspired by Western Novelists Seeks to Build Asia."

23. Jeffrey D. Wilson, "What Does China Want from the Asia Infrastructure Investment Bank?," Indo-Pacific Insights Series (Perth USAsia Centre, May 2017), 4.

24. David Dollar, "The AIIB and the 'One Belt, One Road,'" Brookings, 2015, https://www.brookings.edu/opinions/the-aiib-and-the-one-belt-one-road/.

25. Jin Liqun, "Building Asia's New Bank: An Address by Jin Liqun, President-Designate of the Asian Infrastructure Investment Bank" (Washington, DC: Brookings, October 21, 2015), 10–11, https://www.brookings.edu/wp-content/uploads/2015/10/20151021_asia_infra-structure_bank_transcript.pdf.

26. See Biswa Nath Bhattacharyay, "Estimating Demand for Infrastructure in Energy, Transport, Telecommunications, Water and Sanitation in Asia and the Pacific: 2010–2020," ADBI Working Paper Series (Asian Development Bank, September 2010); Biswa Nath Bhattacharyay and Prabir De, "Restoring the Asian Silk Route: Toward an Integrated Asia," ADBI Working Paper Series (Asian Development Bank, June 2009).

27. Xingqiang (Alex) He, "China in the International Financial System: A Study of the NDB and the AIIB" (Centre for International Governance Innovation, 2016), 4–5; Mike Callaghan and Paul Hubbard, "The Asian Infrastructure Investment Bank: Multilateralism on the Silk Road," *China Economic Journal* 9, no. 2 (2016): 117.

28. Dani Rodrik, "Why Is There Multilateral Lending," in *Annual World Bank Conference on Development Economics 1995*, eds. Michael Bruno and Boris Pleskovic (Washington, DC: The World Bank, 1996).

29. Christopher Kilby, "Donor Influence in Multilateral Development Banks: The Case of the Asian Development Bank," *Review of International Organizations* 1, no. 2 (2006): 173–95.

30. Stephen D. Krasner, "Power Structure and Regional Development Banks," *International Organization* 35, no. 2 (1981): 314.

31. Christopher Kilby, "Donor Influence in Multilateral Development Banks" (Vassar College Economics Working Paper, 2006), http://economics.vassar.edu/docs/working-papers/

VCEWP70.pdf; Daniel Lim and J. R. Vreeland, "Regional Organizations and International Politics: Japanese Influence over the Asian Development Bank and the UN Security Council," *World Politics* 65, no. 1 (2013): 34–72.

32. For the full text of Zheng Xinli's speech, see "Member Newsletter, 2009 Issue 2 [会员通讯 2009 第2期]," China Center for International Economic Exchanges [中国国际经济交流中心], June 3, 2009, http://www.cciee.org.cn/Detail.aspx?newsId=58&TId=106.

33. Cheng Li, "China's New Think Tanks: Where Officials, Entrepreneurs, and Scholars Interact," *China Leadership Monitor*, no. 29 (2009): 2.

34. "Zheng Xinli Author Introduction," China Center for International Economic Exchanges [中国国际经济交流中心], May 4, 2011, http://english.cciee.org.cn/Detail.aspx?newsId=2479&TId=197.

35. "China's Transition at Home and Abroad" (Washington, DC: Brookings, July 21, 2015), 74–77, https://www.brookings.edu/wp-content/uploads/2015/07/20150721_china_transition_transcript.pdf. For the original Chinese, a recording is available on the Brookings website. Zheng's remarks begin at "02:34:00."

36. Wang Lin [王琳], "China Proposes to Build Asia Infrastructure Investment Bank [中国倡议建亚洲基础设施投资银行]," *First Financial Daily* [第一财经日报], October 8, 2013, http://www.yicai.com/news/3036393.html.

37. Hua Shengdun, "AIIB 'Father' Tells of Bank's Birth," *China Daily*, July 24, 2015, http://usa.chinadaily.com.cn/epaper/2015-07/24/content_21395787.htm.

38. Jin Liqun, "Building Asia's New Bank," 6.

39. Jin Liqun, "Bretton Woods," 214–15.

40. Ibid., 216.

41. Xi Jinping, "Chinese President Xi Jinping's Address at AIIB Inauguration Ceremony" (AIIB Inauguration Ceremony, Beijing, January 16, 2016), http://www.xinhuanet.com/english/china/2016-01/16/c_135015661.htm.

42. Jin Liqun, "Building Asia's New Bank," 4–5.

43. "China's Transition at Home and Abroad." The quote here is a translation from the original Chinese, of which a recording is available on the Brookings website. Zheng's remarks begin at "02:34:00."

44. Lai-Ha Chan, "Soft Balancing against the US 'Pivot to Asia': China's Geostrategic Rationale for Establishing the Asian Infrastructure," *Australian Journal of International Affairs* 71, no. 6 (2017): 577.

45. Wilson, "What Does China Want from the Asia Infrastructure Investment Bank?," 7.

46. Jin Liqun, "Building Asia's New Bank" 5.

47. "China's $50 Billion Asia Bank Snubs Japan, India," *Bloomberg*, 2014, http://www.bloomberg.com/news/articles/2014-05-11/china-s-50-billion-asia-bank-snubs-japan-india-in-power-push.

48. Robert Wihtol, "Whither Multilateral Development Finance?" (Asia Development Bank Institute, 2014), http://www.adbi.org/files/2014.07.21.wp491.whither.multilateral.dev.finance.pdf; "China's $50 Billion Asia Bank Snubs Japan, India"; "Lou Jiwei Presided over the Preparatory Work for the Ministerial Dinner Meeting of the AIIB and Delivered a Speech [楼继伟主持筹建亚投行部长级工作晚餐会并致辞]," Ministry of Finance of the People's Republic of China [中华人民共和国财政部], May 3, 2014, http://gss.mof.gov.cn/mofhome/guojisi/zhuantilanmu/yth/201506/t20150617_1257643.html.

49. "Lou Jiwei Answers Reporters' Questions on the Establishment of AIIB [楼继伟就筹建亚洲基础设施投资银行答记者问]," Ministry of Finance of the People's Republic of China [中华人民共和国财政部], December 25, 2015, http://www.mof.gov.cn/zhengwuxinxi/zhengcejiedu/201512cjd/201512/t20151225_1632389.htm. Quoted in Yun Sun, "China and the Evolving Asian Infrastructure Investment Bank," in *Asian Infrastructure Investment Bank: China as Responsible Stakeholder*, ed. Daniel Bob (Washington, DC: Sasakawa USA, 2015), 27–42, https://spfusa.org/wp-content/uploads/2015/07/AIIB-Report_4web.pdf.

50. "Timeline," *China Daily*, October 27, 2014, http://usa.chinadaily.com.cn/epaper/2014-10/27/content_18808521.htm.

51. Bangladesh, Brunei, Cambodia, China, India, Kazakhstan, Kuwait, Laos, Malaysia, Mongolia, Myanmar, Nepal, Oman, Pakistan, the Philippines, Qatar, Singapore, Sri Lanka, Thailand, Uzbekistan, and Vietnam.

52. Quoted in Yun Sun, "How the International Community Changed China's Asian Infrastructure Investment Bank," *The Diplomat*, July 31, 2015, https://thediplomat.com/2015/07/how-the-international-community-changed-chinas-asian-infrastructure-investment-bank/. For full quote and original source, see "Lou Jiwei: The Cutoff for Founding Members of AIIB Is in the End of March [楼继伟:亚投行创始成员国资格确认3月底截止]," *Xinhua [新华网]*, March 6, 2015, http://www.xinhuanet.com/politics/2015lh/2015-03/06/c_1114552782.htm.

53. Jane Perlez, "Stampede to Join China's Development Bank Stuns Even Its Founder," *New York Times*, April 2, 2015.

54. Jin Liqun, "Building Asia's New Bank," 23.

55. Yun Sun, "China and the Evolving Asian Infrastructure Investment Bank," 38.

56. Lingling Wei and Bob Davis, "China Forgoes Veto Power at New Bank to Win Key European Nations' Support," *Wall Street Journal*, March 23, 2015, http://www.wsj.com/articles/china-forgoes-veto-power-at-new-bank-to-win-key-european-nations-support-1427131055; Xingqiang (Alex) He, "China in the International Financial System," 10.

57. Xingqiang (Alex) He, 10.

58. Martin A. Weiss, "Asian Infrastructure Investment Bank (AIIB)" (Congressional Research Service, February 3, 2017), 9; Callaghan and Hubbard, "The Asian Infrastructure Investment Bank," 129.

59. Callaghan and Hubbard, 130.

60. Ibid., 129.

61. Bin Gu, "Chinese Multilateralism in the AIIB," *Journal of International Economic Law* 20, no. 1 (2017): 150.

62. Callaghan and Hubbard, "The Asian Infrastructure Investment Bank," 132.

63. Xingqiang (Alex) He, "China in the International Financial System," 12.

64. Curtis S. Chin, "New Bank Launch Charts Path to Asian-Led Order," *China US Focus*, July 7, 2015, https://www.chinausfocus.com/finance-economy/beyond-the-signing-ceremony-at-a-chinas-own-asian-development-bank/.

65. Weiss, "Asian Infrastructure Investment Bank (AIIB)," 9.

66. Quoted in Yun Sun, "China and the Evolving Asian Infrastructure Investment Bank," 30.

67. "Xi Stresses Implementing Central Economic Policies," *Xinhua*, February 2, 2015, http://www.xinhuanet.com/english/china/2015-02/10/c_127481077.htm. Emphasis added; Wang Lin [王琳], "Fu Ying: AIIB and the Silk Road Fund Support 'One Belt, One Road [傅莹：亚投行、丝路基金支持'一带一路']," *Yicai Wang [一财网]*, March 4, 2015, http://www.yicai.com/news/4581546.html. Quoted in Yun Sun, "China and the Evolving Asian Infrastructure Investment Bank," 30.

68. Chan, "Soft Balancing against the US 'Pivot to Asia,'" 574; Zhong Nan and Cai Xiao, "AIIB Leads Support for Belt and Road Infrastructure Projects," *China Daily*, June 8, 2016, http://www.chinadaily.com.cn/business/2016-06/08/content_25645165.htm.

69. Xingqiang (Alex) He, "China in the International Financial System," 16.

70. Xi Jinping, "Chinese President Xi Jinping's Address at AIIB Inauguration Ceremony."

71. Callaghan and Hubbard, "The Asian Infrastructure Investment Bank," 129.

72. Victoria Ruan, "Former Deputy Finance Minister Jin Liqun Tipped to Become Head of China-Led AIIB," *South China Morning Post*, April 27, 2015, http://www.scmp.com/news/china/policies-politics/article/1754771/former-deputy-finance-minister-jin-liqun-tipped-become; Wei and Davis, "China Forgoes Veto Power at New Bank to Win Key European Nations' Support"; Cary Huang, "Does China Have What It Takes to Lead the AIIB," *South China Morning Post*, May 16, 2015, http://www.scmp.com/news/china/policies-politics/article/1798724/does-china-have-what-it-takes-lead-aiib.

73. Yun Sun, "China and the Evolving Asian Infrastructure Investment Bank," 33.

74. Quoted in Chan, "Soft Balancing against the US 'Pivot to Asia,'" 577.

75. Raphael Minder and Jamil Anderlini, "China Blocks ADB India Loan Plan," *Financial Times*, April 10, 2009.

76. Chan, "Soft Balancing against the US 'Pivot to Asia,'" 580.

77. Ibid., 578; Callaghan and Hubbard, "The Asian Infrastructure Investment Bank," 129.

78. Ren Xiao, "China as an Institution-Builder: The Case of the AIIB," *The Pacific Review* 29, no. 3 (2016): 440.

79. Quoted in Chan, "Soft Balancing against the US 'Pivot to Asia,'" 578.

80. "Foreign Minister Wang Yi Meets the Press," Ministry of Foreign Affairs of the People's Republic of China, March 9, 2016, http://www.fmprc.gov.cn/mfa_eng/zxxx_662805/t1346238.shtml.

81. "Speech by Chinese President Xi Jinping to Indonesian Parliament," ASEAN-China Centre, October 2, 2013, http://www.asean-china-center.org/english/2013-10/03/c_133062675.htm; "Xi Jinping Delivered a Speech in Indonesia's Parliament [习近平在印尼国会发表演讲]," *Sina.com* [新浪财经], October 10, 2013, http://finance.sina.com.cn/china/20131003/132116904825.shtml. The translation slightly differs from the original Chinese, but the English version is what was circulated internationally and so it is cited here.

82. Robert Sutter, *Chinese Foreign Relations: Power and Policy since the Cold War* (Lanham, MD: Rowman & Littlefield, 2009), 297.

83. "China's $50 Billion Asia Bank Snubs Japan, India."

84. Ren Xiao, "China as an Institution-Builder," 436.

85. "China's $50 Billion Asia Bank Snubs Japan, India."

86. "China Finance Minister Raps ADB for Being Bureaucratic," *Nikkei Asian Review*, March 22, 2015, http://asia.nikkei.com/Politics-Economy/International-Relations/China-finance-minister-raps-ADB-for-being-bureaucratic.

87. Jane Perlez, "China Creates a World Bank of Its Own, and the U.S. Balks," *New York Times*, December 4, 2015.

88. Jisi Wang, "One World One Dream?: China and International Order" (Harvard University, April 1, 2015).

89. "A Speech on the Establishment Progress of Asian Infrastructure Investment Bank by Mr. Jin Liqun, Head of the Working Group for Establishment of AIIB," Boao Forum for Asia, May 17, 2015, http://english.boaoforum.org/mtzxxwzxen/14301.jhtml.

90. Paul Pennay, "China Says Western Rules May Not Be Best for AIIB," *Business Spectator*, March 23, 2015, http://www.businessspectator.com.au/news/2015/3/23/china/china-says-western-rules-may-not-be-best-aiib.

91. "CICA Catalogue of Confidence Building Measures" (Conference on Interaction and Confidence-Building Measures in Asia, 2004), http://www.s-cica.org/admin/upload/files/CICA_CATALOGUE_(2004)_-_eng.doc.

92. "CICA Catalogue of Confidence Building Measures."

93. "Secretariat of the Conference on Interaction and Confidence Building Measures in Asia," CICA, n.d., http://www.s-cica.kz/page.php?page_id=9&lang=1.

94. These documents were ostensibly joint documents, but punctuation choices make clear that they were prepared by China. For example, Chinese forms of quotation marks are used throughout rather than Western forms.

95. "The Presentation on the Joint Russian-Chinese Initiative on Strengthening Security in the Asia Pacific Region," 1–2, http://www.s-cica.org/page.php?page_id=24&lang=1&year=2017&month=1&day=0.

96. Ibid., 4.

97. Ibid., 5.

98. "Dai Bingguo's Speech at the 3rd CICA Summit [戴秉国在亚信论坛第三次峰会上发表讲话]," Foreign Ministry of the People's Republic of China [中华人民共和国外交部], 2010, http://www.fmprc.gov.cn/web/gjhdq_676201/gjhdqzz_681964/yzxhhy_683118/xgxw_683124/t707229.shtml.

99. Ibid.

100. "Statement by H.E. Mr. Chen Guoping at CICA Meeting of Ministers of Foreign Affairs."

101. Xi Jinping, "New Asian Security Concept for New Progress in Security Cooperation" (4th Summit of the Conference on Interaction and Confidence Building Measures in Asia, Shanghai, May 21, 2014), http://www.s-cica.org/page.php?page_id=711&lang=1.

102. "Statement by H.E. Mr. Chen Guoping at CICA Meeting of Ministers of Foreign Affairs."

103. "Xi Jinping Holds Talks with President Nursultan Nazarbayev of Kazakhstan," Ministry of Foreign Affairs of the People's Republic of China, September 7, 2013, http://www.fmprc.gov.cn/mfa_eng/topics_665678/xjpfwzysiesgjtfhshzzfh_665686/t1075414.shtml. http://www.fmprc.gov.cn/mfa_eng/topics_665678/xjpfwzysiesgjtfhshzzfh_665686/t1075414.shtml.

104. "China and Kazakhstan Joint Declaration on Further Deepening Comprehensive Strategic Partnership [中哈关于进一步深化全面战略伙伴关系的联合宣言]," *Xinhua* [新华网], September 9, 2013, http://www.xinhuanet.com/world/2013-09/08/c_117273076.htm.

105. See Article 29 of "Declaration of the Fourth CICA Ministerial Meeting" (Conference on Interaction and Confidence-Building Measures in Asia, September 12, 2012), http://www.cica-china.org/eng/zyhyhwj_1/yxhy/yxwzh/t1149048.htm.

106. "China Supports the Development of CICA into a Formal International Organization [中方支持亚信会议发展成为正式国际组织]," China News [中国新闻网], October 12, 2012, http://www.chinanews.com/gn/2012/10-12/4244549.shtml.

107. Xi Jinping, "New Asian Security Concept for New Progress in Security Cooperation."

108. Ibid.

109. For example, see "Keynote Address by H.E. Mr. Wang Yi at CICA 2016 Ministerial" (Conference on Interaction and Confidence-Building Measures in Asia, 2016), http://www.s-cica.org/page.php?page_id=6026&lang=1.

110. "Working Report on the CICA and Its Future Developments at the Fifth CICA Think Tank Roundtable" (Shanghai: CICA Think Tank Roundtable, April 22, 2016), http://www.cica-china.org/eng/xjzs/yxzglt/t1448504.htm.

111. Ibid.

112. Xi Jinping, "New Asian Security Concept for New Progress in Security Cooperation."

113. "Dai Bingguo's Speech at the 3rd CICA Summit [戴秉国在亚信论坛第三次峰会上发表讲话]"; "Statement by H.E. Mr. Chen Guoping at CICA Meeting of Ministers of Foreign Affairs"; Xi Jinping, "New Asian Security Concept for New Progress in Security Cooperation."

114. "Statement by H.E. Mr. Chen Guoping at CICA Meeting of Ministers of Foreign Affairs."

115. Xi Jinping, "New Asian Security Concept for New Progress in Security Cooperation."

116. Wang Tong, "Statement of Mr. Wang Tong, Counselor of the Embassy of the People's Republic of China at the 25th Anniversary of the CICA Process" (Astana, April 19, 2017), http://www.s-cica.kz/page.php?page_id=6130&lang=1.

117. Xi Jinping, "New Asian Security Concept for New Progress in Security Cooperation."

118. Gong Jianwei, "CICA Day Reception 2014: Statement of Ambassador Gong Jianwei, Executive Director" (CICA, Astana, October 6, 2014), http://www.s-cica.kz/page.php?page_id=828&lang=1.

119. Xi Jinping, "Inaugural Statement by H.E. Mr. Xi Jinping at the 2016 CICA Ministerial" (CICA 2016 Ministerial, Beijing, 2016), http://www.s-cica.org/page.php?page_id=6044&lang=1.

120. Xi Jinping, "New Asian Security Concept for New Progress in Security Cooperation"; "China's Policies on Asia-Pacific Security Cooperation" (State Council Information Affairs Office, January 2017), http://www.scio.gov.cn/32618/Document/1539667/1539667.htm.

121. "China's Policies on Asia-Pacific Security Cooperation."

122. Wang Yi [王毅], "Wang Yi Chairs Informal Meeting of Foreign Ministers of CICA Member Countries [王毅主持亚信成员国外长非正式会晤]" (Informal Meeting of CICA Foreign Ministers at the UN General Assembly, New York, September 20, 2017), http://www.cica-china.org/chn/yxxw/t1495625.htm.

123. Gong Jianwei, "CICA Day Reception 2014: Statement of Ambassador Gong Jianwei, Executive Director"; Gong Jianwei, "Second Conference of CICA Non-Governmental Forum: Statement of Ambassador Gong Jianwei Executive Director, CICA Secretariat" (Beijing, June 28, 2017), http://www.s-cica.kz/page.php?page_id=6150&lang=1.

124. "The Statement of the Chairman of the Fourth CICA Think Tank Roundtable on Asian Security Cooperation: Contexts, Missions and Prospects" (Shanghai: CICA Think Tank

Roundtable, December 17, 2015), http://www.cica-china.org/eng/xjzs/yxzglt/t1448497. htm.

125. Gong Jianwei, "Address by Ambassador Gong Jianwei at the 25th Anniversary of the CICA Process" (25th Anniversary of the CICA Process, Astana, April 19, 2017), http://www.s-cica.kz/page.php?page_id=6108&lang=1.2017.

126. Wang Yi [王毅], "Wang Yi Chairs Informal Meeting of Foreign Ministers of CICA Member Countries [王毅主持亚信成员国外长非正式会晤]."

127. "China's Policies on Asia-Pacific Security Cooperation." Numbers added.

128. Ma Chunshan, "What Is CICA (and Why Does China Care about It?)," *The Diplomat*, May 17, 2014.

129. This quote, which is representative of the framing in almost all previous speeches, is from the 2012 address by Chen Guoping. "Statement by H.E. Mr. Chen Guoping at CICA Meeting of Ministers of Foreign Affairs."

130. Gong Jianwei, "Statement of Executive Director Gong Jianwei at the Xiangshan Forum," http://www.s-cica.kz/page.php?page_id=843&lang=1.

131. "Keynote Address by H.E. Mr. Wang Yi at CICA 2016 Ministerial"; Wang Yi [王毅], "Wang Yi Chairs Informal Meeting of Foreign Ministers of CICA Member Countries [王毅主持亚信成员国外长非正式会晤]."

132. "CICA at 25."

133. Chen Dongxiao, "Prospects and Paths of CICA's Transformation," *China Quarterly of International Strategic Studies* 1, no. 3 (2015): 453.

134. Chen Guoping, "Vice Minister Cheng Guoping's Speech at the Opening Ceremony of the Meeting of CICA Senior Officials Committee" (CICA Senior Officials Committee, Yangzhou, November 6, 2014), http://www.cica-china.org/eng/yxxw_1/t1212946.htm.

135. "Shanghai Declaration of the Launching of CICA Think Tank Roundtable" (Conference on Interaction and Confidence-Building Measures in Asia, March 22, 2014), http://www.cica-china.org/eng/xjzs/yxzglt/t1448473.htm.

136. "Keynote Address by H.E. Mr. Wang Yi at CICA 2016 Ministerial."

137. Xi Jinping, "New Asian Security Concept for New Progress in Security Cooperation."

138. Chen Dongxiao, "Prospects and Paths of CICA's Transformation," 459.

139. "CICA at 25."

Chapter 10

1. Hu Jintao [胡锦涛], *Hu Jintao Selected Works* [胡锦涛文选], vol. 3 [第三卷] (Beijing: People's Press [人民出版社], 2016), 241. The original uses the phrase 周边, which is translated as periphery elsewhere in the book with the exception of this epigraph given contextual limitations.

2. Wang Jisi [王缉思], "Wang Jisi: 'Marching Westward': The Rebalancing of China's Geostrategy [王缉思: '西进', 中国地缘战略的再平衡]," *Global Times* [环球网], October 17, 2012, http://opinion.huanqiu.com/opinion_world/2012-10/3193760.html.

3. Ibid.

4. Hu Jintao [胡锦涛], *Hu Jintao Selected Works* [胡锦涛文选], 2016, vol. 3 [第三卷], 241.

5. Ibid., vol. 2 [第二卷], 518. Emphasis added.

6. Ibid., vol. 3 [第三卷], 234–46.

7. Ibid., vol. 2 [第二卷], 518.

8. Ibid., vol. 3 [第三卷], 241.

9. Ibid., vol. 3 [第三卷], 234.

10. Ibid., vol. 3 [第三卷], 239.

11. "China's Peaceful Development" (Beijing: Information Office of the State Council, September 2011), http://english.gov.cn/archive/white_paper/2014/09/09/content_281474986284646.htm.

12. This could plausibly be translated as "a priority direction," but the language clearly indicates centrality based on its usage in other contexts. See Wang Yi [王毅], "Speech by Minister Wang Yi at the Luncheon of the 2nd World Peace Forum [王毅部长在第二届世界和平论坛午餐会上的演讲]," Foreign Ministry of the

People's Republic of China [中华人民共和国外交部], June 27, 2013, https://www.fmprc.gov.cn/web/wjbz_673089/zyjh_673099/t1053901.shtml. See also Wang Yi [王毅], "Insist on Correct View of Righteousness and Benefits, Actively Play the Role of Responsible Great Powers: Deeply Comprehend the Spirit of Comrade Xi Jinping's Important Speech on Diplomatic Work [人民日报：坚持正确义利观 积极发挥负责任大国作用：深刻领会习近平同志关于外交工作的重要讲话精神]," *People's Daily Online* [人民网], September 10, 2013, http://opinion.people.com.cn/n/2013/0910/c1003-22862978.html.

13. Xi Jinping [习近平], *Xi Jinping: The Governance of China* [习近平谈治国理政], vol. 1 (Beijing: Foreign Language Press [外文出版社], 2014), 296.

14. Yan Xuetong [阎学通], "Yan Xuetong: The Overall 'Periphery' Is More Important than the United States [阎学通：整体的'周边'比美国更重要]," *Global Times* [环球时报], January 13, 2015, http://opinion.huanqiu.com/1152/2015-01/5392162.html.

15. "The Central Conference on Work Relating to Foreign Affairs Was Held in Beijing," Ministry of Foreign Affairs of the People's Republic of China, November 29, 2014, http://www.fmprc.gov.cn/mfa_eng/zxxx_662805/t1215680.shtml.

16. Li Keqiang, "Full Text: Report on the Work of the Government (2014)," http://english.gov.cn/archive/publications/2014/08/23/content_281474982987826.htm.

17. "China's White Paper on Asia-Pacific Security Cooperation Policies [中国的亚太安全合作政策白皮书]" (Beijing: State Council Information Office [国务院新闻办公室], January 2017), http://www.scio.gov.cn/zfbps/32832/Document/1539907/1539907.htm.

18. Hu Jintao [胡锦涛], *Hu Jintao Selected Works* [胡锦涛文选], 2016, vol. 3 [第三卷], 237.

19. Ibid., vol. 3 [第三卷], 237.

20. Ibid., vol. 3 [第三卷], 241.

21. Ibid., vol. 3 [第三卷], 241.

22. Ibid., vol. 3 [第三卷], 241.

23. Ibid., vol. 3 [第三卷], 242.

24. Ibid., vol. 3 [第三卷], 239, 241.

25. "China's Peaceful Development."

26. Ibid.

27. Xi Jinping [习近平], *Xi Jinping: The Governance of China* [习近平谈治国理政], vol. 1, 296–99.

28. Ibid., vol. 1, 296–99.

29. Ibid., vol. 1, 296–99.

30. Ibid., vol. 1, 296–99.

31. Ibid., vol. 1, 296–99.

32. Xi Jinping [习近平], "Chairman Xi Jinping's Opening Remarks at the Roundtable Summit of the 'Belt and Road' International Cooperation Summit Forum [习近平主席在'一带一路'国际合作高峰论坛圆桌峰会上的开幕辞]," Ministry of Commerce of the People's Republic of China, May 15, 2017, http://www.mofcom.gov.cn/article/i/jyjl/l/201705/20170502576387.shtml.

33. Xi Jinping, "Jointly Shoulder Responsibility of Our Times, Promote Global Growth" (World Economic Forum, Davos, January 17, 2017), http://www.xinhuanet.com/english/2018-09/03/c_137441987.htm.

34. Devin Thorne and David Spevack, "Harbored Ambitions: How China's Port Investments Are Strategically Reshaping the Indo-Pacific" (Washington, DC: Center for Advanced Defense Studies, 2017), 65.

35. Maria Abi-Habib, "How China Got Sri Lanka to Cough Up a Port," *New York Times*, June 25, 2018, https://www.nytimes.com/2018/06/25/world/asia/china-sri-lanka-port.html.

36. David Dollar, "The AIIB and the 'One Belt, One Road,'" Brookings, 2015, https://www.brookings.edu/opinions/the-aiib-and-the-one-belt-one-road/.

37. Abi-Habib, "How China Got Sri Lanka to Cough Up a Port."

38. Ibid.

39. Ibid.

40. Xi Jinping [习近平], *Xi Jinping: The Governance of China* [习近平谈治国理政], vol. 1, 296–99.

41. See Chapter 9.

42. Robert A. Manning and Bharath Gopalaswamy, "Is Abdulla Yameen Handing Over the Maldives to China?," *Foreign Policy*, March 21, 2018.

43. "China's Foreign Ports," *The Economist*, June 18, 2013, International edition, http://www.economist.com/news/international/21579039-chinas-growing-empire-ports-abroad-mainly-about-trade-not-aggression-new-masters.

44. Ibid.

45. Ibid.

46. Fumbuka Ng, "Tanzania Signs Port Deal with China Merchants Holdings," *Reuters*, May 30, 2013, http://www.reuters.com/article/2013/05/30/tanzania-china-infrastructure-idUSL5N0EB3RU20130530.

47. I thank Tarun Chhabra for suggesting this point.

48. Abi-Habib, "How China Got Sri Lanka to Cough Up a Port."

49. Ibid.

50. He (合) Lian (联), "The Development of Plans for the Construction of the Maritime Silk Road of the 21st Century Is Accelerating" [21世纪海上丝绸之路建设规划正加快制定], *China Securities Journal* (中国证券报), April 16, 2014, http://www.cs.com.cn/app/ipad/ipad01/01/201404/t20140416_4364603.html.

51. "China Accelerates Planning to Re-Connect Maritime Silk Road," *China Daily*, April 16, 2014, http://www.chinadaily.com.cn/china/2014-04/16/content_17439523.htm.

52. Personal interview with a high-level diplomat from an ASEAN state who had met with senior PLA officials about the Belt and Road.

53. Abi-Habib, "How China Got Sri Lanka to Cough Up a Port."

54. Zhou Bo, "The String of Pearls and the Maritime Silk Road," China US Focus, February 11, 2014, http://www.chinausfocus.com/foreign-policy/the-string-of-pearls-and-the-maritime-silk-road/.

55. "East African Port Construction Expected to Be Chinese Supply Base" [东非建港口料华舰补给基地], *Mingpao* {明報}, March 25, 2013, http://www.mingpaovan.com/htm/News/20130325/vab1h.htm?m=0.

56. Ibid.

57. Henry Farrell, "Russia Is Hinting at a New Cold War over SWIFT. So What's SWIFT?," *Washington Post*, January 28, 2015, https://www.washingtonpost.com/news/monkey-cage/wp/2015/01/28/russia-is-hinting-at-a-new-cold-war-over-swift-so-whats-swift/?noredirect=on&utm_term=.29c15baefc36.

58. Hongying Wang, "China and the International Monetary System: Does Beijing Really Want to Challenge the Dollar," *Foreign Affairs*, December 19, 2017, https://www.foreignaffairs.com/articles/asia/2017-12-19/china-and-international-monetary-system.

59. Gregory Chin, "China's Rising Monetary Power," in *The Great Wall of Money: Power and Politics in China's International Monetary Relations*, eds. Eric Helleiner and Jonathan Kirshner (Ithaca, NY: Cornell University Press, 2014), 190–92. See also Wang, "China and the International Monetary System."

60. Chin, "China's Rising Monetary Power," 192.

61. Hu Jintao [胡锦涛], *Hu Jintao Selected Works* [胡锦涛文选], 2016, vol. 3 [第三卷], 280.

62. Chin, "China's Rising Monetary Power," 192.

63. <<<REFO:BK>>>Hu Jintao [胡锦涛], Hu Jintao Selected Works [胡锦涛文选], 2016, vol. 3 [第三卷], 139.

64. Ibid., vol. 3 [第三卷], 281.

65. Ibid., vol. 3 [第三卷], 281–82.

66. Ibid., vol. 3 [第三卷], 218; Chin, "China's Rising Monetary Power," 196–98.

67. Chin, "China's Rising Monetary Power," 195.

68. Jonathan Kirshner, "Regional Hegemony and an Emerging RMB Zone," in *The Great Wall of Money: Power and Politics in China's International Relations*, eds. Eric Helleiner and Jonathan Kirshner (Ithaca, NY: Cornell University Press, 2014), 223.

69. Quoted in ibid., 223.

70. Ibid., 215.
71. Eswar Prasad, *Gaining Currency: The Rise of the Renminbi* (Oxford: Oxford University Press, 2017).
72. Ibid., 103.
73. Huileng Tan, "China's Currency Is Still Nowhere Near Overtaking the Dollar for Global Payments," *CNBC*, February 2, 2018, https://www.cnbc.com/2018/02/02/china-currency-yuan-the-rmb-isnt-near-overtaking-the-us-dollar.html.
74. James Kynge, "Renminbi Tops Currency Usage Table for China's Trade with Asia," *Financial Times*, May 27, 2015, https://www.ft.com/content/1e44915c-048d-11e5-adaf-00144feabdc0.
75. Kirshner, "Regional Hegemony and an Emerging RMB Zone," 214.
76. See ibid., 236–37.
77. "SWIFT History," SWIFT, 2018, https://www.swift.com/about-us/history.
78. Ibid.
79. Philip Blenkinsop and Rachel Younglai, "Banking's SWIFT Says Ready to Block Iran Transactions," *Reuters*, February 17, 2012, https://www.reuters.com/article/us-iran-sanctions-swift/bankings-swift-says-ready-to-block-iran-transactions-idUSTRE81G26820120217.
80. "Payments System SWIFT to Cut Off Iranian Banks," *Reuters*, March 15, 2012, https://www.reuters.com/article/us-eu-iran-sanctions/payments-system-swift-to-cut-off-iranian-banks-idUSBRE82E0VR20120315.
81. Jeremy Wagstaff and Tom Begin, "SWIFT Messaging System Bans North Korean Banks Blacklisted by UN," *Reuters*, March 8, 2017, https://www.reuters.com/article/us-northkorea-banks-swift/swift-messaging-system-bans-north-korean-banks-blacklisted-by-u-n-idUSKBN16F0NI.
82. Farrell, "Russia Is Hinting at a New Cold War over SWIFT."
83. "Russia's Banking System Has SWIFT Alternative Ready," *RT*, March 23, 2017, https://www.rt.com/business/382017-russia-swift-central-bank/.
84. Leonid Bershidsky, "How Europe Can Keep the Money Flowing to Iran," *Bloomberg*, May 18, 2018, https://www.bloomberg.com/view/articles/2018-05-18/how-europe-can-keep-money-flowing-to-iran. See also "Iran nachal podgotovku predlozhenii po ispol'zovaniyu kriptovalyut v tovaroobmene s RF," *Interfax*, May 15, 2018, http://www.interfax.ru/business/612729. Natasha Turak, "Russia's Central Bank Governor Touts Moscow Alternative to SWIFT Transfer System as Protection from US Sanctions," *CNBC*, May 23, 2018, https://www.cnbc.com/2018/05/23/russias-central-bank-governor-touts-moscow-alternative-to-swift-transfer-system-as-protection-from-us-sanctions.html.
85. Zhenhua Lu, "US House Committee Targets Major Chinese Banks' Lifeline to North Korea," *South China Morning Post*, September 13, 2017, https://www.scmp.com/news/china/policies-politics/article/2110914/us-house-committee-targets-major-chinese-banks-lifeline.
86. Michelle Chen and Koh Gui Qing, "China's International Payments System Ready, Could Launch by End-2015," *Reuters*, March 9, 2015, http://www.reuters.com/article/2015/03/09/us-china-yuan-payments-exclusive-idUSKBN0M50BV20150309.
87. Don Weinland, "China's Global Payment System CIPs Too Costly for Most Banks—For Now," *South China Morning Post*, October 17, 2015, https://www.scmp.com/business/banking-finance/article/1868749/chinas-global-payment-system-cips-too-costly-most-banks-now.
88. Gabriel Wildau, "China Launch of Renminbi Payments System Reflects SWIFT Spying Concerns," *Financial Times*, October 8, 2015, https://www.ft.com/content/84241292-66a1-11e5-a155-02b6f8af6a62.
89. Prasad, *Gaining Currency*, 116.
90. *China and the Age of Strategic Rivalry* (Ottawa: Canadian Security Intelligence Services, 2018), 113–22.
91. Stefania Palma, "SWIFT Dips into China with CIPS," *The Banker*, July 1, 2016, https://www.thebanker.com/Global-Transaction-Banking/Swift-dips-into-China-with-CIPS.
92. "Beijing's International Payments System Scaled Back for Launch," *South China Morning Post*, July 23, 2015, https://www.scmp.com/business/money/article/1838428/beijings-international-payments-system-scaled-back-launch.
93. Wildau, "China Launch of Renminbi Payments System Reflects SWIFT Spying Concerns."
94. *China and the Age of Strategic Rivalry*, 113–22.

95. Wildau, "China Launch of Renminbi Payments System Reflects SWIFT Spying Concerns."

96. Bershidsky, "How Europe Can Keep the Money Flowing to Iran."

97. "EU Criticizes Role of US Credit Rating Agencies in Debt Crisis," *Deutsche Welle*, July 11, 2011, https://www.dw.com/en/eu-criticizes-role-of-us-credit-rating-agencies-in-debt-crisis/a-15225330.

98. Huw Jones and Marc Jones, "EU Watchdog Tightens Grip over Use of Foreign Credit Ratings," *Reuters*, November 17, 2017, https://www.reuters.com/article/us-britain-eu-creditratingagencies/eu-watchdog-tightens-grip-over-use-of-foreign-credit-ratings-idUSKBN1DH1J1.

99. "China's Finance Minister Accuses Credit Rating Agencies of Bias," *South China Morning Post*, April 16, 2016, https://www.scmp.com/news/china/economy/article/1936614/chinas-finance-minister-accuses-credit-rating-agencies-bias; Joe McDonald, "China Criticizes S&P Rating Cut as 'Wrong Decision,'" *Associated Press*, September 22, 2017, https://apnews.com/743f86862f5a4b85844dcc10f96e3f8c.

100. Guan Jianzhong, "The Strategic Choice of Chinese Credit Rating System," Dagong Global (via Internet Archive), 2012, https://web.archive.org/web/20160805110146/http://en.dagongcredit.com/content/details58_6631.html.

101. Ibid.

102. "Man in the Middle," *South China Morning Post*, April 26, 2014, https://www.scmp.com/business/china-business/article/1497241/man-middle.

103. Ibid.

104. Liz Mak, "China's Dagong Global Credit Mounts Challenge to 'Big Three' Rating Agencies," *South China Morning Post*, August 7, 2016, https://www.scmp.com/business/banking-finance/article/2000489/chinas-dagong-global-credit-mounts-challenge-big-three.

105. Reports of Guan's government ties are discussed in Christopher Ricking, "US Rating Agencies Face Chinese Challenge," *Deutsche Welle*, November 19, 2012, https://www.dw.com/en/us-ratings-agencies-face-chinese-challenge/a-16389497; Guan Jianzhong, "The Strategic Choice of Chinese Credit Rating System."

106. Asit Ranjan Mishra, "China Not in Favor of BRICS Proposed Credit Rating Agency," *Livemint*, October 14, 2014, https://www.livemint.com/Politics/btAFFggl1LoKBNZK0a45fJ/China-not-in-favour-of-proposed-Brics-credit-rating-agency.html.

107. "Corporate Culture," Dagong Global (via Internet Archive), 2016, https://web.archive.org/web/20160704062906/http://en.dagongcredit.com:80/about/culture.html.

108. "About Us," Dagong Global (via Internet Archive), 2016, https://web.archive.org/web/20160326131607/http://en.dagongcredit.com/about/aboutDagong.html.

Chapter 11

1. Fu Ying, "The US World Order Is a Suit That No Longer Fits," *Financial Times*, January 6, 2016, https://www.ft.com/content/c09cbcb6-b3cb-11e5-b147-e5e5bba42e51.

2. Xi Jinping [习近平], "Xi Jinping Delivered an Important Speech at the Opening Ceremony of the Seminar on Learning and Implementing the Spirit of the Fifth Plenary Session of the 19th Central Committee of the Party [习近平在省部级主要领导干部学习贯彻党的十九届五中全会精神专题研讨班开班式上发表重要讲话]," *Xinhua [新华]*, January 11, 2021, http://www.xinhuanet.com/politics/leaders/2021-01/11/c_1126970918.htm.

3. Zheping Huang, "Xi Jinping Just Showed His Power by Making China's Elite Sit through a Tortuously Long Speech," *Quartz*, October 10, 2017, https://qz.com/1105235/chinas-19th-party-congress-xi-jinping-just-showed-his-power-by-making-chinas-elite-sit-through-a-tortuously-long-speech/.

4. Xi Jinping [习近平], "Secure a Decisive Victory in Building a Moderately Prosperous Society in All Respects and Strive for the Great Success of Socialism with Chinese Characteristics for a New Era [决胜全面建成小康社会 夺取新时代中国特色社会主义伟大胜利]," 19th Party Congress Political Report (Beijing, October 18, 2017).

5. Ibid.

6. Fu Ying, "The US World Order Is a Suit That No Longer Fits."

7. Chen Xiangyang, "China Advances as the US Retreats," *China US Focus*, January 23, 2018, https://www.chinausfocus.com/foreign-policy/china-advances-as-the-us-retreats.

8. Yang Jiechi [杨洁篪], "Promote the Construction of a Community of Common Destiny for Mankind [推动构建人类命运共同体]," *People's Daily* [人民日报], November 19, 2017, http://cpc.people.com.cn/n1/2017/1119/c64094-29654801.html.

9. "Xi Jinping's First Mention of the 'Two Guidances' Has Profound Meaning [习近平首提'两个引导'有深意]," *Study China* [学习中国], February 21, 2017, https://web.archive.org/web/20171219140753/http://www.ccln.gov.cn/hotnews/230779.shtml. This commentary on Xi Jinping's speech was published by the leadership of the China Cadre Learning Network [中国干部学习网], which publishes material for circulation to Party cadres.

10. Xi Jinping [习近平], *Xi Jinping: The Governance of China, Volume 3* [习近平谈治国理政], vol. 3 [第三卷] (Beijing: Foreign Language Press [外文出版社], 2020), 77. Emphasis added.

11. Robert E. Kelly, "What Would Chinese Hegemony Look Like?," *The Diplomat*, February 10, 2014, https://thediplomat.com/2014/02/what-would-chinese-hegemony-look-like/; Nadège Rolland, "China's Vision for a New World Order" (Washington, DC: National Bureau of Asian Research, 2020), https://www.nbr.org/publication/chinas-vision-for-a-new-world-order/.

12. Yuan Peng [袁鹏], "Financial Crisis and U.S. Economic Hegemony: An Interpretation of History and Politics [金融危机与美国经济霸权:历史与政治的解读]," *Contemporary International Relations* [现代国际关系], no. 5 (2009).

13. Yang Jiechi [杨洁篪], "Continue to Create New Prospects for Foreign Work under the Guidance of General Secretary Xi Jinping's Diplomatic Thoughts [在习近平总书记外交思想指引下不断开创对外工作新局面]," Foreign Ministry of the People's Republic of China [中华人民共和国外交部], January 14, 2017, https://www.fmprc.gov.cn/ce/ceus/chn/zgyw/t1430589.htm.

14. "Xi Jinping's First Mention of the 'Two Guidances' Has Profound Meaning [习近平首提'两个引导'有深意]." This site is part of the China Cadre Learning Network [中国干部学习网] for Party cadres. See also the Xinhua readout, which contains other portions. Xi Jinping [习近平], "Xi Jinping Presided over the National Security Work Symposium [习近平主持召开国家安全工作座谈会]," *Xinhua* [新华], February 17, 2017, http://www.xinhuanet.com//politics/2017-02/17/c_1120486809.htm.

15. "Xi Jinping's First Mention of the 'Two Guidances' Has Profound Meaning [习近平首提'两个引导'有深意]." This site is part of the China Cadre Learning Network [中国干部学习网] for Party cadres. Emphasis added.

16. This commentary was written by the editor of the China Cadre Learning Network [中国干部学习网], a website organized by the Central Party School to provide insight on key ideological questions, and was also posted to Chinese state media, including the website of the *People's Daily*.

17. "Xi Jinping's First Mention of the 'Two Guidances' Has Profound Meaning [习近平首提'两个引导'有深意]." This site is part of the China Cadre Learning Network [中国干部学习网] for Party cadres.

18. Xi Jinping [习近平], "Secure a Decisive Victory in Building a Moderately Prosperous Society in All Respects and Strive for the Great Success of Socialism with Chinese Characteristics for a New Era. [决胜全面建成小康社会 夺取新时代中国特色社会主义伟大胜利]."

19. Xi Jinping [习近平], "Xi Jinping Met the 2017 Ambassadorial Conference and Delivered an Important Speech [习近平接见2017年度驻外使节工作会议与会使节并发表重要讲话]," *Xinhua* [新华], December 28, 2017, http://www.xinhuanet.com/2017-12/28/c_1122181743.htm.

20. Ibid.

21. Ibid.

22. Ibid.

23. Zhu Feng [朱锋], "A Summary of Recent Academic Research on 'Great Changes Unseen in a Century' [近期学界关于'百年未有之大变局'研究综述]," *People's Forum - Academic Frontier* [人民论坛 - 学术前沿], no. 4 (2019). Zhu Feng published this piece in a social science journal published by the Chinese Communist Party's flagship newspaper *People's Daily* [人民日报].

24. Li Jie [李杰], "Deeply Understand and Grasp the World's 'Big Changes Unseen in a Century' [深刻理解把握世界"百年未有之大变局"]," *Study Times* [学习时报], September 3, 2018, https://web.archive.org/web/20200624172344/http://www.qstheory.cn/llwx/ 2018-09/03/c_1123369881.htm. This piece was initially published in the Party School journal *Study Times* [学习时报] and then posted on the *Seeking Truth* [求是] site.

25. Zhang Yuyan [张宇燕], "Understanding the Great Changes Unseen in a Century [理解百年未有之大变局]," *International Economic Review* [国际经济评论], September 18, 2019, http://www.qstheory.cn/llwx/2019-09/18/c_1125010363.htm.

26. Du Qinghao [杜庆昊], "Great Changes Unseen in a Century in Historical Perspective [大历史视野中的 '百年未有之大变局']," *Study Times* [学习时报], March 11, 2019, http://www.qstheory.cn/llwx/2019-03/11/c_1124218453.htm.

27. Wu Xinbo [武心波], "The Great Changes Unseen in a Century and Sino-Japanese Relations Have Bright Spots and Dark Spots [百年未有大变局，中日关系有'明"暗']," *Liberation Daily* [解放日报], January 15, 2019.

28. Zhu Feng [朱锋], "A Summary of Recent Academic Research on 'Great Changes Unseen in a Century' [近期学界关于'百年未有之大变局'研究综述]."

29. Luo Jianbo [罗建波], "From the Overall Perspective, Understand and Grasp the World's Great Changes Unseen in a Century [从全局高度 理解和把握世界百年未有之大变局]," *Study Times* [学习时报], June 7, 2019, http://theory.people.com.cn/n1/2019/0607/ c40531-31125044.html.

30. Gao Zugui [高祖贵], "The Rich Connotation of the Great Changes Unseen in a Century [世界百年未有之大变局的丰富内涵]," *Study Times* [学习时报], January 21, 2019, http://theory.people.com.cn/n1/2019/0121/c40531-30579611.html.

31. For a remarkable roundtable set of perspectives on this concept including several leading Chinese thinkers, see Zhang Yunling [张蕴岭] et al., "How to Recognize and Understand the Century's Great Changes [如何认识和理解百年大变局]," *Asia-Pacific Security and Maritime Research* [亚太安全与海洋研究], no. 2 (2019), http://www.charhar.org.cn/ newsinfo.aspx?newsid=14706.

32. Ibid.

33. Nie Wenjuan, "US vs. China: Which System Is Superior?," *China-US Focus*, April 29, 2020, https://www.chinausfocus.com/society-culture/us-vs-china-which-system-is-superior.

34. Wu Baiyi, "American Illness," *China-US Focus*, June 17, 2020, https://www.chinausfocus. com/society-culture/american-illness.

35. Cui Hongjian [崔洪建], "What Does 'Populism,' Found in So Many Headlines, Actually Mean? [频频上头条的'民粹主义'到底是什么意思]," China Institute of International Studies [中国国际问题研究院], March 10, 2018, https://web.archive.org/web/ 20180325192425/http://www.ciis.org.cn/chinese/2018-03/12/content_40248594.htm. The author was previously a diplomat before working at the China Institute of International Studies.

36. Zhang Yunling [张蕴岭] et al., "How to Recognize and Understand the Century's Great Changes [如何认识和理解百年大变局]."

37. Zhu Feng [朱锋], "A Summary of Recent Academic Research on 'Great Changes Unseen in a Century.' [近期学界关于'百年未有之大变局'研究综述]."

38. "Xi Jinping's First Mention of the 'Two Guidances' Has Profound Meaning [习近平首提'两个引导'有深意]."

39. Zhang Yuyan [张宇燕], "Understanding the Great Changes Unseen in a Century [理解百年未有之大变局]."

40. Zhang Yunling [张蕴岭] et al., "How to Recognize and Understand the Century's Great Changes [如何认识和理解百年大变局]."

41. Ibid.Zhang Yunling [张蕴岭] et al.

42. "Deeply Understand the Big Test of Epidemic Prevention and Control [深刻认识疫情防控这次大考]," *People's Daily* [人民日报], April 23, 2020.

43. Chen Qi [陈琪], "The Impact of the Global Coronavirus Pandemic on the Great Changes Unseen in a Century [全球新冠疫情对百年未有大变局的影响]," Ministry of Commerce of the People's Republic of China [中华人民共和国商务部], April 22, 2020, http://chinawto.mofcom.gov.cn/article/br/bs/202004/20200402957839.shtml.

44. "Peking University Center for American Studies Successfully Held an Online Seminar on U.S. and China Relations under the Global Pandemic [北京大学美国研究中心成功举办'全球疫情下的美国与中美关系'线上研讨会]," School of International Studies, Peking University [北京大学国际关系学院], April 13, 2020, https://www.sis.pku.edu.cn/news64/1324227.htm.

45. Chen Jimin, "COVID-19 Hits International System," *China-US Focus*, April 27, 2020, https://www.chinausfocus.com/foreign-policy/covid-19-hits-international-system.

46. Wu Baiyi, "American Illness."

47. "Deeply Understand the Big Test of Epidemic Prevention and Control [深刻认识疫情防控这次大考]."

48. Yuan Peng [袁鹏], "The Coronavirus Pandemic and the Great Changes Unseen in a Century [新冠疫情与百年变局]," *Contemporary International Relations* [现代国际关系], no. 5 (June 2020): 1–6.

49. Shi Zehua [史泽华], "Why Has American Populism Risen at This Time [美国民粹主义何以此时兴起]," *U.S.-China Perception Monitor* [中美印象], May 4, 2016, http://www.uscnpm.com/model_item.html?action=view&table=article&id=10182.

50. Cui Hongjian [崔洪建], "What Does 'Populism,' Found in So Many Headlines, Actually Mean? [频频上头条的'民粹主义'到底是什么意思]."

51. Zhang Yunling [张蕴岭] et al., "How to Recognize and Understand the Century's Great Changes [如何认识和理解百年大变局]."

52. Jin Canrong [金灿荣], "Great Changes Unseen in a Century and China's Responsibility [百年未有之大变局与中国担当]," *Liberation Army Daily* [解放军报], December 11, 2019, http://www.mod.gov.cn/jmsd/2019-12/11/content_4856573.htm. The article, originally published in *Liberation Army Daily*, was also published on the official Ministry of Defense website.

53. Nie Wenjuan, "US vs. China"

54. Wu Baiyi, "American Illness."

55. Ibid.

56. Jin Canrong [金灿荣], "Looking at the World Forum, Jin Canrong: Great Changes in the World in the Next Ten Years [观天下讲坛|金灿荣：未来10年的世界大变局]," *Guancha* [观察], August 1, 2017, https://www.guancha.cn/JinCanRong/2017_08_01_420867_s.shtml.

57. "The Central Economic Work Conference Was Held in Beijing Xi Jinping and Li Keqiang Delivered an Important Speech [中央经济工作会议在北京举行 习近平李克强作重要讲话]," *Xinhua* [新华], December 21, 2018, http://www.xinhuanet.com/2018-12/21/c_1123887379.htm.

58. Xi Jinping [习近平], *Xi Jinping: The Governance of China* [习近平谈治国理政], vol. 3, [第三卷], 294.

59. Ren Jingjing [任晶晶], "Strive to Realize the Great Rejuvenation of the Chinese Nation in the 'Great Changes Unseen in a Century' [在'百年未有之大变局'中奋力实现中华民族伟大复兴]," *Journal of Northeast Asia Studies* [东北亚学刊], 2019.

60. Zhang Yunling [张蕴岭], "An Analysis of the 'Great Changes Unseen in a Century' [对'百年之大变局'的分析与思考]," Journal of Shandong University [山东大学学报], no. 5 (2019): 1–15.

61. Ibid.

62. Lu Hui, "Commentary: Milestone Congress Points to New Era for China, The World," *Xinhua*, October 24, 2017, http://www.xinhuanet.com/english/2017-10/24/c_136702090.htm.

63. Li Jie [李杰], "Deeply Understand and Grasp the World's 'Big Changes Unseen in a Century.' [深刻理解把握世界'百年未有之大变局']."

64. Ren Jingjing [任晶晶], "Strive to Realize the Great Rejuvenation of the Chinese Nation in the 'Great Changes Unseen in a Century.' [在'百年未有之大变局'中奋力实现中华民族伟大复兴]."

65. Ibid.

66. Ibid.

67. Xi Jinping [习近平], "Xi Jinping: Follow the Trend of the Times to Achieve Common Development [习近平：顺应时代潮流 实现共同发展]" (Speech at the BRICS Business

Forum, Johannesburg, South Africa, July 25, 2018), http://cpc.people.com.cn/n1/2018/0726/c64094-30170246.html.

68. Xi Jinping [习近平], "Xi Jinping Met the 2017 Ambassadorial Conference and Delivered an Important Speech [习近平接见2017年度驻外使节工作会议与会使节并发表重要讲话]."

69. Xi Jinping [习近平], "Xi Jinping Delivered an Important Speech at the Opening Ceremony of the Training Class for Young and Middle-Aged Cadres at the Central Party School (National School of Administration) [习近平在中央党校（国家行政学院）中青年干部培训班开班式上发表重要讲话]" (Central Party School, September 3, 2019), http://www.gov.cn/xinwen/2019-09/03/content_5426920.htm.

70. "The Central Economic Work Conference Was Held in Beijing Xi Jinping and Li Keqiang Delivered an Important Speech [中央经济工作会议在北京举行 习近平李克强作重要讲话]."

71. "China and the World in the New Era [新时代的中国与世界]," White Paper [白皮书] (State Council Information Office [国务院新闻办公室], 2019).

72. Zheng Jialu [郑嘉璐], "This Is China's Best Strategic Opportunity Since the End of the Cold War—Interview with Professor Yan Xuetong, Dean of the Institute of International Relations, Tsinghua University [当前是冷战结束以来中国最好的战略机遇—专访清华大学国际关系研究院院长阎学通教授]," *Window on the South* [南风窗], October 9, 2018, https://www.nfcmag.com/article/8372.html.

73. Ibid.

74. Ibid.

75. Ibid.

76. Wu Xinbo [武心波], "The Great Changes Unseen in a Century and Sino-Japanese Relations Have Bright Spots and Dark Spots [百年未有大变局，中日关系有'明'暗']."

77. Xi Jinping [习近平], *Xi Jinping: The Governance of China* [习近平谈治因理政], vol. 3, [第三卷], 294.

78. Liu Jianfei [刘建飞], "How Do Leading Cadres Recognize the World's 'Great Changes Unseen in a Century' [领导干部如何认识世界百年未有之大变局]," *China Party and Government Cadres Tribune* [中国党政干部论坛], October 25, 2019, https://www.ccps.gov.cn/zt/dxxylldlzt/202004/t20200424_139781.shtml.

79. Ren Jingjing [任晶晶], "Strive to Realize the Great Rejuvenation of the Chinese Nation in the 'Great Changes Unseen in a Century.' [在'百年未有之大变局'中奋力实现中华民族伟大复兴]."

80. Zhu Feng [朱锋], "A Summary of Recent Academic Research on 'Great Changes Unseen in a Century.' [近期学界关于'百年未有之大变局'研究综述]."

81. Fang Xiao [方晓], "Innovative Partnership Networks: To Create Growth Point for a Global Partnership Network [创新伙伴关系：打造全球伙伴关系的新增长点]," *International Studies* [国际问题研究], no. 6 (2019): 41–55.

82. Liu Jianfei [刘建飞], "How Do Leading Cadres Recognize the World's Great Changes Unseen in a Century [领导干部如何认识世界百年未有之大变局]."

83. Ibid.

84. Xi Jinping [习近平], "Xi Jinping Delivered an Important Speech at the Opening Ceremony of the Training Class for Young and Middle-Aged Cadres at the Central Party School (National School of Administration) [习近平在中央党校（国家行政学院）中青年干部培训班开班式上发表重要讲话]."

85. Xi Jinping [习近平], "Xi Jinping Delivered an Important Speech at the Opening Ceremony of the Seminar on Learning and Implementing the Spirit of the 5th Plenary Session of the 19th Central Committee of the Party [习近平在省部级主要领导干部学习贯彻党的十九届五中全会精神专题研讨班开班式上发表重要讲话]." Emphasis added.

Chapter 12

1. "Woman Accused of Gross Slander—DN Spread the Story Using Metoo, China's Ambassador in Interview, Public Service Debates Public Service [Kvinna åtalad för grovt förtal—DN spred historien under metoo, Kinas ambassadör i intervju, public service debatterar public

service]," Sveriges Radio, November 30, 2019, https://sverigesradio.se/sida/avsnitt/1421039?programid=2795.

2. Stephen Chen, "China Launches Its First Fully Owned Overseas Satellite Ground Station near North Pole," *South China Morning Post*, December 16, 2016, https://www.scmp.com/news/china/policies-politics/article/2055224/china-launches-its-first-fully-owned-overseas-satellite.

3. A recording can be found here: "Woman Accused of Gross Slander—DN Spread the Story Using Metoo, China's Ambassador in Interview, Public Service Debates Public Service."

4. Jonathan Kearsley, Eryk Bagshaw, and Anthony Galloway, "'If You Make China the Enemy, China Will Be the Enemy': Beijing's Fresh Threat to Australia," *Sydney Morning Herald*, November 18, 2020, https://www.smh.com.au/world/asia/if-you-make-china-the-enemy-china-will-be-the-enemy-beijing-s-fresh-threat-to-australia-20201118-p56fqs.html.

5. Hal Brands, "What Does China Really Want?: To Dominate the World," *Japan Times*, May 22, 2020, https://www.japantimes.co.jp/opinion/2020/05/22/commentary/world-commentary/china-really-want-dominate-world/.

6. "Xi Jinping's First Mention of the 'Two Guidances' Has Profound Meaning [习近平首提'两个引导'有深意]," *Study China [学习中国]*, February 21, 2017, https://web.archive.org/web/20171219140753/http://www.ccln.gov.cn/hotnews/230779.shtml. This commentary on Xi Jinping's speech was published by the leadership of the China Cadre Learning Network [中国干部学习网], which publishes material for circulation to Party cadres.

7. Xi Jinping [习近平], "Xi Urges Breaking New Ground in Major Country Diplomacy with Chinese Characteristics [努力开创中国特色大国外交新局面]," Xinhua [新华网], June 22, 2018, http://www.xinhuanet.com/politics/2018-06/23/c_1123025806.htm.

8. "Xi Jinping: Promoting Belt and Road Cooperation to Deeply Benefit the People [习近平：推动共建'一带一路'走深走实造福人民]," *Xinhua [新华网]*, August 27, 2018, http://www.xinhuanet.com/politics/2018-08/27/c_1123336562.htm.

9. "China and the World in the New Era [新时代的中国与世界]," White Paper [白皮书] (State Council Information Office [国务院新闻办公室], 2019).

10. Wang Junsheng [王俊生] and Qin Sheng [秦升], "Seize the Opportunity from the 'Great Changes Unseen in a Century' [从'百年未有之大变局'中把握机遇]," *Red Flag Manuscripts [红旗文稿]*, April 10, 2019, http://www.qstheory.cn/dukan/hqwg/2019-04/10/c_1124344744.htm. *Red Flag Manuscripts* is published biweekly by *Qiushi*, and this article appeared in print.

11. Zhang Yunling [张蕴岭], "An Analysis of the 'Great Changes Unseen in a Century' [对'百年之大变局'的分析与思考]," *Journal of Shandong University [山东大学学报]*, no. 5 (2019): 1–15.

12. Yuan Peng [袁鹏], "The Coronavirus Pandemic and the Great Changes Unseen in a Century [新冠疫情与百年变局]," *Contemporary International Relations [现代国际关系]*, no. 5 (June 2020): 1–6.

13. Yang Jiechi [杨洁篪], "Continue to Create New Prospects for Foreign Work under the Guidance of General Secretary Xi Jinping's Diplomatic Thoughts [在习近平总书记外交思想指引下不断开创对外工作新局面]," Foreign Ministry of the People's Republic of China [中华人民共和国外交部], January 14, 2017, https://www.fmprc.gov.cn/ce/ceus/chn/zgyw/t1430589.htm.

14. "Xi Jinping's First Mention of the 'Two Guidances' Has Profound Meaning [习近平首提'两个引导'有深意]." Emphasis added.

15. Ibid. Emphasis added.

16. That is, he listed promoting "the community of common destiny for mankind," expanding China's "global partnership network," enlarging "the country's 'circle of friends,'" and promoting BRI.

17. Xi Jinping [习近平], "Xi Urges Breaking New Ground in Major Country Diplomacy with Chinese Characteristics [努力开创中国特色大国外交新局面]."

18. Wang Yi [王毅], "Speech at the Opening Ceremony of the 2018 Symposium on the International Situation and China's Diplomacy [在2018年国际形势与中国外交研讨会开幕式上的演讲]," Foreign Ministry of the

People's Republic of China [中华人民共和国外交部], December 11, 2018, https://www.fmprc.gov.cn/web/wjbzhd/t1620761.shtml.

19. Ibid.

20. "China and the World in the New Era [新时代的中国与世界]."

21. Liu Jianfei [刘建飞], "How Do Leading Cadres Recognize the World's Great Changes Unseen in a Century [领导干部如何认识世界百年未有之大变局]," *China Party and Government Cadres Tribune* [中国党政干部论坛], October 25, 2019, https://www.ccps.gov.cn/zt/dxxylldlzt/202004/t20200424_139781.shtml.

22. Li Jie [李杰], "Deeply Understand and Grasp the World's 'Big Changes Unseen in a Century' [深刻理解把握世界'百年未有之大变局']," *Study Times* [学习时报], September 3, 2018, https://web.archive.org/web/20200624172344/http://www.qstheory.cn/llwx/2018-09/03/c_1123369881.htm.

23. Zhang Yunling [张蕴岭] et al., "How to Recognize and Understand the Century's Great Changes [如何认识和理解百年大变局]," *Asia-Pacific Security and Maritime Research* [亚太安全与海洋研究], no. 2 (2019), http://www.charhar.org.cn/newsinfo.aspx?newsid=14706.

24. Jin Canrong [金灿荣], "Looking at the World Forum, Jin Canrong: Great Changes in the World in the Next Ten Years [观天下讲坛|金灿荣：未来10年的世界大变局]," *Guancha* [观察], August 1, 2017, https://www.guancha.cn/JinCanRong/2017_08_01_420867_s.shtml.

25. Jin Canrong [金灿荣], "Great Changes Unseen in a Century and China's Responsibility [百年未有之大变局与中国担当]," *Liberation Army Daily* [解放军报], December 11, 2019, http://www.mod.gov.cn/jmsd/2019-12/11/content_4856573.htm.

26. Wang Junsheng [王俊生] and Qin Sheng [秦升], "Seize the Opportunity from the 'Great Changes Unseen in a Century.' [从'百年未有之大变局'中把握机遇]."

27. Ren Jingjing [任晶晶], "Strive to Realize the Great Rejuvenation of the Chinese Nation in the 'Great Changes Unseen in a Century' [在'百年未有之大变局'中奋力实现中华民族伟大复兴]," *Journal of Northeast Asia Studies* [东北亚学刊], 2019.

28. "China and the World in the New Era [新时代的中国与世界]."

29. Kristine Lee and Alexander Sullivan, "People's Republic of the United Nations: China's Emerging Revisionism in International Organizations" (Washington, DC: Center for a New American Security, May 2019).

30. "China and the World in the New Era [新时代的中国与世界]."

31. Courtney Fung and Shing-Hon Lam, "China Already Leads 4 of the 15 U.N. Specialized Agencies—and Is Aiming for a 5th," *Washington Post*, March 3, 2020, https://www.washingtonpost.com/politics/2020/03/03/china-already-leads-4-15-un-specialized-agencies-is-aiming-5th/.

32. Ibid.

33. See minute 24 of *"Lectures" Former UN Deputy Secretary-General Wu Hongbo: Excellent Diplomats Must Have Strong Patriotism and Enterprising Spirit 2018-12-22 | CCTV "Lectures" Official Channel [《开讲啦》 前联合国副秘书长吴红波：优秀的外交官要有强烈的爱国心和进取精神 20181222 | CCTV《开讲啦》官方频道]* (CCTV, 2018), https://www.youtube.com/watch?v=pmrI2n6d6VU&t=24m56s.

34. Nicola Contessi, "Experiments in Soft Balancing: China-Led Multilateralism in Africa and the Arab World," *Caucasian Review of International Affairs* 3, no. 4 (2009): 404–34.

35. Jakub Jakóbowski, "Chinese-Led Regional Multilateralism in Central and Eastern Europe, Africa and Latin America: 16 + 1, FOCAC, and CCF," *Journal of Contemporary China* 27, no. 113 (April 11, 2018): 659–73.

36. For example, see "Joint Declaration of China-Latin America and the Caribbean Countries Leaders' Meeting in Brasilia" (Brasilia: China-Latin America and the Caribbean Countries, July 17, 2014), http://www.itamaraty.gov.br/images/ed_integracao/docs_CELAC/DECLCHALC.2014ENG.pdf; "Declaration of Action on China-Arab States Cooperation under the Belt and Road Initiative" (Beijing: China-Arab States Cooperation, July 10, 2018), http://www.chinaarabcf.org/chn/lthyjwx/bzjhywj/dbjbzjhy/P020180726404036530409.

pdf; "Beijing Declaration of the First Ministerial Meeting of the CELAC-China Forum" (Beijing: China-CELAC Forum, January 23, 2015), http://www.chinacelacforum.org/eng/zywj_3/t1230938.htm.

37. "Joint Statement of the Extraordinary China-Africa Summit on Solidarity Against COVID-19," Ministry of Foreign Affairs of the People's Republic of China, June 17, 2020, https://www.fmprc.gov.cn/mfa_eng/zxxx_662805/t1789596.shtml.

38. For the various letters containing signatories critiquing and supporting China on human rights, see Nick Cumming-Bruce, "China Rebuked by 22 Nations Over Xinjiang Repression," *New York Times*, July 10, 2019, https://www.nytimes.com/2019/07/10/world/asia/china-xinjiang-rights.html; Catherine Putz, "Which Countries Are for or against China's Xinjiang Policies?," *The Diplomat*, July 15, 2019, https://thediplomat.com/2019/07/which-countries-are-for-or-against-chinas-xinjiang-policies; Roie Yellinek and Elizabeth Chen, "The '22 vs. 50' Diplomatic Split between the West and China over Xinjiang and Human Rights," *China Brief* 19, no. 22 (December 31, 2019), https://jamestown.org/program/the-22-vs-50-diplomatic-split-between-the-west-and-china-over-xinjiang-and-human-rights/; "Ambassadors from 37 Countries Issue Joint Letter to Support China on Its Human Rights Achievements," *Xinhua*, July 13, 2019, http://www.xinhuanet.com/english/2019-07/13/c_138222183.htm.

39. "The Overwhelming Majority of Countries Resolutely Oppose the United States and Other Countries Interfering in China's Internal Affairs with Xinjiang-Related Issues [绝大多数国家坚决反对美国等国借涉疆问题干涉中国内政]," *People's Daily* [人民日报], October 31, 2019, http://world.people.com.cn/n1/2019/1031/c1002-31429458.html.

40. Data from CNKI.

41. Xi Jinping [习近平], "Secure a Decisive Victory in Building a Moderately Prosperous Society in All Respects and Strive for the Great Success of Socialism with Chinese Characteristics for a New Era [决胜全面建成小康社会 夺取新时代中国特色社会主义伟大胜利]," 19th Party Congress Political Report (Beijing, October 18, 2017); "China and the World in the New Era [新时代的中国与世界]."

42. "China and the World in the New Era [新时代的中国与世界]."

43. Declaration [宣言], "Seize the Promising Period of Historical Opportunity [紧紧抓住大有可为的历史机遇期]," *People's Daily* [人民日报], January 15, 2018, http://opinion.people.com.cn/n1/2018/0115/c1003-29763759.html.

44. Ren Jingjing [任晶晶], "Strive to Realize the Great Rejuvenation of the Chinese Nation in the 'Great Changes Unseen in a Century.' [在'百年未有之大变局'中奋力实现中华民族伟大复兴]."

45. Nie Wenjuan, "US vs. China: Which System Is Superior?," *China-US Focus*, April 29, 2020, https://www.chinausfocus.com/society-culture/us-vs-china-which-system-is-superior.

46. This sentiment can be found in several pieces, including: Zhang Yunling [张蕴岭] et al., "How to Recognize and Understand the Century's Great Changes [如何认识和理解百年大变局]." See also Ren Jingjing [任晶晶], "Strive to Realize the Great Rejuvenation of the Chinese Nation in the 'Great Changes Unseen in a Century' [在'百年未有之大变局'中奋力实现中华民族伟大复兴]"; Zhang Yunling [张蕴岭], "Zhang Yunling: Analysis and Thinking on the 'Great Changes Not Seen in a Century' [张蕴岭：对'百年之大变局'的分析与思考]," *Qiushi Online* [求是网], October 8, 2019, http://www.qstheory.cn/international/2019-10/08/c_1125078720.htm.

47. Yuan Peng [袁鹏], "The Coronavirus Pandemic and the Great Changes Unseen in a Century. [新冠疫情与百年变局]."

48. Charles Rollet, "Ecuador's All-Seeing Eye Is Made in China," *Foreign Policy*, August 9, 2018, https://foreignpolicy.com/2018/08/09/ecuadors-all-seeing-eye-is-made-in-china/; Josh Chin, "Huawei Technicians Helped African Governments Spy on Political Opponents," *Wall Street Journal*, August 15, 2019, https://www.wsj.com/articles/huawei-technicians-helped-african-governments-spy-on-political-opponents-11565793017; Nick Bailey, "East African States Adopt China's Playbook on Internet Censorship" (Washington, DC: Freedom House, October 24, 2017), https://freedomhouse.org/article/east-african-states-adopt-chinas-playbook-internet-censorship.

49. Qiushi published key excerpts of Xi's remarks on the fourth industrial revolution here: "What Is the Fourth Industrial Revolution?: Xi Jinping Described Its Blueprint Like This [第四次工业革命什么样？习近平这样描绘蓝图!]," *Qiushi Online* [求是网], July 27, 2018, http://www.qstheory.cn/zhuanqu/2018-07/27/c_1123186013.htm.

50. Xi Jinping [习近平], "Xi Jinping: Follow the Trend of the Times to Achieve Common Development [习近平：顺应时代潮流 实现共同发展]" (Speech at the BRICS Business Forum, Johannesburg, South Africa, July 25, 2018), http://cpc.people.com.cn/n1/2018/0726/c64094-30170246.html.

51. Wang Junsheng [王俊生] and Qin Sheng [秦升], "Seize the Opportunity from the 'Great Changes Unseen in a Century.' [从'百年未有之大变局'中把握机遇]."

52. Li Jie [李杰], "Deeply Understand and Grasp the World's 'Big Changes Unseen in a Century.' [深刻理解把握世界"百年未有之大变局"]."

53. Ibid.

54. Ibid.

55. Ibid.

56. Julian Baird Gewirtz, "China's Long March to Technological Supremacy," *Foreign Affairs*, August 7, 2019, https://www.foreignaffairs.com/articles/china/2019-08-27/chinas-long-march-technological-supremacy.

57. "China and the World in the New Era [新时代的中国与世界]."

58. Li Jie [李杰], "Deeply Understand and Grasp the World's 'Big Changes Unseen in a Century.' [深刻理解把握世界"百年未有之大变局"]."

59. Ibid.

60. Ibid.

61. Jin Canrong [金灿荣], "Jin Canrong: The Fourth Industrial Revolution Is Mainly a Competition between China and the United States, and China Has a Greater Chance of Winning [金灿荣：第四次工业革命主要是中美之间的竞争，且中国胜算更大]," *Guancha* [观察], July 29, 2019, https://www.guancha.cn/JinCanRong/2019_07_29_511347_s.shtml.

62. Zhang Yunling [张蕴岭] et al., "How to Recognize and Understand the Century's Great Changes [如何认识和理解百年大变局]."

63. Zhu Feng [朱锋], "A Summary of Recent Academic Research on 'Great Changes Unseen in a Century' [近期学界关于'百年未有之大变局'研究综述]," *People's Forum—Academic Frontier* [人民论坛—学术前沿], no. 4 (2019).

64. Zhang Yuyan [张宇燕], "Understanding the Great Changes Unseen in a Century [理解百年未有之大变局]," *International Economic Review* [国际经济评论], September 18, 2019, http://www.qstheory.cn/llwx/2019-09/18/c_1125010363.htm.

65. Yuan Peng [袁鹏], "The Coronavirus Pandemic and the Great Changes Unseen in a Century [新冠疫情与百年变局]."

66. Ibid.

67. Khan Beethika, Carol Robbins, and Abigail Okrent, "The State of U.S. Science and Engineering 2020" (Washington, DC: National Science Foundation, 2020), https://ncses.nsf.gov/pubs/nsb20201/global-r-d.

68. Arthur Herman, "The Quantum Computing Threat to American Security," *Wall Street Journal*, November 10, 2019, https://www.wsj.com/articles/the-quantum-computing-threat-to-american-security-11573411715.

69. Ashwin Acharya and Zachary Arnold, "Chinese Public AI R&D Spending: Provisional Findings" (Washington, DC: Center for Security and Emerging Technology, 2019), https://cset.georgetown.edu/wp-content/uploads/Chinese-Public-AI-RD-Spending-Provisional-Findings-1.pdf.

70. Zhang Yunling [张蕴岭] et al., "How to Recognize and Understand the Century's Great Changes [如何认识和理解百年大变局]."

71. "Li Keqiang: Internet + Double Innovation + Made in China 2025 Will Give Birth to a 'New Industrial Revolution' [李克强：互联网+双创+中国制造2025催生一场"新工业革命"]," *Xinhua* [新华], October 15, 2015, http://www.xinhuanet.com/politics/2015-10/15/c_1116825589.htm.

72. "Made in China 2025: Global Ambitions Built on Local Protections" (Washington, DC: United States Chamber of Commerce, 2017), https://www.uschamber.com/sites/default/files/final_made_in_china_2025_report_full.pdf.

73. Anjani Trivedi, "China Is Winning the Trillion-Dollar 5G War," *Washington Post*, July 12, 2020, https://www.washingtonpost.com/business/china-is-winning-the-trillion-dollar-5g-war/2020/07/12/876cb2f6-c493-11ea-a825-8722004e4150_story.html.

74. Jin Canrong [金灿荣], "Jin Canrong: The Fourth Industrial Revolution Is Mainly a Competition Between China and the United States, and China Has a Greater Chance of Winning [金灿荣：第四次工业革命主要是中美之间的竞争，且中国胜算更大]."

75. Ibid.

76. Ibid.

77. Ibid.

78. Jin Canrong [金灿荣], "Great Change Unseen in a Century: In the Sino-American Chess Game, Who Controls the Ups and Downs [百年未有之大变局 中美博弈谁主沉浮]," *China Youth Daily* [中国青年报社], August 14, 2019, https://baijiahao.baidu.com/s?id=1641695768001946785&wfr=spider&for=pc. The article was reposted at the link provided here.

79. Joe McDonald, "Companies Prodded to Rely Less on China, but Few Respond," *Associated Press*, June 29, 2020, https://apnews.com/bc9f37e67745c046563234d1d2e3fe01; "Supply Chain Challenges for US Companies in China" (Beijing: AmCham China, April 17, 2020), https://www.amchamchina.org/about/press-center/amcham-statement/supply-chain-challenges-for-us-companies-in-china.

80. Damien Ma (@damienics), Twitter Post, June 30, 2020, 4:54 p.m., https://twitter.com/damienics/status/1278114690871300101?s=20.

81. Lindsay Gorman, "The U.S. Needs to Get in the Standards Game—With Like-Minded Democracies," *Lawfare*, April 2, 2020, https://www.lawfareblog.com/us-needs-get-standards-game%E2%80%94-minded-democracies.

82. "Take action and fight to the death to win Lenovo's honor defense war! [行动起来，誓死打赢联想荣誉保卫战！]," WeChat Post, May 16, 2018, https://mp.weixin.qq.com/s/JDlmQbGFkxu-_D2jsqNz3w.

83. Frank Tang, "Facebook's Libra Forcing China to Step Up Plans for Its Own Cryptocurrency, Says Central Bank Official," *South China Morning Post*, July 8, 2019, https://www.scmp.com/economy/china-economy/article/3017716/facebooks-libra-forcing-china-step-plans-its-own.

84. Fung and Lam, "China Already Leads 4 of the 15 U.N. Specialized Agencies—and Is Aiming for a 5th"; Raphael Satter and Nick Carey, "China Threatened to Harm Czech Companies Over Taiwan Visit: Letter," *Reuters*, February 19, 2020, https://www.reuters.com/article/us-china-czech-taiwan/china-threatened-to-harm-czech-companies-over-taiwan-visit-letter-idUSKBN20D0G3.

85. Jack Nolan and Wendy Leutert, "Signing Up or Standing Aside: Disaggregating Participation in China's Belt and Road Initiative," *Global China: Assessing China's Growing Role in the World* (Washington, DC: Brookings Institution, 2020), https://www.brookings.edu/articles/signing-up-or-standing-aside-disaggregating-participation-in-chinas-belt-and-road-initiative/.

86. Xi Jinping [习近平], "Secure a Decisive Victory in Building a Moderately Prosperous Society in All Respects and Strive for the Great Success of Socialism with Chinese Characteristics for a New Era [决胜全面建成小康社会 夺取新时代中国特色社会主义伟大胜利]"; "China's National Defense in the New Era [新时代的中国国防]," White Paper [白皮书] (Beijing: 国务院新闻办公室, 2019).

87. Taylor Fravel, "China's 'World Class Military' Ambitions: Origins and Implications," *Washington Quarterly* 43, no. 1 (2020): 91–92.

88. Ibid. 96.

89. "China and the World in the New Era [新时代的中国与世界]."

90. See the three most recent Defense White Papers: "The Diversified Employment of China's Armed Forces [中国武装力量的多样化运用]," White Paper [白皮书] (Beijing: State Council Information Office [国务院新闻办公室], 2013); "China's Military

Strategy [中国的军事战略]," White Paper [白皮书] (State Council Information Office [国务院新闻办公室], 2015); "China's National Defense in the New Era [新时代的中国国防]."

91. See the three most recent Defense White Papers: "The Diversified Employment of China's Armed Forces [中国武装力量的多样化运用]"; "China's Military Strategy [中国的军事战略]"; "China's National Defense in the New Era [新时代的中国国防]."

92. Xi Jinping [习近平], "To Prevent and Resolve Major Risks in Various Domains, Xi Jinping Has Clear Requirements [防范化解各领域重大风险，习近平有明确要求]," *Xinhua* [新华网], January 22, 2019, http://www.xinhuanet.com/2019-01/22/c_1124024464. htm; "China's National Defense in the New Era [新时代的中国国防]."

93. Wang Yi, "Wang Yi Address to the CSIS Statesmen Forum" (Washington, DC, February 25, 2016), https://csis-prod.s3.amazonaws.com/s3fs-public/event/160225_statesmen_forum_wang_yi.pdf. See also Su Zhou, "Number of Chinese Immigrants in Africa Rapidly Increasing," *China Daily*, January 14, 2017, http://www.chinadaily.com.cn/world/2017-01/14/content_27952426.htm; Tom Hancock, "Chinese Return from Africa as Migrant Population Peaks," *Financial Times*, August 28, 2017, https://www.ft.com/content/7106ab42-80d1-11e7-a4ce-15b2513cb3ff.

94. Murray Scott Tanner and Peter W. Mackenzie, "China's Emerging National Security Interests and Their Impact on the People's Liberation Army" (Arlington, VA: Center for Naval Analyses, 2015), 32.

95. Ibid., 36.

96. "How Is China's Energy Footprint Changing?," *ChinaPower* (blog), February 15, 2016, https://chinapower.csis.org/energy-footprint/.

97. Liang Fang (梁芳), "What Are the Risks to the 'Maritime Silk Road' Sea Lanes? [今日'海上丝绸之路'通道风险有多大？]," *Defense Reference* [国防参考], March 13, 2015, http://www.globalview.cn/html/strategy/info_1707.html.

98. Wang Yi, "Wang Yi Address to the CSIS Statesmen Forum."

99. Xi Jinping [习近平], "Secure a Decisive Victory in Building a Moderately Prosperous Society in All Respects and Strive for the Great Success of Socialism with Chinese Characteristics for a New Era [决胜全面建成小康社会 夺取新时代中国特色社会主义伟大胜利]."

100. "China's National Defense in the New Era [新时代的中国国防]."

101. "China's Military Strategy [中国的军事战略]."

102. "China's National Defense in the New Era [新时代的中国国防]."

103. "Foreign Minister Wang Yi Meets the Press," Ministry of Foreign Affairs of the People's Republic of China, March 9, 2016, http://www.fmprc.gov.cn/mfa_eng/zxxx_662805/t1346238.shtml; Ankit Panda, "After Djibouti Base, China Eyes Additional Overseas Military 'Facilities,'" *The Diplomat*, March 9, 2016, https://thediplomat.com/2016/03/after-djibouti-base-china-eyes-additional-overseas-military-facilities/.

104. Adam Ni, Twitter post, April 20, 2019, 8:32 AM ET, https://twitter.com/adam_ni/status/1119579479087747072/photo/1.

105. Mathieu Duchâtel, "Overseas Military Operations in Belt and Road Countries: The Normative Constraints and Legal Framework," in *Securing the Belt and Road Initiative: China's Evolving Military Engagement along the Silk Roads* (Washington, DC: National Bureau of Asian Research, 2019), 11.

106. Maria Abi-Habib, "How China Got Sri Lanka to Cough Up a Port," *New York Times*, June 25, 2018, https://www.nytimes.com/2018/06/25/world/asia/china-sri-lanka-port.html.

107. Saikiran Kannan, "How China Has Expanded Its Influence in the Arabian Sea," *India Today*, May 15, 2020, https://www.indiatoday.in/world/story/how-china-has-expanded-its-influence-in-the-arabian-sea-1678167-2020-05-15.

108. Jacob Gronholt-Pedersen, "China Withdraws Bid for Greenland Airport Projects: Sermitsiaq Newspaper," *Reuters*, June 4, 2019, https://www.reuters.com/article/us-china-silkroad-greenland/china-withdraws-bid-for-greenland-airport-projects-sermitsiaq-newspaper-idUSKCN1T5191.

109. Jeremy Page, Gordon Lubold, and Rob Taylor, "Deal for Naval Outpost in Cambodia Furthers China's Quest for Military Network," *Wall Street Journal*, July 22, 2019, https://

www.wsj.com/articles/secret-deal-for-chinese-naval-outpost-in-cambodia-raises-u-s-fears-of-beijings-ambitions-11563732482.

110. Ben Blanchard, "China Downplays Solomon Island Lease Debacle, Tells U.S. to Stay Out," *Reuters*, October 29, 2019, https://www.reuters.com/article/us-china-solomonislands/china-downplays-solomon-island-lease-debacle-tells-u-s-to-stay-out-idUSKBN1X80YR.

111. Dennis J. Blasko and Roderick Lee, "The Chinese Navy's Marine Corps, Part 2: Chain-of-Command Reforms and Evolving Training," *Jamestown China Brief* 19, no. 4 (2019), https://jamestown.org/program/the-chinese-navys-marine-corps-part-2-chain-of-command-reforms-and-evolving-training/.

112. Minnie Chan, "Chinese Navy Set to Build Fourth Aircraft Carrier, but Plans for a More Advanced Ship Are Put on Hold," *South China Morning Post*, November 28, 2019, https://www.scmp.com/news/china/military/article/3039653/chinese-navy-set-build-fourth-aircraft-carrier-plans-more.

113. Christopher D. Yung, "'Building a World Class Expeditionary Force'" (The US-China Economic And Security Review Commission, Washington, DC, June 20, 2019), https://www.uscc.gov/sites/default/files/Yung_USCC%20Testimony_FINAL.pdf.

114. Trym Aleksander Eiterjord, "Checking In on China's Nuclear Icebreaker," *The Diplomat*, September 5, 2019, https://thediplomat.com/2019/09/checking-in-on-chinas-nuclear-icebreaker/.

Chapter 13

1. Harold Karan Jacobson and Michel Oksenberg, *China's Participation in the IMF, the World Bank, and GATT: Toward a Global Economic Order* (Ann Arbor: University of Michigan Press, 1990), 139.

2. Andrew W. Marshall, "Long-Term Competition with the Soviets: A Framework for Strategic Analysis" (Arlington, VA: RAND, 1972), viii.

3. Kenneth Waltz, *Theory of International Politics* (Long Grove, IL: Waveland Press, 2010 [1979]); David Lake, *Hierarchy in International Relations* (Ithaca, NY: Cornell University Press, 2009).

4. Paul Musgrave and Dan Nexon, "Defending Hierarchy from the Moon to the Indian Ocean: Symbolic Capital and Political Dominance in Early Modern China and the Cold War," *International Organization* 73, no. 3 (2018): 531–626; Alex D. Barder, "International Hierarchy," in *Oxford Research Encyclopedia of International Studies* (Oxford: Oxford University Press, 2015).

5. Robert Gilpin, *War and Change in World Politics* (Cambridge: Cambridge University Press, 1981), 26.

6. Ibid., 44; Evan A. Feigenbaum, "Reluctant Stakeholder: Why China's Highly Strategic Brand of Revisionism Is More Challenging Than Washington Thinks," April 27, 2018, https://carnegieendowment.org/2018/04/27/reluctant-stakeholder-why-china-s-highly-strategic-brand-of-revisionism-is-more-challenging-than-washington-thinks-pub-76213.

7. Michael Lind, "The China Question," *Tablet*, May 19, 2020, https://www.tabletmag.com/sections/news/articles/china-strategy-trade-lind.

8. Yuan Peng [袁鹏], "The Coronavirus Pandemic and the Great Changes Unseen in a Century [新冠疫情与百年变局]," *Contemporary International Relations* [现代国际关系], no. 5 (June 2020): 1–6; Robert E. Kelly, "What Would Chinese Hegemony Look Like?," *The Diplomat*, February 10, 2014, https://thediplomat.com/2014/02/what-would-chinese-hegemony-look-like/; Nadège Rolland, "China's Vision for a New World Order" (Washington, DC: National Bureau of Asian Research, 2020), https://www.nbr.org/publication/chinas-vision-for-a-new-world-order/.

9. Charles Glaser, "A U.S.-China Grand Bargain?: The Hard Choice between Military Competition and Accommodation," *International Security* 39, no. 4 (2015): 86, 49–90.

10. Barry R. Posen, "Pull Back: The Case for a Less Activist Foreign Policy," *Foreign Affairs* 92, no. 1 (2013).

11. Michael D. Swaine, Jessica J. Lee, and Rachel Esplin Odell, "Towards and Inclusive and Balanced Regional Order: A New U.S. Strategy in East Asia" (Washington, DC: Quincy

Institute, 2021), 8–9, https://quincyinst.org/wp-content/uploads/2021/01/A-New-Strategy-in-East-Asia.pdf.

12. Glaser, "A U.S.-China Grand Bargain?," 50.

13. Lyle Goldstein, "How Progressives and Restrainers Can Unite on Taiwan and Reduce the Potential for Conflict with China" (Washington, DC: Quincy Institute, April 17, 2020), https://responsiblestatecraft.org/2020/04/17/how-progressives-and-restrainers-can-unite-on-taiwan-and-reduce-the-potential-for-conflict-with-china/.

14. Peter Beinart, "America Needs an Entirely New Foreign Policy for the Trump Age," *The Atlantic*, 2018, https://www.theatlantic.com/ideas/archive/2018/09/shield-of-the-republic-a-democratic-foreign-policy-for-the-trump-age/570010/.

15. Chas W. Freeman, "Beijing, Washington, and the Shifting Balance of Prestige" (Newport, RI: China Maritime Studies Institute, 2011), https://mepc.org/speeches/beijing-washington-and-shifting-balance-prestige.

16. Bruce Gilley, "Not So Dire Straits: How the Finlandization of Taiwan Benefits U.S. Security," *Foreign Affairs* (January/February 2010).

17. Glaser, "A U.S.-China Grand Bargain?," 57, 72.

18. Paul Kane, "To Save Our Economy, Ditch Taiwan," *New York Times*, November 10, 2011, https://www.nytimes.com/2011/11/11/opinion/to-save-our-economy-ditch-taiwan.html.

19. Goldstein, "How Progressives and Restrainers Can Unite on Taiwan and Reduce the Potential for Conflict with China."

20. Glaser, "A U.S.-China Grand Bargain?," 86; Goldstein, "How Progressives and Restrainers Can Unite on Taiwan and Reduce the Potential for Conflict with China," 61.

21. Lyle J. Goldstein, *Meeting China Halfway: How to Defuse the Emerging US-China Rivalry* (Washington, DC: Georgetown University Press, 2015), 61.

22. James Steinberg and Michael E. O'Hanlon, *Strategic Reassurance and Resolve: U.S.-China Relations in the Twenty-First Century* (Princeton: Princeton University Press, 2014), 5.

23. Michael O'Hanlon and James Steinberg, *A Glass Half Full?: Rebalance, Reassurance, and Resolve in the U.S.-China Strategic Relationship* (Washington, DC: Brookings Institution Press, 2017), 21–23.

24. Goldstein, *Meeting China Halfway*.

25. Ananth Krishnan, "From Tibet to Tawang, A Legacy of Suspicion," *The Hindu*, October 22, 2012, https://www.thehindu.com/opinion/op-ed/from-tibet-to-tawang-a-legacy-of-suspicions/article4019717.ece.

26. Jane Perlez, "Calls Grow in China to Press Claim for Okinawa," *New York Times*, June 13, 2013, https://www.nytimes.com/2013/06/14/world/asia/sentiment-builds-in-china-to-press-claim-for-okinawa.html.

27. Eduardo Baptista, "Why Russia's Vladivostok Celebration Prompted a Nationalist Backlash in China," *South China Morning Post*, July 2, 2020, https://www.scmp.com/news/china/diplomacy/article/3091611/why-russias-vladivostok-celebration-prompted-nationalist.

28. Beinart, "America Needs an Entirely New Foreign Policy for the Trump Age."

29. *Deng Xiaoping Selected Works* [邓小平文选], 2nd ed., vol. 3 [第三卷] (Beijing: People's Press [人民出版社], 1993), 320.

30. Ibid., *Deng Xiaoping Selected Works* [邓小平文选], vol. 3 [第三卷], 324–27.

31. For Jiang's 8th Ambassadorial Conference address, see Jiang Zemin [江泽民], *Jiang Zemin Selected Works* [江泽民文选], vol. 1 [第一卷] (Beijing: People's Press [人民出版社}, 2006), 311–17.

32. Hu Jintao [胡锦涛], *Hu Jintao Selected Works* [胡锦涛文选], vol. 2 [第二卷] (Beijing: People's Press [人民出版社], 2016), 503–4.

33. Zong Hairen [宗海仁], *China's New Leaders: The Fourth Generation* [中國掌權者: 第四代] (New York: Mirror Books [明鏡出版社], 2002).

34. Yan Xiaofeng [颜晓峰], "Take the Strategic Initiative in the Great Changes Unseen in a Century [在百年未有之大变局中打好战略主动仗]," *Qiushi Red Flag Manuscripts* [红旗文稿], February 26, 2019, http://www.qstheory.cn/dukan/hqwg/2019-02/26/c_1124163834.htm?spm=zm5062-001.0.0.1.Cr0LbB. *Red Flag Manuscripts* is published bi-weekly by *Qiushi*, and this article appeared in print.

35. Fu Ying [傅莹], "Sino-American Relations after the Coronavirus [新冠疫情后的中美关系]," *China-US Focus*, June 26, 2020, http://cn.chinausfocus.com/foreign-policy/20200629/41939.html.

36. Jiang Zemin [江泽民], *Jiang Zemin Selected Works* [江泽民文选], vol. 3 [第三卷], 448–49.

37. For Hu's speech, see Literature Research Office of the Chinese Communist Party Central Committee [中共中央文献研究室], *Selection of Important Documents since the 15th Party Congress* [十五大以来重要文献选编], vol. 2 (Beijing: People's Publishing House [人民出版社], 2001), 1205–27.

38. Nicholas Kristof, "Looking for a Jump-Start in China," *New York Times*, January 5, 2013, https://www.nytimes.com/2013/01/06/opinion/sunday/kristof-looking-for-a-jump-start-in-china.html.

39. Goldstein, *Meeting China Halfway*, 335–36.

40. Edward Cunningham, Tony Saich, and Jesse Turiel, "Understanding CCP Resilience: Surveying Chinese Public Opinion through Time" (Cambridge, MA: Ash Center for Democratic Governance and Innovation, Harvard Kennedy School, July 2020), https://ash.harvard.edu/publications/understanding-ccp-resilience-surveying-chinese-public-opinion-through-time; Lei Guang et al., "Pandemic Sees Increase in Chinese Support for Regime" (San Diego: China Data Lab at University of California at San Diego, June 30, 2020), http://chinadatalab.ucsd.edu/viz-blog/pandemic-sees-increase-in-chinese-support-for-regime-decrease-in-views-towards-us/.

41. "Interview: 'You Can Criticize The CCP, but You Must Not Criticize Xi Jinping,'" *Radio Free Asia*, August 18, 2020, https://www.rfa.org/english/news/china/interview-caixia-08182020152449.html.

42. Hal Brands and Zack Cooper, "After the Responsible Stakeholder, What?: Debating America's China Strategy," *Texas National Security Review* 2, no. 1 (2019), https://tnsr.org/2019/02/after-the-responsible-stakeholder-what-debating-americas-china-strategy-2/.

43. Aaron Friedberg, "An Answer to Aggression: How to Push Back Against Beijing," *Foreign Affairs* 99, no. 5 (2020): 150–64; Matthew Kroenig and Jeffrey Cimmino, "Global Strategy 2021: An Allied Strategy for China" (Washington, DC: Atlantic Council, 2020); Kurt M. Campbell and Jake Sullivan, "Competition without Catastrophe: How America Can Both Challenge and Coexist with China," *Foreign Affairs* 98, no. 5 (2019): 96–110; Melanie Hart and Kelly Magsamen, "Limit, Leverage, and Compete: A New Strategy on China" (Washington, DC: Center for American Progress, April 3, 2019); Orville Schell and Susan L. Shirk, "Course Correction: Toward an Effective and Sustainable China Policy" (New York and San Diego: Asia Society and UCSD 21st Century China Center, 2019); Ely Ratner et al., "Rising to the China Challenge: Renewing American Competitiveness in the Indo-Pacific" (Washington, DC: Center for a New American Security, 2019).

44. Andrew F. Krepinevich, "Preserving the Balance: A U.S. Eurasia Defense Strategy" (Washington, DC: Center for Strategic and Budgetary Assessments, January 19, 2017), https://csbaonline.org/uploads/documents/Preserving_the_Balance_%2819Jan17%29HANDOUTS.pdf.

45. "GDP, (Current US$)," World Bank Open Data, 2020, https://data.worldbank.org/indicator/ny.gdp.mktp.cd.

46. Ben Carter, "Is China's Economy Really the Largest in the World?," BBC, December 15, 2014, http://www.bbc.com/news/magazine-30483762.

47. Michael J. Green, *By More than Providence: Grand Strategy and American Power in the Asia Pacific Since 1783* (New York: Columbia University Press, 2017).

48. Stephen Biddle and Ivan Oelrich, "Future Warfare in the Western Pacific: Chinese Antiaccess/Area Denial, U.S. AirSea Battle, and Command of the Commons in East Asia," *International Security* 41, no. 1 (2016): 7–48.

49. Michael Beckley, "Plausible Denial: How China's Neighbors Can Check Chinese Naval Expansion," *International Security* 42, no. 2 (2017); Eugene Gholz, Benjamin Friedman, and Enea Gjoza, "Defensive Defense: A Better Way to Protect US Allies in Asia," *Washington Quarterly* 42, no. 4 (2019): 171–89.

50. Ratner et al., "Rising to the China Challenge," 29.

51. Ben Kesling and Jon Emont, "U.S. Goes on the Offensive against China's Empire-Building Funding Plan," *Wall Street Journal*, April 9, 2019, https://www.wsj.com/articles/u-s-goes-on-the-offensive-against-chinas-empire-building-megaplan-11554809402.

52. For an overview of some of these cases, see Dan Kliman et al., "Grading China's Belt and Road" (Washington, DC: Center for a New American Security, 2019), https://s3.amazonaws.com/files.cnas.org/CNAS+Report_China+Belt+and+Road_final.pdf; Edward Cavanough, "When China Came Calling: Inside the Solomon Islands Switch," *The Guardian*, December 9, 2019, https://www.theguardian.com/world/2019/dec/08/when-china-came-calling-inside-the-solomon-islands-switch; "Maldives' Defeated President, Abdulla Yameen, Accused of Receiving US$1.5 Million in Illicit Payments before Election," *South China Morning Post*, October 3, 2018, https://www.scmp.com/news/asia/south-asia/article/2166728/maldives-defeated-president-abdulla-yameen-accused-receiving.

53. "'Let's Talk'—Former UN Deputy Secretary-General Wu Hongbo: Excellent Diplomats Must Have Strong Patriotism and Enterprising Spirit, December 22, 2018 | CCTV 'Let's Talk' Official Channel [《开讲啦》我的时代答卷 前联合国副秘书长吴红波：优秀的外交官要有强烈的爱国心和进取精神 20181222|CCTV《开讲啦》官方频道]," YouTube, December 22, 2018, https://www.youtube.com/watch?v=pmrI2n6d6VU&t=24m56s.

54. Courtney Fung and Shing-Hon Lam, "China Already Leads 4 of the 15 U.N. Specialized Agencies—and Is Aiming for a 5th," *Washington Post*, March 3, 2020, https://www.washingtonpost.com/politics/2020/03/03/china-already-leads-4-15-un-specialized-agencies-is-aiming-5th/.

55. Tian Yuhong [田玉红], "China Radio International's Tian Yuhong: From Adding Together to Fusing Together to Restructure a New Type of International Media Structure [国际广播电台田玉红: 相加到相融重构新型国际传媒]," *Sohu [搜狐]*, December 13, 2019, https://m.sohu.com/n/475699064/?wscrid=95360_6.

56. Ratner et al., "Rising to the China Challenge," 15–16.

57. Ibid., 15–16.

58. Brendan Greeley, "How to Diagnose Your Own Dutch Disease," *Financial Times*, 2019, https://ftalphaville.ft.com/2019/03/13/1552487003000/How-to-diagnose-your-own-Dutch-disease/.

59. Frank Tang, "Facebook's Libra Forcing China to Step Up Plans for Its Own Cryptocurrency, Says Central Bank Official," *South China Morning Post*, July 8, 2019, https://www.scmp.com/economy/china-economy/article/3017716/facebooks-libra-forcing-china-to-step-plans-its-own.

60. Michael E. O'Hanlon, *The Senkaku Paradox: Risking Great Power War Over Small Stakes* (Washington, DC: Brookings Institution Press, 2019).

61. David Simchi-Levi and Edith Simchi-Levi, "We Need a Stress Test for Critical Supply Chains," *Harvard Business Review*, April 28, 2020, https://hbr-org.cdn.ampproject.org/c/s/hbr.org/amp/2020/04/we-need-a-stress-test-for-critical-supply-chains; Bill Gertz, "China Begins to Build Its Own Aircraft Carrier," *Washington Times*, August 1, 2011.

62. "The Importance of International Students to American Science and Engineering" (National Foundation for American Policy, October 2017), http://nfap.com/wp-content/uploads/2017/10/The-Importance-of-International-Students.NFAP-Policy-Brief.October-20171.pdf. Boris Granovskiy and Jill H. Wilson, "Foreign STEM Students in the United States" (Washington, DC: Congressional Research Service, November 1, 2019), https://crsreports.congress.gov/product/pdf/IF/IF11347. The report notes that, "According to the National Science Foundation's 2017 survey of STEM doctorate recipients from U.S. IHEs, 72% of foreign doctorate recipients were still in the United States 10 years after receiving their degrees. This percentage varied by country of origin; for example, STEM graduates from China (90%) and India (83%) stayed at higher rates than European students (69%)."

63. Remco Zwetsloot, "Keeping Top AI Talent in the United States: Findings and Policy Options for International Graduate Student Retention" (Washington, DC: Center for Security and Emerging Technology, 2019), https://cset.georgetown.edu/wp-content/uploads/Keeping-Top-AI-Talent-in-the-United-States.pdf.

64. James Pethokoukis, "Jonathan Gruber on Jump-Starting Breakthrough Science and Reviving Economic Growth: A Long-Read Q&A," American Enterprise Institute, June 3, 2019, https://www.aei.org/economics/johnathan-gruber-on-jump-starting-breakthrough-science-and-reviving-economic-growth-a-long-read-qa/.

65. Anthony M. Mills and Mark P. Mills, "The Science before the War," *The New Atlantis*, 2020.

66. Pethokoukis, "Jonathan Gruber on Jump-Starting Breakthrough Science and Reviving Economic Growth."

67. Michael Brown, Eric Chewning, and Pavneet Singh, "Preparing the United States for the Superpower Marathon with China" (Washington, DC: Brookings Institution, 2020), https://www.brookings.edu/wp-content/uploads/2020/04/FP_20200427_superpower_marathon_brown_chewning_singh.pdf.

68. Matt Stoller, *Goliath: The 100-Year War between Monopoly Power and Democracy* (New York: Simon & Schuster, 2019).

69. Alison Snyder, "Allies Could Shift U.S.-China Scientific Balance of Power," *Axios*, June 18, 2020, https://www.axios.com/scientific-research-expenditures-america-china-743755fe-3e94-4cd3-92cf-ea9eb1268ec2.html.

70. Ratner et al., "Rising to the China Challenge."

71. Lindsay Gorman, "The U.S. Needs to Get in the Standards Game—With Like-Minded Democracies," *Lawfare*, April 2, 2020, https://www.lawfareblog.com/us-needs-get-standards-game%E2%80%94-minded-democracies.

Conclusion

1. Samuel P. Huntington, "The U.S.—Decline or Renewal?," *Foreign Affairs*, 1988, https://www.foreignaffairs.com/articles/united-states/1988-12-01/us-decline-or-renewal.

2. Elmo R. Zumwalt, *On Watch* (New York: Quadrangle, 1976), 3–22.

3. Niall Ferguson, *Kissinger, 1923–1968: The Idealist* (New York: Penguin, 2015), 183.

4. Zumwalt, *On Watch*, 319.

5. Ibid.

6. Bernard Gwertzman, "The Gloomy Side of the Historian Henry A. Kissinger," *New York Times*, April 5, 1976, https://www.nytimes.com/1976/04/05/archives/the-gloomy-side-of-the-historian-henry-a-kissinger.html.

7. Ibid.; "Partial Transcript of an Interview with Kissinger on the State of Western World," *New York Times*, October 13, 1974, https://www.nytimes.com/1974/10/13/archives/partial-transcript-of-an-interview-with-kissinger-on-the-state-of.html; Henry A. Kissinger, *The Necessity for Choice: Prospects of American Foreign Policy* (New York: Harper, 1961), 2–3.

8. Much of the text following this paragraph is adapted from Kurt M. Campbell and Rush Doshi, "The China Challenge Can Help America Avert Decline," *Foreign Affairs*, December 3, 2020, https://www.foreignaffairs.com/articles/china/2020-12-03/china-challenge-can-help-america-avert-decline.

9. Huntington, "The U.S.—Decline or Renewal?"

10. Ruchir Sharma, "The Comeback Nation," *Foreign Affairs* 99, no. 3 (2020): 70–81.

11. David Pilling, "'Everybody Has Their Eyes on America': Black Lives Matter Goes Global," *Financial Times*, June 21, 2020, https://www.ft.com/content/fda8c04a-7737-4b17-bc80-d0ed5fa57c6c.

12. Jill Lepore, "A New Americanism," *Foreign Affairs* 98, no. 2 (2019): 10–19.

13. John F. Kennedy, "Remarks of Senator John F. Kennedy at Municipal Auditorium, Canton, Ohio" (Canton, Ohio, September 27, 1960), https://www.jfklibrary.org/archives/other-resources/john-f-kennedy-speeches/canton-oh-19600927.

INDEX

For the benefit of digital users, indexed terms that span two pages (e.g., 52–53) may, on occasion, appear on only one of those pages.